OXFORD THEOLOGICAL MONOGRAPHS

OXFORD THEOLOGICAL MONOGRAPHS

'WORKING THE EARTH OF THE HEART'
The Messalian Controversy in History, Texts, and Language to AD 431
Columba Stewart, OSB (1991)

THE LORDSHIP OF CHRIST
Ernst Käsemann's Interpretation of Paul's Theology
David V. Way (1991)

BEAUTY AND REVELATION IN THE THOUGHT OF SAINT AUGUSTINE
Carol Harrison (1992)

THE MURATORIAN FRAGMENT AND THE DEVELOPMENT OF THE CANON
Geoffrey Mark Hahneman (1992)

CHRISTOLOGY AND COSMOLOGY
Models of Divine Activity in Origen, Eusebius, and Athanasius
J. Rebecca Lyman (1993)

KIERKEGAARD AS NEGATIVE THEOLOGIAN
David Law (1993)

EARLY ISRAELITE WISDOM
Stuart Weeks (1994)

THE FATHERHOOD OF GOD FROM ORIGEN TO ATHANASIUS
Peter Widdicombe (1994)

RIGHT PRACTICAL REASON
Aristotle, Action, and Prudence in Aquinas
Daniel Westberg (1994)

JOHN NEWTON AND THE ENGLISH EVANGELICAL TRADITION
Between the Conversions of Wesley and Wilberforce
D. Bruce Hindmarsh (1996)

ST GREGORY OF NAZIANZUS
POEMATA ARCANA
C. Moreschini and D. A. Sykes (1997)

Anglican Evangelicals

Protestant Secessions from the *Via Media*, *c*.1800–1850

GRAYSON CARTER

UNIVERSITY PRESS

OXFORD
UNIVERSITY PRESS

Great Clarendon Street, Oxford OX2 6DP

Oxford University Press is a department of the University of Oxford.
It furthers the University's objective of excellence in research, scholarship,
and education by publishing worldwide in

Oxford New York
Athens Auckland Bangkok Bogotá Buenos Aires Calcutta
Cape Town Chennai Dar es Salaam Delhi Florence Hong Kong Istanbul
Karachi Kuala Lumpur Madrid Melbourne Mexico City Mumbai
Nairobi Paris São Paulo Shanghai Singapore Taipei Tokyo Toronto Warsaw
and associated companies in Berlin Ibadan

Oxford is a registered trade mark of Oxford University Press
in the UK and certain other countries

Published in the United States
by Oxford University Press Inc., New York

First published 2001

British Library Cataloguing in Publication Data
Data available

Library of Congress Cataloging in Publication Data
Data applied for

ISBN 0-19-827008-9

1 3 5 7 9 10 8 6 4 2

Typeset by Best-set Typesetter Ltd., Hong Kong
Printed in Great Britain
on acid-free paper by
Biddles Ltd., Guildford and King's Lynn

to John Walsh
with abiding gratitude

ACKNOWLEDGEMENTS

The completion of this study has been made possible through the various expressions of kindness, encouragement, and practical assistance received from institutions, friends, scholars, and acquaintances in Great Britain, Ireland, and the United States.

In particular, gratitude must be expressed to the librarians and staff of the following institutions, all of whom gave freely and generously of their time and talents: the Bishop Payne Library at the Virginia Theological Seminary, Alexandria, Virginia; the Bodleian Library, Oxford; Brasenose College Library, Oxford; the Bristol City Record Office, Bristol; the British Library, London; the Cambridge University Library, Cambridge; Christ Church Library, Oxford; the Davis Memorial Library at Methodist College, Fayetteville, North Carolina; the Devon County Library, Exeter; the Devon and Exeter Institute, Exeter; the Devon Record Office, Exeter; the Devon Record Office, Plymouth; the Exeter Cathedral Library, Exeter; Exeter College Library, Oxford; the Gloucestershire County Record Office, Gloucester; the Hampshire County Library, Winchester; the Hampshire County Record Office, Winchester; the Henry E. Huntington Library, San Marino, California; the John Rylands University Library, Manchester; Lambeth Palace Library, London; the Leicestershire Record Office, Leicester; the Library of Congress, Washington, DC; the Oxfordshire Record Office, Oxford; Pusey House Library, Oxford; the Somerset County Library, Taunton; the Somerset Record Office, Taunton; the Surrey Record Centre, Woking; the William R. Perkins Library and the Divinity School Library, Duke University; and the Wiltshire County Record Office, Trowbridge. Captain Gerard Noel provided access to the Noel family papers in his private possession. The Revd Iain H. Murray furnished copies of the letters of Henry Bulteel in his possession. Mrs Retta T. L. Casbard of the Albury Historical Society supplied local historical material on Henry Drummond. Miss Melanie Barber provided copies of materials contained in the Blomfield papers at Lambeth Palace Library. Mr John Leach helped to unravel the details of James Shore's later career as proprietor of a Derbyshire health spa. Dr John Orbell and his staff at Baring Brothers provided assistance to my research into the Baring family and allowed open access to the bank's extensive archival collection. The University Church at Oxford, St. Mary the Virgin, supplied office accommodation during a busy period of editing and checking footnotes in the summer of 1998, and my thanks must be expressed to the vicar, the Revd Canon Brian Mountford, who has provided much support for the completion of this study. Richard Sharp very kindly provided expert assistance in selecting a suitable illustration for the dust jacket. The valuable assistance of Georga Godwin at Oxford University Press has been greatly appreciated by the author thoughout the final stages of preparation of this work.

There are many individuals who are owed a special debt for their assistance—practical and otherwise—in the preparation of this study. My initial interest in the subject was kindled through the friendship of Dr Wes Balda, and I will always remain grateful for his influence in my life. This early curiosity about 'serious religion' in England was nurtured at Fuller Seminary in California, to which I am indebted for the rigorous intellectual and academic preparation I received there from (among others) Dr James E. Bradley, Dr Geoffrey W. Bromiley, Dr Richard A. Muller, and Dr Lewis B. Smedes. During the same period, I spent many pleasurable hours of study at the Henry E. Huntington Library in nearby San Marino, where the influence of a small group of English historians, including the late Professor Leland Carlson, Professor Patrick Collinson, and Dr Michael E. Moody made an abiding impression upon my life and scholarship. While undertaking research at Oxford I enjoyed the companionship of a remarkable group of fellow graduate students, whose work is now beginning to reshape, in important and varied ways, our understanding of eighteenth- and nineteenth-century ecclesiastical history. Each has contributed freely of his time, friendship, and immense knowledge of ecclesiastical history (often through the pages of his own work), and my abiding gratitude to them must be acknowledged. They include Dan Brunner, Arthur Burns, Peter Doll, Jim Gerrard, Bruce Hindmarsh, Peter Nockles, Colin Podmore, Richard Sharp, Mark Smith, John Wolffe, and Chris Zealley.

Other individuals who have contributed to the completion of

this study include Dr P. H. A. M. Abels, the Revd Jonathan Burnham, Professor Richard Carwardine, Dr Tim Grass, Dr Craig C. Hill, the late Revd Professor Peter Hinchliff, the Revd and Mrs Vernon Orr, the Revd John S. Reynolds, the Rt Revd Geoffrey Rowell, Mr Brian Snell, and Dr Timothy Stunt. Dr David Bebbington must be singled out for special recognition. I remain much indebted to each. Of course, all remaining errors and mistakes are entirely my own.

My mother (and late) father have also been a valued source of love and encouragement throughout the various stages of this study. Likewise my wife, Catherine, and our two children, Katie and Geoffrey, whose love and support have sustained me through many long hours of travel, research, writing, and preparation.

My greatest debt, however, remains to Dr John Walsh of Jesus College, Oxford, who first suggested that I undertake a study of this topic—albeit in modified form—and supervised it as an Oxford doctoral thesis. His encouragement, approachability, persistence, determination, and, most especially, his knowledge and love of the study of English Evangelicalism, have been paramount in the completion of this work. As a scholar, mentor, and friend, my debt to him remains immeasurable. That debt has been acknowledged, only in part, in the dedication of this study.

Several bodies have provided generous financial assistance, without which the completion of this work would have been impossible. These include an Overseas Research Students' Award made by the Committee of Vice-Chancellors and Principals of the Universities of the United Kingdom, a grant from the Denyer and Johnson Fund of the Faculty of Theology of the University of Oxford, and a grant from the Squire Marriott Fund also of the Faculty of Theology.

Grayson Carter

Methodist College
Fayetteville, NC
Advent, 1998

CONTENTS

LIST OF ABBREVIATIONS

Al. Cant.	John and J. A. Venn (eds.), *Alumni Cantabrigienses: A Biographical List of All Known Students, Graduates and Holders of Offices at the University of Cambridge, from the Earliest Times to 1900*. Part I: *From the Earliest Time to 1751* (Cambridge, 1922–7). Part II: *From 1752 to 1900* (Cambridge, 1940–54).
Al. Dub.	George Dames Burtchaell and Thomas Ulick Sadleir (eds.), *Alumni Dublinenses: A Register of the Students, Graduates, Professors and Provosts of Trinity College in the University of Dublin (1593–1860)* (Dublin, 1924).
Al. Ox.	Joseph Foster (ed.), *Alumni Oxonienses: The Members of the University of Oxford, 1500–1714: Their Parentage, Birthplace, and Year of Birth, with a Record of their Degrees* (Oxford, 1891–1). *The Members of the University of Oxford, 1715–1886: Their Parentage, Birthplace, and Year of Birth, with a Record of their Degrees* (Oxford, 1888).
Hansard	*The Parliamentary History of England From the Earliest Period to the Year 1803* (1819). *The Parliamentary Debates: Forming a Continuation of the Work Entitled 'The Parliamentary History of England from the Earliest Period to the Year 1803'* (1820–30); and *Hansard's Parliamentary Debates: Third Series, Commencing with the Accession of William IV* (1831–91).
AR	The *Annual Register.*
BDE	Donald M. Lewis (ed.), *The Blackwell Dictionary of Evangelical Biography* (Oxford, 1995).
BMag	The *Baptist Magazine.*
Bod	Bodleian Library, Oxford.
BQ	The *Baptist Quarterly.*
CG	The *Christian Guardian.*
CO	The *Christian Observer.*
CMS	The Church Missionary Society.
CW	William Kelly (ed.), *The Collected Writings of J. N. Darby*, 2nd edn. (Kingston-on-Thames, 1956).

DNB	The *Dictionary of National Biography*.
EC	The *English Churchman*.
EdR	The *Edinburgh Review*.
EM	The *Evangelical Magazine*.
ER	The *Eclectic Review*.
Fry	The Diary of Alfred C. Fry in the Christian Brethren Archive at the John Rylands University Library, Manchester.
GM	The *Gentleman's Magazine*.
GS	The *Gospel Standard*.
HD	MSS St. Edmund Hall 67/1–20, *The Diary of the Revd John Hill, Vice-Principal of St. Edmund Hall, Oxford*, on deposit at the Bodleian Library, Oxford.
JEH	The *Journal of Ecclesiastical History*.
JRH	The *Journal of Religious History*.
New DNB	The *New Dictionary of National Biography* (Oxford, in preparation).
Non	The *Nonconformist*.
QR	The *Quarterly Review*.
RO	Record Office.
VE	*Vox Evangelica*.
WE	William Burton (ed.), *Essays and Correspondence, Chiefly on Spiritual Subjects, by the Late John Walker* (1838).

NOTES ON THE TEXT

1. The term 'Evangelical' refers to adherents of 'serious religion' within the Church of England and the Church of Ireland; 'evangelical' refers to adherents of a similar theological persuasion within Protestant Nonconformity; 'churchman' refers to members—clerical or lay, male or female—of the Church of England or the Church of Ireland; 'Dissent' and 'Nonconformity' are employed interchangeably and refer to adherents of Protestant denominations only, not including members of the Roman Catholic Church.
2. In quotations and references, capitalization and punctuation have sometimes been standardized in keeping with modern English idiom.
3. The place of publication for works cited in footnotes and the bibliography is London unless otherwise specified.

Evangelical religion has been the fashion: the tide is turned; and much that had floated forward on its surface, is now floating backward wither it set out. Many that called themselves evangelical, and seemed to delight in the truth that is so designated, have now disowned the word, and grown, at least, indifferent to the doctrine. There is every appearance that the world will get back its own—some landed and some wrecked upon its familiar shores, where they will find themselves, alas! how much at home!

Fast fixed, meantime, upon the rock of ages, the Church of Christ remains: firm, immutable and separate as ever: she has not neared the world; and however in calm times the world has poured its multitudes upon her borders, the distance is ever and exactly what it was . . . They who have built their house upon that Rock, will be as surely found upon it, when the current turns, as when the floating multitude came in upon them; for what was but a fashion of the times to others, is life and peace to them. Of those whom we now see departing from us, we believe and are assured that we shall see many back: but with what loss returning!

Caroline Wilson, *The Inquirer in Oxford* (1839), iv–v.

Introduction

Though the Evangelical Revival was cradled in the Church of England, its relationship to its mother Church was not always an easy one. From the outset its presence aroused hostility. There were persistent claims that Evangelicals were suspect as churchmen; that they were half-hearted in their attachment to the Establishment, if not downright disloyal. Their theology aroused uncomfortable memories of militant Puritanism: solifidian theories of justification by faith alone, 'enthusiastic' views of the need for drastic regeneration by the Holy Spirit, potentially antinomian ideas of predestination and final perseverance—all these had uncomfortable resonances of a bygone fanaticism which should by now have been laid to rest.

Evangelical ecclesiology was regarded with similar suspicion, for it placed paramount stress on the overriding claims of the invisible 'Church of Christ', the redeemed body of all elect souls gathered out of the world from all churches and nations. The promotion of this invisible body was seen by Evangelicals as the object of all their work, taking precedence, in the last resort, over attachment to any visible, terrestrial church. Many churchmen feared that this ecclesiological premiss would encourage dangerous contacts with Protestant Dissent, and perhaps even lead to social unrest. If the only abiding spiritual categories were those which separated the regenerate from the unregenerate, was it not probable that Evangelical clergymen would have far more in common with like-minded Dissenters than with allegedly 'unregenerate' clergymen of their own Church? The co-operation of 'Gospel clergymen' with Methodists and Nonconformists in voluntary associations like the Bible Society only served to increase this suspicion.

By the end of the eighteenth century, the course of the Revival seemed to have confirmed some of these fears as several large 'Gospel' groupings moved out of the orbit of the National Church. The Countess of Huntingdon's Connexion had formally seceded from the Church in 1781, by which time many of Whitefield's Calvinistic Methodist societies had already slipped more quietly into Dissent. The Wesleyan Methodists remained formally in the Church until Wesley's death in 1791, and retained an anomalous stance towards it thereafter, but were clearly destined for separate existence well before the end of the century despite their founder's claim to 'live and die a member of the Church of England'. The para-church organizations built-up by the clerical leaders of 'Methodism' in its various forms, professed sympathy for the Church, but operated increasingly outside its control and authority. Though there was deep respect for the Reformation formulae of the Church of England, it seemed to many Methodist leaders that the great majority of the clergy no longer professed them and opposed those who did. Though the Church of England with its high prestige, social hegemony, and vast endowments, seemed by far the best instrument for any campaign of national regeneration, the Establishment also placed daunting legal and administrative hindrances in the way. By the onset of the nineteenth century, not a few mission-minded clergymen had come to believe that they could operate far more effectively outside the parameters of the Establishment than within it.

At the same time, however, an increasingly large body of 'Gospel clergymen' had moved in the opposite direction, to become far more firmly attached to the order and authority of the National Church, by law established. They distanced themselves from the 'irregularity' of the Methodists, and saw predecessors like William Grimshaw of Haworth, or John Berridge of Everton, who indulged in occasional bouts of field-preaching, as sadly misguided. By 1800, it had become clear that 'irregularity' produced more Dissenters than churchmen, and that 'connexions' like Wesley's could not be contained within the church as it was at present constituted. The great majority of Evangelical clergymen were by now firm 'regulars', with a loyalty to the principle of order in both Church and State that had been stiffened by the anti-'Jacobin' reaction of the 1790s. They were confident that they could capture the apparatus of the Established Church far more easily by quiet, orderly infiltration, than by 'irregular' militancy. With a firm foothold in Oxford and Cambridge, with their nationwide network of voluntary societies, and with spokesmen like William Wilberforce and Hannah More, they believed that they had far more to gain by working with the grain of establishment sentiment than by opposing it. By the early nineteenth century, the dominant tone of Anglican Evangelicalism was captured by the title of a well-known work by James Bean: *Zeal Without Innovation*.[1]

But though clerical Evangelicalism was by now safely corralled within the canonical bounds of the Church, this did not mean that all tension between the claims of the Gospel and the claims of the Establishment had vanished. There was a great fund of Anglican loyalism among the Evangelical clergy during the first half of the nineteenth century, but it was by no means total and it was always subject to potential strain. Much writing on Evangelicalism has assumed too easily that the views of moderates like those around Charles Simeon at Cambridge, or Wilberforce at Clapham, or those of the 'Christian Observer school', were those of all Evangelicals. Evangelical praise for the Church–State connection, and professions of contentment with the formularies of the Church—especially its liturgy—often concealed doubts, and should not be taken too easily at face value. Recent scholarship on early nineteenth-century Evangelicalism, such as that by Ian Bradley on the Clapham Sect, Clyde Ervine's close study of the variant views of clerical leaders on some key issues of theology, and David Bebbington's major study of Evangelicalism in modern Britain, have revealed the diversity of outlook which lurked beneath the apparent unities of 'vital religion'.[2] This was especially the case after the mid-1820s, when a stern reaction arose to the alleged worldliness and accommodationism of moderate leaders.

This study aims to explore still further the complexities of Evangelicalism by looking at those clergymen who were so discontented with the status quo in the Established Church that they were propelled into outright secession. There were far more of these than have been realized—indeed, they numbered well over a hundred in the period between 1800 and 1850.[3] Save for a brief article by Harold Rowdon, or for the briefest of allusions in academic works (often in footnotes), their existence has been virtually

[1] See J. D. Walsh, 'The Anglican Evangelicals in the Eighteenth Century', in M. Simon (ed.), *Aspects de l'Anglicanisme* (Paris, 1974), 102.

[2] Ian Bradley, *The Call to Seriousness: The Evangelical Impact on the Victorians* (1976); W. J. C. Ervine, 'Doctrine and Diplomacy: Some Aspects of the Life and Thought of the Anglican Evangelical Clergy, 1797 to 1837', Ph.D. thesis (Cambridge, 1979); D. W. Bebbington, *Evangelicalism in Modern Britain* (1989).

[3] See Appendix.

ignored.[4] Yet they are surely worthy of study. Those who made their exit to the right of the Anglican stage by seceding to the Church of Rome have attracted a great deal of attention, particularly those who went with Newman or Manning: those who made a leftward exit into Protestant Dissent have attracted almost no scholarly attention. This is regrettable, for although these Protestant seceders constituted only a small fraction of the Anglican clerical body, their existence is a tribute to the anxieties which Evangelicals—as well as Tractarians—experienced about the viability of the famous Anglican *via media*. If Newman seceded because he thought the Church of England to be insufficiently catholic, a number of fervent fellow clergymen departed because they took the opposite view and found the Established Church too unreformed and popish. There was unanimity here among the rival types of secessionists as well as their obvious divergence; a 'Romeward' seceder like Manning and a high Calvinist seceder like J. C. Philpot were agreed in regarding the Church of England as a highly imperfect and artificial amalgam of irreconcilable elements held together by a crude Erastianism. Both saw it as lacking in firm discipline and deplorably subject to exploitation by worldly, secular-minded interests.

The Evangelical seceders are of significance because they often articulated anxieties—and sometimes expectations—which troubled many of their brethren who did not leave the Church. There was much about the government and liturgy of the Church which worried conscientious exponents of 'vital religion', but which was suppressed or expressed privately. The seceders brought these tensions out of the closet and into the open. By examining them, a further picture can be gained of the complexities of Anglican Evangelicalism which may help to offset the rather homogenized and consensual picture which many accounts still present.

The main focus of this study is on the period between 1800 and 1850, especially that of the 1830s and 1840s which produced the greatest number of secessions. There is, however, an introductory chapter which sets out the 'normative' Evangelical ecclesiological position, followed by a chapter summarizing some of the impulses for secession visible in the late eighteenth century. Between these early seceders and those of the first decades of the nineteenth

[4] H. H. Rowdon, 'Secession from the Established Church in the Early Nineteenth Century', in *VE* (1964), 76–88.

century, there are obvious similarities. Some of the same recurrent trigger mechanisms for secession are visible in both periods: dissatisfaction with the worldliness fostered by the patronage system, and the dubious connection of the Church with politics; impatience at the restraints imposed on evangelism by canon law and by the authority of the bishops; grave doubts about some of the Prayer Book rubrics and ceremonies; a proclivity to a high Calvinism which emphasized the need for the separation of the elect from spiritual contact with reprobates. The importance of any of these factors varied between individuals: by no means all seceders, as we shall see, left the Church of England for the same reason.

There was also a difference of emphasis between the early period and that under discussion. The eighteenth-century clerical seceders were few in number and often moved by despair at the sluggishness and inertia of the Church authorities; some of the most prominent of those who left in the 1830s and 1840s, however, were moved by a different consideration—not so much by the inertia of their fellow churchmen as by their misguided activism. They were aghast at the progress of the Oxford Movement and at the threat which popery, both within the Church and outside it, posed to their hopes of making the doctrines of the Reformation once again triumphant in the Church. Ironically, like their Tractarian opponents, they were almost as worried by the currents of theological liberalism which seemed to threaten the scriptural foundation of the Gospel: they watched with alarm as Whig governments appointed Broad Churchmen like Renn Dickson Hampden to high positions. Also like their Tractarian opponents, some Evangelicals began to question the value of the Church–State connection after the 'constitutional revolution' of 1828–32 seemed to destroy the Anglican character of Parliament, and render the Church vulnerable to the political hostility of Roman Catholics, Dissenters, and secular radicals. This period too saw an upsurge of theological currents which made some Evangelicals dissatisfied with the state of their Church. High Calvinism, millenarian excitement, a romantic, primitivistic yearning to regain the simplicity of the apostolic church—all these took their toll and eroded the loyalty of Evangelical clergymen in this troubled time.

This is in many ways an exploratory study, and, of necessity, it is not an exhaustive one. No doubt much work remains to be done on the subject of Evangelical secessions, as well as on the complex issue of the Evangelicals' relationship with the Established Church. Though there were some group secessions, many Evangelical clerical seceders went out of the Church as isolated individuals, and a good deal probably remains to be uncovered about their particular case histories from local sources. It is highly likely that there were a number of quiet seceders who left no trace on the obvious sources; men who wrote no pamphlets and excited no publicity. Had they departed *en masse*, like the Western Schism, or the Scots ministers of the great Disruption, they would have been much more easily pinned down.

In completing this study, the author has been compelled to cut what is only a swath through the tangled undergrowth of this particular tract of Anglican history. For the most part, consideration of the many lay seceders from the Church of England has been omitted, though some of the more prominent of these appear from time to time. This is essentially a study of *clerical* secessions and attitudes towards the Church. Attention has been focused largely on particular episodes which illustrate the main issues involved. No doubt, over time some of the more obscure spaces of the canvas will be filled in by others, especially through local history. The sources which have been consulted, however, have provided a good deal of coverage: there is a very large quantity of printed source material available in the shape of sermons, tracts, and biographies, which were consulted for the most part in the Bodleian Library, Oxford, the British Library, and the Cambridge University Library. Religious and secular periodicals of the period yielded a substantial quantity of additional information, especially the files of the *Christian Observer*, the *Record*, and the *Christian Guardian*. Moreover, a rich vein of local historical material has been consulted at county record offices, especially in the West Country. Finally, the picture has been filled out at several points by a number of other interesting manuscript sources, notably the diaries of John Rashdall and John Hill, both on deposit at the Bodleian Library; the Noel family papers in possession of Captain Gerard Noel of Essex, and those Noel family papers at the Leicestershire County Record Office; the Blomfield Papers at Lambeth Palace Library; and the diary of Alfred C. Fry on deposit in the Christian Brethren Archive at the John Rylands University Library in Manchester.

1

Evangelicals and the Established Church

The chief origins of the Evangelical Revival are to be found in the Church of England. To the surprise of Nonconformists, the religious revival for which many of them had prayed descended in the 1730s not in their godly meeting houses where the old reformed Calvinism survived, but within a Church of England which seemed to have apostatized from the 'doctrines of grace'. In England, it was clergyman like John and Charles Wesley, George Whitefield, James Hervey, and in Wales, Anglicans like Daniel Rowland and the layman Howell Harris who set the new Evangelical movement in motion.

In time, the forces of renewal often proved too strong to be contained in the structures of the Established Church: the new wine spilled over the rim of the old bottles as 'connexions' which began inside the National Church moved across its frontiers into separatism. The 'Inghamites', the Countess of Huntingdon's Connexion, Wesleyan Methodism, Welsh Calvinistic Methodism, and other smaller groupings all moved along a trajectory that led them towards Dissent, though not without a number of anomalous intermediate stages.

Yet, a sizeable proportion of the growing band of 'Gospel clergymen' still stayed within the Church into which they were ordained. These came to be known as Evangelical clergymen—a title which will be attributed to them throughout this study—and they were, at least by the late eighteenth century, taxonomically distinguished from the 'Methodism' of the more irregular evangelical bodies. In historical categorization, 'Evangelical' has come to be equated with this large body of Christians who subscribed to a theology and spirituality characterized—in David Bebbington's recent account—by the general evangelical attributes of conversionism, activism, biblicism, and crucicentrism, but who practised their piety within the State Church.[1]

For many, conformity to the rubrics, liturgy, and canons of the Church came easily: to others, who will be the main subject of this study, it did not, but was accompanied by anxiety, tension, and, in some cases, schism. Before embarking on the tangled story of the minority of the outright seceders from the Church, it is necessary to examine the views of the establishmentarian majority, who saw no insuperable obstacle between themselves and loyalty to the Church of England by law established, or to its formularies.

It has often been said that the early Evangelicals were not intellectuals.[2] Being primarily concerned with soul-saving—the 'one thing needful'—it is said that they possessed no deep interest in the close study of theology, metaphysics, history, or ecclesiology. This is true only in a limited sense, for the movement was capable of throwing up a homespun biblical commentator like Thomas Scott, a church historian like Joseph Milner, and a moralist like Thomas Gisborne. If Evangelicalism produced few students of ecclesiology to compare with those of the Oxford Movement, nevertheless Evangelicals, as aggressive and innovative evangelists, were forced constantly to come to terms with ecclesiological issues in ways seldom faced by the ordinary incumbent who took the existing ecclesiastical order and status quo for granted. The active commitment to soul-saving itself raised questions. How far was a godly clergyman to be constrained by canons that appeared to hinder the preaching of God's Word to all people? How far was the duty of obedience to bishops to be carried when it inhibited the welfare of souls who were perishing? Was the liturgy of the Church sufficiently consonant with Scripture to be accepted and used without danger or serious hesitation? What was the relationship of converted souls, at present a small minority in the

[1] See D. W. Bebbington, *Evangelicalism in Modern Britain* (1989), 3. An earlier statement of Evangelical doctrines can be found in the diary of Henry Thornton. See Add. MSS 7674, Thornton Family Papers, I/R, 7 Jan. 1795, Cambridge University Library.

[2] W. E. Gladstone, *Gleanings of Past Years* (1879), v.11; 'The Evangelical Movement: Its Parentage, Progress, and Issue', in *British Quarterly Review* (July and Oct. 1879), 14; W. H. B. Proby, *Annals of the 'Low Church' Party in England*, (1888), i.348–9; C. K. F. Brown, *A History of the English Clergy, 1800–1900* (1953), 169–70; John E. Linnan, 'The Evangelical Background of John Henry Newman, 1816–26', Th.D. thesis (Louvain, 1965), i.188–9.

National Church, to the apparently unregenerate majority with whom they associated in the open community of the parish church? What was the 'Church of Christ' and what were its relations to the terrestrial Church of England? At a more pragmatic level still, did the Establishment to which all Evangelicals belonged and from which the 'Gospel clergy' drew their income, do more harm than good to the cause of 'serious religion' by associating the Church with the world of high politics and local lay patronage? Such questions were not only theoretical issues but matters of great pastoral concern to an Evangelical incumbent. They frequently acquired salience in particularly contentious situations—as when a zealous evangelist collided with a prickly bishop or an unsympathetic patron, or when Evangelicals sat down to ponder the propaganda of Nonconformists against the Established Church. These issues demanded some kind of an answer.

Central to Evangelical ecclesiology was the idea of the 'Church of Christ', the invisible body of all regenerate souls to which alone could be given the adjectives, 'one, holy, and catholic'.[3] Here, at the theoretical level, all Evangelicals were agreed. While they prized the visible Church into which they were ordained, Evangelicals maintained that its interests should be subordinated to those of the real church, the 'Church of Christ', or the invisible body of all believers. John Newton, who settled at Olney and London as a 'regular' parish clergy after contemplating a career in Dissent, agreed: the invisible church, he insisted, was God's 'peculiar kingdom, which He has established distinct from the kingdoms of this world, though diffused and extended among them, and which, in due time, like leaven, will pervade and assimilate them all to Himself'.[4] So too did the impeccably 'regular' Thomas Robinson of Leicester, who described the true 'Church of Christ' as 'one compact well-ordered society', united 'under one common Head, actuated by one Spirit, having the same hopes and enjoyments, and directed by the same laws and principles'. Its membership was composed of those 'of every age and place, . . . far removed from and unknown to each other, diversified by

[3] John H. Overton, *The English Church in the Nineteenth Century* (1894), 97; Yngve Brilioth, *The Anglican Revival* (1925), 41.

[4] John Newton, 'The Lord Reigneth', in *The Works of the Revd John Newton*, ed. Richard Cecil (1824), iv.405.

a thousand external modes and customs, and divided into a thousand denominations'.[5]

What then was a visible church? The Evangelicals gratefully cited the nineteenth Article which had defined it as, 'a congregation of faithful men, in which the pure Word of God is preached, and the sacraments duly ministered according to Christ's ordinance, in all those things that of necessity are requisite to the same'. Much, of course, depended on the definition of such key phrases as 'faithful', 'pure', and 'duly ministered'. Most Evangelicals had no difficulty in accepting that their own Church, whatever its defects in practice, was fundamentally sound and based on the attributes set out in this Article. The Church of England as it now stood, claimed Thomas Robinson, was a body in which 'the truth of the Gospel is maintained, in all its essential points, where the sacraments are duly administered', and where 'the pastoral office has its regular and proper exercise'.[6] The Church of England rested on the bedrock of scriptural fundamentals. Whether or not the majority of the clergy were loyal in advancing these attributes was far more problematic, but it was not difficult for early Evangelicals to regard the growing number of 'Gospel clergy' as proof that there was at very least a righteous remnant in the Church of England which was the harbinger of far better things to come.

More difficult was the prickly question of church membership. Only 'real' Christians were members of the 'Church of Christ'. These were defined in somewhat varied terms, though the criteria for membership—conversion and regeneration—were clear enough. These 'real believers' were variously defined as the body of those called out of—and separated from—'the world';[7] as a congregation of God's faithful and elect;[8] and as a collection of true and faithful believers who have been called to eternal life by the Holy Spirit, and who concur on the fundamentals of the Christian faith.[9] Most Evangelicals also generally believed that

[5] Thomas Robinson, *The Christian System*, 3rd edn. (1825), iii.324–5.

[6] Ibid. 334; *CO* (1804), 28.

[7] Robinson, *The Christian System*, iii.324.

[8] *CO* (1804), 352; (1841), 270.

[9] Richard Hill, *An Apology for Brotherly Love, and for the Doctrines of the Church of England* (1798), 25–6, 156–7.

membership in the visible church was properly initiated by the sacrament of baptism, rightly received.[10]

But what was the relation of the 'real' to the merely 'nominal' Christians with whom they were associated in their membership of the National Church? As John Overton put it sharply in his influential work, *The True Churchmen Ascertained*: 'Either . . . the Church of England considers *all* persons real Christians who are comprehended within her external pale, or she considers only *some* of her visible members entitled to this character, and the rest mere nominal and professed Christians.'[11] Though operating within the structure of an Established Church which was open to all who had been baptized, and whose rubrical offices—such as those for baptism, marriage, and burial—were used indiscriminately for all, whether godly Evangelicals or unrepentant sinners, the Evangelicals inclined towards Overton's second category. They accepted that the elect were ultimately not to be infallibly distinguished from the regenerate in the terrestrial church: such judgment pertained ultimately to God (though strong assumptions could no doubt be made by an experienced pastor as to the true spiritual state of some individual members of a congregation). Here they had the teachings of the Protestant reformer John Calvin behind them. Everyone should understand, Calvin had maintained, that the visible church must be 'composed of good and bad men mingled together'.[12] Unlike the pastors of the 'gathered' churches of the Independents and Baptists, Anglican Evangelicals were generally committed to the principle that the wheat must be allowed to grow with the tares: that there could be no separation of 'visible saints' from the unregenerate lump. The presence of unregenerate individuals in the community of a church was no cause for secession from it. The ministry of the Word and administration of the sacraments, as Calvin had declared, 'have too much influence in preserving the unity of the church, to admit of its being destroyed by the guilt of a few impious men.'[13] Overton

[10] John Overton, *The True Churchmen Ascertained* (York, 1801), 103–4, 106; John H. Pratt (ed.), *Eclectic Notes* (1856), 368–72; Arthur Pollard and Michael Hennell (eds.), *Charles Simeon* (1959), 106–12; Hugh McNeile, *Lectures on the Church of England* (1840), 13–27; Thomas Scott, *Essays on the Most Important Subjects in Religion*, 10th edn. (1823), 212–13.

[11] Overton, *The True Churchmen Ascertained*, 102.

[12] John Calvin, *Institutes of Christian Religion* (Philadelphia, 1932), ii.235.

[13] Ibid. 238.

agreed that 'in the visible church the evil be ever mingled with the good.'[14] John Newton described the visible church in terms of a threshing-floor on which chaff is mingled with the wheat, or as a fisherman's net enclosing a great multitude of fish both good and bad.[15]

Evangelicals became indignant when High Churchmen like Charles Daubeny, and others, denounced them as 'Dissenters in the Church' whose loyalty to the Establishment was weak and grudging, and whose real place was with the Nonconformists outside her walls.[16] Much of the force of this accusation lay in the association of Evangelicals as a whole with the irregularity of the Methodists, and those early 'Gospel clergy' like William Grimshaw or John Berridge who were prepared to copy Wesley or Whitefield to the extent of field-preaching in other men's parishes. Though (as we shall see) irregularity still persisted here and there, this charge was manifestly unfair by the late eighteenth century, when most Evangelical parish clergy were scrupulously 'regular', dissociated themselves from Methodism, and kept their ministrations to their own parishes. But the charge of being 'Dissenters in disguise' also rested on the suggestion that the 'Gospel clergy' were grudging or secretly hostile in their attitude to much in the Church's polity and formularies. This was vehemently denied by the 'regular' Evangelicals. Overton's *The True Churchmen Ascertained*, repeated the claim, often made in the eighteenth century, that the Evangelical clergy were not merely clandestine Dissenters, but were actually 'the *true* churchmen', since they alone subscribed to the Calvinistic Thirty-Nine Articles and the homilies which explained them, in clear and unambiguous terms.[17] If the prime essential of true churchmanship was purity of doctrine, then the 'Gospel clergy' who accepted unequivocally the pure teachings of the Reformation were the true successors of Cranmer, Jewel, and the other Protestant teachers who founded the present reformed Church of England. If the test of Anglican orthodoxy was a doctrinal test, it was Daubeny and his staunch

[14] Overton, *The True Churchmen Ascertained*, 103.

[15] Newton, 'The Lord Reigneth', iv.406.

[16] Charles Daubeny, *A Guide to the Church* (1798); *Vindiciae Ecclesiae Anglicane* (1803); *On the Nature, Progress, and Consequences of Schism* (1818); Thomas Kipling, *The Articles of the Church of England Proved Not to be Calvinistic* (Cambridge, 1802).

[17] Overton, *The True Churchmen Ascertained*, pp. iv, xi, 397.

High Church allies who were the 'true Dissenters', for they had apostatized from the plain and unequivocal meaning of the Articles.[18]

By the end of the eighteenth century, especially after the outbreak of the French Revolution had created a conservative backlash in England, Evangelicals went out of their way to distance themselves from disorderly Methodism and Dissent, and to underline their devotion to the formularies and order of the Church. Various apologists praised the episcopal polity of the Church of England. Though episcopacy was not essential, for it pertained to the *bene esse* rather than the *esse* of the Church,[19] it was ancient, of apostolic origin, and, with its principle of hierarchy, far more suited to the ordering of fallen human nature than the 'republican' synodical system of the Presbyterians.[20] Before allowing her house guest, William Magee, the moderate Evangelical archbishop of Dublin, to depart from Barley Wood, Hannah More insisted upon an episcopal blessing, which she got.[21] In some quarters of the Evangelical world, in fact, the principle of apostolicity as a foundation for holy orders seems to have been held with a fervour which might have surprised later and post-Tractarian generations. In 1804, a correspondent of the major Evangelical publication, the *Christian Observer*, echoing the eighteenth-century High Churchman Jones of Nayland, claimed that the Church had been governed by bishops, priests, and deacons from apostolic times: where these orders were to be found duly appointed, *the Word preached*, and the sacraments administered, there the 'Church of Christ' was to be found, with its form and authority.[22] As late as 1836, in reviewing the Oxford *Tracts*, the *Christian Observer* reaffirmed its belief in the apostolic nature of the Anglican priesthood: 'The papists are continually renewing their charge of the invalidity of the claim of the Church of England to the seal of

[18] See also *CO* (1818), 12.

[19] Cf. Norman Sykes, *Old Priest and New Presbyter* (Cambridge, 1956), 5, 85–117.

[20] See *CO* (1803), 709–10; (1804), 1–4, 129–33; (1839), 287. See also Thomas Gisborne, *Familiar Survey of the Christian Religion* (1799), 347.

[21] William Magee, *The Works of the Most Reverend William Magee, D.D.*, ed. A. H. Kenny (1842), i, p. lxxiii. Magee's churchmanship remains subject to some scholarly debate. See Peter Nockles, 'Church or Protestant Sect? The Church of Ireland, High Churchmanship, and the Oxford Movement, 1822–1869', in the *Historical Journal*, 41/2 (1998), 461.

[22] *CO* (1804), 28; 352; (1805), 716. See also Robinson, *The Christian System*, iii.335; Gisborne, *Familiar Survey*, 354–5; T. R. Birks, *Memoir of the Revd Edward Bickersteth*, 2nd edn. (1852), i.99.

apostolic succession . . . We see no reason to doubt that the present bishops and clergy of the Church of England are descended in an unbroken line from the apostles of Christ, in a regular transmission of the ministerial function.'[23]

The Thirty-Nine Articles and the homilies also gained the warm assent of Evangelicals. Not only did several of the Articles appear to reflect the moderately 'Calvinistic' theology held by most Evangelicals, but they also expressed the fundamental principle of the reformers in ways that avoided extremes and kept to the true *via media* of the English Church.[24] The catechism was accepted equally warmly: it was so phrased as to do immense good.[25] The Anglican formularies were seen not only as scriptural,[26] but as an effective prophylactic against the introduction of heresy into the Church.[27]

Evangelical approval of the liturgy was fervent, though not without some qualifications which were often unexpressed, at least in public. Any doubts about its perfection were, however, counterbalanced by the suspicion that Prayer Book reform, if it came, might be pushed through by liberals such as the Feathers Tavern petitioners in the 1770s, or by extreme High Churchmen who would attempt to reform it along popish lines.[28] Henry Venn described the Anglican liturgy as the most excellent yet devised in Christendom and feared its possible alteration.[29] The *Christian Observer* maintained 'a filial veneration' for the liturgy, its editors declaring their joy in using the same words of prayer as their forefathers. The liturgical form of worship was sharply contrasted to that of extempore prayer, and praised for allowing less dependence upon man and more upon the Holy Spirit, and for affording little scope for personal display or for criticism of the

[23] *CO* (1836), 562; (1831), 383–4; (1834), 100. Cf. John Wesley, *The Letters of John Wesley*, ed. John Telford (1931), vii.284; Gisborne, *Familiar Survey*, 349–50.

[24] Hannah More, 'Hints Towards Forming the Character of a Young Princess', in *The Works of Hannah More* (1834), iv.351–2; T. R. Birks, *The Present Crisis* (1854), 9–10.

[25] See *CO* (1808), 764–6.

[26] John Morison, *The Fathers and Founders of the London Missionary Society*, 2nd edn. (1844), 26; Gisborne, *Familiar Survey*, 354–5; Birks, *Memoir of Edward Bickersteth*, i.99.

[27] Gisborne, *Familiar Survey*, 354–5.

[28] See William Goode, *Rome's Tactics* (1867), 98–100.

[29] Henry Venn, *The Life and a Selection of the Letters of the Late Revd Henry Venn, M.A.*, ed. Henry Venn, 2nd edn. (1835), 175–6. T. T. Biddulph, *Essays on Some Select Parts of the Liturgy of the Church of England* (Bristol, 1798); Basil Woodd, *The Excellence of the Liturgy* (1810); the *Pamphleteer*, 1812, 159–83; Birks, *Memoir of Edward Bickersteth*, i.99.

officiating clergyman.[30] The practice of common prayer was seen as essential to public worship: Hugh Stowell extolled the excellencies of the liturgy and criticized those who came to church primarily to hear the sermon.[31] Charles Simeon, who was wont to proclaim, 'the Bible first, the Prayer Book next, and all other books and doings in subordination to both',[32] lauded the Anglican prayers as his personal 'marrow and fatness'.[33] He advised the young men at his famous conversation parties: 'pray the prayers and don't read them only; adhere sacredly to the directions of the rubric, except where they have become obsolete, and the resumption of them would clearly do harm.'[34] When William Ward, bishop of Sodor and Man, chanced upon a communion service at Holy Trinity, Simeon instinctively administered both elements to him alone before administering to the remainder of the congregation, justifying his action on the basis of strict adherence to the Prayer Book rubric.[35] Though the wording of the burial service worried some scrupulous Evangelicals, most accepted it. While extolling the benefits of the Prayer Book in a lecture at Great St. Mary's, Simeon defended the use of the burial service over an unrepentant man, 'because we speak not of *his*, but of *the*, resurrection to eternal life; and because, where we do not absolutely *know* that God has *not* pardoned a person, we may entertain *some* measure of hope that he *has*.'[36] He similarly accepted the rubric for baptism, urging that the remission of our sins and the regeneration of our souls was attendant on it—cautioning, however, that the Prayer Book insisted upon a further change in a believer's heart.[37]

There were, as we shall see again and again, barely concealed difficulties in the liturgy. Evangelicals willingly conceded that it was a human composition and as such imperfect.[38] Some disliked the Athanasian Creed. Simeon admitted that some scrupulous

[30] *CO* (1820), 76.

[31] Hugh Stowell, *The Excellencies of the English Liturgy* (1865), 4.

[32] Charles Smyth, *Simeon and Church Order* (Cambridge, 1940), 291.

[33] William Carus, *Memoirs of the Life of the Revd Charles Simeon, M.A.*, 3rd edn. (1848), 210.

[34] Abner William Brown, *Recollections of the Conversation Parties of the Revd Charles Simeon, M.A.* (1863), 12.

[35] Ibid. 12–13.

[36] Charles Simeon, *The Excellency of the Liturgy* (Cambridge, 1812), 44.

[37] Ibid. 47–51.

[38] Brown, *Recollections*, 221; *CO* (1805), 732; Hannah More, *Remarks on the Speech of M. Dupont* (1793), 20.

Christians had seceded from the Church because of the defects in the Prayer Book, 'in the hope of finding a purer worship elsewhere'.[39] Even among the clergy loyal to the Church, it was often conceded that popish survivals still remained which ought one day to be removed.[40] These comments became more open after the onset of the Oxford Movement, when it became apparent that these 'blemishes' were being exploited by Tractarians and Ritualists. This unease led to the publication of at least twenty revisions of the Prayer Book between 1842 and 1894, mostly by embattled ultra-Evangelicals.[41]

Despite the presence of minor imperfections in the Church and its formularies, most Evangelicals remained adamant that secession to Protestant Dissent was unjustified. Although their catholic spirit could readily countenance fellowship with evangelical Dissenters, they regarded the Church as immeasurably superior to Nonconformity. Dissent was seen as unbalanced and prone to constant schism. In its chapels, Simeon and others alleged, the congregation held a dangerous whip hand over its minister, whose salary it provided, and so prevented him from preaching the Gospel fearlessly in the way possible to the clergy in a State Church whose incomes came from endowments and tithes.[42]

The Dissent of evangelical Christians was seen as essentially unnecessary.[43] It was not to be compared to the separation of the Church of England from the Church of Rome which had apostatized from the faith, for the foundations of the English Church were pure and reformed. Those who went over to Dissent were schismatics who divided the body of Christ. None the less, the Evangelical clergy urged their people to treat Dissenters with charity and kindliness and not to anathematize them in the style of some High Churchmen. Since much Dissent stemmed from the lack of 'real' religion in the Church, the best way to prevent its further progress was for the Established clergy to out-preach their rivals by a fervent exposition of the Gospel.[44]

[39] Simeon, *The Excellency of the Liturgy*, 71–8.

[40] John Scott, *Reformation, Not Subversion* (1831).

[41] See A. Elliott Peaston, *The Prayer Book Revisions of the Victorian Evangelicals* (Dublin, 1963), 2.

[42] Brown, *Recollections*, 221–2.

[43] Pratt, *Eclectic Notes*, 3–6.

[44] Ibid. 180–3.

I

However loyal they might be to the Church of England and its formularies, it was impossible for Evangelicals to ignore the issue of establishment, especially when the campaign for Test Act repeal surfaced once more in the 1780s, and when active political campaigns for disestablishment followed in the wake of the Reform Bill crisis in the 1830s.[45] By nature, Evangelicals were happiest when engaged in 'soul-saving'; like Hannah More they regarded 'the unpleasant and boundless fields of controversy' accompanying the establishment debate as best left to others, since engagement in controversy only embittered relations with the Dissenters whom they were trying to woo. 'Far be it from me', she wrote, 'to stand forth the fierce champion of a liturgy, or the prejudiced advocate of forms and systems. A sincere member of the establishment myself, I respect its institutions without idolatry, and acknowledge its imperfections without palliation.'[46] When Evangelicals did comment on the issue, their statements were usually defensive and pragmatic, more concerned with the pastoral utility of a national religious provision than with the claim that the Church of England had any exclusive right to the promulgation of religious truth. Yet the increasing stridency of political Dissent, especially after the formation of the Anti-State Church Association (later the Liberation Society) in 1844, forced them into periodic defence of their position.

Evangelicals defined establishment in a number of different, though usually not discordant terms. One of the most succinct yet comprehensive definitions was provided by the *Christian Observer* in 1839. A valid establishment was one founded on:

> Articles of belief and sacramental institutions, as well as moral principles, collected and arranged out of the inspired volume, and deriving their authority from their incontrovertible accordance with its announcements. There must also be a body of men, including a gradation of officers, whose business it is to teach the truths—to administer the ordinances, and to inculcate the precepts, thus drawn forth from the volume of inspiration. To these men . . . will belong the duty of setting forth

[45] For a survey of the disestablishment campaign, especially in its later stages, see William H. Mackintosh, *Disestablishment and Liberation* (1972).

[46] Hannah More, *An Estimate of the Religion of the Fashionable World*, 3rd edn. (1791), 4–5.

national Articles of faith . . . and of determining rites, ceremonies, and functional polity . . . Towards the effective workings of a system, which is thus to be co-extensive with the community by which it has been adopted, an adequate provision for its ministers and the maintenance of public worship are indispensably necessary.[47]

The Evangelicals' defence of their own establishment drew on a wide variety of arguments, some of them derivative and commonplace, others stemming more directly from Evangelical piety. Inevitably, the arguments from Scripture had their place, for no major commitment could be undertaken without the confidence that it had biblical sanction of some kind.[48] The English Church was established, claimed Charles Girdlestone, the Evangelical vicar of Sedgley, 'not only by the law of the land, but by the Gospel of Jesus Christ. Its ministers have that appointment which at the first came from Him.'[49] As we shall see, the argument from Scripture was not entirely straightforward, since disestablishmentarian Dissenters were capable of using it to oppose the Church–State connection. The religious opponents of establishment understandably made much of the lack of government support in the New Testament era and in the centuries of persecution that followed it, pointing out that the Church was most pure while it was free of State control: it was Constantine's elevation of Christianity into a State religion that had corrupted it into a worldly institution. For their part, Evangelicals often based their reply on the precedents of the Old Testament.[50] Here in ancient Israel could be found the close, covenanted union of Church and State. Hugh McNeile developed the idea that since God had appointed those in power—notably the Crown as head of the Church—the State maintained a concomitant and sacred duty to promote Christianity.[51] When this contractual obligation was fulfilled, God would grant His favour and protection to the State.[52] To Evangelicals steeped in the parallelism between ancient

[47] *CO* (1839), 287. [48] *CO* (1826), 343.

[49] Charles Girdlestone, *Church Rates Lawful, But Not Always Expedient* (1833), 11. See also *Three Letters on Church Reform* (1832–4).

[50] Thomas Scott, *A Letter* (Kilkenny, 1816), 21–2; *CG* (1824), 385–6; the *Record*, 19 Feb. 1849; William Marsh, *The Church and the State* (1849), p. xiii.

[51] Hugh McNeile, *Letters to a Friend* (1834), 17; *The Church and the Churches* (1846), 532, 547–8, 558 n; Daniel Wilson, *A Farewell Charge*, 2nd edn. (1845), 24–5; the *Record*, 23 July 1838.

[52] R. B. Seeley, *Essays on the Church* (1834), 103; More, 'Hints', *The Works*, iv.348.

Israel and modern England—the 'elect nation' favoured of God—the idea of the covenanted people came easily, as it had done to their forebears. The divine blessings were seen to flow from the contractual relationship with Jehovah. The establishment and maintenance of true religion would advance the authority and stability of the State, check lawlessness and insubordination, and encourage patriotic love of country.[53] By ensuring that the State had a moral and spiritual basis in the Christian faith, establishment would control arrogance and pride among the governors of the realm and encourage them to seek God's will in affairs of State. Only religion, firmly grounded in State sustenance, could restrain sinful human nature and place before the conscience those offers of eternal reward and punishment that would stabilize society and preserve it from anarchy and lawlessness.

More important than arguments from civil prudence were those based on the spiritual and pastoral benefits of establishment. The huge advantages to be gained from the nationwide coverage of the parochial system were well appreciated.[54] Moreover, the existence of legally binding rubrics and confessional doctrines ensured continuity of pure teaching in a parish and helped to prevent schism.[55] The Scottish evangelical Thomas Chalmers, perhaps the greatest influence of his day on the issue, claimed that establishment provided 'ducts of conveyance' for irrigating the nation with divine grace through the reading and the preaching of Scripture.[56] Thanks to provision of clergy and churches across the whole landscape of England, Wales, and Ireland by the State, no person could be considered as outside the ministrations of the Established Church. The contrary principle of voluntarism was described by the *Christian Observer* as 'infidel and practically

[53] See Wilson, *A Farewell Charge*, 24–5; Samuel Charles Wilks, *Correlative Claims and Duties*, (1821), 25; Marsh, *The Church and the State*, p. xxi; *CO* (1823), 722; Robinson, *The Christian System*, iii.337; McNeile, *Lectures on the Church of England*, 160–1; McNeile, *Letters to a Friend*, p. xii; C. Marsh, *The Life of the Revd William Marsh, D.D.* (1867), 154; More, 'Hints', *The Works*, iv.354. See also Joseph Milner, *The History of the Church of Christ* (York and Cambridge, 1794–1809), ii.232.

[54] Scott, *A Letter*, 30; More, 'Hints', *The Works*, iv.349–50; Wilks, *Correlative Claims and Duties*, 25–38; the *Record*, 18 Oct. 1830.

[55] Robert Isaac Wilberforce and Samuel Wilberforce, *The Life of William Wilberforce* (1838), ii.27; James Bean, *Zeal Without Innovation* (1808), 24; Wilks, *Correlative Claims and Duties*, 69–109; *CO* (1808), 223–6.

[56] Thomas Chalmers, 'Lectures on the Establishment and Extension of National Churches', 1838, in *The Collected Works of Thomas Chalmers* (Glasgow, 1835–42), xvii.196.

ineffective'.[57] On the basis of Chalmers's famous lectures on establishments, the Evangelicals argued that under a voluntarist system of 'ecclesiastical free trade', religion only went to those who demanded it and were prepared to pay for it, and not to the mass of spiritually destitute who, bound by their sinfulness, did not demand it, even though they needed it most. Only that religion which was provided by an establishment could seek out irreligion in its darkest pockets and corners.[58]

Evangelicals had little time for those who praised the American 'experiment' of separating Church and State. Many Dissenters, on the other hand, held up the example of the United States as a model of Church–State relations. Since the American constitution had prohibited federal support for any religious confession, religion had not withered but had prospered: evangelical piety, it seemed, flourished far more under a system of free, unfettered competition then it did in Europe, where crippling legal constraints and corrupt political association with an aristocratic ruling order held it back. Evangelicals rejected this thesis.[59] Only a national establishment could provide religious instruction for the mass of those too poor to pay for it, or cope with the vast areas of rural England virtually unserved by voluntarism.

There were other less visible but still important advantages of establishment. The legal, parliamentary foundation of the Church's teaching meant that her sacred formularies would be constitutionally preserved against the encroachments of religious heresy, whether socinian or popish.[60] Continuity of teaching would be maintained.[61] Though the Anglican Establishment had no monopoly of religious truth (for the Reformation doctrines could also be found among Methodists and Dissenters, as well as in the Scots Kirk), Evangelicals supported it because it seemed to them to rest on the bedrock of Reformation truth. Without this guarantee of doctrinal purity, the principle of establishment by itself would have had little intrinsic appeal.

[57] *CO* (1839), 287. See also More, 'Hints', *The Works*, iv.348.

[58] See Wilberforce, *Life of William Wilberforce*, ii.401.

[59] *CO* (1807), 54; (1826), 343–4; Wilson, *A Farewell Charge*, 25.

[60] McNeile, *Letters to a Friend*, p. xiii; Marsh, *The Church and the State*, pp. ix, xxi;. Gisborne, *Familiar Survey*, 354–5; More, 'Hints', *The Works*, iv.349, 354; *CO* (1832), 561; Ian S. Rennie, 'Evangelicalism and English Public Life, 1832–50', Ph.D. thesis (Toronto, 1962), 310.

[61] Wilberforce, *Life of William Wilberforce*, ii.401; *CO* (1806), 630; (1821), 625; (1835), 84.

The Evangelicals' commitment to the principle of establishment was sufficiently pronounced to convince Charles Simeon, amongst others, to conform to the Kirk (rather than the Episcopal Church) while travelling in Scotland.[62] Nevertheless this basic loyalty did not preclude some reservations about both the concept and the workings of the Church–State connection. Hannah More, Thomas Gisborne, and others admitted that establishments, as human institutions, are necessarily imperfect.[63] As Henry Ryder, the first Evangelical bishop, warned his clergy, 'committed to earthen and tainted vessels, the administration of the "sincere milk of the Word" cannot fail to contract a stain from the vehicles in which it is dispensed'.[64]

As the great Scottish Disruption illustrated, the issue of State 'intrusion' was the point at which an Evangelical's duty as a member of the Establishment could most sharply conflict with his conscience and his right of private judgement. How should an Evangelical respond when the State attempted to impose an unsuitable clergyman upon a parish, or even a 'heretical' doctrine opposed by Scripture? Who was to formulate Christian doctrine, the State or the Church? As Thomas Scott succinctly put it: 'we may lawfully worship, and officiate as ministers, in an *establishment*; provided that establishment does not require of us things in other respects contrary to our consciences.'[65] The real problem, in the opinion of Hugh McNeile, came when the State transgressed the scriptural limits of its authority in doctrinal matters. This, far more than obedience in matters comparatively indifferent, such as those of ritual, was the crux:

> The Church has scriptural authority to decree rites and ceremonies, *in addition* to what is contained in Scripture, provided there be nothing in them '*contrary* to God's Word written'. But the Church has no authority to enforce any doctrine in addition to what is contained in Holy Scripture. Doctrines in addition to the Bible must be rejected for conscience sake. But ceremonies in addition to, and not in opposition to the Bible,

[62] Carus, *Memoirs of Charles Simeon*, 90; Anon., *A Brief Memoir of the Late Revd William Richardson*, 2nd edn. (1822), 30 n.

[63] More, *Remarks on the Speech of M. Dupont*, 17; Gisborne, *Familiar Survey*, 355–6; Scott, *A Letter*, 20–1.

[64] Henry Ryder, *A Charge* (Stafford, 1828), 7.

[65] Scott, 'A Letter', in Peter Roe (ed.), *The Evil of Separation from the Church of England Considered* (Kilkenny, 1815), 29.

if decreed by the ruler, must be received, adopted, and practiced, for conscience sake.[66]

Fortunately for the Evangelical clergy, he added, 'this distinction is fully recognized, and very happily expressed', in the twentieth Article of the Church of England.[67] Thomas Chalmers, who led the opposition to State intrusion in Scotland at the time of the Disruption, agreed that although the Church should willingly and rightfully receive all its maintenance from the civil power, 'it follows not that it therefore receives its theology from the same quarter; or that this theology should acquire thereby the slightest taint of infusion of secularity.'[68] Despite such resolves, most English Evangelicals (as we will see) capitulated to repeated examples of State intrusion during the first half of the nineteenth century. But not all. The question of unacceptable Erastianism set in motion the reluctant secession of a number of 'Gospel clergy' from the Church.

II

Few eighteenth-century Evangelicals needed to articulate their views on the establishment in any sustained and formal manner. For the most part, the principle of establishment was taken for granted, assumed rather than actively contemplated. The early decades of the Evangelical Revival were not years in which the Church perceived itself to be under siege. There was little challenge from Dissent—declining or stagnant until the 1780s—while Methodism under Wesley remained within the boundaries of the Established Church. Then, however, in the 1790s, a sharper degree of self-consciousness entered into the Evangelical view of establishment. The Dissenting campaign for repeal of the Test and Corporation Acts between 1787 and 1790 created something of a panic concerning the future of the old order in Church and State, particularly as some of its leaders were 'rational Dissenters' like Capell Lofft whose views on the Trinity were suspect.[69] The connection of Unitarianism with democratic politics and

[66] McNeile, *Letters to a Friend*, 46–7.

[67] Ibid. 47. This Article granted to the Church power to decree rites or ceremonies, and authority in controversies of faith. At the same time, it prohibited the Church from advancing any doctrine that is contrary to God's written Word.

[68] Chalmers, *Lectures on the Establishment and Extension of National Churches*, xvii.197.

[69] Norman Sykes, *Church and State in England in the XVIII Century* (Cambridge, 1934), 341–2.

'Jacobinism' in activists like Joseph Priestley and renegade Anglicans such as Gilbert Wakefield and John Horne Tooke increased the alarm. So too did the remarkable upsurge of Methodism and evangelical Nonconformity in the 1790s. Suddenly it seemed not impossible that, if this trend continued, the Church of England might become a minority body—like the Church of Ireland—and be doomed to disestablishment on numerical grounds.

The 1790s and the Napoleonic wars produced a flurry of Evangelical affirmations in defence of the Church of England, its Thirty-Nine Articles, its liturgy, and its civil connection. Hannah More's influential work *Village Politics* (1793) extolled the benevolent virtues of a strict social and religious hierarchy in which the parish church—undergirded by its Established status—played a vital role. Joseph Milner's celebrated *Church History* (1794–1809) claimed that the supreme civil power had a right to establish 'the true religion by positive institutions', to ensure 'public respect to these institutions by penal laws', and to 'restrain and punish the propagators of irreligious opinions'.[70]

In the post-war years Evangelical fears for the future of establishment seemed to have receded somewhat, though there still seemed a possibility that godless English radicals might one day pull down throne and altar. The potential challenge of evangelical Dissent seems temporarily to have diminished. It became clear that Wesleyan Methodism—by far the largest grouping outside the Church—was still in favour of the Establishment principle: under the control of Jabez Bunting and his allies it was not disposed to threaten the existing order in Church or State.[71] Dissent in general seemed politically innocuous. When Nonconformist disabilities under the Test and Corporation Acts were lifted in 1828, Evangelicals for the most part shared the view of Parliament and the episcopate that Nonconformity presented little threat to the Anglican Establishment. Few heeded the warnings of the high Tory Evangelical Sir Robert Harry Inglis that the Tests should be retained as a bulwark against any further attack on the Church.[72]

This complacency was rudely shattered by the sudden resurgence of political Dissent in the Reform Bill crisis. Dissenting

[70] Milner, *The History of the Church of Christ*, ii.232.

[71] David Hempton, *Methodism and Politics in British Society 1750–1850* (1984), 185–90.

[72] Rennie, 'Evangelicalism and English Public Life', 111.

demands for complete equality and for disestablishment came to many Evangelicals as a bolt of lightening from a clear sky. The editors of the *Record*, for instance, declared that they would never have supported repeal of the Tests if they had 'believed that it added any real power to the Dissenters to the disadvantage of the Church'; still less if they had thought 'that it was tantamount to a casting off of the allegiance which this Kingdom professed to Christ and His religion.'[73] The attack on the establishment principle was no longer led by 'radical Dissenters', but by evangelical Dissenters—the very Christians with whom Evangelicals rubbed shoulders at Bible Society or anti-slavery meetings—devout men like Edward Miall and Thomas Binney. It was all the more disturbing for that.

What made the polemic of the evangelical opponents of establishment particularly alarming was their apparent link with dangerous democratic movements, particularly to the pressure-group politics of the middle-class radicals of the Anti-Corn Law League. Their willingness to co-operate with Roman Catholics, socinians, and other secular radicals, who were sometimes anti-clerical or even (like the Owenites) anti-Christian, in bringing down the Church only served to convince Evangelicals that disestablishment might be the prelude to national apostasy and godlessness.[74] The Evangelicals' defence of establishment, therefore, was prompted by fears about the destructive potential of the campaigners against the great institutions of Church and State, as well as by their positive belief in the superiority of the Church and its civil connection. They came to see disestablishment not as a movement which aimed to restore civil and religious rights, but as a force for irreligion.

Though agreed on the need to preserve the Established Church, Evangelicals differed over the best way to achieve their objective. Especially from the late 1820s the movement tended (as we will see) to fragment into divergent sub-groupings, between which there was a marked degree of friction. This cleavage was especially apparent between the so-called 'Recordites'—who followed the lead of the ultra-Protestant and conservative periodical the *Record*—and those more moderate Evangelicals whose views

[73] The *Record*, 29 July 1828.

[74] Hugh McNeile, *Speech* (Edinburgh, 1844), 4, 6–15; the *Record*, 18 Oct. 1830. See also *CO* (1837), 62–3. Hugh Stowell, 'Speech' (1843), in the *Pulpit*, 43, 440.

were expressed by the *Christian Observer*, organ of the pragmatic Clapham coterie. The liberal leanings of the 'Christian Observer school'—which favoured the passage of both the Catholic Emancipation and the Reform Bills—were rejected by the 'Recordites', who demanded a more resolute opposition to the solvent acids of political liberalism: a more dogmatic and Calvinistic theology than that offered by Charles Simeon and his like, and a more vigorous defence of the existing order in Church and State. At the opposite extreme to the *Record*—and far removed from the moderate, Whiggishly-inclined establishmentarianism of the *Christian Observer*—was the small party gathered around the mercurial Evangelical philanthropist Sir Culling Eardley. In December 1839, Sir Culling, who came to believe that disestablishment would be beneficial for the Church as well as an aid in evangelism, founded the Voluntary Church Association, a body committed to uniting churchmen and Dissenters in campaigning for the disestablishment of the Church of England.[75] The Association, which was firmly denounced by the *Christian Observer* and by many other Evangelicals,[76] issued a series of tracts to further their cause, as well as a monthly paper, the *Voluntary* (which merged, after 1846, with the *Christian Examiner*).

In 1832 the Christian Influence Society, dominated by the 'Recordite' Alexander Gordon, was founded in order 'to give a right direction to the public mind on the subject of religion and morals and the general state of society'.[77] It encouraged a number of Evangelicals (by no means all of them 'Recordites') to publish works defending the Church and its civil connection, and there were numerous responses, most notably William Dealtry's *The Importance of the Established Church* (1832), and *An Argument for a Church Establishment* (1833) by William Scholefield, Regius Professor of Greek at Cambridge.

Both writers made full use of the pragmatic, pastoral arguments for establishment, many of which were familiar enough. Rhetorically, Dealtry placed the counterfactual hypothesis before his readers: what would England be like *without* a State religion? He

[75] G. I. T. Machin, *Politics and Churches in Great Britain 1832 to 1868* (Oxford, 1977), 107; Mackintosh, *Disestablishment and Liberation*, 8.

[76] *CO* (1846), 604–11.

[77] In addition to the less important Established Church Society, also founded by Evangelicals two years later. See Rennie, 'Evangelicalism and English Public Life', 300.

was in no doubt of the answer: it would be a moral desert, punctuated only by a few haphazardly scattered oases. Moreover, a legally constituted National Church, whose doctrinal formulae were guaranteed by act of Parliament, would be unlikely to defect from the principles of the Gospel. Voluntary churches, on the other hand, could and did apostatize—witness the declension of the old Presbyterian churches into Unitarianism. As long as the Church of England remained established, it would remain 'the depository of that sacred fire which she received from the altar of the Lord.'[78]

Scholefield, exulting in the universal pastoral superintendence conferred by establishment, argued that the withdrawal of that nationwide clerical coverage would lead England back to virtual paganism, especially in the great cities.[79] He rejected the claim of the voluntaries that the vigorous state of religion in the United States proved the efficacy of the separation of Church and State. Most existing evidence, he argued, was drawn from the state of religion in some of the great American cities: it ignored the appalling spiritual destitution of the myriad scattered and isolated settlements in its villages and forests.[80]

The most celebrated exponent of the case for establishment on the ground of pastoral utility was Thomas Chalmers, whom the Christian Influence Society induced to deliver his celebrated *Lectures on the Establishment and Extension of National Churches* during April and May 1838.[81] 'It may be well in commerce, that markets should be left to find their own spontaneous level', Chalmers asserted in the second of his lectures, 'but it is not well that matters should thus be left in Christianity—else no attempt will be made, either to instruct the poor or to reclaim the profligate.'[82] Government had a duty to encourage the spread of Christianity throughout the land; voluntarism could not take over this responsibility, for it functioned only to meet the demands of those who already possessed religious concern and the means to afford pew rents, while neglecting the

[78] William Dealtry, *The Importance of the Established Church* (1832), p. xviii. Dealtry was John Venn's successor as rector of Clapham and later became Archdeacon of Surrey.

[79] James Scholefield, *An Argument for a Church Establishment* (Cambridge, 1833), 11.

[80] Ibid. 16.

[81] See Stewart J. Brown, *Thomas Chalmers and the Godly Commonwealth in Scotland* (Oxford, 1982), 269–71.

[82] Chalmers, 'Lectures on the Establishment', in *The Collected Works of Thomas Chalmers*, xvii.246.

irreligious, the ignorant, and the poor. Religion was not like trade, which followed the laws of supply and demand, for those who needed it most—the poor and the ignorant—demanded it least. The premiss for 'ecclesiastical free trade' was a flawed one: it left out the vital fact of human depravity and natural dislike of God's Word. Chalmers's most impassioned argument was directed against the government's rejection of Church extension—an issue on which the Kirk enjoyed the support of the great mass of the Scottish people. He warned that such insensitivity to the unfranchised poor, who were often ignored by Parliament, would not be tolerated by the Established clergy, who would continue to fight on their behalf to ensure the extension of religion.

Chalmers's six lectures were a celebrated success,[83] though the backlash was swift and severe. William Gladstone (now a High Churchman) published a work on establishment which was decidedly unsympathetic to Chalmers's use of severely utilitarian arguments on behalf of establishment.[84] The various 'voluntary' journals were, of course, highly critical of the lectures, and the Dissenting Deputies quickly set up a subcommittee to present the counter case for voluntarism.[85] Ralph Wardlaw, an able Scottish Congregational minister from Glasgow, was appointed by the Deputies to deliver a series of lectures in reply to Chalmers, and these were delivered in London in April and May 1839 to equally large and enthusiastic audiences.[86]

Wardlaw set out his argument by juxtaposing the unscriptural nature and intrinsic unfairness of establishment, against the scriptural nature and numerous advantages of voluntarism. The principle of establishment, whether defined by Chalmers in terms of pastoral utility, or Gladstone in terms of a *national personality*, or

[83] See Owen Chadwick, 'Chalmers and the State', in A. C. Cheyne (ed.), *The Practical and the Pious* (Edinburgh, 1985), 65–83. See also W. Hannah, *Memories of Dr Chalmers* (Edinburgh, 1849–52), iv.37–46.

[84] W. E. Gladstone, *The State in its Relations with the Church* (1838). Although welcomed by some Evangelicals as an aid to the campaign, the work was censured by others, including the *CO* (1839), 126, 286), for exalting episcopal churches above established (but non-episcopal) bodies, such as the Scottish Kirk. See also John Morley, *The Life of William Ewart Gladstone* (1903), i.171–2.

[85] Bernard Lord Manning, *The Protestant Dissenting Deputies* (Cambridge, 1952), 389; *Voluntary Church Magazine* (Oct. 1838), 433–41; *Presbyterian Review* (Jan. 1840), 398–429.

[86] Manning, *The Protestant Dissenting Deputies*, 390. Wardlaw's lectures were quickly published, with over 11,000 copies being printed. See ibid. 390–1; Ralph Wardlaw, *National Church Establishments Examined* (1839).

Coleridge in terms of a *national civilization establishment*, should be rejected by Christians as unsound and contradictory. The voluntary principle, on the other hand, was instinctive to a man's nature; a matter of free will and not coercive; it exemplified the inner spiritual freedom set out in the New Testament as the model for the Christian church; and was more likely to provide the English Church with increased efficiency, spiritual purity, and independence from civil intrusion.

Sensing that they had lost the momentum in the debate over establishment, the Christian Influence Society arranged for another set of lectures to be delivered during March 1840 in the same rooms as Chalmers's earlier triumph. Hugh McNeile, the combative Irish Evangelical perpetual curate of St. Jude's, Liverpool, was one of the most articulate and prolific defenders of establishment in England.[87] His *Lectures on the Church of England* succeeded in raising the debate to the higher ground occupied by Wardlaw by setting forth the biblical and historical basis of the English establishment.[88] He underscored the claim that the establishment of the Church of England rested not merely on its utility—as Chalmers had demonstrated—but on *truth*.[89] Its clergy were part of a great historical succession traceable back to apostolic times,[90] its liturgy was an aid to worship,[91] its formularies ensured continuance of proper doctrine,[92] and its endowments gave the means of disseminating the Gospel in places untouched by voluntarism.[93] 'We recognize a commandment to baptize *nations*,' he claimed, 'to cast a net which enclosed not good fish only, but bad also . . . We recognize, therefore, a demand for *outward means*, not upon a congregational scale only, but on a national scale.'[94] This great task was beyond the reach of the

[87] Besides those works cited above see Hugh McNeile, 'The True Scriptural Ground and Limits of Church Authority' (1830), in the *Pulpit*, 14: 293–9; 'The Danger of the Church of Ireland' (1832), in the *Pulpit*, 19: 17–26; 'Church Reform' (1832), in the *Pulpit*, 19: 254–62; 'The Constitutional and Ritual of the Church of England Defended' (1834), in the *Pulpit*, 23: 241–50; 'Church Endowments Defended Both Upon Scriptural and Secular Grounds' (1834), in the *Pulpit*, 23: 289–304; 'Church Endowments Defended' (1834), in the *Pulpit*, 30: 321–33; *The Church Establishment* (1837); 'The Scriptural Warrant for an Established Church' (1837), in the *Pulpit*, 30: 269–79; *The Church and the Churches* (1846).

[88] McNeile, *Lectures on the Church of England*. For the Dissenting response see George Redford, *Christianity Against Coercion* (1840).

[89] McNeile, *Lectures on the Church of England*, 5, 147–99.

[90] Ibid. 56–62.

[91] Ibid. 104–13. [92] Ibid. 113–16, 272. [93] Ibid. 204–8. [94] Ibid. 165.

voluntary principle. McNeile dismissed Wardlaw's claim that the Jewish theocracy was no precedent for a modern constitutional monarchy in a liberal state: that Israel showed a national establishment 'so peculiar and *unique* as to place it beyond the reach of imitation'.[95] Far from it. The ancient Jewish state was, *pari passu*, always a paradigm for the modern Christian state. National worship and a national priesthood remained the model which, though in modern variations and forms, must be accepted as the divine model.[96]

III

With such arguments, the great mass of Evangelicals remained content. The patriarchal theocratic argument helped to satisfy the high Tories of a paternalist cast of thought, while the argument from utility convinced those who were more in tune with the pragmatic liberalism of the age of Russell and Peel. Yet, as we shall see, not all Evangelicals were convinced. The scriptural case for establishment was as vigorously denied—by impeccably evangelical Dissenters who were manifestly members of the 'Church of Christ'—as it was affirmed by the Evangelicals of the Church. The battle of texts was inconclusive. The argument from utility was even more keenly two-edged. If establishments were said to promote the extension of the Gospel, it was by no means clear that the existing establishment of the Church of England did not also hinder evangelism, tying it to a corrupt patronage system in Church and State, and preventing the evangelization of the people by its stiff-necked legalism. Perhaps the example of the United States was more valid than churchmen cared to admit? The basic weakness in the ideological defence of establishment by Evangelicals was (at least in the view of many High Churchmen) that at its heart it had a comparatively low theory of the terrestrial or 'visible' churches. The interests of the invisible 'Church of Christ' remained always paramount. No terrestrial church form, no particular polity or order, was exclusive or even *jure divino*. Evangelicals admitted that the existing Church of England, though it rested on excellent foundations, was very far from perfect and in need of considerable reform. Hugh McNeile

[95] Ibid. 171.

[96] See also T. R. Birks, *The Christian State: Or the First Principles of National Religion* (1847).

admitted in his defence of the Church that some clergy did not live up to their calling, that the appointment of bishops smacked of Erastianism, and that the liturgy contained embarrassing blemishes (which, he suggested, should be put in brackets and allowed to be omitted by scrupulous Evangelicals).[97] It remained a legitimate inference from Evangelical ecclesiology that if the Gospel could be proclaimed more effectively outside the establishment, or in a regime in which Church and State were separated, then the zealous Christian might have to abandon a moribund State Church. As we shall see, not a few 'Gospel clergymen' accepted the logic of this position.

[97] McNeile, *Lectures on the Church of England*, 245–9, 262.

2
The Impulse to Secession

Very few of the early leaders of the Evangelical Revival were separatists in principle. They accepted the idea of a National Church by law established, and firmly rejected the separatist idea of true churches as small local bodies of 'visible saints' gathered out of the unregenerate world. The early Methodist leaders believed that a national reformation would be best accomplished by a revival within the National Church; their aim was to leaven the Anglican lump, not to found a new denomination. Wesley thought that the Puritans had failed to regenerate the country because they had hived off the 'godly ones' into conventicles, abandoning the task of converting the whole nation to concentrate on the sanctification of the small minority of their own sectarian 'saints'. If the converts of the Revival were to follow the same course, he argued, they would dwindle into narrow sectarianism and marginality.[1] Thus Wesley's deep loyalty to the Church was partly due to his belief that its parochial structure would be of great assistance in transforming the nation's spiritual state.[2] Most Evangelicals also found Puritan scrupulosity over issues of ritual and liturgy difficult to comprehend. It was for Wesley a weakness in the godly men of the seventeenth century that they spent 'much of their time and strength in disputing about surplices and hoods, or kneeling at the Lord's Supper'.[3]

In some important respects it was easier for a vigorous conversionist reforming group to exist in the eighteenth-century Church than it had been in the late seventeenth. There were few checks from the authorities in Church and State. By the time the Revival broke out in the late 1730s, moderation and Latitudinarianism

[1] *The Works of John Wesley*, ed. Thomas Jackson, 3rd edn. (1831), vii.278, 427–8.

[2] See John Wesley, 'Reasons Against a Separation From the Church of England' (1758), in *CO* (1805), 139–43; Frank Baker, *William Grimshaw 1708–63* (1963), 250–1.

[3] Entry of 13 Mar. 1747, in *The Journal of John Wesley*, ed. Nehemiah Curnock (1938), iii.286.

were in the ascendant. Walpole and the Pelhams, like their Whig episcopate, were disinclined to stir up Church affairs by high-handed actions: sleeping dogs were left to lie, as far as possible, in Church and State. The religious temperature dropped. The absence of Convocation after 1717 removed an arena of clerical controversy, and thus made partisanship and group intolerance harder to sustain. The decentralization of the Church made collective condemnation very difficult to mount. Episcopal discipline was usually mild. Heterodox clerics were generally ignored and left alone. Spectacularly irregular reformers like Wesley and—even more so—Whitefield remained largely immune from prosecution, let alone expulsion, and died as fully accredited clergymen of the Established Church.

Nevertheless, the role of the Evangelical clergyman in the eighteenth-century Church was not an easy one. If episcopal prosecution was seldom forthcoming, it was always there, in reserve, as a threat. Evangelicals found themselves ostracized by colleagues and ridiculed by neighbours. Not infrequently they were attacked in visitation sermons as they sat silent beneath the pulpit. They were often cut off from patronage: many served as low-paid curates or in obscure parishes. Their Calvinistic doctrine was often denounced as 'enthusiasm'. Though reformed theology had been dominant in the Church until the Restoration, it had been largely overlaid after 1660 by Arminianism, whether that of Laudian High Churchmen, or Latitudinarians. When the Evangelicals attempted to restore a Calvinistic interpretation of the Articles they were continually told by those in authority that their theology was un-Anglican; it was the teaching of seventeenth-century Puritan regicides and modern Dissenters, but not that of the Church of England. It is hardly surprising therefore that many early Evangelicals were seized from time to time by a strong sense of loneliness and isolation, which strained their sense of loyalty to the Church to which they belonged.

The most obvious point of conflict between early Evangelical clergymen and the Establishment came over the issue of Church order.[4] The call to 'go into all the world and preach the Gospel to the whole creation' was not easily obeyed within the legal confines of the Church of England, and early Evangelical clergymen

[4] See Roger H. Martin, *Evangelicals United: Ecumenical Stirrings in Pre-Victorian Britain, 1795–1830* (1983), 6–8.

often found themselves driven to adopt evangelistic expedients which conflicted with existing Anglican practice or rule.[5] Extempore prayer; the formation of 'religious societies' often owing no allegiance to the parish clergy or diocesan bishop; irregular preaching in fields, barns, hired rooms, or private houses; even—in the case of the Methodists—the building of preaching-houses and the authorization of lay preachers—all these pragmatic expedients involved conflict with the legal structures of the Established Church. Theologically, clerical irregularity could be justified on the basis of a separation of doctrine and ecclesiastical order, many Evangelicals contending that primary loyalty must be given not to any particular denomination, but to the invisible church, the 'Church of Christ', the 'community of saints'.[6]

The 'Gospel clergymen' who participated in these expedients can be placed in two broad categories: irregulars and half-regulars. The irregulars were unbeneficed clergy, like Wesley and Whitefield, who engaged in itinerant preaching, officiated cheerfully in unlicensed and unconsecrated chapels, and set about establishing their own 'religious societies' in a nationwide 'connexion' which took no orders from parish clergy or diocesan bishops.[7] Despite pleas by Wesley and others to 'keep to the Church', in many cases this proved difficult, if not impossible. Societies quickly evolved into full-fledged churches. Connexions hardened into virtual denominations. The irregular Methodist clergy led their groups slowly, but inexorably, out of the Church of England. Some of the English Calvinist Methodist societies broke off into Nonconformity at an early state, possibly because of Whitefield's absences in America and his early death. Some of Lady Huntingdon's chaplains formally seceded in 1781–2.[8] The

[5] Such expedients have been closely studied in several important works. See Charles Smyth, *Simeon and Church Order* (Cambridge, 1940); J. D. Walsh, 'The Yorkshire Evangelicals in the Eighteenth Century', Ph.D. thesis (Cambridge, 1956); Frank Baker, *John Wesley and the Church of England* (1970). They were not accepted by all early Evangelicals, a number of whom, such as Walker of Truro, disagreed with Wesley over the issue of irregularity. See C. J. Abbey and J. H. Overton, *The English Church in the Eighteenth Century*, 2nd edn. (1902), 324, 378.

[6] See Walsh, 'The Yorkshire Evangelicals', 60.

[7] See John Walsh, 'Religious Societies, Methodist and Evangelical, 1738–1800', in W. J. Sheils and Diana Wood (eds.), *Studies in Church History: Voluntary Religion* (Oxford, 1986); John Wesley, *A Plain Account of the People Called Methodists* (Bristol, 1749).

[8] See Edwin Welch, *Spiritual Pilgrim: A Reassessment of the Life of the Countess of Huntingdon* (Cardiff, 1995), 157–61.

Wesleyans remained formally within the Church of England until Wesley's death in 1791, and drifted only slowly away from it thereafter. The Welsh Calvinistic Methodists, under the leadership of Thomas Charles of Bala, resisted separation until 1811 when eight of their foremost lay preachers were ordained and the connexion formally seceded.

In addition to full-time unbeneficed itinerants like Wesley and Whitefield, there were a number of half-regulars—clergy who combined a parochial cure of souls with occasional preaching trips into the parishes of their 'unawakened' colleagues. Many of the early evangelists were prepared to set off on field-preaching tours with Methodist leaders, or conducted their own irregular services in neighbouring parishes, including William Grimshaw, John Newton, John Fletcher, and Thomas Haweis.[9] Perhaps the most notorious half-regular of his day was John Berridge, the incumbent of Everton, in Bedfordshire.[10] Although cordially approving of the Anglican formularies—and thankful for a building to preach in and for Church revenue to live on—Berridge lamented the continued existence of many 'dark' parishes, where the Gospel was not preached.[11] Abandoning ecclesiastical order for the 'higher call' of soul-saving, he developed an extensive itinerant ministry throughout the region, preaching in barns, farmhouses, cottages, and in the open air.[12] Another well-known half-regular was Henry Venn, vicar of Huddersfield, in the West Riding,[13] who served as private chaplain to Lady Huntingdon and itinerated at her chapels, in neighbouring parishes, in private houses, in farmers' barns, and at Rowland Hill's Surrey Chapel.[14]

[9] C. G. Brown, 'Itinerancy and Loyalty: A Study in Eighteenth Century Evangelicalism', in *JRH* (June 1971), 235, 237.

[10] See Smyth, *Simeon and Church Order*, 250–1; Marcus Loane, *Cambridge and the Evangelical Secession* (1952), 83.

[11] Smyth, *Simeon and Church Order*, 276–8.

[12] Brown, 'Itinerancy and Loyalty', 233.

[13] See Walsh, 'The Yorkshire Evangelicals', 185–232.

[14] Ibid. 206; *ER* (Dec. 1839), 627–8; Edwin Sidney, *The Life of the Revd Rowland Hill* (1834), 167–8. This clerical irregularity later caused some embarrassment to his son, John Venn (1759–1813), rector of Clapham, who went to great pains to point out his father's increasing commitment to normative churchmanship. See John Venn, *The Life and a Selection From the Letters of the Late Revd Henry Venn, M.A.*, 2nd edn. (1835). Such a claim, which disclosed much about the changes in Evangelical attitudes to clerical irregularity from one generation to another, was later contested by several plausible accounts, and perhaps reflected the younger Venn's fears over the expansion of Dissent and the future of the Church in the early nineteenth century. See A. C. H. Seymour, *The Life and Times of Selina, Countess of Huntingdon* (1844), 6th edn., i.291–3; *ER* (Dec. 1839), 627–8.

Another catalyst in encouraging the work of half-regulars was the formation of the Countess of Huntingdon's Connexion. Like Berridge, the Countess, although warmly attached to the Church, was concerned that the Gospel was not being preached in every parish. She therefore appointed a number of sympathetic clergy as her private chaplains, including Berridge, John Eyre, Haweis, Hill, William Romaine, Venn, and Whitefield.[15] This activity continued until 1781–2, when Lady Huntington was compelled to secede from the Church and seek protection for some seventy-six of her chapels under the provisions of the Toleration Act.[16]

As the Revival progressed, the number of half-regulars rapidly decreased. Ecclesiastical regularity became the norm by the 1770s, or earlier. The reasons for this have been explored in several previous scholarly accounts, and can be briefly summarized.[17] It became increasingly plain to most 'Gospel clergymen' that the Methodists were sliding towards formal Dissent, and thus forfeiting their claim to be a ginger group within the Establishment. The price of irregularity began to appear too high. When a 'new Toryism' began to grow in the age of the American and French Revolutions, young clerical converts were more disposed than their elders to appreciate the importance of order to a well-constituted establishment in Church and State. By the end of the century, regularity had largely triumphed among the 'serious clergy'. The Evangelical clergy who now poured out of Oxford and Cambridge felt confident in their attachment to the Established Church: their numbers were growing, their position was secure, and they hoped, in the not too distant future, to win back the Church as a whole to the once-forgotten principles of the English Reformation.

None the less, despite the triumph of regularity, the position of the 'Gospel clergy' in the late eighteenth-century Church of England remained one of tension, however much that tension could be concealed by affirmations of loyalty to the Establishment. As long as Evangelicalism remained a vigorously evangelistic force in a Church which was deeply antagonistic to the 'enthusiasm' of its conversionist message, it was bound to collide

[15] Seymour, *Selina, Countess of Huntingdon*, i.83; Martin, *Evangelicals United*, 208.

[16] See Edwin Welch (ed.), *Two Calvinistic Methodist Chapels, 1743–1811* (1975), p. xvii, 64; *Spiritual Pilgrim. A Reassessment of the Life of the Countess of Huntingdon*, 157–61.

[17] See Smyth, *Simeon and Church Order*; Walsh, 'The Yorkshire Evangelicals'.

with the prejudices of contemporaries. There were a number of points of potential conflict—both ideological and ecclesiastical—which often forced even loyal establishmentarian Evangelical clerics to consider the grounds for their allegiance to the state church.

One problem was the primary issue of obtaining ordination. Some bishops saw Evangelical ordinands as potential Methodists, prone to irregularity and disobedience. It was usually more convenient and less provocative for bishops to curtail the supply of Evangelical ordinands than to attempt the prosecution of troublesome clerics already in holy orders. They feared them as concealed Dissenters; a Trojan horse of Puritan separatism in the bosom of the Establishment. Another problem was episcopal discipline, which could be brought to bear on disorderly Evangelicals. In their plain sense, the canons of the Church of England appeared to prohibit all evangelistic activity outside a clergyman's own parish (and even a few within it), and thus were seen by some Evangelicals as unjustified encumbrances upon evangelism and the pastoral ministry.[18] When violations of Church order occurred they were generally overlooked by the bishops, who on the whole showed remarkable restraint in enforcing canonical obedience—a reluctance which was perhaps accentuated by the fact that the costs of any litigation had to come from their own pockets.[19] On occasion, however, Evangelicals who engaged in irregular forms of ministry were formally disciplined by their diocesan, including Benjamin Ingham, Thomas Haweis, John Bradford, and William Gunn.[20] At Oxford, in a celebrated case during the 1760s, six Methodist undergraduates were expelled from St. Edmund Hall,[21] while in Wales Daniel Rowland had his licence withdrawn by the bishop of St. David's in 1763.[22] Such disciplinary actions, though

[18] Canons seventy-one and seventy-three were particularly prohibitive. See C. H. Davis, *The English Church Canons of 1604* (1869), 70–3; Gerald Bray, *The Anglican Canons 1529–1947* (1998).

[19] Peter Virgin, *Church in an Age of Negligence* (Cambridge, 1989), 160.

[20] See D. F. Clarke, 'Benjamin Ingham (1712–1772), with Special Reference to his Relations with the Churches . . . of His Time', M.Phil. thesis (Leeds, 1971); Arthur Skevington Wood, *Thomas Haweis, 1734–1820* (1957), 79–80; Ralph F. Chambers and Robert W. Oliver, *The Strict Baptist Chapels of England* (1952), i.72; *EM* (1807), 44–5.

[21] See S. L. Ollard, *The Six Students of St. Edmund Hall Expelled From the University of Oxford in 1768* (1911).

[22] See Eifion Evans, *Daniel Rowland and the Great Evangelical Awakening in Wales* (Edinburgh, 1985), 325.

they did not generally affect the regular Evangelical clergy, nevertheless gave cause for unease. A final anxiety-inducing factor was the Church's patronage system. During much of the eighteenth century, there had been great resentment at the exclusion of many 'Gospel clergymen' from preferment. This discrimination continued to anger Evangelicals in the early nineteenth century, even though they were starting to dig themselves into some important livings, and were learning to use the anomalies of the patronage system for their own benefit.[23]

I

The issue of patronage lay behind one of the endemic problems faced by Evangelicals: that of maintaining a succession of 'Gospel clergy' in a parish—a difficulty which led to the secession of large numbers of laity from the Church.[24] At the heart of the matter lay the inability of Evangelicals to ensure the succession of an 'Gospel incumbent' after the death, retirement, or transfer to another parish of their present clergyman. Advowsons were legally held by a variety of patrons, and could be purchased by Oxford and Cambridge colleges, city companies, or by anyone prepared to acquire patronage rights on the open market. In practice, they were often held by wealthy and powerful patrons who deferred to the interests of political or family connection when making appointments.

For many Evangelicals, this practice posed a serious dilemma. John Berridge complained in 1777 that the arrival of a non-Evangelical successor often compelled many parishioners to secede to evangelical Dissent. He speculated that although God was calling more Evangelicals into the Church, many more adherents of 'vital religion' might one day be forced to secede *en masse* because of the difficulties associated with patronage and succession.[25] William Grimshaw was so distrustful of his own patron that in 1758 he built a Methodist chapel in his parish for his congregation's 'dual

[23] For further exploration of this issue see Anon., *A Brief Memoir of the Revd William Richardson*, 2nd edn. (1822), 47; David Simpson, *Plea for the Church* (1797); Rowland Hill, *Journal of a Tour Through the North of England and Parts of Scotland* (1799), 106–9 n.; Rowland Hill, *Spiritual Characteristics Represented in an Account of a Most Curious Sale of Curates by Public Auction* (1803).

[24] The so-called 'problem of continuity' has been well documented in various scholarly accounts of the Revival. See Smyth, *Simeon and Church Order*, 201–47.

[25] *The Works of the Revd John Berridge, A.M.*, ed. Richard Wittingham, (1838), 517–18.

use' (or 'singular use' if the parish fell into theological 'darkness') after his death.[26] Edward Bickersteth, an occasional attender on the ministry of the Dissenter William Jay at Bath, argued that it was 'a positive duty to go where Christianity, and not mere morality, is preached', even if this entailed attending a ministry outside the Church.[27] After Henry Venn left Huddersfield in 1771, the large congregation rapidly evaporated when the patrons appointed a stiff anti-Evangelical, of whom a disgusted parishioner remarked 'they might as well have put a poker in't pulpit'.[28] Many others left either because they believed they had been 'abandoned' by the Church, particularly within the new urban industrialized areas where Church extension could not keep pace with the rapid migration, or because evangelical Dissent offered an attractive alternative to local Anglican listlessness and heterodoxy.[29] In 1796, a group of Evangelicals in Camberwell, alarmed that the Gospel was no longer preached in the parish, built a chapel from their own resources. As the bishop and vicar refused to consent to its licensing, it was registered under the Toleration Act as a Dissenting meeting house known as Camden Chapel.[30] Other examples of London chapels established under similar circumstances include Orange Street Chapel, Islington Chapel, Stockwell Chapel, and Union Chapel, Islington.[31] A similar situation developed in the parish of St. Giles', Reading, where, as a consequence of problems associated with succession, four major schisms occurred between 1774 and 1821.[32] Although High Churchmen responded to such developments by appealing to the interests of the Church, and by advocating the passage of new

[26] Grimshaw was the well-known incumbent of Haworth, Yorkshire. See Baker, *William Grimshaw*, 252.

[27] See T. R. Birks, *Memoir of the Revd Edward Bickersteth*, 2nd edn. (1852), i.43; *CO* (1807), 303.

[28] Quoted in Walsh, 'Religious Societies', 296.

[29] See Walsh, 'The Yorkshire Evangelicals', 84. Robert Robinson (1735–90) was an example of this second pattern. See *Select Works of the Revd Robert Robinson of Cambridge*, ed. William Robinson (1861); *EM* (1794), 72.

[30] Basil F. L. Clarke, *The Building of the Eighteenth-Century Church* (1963), 197–8. Henry Melville, minister from 1829–43, finally convinced Bishop Blomfield to license the chapel, and it was consecrated in 1844.

[31] See Henry Allon, *Memoir of James Sherman* (1863), 127.

[32] For details of the various secessions at St. Giles' see Smyth, *Simeon and Church Order*, 201–47. See also Edward Barry, *The Friendly Call of Truth and Reason to a New Species of Dissenter* (Reading, 1799); John Mann, *The Stranger in Reading* (Reading, 1810); Allon, *Memoir of the Revd James Sherman*, 157; Henry Gauntlett [Detector], *Letters to the Stranger in Reading* (1810).

legislation which would advance the Church's effectiveness and strengthen its defences, their pleas failed to stem the steady flow of lay Evangelical seceders into the ranks of Protestant Dissent.

Continuity of Evangelical ministry was a problem whose severity was to diminish with the passage of time. As Evangelicalism gained in respectability, attracting increasing numbers of patrons, lay and clerical, the issue was in general less keenly felt. But it did not entirely vanish, for the vagaries of the patronage system, with its dependence on the changing personal whim of patrons (be they layman or bishop), continued to emphasize the lottery element in the appointment of the Church's pastors.

II

Behind all the debates on the issue of Church order within the Evangelical camp were two priorities which needed to be kept in balance. On the one hand, there were immortal souls to be saved; an obligation so overwhelming and sacred that it might seem that all other obligations necessarily yielded to it. Surely, the interests of the 'Church of Christ', the invisible body of all regenerate saints, were paramount? Yet, on the other hand, stood loyalty to the order and discipline of the branch of the visible Church, a Church to which Evangelicals owed the duty of canonical obedience, sacralized in their ordination oath of obedience to the bishop. To undermine that order for the short-term advantage of irregular preaching was to take an incalculable step into the dark. Would not repeated breaches of discipline gravely weaken the whole structure of the National Establishment and—in the long term—promote Dissent and religious anarchy? The alternatives were put by T. D. Whitaker, strong Tory but fervent Evangelical: 'on the one hand, men are not to be left to perish in ignorance in order to preserve an Establishment; and on the other, they are not deliberately to be driven into schism to save their souls.'[33]

Balancing the demands of the visible Church of England against those of the invisible 'Church of Christ' could be an agonizing task. Not surprisingly it was an issue which received very different pastoral responses. The irregulars and half-regulars saw the needs of the 'Church of Christ' as paramount. The ultimate end of the Church, they argued, was to save souls, and its

[33] T. D. Whitaker, *An History of Whalley*, 4th edn. (1872–6), 251.

structures were to be regarded as pragmatic instruments for the achievement of this end. As Wesley put it: 'What is the end of all ecclesiastical order? Is it not to bring souls from the power of Satan to God, and to build them up in His fear and love? Order, then, is so far valuable as it answers these ends; and if it answers them not, it is nothing worth.'[34] The case for irregularity rested on a separation of the doctrine from ecclesiastical order, and the maintenance of any particular party or ecclesiastical system must be seen as subordinate to the advancement of the Gospel. 'What is it you have "deliberately engaged yourself to defend"?' Wesley asked the earl of Dartmouth. 'The constitution of the Church of England. And is not her doctrine a main part of this constitution? A far more essential part thereof than any rule of external order?'[35] As the Church's *raison d'être* was evangelism and soul-winning, its legal and administrative apparatus (including order) must be subservient to that purpose. The dictum of the Puritan Richard Baxter, 'it's better that men should be disorderly saved than orderly damned, and that the Church be disorderly preserved than orderly destroyed' was only too applicable.[36] As Wesley claimed, 'I would observe every punctilio of order, except where the salvation of souls is at stake. Then I prefer the end before the means.'[37] John Berridge advised young preachers in 1775, 'Ask no man's leave to preach Christ; that is unevangelical and shameful. Seek not much advice about it; that is dangerous . . . If you are determined to be evangelically regular, i.e. secularly irregular; then expect, wherever you go, a storm will follow . . . which might frighten you, but will bring no real harm.'[38] On such an assumption the irregular Evangelical was seen as a better churchman than either his Latitudinarian colleague, who kept to the Church's order but betrayed its doctrine, or his High Church colleague, who kept to both order and doctrine but abandoned the Church's imperative to save souls.

The response of the regulars was to remain true to the constitution of the visible Church to which they belonged. They too used pragmatic arguments, but on the side of order. The Church

[34] Letter of 25 June 1746, in *The Letters of the Revd John Wesley, A.M.*, ed. John Telford (1931), ii.77–8.
[35] Ibid. letter of 10 Apr. 1761, iv.148.
[36] Richard Baxter, *Five Disputations of Church-Government and Worship* (1659), 165.
[37] Quoted in *The Letters of John Wesley*, ed. Telford, iv.146.
[38] Quoted in Smyth, *Simeon and Church Order*, 249.

of England was not only properly constituted, with its admirable liturgy and Reformed Articles, but, as a National, Established body was by far the most effective agency for a nationwide campaign of evangelism. To weaken her strength in the pursuit of short-term gains would be extremely dangerous. It was far better to work from within the Establishment and its orderly system than to operate outside it. The quiet successes of field-preaching were bought at too high a price—that of alienating the sympathy of the clergy and the great mass of loyal Anglicans. It was far better to stay within the framework of Church order and labour excessively in order to capture it intact for the Gospel.

III

By 1800, among Evangelicals at large the regulars were overwhelmingly in the ascendant. Irregularity was frowned on and its few remaining practitioners were soon to be strongly criticized in the pages of the *Christian Observer*.[39] In England few new unbeneficed roving irregulars were produced: Wesley and Whitefield were now increasingly regarded as archaic figures of the past. Though a few half-regulars—like Thomas Haweis—still existed, they were isolated figures. In most ways, the battle for Church order in the Evangelical soul had been won decisively by the regulars. There were many factors behind this victory. The outbreak of the American and French Revolutions, and the fear of political radicalism at home, had set in motion a conservative neo-Toryism which affected the Church as strongly as any institution, and encouraged high views of the need for hierarchy, authority, obedience, and tradition.[40] The alarming growth of Methodism and evangelical Nonconformity in the 1790s seemed to threaten the future of the Established Church: if Dissent continued to expand at this rate, would the Church not soon be a vulnerable minority institution like her offspring the Church of Ireland? Many Evangelicals now felt guilty at the way in which the irregularity of their own colleagues had encouraged this upsurge in Dissent. Too many of those who had been converted by irregular preaching had joined Dissent rather than the Church. 'The

[39] *CO* (1802), 162.

[40] See Walsh, 'The Yorkshire Evangelicals', 327–67; N. Murray, 'The Influence of the French Revolution on the Church of England and its Rivals, 1789–1803', D.Phil. thesis (Oxford, 1975).

clergyman beats the bush and the Dissenters catch the game', complained Charles Simeon, expressing the view of many of his colleagues.[41]

The need for irregularity seemed less now that 'serious religion' had gained a substantial bridgehead in the Establishment. By the onset of the nineteenth century, Evangelicals no longer felt themselves massively outnumbered. They had a growing hold on the middle classes. The 'problem of continuity' seemed less urgent, for it was being addressed by the advancement of Evangelical patronage. Perhaps the first Evangelical systematically to engage in such trade was John Thornton, the great 'Russian merchant', who used a portion of his enormous wealth to purchase advowsons.[42] Another was William Marsh, the influential incumbent of St. Peter's, Colchester.[43] The most vigorous and successful Evangelical investor in patronage, however, was Charles Simeon, who, prior to his death in 1836, acquired some twenty-one separate advowsons. Many of these were key parishes in large towns, some with multiple rights of presentation.[44] These were then placed under the care of a trust, which was charged with procuring further rites of patronage by purchase or by gift. As the Church moved into the nineteenth century, this work of acquiring advowsons in key towns and cities, as Simeon intended, created a number of 'spheres of influence', in which Evangelicals could labour with the assurance that their efforts to advance the Gospel would not be undermined by an unsympathetic successor.[45]

Another important change was the ability of moderate Evangelicals to secure ordination in the Church. Several bishops, in particular Beilby Porteus of London, Shute Barrington of Durham, Thomas Burgess of St. David's, and William Lort Mansel of Bristol, regularly ordained moderate Evangelicals.[46] An

[41] William Carus, *Memoirs of the Life of the Revd Charles Simeon, M.A.* (1847), 139.

[42] See Anon., 'Incidents in the Life of John Thornton, Esq., the Philanthropist', in *Congregational Magazine* (1842), 825; Venn, *Life of Henry Venn*, 491–2. His son, Henry, advanced the work after his father's death in 1790. See Carus, *Memoirs of Charles Simeon*, 368–9, 380–2; Cf. Evans, *Daniel Rowland*, 326.

[43] C. Marsh, *The Life of the Revd William Marsh* (1867), 12–13.

[44] Smyth, *Simeon and Church Order*, 246n.

[45] See W. D. Balda, '"Spheres of Influence": Simeon's Trust and its Implications for Evangelical Patronage', Ph.D. thesis (Cambridge, 1981).

[46] See Smyth, *Simeon and Church Order*, 245.

even more significant sign of the Evangelicals' ability to gain ordination was the appointment of Henry Ryder in 1815, as the first Evangelical bishop, for this marked the beginning of the movement's direct access to episcopal influence.[47] In spite of this advance, however, there remained a few bishops opposed to the ordination of Evangelicals. The best known among these was Herbert Marsh of Peterborough, who required all candidates for ordination to face his so-called 'Cobwebs to catch Calvinists'—a notorious list of eighty-seven questions devised to expose latent 'enthusiasts'.[48]

But if early nineteenth-century bishops were more accommodating to 'Gospel clergy' in some respects, they were also sterner in others. Even before the Church reforms of the 1830s, there were signs of a tighter episcopal control of clerical irregularity. While the eirenical bishop Porteus showed kindliness and understanding to Evangelicals, and was an admirer of Wilberforce and a friend of Hannah More, he was still swift to inhibit the Revd Dr Draper from preaching in the diocese of London in 1809 on the grounds that he had accepted the Presidency of Cheshunt College, the training centre for lay preachers in Lady Huntingdon's Connexion.[49] No such action had been taken against John Fletcher in a similar situation at Trevecca in earlier years. Similar treatment was meted out to the Revd Isaac Bridgman in 1823 when he began to itinerate in Gloucester diocese, in the old Rowland Hill style. Writing in the 1840s, William Carus noted in his *Memoirs of Charles Simeon* the contrast between the old days and the new. 'For many years it was not deemed irregular, even by the bishops, for clergymen to preach in Lady Huntingdon's chapels, provided the prayers were said. Preaching in barns, or other places, was viewed much in the same light. It was not until a comparatively recent period that the bishop's licence was deemed absolutely necessary.'[50]

By the 1820s—perhaps earlier—there were signs that the abuses

[47] See G. C. B. Davies, *The First Evangelical Bishop* (1957).

[48] See *DNB*. Marsh was criticized in the House of Lords for this heavy-handedness, and by Sydney Smith in the pages of the *Edinburgh Review*. See *EdR* (1822), 432–49. Cf. the *Record*, 14 June 1849.

[49] See Robert Hodgson, *Life of Beilby Porteus* (1811), 266–74.

[50] Carus, *Memoirs of Charles Simeon*, 277–8.

which had limited the effectiveness of the Church during the eighteenth century were beginning to be reformed.[51] Episcopal superintendence of the clergy increased; pluralism and non-residence began to be weeded out, and the lot of curates improved; parsonages and churches were rebuilt, or modernized; and diocesan administration was improved as the office of rural dean was revived in some dioceses, bringing the localities under closer episcopal surveillance.[52] Above all else, the rise of Tractarianism during the 1830s increased the polarization between Evangelicals and High Churchmen, leading indirectly to tighter ecclesiastical control and discipline, and even, in some instances, to prolonged conflict and litigation.

None the less—as we shall see repeatedly in the pages to come—doubts about the efficiency of the Established Church as an agency of soul-saving did not altogether vanish. The old patronage system retained much of its hold on the Church: bishops were still appointed by politicians, while parsons could be appointed by laymen of dubious spiritual credentials. In some respects the issue of crown patronage was *more* sensitive in the 1830s than before, since thanks to the repeal of the Test and Corporation Acts and to the enactment of Catholic Emancipation, Parliament could no longer be considered a 'lay synod of the Church of England': Church appointments in the name of 'the Crown' could henceforth, at least in theory, be made by politicians of all faiths or of no faith. There were still devout Anglican clergymen who came to feel that the legal and disciplinary trammels of establishment tragically hampered the work of evangelism, and should be disregarded on that account. By the 1840s this anxiety was becoming acute, as the extent of urban de-Christianization became apparent. An Evangelical churchman like Baptist Noel could still respond to the appalling spectacle of 'spiritual destitution' in London and the great manufacturing cities much as John Wesley had responded to neglected rural-industrial communities like those of Kingswood colliers or Cornish tinners in the 1740s, seeing the situation as one of acute crisis in which

[51] See G. F. A. Best, *Temporal Pillars* (Cambridge, 1964); John Walsh, Colin Haydon, and Stephen Taylor (eds.), *The Church of England, c.1689–c.1833: From Toleration to Tractarianism* (Cambridge, 1993).

[52] See R. Arthur Burns, 'The Diocesan Revival in the Church of England, *c.*1825–1865', D.Phil. thesis (Oxford, 1990).

many of the ordinary restrictions of canon law and legality should be suspended or scrapped.

IV

None the less, in the nineteenth century, Church order was no longer the chief catalyst for disaffection with the Establishment. Instead, doctrinal differences, particularly those relating to the Anglican liturgy, played a larger part as a trigger for individual secessions. Theological 'extremism' was probably a more significant irritant than pastoral exasperation. This, too, had its roots in the eighteenth century. As we have seen, the normative Evangelical view of the Prayer Book was one of reverence. But the admiration was not total. There were still apparent relics of a popish past to be seen in the liturgy. Although many Evangelicals concurred with Rowland Hill that the liturgy was 'a public blessing to the nation',[53] and although many of the Evangelical seceders continued to use it after leaving the Church (while omitting what they regarded to be its popish or Arminian vestiges),[54] a number of others strongly objected to one or more aspects of it. Why sensitivity to theological error in the liturgy became acute in the early years of the nineteenth century remains uncertain. Among other influences, of course, the increased strife and controversy between Evangelicals and High Churchmen brought certain aspects of the liturgy into higher profile, and gave prominence to the 'Catholic' nature of the Prayer Book. Liberal plans for Prayer Book reform may also have focused Evangelical attention on the shortcomings of the liturgy. In either case, Evangelicals became concerned over the issue of whether portions of the liturgy were doctrinally unsound, or their Protestant nature corrupted and distorted by modern practice. The Anglican baptismal and burial services serve as good examples of such concern, leading to considerable intra-party strife.

From an early date, Evangelical discontent over the wording of the burial service can be found. Every 'Gospel clergyman' was

[53] Quoted in Sidney, *Life of Rowland Hill*, 440–1.

[54] Although this practice was of questionable legality, no seceder was prosecuted in the ecclesiastical courts over this, and it was even defended by some Evangelical clergy: Henry Venn encouraged his old parishioners at Huddersfield to continue to use the liturgy in their new meeting house, for it was full of sound doctrines and teachings. See Venn, *Life of Henry Venn*, 174–5; Gauntlett [Detector], *Letters to the Stranger in Reading*, 71.

called upon to bury baptized parishioners who, on any normal construction, could be presumed to be unrepentant and were sometimes gross sinners who had died in a state of virtual self-excommunication. Despite their estrangement from the faith and practice of the Church, the sixty-eighth canon obliged all clergy to provide a Christian burial service for them *and* to inter their corpses in consecrated ground.[55] 'We commit his body to the ground,' the canon read, 'in sure and certain hope of the resurrection to eternal life, through our Lord Jesus Christ.' Was it not hypocrisy, or worse, to pronounce this optimistic message over the corpse of unrepentant sinners? To some sensitive Evangelicals, the compulsion to read the rubric demanded hypocrisy and was an unscriptural perversion of a sacred rite. By the implicit assumption that all those buried were regenerate souls, parochial discipline was destroyed, awkward questions were raised about the efficacy of paedobaptism, and the distinction between elect and reprobate was blurred. Consequently, the 'Church of Christ' was reduced to little more than the 'church of the world'. These doubts about the burial rubric worried some early Evangelicals. Walker of Truro, for instance, was embroiled in an unpleasant controversy over his refusal to bury a notorious drunkard, which led to his estrangement from much of his congregation as well as the local squire.[56] William John Brook, several years after becoming curate at St. Nicholas, Brighton, in 1800, was required to read the burial service over a baptized parishioner who had, as he put it, 'died in sin' and 'without a hope' of gaining eternal life. Brook found this task so revolting that he immediately seceded from the Church, to end his days as minister to the high Calvinist Providence Chapel, Brighton, where he laboured until his early death in 1811.[57]

Rather surprisingly, the baptismal rubric—which troubled the consciences of many nineteenth-century Evangelicals—caused rather less anxiety to those of the eighteenth. The declaration 'seeing now . . . that this child is regenerate', and the prayer

[55] See Davis, *The English Church Canons of 1604*, 66–7.

[56] See Edwin Sidney, *The Life, Ministry, and Selections from the Remains, of the Revd Samuel Walker, B.A.*, (1835), 13–14.

[57] John White Middelton, *An Ecclesiastical Memoir of the First Four Decades of the Reign of George the Third* (1822), 218; Thomas Wright, *The Life of William Huntington, SS* (1909), 129–30; Chambers and Oliver, *The Strict Baptist Chapels of England*, ii.122.

towards the end of the service thanking God 'that it hath pleased thee to regenerate this infant with thy Holy Spirit', could be seen as an affirmation of an *ex opere operato* theory of baptismal regeneration and a denial of the Evangelical conviction that regeneration normally accompanied conversion. Doubts about the rubric occasionally surfaced and were instrumental in causing the secession of Isaac Slee, who ended his days as a Baptist minister in Haworth, Yorkshire, in 1784.[58]

Another Evangelical who objected to certain aspects of the liturgy was David Simpson of Macclesfield. In 1797, he complained that there were 'not a few persons' who objected to the unscriptural wording of a number of Prayer Book rubrics, including those for baptism, confirmation, the service of the sick, holy communion, ordination, and burial. 'It seemed a hardship to the enlightened and conscientious part of the clergy', he wrote, to comply with forms which so controverted the Reformation doctrine of the Articles. 'When we baptize children, we thank God that it hath pleased Him to regenerate them with the Holy Spirit, to receive them for His own children by adoption, and to incorporate them into His holy church.' When the same children were presented to the bishop for confirmation, he also addressed the divine being as having 'vouchsafed to regenerate them by water and the Holy Ghost, and as having given unto them the forgiveness of all their sins', while many of them were as vile young rogues as ever existed. Thus, he complained, 'when we come to bury them, we dare do no other then send them all to heaven, though many of those we commit to the earth have been as wicked in life as men well can be this side of hell. This surely is a great hardship. Yet we have no remedy. We must do it, or forfeit our roast beef and plum pudding.'[59] Simpson planned to secede in 1799, but died before he could do so.

His was an extreme voice. Yet, as we shall see, Simpson's doubts about the liturgy were to surface again and again in the early nineteenth century, especially during the 1830s and 1840s when the Oxford Movement was drawing attention to the 'Catholic' implications of the Anglican liturgy. By the time of the Gorham crisis, Evangelicals were murmuring audibly about Prayer Book reform.

[58] See Cecil Edgar Shipley, *The Baptists of Yorkshire* (Bradford, 1912), 185.

[59] D. Simpson, *A Plea for Religion*, 5th edn. (1808), 150, 155–6.

Why this had not often been the case in the eighteenth century remains an open question. Perhaps the early Evangelicals were too absorbed in 'the one thing needful'—the saving of souls? Perhaps it was because, like Wesley, many had been raised within the High Church tradition and continued to admire its orthodoxy? It is also likely that (as discussed earlier) early Evangelicals opposed liturgical reform on the grounds that any alterations at that time would more probably be not in a reformed, but in a liberal or High Church direction.

V

A further cause of theological friction between the early Evangelicals and their Church lay in the 'Calvinism' to which most of them subscribed. Though a predestinarian theology might appear to be plainly deducible from some of the Articles, it had been eclipsed after the Restoration, and its revival within the National Church was vigorously opposed. 'Calvinism', like 'Methodism', was a blanket term when used pejoratively, and was employed to convey many disparate theological modes—including (ironically) Wesley's 'Arminianism', which some misinformed critics considered to be Calvinistic. The prevailing suspicion of predestinarian Calvinism was fuelled by a number of connected anxieties. It was now seen as the creed of sectaries and Cromwellian levellers and regicides, conducive to fanatical theories of the need for a 'dominion of grace' of the elect over the reprobate. It was seen as pastorally disruptive, skimming off the predestined saints from the mass of the unregenerate in ways which divided a parish in two, and negated the conception of an Anglican clergyman as equal pastor of all the souls within his cure. The doctrine of predestination was believed to encourage despair among those who thought themselves 'elect'. Calvinists who carried their fatalistic doctrine of grace to its logical conclusion (it was claimed) often fell into the foulest sin, convincing themselves that as privileged members of the elect, they could not fall from grace and so could commit sin with impunity: whatever they did, they would 'finally persevere'. The essence of Calvinism, charged John Wesley in a famous epigram, was that a man was either saved do what he *would*, or damned do what he *could*.[60]

[60] See John Wesley, 'The Consequence Proved', in *Works of John Wesley*, ed. Jackson, x.370.

Most Calvinist Evangelicals rebuffed charges like these without too much loss of confidence. They were fortified by the belief that the Articles were clearly on their side, at least if taken in their plain and literal sense. They were confident that their teachings were those of most English reformers and the majority of divines in the Church of England until the Civil War. The predominant tone of Evangelical Calvinism was one of moderation. Its exponents attempted to avoid the over-systematization of the Puritans. They tried to stick to the simple formulations of Scripture, avoiding speculative theories about free will and necessity. They avoided so-called 'double predestination'; accepting predestination to life as a doctrine clearly set out in the New Testament, but refusing to preach predestination to death on the grounds that it was not plainly advanced in the Scriptures. They tried to formulate a doctrine of grace which made God totally responsible for man's salvation and man alone responsible for his damnation. They embraced the notions of total depravity, particular election, justification by faith alone through grace, and final perseverance,[61] but adhered to these doctrines not with rigid dogmatism, but with flexibility. Richard Cecil argued that Scripture must be interpreted as it was found, without attempting to force it into a particular system.[62] In other words, when the Bible—and the Articles, canons, and Prayer Book—revealed 'Calvinistic' doctrines (such as predestined election), they should be accepted as such; when 'Arminian' (such as the injunction to work out our own salvation in fear and trembling), likewise. With this approach, the Calvinistic emphasis on the sovereignty of God's grace would be complemented by the Arminian emphasis on man's responsibility, avoiding antinomianism on the one hand and pelagianism on the other.[63] Charles Simeon was the most celebrated exponent of this 'middle-way Calvinism'. Writing of himself in the preface to one of his most popular works, he declared that he:

> takes his religion from the Bible; and endeavours as much as possible, to speak as that speaks . . . He does not hesitate to lay the whole blame of men's condemnation on their own depraved will . . . [and] does not scruple to state . . . 'that we have no power to do good works . . . without

[61] See Walsh, 'The Yorkshire Evangelicals', 1–10.

[62] Josiah Pratt (ed.), *The Remains of the Revd Richard Cecil, M.A.*, 8th edn. (1825), 297.

[63] See W. J. C. Ervine, 'Doctrine and Diplomacy: Some Aspects of the Life and Thought of the Anglican Evangelical Clergy, 1797 to 1837', Ph.D. thesis (Cambridge, 1979), 35.

the grace of God by Christ preventing us that we may have a good will' . . . He is aware, that advocates for this or that system . . . will be ready to condemn his as inconsistent . . . [but] it is possible that the truth may lie, not exclusively in either, nor yet in a confused mixture of both, but in the proper and seasonable application of them both.[64]

By the early nineteenth century, it seems to have been uncommon for Evangelicals to preach sermons on predestination. Though widely accepted as a biblical truth, predestined election was seen as a non-essential, and as a truth better kept for the private encouragement of saints rather than one to be propagated from the pulpit. One reason for this reticence in advancing predestinarian doctrine was that it might encourage antinomianism among the unwary, for moderate Evangelicals were uneasily aware that there were many high or hyper-Calvinists who carried the doctrine of predestination to lengths which encouraged immorality and fatalism. Henry Venn found this distortion of the doctrine rampant among the Dissenters of some of the East Anglian villages around his parish of Yelling. 'A false, libertine Calvinism' of this type, he complained, 'stops up every avenue: sin, the law, holiness, experience, are all nothing. Predestination cancels the necessity of any change, and dispenses at once with all duty.'[65]

To the embarrassment of most Evangelicals, doctrines like these were not only the property of rural Nonconformists: they had a well-publicized foothold in the ranks of the 'Gospel clergy' themselves. Though hyper-Calvinists were few in number they were active, especially in London and in the West of England. John Bradford seceded from the Church in 1778. He then served, for a time, in Lady Huntingdon's Connexion, before becoming an independent Calvinistic minister in South Wales, Birmingham, and finally London, where he served at City Chapel, Grub Street. On one occasion, while preaching at Spa Fields Chapel, he caused a sensation by proclaiming 'that the believer was not only delivered from the moral law as a covenant of works, but also as a rule of life; and that the Christian had no more to do with it, nor any more attention to pay to it, than to the Koran of the Arabian

[64] Charles Simeon, *Helps to Composition, or One-Hundred Skeleton Sermons* (Cambridge, 1801), pp. v–vi.

[65] See Venn, *Life of Henry Venn*, 34.

impostor'.[66] An especial *bête noire* of the moderate Calvinists was Robert Hawker, vicar of Charles, near Plymouth, from 1784 to 1827, who popularized extreme Calvinism in a series of sermons and cheap tracts.[67] So extreme was his teaching that William Wilberforce would not allow his children to go to services at the Lock Hospital in London when Hawker was preaching, lest they drink in his 'poison'.[68] The origins of Hawkerite teaching can be traced to a long ultra-Calvinist tradition running back at least to the early seventeenth century. The hyper-Calvinists carried the doctrine of divine sovereignty to such lengths as virtually to eliminate human agency in things spiritual. They spoke of 'eternal justification' by a divine covenant before creation itself: worse, they taught the doctrine of 'eternal sanctification'—that all the sins of an elect soul were blotted out before they were even committed. For the ultra-Calvinist there was no such thing as spiritual growth. From his birth, the predestined chosen one was clothed in Christ's perfect holiness: whatever his sins or infirmities, they were already expunged from the sight of God.[69]

The hyper-Calvinist held that the moral law had no binding force on the true Christian. Thanks to the 'finished work of Christ', the sinful acts of an elect soul were not debited to his account. The moral law was not a rule of life for the Christian; he would follow it voluntarily out of an interior principle of love, but he was no longer bound by it. And if he broke it, he need feel no anxiety about his spiritual safety. The Gospel *freed* men from the obligation to obey the law; they should no longer strive to please God by commutative acts or 'good works'. There was only one command in the Gospel, and it was not '*work*' but '*believe*'. The proof of election did not lie in any outward proofs of faith. The true believer knew that he was one of the predestined elect not from any signs of increasing holiness in his life, but from the assurances of an interior conviction that he was God's chosen one. Here, in the opinion of most Evangelicals, the hyper-Calvinists lapsed into the old heresy of antinomianism, which had plagued

[66] See A Friend, *Memoirs of the Life of the Revd Thomas Wills, A.B.* (1804), 213–14; Welch, *Spiritual Pilgrim. A Reassessment of the Life of the Countess of Huntingdon*, 186.

[67] See J. Williams (ed.), *The Works of Robert Hawker, D.D.* (1831).

[68] Robert Isaac and Samuel Wilberforce, *The Life of William Wilberforce* (1838), iii.473.

[69] See J. D. Walsh, MS 'Calvinism'. Cf. Peter Toon, *The Emergence of Hyper-Calvinism in English Nonconformity 1689–1765* (1967), 144–5.

English Calvinists for over two hundred years.[70] Advanced during the early seventeenth century by John Eaton, Tobias Crisp, John Saltmarsh, and Robert Lancaster, among others, antinomianism declined until the republication of Crisp's works in 1689–90, when it enjoyed a considerable revival among Nonconformists.[71] In particular, there was a collective outbreak in 1719 in Exeter (always a seedbed for high Calvinist teaching, as we shall see), involving at least three separate Nonconformist congregations spread over a wide area of the West Country.[72] For the most part, ultra-Calvinists were 'theoretical antinomians' who did not allow their belief in the freedom of Christians from the obligations of the moral law to influence their conduct in the direction of immorality. But this was not always so, and examples could easily be found of 'practical antinomians': Calvinist extremists who lapsed cheerfully into sin—usually sexual—under the belief that they were eternally sanctified.[73]

By the close of the eighteenth century, hyper-Calvinism had again gained ground amongst Nonconformists, so much so that it had become, in the alarmed opinion of the Dissenting historians Bogue and Bennett, 'the most prevailing evil of the day'.[74] This 'poison', however, far from being confined to Dissenters, was also being imbibed in increasing portions by Evangelicals. The reasons behind this are difficult to determine. It is likely that there was some seepage of antinomian ideas from Dissent to Anglican Evangelicalism, for the areas especially affected—Ireland and the English West Country—had a long Puritan-Nonconformist tradition of hyper-Calvinism. In part, the exaggerated Calvinism of Hawker represented an extreme reaction against the repeated assaults of the High Church polemicists such as Richard Mant, who were launching virulent attacks against a Protestant interpretation of the Articles and Prayer Book.[75] The sharpening of the conflict between Church parties in the 1830s may well have

[70] See Toon, *The Emergence of Hyper-Calvinism*, 28.

[71] Dewey D. Wallace, Jr., *Puritans and Predestination: Grace in English Protestant Theology, 1525–1695* (Chapel Hill, NC, 1982), 113; Christopher Hill, 'Dr Tobias Crisp, 1600–43', in *Balliol Studies*, ed. John Prest (Oxford, 1982), 55–76.

[72] Toon, *The Emergence of Hyper-Calvinism*, 37–8. These congregations supported 4 ministers, and were controlled by a committee of 13 laymen.

[73] See Joseph Hart, *Hymns* (1759), 5–6.

[74] James Bogue and James Bennett, *History of Dissenters* (1808–12), iv.392–6.

[75] See Richard Mant, *An Appeal to the Gospel* (Oxford, 1812).

encouraged more rigid and systematic ideas of predestination in the Evangelical ranks. Increasing tension seems to have produced extremism.

Not surprisingly, extreme Calvinism of this type was denounced not only by those outside the Evangelical Revival, but by many embarrassed moderate Evangelicals. Thomas Scott, for one, conducted a long campaign against the antinomian tendencies of high Calvinism, most notably in his widely read *Treatise on Growth in Grace* (1787). Hyper-Calvinism was all the more threatening because it represented not so much an outright denial of the Evangelical 'doctrines of grace' as an exaggeration or perversion of them. It seemed to run counter to the activist strain in Gospel teaching that characterized mainstream Evangelicalism. Extreme predestinarianism was frequently opposed to the evangelism and the missionary outreach of the Revival: what use was it preaching to the unconverted and offering God's grace to all (ran the argument of the 'hypers'), if the fate of every soul had been sealed before eternity? To urge repentance and conversion on sinners was to imply that God's grace was not sovereign and that salvation was attainable by an act of human will. The presence of men like Hawker among the 'Gospel clergy' posed a grave problem to Evangelicals, not so much because hyper-Calvinism won large numbers of converts (its theology militated against mass proselytism), but because it brought the Evangelical Gospel into disrepute and gave great polemical advantage to opponents of the Revival. To its opponents, it lent substance to the constant argument that the tendency of Evangelicalism was in an antinomian direction.

High and hyper-Calvinists were strongly represented among Evangelical clergy seceding from the Church of England, as we shall see in the following chapters. Why was this? There would seem to be no obvious connection between a high predestinarian theology and separatism: many extreme Calvinists—like Hawker himself—were content to remain within the Anglican Establishment and to conduct an energetic parish ministry within it. Yet there can be little doubt that high or hyper-Calvinists were more susceptible to the lure of secession than most of their Evangelical colleagues. In the late eighteenth century two well-known seceders, John Bradford and William John Brook, abandoned Anglicanism to take up their ministry in hyper-Calvinist chapels, becoming allies of the celebrated William Huntington, coal-heaver turned preacher, who held a role in Nonconformist circles rather similar to that of Hawker in the Church of England, as the mentor and publicist of 'hyperism'. Many more were to follow in their footsteps during the first half of the nineteenth century.

Several reasons can be suggested for the link between extreme Calvinism and separatism. First, the mere espousal of such *outré* views cut a clergyman off from his fellows and brought ostracism and vilification, not only from his 'carnal' colleagues, but still more from angry Evangelicals. If 'hyperism' was weak and derided in the Church, it had a long and not unrespectable foothold in Dissent, particularly among the Strict Baptists in whose chapels high Calvinism flourished. It was tempting for a clergyman wearied of controversy over his alleged antinomianism to leave a troubled parish for a quieter, more congenial billet among Nonconformist friends and admirers. Secondly, there was a barely submerged tendency in high Calvinist theology itself towards the separatist theory of the 'gathered church'. There was much in the teaching of ultra-Calvinism to encourage ideas of the elect as an eternally privileged, sanctified body, totally and utterly distinct from the mass of unregenerates. Why should God's chosen ones associate promiscuously in worship with those who were eternally cast off by Him? Why should God's children not assemble together in their own meetings, to hear the pure Word, untrammelled by contact with the impure?[76] The demands of fellowship with like-minded souls could easily encourage secession from the parish Church, which was open to believers and non-believers, saints and worldlings, alike. A separated church in which the elect were visibly set apart from the world would symbolize the eternal distinction separating the children of light and the children of darkness.

VI

These, then, were some of the impulses which from an early date produced dissatisfaction with the status quo of the Church of England among some 'Gospel clergymen'. Their relative salience in any individual secession, or in group secessions, varied from case to case. Doubts about the liturgy, frustrations about the way

[76] See Walsh, MS 'Calvinism'.

in which the legal trammels of establishment hindered the work of evangelism, personal collisions with Church authorities, and leanings to high Calvinism; each of these could set in motion a determination to leave a Church that appeared irredeemably fallen. In some, one consideration predominated; in others, another. At times they were combined.

This study is concerned with the course of Evangelical secessions in the first half of the nineteenth century. It is difficult to formulate a precise estimate of the number of these seceders.[77] Two contemporary accounts shed light on this question by claiming that about a hundred Evangelical clergymen seceded into the Nonconformist ministry during the first half of the nineteenth century,[78] a figure which represents approximately two per cent of the Evangelical clergy, if Conybeare's celebrated 1853 estimate of the numerical strength of the various Church parties is accepted.[79] This study has identified well over a hundred Evangelical clergymen who seceded from the Church of England into Protestant Dissent, mostly during the first half of the nineteenth century, in addition to a number of prominent Evangelical lay seceders.[80]

The great bulk of Evangelical clergy, it is clear, avoided secession and remained within the Established Church. Most condemned secession unequivocally.[81] Numerically, therefore, the

[77] See H. H. Rowdon, 'Secession From the Established Church in the Early Nineteenth Century', in *VE* (1964), 76–88.

[78] James Shore, *The Case of the Revd James Shore, M.A., by Himself* (1849), 23; *Non*, 21 Mar. 1849, 221.

[79] See W. J. Conybeare, 'Church Parties', in *EdR* (1853), 338. Conybeare claimed that of 18,000 Established clergy, 5,800 were adherents of 'serious religion'. More than 100—or over 2%—of these seceded into the Nonconformist ministry. In comparison, slightly fewer Tractarians seceded to Rome, but they represented a larger percentage of the Catholic party. According to George Herring, 96 Tractarians seceded to Rome prior to 1853, or 9.6% of Conybeare's estimated 1,000 Tractarian clergy. See George W. Herring, 'Tractarianism to Ritualism', D.Phil. thesis (Oxford, 1984), 45, and Appendix.

[80] See Appendix, 1.

[81] The Eclectic Society referred to it as an unscriptural apostasy, which diminished affection and humility; weakened the strength of the Church; relaxed order, government, and discipline; produced a party spirit, bigotry, and uncharitableness; and advanced evil. See J. H. Pratt (ed.), *Eclectic Notes* (1856), 3. High Churchmen were equally harsh in their denunciations of secession. See George Isaac Huntingford, *A Call for Union with the Established Church* (Winchester, 1800); John Randolph, *A Charge Delivered to the Clergy of the Diocese of London* (1810); William Phelan, *The Bible, Not the Bible Society* (Dublin, 1817), 95. Secession was, however, defended by some Evangelicals. In 1803, an Evangelical layman published a work which vigorously defended Evangelical seceders against the charge of schism. See Ambrose Sherle, *Charis: Or, Reflections, Chiefly, Upon the Office of the Holy Spirit in the Salvation of Men* (1803), 117–27.

seceders remained a small group, albeit an important one for their publicity value, since they aroused much anger among churchmen and much sympathy among Dissenters, for whom their propaganda value in the campaign against the Establishment was considerable. But their importance does not cease here. Much of the significance of Evangelical secession lies not in the numbers involved, but in the insight it provides into the difficulties and doubts—usually submerged in published sermons or biographies—which assailed many Evangelicals who tried to reconcile their churchmanship with their evangelistic fervour, spiritual experiences, and formal theology. The seceders made explicit, and carried to great lengths, doubts which clearly surfaced in a great many Evangelical minds. They are to Evangelicalism what the Rome-ward seceders of the Oxford Movement were to the English High Church tradition—an example of what could become of a grouping within the Church which found the *via media* unsatisfactory and determined to seek a more coherent and extreme position, unhampered by English moderation and compromise.

As the spiritual climate in England began to heat up in the early nineteenth century, Anglican moderation proved increasingly unattractive for some 'Gospel clergy', who needed more rigid and identifiable boundaries between the elect and the non-elect. Consequently, Evangelicalism began to fragment into various—and often hostile—camps. An early example occurred in Ireland, where two prominent clergymen, propelled by their Calvinistic principles, seceded, set up their own separate connexions, and waged spiritual warfare on their rivals, and each other. Before long, this separatist impulse was visible in England as well, where it began to percolate in Evangelical circles, finding expression in the eruption of the so-called Western Schism in 1815. Shortly afterwards, the emergence of the 'Recordites' can be seen—a small, but highly influential, body of conservative Evangelicals more doctrinaire, and sometimes Calvinistically more advanced, than their contemporaries—which intensified intramural tensions within the Evangelical world.[82] The 'Recordites' were, as a rule, firm supporters of the Established Church, but their tendency to a stern, dogmatic, and Puritan spirituality helped on

[82] Their organ, the *Record*, began publication on 1 Jan. 1828.

secessionist tendencies concealed in the larger Evangelical movement.

In the late 1820s and 1830s several new doctrinaire groupings appeared, creating turbulence among the more earnest devotees of 'vital religion'. One segment gathered round Edward Irving and the so-called Albury Circle; another round John Nelson Darby and the early Christian Brethren; and a third arose in Oxford where high Calvinist doctrine helped to inspire the secession of several prominent Evangelicals, including Henry Bulteel, J. C. Philpot, and William Tiptaft. These events helped (as we will see) to alienate a number of moderate Evangelicals from their party and even, over time, from their Church. The fragmentation of Evangelicalism, and the eruption of extremist deviations, helped, by a reactive process, to act as one of the triggers of the Oxford Movement, and aided the polarization of the Church of England in the decades that followed.

3

Thomas Kelly and John Walker, and the Revival of 'Apostolic' Practices within Irish Evangelicalism

At the outset of the nineteenth century, Evangelicalism was in the ascendant: it was fast stabilizing and consolidating, less prone to extreme forms of speculative Calvinism, more 'regular' in its adherence to the norms of Anglican churchmanship, and increasingly respected within fashionable circles. Nevertheless, it still had its unacceptable face, for a small number of 'irregular' and doctrinally extreme 'Gospel clergymen' remained on the scene, keeping within the bounds of the Establishment, but ministering outside its normal confines and conventions. While a few examples of *outré* clergy could still be found in England, during the first decade of the nineteenth century they became more noticeable in and around Dublin. Here, a revival of so-called 'apostolic' practices occurred around 1803, accompanied by determined separatism, anti-Erastianism, anti-clericalism, and high Calvinism. This movement quickly led to the secessions of two of the most prominent Irish Evangelicals from the Church of Ireland, as well as to the creation of two new religious 'connexions' which rivalled—and often vehemently opposed—both the Anglican Establishment and one another. This chapter will examine the ethos of this Irish revival and its repercussions on Anglicanism on both sides of the Irish Sea.[1]

[1] This study attempts to build on recent scholarly investigations into Irish Evangelicalism. See Alan Acheson, 'The Evangelicals in the Church of Ireland, 1784–1859', Ph.D. thesis (Queen's University, Belfast, 1967); Desmond Bowen, *The Protestant Crusade in Ireland, 1800–70* (Dublin, 1978); Irene Hehir, 'New Lights and Old Enemies: The Second Reformation and the Catholics of Ireland, 1800–35', MA diss. (Wisconsin, 1983); David Hempton, 'Methodism in Irish Society, 1770–1830', in *Transactions of the Royal Historical Society* (1986), 117–42; Joseph Liechty, 'Irish Evangelicalism', Ph.D. thesis (Maynooth, 1987); Myrtle Hill, 'Evangelicalism and the Churches in Ulster Society: 1770–1850', Ph.D. thesis (Queen's University, Belfast, 1987); Joseph Liechty, 'The Popular Reformation Comes to Ireland: The Case of John Walker and the Foundation of the Church of God, 1804', in R. V. Comerford (ed.), *Religion, Conflict and Coexistence in Ireland* (Dublin, 1990), 159–87;

The unsettled life of Evangelicalism in Dublin reflected the wider unease of Anglicanism in what was in some respects an alien and certainly a difficult environment. The Church of Ireland, as the religion favoured by the Anglo-Irish educated middle class, was not, as a rule, the religion of the poor.[2] Although enjoying some success in ministering to the spiritual needs of the minority governing classes, and in producing a number of notable individuals, in the eyes of the Celtic peasantry it remained a symbol of Anglo-Saxon supremacy and domination; the so-called 'handmaid of the Ascendancy'.[3] It was unable to compete effectively with the Roman Catholic priests for the affections of the people, or resist the temptations which accompanied its social elevation and legal establishment.[4]

During the late eighteenth century, the state of Irish Anglicanism had become, at least in the view of the High Church polemicist Richard Mant, 'very low indeed', resembling 'the wilderness, the solitary place, and the desert realized.' This was 'a season of *supineness* and *inaction*'[5] with regard to religion, where Protestants and Roman Catholics were divided into separate cultures, where the dissemination of French revolutionary principles was feared equally by the politicians and the leaders of the two rival religious camps,[6] and where the Anglican clergy languished in relative prosperity and indolence.

In the north, Anglicanism and Presbyterianism vied for political and social supremacy, each despising the other while remaining tied to an unholy alliance against the omnipresent Church of Rome.[7] As pressure mounted to enact Catholic Emancipation, Protestant and Catholic tensions in Ulster increased, making social integration even more difficult in some respects than in the south.

Desmond Bowen, *History and Shaping of Irish Protestantism* (New York, 1995); David Hempton, *Religion and Political Culture in Britain and Ireland* (Cambridge, 1996); Alan Acheson, *A History of the Church of Ireland, 1691–1996* (Dublin, 1997).

[2] See James Anthony Froude, *The English in Ireland in the Eighteenth Century* (1872–4), i.157.

[3] J. K. L. [James Doyle], *Letters on the State of Ireland* (Dublin, 1825), 69. Doyle was the Roman Catholic Bishop of Kildare and Leighlin.

[4] Froude, *The English in Ireland in the Eighteenth Century*, i.157.

[5] Richard Mant, *History of the Church of Ireland* (1840) ii.779.

[6] See Bowen, *The Protestant Crusade in Ireland*, 1–26. Maynooth College was founded in 1795, in part to protect the Irish Catholic clergy from radical French teachings.

[7] Bowen, *The Protestant Crusade in Ireland*, 29–34.

Nor did the spiritual climate of Ireland improve significantly after the Act of Union in 1800–1.[8] 'At that time religion was at a low ebb in the Church of Ireland', claimed the Scottish evangelical Alexander Haldane, and Evangelicals were frequently made the objects of ridicule and reproach.[9] Although increasingly native-born and middle-class, the clergy of the Church of Ireland were still typically younger sons of the Anglo-Irish aristocracy and landed gentry, who continued to monopolize the Established Church's wealthy livings while doing little to promote its welfare, 'either by their liberality or their labour'.[10] Often well-educated, refined, and hospitable, the clergy were seen by the Protestant landowning class as a welcome cultural oasis in the midst of a spiritual and social desert.[11] But although sometimes enthusiastic about advancing Protestantism, far too often the Irish Anglican clergy were impotent and demoralized, living and working in isolation from the social and spiritual life of the encircling Roman Catholic majority. As the Victorian novelist and satirist Anthony Trollope (who had extensive first-hand knowledge of the state of religion in Ireland) claimed during the run-up to Irish disestablishment:

> Of all men the Irish beneficed clergyman is the most illiberal, the most bigoted, the most unforgiving, the most sincere, and the most enthusiastic . . . Soured by the misfortunes of his own position, conscious that something is wrong, though never doubting that he himself is right, aware of his own unavoidable idleness, aware that when he works he works to little or no effect . . . It is a lifelong grief to him that in his parish there should be four hundred and fifty nominal Roman Catholics, and only fifty nominal members of the Church of England. But yet he is staunch. There is a good day coming, though he will never see it.[12]

Moreover, the Anglican episcopal bench in Ireland was often not very effectual. Generally obtaining preferment not through ability or vigour, but through the old channels of social or political connection, the bishops expected to pass from small 'rearing

[8] This united the Church of England and the Church of Ireland into one spiritual and political body.

[9] Alexander Haldane, *Memoirs of the Lives of Robert Haldane of Airthrey, and of His Brother, James Alexander Haldane*, 3rd edn. (1853), 343.

[10] James Godkin, *Ireland and her Churches* (1867), 217.

[11] R. W. Martin, *Ireland Before and After the Union* (1848), 367.

[12] Anthony Trollope, *Clergymen of the Church of England* (1866), 115–16. See also *The McDermots of Ballycloran* (1847).

dioceses' to richer and more powerful appointments unless convicted of a gross neglect of duty.[13] The collective wealth of the bench was dangerously blatant, its bishops described by one Victorian critic sweepingly as 'a sort of Levitical tribe, far better endowed than any other priestly order ever was in the history of the world'.[14] Although in 1815 membership in the Church of Ireland was less than the population of the diocese of Durham (comprising some ten per cent of the Ireland's total population), it was nevertheless governed by no fewer than four archbishops and twenty-two bishops. Its annual revenues totalled some £800,000, three-quarters of which came from tithes mostly paid by the more than six million Irish Catholics.[15]

Despite this atmosphere of privilege and torpor, Irish Evangelicalism began to gain momentum through its fervour.[16] 'Gospel clergymen', lauded by the religious writer Alexander Knox (High Churchman though he was), enjoyed considerable success in advancing the 'doctrines of grace' within the spiritual void left vacant in the aftermath of the French Revolution. 'In Ireland', Knox assured his friend Dr Alcock in 1802, 'things are better. All good, there, is not confined to Methodists, nor the methodistical. We have, there, many who, though not at all methodistical, have religion sincerely at heart, and have hearts finely formed for liberality.'[17] Moderate in their Calvinism, and less rigidly attached to the Establishment than their English counterparts,[18] the Irish Evangelical clergy operated freely within the parochial and extra-parochial circles of Dublin's blossoming revival. From here they corresponded with prominent English Evangelicals, inviting them to visit and preach in their churches, and made frequent reciprocal visits across the Irish Sea.

In this work, Evangelicalism was greatly aided by Irish Methodism. Both had established a foothold in Ireland during the eighteenth century, with Methodism predominating well into the

[13] Bowen, *The Protestant Crusade in Ireland*, 40.

[14] Godkin, *Ireland and Her Churches*, 526.

[15] See T. H. Lister, 'State of the Irish Church', in *EdR* (1835), 502–9.

[16] See Walter Alison Phillips (ed.), *History of the Church of Ireland* (Oxford and London, 1933), iii.333.

[17] Quoted in *Remains of Alexander Knox, Esq.* (1834–7), iv.104. See also iv.501.

[18] In his visitation charge of 1822, when clerical 'irregularity' had become increasingly uncommon within English Evangelical circles, Archbishop Magee of Dublin was compelled to take up this theme at length. See William Magee, *A Charge to the Clergy* (Dublin, 1822), 23–5.

1800s. Subsequently, they grew side by side, Evangelicalism finding its greatest influence amongst the landed gentry and Dublin's influential middle classes, while Methodism was most effective amongst the lower orders in town and country. The social effects of their teachings, however, were much the same, with their respective followers, according to one Victorian account, 'in habits and demeanor strict; . . . active in repressing vice and irreligion, and zealous to promote works of benevolence and charity'.[19]

Precise estimates of the size of the two movements are difficult to make. In 1791, at the time of Wesley's death, there were twenty-nine circuits, sixty-seven Methodist preachers, and fourteen thousand Irish members,[20] including some 'Church' Methodists who continued to receive the sacraments at the Established Church and who were, therefore, often indistinguishable from Evangelicals.[21] By 1802, there were one hundred and twenty-two Wesleyan meeting houses in Ireland. Fourteen years later, the movement had grown to forty-eight circuits, one hundred and thirty-three preachers, and nearly twenty-nine thousand members.[22] By contrast, the Evangelical party at this time was relatively small; one account estimated its strength in 1797 at twenty-nine clergymen.[23] Through the early to mid-nineteenth century Anglican Evangelicalism steadily gained influence in the Church of Ireland, benefiting greatly not only from its social and established status, but also from the pervasive challenge of the old enemy, Roman Catholicism.[24] It was commonly accepted by most Irish Protestants outside Ulster that it would be disastrous for Protestantism to splinter into smaller groups, as in the north. This belief hindered orthodox Dissent from expanding as rapidly in Ireland (outside the northern counties) during this period, as it did in England,[25] leaving the Evangelicals to advance the 'doctrines

[19] See J. T. Ball, *The Reformed Church of Ireland*, 2nd edn. (London and Dublin, 1890), 269–70. See also Acheson, *A History of the Church of Ireland*, 100–5.

[20] Godkin, *Ireland and Her Churches*, 106.

[21] Bowen, *The Protestant Crusade in Ireland*, 34.

[22] Godkin, *Ireland and Her Churches*, 106.

[23] See Maiben C. Motherwell, *A Memoir of The Late Albert Blest* (Dublin, 1843), 64.

[24] See Donald H. Akenson, *The Church of Ireland* (New Haven, 1971), 132; Acheson, *A History of the Church of Ireland*, 120–1, 126–7, 155–60.

[25] In 1816, there were 7,490 Nonconformists in Dublin: 2,200 Orthodox Presbyterians, 760 Unitarians, 140 Presbyterian Seceders, 1,700 Independents, 1,420 Methodists, 230 Moravians, 150 Baptists, 650 Quakers, and 240 miscellaneous Dissenters (including 'Kellyites' and 'Walkerites'). See Godkin, *Ireland and Her Churches*, 106.

of grace' without much hindrance from their Protestant 'allies'.[26]

The influence of Evangelicalism in Ireland was disproportionate to its numerical strength, and even some critics of 'serious religion' were impressed by its success. William Magee, the moderately Evangelical Archbishop of Dublin, reported to the House of Lords in 1825 that there had 'been lately an excitement of attention to the subject of religion throughout the people, such as perhaps there has not been before at any period since the Reformation. In truth, with respect to Ireland, the Reformation may, strictly speaking, be truly said only now to have begun.'[27] Gladstone claimed that the Irish Evangelical party made, if not earlier, then greater, progress than its English counterpart, for its growth was aided by the highly political nature of the local religious climate.[28] In Ireland, as elsewhere during this period, Anglicanism tended to move along its Protestant–Catholic poles in direct response to the religious orthodoxy of its major competitor (or opponent). Where Roman Catholicism was in the ascendancy, as in Ireland, or where it was influential, as in Liverpool, more overtly Reformed forms of Anglicanism predominated; alternatively, where Protestantism was in the ascendancy, as in much of Scotland, Anglicanism tended toward more Catholic forms of expression. This inherent counter-effect within Anglicanism was not lost on the Irish Evangelical clergy, whose advancement of the 'doctrines of grace' was enthusiastically welcomed by many Protestants as a prophylactic against religious and social dominance by Rome.

In a receptive spiritual climate, Evangelicals came to exert a powerful influence within the Church of Ireland, and within

[26] Even by 1850, there were only 24 Congregational, 16 Baptist, and 12 Brethren chapels in Ireland. See William Urwick, *Brief Sketch of the Religious State of Ireland* (Dublin, 1852), 16.

[27] William Magee, *The Evidence of His Grace the Archbishop of Dublin, Before the Select Committee of the House of Lords, on the State of Ireland* (Dublin, 1825), 9–10. After a celebrated career at Trinity College, Dublin, Magee (1766–1831) became rector of Cappagh, County Tyrone, and Killeleagh, County Down, and was once considered by Spencer Perceval for the vacant see of Oxford. He was successively Bishop of Raphoe (1819–22), and Archbishop of Dublin (1822–31). For a more thorough discussion of the influence of the Protestant cause in Ireland at this time see Joseph Liechty, 'The Problem of Sectarianism and the Church of Ireland', in Alan Ford, James McGuire, and Kenneth Milne (eds.), *As by Law Established: The Church of Ireland Since the Reformation* (Dublin, 1995), 220.

[28] W. E. Gladstone, 'The Evangelical Movement: its Parentage, Progress, and Issue', in *QR* (1879), 10.

Irish society at large. This can be seen within such national institutions as Trinity College, Dublin, where several 'Gospel clergymen' became distinguished fellows;[29] and on the Episcopal bench, to which were elevated a number of accomplished Evangelicals—such as Robert Daly and Power le Poer Trench—to positions of leadership.[30] It can also be seen in Irish family life (especially among the aristocracy), where a large Evangelical network developed, and in the extensive operations of numerous voluntary societies in Ireland, many of which were dominated by Evangelicals.[31]

In the 1790s there were traumatic upheavals in Ireland as the spirit of revolution spread, stimulated by French example. The formation of the United Irishmen, and the insurrection and massacre at Wexford and elsewhere in 1798, sent profound shock waves through the country. Here, without doubt, was an atmosphere favourable to the growth of 'serious religion'.[32] As one contemporary account wrote, 'we live in an age when not only the pillars of government, but the adamantine foundations of religion itself, shaken as it were by an earthquake, tremble to its base.'[33] A revitalized Protestantism founded on faith and conversion, with implications for the transformation of the 'inner' man, offered a twofold attraction. First, the personal, experiential piety of Evan-

[29] Liechty, 'Irish Evangelicalism', 124. Of the 29 Evangelicals serving in the Church of Ireland in 1797, almost all had attended Trinity College.

[30] Daly (1783–1872), a graduate of Trinity College, Dublin, was successively Dean of St. Patrick's, Dublin (1842–3), and Bishop of Cashel, Emly, Waterford, and Lismore (1843–72). Trench (1770–1839), also a graduate of Trinity College, Dublin, was successively Bishop of Waterford (1802–10), Elphin (1810–19), and Archbishop of Tuam (1819–39). Some confusion surrounds the issue of Trench's adherence to Evangelicalism. Donald Akinson denies Trench's Evangelical connections. See Akinson, *The Church in Ireland*, 133. The author of Walker's entry in the *DNB* (and other scholars), however, acknowledge his continued adherence to 'serious religion'. While opposed to the extreme doctrines of grace, Trench actively promoted the interests of Evangelicalism on a number of various levels, including the Bible Society, the Church Missionary Society, and the Irish Society, in which he served a lengthy term as President. Upon his death, the well-known Evangelical Peter Roe described him as 'an honoured instrument in the promotion of Evangelical religion'. See Joseph D'Arcy Sirr, *A Memoir of the Honourable and Most Reverend Power Le Poer Trench* (Dublin, 1845), 61, 459, 487, 791; Acheson, *A History of the Church of Ireland*, 127.

[31] Ibid. 121, 124–5, 127–8.

[32] For more information on the Wexford Rising and the accompanying civil unrest in Ireland during the 1790s see J. C. Beckett, *The Making of Modern Ireland 1603–1923* (1966), 263–5; Marianne Elliott, 'Ireland and the French Revolution', in H. T. Dickinson (ed.), *Britain and the French Revolution* (1989), 83–101.

[33] *Ireland's Mirror, or A Chronicle of the Times* (Dublin, 1804–5), i, p. iii.

gelical religion gave solace in a period of acute anxiety. Second, the evangelistic energies of the Revival offered a possible way of dealing with the insurgency of the rebellious Roman Catholic majority: it was hoped that the conversion of the peasantry to 'vital religion' might bring about the social stability which force of arms could not achieve. Many landlords previously opposed to methodistical 'enthusiasm' now welcomed travelling preachers. Consequently, from the 1790s began what Desmond Bowen has appropriately christened 'the Protestant Crusade' for the spiritual conquest of the Irish people.

However, the alarms of the Revolutionary era could have two potentially contradictory results. On the one hand, it could assist the creation of a pan-evangelical movement, similar to that on the mainland in which various religious groups united to promote the Gospel; not only to galvanize 'nominal' Protestant churchgoers, but also to convert the mass of Roman Catholics. In such a framework, converted Evangelicals of all persuasions could co-operate against the Roman menace which surrounded them. In unity lay strength. Yet there was also a countervailing force which promoted schism and theological extremism. The links between social or political movements and religious attitudes are often obscure, but it is likely that the trauma of the Revolutionary era had a catalytic effect on some Evangelical minds in very different ways: while it provoked evangelism in some quarters, it also excited millennialism in others. In some minds the political-religious tensions of the period aroused yet another reaction: a desire for purist separatism, a drawing apart of the chosen few into a tight-knit brotherhood which cut itself off from the wicked and turbulent world which threatened it.

The 'Protestant crusade' encouraged several developments on the Irish religious scene. One of the most significant was the establishment of religious societies, or special interest groups organized to promote a specific goal.[34] These included the General Evangelical Society in Dublin, formed in 1787; the Ulster Evangelical Society, formed in 1798; the Hibernian Bible Society, formed in 1806; and the Hibernian Church Missionary Society, formed in

[34] See Akenson, *The Church of Ireland*, 134; Phillips, *History of the Church of Ireland*, iii.335–6, 349–51. Some were pan-evangelical, in that they included both churchmen and Dissenters; while others, like the Hibernian Church Missionary Society, were strictly Anglican in membership.

1814.[35] These voluntary societies had a number of advantages over the parochial ministry, upon which the Irish Evangelicals were quick to capitalize. Though parishes were fixed geographically, the societies were inter-diocesan; ecclesiastical boundaries were largely irrelevant to them and their members.[36] Thus, they served as a means by which Evangelicals could engage in 'quasi-irregular' itinerant ministries, not tied to parish limits, and able to penetrate evangelistically into 'dark' parishes without incurring criticism or canonical censure. Moreover, the societies were not under the authority of diocesan bishops or the Established Church, but were semi-autonomous bodies controlled by boards of governors. These boards were generally composed of clergy *and* laymen, churchmen *and* Dissenters, with the Anglican clergy sometimes in the minority. Thus, a society's evangelistic efforts could benefit from its Anglican connections (in such things as employing the Church's formularies and rubrics), or it could ignore them, whichever proved most advantageous in a given situation. Either way, these powerful associations had the result of softening the boundaries between Church and Dissent. The Evangelicals engaged in them were unlikely to be stiff churchmen. Their attachment to the Established religion was somewhat more shallowly rooted than usual. At the same time, however, in at least one way these societies contributed to an escalation of Anglican–Nonconformist tensions: they provoked High Churchmen who were quick to denounce any enterprise (or body) which involved co-operation between Church and Dissent. Thus, the efforts of Evangelicals to strengthen the Establishment through evangelism and through developing links with orthodox Nonconformists, sometimes led—ironically—to its weakening.

Another effect of the 'Protestant crusade' in Ireland was the opening of private homes in Dublin and elsewhere to the ministry of Evangelicals, Methodists, and Moravians—a development which, although 'irregular', attracted a large number of important middle-class converts to the cause of 'serious religion'.[37] Even more influential was the building of several private evangelical

[35] Liechty, 'Irish Evangelicalism', 6, 56. [36] Akinson, *The Church in Ireland*, 134.

[37] See A. C. H. Seymour, *The Life and Times of Selina, Countess of Huntingdon* (1839–40), ii.215–16.

chapels operating on the fringes of the Established Church, such as York Street and Plunket Street Chapels, Dublin.[38] By far the most significant of Dublin's 'extra-parochial' preaching houses was Bethesda Chapel, in Dorset Street, which became so influential that it was known locally as the 'cathedral' of Irish Evangelicalism.[39]

Bethesda had been opened in June 1786, 'according to the forms of the Episcopal Church',[40] with Edward Smyth, a close associate of Wesley and an Arminian, and William Mann, a moderate Calvinist, serving as its first chaplains.[41] William Smyth, a local lay patron who was anxious to establish an Evangelical presence in Dublin, had personally financed the chapel's construction,[42] having been led to believe that it would be licensed by his uncle, the archbishop of Dublin, as a chapel-of-ease; however, his uncle's premature death and the unwillingness of his successor, John Cradock, to sanction the establishment of a 'Gospel chapel' in his diocese, prevented this from occurring and Bethesda instead became a Dissenting meeting house protected by the Toleration Act.[43] Despite this unforeseen development, Bethesda continued to stand in close connection with the Established Church, its deed of trust stipulating that its trustees and chaplains be drawn from the Evangelical clergy. This created a most ambiguous situation in that several episcopally ordained Evangelicals were not only officiating in what was technically a Dissenting meeting house, but were also trustees of its affairs. In 1821, John Beresford,

[38] York Street Chapel had been established in 1808 by a group of local evangelical businessmen, and could accommodate over sixteen hundred worshippers. See Liechty, 'Irish Evangelicalism', 68–9, 328–31; Godkin, *Ireland and her Churches*, 105; Anon., *Life and Letters of William Urwick, D.D., of Dublin* (1870), 280–1. Plunket Street Chapel was associated with the Countess of Huntingdon's Connexion, William Cooper serving as minister. See William Urwick, 'Memoir of the Late Revd Thomas Kelly, of Dublin', in *EM*, (Feb. 1856), 64; Acheson, 'The Evangelicals in the Church of Ireland', 19; Godkin, *Ireland and Her Churches*, 104–5.

[39] Bowen, *The Protestant Crusade in Ireland*, 68; Richard Sinclair Brooke, *Recollections of the Irish Church* (1877), 18; Acheson, *A History of the Church of Ireland*, 98–9. See also Akinson, *The Church in Ireland*, 132. Bethesda was occasionally referred to as Lock Chapel, a reference to the adjoining penitentiary.

[40] C. H. Crookshank, *Memorable Women of Irish Methodism in the Last Century* (1882), 112. The foundation stone at Bethesda had been laid in July 1784. The chapel was destroyed by fire in 1839, Bethesda Church being erected in its place.

[41] Seymour, *Selina, Countess of Huntingdon*, ii.202; Liechty, 'Irish Evangelicalism', 331–2.

[42] Crookshank, *Memorable Women*, 112. Seymour, *Selina, Countess of Huntingdon*, ii.202.

[43] See Acheson, 'The Evangelicals in the Church of Ireland', 27–32, Appendix A.

Archbishop of Dublin, declined the petition of a number of eminent Evangelical laymen to license Bethesda because he opposed the Calvinistic doctrines preached there.[44] This irregular situation continued until 1825, when Bethesda was licensed as a proprietary chapel of the Church of Ireland by Archbishop William Magee.[45]

In spite of its anomalous early status on the fringes of the Established Church, Bethesda soon became the centre of the Irish Evangelical movement;[46] it was a venue for such well-known 'Gospel clergymen' as the Arminian John Wesley and the moderate Calvinist Rowland Hill during their visits to Ireland.[47] The ministry at Bethesda proved so popular and influential that the provost of Trinity College soon inhibited undergraduates from attending its services, while the unsympathetic bishop of Cashel regarded attendance (let alone preaching) at Bethesda as a test of disloyal churchmanship in those seeking ordination or preferment.[48] With the resignation of both Smyth and Mann in 1794, however, the nature of Bethesda chapel began to alter. Perhaps reflecting larger changes within Irish Evangelicalism as it gained confidence and moved increasingly away from its Methodist cradle, the Chapel became more rigidly Calvinistic, more separatist, and less attached to the formularies of the Established Church. The Scottish high Calvinist James Alexander Haldane was warmly received by John Walker and Walter Maturin, Bethesda's new chaplains, when visiting Dublin during the summer of 1804, and preached frequently from its pulpit.[49] In the course of time, these changes had a profound effect upon the prosperity of both Bethesda and Irish Evangelicalism itself.

[44] Acheson, *A History of the Church of Ireland*, 137. Beresford did not, as Acheson suggests, become Archbishop of Armagh until 1822.

[45] See Acheson, 'The Evangelicals in the Church of Ireland', 162; idem. *A History of the Church of Ireland*, 157.

[46] Seymour, *Selina, Countess of Huntingdon*, ii.230–1. Stokes characterized Bethesda as 'the headquarters of the followers of Whitefield and Lady Huntingdon in Dublin'. See G. T. Stokes, 'John Nelson Darby', in the *Contemporary Review* (1855), 539. Alexander Haldane referred to Bethesda as 'a beacon-light in the midst of darkness'. See Haldane, *Memoirs of Robert and James Alexander Haldane*, 343.

[47] Seymour, *Selina, Countess of Huntingdon*, ii.206, 219, 225. Wesley preached at Bethesda in 1787, some four years before his death.

[48] Liechty, 'Irish Evangelicalism', 332.

[49] Haldane, *Memoirs of Robert and James Alexander Haldane*, 343.

I

For all its growth and increasing prominence, the Irish Evangelical movement was not without its concomitant difficulties. Even more than in England, there remained an undercurrent of Protestant extremism, encouraged by religious dogmatism in Scotland and Ulster. Irish Evangelicalism was not entirely successful in resisting clerical irregularity, or in adhering to the moderate version of the 'doctrines of grace' which had now united most English Evangelicals into a coherent, respectable, and influential party. Consequently, the cause of 'vital religion' in Ireland suffered a damaging reversal at the beginning of the nineteenth century: the almost simultaneous secession of Thomas Kelly and John Walker, two of the most gifted and energetic clergymen of their generation, whose loss to the Established Church and to the Irish Evangelical movement encouraged outbreaks of theological extremism and sent shudders through religious circles on both sides of the Irish Sea.

Thomas Kelly was born in Dublin in 1769, the son of Thomas Kelly, a wealthy and prominent Dublin lawyer.[50] An amiable and buoyant young man,[51] he entered Trinity College, Dublin, in 1785, intending to practise law, and it was here that his friendship with his contemporary John Walker developed.[52] Then, coming under the influence of the Hutchinsonians,[53] Kelly became an ascetic, so reducing himself by fasting that he jeopardized his own life.[54] The preaching and writings of William Romaine impressed him with the awfulness of eternity, and a few remarks from John Walker completed his determination to devote himself entirely to spiritual matters.[55] In 1792, therefore, against the wishes of his

[50] Kelly's father, the Rt. Hon. Chief Baron Kelly, was a judge of the Irish Court of Common Pleas. See Frederic Boase, *Modern English Biography*, 2nd edn. (1965), v.806; Brooke, *Recollections of the Irish Church*, 193. Kelly junior was perhaps best known as the author of some 765 hymns. See Thomas Kelly, *Hymns on Various Passages of Scripture* (Dublin, 1804); *Hymns Adapted for Social Worship* (Dublin, 1811); and *Hymns Not Before Published* (Dublin, 1815).

[51] Urwick, 'Memoir of Thomas Kelly', 61. Cf. Anon., *Life of William Urwick.*

[52] Walker graduated from Trinity College in 1789. See *Al. Dub.*, 458; Brooke, *Recollections of the Irish Church*, 193.

[53] Or that body which formed around the High Church religious figure, John Hutchinson (1674–1737).

[54] See Urwick, 'Memoir of Thomas Kelly', 62.

[55] See ibid. 61–2; D. E. Jenkins, *The Life of the Revd Thomas Charles B.A. of Bala* (Denbigh, 1908), iii.175.

father, he abandoned the law and was ordained, together with his friends Walker, Walter Shirley, and Henry Maturin, in the Established Church.[56]

In early 1794, intent on advancing 'free grace' within Dublin's numerous but somewhat comatose Churches, the four friends arranged with another ally, the curate of St. Luke's, Dublin, to preach in succession each Sunday afternoon at the Church.[57] This initiative produced much local excitement and made a rapid impact on the artisans of that manufacturing district.[58] Before long, however, the rector got wind of their activities. Dismissing their extempore preaching as being 'tantamount to Methodism and Dissent',[59] he silenced the four and reported them to the archbishop.[60] During this period, Kelly also celebrated communion at small, private gatherings of Evangelicals: though he knew this practice was proscribed by canon law, he held it to be established—and therefore permitted—by Jesus' 'great commission'.[61] His episcopal superiors saw matters in a different light. Robert Fowler, the Archbishop of Dublin, summoned Kelly and his three friends to answer charges of irregularity and preaching 'strange and pernicious doctrines'.[62] Though claiming that they taught only those doctrines set out in the Articles, Fowler remained unimpressed; all four were swiftly inhibited from further ministry in the diocese of Dublin.[63]

Like the Methodists a generation earlier, these young Evangelical clergymen were driven to minister in Dissenting chapels, in private houses, in the open air, or in other dioceses. Some moved on to a ministry in Dublin's private chapels, while Kelly, at first continuing at a local 'drawing-room meeting' at the home of Alderman Hutton,[64] soon abandoned Dublin for his father's

[56] Jenkins, *Life of Thomas Charles*, iii.175; C. H. Crookshank, *History of Methodism in Ireland* (1886), ii.67.

[57] Urwick, 'Memoir of Thomas Kelly', 63; Anon, *Life of William Urwick*, 281.

[58] Jenkins, *Life of Thomas Charles*, iii.175.

[59] Brooke, *Recollections*, 193; Urwick, 'Memoir of Thomas Kelly', 63.

[60] Jenkins, *Life of Thomas Charles*, iii.175; Motherwell, *Memoir of Albert Blest*, 71–2. See also Seymour, *Selina, Countess of Huntingdon*, ii.213–14.

[61] John Hall, *The Memory of the Just: A Tribute to the Memory of the Late Thomas Kelly* (Dublin, 1855), 17–18. See also Haldane, *Memoirs of Robert and James Alexander Haldane*, 343.

[62] Urwick, 'Memoir of Thomas Kelly', 63; Acheson, *A History of the Church in Ireland*, 114.

[63] Crookshank, *History of Methodism in Ireland*, ii.67.

[64] Urwick, 'Memoir of Thomas Kelly', 64. See also Brooke, *Recollections of the Irish Church*, 16.

country house in Queen's County, afterwards taking up a cure of souls in the nearby parish of Athy.[65] Here his preaching proved highly popular, and led to co-operation with the local Wesleyan Methodists and Independents in advancing the 'doctrines of grace'. Opposition to this 'irregularity' from the ecclesiastical authorities, however, soon led Kelly to abandon all hope of preferment in the Church of Ireland.[66] In 1794 he married a Miss Tighe of Rosanna, who contributed a substantial sum to his already considerable fortune.[67] He then migrated to Blackrock, outside Dublin, where he officiated at a small chapel-of-ease constructed from his own resources. Kelly's genius for preaching and organization soon attracted a sizeable congregation at the chapel, which served as the focal point of his powerful, if unsettled, ministry for many years.[68]

During this period Kelly preached wherever he was called: at Bethesda Chapel, at St. Mary's, Kilkenny, or in neighbouring parishes, either on his own or in partnership with the English Evangelical Rowland Hill, whose pan-evangelical fervour he now shared, or with the Scottish high Calvinist Robert Haldane.[69] By 1802, he had formed his own preaching connexion, in partnership with the Countess of Huntingdon and the Independents, which supplied preachers for the work of the local interdenominational General Evangelical Society. As they set off on their itinerant tours, Kelly's preachers were reminded that they were not being sent out 'as the agents of *any* party in the "Church of Christ" '; their only purpose was to 'declare the pure and simple Gospel to all who are willing to hear it'.[70]

Kelly was too wealthy and temperamentally too independent to remain subject to those, like Fowler and most of the Irish episcopal bench, whom he did not respect, and too sensitive to subject

[65] Jenkins, *Life of Thomas Charles*, iii.175; Crookshank, *History of Methodism in Ireland*, ii.67, 71.

[66] See Jenkins, *Life of Thomas Charles*, iii.175.

[67] Ibid., ii.67. Kelly's wife was the only child of Sir William and Lady Betty Fownes, and upon their death, she inherited their considerable fortune and estates. See Seymour, *Selina, Countess of Huntingdon*, ii.213.

[68] Crookshank, *History of Methodism in Ireland*, ii.67.

[69] See Seymour, *Selina, Countess of Huntingdon*, ii.219, 225; John Scott (ed.), *Letters and Papers of the Late Revd Thomas Scott, D.D.* (New Haven, 1826), 185; Haldane, *Memoirs of Robert and James Alexander Haldane*, 499–500; Samuel Madden, *Memoir of the Life of the Late Peter Roe, A.M.* (Dublin, 1842), 57.

[70] *Hibernian Evangelical Magazine* (1802), 183.

himself to further episcopal discipline.[71] In 1803, therefore, he formally seceded from the Established Church, concluding that his evangelistic talents would be more effective within his own connexion.[72] This decision was partly based upon the belief that a national establishment of religion, 'whatever truth might be embodied in its confessions and its ritual, could not, *as a system*, be so modified as to bring into operation the principles of the New Testament'.[73] Kelly concluded that he must secede or forever be identified with the abuses of the Established Church. He later justified his decision in terms of his pan-evangelical ecclesiology. By seceding from the Church of Ireland he would maintain closer fellowship with the members of the larger 'Church of Christ'. He could, he argued:

> Avow a personal fellowship . . . with every minister of the . . . Church who cordially holds, faithfully preaches, and consistently exemplifies . . . justification 'by the grace of God . . .' I can see . . . the multiplication of faithful and zealous preachers of this doctrine in the . . . Establishment . . . [which] with me, is but one species of a genus . . . I do not dissent from the sound doctrine embodied in certain Articles . . . neither do I dissent from the persons, whether clergymen or others, who love our Lord Jesus Christ in sincerity.[74]

At his own expense, Kelly then set about establishing meeting houses affiliated as 'Kellyites', as his connexion quickly became known throughout Ireland and England.[75] Some of his pulpits were filled by laymen and local ministers, others with students from the Haldanes' academy in Scotland.[76] Although the precise location and numerical strength of the 'Kellyites' remains uncertain, congregations were known to exist at New Ross, Waterford, Blackrock, Dublin, Athy, Kilkenny, Cork, Limerick,[77] Portarlington, and Wexford.[78] Here and elsewhere Kelly proved a popular preacher, gaining the respect of many throughout Ireland and

[71] Brooke, *Recollections of the Irish Church*, 17.

[72] Acheson, 'The Evangelicals in the Church of Ireland', 32.

[73] See Motherwell, *Memoir of Albert Blest*, 79.

[74] Quoted in Urwick, 'Memoir of Thomas Kelly', 65.

[75] Brooke, *Recollections of the Irish Church*, 193.

[76] Urwick, 'Memoir of Thomas Kelly', 65.

[77] Jenkins, *Life of Thomas Charles*, iii.175; Robert Milne, *An Attempt to Defend the Church of England*. (Dublin, 1817), 7; Crookshank, *History of Methodism in Ireland*, ii.67.

[78] H. H. Rowdon, 'Secession From the Established Church in the Early Nineteenth Century', in *VE* (1964), 78.

Britain. In 1807, during a visit to Ireland (discussed below), the Welsh Evangelical Thomas Charles lodged with Kelly's father in Dublin. Although alarmed by the generally low state of 'serious religion' in Ireland, Charles nevertheless waxed lyrical about the Judge's son, describing him as 'a very pious clergyman'. The younger Kelly spoke of visiting Wales and Chester in the following October, Charles reported, 'and I will do all I can to prevail on him to visit Liverpool. He is a much *respected* character by *all*, his ministry has been much blessed.'[79]

The 'Kellyites' theological and doctrinal principles remain cloudy, partly because Kelly was unconcerned about defining them in the context of heated controversy, which might hinder his evangelistic efforts. His focus lay on the 'one thing needful'. Moreover, his movement was less radical than the parallel connexion formed by his friend and rival John Walker (discussed below). What can be ascertained is that Kelly wished it to resemble the 'apostolic' model: baptism and communion were recognized as sacraments; two orders of ecclesiastical offices were established, elders and deacons; and informal ordination, which was open to every qualified member, was seen as a prerequisite to holding office or a position of trust.[80] Worship was not, however, as in Walker's body, thrown open to anyone wishing to speak, but conducted by members according to a prearranged plan, allowing some limited opportunity for extempore prayer and preaching. Baptism was made strictly on profession of faith.[81] These doctrinal positions bore considerable resemblance to those of the Irish Independents, as Kelly was repeatedly informed by William Urwick, the well-known Congregationalist minister of York Street Chapel, Dublin.[82]

As a moderate Calvinist, Kelly attempted to occupy the 'middle ground' between what he considered to be the doctrinally 'unreformed' religious Establishment and the more extreme forms of speculative Calvinism, such as that advanced by Walker and his followers. He dismissed a suggestion that the 'Kellyites' should unite with the 'Walkerites' because he objected to Walker's

[79] Charles to Thomas Rice Charles, 20 Aug. 1807, in Jenkins, *Life of Thomas Charles*, iii.174.

[80] Hall, *The Memory of the Just*, 19, 22.

[81] William Blair Neatby, *A History of the Plymouth Brethren* (1901), 27–8.

[82] Anon., *Life of William Urwick*, 280–1.

teaching that the Arminian John Wesley was in Hell.[83] Despite the success of his movement, Kelly remained a somewhat aloof figure in the 'Gospel world'. Though numerous attempts to enlist his aid either in the larger Evangelical movement or in the disestablishment campaign were made, he refused to be drawn away from his work in extending the influence and spiritual life of his own connexion.[84]

When Kelly eventually deigned to respond in print to critics of his secession,[85] he claimed that his doctrines had been unchanged since the date of his ordination. He denied that his separation from the Established Church posed any threat to the State;[86] indeed, he urged that secession based upon truly spiritual principles must lead Christians to become, as in apostolic times, loyal and peaceful members of the community.[87] Since the early Church had been founded upon the principles of selection and spirituality,[88] and since the Church of Ireland had lost both of these attributes, it neither was, nor could be, based upon the same ancient model. The Established Church, he concluded, had therefore apostatized from Christian orthodoxy because it had substituted the doctrine of comprehension for that of 'selection', and because it had embraced liberalism and secularism at the expense of true spirituality.[89]

Kelly's tract provoked a number of lively responses. The well-known English Evangelical and biblical commentator Thomas Scott published a riposte supporting the principle of religious establishments and denouncing many of Kelly's assertions.[90] The claim that it was the absence of establishment in the apostolic church which had encouraged its rapid growth and preserved its

[83] See Neatby, *A History of the Plymouth Brethren*, 27.

[84] Alan Acheson claims that there is no evidence that Kelly led even one person to secede from the Established Church, implying that his followers were drawn either from Protestant Dissent (including Methodism), from Roman Catholicism, or from the unchurched. See Acheson, 'The Evangelicals in the Church of Ireland', 122. Cf. Richard Sinclair Brooke, *Recollections of the Irish Church*, 194.

[85] Thomas Kelly, *A Plea for Primitive Christianity: In Answer to a Pamphlet by the Revd Peter Roe, Entitled, 'The Evil of Separation from the Church of England'* (Dublin, 1815). For a response to this see Milne, *An Attempt to Defend the Church of England.*

[86] Kelly, *A Plea for Primitive Christianity*, 2–3.

[87] Ibid. 4. [88] Ibid. 8–9. [89] Ibid. 9–10.

[90] Thomas Scott, *A Letter to the Revd Peter Roe* (Kilkenny, 1816). See also William Burgh, *Dissent From the Church of England Shewn to be Unwarrantable*, 2nd edn. (Dublin, 1833). Kelly responded to Burgh's attack in *A Letter to the Revd William Burgh* (Dublin, 1833).

doctrinal purity was energetically taken up, Scott pointing out the historical irrelevance of such a suggestion. How could such a tiny movement as the Christianity of the Acts of the Apostles have been 'established' by the hostile, pagan Roman emperors of the first century AD? Equally absurd was Kelly's claim that the Irish bishops might expel the Evangelical clergy: this was politically impracticable, and, if attempted, would ruin the Church of Ireland.[91]

In the aftermath of this exchange, Power Le Poer Trench, the moderate Evangelical Archbishop of Tuam, wrote twice to Kelly attempting to draw him back into the fold of the Established Church.[92] After being rebuffed on both occasions, Trench replied: 'It is clear to me . . . that your objection is not to the doctrines or discipline of our Established Church, but to all establishments as such.'[93] Trench urged Kelly to consider the views of Joseph Milner and Thomas Chalmers, who had both penned famous works defending establishment on grounds of history and utility, and accept arguments in favour of a state church.[94] Kelly replied that he did not object to the existence of establishments *per se*, but to any religious institution which might compel its members to abandon the principle of private judgement. He conceded that an establishment might conceivably exist in which Christians were not inhibited from professing their own principles, but he clearly did not regard the Irish Church as falling into this category for it had apostatized from the teachings of the New Testament. Should, therefore, the Church of Ireland be disestablished? Unlike many nineteenth-century Nonconformists (and unlike many of the Evangelical seceders), Kelly expressed no interest in the separation of Church and State as a political issue. Nor would he allow his secession from the Church to separate him from those true believers who chose to remain within it.[95]

[91] Scott, *A Letter*, 4–6.

[92] See Trench to Kelly, 16 Oct. 1820, in Sirr, *Memoir of Power Le Poer Trench*, 728–31. By one account, Peter Roe also made repeated attempts to entice Kelly back into the Church. See Brooke, *Recollections of the Irish Church*, 194.

[93] See Trench to Kelly, 21 Dec. 1820, in Sirr, *Memoir of Power Le Poer Trench*, 730.

[94] Ibid. 731. See Joseph Milner, *The History of the Church of Christ* (York and Cambridge, 1794–1809), especially the chapter 'Reflections on Ecclesiastical Establishments'; Thomas Chalmers, *The Christian and Civic Economy of Large Towns* (Glasgow, 1821–6), i.91, 93. Chalmers's essays had previously been published in separate form, at first in the *Edinburgh Review* and later independently. See Stewart J. Brown, *Thomas Chalmers and the Godly Commonwealth in Scotland* (Oxford, 1982), 144.

[95] Sirr, *Memoir of Power Le Poer Trench*, 731.

Kelly's unwillingness to issue a blanket condemnation of the Irish Church, or to agitate for its disestablishment, tended to moderate the impact of his secession. On the surface, this appears a mere episode; when, however, the 'Kellyite' schism is seen within its larger context as a group separation occurring simultaneously with the more spectacular departure of John Walker, it takes on added significance. Together, the two secessions sent shudders of alarm through both the Irish Church and Evangelicalism at large.

Though Kelly's schism drew unwelcome attention to the discontent of Evangelical 'ultras', it did not give the new connexion enough publicity to attract large numbers or ensure its permanence, for by 1856 many of his chapels had closed. Congregations still met at Blackrock, Waterford, New Ross, Athy, and perhaps elsewhere, but by now the number of adherents had shrunk considerably. He continued to minister to the congregations at Blackrock and Athy until his death in May 1855, but whether—and for how long—they continued after that time remains uncertain.[96] Curiously, in 1846, some nine years before Kelly's death, the *Dublin University Magazine* reported that he was said to have declared 'that if Dr Magee had been archbishop before his secession from the Church, he never would have been a separatist'. It then claimed, probably erroneously, that Magee (who died in 1831) had actually secured Kelly's readmission to the Church.[97] No other evidence exists to support this assertion, and it seems unlikely that the *Evangelical Magazine* (an organ of Protestant Dissent) would have lauded Kelly's achievements after his demise, had he in fact returned to the Church.[98] In any case, the rapid decline of Kelly's connexion may have been due to its rather chaotic organizational structure, which rejected any hint of formal ministry. Another factor may have been Kelly's tendency, during his later years, to live a rather retired and studious life, spending less time preaching and itinerating about the Irish countryside. The decline of the 'Kellyites' may also have been accelerated by the rapid growth of 'serious religion' within the Irish Establishment, or competition from new sects like the Christian Brethren, which began to emerge in and

[96] See Jenkins, *Life of Thomas Charles*, iii.175; Urwick, 'Memoir of Thomas Kelly', 65–6. See also the *Primitive Wesleyan Methodist Magazine* (1856), 80–4.

[97] See *Dublin University Magazine* (Dec. 1846), 761.

[98] See Urwick, 'Memoir of Thomas Kelly', 61–71.

around Dublin during the late 1820s. Whatever the causes, Kelly's secession and the establishment of his connexion were by no means without significance, for they drew attention to some of the difficulties encountered by 'Gospel clergymen' on both sides of the Irish Sea in adhering to the Anglican Establishment, and gave added weight to the more spectacular exit of John Walker from the Church.

II

The secession of Kelly's friend, colleague, and sometimes rival, the more volatile and vitriolic John Walker, was of considerable significance to the cause of 'serious religion' in Ireland.[99] It led to the establishment of the first indigenous Irish Dissenting body;[100] it robbed the forces of Irish Evangelicalism of its most popular, and perhaps most able, commander;[101] and it encouraged the revival of 'apostolic' practices, with an accompanying separatism and high Calvinism, within the Evangelical ranks. It also brought about—by abreaction—increased discipline and clerical 'order' among those Evangelicals who remained within the Irish Church;[102] it helped to discredit 'vital religion' when it was beginning to win converts within fashionable circles; and, perhaps most serious of all, it damaged the mission of the Church of Ireland by providing Roman Catholics with a sensational and well-publicized example of Protestant schism and division.

Walker was born in 1768 in County Roscommon, the son of the Evangelical clergyman Matthew Clericus Walker.[103] He entered Trinity College, Dublin, in 1786,[104] and was later ordained, quickly establishing such a reputation within Dublin's burgeoning Evangelical movement as a popular and effective

[99] For biographical information on Walker see *DNB*; James Wills and Freeman Wills, *The Irish Nation: Its History and Its Biography* (Edinburgh, London, and Dublin, 1875), iv.452–6; John S. Crone (ed.), *A Concise Dictionary of Irish Biography*, 2nd edn. (Dublin, 1937), 258; Alfred Ware, *A Compendium of Irish Biography* (Dublin, 1878), 544; Henry Boylan, *A Dictionary of Irish Biography*, 2nd edn. (Dublin, 1979), 360–1; Liechty, 'Irish Evangelicalism', 313–89.

[100] Liechty, 'Irish Evangelicalism', 42.

[101] See Wills and Wills, *The Irish Nation*, iv.453–4.

[102] See Magee, *A Charge to the Clergy*, 23–5.

[103] *DNB*. The family later moved to County Tipperary. See Liechty, 'Irish Evangelicalism', 314.

[104] *Al. Dub.*, 847. He was, at graduation, classics gold medalist; in 1791 he was elected a fellow of Trinity; in 1799 he was Donnellon lecturer. See also Crookshank, *History of Methodism in Ireland*, ii.67.

clergyman that he was later described by a contemporary as 'the father of what religion was then in the Church'.[105] In 1792, James Garie, a chaplain in Lady Huntingdon's Connexion, greeted his arrival in Dublin ecstatically, exclaiming that 'the Lord has in some measure appeared for his cause in this city, by raising up Mr Walker . . . to preach in the churches with much zeal, simplicity, and clearness.'[106] Walker's power and popular appeal derived from the fusion of two contradictory characteristics. On the one hand, he was a man of decided opinions, who appeared to the public as a stern and uncompromising controversialist, doing battle at various times with the Established Church, the Methodists, the Haldane brothers, the Baptists, Dissenters in general, with Alexander Knox and his circle, and, finally, with his erstwhile Evangelical allies.[107] Yet, paradoxically, he was also a shy and sensitive scholar with little interest in politics, and with a noticeable speech impediment.[108] Bearing a remarkable resemblance to another Irish Evangelical who was to burst on the scene a few years later, John Nelson Darby, Walker blended religion and scholarship, dogmatism and liberality, sternness and sensitivity, in a complex and explosive mixture.[109]

At the time of his inhibition (together with Kelly) by Archbishop Fowler, Walker made clear his contempt for the Established clergy. In a sermon he complained that, for preaching the 'doctrines of grace' he was denounced as a Methodist, an enthusiastic, or an antinomian. To the question, 'considered so by whom?', he had a ready reply. 'By men who call themselves believers.—Believers! no; they are baptized infidels.'[110] He then began itinerating around the Irish countryside, fully aware that this might provide his superiors with new grounds of attack, though the threat did little to dampen his sense of Providential guidance.[111] Meanwhile he pursued his teaching duties at Trinity College, where he had a following amongst the students, gathering them around him to pray and read the Bible;[112] he also taught Sunday school on Abbey Street, entertained visiting Evangelical digni-

[105] See J. H. Singer, *Brief Memorials of B. W. Mathias* (Dublin, 1842), 204.

[106] Quoted in Seymour, *Selina, Countess of Huntingdon*, ii.214–15.

[107] Liechty, 'Irish Evangelicalism', 315. [108] Ibid. 316, 334. [109] Ibid. 322.

[110] Walker, *Substance of a Charity Sermon* (Dublin, 1796), 14.

[111] See Urwick, 'Memoir of Thomas Kelly', 64.

[112] Charles A. Cameron, *History of the Royal College of Surgeons* (Dublin, London, and Edinburgh, 1886), 486.

taries,[113] and hurled himself into several pan-evangelical enterprises.[114] In 1796, he published two works calling attention to the desperate spiritual needs of the Church of Ireland, which quickly gained the attention of Evangelical leaders in England.[115] Between 1795 and 1800, Walker served as a director of the pan-evangelical London Missionary Society.[116] In about 1799, he established the Evangelical Society, another pan-evangelical body working in and around Dublin.[117] Writing to his former student Benjamin Mathias, Walker noted that this body has been 'a rallying point for all lively and liberal Christians of all parties, not for bringing them out from their several denominations, but in bringing them to act in brotherly concert in them.'[118] He was, as David Hempton has observed, 'an arch-critic of everyone's religious opinions but his own'.[119] Later, he warned Mathias that the Established Church had become 'too contracted' and instead urged him to begin to pray for the larger 'Church of Christ'. 'I can bring promises with me to the throne of grace for that, which I cannot use for any particular church with certainty. *Entre nous*, I am apt to think that the revival which appears about to take place in our Church is preparatory to its dissolution as an establishment.'[120]

During the mid-1790s, Walker and his friend, the moderate Calvinist Walter Maturin, were appointed to replace Smyth and Mann as co-chaplains at Bethesda Chapel.[121] This arrangement lasted for three years, after which Maturin became rector of Raphoe, with Walker being left in sole charge of the chapel's

[113] Liechty, 'Irish Evangelicalism', 125–6.

[114] See Motherwell, *Memoir of Albert Blest*, 63.

[115] Walker, *Substance of a Charity Sermon: The Church in Danger* (Dublin, 1796). Rowland Hill wrote admiringly about Walker's natural talent, characterizing him as 'that most valuable servant of God'. See Rowland Hill, *Journal of a Tour Through the North of England and Parts of Scotland* (1799), 6. During his travels in Ireland, Hill achieved considerable popular standing. See Seymour, *Selina, Countess of Huntingdon*, ii.219, 225.

[116] See Roger H. Martin, *Evangelicals United: Ecumenical Stirrings in Pre-Victorian Britain, 1795–1830* (1983), 60.

[117] See Singer, *Brief Memorials of B. W. Mathias*, 35.

[118] Walker to Mathias, *c.*1799, ibid. 36.

[119] Hempton, 'Methodism in Irish Society', 117.

[120] Walker to Mathias, Nov. 1799, in Singer, *Brief Memorials of B. W. Mathias*, 38–9.

[121] Crookshank, *History of Methodism in Ireland*, ii.67; Acheson, 'The Evangelicals in the Church of Ireland', 32; Haldane, *Memoirs of Robert and James Alexander Haldane*, 343. Thomas Kelly, George Carr (both later seceders), and Dr Thorpe often assisted at Bethesda.

influential ministry.[122] Here, he quickly rose to prominence as the leading figure in Irish Evangelicalism, exerting his powerful personality on the cause of 'serious religion' in and around Dublin. Within a few short years, however, it became evident that a pronounced shift was taking place in his conception of what 'the Gospel' entailed.

The course of this change can be clearly traced. As we have seen, in 1799 Walker remarked ominously that he had come to see the Evangelical movement as a means of preparing the Church of Ireland for the inevitable—and beneficial—disestablishment that awaited it.[123] In the following year, he accused the middle and higher classes of a cold indifference in worship that he believed was responsible for sapping the moral fibre of the nation.[124] Two years later, he delivered a scathing attack on Wesleyan Methodism, which hinted at the growing radicalism of his ecclesiology and the soaring levels to which his high Calvinism would reach.[125] Here were clear signs of increasing disillusionment with the existing 'Gospel world' in Ireland.

Walker began his attack on the Methodists—and on Arminianism in general—by presenting a sharply dualistic vision of the current religious world. There were, he held, two distinct groupings to be discerned:

> Those who through grace are 'on the Lord's side', and those who are of the world. The former are scattered through various outward churches, under various names: but they are all one body, having one Lord, one faith, one hope. Nothing but blind bigotry suggests that they are to be found only under one denomination . . . They are daily discovering themselves to be brethren, and acting in brotherly concern for the advancement of that one cause.[126]

Walker rounded on Wesleyan Methodism as a body, castigating it as an agency of religious tyranny, encouraging 'idolatrous attachment to men and submission to human authority'.[127] He saw Wesley as a domineering autocrat who had enslaved his adherents

[122] Liechty, 'Irish Evangelicalism', 334.

[123] See Walker to Mathias, Nov. 1799, in Singer, *Brief Memorials of B. W. Mathias*, 39.

[124] Walker, *A Sermon, General Fast* (Dublin, 1800).

[125] Walker, *An Expostulatory Address to the Members of the Methodist Society in Ireland* (1802), in *WE* i.1–32. For a modern review of this work and its impact upon Methodism in Ireland see Hempton, 'Methodism in Irish Society'.

[126] *WE* i.7–8. [127] Ibid. 8.

in spiritual bondage.[128] His Arminian doctrines of faith, grace, justification, and sanctification were a 'mass of the most dangerous errors', designed to sanction a system not of true spiritual assurance, but of merely human feelings.[129] Sanctification should be regarded not as a gradual process, but as an immediate divine act which brings Christians into a particular relationship with God, in which they become a holy nation and a peculiar people,[130] and which occurs at the precise moment of conversion.[131] The natural man is both a voluntary agent and the slave of sin; though no mere machine, devoid of free will, he remains enslaved by evil until converted.[132]

One of the principal results of Walker's attack on Methodism was the able response it provoked from Alexander Knox, Wesley's Irish admirer and Lord Castlereagh's private secretary.[133] Knox praised the 'practical effects' of Methodism, especially amongst the lower orders, and stated that he could not view the movement 'in any other light than as a gracious appointment of Providence, for evangelizing the poor'.[134] The utilitarian tone of Knox's argument made little impression on Walker, however, who quickly turned his polemic against Knox, defending in no uncertain terms the scriptural basis of free grace and election, and the Calvinistic nature of the Articles.[135] The clash took its toll on Walker's health, however, compelling him, during the summer of 1802, to abandon Dublin for the healing waters of Buxton, in Derbyshire, where he seems to have made a speedy recovery from 'a tendency to paralysis or apoplexy, combined with flying gout'. Soon, he was preaching at the house of a local farmer where he attracted so much attention that, on the following Sunday, 'the place was crowded, and many outside'. He also preached at the parish church at Fairfield and, during the evenings, in the local hills.[136] These successes convinced Walker (if any proof was necessary) that while membership in the Establishment had its advantages, the primary task of 'soul-saving' could sometimes be undertaken more effectively when free from its canonical restrictions.

128 Ibid. 10. 129 Ibid. 10, 16. 130 Ibid. 14–15. 131 Ibid. 19.

132 Ibid. 28.

133 Alexander Knox, *Remarks on an Expostulatory Address to the Members of the Methodist Society* (Dublin, 1802).

134 Ibid. 29.

135 Walker, 'A Series of Letters to Alexander Knox', 1802, in *WE* i.33–174.

136 See Singer, *Brief Memorials of B. W. Mathias*, 59–63.

During this period, Walker's ecclesiology was undergoing rapid refinement. He had come to believe that God's kingdom was not of this world, but distinct and independent from every political regulation of man. A religious establishment, he now held, was a merely political institution; the great mass of those connected with it were persons who gave no evidence of belonging to the kingdom of God. Christ's disciples were not the citizenry of the State, but a people chosen out of a world which hated and despised them. Though still valuing his position in the Established Church for the opportunities it provided for reaching multitudes who would otherwise remain ignorant, Walker had now come to believe that he would eventually be expelled from it.[137]

Was he a hypocrite in remaining inside an imperfect establishment? No, Walker replied. All establishments offered secular temptations to Christians: such temptations were endemic to every institution. The root of the danger lay not in the existence of an establishment *per se*, but in the human—and therefore corrupted—nature of an establishment. The true brethren, those who were members of the 'Church of Christ', might continue to be unharmed by the worldliness of an Established Church and would continue in truth and grace despite the civil connection of the Church to which they belonged.

Walker considered the possibility of seceding, but was reluctant to abandon a position in which he saw himself providentially placed; by so doing he might excite unseemly controversy. For the time being, therefore, he decided to remain a clergyman of the Church of Ireland.[138] If he should be expelled from it, the reasons for his ejection would focus public attention on the principles for which he stood, and justify his separation. While looking cheerfully towards the prospect of expulsion, for the time being he demurred from actively seceding.[139]

Although these shifts in Walker's religious perception offended some, he became increasingly indifferent to criticism; indeed, he now denounced not only 'nominal' Christians, but many professed Evangelicals as traitors to the 'apostolic' faith:

> Within the past few years various trying circumstances concurred to open my eyes on the real character of that part of the religious world,

[137] Walker, 'An Address to Believers' (1804), in *WE* i.175–213.
[138] Ibid. 193–4. [139] Ibid.

which goes under the name of *evangelical*; and brought to my attention the awful evils that reign in the majority of that class of professors . . . My attention was thus forced to the melancholy contrast, between that way in which Christians were walking in these days, and walked in the days of the apostles. I began increasingly to remark how the disciples, in the apostolic churches, *walked together* as brethren, closely united with each other, and separated from them that believeth not.

Since the commencement also of the public controversy in which I was engaged, in consequence of my *Expostulatory Address to the Methodists*; I have had increasing opportunities of observing how few of those, who profess what is called *evangelical* doctrine, understand or believe the Apostolic Gospel . . . I saw more and more clearly that the little flock of genuine disciples had been awfully scattered among the heathen, and had been in consequence too much 'learning their works'; that they ought to be collected together as of old, and called back—both for their own profit and for the glory of their Lord—to walk together according to the apostles rule.[140]

Walker discussed his views with sympathetic Evangelicals, and published them in a small pamphlet.[141] Nine months later, together with eight like-minded brethren, he began an attempt to live in an everyday manner under a scriptural and 'apostolic' rule.[142] He began to advance a radical 'primitivism' which in some respects foreshadowed the views advanced by a number of other Evangelical seceders, including John Nelson Darby, Edward Irving, Theodosia Powerscourt, and the members of the Western Schism.

Walker had come to believe that an important aspect of this 'apostolic' rule was 'marked separatism'; worshipping apart from those outside the 'apostolic' faith and practice. True brethren were called to walk as those who are not of the world; they were chosen out of the world and crucified to the world, strangers and pilgrims upon earth whose life is hid with Christ in God. They were called to come out and be *separate*, as a *peculiar people*.[143] At first, his separatism remained primarily theoretical; he believed that it was not inconsistent with Christian duty to remain within the Established Church.[144] An establishment was merely:

[140] Ibid. 196–7.

[141] Walker, *Hints on Christian Fellowship* (Dublin, 1804).

[142] Walker, 'An Address to Believers', i.197; 'A Brief Account of the People Called Separatists' (1821), in *WE*, i.556–650.

[143] Walker, 'An Address to Believers', i.185–6.

[144] Ibid. i: 197.

a provision made by the State, for the religious instruction and edification of the inhabitants . . . according to certain prescribed forms and regulations, which were to be observed by its officiating ministers in their *public* exercises, in the places publicly allotted by the State for their ministrations, and at times appointed by public authority and usage: but . . . without any design originally to abridge their Christian liberty in other respects.[145]

But there was a rider to this. If the regulation of *public* worship was the only concern of the State in the area of devotion, it followed that the State should grant latitude towards all private ministrations, such as Bible readings and preaching in private houses—the kind of activities often undertaken in Evangelical parishes by voluntary societies. Only if this prerogative of private association was abrogated, and the official rubrics made obligatory for all forms of devotion, did acceptance of the establishment principle become unlawful for true Christians. At this stage in his ecclesiological development, Walker seems to envision an established *ecclesia* which allows full freedom to the *ecclesiolae*, or voluntary associations of the regenerate within its bosom. While, in fact, the religious societies came close to doing this in many Evangelical parishes during the late eighteenth and early nineteenth centuries, they shied away from admitting it too publicly for fear of raising the hackles of High Church bishops.[146]

At the same time, although Walker was advocating only a form of 'semi-separatism', he was clearly moving on towards a more radical ecclesiology which in some ways resembled that of the sixteenth-century English Puritans.[147] He soon began to prohibit so-called 'mixed communion' (the practice of 'believers' and 'non-believers' uniting in worship) at Bethesda. Although he did not see united worship as intrinsically unlawful, he feared that it might give outsiders a false impression of the nature of the true 'Church of Christ'.[148] He even considered removing the chapel's pews, or at least establishing pews for the regenerate *only*, arguing that as long as believers and unbelievers could sit together, 'the true

[145] Walker, 'An Address to Believers', i.198.

[146] See John Walsh, 'Religious Societies: Methodist and Evangelical 1738–1800', in W. J. Sheils and Diana Wood (eds.), *Voluntary Religion: Studies in Church History* (Oxford, 1986), 279–302.

[147] For a discussion on the origins of separatism in English Puritanism see Patrick Collinson, 'The English Coventicle', in Sheils and Wood, *Voluntary Religion*, 245–59.

[148] Walker, 'An Address to Believers', i.199.

church were not sufficiently outwardly separated as a body'.[149] Over time, he began to regard 'apostolic' principles as incompatible with a civil establishment of religion. If such establishments were contrary to the nature and laws of Christ's kingdom, he now believed, adherence to Scripture mandated outright secession from the Irish Church.[150] Yet, he also concluded that it would be equally wrong to affiliate with Protestant Dissent, which was just as corrupt, or indeed to associate with any existing religious body.[151] Employing what he saw as the 'rule of the apostles', he determined that Bethesda should become an independent body, unconnected in any formal way with other believers, with himself as its anointed head.[152] Within its walls true Christians would unite with the 'mixed multitude of pagans' (that is nominal Christians) in the public reading and expounding of the Scriptures, but not in the singing of hymns or in prayer, which were reserved only for those acknowledged as *authentic* brethren. For how, Walker inquired, could unbelievers 'call on Him, in whom they have not believed'?[153]

The events leading up to Walker's formal separation from the Established Church are not altogether clear. Peter Roe, the influential Evangelical incumbent of St. Mary's, Kilkenny, described Walker's secession as taking place soon after he had given public notice that he would preach at some market-house in the north, and did so. When this came to the attention of John Kearney, the provost of Trinity College, Walker was summoned to appear before the governing body to answer 'such charges as might be brought against him'.[154] On 8 October 1804, before the appointed hour, he wrote to Kearney announcing that he was not only seceding from the Church but also resigning his fellowship. Not content with a simple letter of resignation, Walker set out the reasons for his decision, to mark publicly those principles he could no longer retain with a clear conscience.[155] At this stage (according to an

[149] Singer, *Brief Memorials of B. W. Mathias*, 118.

[150] Walker, 'An Address to Believers', i.200–5.

[151] Singer, *Brief Memorials of B. W. Mathias*, 102.

[152] J. H. Overton was incorrect in claiming that Walker and his followers remained members of the Established Church. See J. H. Overton, *The English Church in the Nineteenth Century* (1894), 315.

[153] Walker, 'An Address to Believers', i.209.

[154] See Madden, *Memoir of Peter Roe*, 141.

[155] See Walker, 'An Address to Believers', i.205–6.

account which differs slightly from Roe's), Kearney sent for him, tearfully urging retraction, or at least reconsideration, but Walker remained adamant, fearing that delay might suggest indecision. On the following day, after consulting with the two deans, Kearney expelled him.[156] Far from being upset by this, Walker appeared to welcome his brusque expulsion as a mark of true discipleship and divine favour.[157] He then extended the scope of his separation by resigning from three pan-evangelical societies.[158] From now on he supported himself and his family by collecting pew rents and voluntary tithes from the congregation at Bethesda, by preparing private students for university admission, by publishing a few classical commentaries, and by offering public lectures on university subjects.[159]

III

After his secession, Walker faced a potentially explosive atmosphere at Bethesda. Controlled by Evangelical trustees decidedly unsympathetic to high Calvinism and anti-Erastianism, and with a majority of the congregation now excluded from participation in full worship, Bethesda was a bitterly divided house with an uncertain future. On 15 October 1804, Walker wrote to Benjamin Williams Mathias, his former student and now head of the trustees, informing him of his secession and warning that he could no longer continue with 'the usual forms of divine service' at the chapel.[160] This ambiguous declaration met with little support from the trustees, who were concerned that Walker's new doctrines would continue to divide the congregation and erode still further the chapel's already tenuous relationship with the Established Church. Walker was swiftly compelled to resign as chaplain. He

[156] See Walker, *Supplementary Annotations on Livy* (Glasgow, 1822), pp. xii–xiii.

[157] Walker, 'An Address to Believers', i.205–6.

[158] Ibid. 206. These were: the General Evangelical Society of Dublin, the Society for Distributing Evangelical Tracts, and the Association Incorporated for Promoting Religion and Virtue.

[159] *DNB*; Liechty, 'Irish Evangelicalism', 317. In 1822 Walker placed an advertisement for two or three private students whom he was willing to receive into his home at 8 Camden Street, Camden Town, for tuition. He denied, however, any intention to proselytize his students. See Walker, *Supplementary Annotations on Livy*.

[160] See Singer, *Brief Memorials of B. W. Mathias*, 90–1. Mathias had graduated from Trinity College, Dublin, in 1796. In the following year he was ordained to the curacy of Rathfryland, Co. Down, by Dr John Porter, Bishop of Killala. See *DNB*; W. D. Killen, *The Ecclesiastical History of Ireland* (1875), ii.382.

was succeeded by Mathias who appears to have implemented a rather exact form of churchmanship at Bethesda.[161]

This upheaval produced predictable havoc amongst the congregation. Some fifty members of the original body remained with Mathias, forty-two seceded with Walker, with the remainder abandoning both, seeking fellowship elsewhere.[162] At least one clergyman, a Mr Robinson (perhaps the assistant curate of Newry) also seceded.[163] With this small core of followers, Walker established the first congregation of his connexion in Stafford Street, Dublin, which he unashamedly christened the 'Church of God'.[164] It met with a mixed, though not indifferent, public response. A Dublin magistrate hotly argued that the 'Government ought to *exterminate from society* such [false religious] principles.'[165] An anonymous critic suggested that the best response to Walker's supporters would be 'a straight jacket—a shaven head, some clean straw—and a dark room in Swift's Hospital', though on reflection he admitted that persecution would only give a measure of dignity to their 'nonsense', and that the best course was 'refutation and ridicule'.[166] Several Evangelical families were devastated when the 'Walkerite' members refused to worship or enter into any form of fellowship with their relations.[167] Moreover, and not surprisingly, Walker's rigidly separatist views shocked the exponents of a united, pan-evangelical Protestant movement in Ireland.

Walker's secession was followed by much Evangelical breast beating. Peter Roe regarded the loss of Walker, and the establishment of the 'Separatists', as truly lamentable and highly damaging to the Church and the Gospel cause.[168] Henry Maturin wrote that although the number of Evangelical clergy was increasing, the secession of Walker and his followers 'weakens our hands'.[169]

[161] See Phillips, *History of the Church of Ireland*, iii.331–2.

[162] Singer, *Brief Memorials of B. W. Mathias*, 97, 149.

[163] See ibid. 93.

[164] Motherwell, *Memoir of Albert Blest*, 89–90. Walker's connexion was also known as the 'Separatists' and the 'Walkerites'.

[165] See Walker, 'The Petition of Certain Christian People Resident in London' (1822), in *WE* ii.13.

[166] 'A Beneficed Clergyman', *Strictures on a Pamphlet, Entitled the Monstrosities of Methodism* (Dublin, 1808), 2. See also William Cooper, *An Address to the Church Assembling in Plunket-Street, Dublin* (Dublin, 1805); *A Letter to Mr John Walker* (Dublin, 1808); A Member of the Church of Christ in Sligo, *Marked Separation in All Religious Meetings . . . Considered* (Dublin, 1805).

[167] See Liechty, 'Irish Evangelicalism', 375.

[168] Quoted in Madden, *Memoir of Peter Roe*, 142.

[169] Quoted in Acheson, 'The Evangelicals in the Church of Ireland', 127.

The Irish Evangelical Albert Blest gloomily confessed that Walker's secession had forced him to consider the recent advance 'in conveying the leaven of divine truth into the College and the Church, as blasted forever'.[170]

At the same time, notoriety quickly made the 'Church of God' an object of attention in Dublin's fashionable circles. Public interest was aroused by the spectacle of an able and devout scholar sacrificing collegiate honours and distinctions for conscience, while many were intrigued by a body which took with such intense seriousness the scriptural admonitions in Romans 12:2 against being 'conformed to this world'.

IV

Once out of its Anglican cradle, the 'Church of God' quickly began to embrace doctrines which the 'Gospel world' at large deemed unacceptable. Its ecclesiology placed an extreme emphasis on the visible and local church. The fundamental principle of the 'Walkerites' was that they alone had made a full return to 'apostolic' practices. Here, at last, the primitive brotherhood of the first Christians was re-enacted. This new connexion was to be a gathering of believers holding one faith, living under one rule and in the closest brotherhood, at peace with one another, and taught and edified by the spiritual gifts of the elders.[171] The 'Church of God' was inspired by the radical, primitivistic assumption that the Acts of the Apostles had revealed, once and for all, the Christian order in all its fullness, and that such an order could—and should—be reconstituted. 'Are we to hear of these days without looking for their return,' Walker asked? 'God forbid! . . . it is no vain or groundless expectation that primitive Christianity shall yet be revived.'[172]

The members of this new body would manifest the characteristics of Christ's first disciples. The same apostolic Word came to them still, with the same authority as in the first century, containing God's clear commandments for their profit and glory. The church was not called on to make any worldly regulations to

[170] Quoted in Motherwell, *Memoir of Albert Blest*, 168.

[171] Walker, 'An Essay on the Divine Authority of the Apostolic Traditions' (1807), in *WE* i.224–55; 'Remarks on Certain Questions' (1810), in *WE* i.310–32; 'A Brief Account of the People Called Separatists' (1821), in *WE* i.556–60;

[172] Walker, *Substance of a Charity Sermon*, 15.

promote its fraternal union, but simply to adhere to the unchangeable laws of Scripture.[173] It should refuse to subscribe to any oaths.[174] It should sanction no organized body of clergy, lest they become a heretical caste 'of pretended agents between God and the people', dressed up in the 'trappings and claims of the Jewish priesthood'.[175] The church should assemble together on the first day of the week, when its members would take bread and wine as a memorial of Christ's resurrection, would pray and offer praise, read the Scriptures, exhort and admonish one another as brethren 'according to their several gifts and ability', contribute gifts to the poor, and express their fraternal affection by saluting each other with a holy kiss.[176]

An essential element in the 'Separatists'' ecclesiology was a firm rejection of religious establishments. Every attempt, they contended, to dress up Christ's kingdom in a garb which attracted worldly respect and approbation, under the mask of promoting its interests, only served to disguise its true character.[177] The church must instead revert to the 'apostolic' principles of the pre-Constantinian church, for Walker now concluded that it had been the Imperial establishment of Christianity which had led to its disastrous corruption.[178] A State Church was anti-Christian, a thing of this world, the creation of human policy usurping the prerogatives of God.[179]

Even more alarming to mainstream Evangelicals was the pronounced separatism of the 'Church of God'.[180] Its starting point was the assumption of the eternal incompatibility of church and world. As the Gospel was 'peculiarly offensive to the world and peculiarly unintelligible',[181] and as all brethren were 'a despised and suffering people, hated by all men for his name's sake',[182]

[173] Walker, 'A Brief Account of the People Called Separatists', i.557.

[174] In 1822, he had obtained an Act of Parliament exempting the 'Separatists' from taking oaths. See Walker, 'The Petition of Certain Christian People Resident in London', ii.1–22. See also *GM* (1833), ii.540–1.

[175] Walker, 'Thoughts on Religious Establishments' (1810), in *WE* i.333–44.

[176] Walker, 'A Brief Account of the People Called Separatists', i.559–60.

[177] Walker, 'Thoughts on Religious Establishments', i.333.

[178] Ibid. 336. [179] Ibid. 341.

[180] For an attack on the strict separatism of the 'Walkerites' see William Brainwood, *Letters on a Variety of Subjects* (Edinburgh, 1808), 32; T. Brocas, *God: No Respecter of Persons* (1808), 91.

[181] Walker, *Supplementary Annotations on Livy*, p. xiii.

[182] Walker, 'A Brief Account of the People Called Separatists', i.559.

Christians must necessarily live and worship in separation from other so-called believers.[183] This principle was rigorously carried out. During a six week tour of Scotland, in which Walker met with many religious men, he claimed that he did not find one true believer with whom he could unite in fellowship.[184] When his daughter developed friendships with Evangelicals outside the 'Church of God', he told her bluntly that unless she renounced such associations he would be 'obliged (though with a bleeding heart) solemnly to renounce all fellowship' with her, and to despise her 'as one rejecting the Word of the Lord, and savouring not the things that be of God—but the things that be of men'.[185]

The 'Walkerites' adopted other practices which distinguished them from various sections of conventional Evangelicalism. Walker himself attacked the Baptists in print, arguing that there was no scriptural warrant for the adult baptism of a person raised in a Christian home. Baptism by immersion had been perverted by post-apostolic believers and it should return to its Judaic form: administered to entire families—adults *and* children alike—upon the conversion of the head of the house. Since Christ had offered no instruction other than merely affirming the Jewish rite by which he himself had been baptized, it was argued that his followers should do likewise.[186]

As was often the case with intense and rigoristic forms of contemporary evangelical religion, separatism was here combined with high Calvinism. Although not easily defined, Walker's high Calvinism tended (at least in public perception) to dominate the theological orientation of the 'Church of God'. He adamantly opposed any form of Arminianism, and commented disparagingly on what he saw as a Methodist characteristic—the reliance on pangs of human conscience as marks of effectual grace; he warned his readers to 'consider how many evils have arisen from dealing with every man, who has a sudden impulse of alarm in his conscience, as if he were therefore *convinced of sin*: and with every man who, after such an alarm, has a sudden gust of joy, as if he were therefore *justified*'.[187] Emotional epiphenomena like

183 Walker, 'Thoughts on Religious Establishments', i.334.

184 Walker, 'Remarks on Certain Questions', i.310.

185 Walker to his daughter, April 1813, in *WE* ii.199.

186 See Walker, 'Thoughts on Baptism' (1805), in *WE* i.214–23. See also 'Observations on a Letter Addressed to the Author' (1809), in *WE* i.256–309.

187 See Walker, 'An Expostulatory Address', i.24.

these were not to be trusted, as they too often were by Wesleyan exponents of 'Arminianism blasphemy'.[188] 'Being an Arminian', he concluded, 'excludes not a man from being the object of charity—or love—in its various exercises: neither does his being a Turk or an Infidel exclude him. Neither do I conceive . . . that making a general *profession* of Arminian doctrine, precludes a hope, that a man is a real believer of the Gospel. But I am as sure, that a man's being *really* an Arminian precludes that hope . . . The essential character of Arminianism stands in direct opposition to . . . the Gospel . . . Meanwhile I say nothing, but . . . that *no real Arminian is a real believer*.'[189] Walker was anxious to condemn that '*infidel repentance*' which the Arminian claimed for himself, repentance which was no more 'a preliminary to faith, than Murder or Adultery'[190]—sins which in themselves were no more efficacious that the prayers and alms deeds of the unconverted Roman centurion, Cornelius, in Acts 10.[191]

By the time of his secession Walker had become so extreme in his condemnation of 'self-righteousness' among the formally pious, that he informed the congregation at Bethesda that even the prostitutes in attendance (from the adjoining Lock penitentiary and workhouse) were closer to a state of grace and divine acceptance than most of those present.[192] Whatever religious acts they performed no one would come to salvation, except those chosen ones whom Christ 'shall absolutely "bring unto glory" '.[193] This phillipic alarmed Dublin's respectable religious public, especially those who held Arminian or moderate Calvinistic views. No doubt Walker anticipated this. To some of his critics he seemed deplorably antinomian. Yet he cannot be tarred with the stain of antinomianism, except perhaps theoretically.[194] Although he admitted that he was a Calvinist, he denied that he was an extreme Calvinist. Paradoxically, he was wont to dismiss both low (or moderate) and high Calvinism. Moderate Calvinism seemed

[188] See Walker to W. C., 7 May 1829, in *WE* ii.456.

[189] Walker, 'An Expostulatory Address', i.51–2.

[190] Walker, 'A Series of Letters', i.113. [191] Ibid. 154.

[192] See Liechty, 'Irish Evangelicalism', 346.

[193] Walker, 'Remarks Corrective of Occasional Mistranslations in the English Version of the Sacred Scriptures' (1831), in *WE* ii.54–122. See also Walker, 'A Brief Account of the People Called Separatists', i.558.

[194] See *ER* (1838), 523; David Robert Ross, *A Reply to the Author of a Article Entitled 'Sandemanian Theology, John Walker' Which Appeared in the ER of November 1838* (Dublin, 1839), 9.

to him 'contemptible in its philosophy': like many critics, he seems to have seen it as feeble dilution of the biblical doctrine of predestination, a mishmash of Calvinism and Arminianism, 'insidiously ungodly in all its origins and principles'. High Calvinism he accepted as theoretically closer to the Gospel, but none the less potentially vitiated by its diversion of attention away from the objectivity of the revealed Word towards some personal sensation of 'assumed favouritism' that took little account of that dread of sin which marks the true believer.[195] This final reproach Walker reserved for such individuals as James Harington Evans of the Western Schism (discussed in Chapter 4), who believed that through grace they have been made 'less wholly evil' than they really were, even incapable of sinning. Men such as these, Walker concluded, 'know little of the true grace of God.'[196] None the less, the charge of antinomianism remained with Walker throughout his career outside the Church, hampering his witness and tarnishing his reputation as a scholar of the first order.

By 1807, reports of the low state of Irish Protestantism had begun to filter back to the British mainland, producing disquiet in Evangelical circles. In that year, a pan-evangelical body, the Hibernian Society for the Diffusion of Religious Knowledge in Ireland, dispatched a delegation to investigate the condition of religion in the country.[197] Its members were depressed by what they discovered, Thomas Charles of Bala reporting unhappily that 'vital religion' seemed to be in a state of virtual collapse:

> The religious people are sadly divided: hardly two persons think alike, and some persons often change their Sentiments: forever disputing with each other instead of labouring to promote the general cause of religion among them. Cooperites, Walkerites, Haldanites, Kell[y]ites, dispute with one another with great uncharitableness. This has given great offence, and people in general become very indifferent to all religion . . . The popish priests are much more zealous and successful in making proselytes than [the] Protestants: ind[eed the] religious zeal among the Protestants is almost extin[guished].[198]

[195] See Walker, 'A Sufficient Reply to Mr Haldane's Late Strictures Upon the Author's Letters on Primitive Christianity' (1821), in *WE* i.432–506.

[196] Walker to R. L. C., 5 Mar. 1818, in *WE* ii.248.

[197] See Motherwell, *Memoir of Albert Blest*, 190–1.

[198] Charles to Thomas Rice Charles, 6 Aug. 1807, in Jenkins, *Life of Thomas Charles*, iii.166–8, 170.

He was equally alarmed by the lengths to which separatism had gone among some radical groups. 'They administer the Lord's Supper without any minister', Charles noted, and 'will not pray with the ungodly; others will not worship unless the believers sit in *contact* with each other, etc. It were useless to mention all the follies and trifles they dispute about. The baneful effects of these foolish disputes among the religious people we have perceived every where we have been.'[199] Upon returning, the delegates' report revealed that the 'Walkerites', although numerically small, were being assisted by an anonymous, Scottish benefactor (very likely Robert or James Alexander Haldane), and were active in promoting Sunday schools which taught the disreputable doctrine of 'marked separatism'. An advance of their movement, it cautioned, might enact serious damage upon the fragile state of 'serious religion' in Ireland.[200]

V

Walker's voluminous writings, and the controversial literature they provoked, provide some insight into the practices and progress of the 'Church of God'. In about 1818, he was claiming cheerfully that the 'Separatists' had multiplied at a gratifying rate. The Dublin membership sometimes exceeded a hundred, with six or seven little churches meeting in the countryside amounting to about a hundred more. They claimed the allegiance of some dozen Evangelical clergymen who had seceded from the Established Church, and more than twenty former Baptist ministers.[201] In 1821, he published a brief *apologia* for the movement, boasting that the 'Separatists' had been drawn mainly from Dublin's prosperous Evangelical ranks. Yet, despite all the attendant publicity he was forced to admit that they were still:

> a very small sect; very little known, and less liked: nor do they expect ever to be numerous or respectable on earth. Their most numerous church (assembling . . . in Stafford Street, Dublin,) consists perhaps of about one hundred and thirty individuals. They have about ten or twelve smaller churches in different parts of Ireland: and within the last two

[199] Ibid., Charles to David Charles, Aug. 1807.

[200] See Motherwell, *Memoir of Albert Blest*, 192.

[201] Walker to J. H. (*c*.1818), in *WE* ii.243.

years a church in the same connexion has appeared in London, assembling in Portsmouth Street, Lincoln's-Inn-Fields.[202]

Accounts of the 'Church of God' made contrasting claims as to its size and influence. One alleged that outside Ireland it had flourished and increased, especially in the West of England, Exeter, Plymouth, Bristol, and Birmingham.[203] Another claimed that congregations existed in Waterford, Kilkenny, and Cork.[204] A further congregation appears to have been gathered around James Buchanan of Camowen Green, near Omagh.[205]

Walker's followers attempted to live according to a strict 'apostolic' rule. Any teaching unconnected with their sectarian particularities was denounced in the strongest language. When, for example, a small group of 'Separatists' occasionally returned to Bethesda Chapel for a service, they would wait for a reference to some disagreeable teaching, upon which they would march out in a phalanx, 'declaring that this was legal[istic] doctrine, and not such as a Christian could listen to'.[206] Nor were the 'Separatists' immune from internal divisions. In about 1815 a schism developed in the Stafford Street congregation over the long-established practice of 'holy kissing', administered to the occupants of adjoining seats upon arrival and departure. This practice ran into trouble when a newly married woman—not 'one of the initiated'—was greeted in the appropriate fashion by a burly Irish blacksmith and a terrific hubbub ensued, with the 'kissers' opposing the 'anti-kissers'. Eventually the 'kissers', supported by Walker, prevailed, but not before the charge of eroticism (so often levelled against 'enthusiasts') had been raised. Stunned by the allegation, Walker

[202] Walker, 'A Brief Account of the People Called Separatists', i.556–7. See also Wills and Wills, *The Irish Nation*, iv.454. Elsewhere Walker revealed that a congregation had also been formed in Leith. See Walker, *Seven Letters to a Friend on Primitive Christianity* (1834), 107.

[203] Stokes, 'John Nelson Darby', in the *Contemporary Review* (1885), 539–40.

[204] Madden, *Memoir of Peter Roe*, 140, 256–7. Of these, the Dublin and Birmingham congregations continued to exist until at least 1885. See Stokes, 'John Nelson Darby', in the *Contemporary Review*, 539–40.

[205] Buchanan, a protégé of the Haldanes, had formed a religious body in 1807 which developed some formal ties with Walker and his connexion; however, it was less committed to extreme forms of Calvinism and held some Baptist doctrines. In 1816, Buchanan emigrated to America, where, three years later, he became the British consul in New York. See F. Roy Coad, *A History of the Brethren Movement* (Exeter, 1968), 81.

[206] Singer, *Brief Memorials of B. W. Mathias*, 149.

quickly abandoned Dublin for the less quarrelsome atmosphere of London.[207] Here things remained relatively calm until 1829, when open schism erupted between the London and Dublin congregations over the issue of congregational discipline.[208] The 'Separatists' regarded the maintenance of discipline as a divine command, excluding backsliders from fellowship and from receiving the sacrament. When a Dublin member disclaimed subjection to discipline, but was not immediately silenced or expelled (instead becoming the object of lengthy debates), Walker and his London followers were compelled to intervene.

At first, private attempts were made from London to admonish the Dublin brethren and to recall them to the principles of Christian fellowship which they had abandoned. These failed, however, and the discord continued to rage.[209] A small deputation was then formed to consider the matter. A letter was dispatched to the brethren in Dublin, denouncing them for letting the church be turned into 'a theatre for theological controversy and debate', and admonishing them to expel everyone who refused to submit to scriptural discipline.[210] When read out to the brethren in Dublin, the letter was dismissed as 'an officious interference' and 'a usurpation of jurisdiction'.[211] Three divisions quickly emerged: those opposed to such authoritarianism, those who favoured continued debate and consideration, and those in favour of firm discipline. A schism followed when the third group seceded from the other two. Since the disputants remained unrepentant, the London congregation severed its Dublin connection.[212] The disciplinarians eventually managed to reestablish fellowship with their London brethren, but the episode was an embarrassing debacle, confirming Walker's critics in their belief in the dangerous friability of Protestant extremism.[213]

Walker continued to reside in London until very nearly the end of his life. His affection for Ireland and for Trinity College never wavered, however, and in 1833 his old College tried to atone for

[207] *AR* (appendix to chronicle) (1833), 249.

[208] See Walker, 'Statement of the Interruption of Christian Connexion Between the Church in London and the Church in Dublin' (1829), in *WE* ii.23–53. (This teaching was based on 1 Corinthians 5: 11.)

[209] Ibid. 24.

[210] Ibid. 25–6. [211] Ibid. 27. [212] Ibid. 28. [213] Ibid. 31.

its earlier unkindness by granting him a generous pension of six hundred pounds.[214] He returned to Dublin, perhaps to visit, perhaps to reside, but died on 25 October 1833 before he could benefit from the proceeds of his pension.[215]

VI

Despite its aggressive stance towards other religious bodies, its internal divisions, and its failure to gain significant ground as a connexion, the 'Church of God' exerted a marked influence on Evangelicalism in Britain, if less through its small congregations than by the number and loquacity of its opponents. Its impact was variously assessed. One critic complained rather wildly that 'Walkerite' leaders had pursued major Evangelicals through Ireland, England, and Scotland, 'poaching upon their congregations, robbing them of their most devout adherents, and representing themselves as specially spiritual' because of their 'apostolic' freedom from dependence on tithes and endowments.[216] Taking a very different tack, another observer saw the Church's influence as small and on the whole beneficial as a kind of aversion therapy, for though Walker had caused a few unsteady characters to wobble, the debates which he had triggered off had actually strengthened the Establishment, provoking much sober reflection about its advantages.[217]

The most influential critic of the 'Church of God' was Peter Roe,[218] a man sensitive on issues relating to separatism since he had been harried by John Kearney (the Bishop of Ossory), who was suspicious that the pan-evangelical gatherings held at

[214] *DNB*. In 1822, Walker exclaimed 'I have never complained, nor do I now complain; I was expelled from that PROTESTANT University, as a disgrace to it, *for believing the scriptures*; and after I had tendered the *resignation* of my Fellowship.' See Walker, *Supplementary Annotations on Livy*, pp. xiii, xi. In his introduction to *Murray's Compendium*, Walker expressed his hope that his words might serve the students of Trinity College, 'for though no longer connected with that body, I must continue to feel an interest in its true prosperity'. See R. Murray, *Murray's Compendium of Logic* (1847), p. iii.

[215] S. Austin Allibone, *A Critical Dictionary of English Literature and British and American Authors Living and Deceased* (Philadelphia, 1877), iii.2543. See also *GM* (1833), ii.540; the *London Literary Gazette* (1838), 5; and the *AR* (appendix to chronicle) (1833), 249.

[216] See Stokes, 'John Nelson Darby', in the *Contemporary Review* (1885), 539.

[217] John Quarry to Roe (1813), in Madden, *Memoir of Peter Roe*, 257–8.

[218] See Thomas J. Johnson, John L. Robinson, and Robert Wyse Jackson, *A History of the Church of Ireland* (Dublin, 1953), 251; Akinson, *The Church in Ireland*, 132.

Kilkenny might lead to dissent among the local clergy.[219] Though not at all averse to opposing what he saw as the errors of popery, Roe rejected the use of religious controversy as a means to promote 'Gospel principles'. The 'best way to prevent one filling a vassal with chaff', he claimed, 'was to anticipate him by filling it with wheat.'[220] As an occasional itinerant, he was not above attending a Dissenting chapel when visiting in a 'dark' parish, although he remained firmly attached to the Anglican formularies.[221] Prior to Walker's secession, Roe had found much to admire in his teachings, describing his address to the Methodists as 'a work full of logic and *sophistry*, ably written, and containing . . . truths' which few could answer.[222] Within two years, however, this admiration had been destroyed by Walker's secession and doctrinal extremism. Contrasting the dogma of the 'Church of God' with that advanced by the sixteenth-century English separatist Robert Browne, Roe claimed that Walker had come to possess 'the highest, and I believe most extravagant doctrines of Calvinism; deals very much in censure, and in condemning those who differ from him, yet I could also observe with sorrow, very unwarrantable prejudices entertained against those who do not think with him. How many who reprobate the doctrine of infallibility, really believe it, and act upon it.'[223]

In September 1813, the town of Kilkenny was 'invaded' by members of Walker's connexion.[224] This was hardly surprising to Roe, for the 'Separatists' had been advancing throughout the area for some time, targeting the flocks of leading Evangelical

[219] See Madden, *Memoir of Peter Roe*, 411. For a High Church critique, which accused Roe of being a Brownist, see: Anon., *Evil of Separation from the Church of England Considered in a Series of Letters Addressed Chiefly to the Revd Peter Roe, Minister of St. Mary's, Kilkenny* (Kilkenny, 1815).

[220] Madden, *Memoir of Peter Roe*, 411.

[221] Ibid. 96–7, 112–13, 556. See also Killen, *The Ecclesiastical History of Ireland*, ii.386.

[222] Peter Roe, diary entry for 2 Oct. 1802, cited in Madden, *Memoir of Peter Roe*, 116. Roe's admiration for the work continued for many years.

[223] See ibid., pp. viii–ix; Peter Roe's diary entry for 10 Sept. 1804, 140.

[224] In July 1815, Thomas Scott described the 'invaders' of Kilkenny as 'followers of Messrs. Haldane'. Moreover, in his memoirs of the brothers Haldane, Alexander Haldane has described Thomas Kelly as an 'old friend' of Robert Haldane. It seems clear that the two were closely associated in their evangelistic endeavours in Ireland and perhaps also on the Continent, though it remains uncertain to what extent Haldane actively participated in the leadership or congregational life of the 'Kellyites'. Within such a context, Scott's reference to the 'invaders' as the 'followers' of the Haldanes is made clear. See Scott, *Letters and Papers of the Late Revd Thomas Scott, D.D.*, 185; Haldane, *Memoirs of Robert and James Alexander Haldane*, 499–500.

clerics.[225] For a time Roe believed that the seceders would make little headway in Kilkenny, but he eventually realized that a strong counter-attack must be mounted if a major schism in his parish was to be avoided.[226] He then set about collecting a volume of essays written by leading English and Irish Evangelicals strongly opposed to secessionism, including Thomas Scott, Legh Richmond, and Charles Simeon,[227] which he published under the title, *The Evil of Separation from the Church of England Considered.*[228]

Predictably, the work was warmly received by Evangelicals, who were delighted to see an important statement supporting the Church–State connection and validating their position within the Establishment. It was coolly received by some suspicious High Churchmen, however, who criticized it as lukewarm on the value of episcopacy.[229] Roe and his contributors remained undeterred by such criticism, and the work succeeded in persuading the majority of Roe's congregation to remain within the Church of Ireland.[230] Yet the High Church critique served to illustrate the Establishment's internal divisions, providing Walker and his followers with corroboration for their prediction that any house so divided must surely be close to collapse.

The essays themselves ranged in tone from the accommodating to the aggressive. W. D. Hoare, after reminding his readers of the obligations of unity and the advantages of establishment, attacked Walker in strong terms for being more concerned about precise points of sectarian identity than about Christianity itself: his extremism was helping the cause of infidelity.[231] Elsewhere, much was made of the egalitarianism of Walker's connexion,

[225] Madden, *Memoir of Peter Roe*, 255–6.

[226] Ibid. 256, Peter Roe's diary entry for Sept. 1813.

[227] Although Richmond's and Simeon's were published anonymously. The Irish contributors included William Digby, the Archdeacon of Elphin; George Hamilton, the rector of Killermogh; William Napper, the curate of Old Ross; Dr Thomas Grace, the Archdeacon of Ardfert; Robert Shaw; and W. D. Hoare. See Stokes, 'John Nelson Darby', in the *Contemporary Review* (1885), 539; Madden, *Memoir of Peter Roe*, 260; and, Catherine M. Marsh, *The Life of the Revd William Marsh, D.D.* (1867), 114.

[228] Peter Roe, *The Evil of Separation from the Church of England Considered* (Kilkenny, 1815). For a review of this work see *CG* (1818), 346–9. Such was the work's acceptance and popularity that a second edition, corrected and enlarged, was published in England two years later.

[229] See William Phelan, *The Bible, Not the Bible Society* (Dublin, 1817), 110–70.

[230] Madden, *Memoir of Peter Roe*, 259.

[231] W. D. Hoare, 'Extract of a Letter', in Roe, *The Evil of Separation*, 97. See also ibid. 101, Thomas Grace, 'A Letter'.

which was represented as dangerously anarchic and lacking the hierarchical authority of an 'apostolic' ministry: it was especially denounced for allowing unqualified individuals to speak or minister whenever moved by the Spirit.[232]

Evangelical critics sought to place the new schism in a heresiographical tradition, so that it could be the better identified. It was easier to controvert Walkerism once it could be portrayed not as a new and vital movement, but merely as an old heresy revived. The most plausible theory was that in founding the 'Church of God', Walker was only restoring the doctrines of John Glas and Robert Sandeman.[233] This was not surprising, for 'Sandemanianism' had long been rife among some Irish Protestant religious groups, especially the Baptists.[234] Greville Ewing, the Scottish seceder who had turned Independent (and later Congregationalist), had been strongly influenced by the teachings of Glas and Sandeman during the 1790s. His own views were imbibed by the brothers Haldane who, in turn, introduced their own fiery brand of high Calvinism and separatism to Dublin's Bethesda Chapel during the summer of 1801.[235]

Glas was a deposed Scottish clergyman who had formed a religious connexion (known as the 'Glasites') based upon 'apostolic', separatist, and idiosyncratically Calvinistic principles.[236] In 1744, he was joined by Sandeman, his son-in-law, who was responsible for transferring the sect to England and America, where they became known as the 'Sandemanians'.[237] The 'Glasites' practised weekly communion, the so-called 'love-feast', the holy kiss, and the washing of feet. They espoused communal practices which had a radical resonance: a kind of community of goods, weekly

[232] Robert Shaw, 'A Letter', in Roe, *The Evil of Separation*, 123–32.

[233] See *ER* (1838), 519. These accusations may, in part, have been stimulated by a recent attack on 'Sandemanianism'. See Andrew Fuller, 'Strictures on Sandemanianism', in *Twelve Letters to a Friend* (Nottingham, 1810).

[234] See Joshua Thompson, 'Baptists in Ireland, 1792–1922: A Dimension of Protestant Dissent', D.Phil. thesis (Oxford, 1988), 29–30.

[235] See Haldane, *Memoirs of Robert and James Alexander Haldane*, 233–4, 343; M. J. Votruba, 'Observations Concerning Practices of the Lord's Supper', in *Discipliana*, 22 (Mar. 1962), 6. Though the Haldanes expressed disapproval of some aspects of the 'Sandemanians', they accepted a number of their less extreme doctrines.

[236] See *DNB*; *The Works of Mr John Glas* (Edinburgh, 1761).

[237] See *DNB*; Robert Sandeman, *Letters on Theron and Aspasio* (Edinburgh, 1757). A second edition, with an appendix, was published in 1759; and a third edition, with the addition of an enlarged appendix, was published in 1762.

collections for the poor, and abstention from eating blood or strangled meat. In their polity, they maintained a plurality of elders in each congregation, two of whom had to be present during all acts of discipline and in the administration of communion.[238] Their Trinitarian and Christological views were highly unorthodox. Furthermore, they condemned all religious establishments as hostile to Christ's kingdom, and remained strictly separate from all other so-called believers.[239]

The doctrinal resemblances between the 'Glasites' and the 'Church of God' forced Walker repeatedly to contrast his own position with theirs. In this process a number of interesting admissions were made. Walker allowed that he had become acquainted with Sandeman's writings during his correspondence with Alexander Knox in 1802–3.[240] However, although the 'Walkerites' and 'Glasites' concurred on many points,[241] they also differed, especially on their views of assurance and sanctification. In 1818, Walker saw the need to distance himself from Sandeman's teachings, admitting:

> Precious as his vindication of the truth appears against the corruptions and perversions of the popular divines, we conceive that he himself afterwards awfully perverts and corrupts it, in representing the Gospel as calculated to afford a sinner joy at first on believing, only as satisfying him that he *may peradventure* be saved because *any* sinner may be saved, but leaving him doubtful whether he believes it or not, till after a course of painful exertion in the work of faith and labour of love he is led to discover in himself some good evidence of his faith, which affords him personal confidence towards God . . . I do believe that in their body it has been a root of bitterness and leaven of ungodliness.[242]

On another occasion Walker advised an acquaintance (who had separated from the 'Glasites') that his decision appeared 'to have been mercifully ordered', for they seemed to him to possess a system not of divine but of human prescription, 'laid down for

[238] Charles Buck, *A Theological Dictionary*, 2nd edn. (1833), 844–5.

[239] See David Bogue and James Bennett, *History of Dissenters, 1688–1808* (1808–12), iv.107–25.

[240] Walker to J. H., *c.*1818, in *WE* ii.242.

[241] Walker to Anon., Apr. 1804, in *WE* i.407; Walker to R. L. C., 14 Jan. 1818, in *WE* ii.239; Walker to J. H., *c.*1818, in *WE* ii.242; Walker to A. M'I, 12 June 1821, in *WE* ii.338.

[242] Walker to R. L. C., 14 Jan. 1818, in *WE* ii.239–40. See also *WE* ii.258, 274, 282, 286, 293, 389, 418.

them by a man'.[243] Nevertheless, though he criticized their adherence to the practice of sprinkling in baptism,[244] their understanding of the nature of the Church,[245] their exaggerated emphasis on the role of elders in the body,[246] their understanding of the feast of charity, and their views on salutation, he allowed that in all other respects the two connexions maintained no essential differences.[247]

The 'Glasites' and 'Sandemanians' were not the only bodies which encouraged comparisons with Walker's connexion. Coleridge, whose own theological views often appeared perplexing (if not entirely opaque), found Walker's formularies 'hard to understand', speculating that his creed, 'or doctrines of the New Church, as it is called, appears to be a miscellany of Calvinism and Quakerism'.[248] In 1818, an anonymous critic writing in the *Christian Guardian*, a former member of the 'Church of God' but now an Evangelical clergyman, accused the 'Separatists' of holding ultra-Calvinist doctrines indistinguishable from those of the Western seceders.[249] Given the extreme variability of the Seceders' theological positions, this claim was not easy to sustain, and was dismissed by Walker who severely criticized the Western schismatics.[250] It had some plausibility, however, in relation to Walker's views of sanctification. These, it was claimed, encouraged antinomianism by ridiculing 'growth in grace', by advocating an instantaneous and imputed sanctification, and by depreciating the moral law. There were certainly passages in Walker's works which might encourage suspicions like these. In his clash with the Wesleyans he wrote with characteristic confidence: 'According to Scripture, I am not warranted to consider it any part of the work of grace to *mend* our fallen nature. *That* nature is as bad—as wholly evil—in a believer as in an unbeliever . . . as bad

243 Walker to J. H., *c.*1818, in *WE* ii.242.

244 See Walker to R. L. C., 23 Apr. 1818, in *WE* ii.254.

245 Walker to A. M'I., 12 June 1821, in *WE* ii.339.

246 Walker to R. L. C., 14 Jan. 1818, in *WE* ii.239; Walker to J. H., *c.*1818, in *WE* ii.242–3; Walker, 25 Aug. 1823, in *WE* ii.390.

247 Walker to J. H., *c.*1818, in *WE* ii.243.

248 Samuel Taylor Coleridge, *Specimens of the Table Talk of Samuel Taylor Coleridge*, New edn. (1852), 65.

249 See *CG* (1818), 171–3.

250 See Walker to R. L. C., 14 Jan. 1818, in *WE* ii.239–40; Walker to R. L. C., 23 Feb. 1818, in *WE* ii.244; Walker to R. L. C., 5 Mar. 1818, in *WE* ii.246–7; Walker to J. G. S., 12 June 1821, in *WE* ii.324–6.

in Paul the apostle, just finishing his course, and ready to receive the crown of righteousness, as in Saul of Tarsus, a blasphemer.' What then should we understand by being *sanctified*? 'I answer in a word—*separated* unto God, so as to be brought into a particular relation to him.' Walker accepted that by being engrafted into Christ, believers would, in varying degrees, show the fruits of the Spirit as described in Galatians 5:22–3—love, joy, peace, goodness, faith, meekness, and temperance. But, he maintained, 'they mistake the nature of that work . . . who imagine that it is a work which *improves* our corrupt nature.'[251] Walkerite exclusivism also repeatedly confused and even outraged his critics: not only those who held to the principle of a comprehensive National Church, but also those who maintained the pan-evangelical principles of the Bible Society and other evangelical associations. The 'Walkerites'' claims for their own small sect seemed absurd: they anathematized all churches but their own; though rejecting individual perfection, they frequently extolled their own Church as perfectly pure.[252]

VII

During the early nineteenth century, Irish Evangelicalism, although not robust, was relatively prosperous. It was advanced by its adherents as the best means of inculcating new life into the weak and ineffectual Anglican Establishment, and as the most effective prophylactic against Roman domination. By now it had extended beyond the early evangelistic campaigns and Methodist societies established by Wesley to become more respectable, moving more successfully into the Established Church, into Dublin's prosperous middle classes, and even into aristocratic 'ascendancy' circles. From this base, it provided some of the energy, vigour, and combative firepower needed to promote the Church of Ireland's ambitious mission: a thoroughgoing Protestant Reformation through the nation.

This explains why the secessions of Thomas Kelly and John Walker, and the formation of their small, apparently insignificant connexions, were seen as setbacks to the advancement of 'serious religion' and the wider cause of Irish Protestantism. Starting out

[251] Walker, 'An Expostulatory Address', i.13–16.

[252] See *CG* (1818), 172–3. Cf. 'Sandemanian Theology—John Walker', in *ER* (1838), 519–31.

on their careers as respected Evangelical clerics marked out for advancement in the Irish Church, Kelly and Walker had sacrificed much in terms of status and financial gain to satisfy the imperatives of conscience. Initially, the two had been close friends, allies in the fight to advance the 'doctrines of grace' against the Goliath of Irish Catholicism. But their idiosyncrasies had divided them and had diminished, if not destroyed, their influence in mainstream Evangelical circles. The divisions which emerged, both within and between these two 'Gospel connexions', played some part in weakening whatever opportunity the Evangelicals may have had of launching a comprehensive Protestant Reformation in Ireland during the early nineteenth century.

The spectacle of Anglican friability provided by these schisms helped discredit Protestantism as a whole in the eyes of the Roman Catholic majority, to whom the 'Kellyites' and 'Walkerites' offered new proof of the instability of Reformed religion and the lack of any coherent centre of authority. What else was to be expected of a creed based on the potentially anarchic principles of *sola scriptura* and the right of private judgement? As long as liberal Anglicans, High Churchmen, and Roman Catholics had been confronted by an Evangelicalism that was comparatively unified, respectable, theologically moderate, and above all increasingly popular, they were compelled to take notice; but when the movement began to fragment, with talented leaders criticizing the Established Church, seceding into obscure and eccentric forms of Dissent, and separating from all who disputed their claim to exclusive religious insight, the status of Evangelicalism in Ireland was compromised.

Nor was the importance of the 'Kellyite' and 'Walkerite' movements confined to Ireland. As Joseph Liechty has observed, the 'Walkerites', in particular, were 'a small but significant reversal of the usual flow of Protestant influence from Great Britain to Ireland.'[253] Fallout from 'Walkerism' was visible in the Western Schism in 1815, still more among those who established the Plymouth Brethren in the late 1820s. The vision of primal 'apostolical' purity and brotherhood which Kelly and Walker had held up for view as a higher and more fulfilling evangelical path, encouraged others to secede from the Church, to build upon their

[253] See Liechty, 'The Popular Reformation Comes to Ireland', 184.

extreme theology and ecclesiology, to embrace 'apostolic' principles, and to form their own religious connexions. Kelly and Walker were only two amongst a long list of clerical seceders who abandoned the Church during the early nineteenth century, but they were among the more significant. To restless or disgruntled believers they offered a model for an evangelicalism severed from all compromising entanglements with the State and aristocratic patronage, and set apart from an encroaching 'world'—a model which had rejected the social accommodation of a genteel Anglican Evangelicalism and disavowed the compromises of 'moderate' Calvinism. The ridicule and hostility which they suffered only seemed to enhance their claim to apostolic authority: after all, had not the Gospels always stressed that true saints of God would endure such tribulations? The example of the Irish separatists—as we shall see in later chapters—did not go unnoticed by secessionist movements in Ireland and on the British mainland.

4
The Western Schism

The Western Schism, as it was quickly labelled by its critics, has remained an obscure and virtually unexplained footnote in the history of the Church of England ever since its outbreak in 1815.[1] Although episodic clerical secessions from the Church had occurred among Evangelicalism during the previous century, especially within its Methodist branches, such disruptions were surprisingly few and inconsequential. When, therefore, a whole coterie of West Country Anglicans seceded from the Church in sensational fashion, they produced the most noteworthy schism of its kind in England for over a century.[2] The label 'Western Schism' was adapted—perhaps ironically—from the great split experienced by the Roman Catholic Church during the late fourteenth century. Since the Nonjurors, mass clerical secessions from the English Church had been virtually unknown, and the notion of a conspiratorial band of believers propagating new theological 'discoveries' and 'truths' at the expense of accepted Anglican doctrines and traditions, and advocating not only separatism but even disestablishment, was new and startling. Not surprisingly, the publicity which accompanied the Schism prefigured—albeit on a much smaller scale—that aroused by the Tractarian secessions some thirty years later.

Despite fears that the Schism would produce a wave of Evangelical secessions throughout England and Ireland, its influence

[1] Some brief attempts to assemble the details of the Schism have been made. See Sabine Baring-Gould, *The Church Revival* (1914), 95–7; E. H. Broadbent, *The Pilgrim Church*, 3rd edn. (1945), 368–9; Alan Brockett, *Nonconformity in Exeter, 1650–1875* (Manchester, 1962), 162–6, 210–11; L. Pamela Fox, 'The Work of the Reverend Thomas Tregenna Biddulph', Ph.D. thesis (Cambridge, 1953), 108–16; Charles Hole, *A Manual of English Church History* (1910), 391–2; W. H. B. Proby, *Annals of the 'Low Church' Party in England* (1888), i.292; Howard V. Young, Jr., 'The Evangelical Clergy in the Church of England, 1790–1850', Ph.D. diss. (Brown University, 1958), 92–3; W. J. C. Ervine, 'Doctrine and Diplomacy: Some Aspects of the Life and Thought of the Anglican Evangelical Clergy, 1797–1837', Ph.D. thesis (Cambridge, 1979), 70–2.

[2] Charles Smyth, *Simeon and Church Order* (Cambridge, 1940), 254.

was largely confined to the counties of Surrey, Hampshire, Wiltshire, Somerset, Devon, and Gloucestershire. It involved a comparatively small group bound together by close ties of friendship, kinship, and ideology. Its reverberations were also limited by the extremism—and inconsistency—of the principles of its leaders and by their reluctance to advertise their views or engage in public debate. The swift and severe denunciation handed out by its critics may have also played a role in reducing its effects on the evangelical public. Public condemnation indeed was so vehement that it not only gave the Schism dangerous publicity, but proved more significant than the Schism itself.

As criticism of the Schism increased, Evangelicals—and not liberals or High Churchmen—emerged as the chief critics of the Schism.[3] At first glance this may appear surprising, since the seceders had exceptionally good Evangelical credentials and party contacts. Such points in their favour, however, were soon offset by anxiety at the way in which the Schism had presented a distorted version of Evangelical theology—advancing, among other things, unorthodox Trinitarianism and Christology, and antinomianism—and had strained relations between Evangelicals and their fellow Anglicans. It was quickly realized by many 'Gospel clergy' that these eccentricities could be used to tar every advocate of 'serious religion' with the same disreputable brush. Not for the first time Evangelicals found themselves compelled to defend their Anglican orthodoxy on two different fronts, simultaneously asserting their claims to be 'true Churchmen'—the authentic inheritors of the English Reformation—against liberals and High Churchmen, while also attempting to prevent exaggerations of the 'doctrines of grace' by their high Calvinist brethren—'ultra-Evangelicals', as Charles Simeon called them—whose aberrations threatened to bring the entire party into disrepute.

The high predestinarianism, itinerant preaching, and determined separatism visible among the Western Schismatics also seemed to substantiate, in embarrassing fashion, some of the most repetitious charges which had long been levelled against the Evangelical party: that its doctrines were incipiently antinomian; that it encouraged fatalism; and, above all, that it was potentially schismatic: Evangelical clergymen were in reality 'Dissenters in the

[3] See Young, 'The Evangelical Clergy in the Church of England', 94.

church' whose loyalty to the national Establishment was at best lukewarm and suspect. The significance of the Schism, therefore, lay less in the secession of a handful of little-known clergy and lay people from the Church of England, and more in the damage which it inflicted on Evangelical claims to represent Anglican orthodoxy and in the pattern it set for further outbreaks of theological extremism. For this reason it became a significant episode during an uneasy period in Anglican history.

I

The Western Schism arrived at an awkward time. During the first two decades of the nineteenth century, Evangelicals had begun to assert their Anglican credentials with greater success and to gain increased acceptance for their claims to be a legitimate, respectable, and—despite their proselytizing energy—doctrinally moderate element within the Church. Its clergy were by now overwhelmingly 'regular' in their attitudes to Church order; there were now virtually no 'irregulars' like Wesley or Whitefield, while the 'half-regulars' like Rowland Hill, who combined a settled ministry with occasional field-preaching and appearances in Dissenting chapels, were increasingly scarce. Evangelicals, such as those of the dominant 'Christian Observer school', were eager to proclaim their loyalty to the canons and rubrics of the Established Church. Furthermore, the doctrine of the Evangelical clergy was by now overwhelmingly moderate in its Calvinism; mildly predestinarian, practical, and careful to avoid what had become known as the 'rigours of Calvinism', such as twofold predestination. Biblical commentators like Thomas Scott had stressed the need for the pursuit of holiness and growth in grace in the life of the Christian, and rebutted the antinomian tendencies of high Calvinism. The historian Joseph Milner had, with some success, given the Evangelicals a respectable pedigree to be traced back not only to the Reformation, but through the Augustinian tradition of the Middle Ages back to the early Fathers.[4]

Through such patient labours, the nascent Evangelical party sought to attract to its ranks respectable middle class and aristocratic sympathizers who had hitherto been alienated from the Revival by the disorderliness of Methodism. The Western

[4] Joseph Milner, *The History of the Church of Christ* (York and Cambridge, 1794–1809). See also J. D. Walsh, 'Joseph Milner's Evangelical Church History', in *JEH* (1959), 174–87.

Schism threatened this new found respectability. It also revealed to the world, and especially to the 'Gospel world', that the Evangelicals' much-touted attachment to the principles of the Established Church often concealed serious doubts about particular aspects of the Anglican system.

While Simeon and many others had extolled the Prayer Book, there remained, as we have seen, certain popish survivals in its formulae—such as the baptismal and burial rubrics—which most Evangelicals preferred either to ignore or to interpret in their own fashion. As one of the seceders remarked, 'There are few enlightened ministers in the Establishment who have not, at some period or other, found their consciences wounded, from the use of that form of service prescribed for the public baptism of infants.'[5] To these inconsistencies the seceders now drew attention. Meanwhile, the publicity given to the handful of high Calvinists in the Western Schism brought into high relief those aspects of predestinarianism which most Evangelicals had been at pains to avoid.

The extremism of the Western Schismatics provided the spectacle of a group of Evangelicals who were not content with moderation and compromise, but wished to push their Reformed theology to unpalatable limits. By 1815 the Evangelical party had become accustomed to frontal attacks by liberals and High Churchmen, to which they had learned to respond on the whole with dignity and moderation, if not silence. It was an altogether different matter to remain quiet when they saw their own doctrines of grace being perverted by unbalanced and well-connected Evangelicals who seemed expert at attracting adverse publicity to their cause.

II

Like Irvingism and Brethrenism some two decades later, the Western Schism was based on the unusual religious theories of wealthy and well-connected lay Evangelicals in alliance with a small band of like-minded—and sometimes related—clergymen who served under their patronage. The network which held the Schism together in some kind of tenuous collective existence was

[5] Thomas C. Cowan, *A Brief Account of the Reasons Which Have Induced the Revd T. C. Cowan to Secede From the Established Church*, 2nd edn. (Bristol, 1817), 31. For a response see 'A Layman', *The Church of England Vindicated* (Exeter, 1818).

the kinship of the Barings, a family of bankers and merchants. Specialists in lending money to foreign governments, the House of Baring had, by the early nineteenth century, become so influential in world affairs that the Duc de Richelieu, Louis XVIII's Prime Minister, was reputed to have exclaimed, 'There are six great powers in Europe: England, France, Prussia, Austria, Russia, and Baring Brothers'.[6] The founder of this commercial empire (and father of the three leading adherents of the Schism) was Sir Francis Baring, MP and Chairman of the East India Company, who, at his death in 1810, was described by Lord Erskine as 'unquestionably the first merchant of Europe'.[7]

If male patronage made the Schism possible, it was inspired and driven forward—at least according to public perception—by female religious zeal, a factor which rendered it even more suspect in the eyes of many patriarchally minded Evangelicals.[8] As the *Christian Observer* noted drily, '*women* have been foremost in embracing and organizing this lamentable defection from received principles', as one might expect from a sex which lacked the steady judgement and 'cool, discriminating, and enlarged view of things' characteristic of masculinity. Like modern Eves, these 'honourable women' had lured their menfolk from the garden of Gospel truth into a wilderness of error.[9]

Foremost in the launching of the Schism was Harriet Wall, the eldest daughter of Sir Francis Baring and the wife of Charles Wall, partner in the Baring Bank.[10] Intellectually agile and temperamentally cool, Mrs Wall held (according to one of her relations) 'a real superiority over the heated brains and crude notions of her disciples'.[11] She was much given to doctrinal novelties. After her conversion to 'serious religion', which occurred some time before 1815, her home at Albury, Surrey (later well-known as the venue for the Albury conferences and as the spiritual headquarters of the Catholic Apostolic Church), became a focus of local devotional activity. In one of her drawing rooms she organized

[6] See Philip Ziegler, *The Sixth Great Power* (1988), 85.

[7] *GM* (1810), 293.

[8] For an account of Harriet Wall's influence upon the outbreak and progress of the Western Schism see Samuel Nicholson, *Select Remains of the Revd John Mason* (1836); Baring-Gould, *The Church Revival*, 95–7.

[9] *CO* (1819), 33.

[10] For details of Mrs Wall see Grayson Carter, 'Harriet Wall', in *New DNB*; Nicholson, *Select Remains of the Revd John Mason*, pp. ix–x.

[11] Baring-Gould, *The Church Revival*, 96.

twice-daily Scripture readings and prayers, which drew in upwards of a hundred and fifty relatives and neighbours. In the absence of a clergyman, Mrs Wall led these herself. Eventually, fearing that these assemblies might be construed as illegal conventicles, and being unwilling to license her home as a Dissenting meeting house, she began to curtail public admission.[12]

After the sudden death of her husband in 1815, Mrs Wall moved to Everton, near Lymington, Hampshire,[13] to be nearer her brother, Sir Thomas Baring, of Stratton Park, Micheldever,[14] and her son, Charles Baring Wall, of Norman Court, West Tytherley.[15] She then set about converting her rural circle. In this she enjoyed no little success, drawing into her coterie several members of her extended family as well as several neighbouring clergymen. Meeting regularly for discussion, the 'Baring party', as it was soon labelled by its critics, became convinced that some of the doctrines in the Thirty-Nine Articles and Prayer Book were inconsistent with Scripture.[16] This news was quickly disseminated, and understandably so, given the national prominence of the Baring family. The spectacle of young and affluent members of an internationally respected financial house advocating separatism and preaching unorthodox doctrines which looked like sabellian and antinomian heresy, was bound to attract attention.

The principal adherents of the 'Baring party' included (beside Mrs Wall) her brother, Sir Thomas Baring and his wife Mary; another brother, the Hon. and Revd George Baring, until his secession in 1815 vicar of Winterbourne Stoke, Wiltshire, and

[12] Nicholson, *Select Remains of the Revd John Mason*, p. xiii.

[13] Though she retained ownership of her house at Albury until June 1819, when it was sold to Henry Drummond. See MS 1322, Surrey Record Centre.

[14] Sir Thomas Baring (12 June 1772–3 April 1848), MP for Wycombe, 1806–32, and Hampshire, 1832, was the eldest son of Sir Francis Baring, founder of the Baring Bank, Chairman of the East India Company, and a member of at least 47 Evangelical voluntary societies. He was also the father of Charles Baring, the Evangelical Bishop of Gloucester and Bristol, and later Durham. For details on his career see Ford K. Brown, *Fathers of the Victorians* (Cambridge, 1961), 88, 357.

[15] See H. R. Doubleday (ed.), 'Hampshire and the Isle of Wight', in *The Victoria History of the Counties of England*, 2nd edn. (1973), iv.521. Charles Baring Wall (1795–1853) was Lord of the Manor of West Tytherley, Hampshire. A magistrate, he was Liberal MP for Guildford (1819–26, 1830–1, 1832–47); Wareham (1826–30); Weymouth (1831); and Salisbury (1847–53). In 1833 he was tried for indecency, but acquitted. See *AR* (1833), 314–19.

[16] Nicholson, *Select Remains of the Revd John Mason*, p. xv. The seceders were also called the 'New Lights' by some of their critics. See M. Caston, *Independency in Bristol* (London and Bristol, 1860), 156.

curate of Durston, Somerset (where he was the protégé of the non-resident Evangelical, Thomas T. Biddulph), and his wife Harriet;[17] her two younger sisters, Frances Kemp and Lydia Story, who induced their husbands, Thomas Read Kemp, MP, and Philip Lacock Story, to abandon their commercial and political interests and enter the ministry;[18] Thomas Snow, another banker's son and vicar of Micheldever and East Stratton,[19] and his curate George Bevan;[20] and James Harington Evans, curate at nearby Milford and Hordle.[21] They were later joined by Thomas Connolly Cowan, curate of St. Thomas's, Bristol.[22] Another member of the 'Baring party', later to achieve prominence as a founder and financier of the Irvingites, was Henry Drummond, also a banker, an energetically devout, albeit volatile character, who lived at The Grange, Northington, a magnificent neoclassical house and estate which bordered Sir Thomas Baring's extensive estate at Stratton. The details of Drummond's involvement in the Schism are not altogether clear, but it appears that after formally seceding from the Church, probably in 1815 or 1816, he was baptized by immersion.[23]

The doctrinal excesses of the Schism did not appeal to all

[17] For details of George Baring see Grayson Carter, 'George Baring', in *New DNB*; MS D1/2/30/143, Wiltshire RO; Joseph Foster, *Index Ecclesiasticus* (Oxford, 1890), 8; MS EP/A/1/3, Bristol City RO; Ziegler, *The Sixth Great Power*, 47–8, 56.

[18] See Baring-Gould, *The Church Revival*, 95–9. Thomas Read Kemp was Whig MP for Lewes, vice-president of the Church Missionary Society, and owner of a large portion of Brighton, where he built a chapel in which he officiated. For details of Kemp see *DNB*. Philip Lacock Story married Lydia Baring in 1806; there was no issue from the marriage.

[19] Thomas Snow (1786–*c*.1865) of Langton House, Blandford, Dorset, was educated at Sherborne and Queens' College, Cambridge (matriculated 1810, BA 1814). For details of Snow see *Al. Cant.*, v.586; MSS 21M65 A2/4/181, 21M65/B5/1, 21M65 E5/280/1, and 11M52, Hampshire RO.

[20] George Bevan (1782–1819) of Fosbury, Wiltshire, was educated at Trinity College, Cambridge (matriculated 1809, BA 1813), and admitted at Lincoln's Inn on 21 Jan. 1805. For details of Bevan see *Al. Cant.*, i.253; *The Records of the Honourable Society of Lincoln's Inn* (1896), ii.20; *Burke's Landed Gentry*, 18th edn. (1965), i.59; MS 21M65/E1/1, Hampshire RO; *Salisbury and Winchester Journal*, 27 May 1816, 4.

[21] For details of Evans see James Joyce Evans, *Memoir and Remains of the Revd James Harington Evans* (1852); Grayson Carter, 'James Harington Evans', in *New DNB*; *Al. Ox.*, ii.434; MS 21M65/E1/1, Hampshire RO; Arthur J. Willis (ed.), *Winchester Ordinations 1660–1829* (Folkestone, 1964–5), i.126.

[22] Thomas Cowan matriculated at Trinity College, Dublin, in 1793 (BA 1798). For details of Cowen see *Al. Dub.*, 184; MS EP/V/4/45, Bristol City RO.

[23] See Le Roy E. Froom, *The Prophetic Faith of Our Fathers* (Washington, 1946–54), iv.435. Froom claims that Drummond seceded in June 1817, but this is unlikely as he was in Geneva at the time. Drummond's religious life is explored in more detail in Chapter 5.

members of the Baring tribe, however, especially their itinerant preaching and pronounced separatism. The shock to some members of the family is revealed in an exchange of letters between Henry Baring, written in September 1815, and his brother, Sir Thomas Baring. As Henry reported:

> George, the Kemps and Mrs Wall have been within a few miles of us the greatest part of the summer, but as to any communication with them they might as well have been in China. I forget myself, Mrs Wall did call for a few minutes on her way to Fordingbridge to hear George preach but being under an imperious necessity of hearing him again on the following day at nine o'clock in the morning at twenty miles distance she could afford no more time for feelings for which she was once so particularly distinguished. As for George he preaches all around us, and perhaps within sight of our house twice every month, but has never entered our doors. Whatever his doctrines may be, this is miserable practice.[24]

In reply, Sir Thomas expressed sympathy with the new movement. The exasperated Henry, unable to conceal his disappointment at his brother's attitude, told him plainly that he much regretted the outbreak of the Schism and the recent secession of some of its leading adherents because of the injury it might inflict upon the Church. Thomas's condoning their behaviour evidently placed him 'not very far behind them in doctrine'. Though Henry appreciated George's sincerity, he still considered his behaviour 'weak and inconsistent', and, 'if followed up in the manner we have too much reason to fear, disgraceful to his family'. As for George's conscience, 'upon which all this mass of absurdity is made to rest', carry it to its natural conclusions and Joanna Southcott would be made to look like a saint.[25] An astute, if rather harsh judge of character, Henry attributed his younger brother's behaviour to constitutional vanity:

> George the foxhunter and George the Methodist preacher are, in my opinion, precisely the same persons. Humility, it is true, is on his tongue but pride and the love of distinction is equally in his heart. The quiet and useful life of a respectable country clergyman was much too tame and unobtrusive for him, but as the ranting preacher of a wild sect he

[24] Henry Baring to Sir Thomas Baring, 28 Sept. 1815, in MS Northbrook Papers, B3 viii.

[25] Joanna Southcott (1750–1814), a notorious religious fanatic who claimed special prophetic understanding.

will draw upon himself the eyes of the world, which in my opinion is what he chiefly seeks however he may hide his leading motives from others and even from himself. I am only sorry that he did not know himself better than to enter upon a profession from which he now retires in a manner so disgraceful to himself and his family . . . I am much at a loss to conceive what George will do next for it is clear that he cannot be quiet—indeed in his letter to Alexander he tells him it is not his intention to remain in a state of inactivity, which is fearful intelligence to me who lives in the very centre of his absurdities.[26]

During the Schism's initial phase, the seceders were regularly hosted by Sir Thomas Baring at Stratton Park, the young converts travelling to discuss, debate, and settle their new theological discoveries in an atmosphere in which 'vital Christianity could be combined with the refinements of creature comforts and attendance'.[27] Between these gatherings, the seceders dispersed to spread their new doctrines to nearby towns and villages. The reverberations were soon felt throughout the West Country.

Some information regarding the Schism's progress in and around the village of Milford, where James Harington Evans served as curate, has survived. Here, local houses were rented out for the summer season to members of 'the higher circles' who had fallen under the Schism's influence.[28] One unsympathetic critic, a local clergyman, claimed that the seceders' high Calvinism had rapidly divided the local community and undermined social order by its rigoristic separation of the elect from the reprobate. '*Family harmony* withered away', he complained; children began to look upon their parents with pity and contempt, 'as not so far *advanced*, or deeply *experienced*, as themselves; sisters quarrelled with sisters on points of "knotty divinity", and servants regarded their masters as "mere babes" in grace; or rather, as not having any grace at all; groping in "darkness visible" here, and condemned to "utter darkness" hereafter'.[29] There was a dramatic confrontation when George Thompson, the non-resident vicar of Milford, returned unannounced on one particular Sunday during the early days of the Schism intending to preach, to find that Evans had arranged to have a clerical ally officiate at the same service. Evans pleaded

[26] Henry Baring to Sir Thomas Baring (n. d.), in MS 'Northbrook Papers', B3 viii.

[27] Baring-Gould, *The Church Revival*, 96.

[28] Evans, *Memoir of James Harington Evans*, 28–9.

[29] Richard Warner, *Considerations on the Doctrines of the Evangelical Clergy* (Bath, 1817), 60–1.

with Thompson to yield, as his friend had come expressly to preach and was expected by the large congregation; when this was refused, Evans's unidentified friend made his way to the church porch, where he announced loudly: 'Ye who are inclined to remain in darkness continue in the church, but you who wish to *hear the Gospel*, follow me.' The church then emptied. Thompson preached to nearly naked walls, while his rival addressed a large crowd in the nearby fields.[30]

Another account described vividly how the antinomian preaching of one of the seceders in an unnamed West Country town alienated the inhabitants, first from their own teachers and later from religion altogether:

> By exalting *faith* and decrying *works*, as all emanating from the *law*, with which Christians . . . had nothing to do, he produced a complete revolution in the place. This success he acquired by his appeal to the corrupt passions, by telling his hearers that all who thought as he did, were decreed to eternal life; and that, being interested in the decrees, the fluctuation of frames and feelings, sins, and frailties, however great, could not, in the least, counteract designs which were settled from all eternity . . . God was not constrained by merit, nor restrained by demerit . . . [and that] sin could not hurt them.[31]

When a notorious drunkard heard this, he at once exclaimed, 'this is the preaching for me!' The effect of the message was weakened soon afterwards, however, when the preacher suddenly disavowed his errors and promised henceforth to promote 'the true sentiments of the Bible' as an act of contrition for his past sins.[32] If perhaps exaggerated, such local accounts nevertheless highlight the extremes and volatility which were to characterize the Schism throughout not only its initial phase, but much of its history.

III

The initial phase of the Schism was sensational, but short-lived. Soon the focus and energy of the movement began to spread westward under the leadership and patronage of George Baring, and a second—and more peripatetic—phase of the Schism was initiated. After Baring's secession in 1815, he purchased Walford

[30] Ibid. 61–2.

[31] See Joseph Cottle, *Strictures on the Plymouth Antinomians*, 2nd edn. (1824), 31.

[32] Ibid. 32.

House, outside Taunton and hard by Thomas Biddulph's parish at Durston, which served as the headquarters of the Schism during its second phase. He then invited Bevan, Snow, and Evans to reside with him and to establish a new ministry in and around Taunton.[33]

At first, Baring preached in a hired room at 54 East Street, Taunton.[34] Here, according to one local account, 'the novelty of the scene, the respectability of the parties, and the style of their preaching, attracted a numerous congregation.'[35] Those attending the initial service included a correspondent from the *Taunton Courier*, who documented how Baring impressed upon the minds of the crowd that it was not any hostile feeling to the Church or its members that had prompted his secession, but 'the apostolic idea of his duty to become a "helper of the joy" of the believers in Christ'.[36] This early success prompted Baring, in April 1816, to purchase the Octagon Chapel in Middle Street, Taunton, from the Wesleyan Methodists and reopen it under the unusual denominational standard of 'Trinitarian and Particular Baptists'.[37] As the party had now come to embrace the doctrine of believers' baptism,[38] Baring baptized Snow, Bevan, and several others by immersion at the chapel on 15 May; several weeks later, Baring, together with his wife and a number of others, were baptized, in the same fashion, by Bevan.[39] In this old Nonconformist stronghold, the seceders' high Calvinism and strange—and unorthodox—views on the Trinity proved attractive to a number of the inhabitants.[40] The novelty value of this Taunton phase of the Schism seems to have worn off rather quickly, however, and, despite their local success in attracting publicity and adherents to their cause, the *quadrumvirate* soon began to split up.

Around November 1816, the third—and final—phase of the Schism began to emerge, as Evans moved to London and Snow

33 The *Hampshire Chronicle*, 22 Jan. 1816; 5 May 1817.

34 See the *Salisbury and Winchester Journal*, 1 Jan. 1816, 4: 22 Jan. 1816, 4; the *Taunton Courier*, 11 Jan. 1816; James Savage, *History of Taunton* (Taunton, 1822), 192.

35 Nicholson, *Select Remains of the Revd John Mason*, p. xvi.

36 The *Taunton Courier*, 11 Jan. 1816.

37 Ibid., 27 June 1816; the *Bristol Gazette*, 25 Apr. 1816; Brockett, *Nonconformity in Exeter*, 165. The Octagon Chapel had been opened by John Wesley in March 1776.

38 Nicholson, *Select Remains of the Revd John Mason*, p. xvii.

39 The *Taunton Courier*, 27 June 1816; the *Salisbury and Winchester Journal*, 24 June 1816, 4.

40 Brockett, *Nonconformity in Exeter*, 165.

migrated to Cheltenham (both under the patronage of Mrs Wall), while Baring and Bevan remained—for the time being—at the Octagon Chapel where they propagated their new doctrines and itinerated in the surrounding countryside.[41] Harriet Baring, it appears, also began to preach, going about with her harp into the local cottages, the country folk gathering opened eyed and mouthed to catch a glimpse at the so-called 'wonderful lady'.[42] Baring and Bevan were soon joined in Taunton by John Mason, a domestic servant of Mrs Wall, who had proved particularly adept at local preaching.[43] Mason preached, at first, at Shrewton, Wiltshire, where, in July 1816 a congregation had been established by the seceders and a chapel opened, but yet remained without a resident minister;[44] sometime during 1817 he moved to Taunton where he began to preach in a number of local villages.[45]

The rapid fragmentation of the Schism's original leadership revealed something of its youthful effervescence and doctrinal restlessness. To the outside world, however, the dispersal may have suggested that something approaching a missionary campaign had begun, and that the Schism was being deliberately exported to new centres where it could spread, infecting unsuspecting believers and feeding on existing Anglican and Nonconformist congregations.

The Schism continued to gain momentum during its third phase, its high Calvinism, sabellianism, and separatism proving attractive in the volatile religious atmosphere of the West Country. Nowhere was this momentum so great as in the traditional Nonconformist stronghold of Exeter, where the doctrinal eccentricity

[41] See Fox, 'Thomas Tregenna Biddulph', 110; Evans, *Memoir of James Harington Evans*, 113; the *Salisbury and Winchester Journal*, 29 July 1816, 4. The *Journal* also claimed that a Mr Capper had contributed to the cost of Snow's chapel.

[42] Jane Miriam Crane, *Records of the Life of the Revd Wm. H. Havergal, M.A.*, 2nd edn. (1882), 14.

[43] Mason had been a farm labourer at Norman Court, one of the Walls' country houses. After his conversion to 'serious religion' he abandoned the Church because, as he put it, 'the Gospel was not preached there', and was baptized at the Baptist chapel at Broughton. Subsequently promoted to footman, Wall persuaded him to abandon his intentions to enter the Baptist academy at Bristol. See Nicholson, *Select Remains of the Revd John Mason*, pp. xvii–xviii.

[44] The *Salisbury and Winchester Journal*, 22 July 1816, 4.

[45] Nicholson, *Select Remains of the Revd John Mason*, pp. xix–xx; the *Taunton Courier*, 27 Nov. 1817, 8.

of the Western Schismatics made a rapid impression on the religious life of the city. Samuel Kiplin, a prominent local figure and minister of South Street Baptist Chapel, gave an emotional account of the upheaval which ravaged his own congregation. He characterized the Schism as an explosion of antinomian enthusiasm, breeding sectarianism and dissension. 'Discord and separation entered every church and congregation. No human efforts could stem the torrent; it proceeded rapidly, until harmony fled.'[46] Unable 'to bear the boisterous contention of these unscriptural ferments' within his own chapel, Kiplin tendered his resignation on 5 January 1817 and fled the scene.[47] In an explanatory letter to his congregation, he confessed: 'I no more come among you as a pastor highly esteemed for his works sake, but as a criminal to be judged by the standard orthodoxy of the times.' When urged to reconsider, he replied: 'shackled and fettered I will not attempt to go on'.[48] His friends persisted, however, eventually gaining a large majority of the congregation in favour of his restoration. On 9 March, Kiplin accepted their invitation on condition that the malcontents withdraw from their communion.[49] Consequently, on 31 March 1817 seventy-two members of South Street Chapel seceded: thirteen affiliating with various local bodies, the remainder forming their own congregation in a hired room in Bartholomew Street.[50]

Initial pastoral oversight of this new body was provided by George Baring, who, in the same month that Kiplin had been driven from his pulpit, had purchased Northbrook House outside Exeter to serve as the headquarters of the Schism in south Devon.[51] It was not long before Baring became permanent minister to the body which had seceded from South Street Chapel,

[46] Anon., *Memoir of the Revd Samuel Kiplin* (Exeter, 1832), 21–2. See also Arthur Gabb, *A History of Baptist Beginnings with an Account of the Rise of Baptist Witness in Exeter, and the Founding of South Street Church* (Exeter, 1954), 45–6; H. E. Bickers, *A Brief History of the Baptist Church now Meeting in South Street Chapel, Exeter, From the Year 1656* (Exeter, 1906), 23.

[47] Anon., *Memoir of Samuel Kiplin*, 21–2; Brockett, *Nonconformity in Exeter*, 162.

[48] 1 May 1817. See Brockett, *Nonconformity in Exeter*, 162.

[49] Ibid.; Anon., *Memoir of Samuel Kiplin*, 21–1.

[50] MSS 76/44/1/2; 76/44/1/2/1, 'Minute Book', Bartholomew Street Chapel, Devon RO.

[51] Baring also officiated during January and February at the spacious chapel on Princes Street, Plymouth dock. See *Woolmer's Exeter and Plymouth Gazette*, 11 Jan. 1817; the *Salisbury and Winchester Journal*, 13 Jan. 1817, 4.

turning over responsibility of the Octagon Chapel to Mason, while Bevan moved to London.[52] The Bartholomew Street congregation now became the axis of the Western Schism, the final chapter of its history being closely associated with the congregation's early successes and failures.

Although Exeter had now become the focus of his attention, Baring continued his itinerant ministry throughout the West Country, generating no little amount of attention and controversy. In May 1817, for instance, he preached at Southampton to crowded rooms;[53] in the same month, he preached at Salisbury to an audience so large that many were forced to use ladders to climb into the building through the windows.[54] His high Calvinism is suggested by an account of this sermon which claimed that he preached and prayed for the elect only—a message which seemed to some 'destitute of Christian modesty and charity', while inflicting 'great pain to the sober and humble minded'. With some plausibility this observer claimed that the seceders drew their support only from the restless and discontented in the religious world—'those who are tossed about with every wind of doctrine'—while having little appeal to the 'established believer'.[55] There can be little doubt that the spectacle of well-born Anglican seceders had considerable curiosity value for Dissenting chapelgoers. When, in the following month, Baring preached at a meeting-house in Exmouth, the size of the congregation was so great he was obliged to move out into the open air.[56] During July and August he baptized several new converts into the Exeter body, and on 28 August he purchased a site on Bartholomew Street which would provide a permanent—and expanded—base of operations in Devon.[57] On 26 November 1817 he held a service of baptism at Gideon Chapel, Bristol, where a large crowd gathered, drawn in part by the publicity given to the recent secession of Thomas Cowan from the Church of England.[58] At this service, Cowan was baptized by

[52] Nicholson, *Select Remains of the Revd John Mason*, p. xx.

[53] The *Salisbury and Winchester Journal*, 5 May 1817, 4.

[54] Anonymous clergyman to J. Randall, 2 May 1817, in Charles Hole, *The Life of William Whitmarsh Phelps* (Reading, 1871–3), i.139.

[55] Ibid. [56] *Woolmer's Exeter and Plymouth Gazette*, 28 June 1817.

[57] MS 76/44/1/2/2, 'Minute Book', Bartholomew Street Chapel; *Woolmer's Exeter and Plymouth Gazette*, 28 June 1817.

[58] *Woolmer's Exeter and Plymouth Gazette*, 6 Dec. 1817; Fox, 'Thomas Tregenna Biddulph', 110–11. Gideon Chapel was also known as Pithay meeting house.

Baring along with some sixty others, including around twenty members of St. Thomas's (Cowan's former parish), many other candidates reportedly being anxious to join them.[59] Back in Exeter, on New Year's Day 1818, Baring combined philanthropy with an attempt to achieve some standing in the community, by giving away six hundred loaves of bread and eight hundred pounds of beef to the poor who came properly recommended.[60] On 16 August 1818 Baring's ambitious new edifice on Bartholomew Street, accommodating upwards of a thousand worshippers and costing nearly £4,000 to build, was dedicated. Thomas Read Kemp preached in the morning, George Bevan in the afternoon, and Thomas Cowan in the evening.[61] Seven months later, in March 1819, Baring formulated the fourteen doctrinal points upon which his new body would operate. He astonished the religious world by a bold affirmation of Trinitarian heterodoxy—and especially astonished the city of Exeter, which had often been riven by controversies on the issue. The Christological implication of sabellianism were readily apparent in his first two propositions, which called for 'the unity of Jehovah in person, name, and being—the one God the Father'; and, 'the preexistence of the man Christ Jesus, having all his spiritual posterity in himself, and in union with the one God before the foundation of the world'.[62] A further proposition proclaimed the hyper-Calvinist idea of eternal sanctification—the believer's eternal redemption from sin, the law, death, and hell. Baptism in the chapel was by immersion and administered solely to believers, and only those who had been properly baptized could exercise authority (i.e. choosing new ministers, deacons, and public servants).[63]

[59] *Woolmer's Exeter and Plymouth Gazette*, 6 Dec. 1817; Fox, 'Thomas Tregenna Biddulph', 110–11.

[60] The *Salisbury and Winchester Journal*, 12 Jan. 1818, 4.

[61] Construction was financed by Baring and Wall. See Brockett, *Nonconformity in Exeter*, 165; Nicholson, *Select Remains of the Revd John Mason*, p. xxii; the *Bristol Gazette*, 4 Feb. 1819; MS 76/44/1/2/2, 'Minute Book', Bartholomew Street Chapel.

[62] MS 76/44/1/2/3–5, 'Minute Book', Bartholomew Street Chapel. See also Havergal to Tebbs, *c.*1816, in Crane, *Life of Wm. Havergal*, 17, in which Havergal (Baring's successor at Durston) claimed to have 'positive evidence' that Baring taught that 'the Holy Spirit is not a party concerned in the Covenant of Redemption', which 'virtually denies the Divinity of the Eternal Spirit, and is awfully consistent with a scheme that admits of sanctification only by imputation'.

[63] MS 76/44/1/2, 'Minute Book', Bartholomew Street Chapel.

The Bartholomew Street flock was a dangerously mixed body. While some of the members accepted Baring's more unusual doctrines, others rejected them, though often deterred from expressing disapproval by respect for their minister's wealth and social rank. This initial quiet did not continue. Circumstances quickly conspired to bring the Exeter phase of the Schism to a premature conclusion. Despite the accession of several members of the Baring tribe to the cause, it soon became clear that other family members were deeply embarrassed by the adverse publicity to the family name which had been brought by the Schism. For a banking family dependent on a reputation for stability and good sense, this kind of escapade seemed highly damaging. Events were brought to a head during the spring of 1819 when George suddenly abandoned Exeter for the Continent, presumably on orders from his family.[64] At first, he lived in Baden-Baden;[65] eventually, he settled in a villa in Florence, where, in September 1828, Henry Fox found him puffing cigar smoke at Lady Dudley and decidedly the worse for drink, surrounded by his daughters, 'tall, raw-boned, vulgar misses', as he described them, 'very underbred and unladylike in their conversation and manners'.[66]

Baring's forced exile, however, did little to curtail his profligate lifestyle and he was eventually compelled to declare bankruptcy.[67] Back in England, his family attempted to redeem the situation by applying to Lord Lansdowne, the former Chancellor of the Exchequer and son of the First Marquis of Lansdowne (who had been an important patron of Sir Francis Baring), but nothing of advantage appears to have arisen from this entreaty. Sir Thomas Baring, by now well out of sympathy with George and with the excesses of the Schism, was for letting his brother stew in his own juice; Alexander, on the other hand, fearing that the disgrace of George's bankruptcy might damage the family reputation and the family business, insisted that it 'must be cleared'. His family, Alexander insisted, should rally round their 'unfortunate member', and Thomas, as head of the family, should make the necessary arrangements to smooth things over.[68]

[64] See *Woolmer's Exeter and Plymouth Gazette*, 30 Jan. 1819; Ziegler, *The Sixth Great Power*, 47–8.

[65] MS 76/44/1/1/1–16, 'Minute Book', Bartholomew Street Chapel.

[66] Earl of Ilchester (ed.), *The Journal of the Hon. Henry Edward Fox* (1946), 318–19.

[67] See Alexander Baring to Sir Thomas Baring, *c.*10 June 1827, *Northbroke Papers*, E7 d.

[68] Ibid.

With George's exile to the Continent, the Western Schism had, to all intents and purposes, run its course. Mason was summoned from Taunton to Exeter and given a life interest in the Bartholomew Street Chapel and the adjoining residence.[69] The Octagon Chapel was closed sometime after 1822, and eventually taken over by the Plymouth Brethren.[70] Mason, who was 29 years old at the time of his moving to Exeter, initially maintained the same Christological and Trinitarian doctrines as his mentors; by 1821, however, 'his mind was in a wavering state', torn between doctrinal orthodoxy and the excesses of the 'Baring party'.[71] Within four years, he came to reject the Schism's heterodoxy, publishing an account of his revised position in the *New Baptist Magazine*.[72] Since the 'Baring party' remained divided over the doctrine of particular redemption, maintained no biblical order or discipline, showed little brotherly love, and failed to hold regular communion services, he concluded that he must now separate from it.[73] Mason then wrote to Baring offering to resign as minister of the Bartholomew Street Chapel; Baring responded with a long letter defending his doctrinal views, but stating his willingness to allow Mason to continue as minister, which he did until his premature death in 1835.[74] The chapel was then purchased from Baring by the members of the congregation for £1,000.[75] Perhaps predictably, its devotional life was repeatedly hampered by a spirit of sectarian conflict which produced a series of further schisms—the largest, in 1840, into Plymouth Brethrenism.[76] It was claimed that Baring eventually returned to the Established Church, but this remains uncertain.[77] He died on 4 October 1854 at Cumberland Villa, Shirley, near Southampton, having

[69] Nicholson, *Select Remains of the Revd John Mason*, p. xxix.

[70] In 1826, the Octagon Chapel was reopened by the Wesleyan Methodists. See Savage, *History of Taunton*, 192–3; the *Taunton Courier*, 26 July 1826. In 1832, it was sold to an unknown buyer for some £360 and used by various religious groups before becoming a Brethren assembly. See MS 'Octagon Chapel', Somerset Local Studies Library, Taunton.

[71] Nicholson, *Select Remains of the Revd John Mason*, p. xxv.

[72] John Mason, 'Reasons for Withdrawing From a Church Not Constituted Agreeably to the Rule of the Word of God', in *New Baptist Magazine*, 1825, 486–9. See also John Mason, *On the Godhead, Distinction, Unity, and Worship of the Father, the Son, and the Spirit* (Exeter, 1826).

[73] Mason, *Reasons for Withdrawing*, 486–9.

[74] Nicholson, *Select Remains of the Revd John Mason*, pp. xxix–xxx, xxxviii.

[75] MSS 76/44/1/1/1–26; 76/44/1/2/23, 'Minute Book', Bartholomew Street Chapel.

[76] MSS 76/44/1/2/25–9, 'Minute Book', Bartholomew Street Chapel; A. E. Knapman, *A History of St Thomas' Baptist Church, Exeter, 1817–1967* (Exeter, 1967), 3–5.

[77] Havergal to Tebbs (n. d.), in Crane, *Life of Wm. Havergal*, 96–7, 166.

apparently returned to England sometime after the death of his wife in Bologna in May 1833.[78]

IV

So far, this study has concentrated chiefly on George Baring, the leader and principal patron of the Schism, but the spiritual odyssey of his fellow seceders is also worthy of consideration. Most significant among these was James Harington Evans.[79] Having been brought up in the orderly peace of Salisbury Cathedral close, where his father was priest-vicar and headmaster of the Grammar School, Evans would not have appeared a radical schismatic. He was academically able—a fellow of Wadham College, Oxford, at 20—and a keen oarsman, but none the less given to the pangs of early guilt so characteristic of evangelical converts. In his early days he was unusually shy and had to fortify himself with wine from a hip flask before preaching a sermon. Helped by Philip Doddridge's *On the Rise and Progress of Religion in the Soul* (1745) and other works, he passed through a classic conversion experience at the age of 27, after the deaths of his mother and an infant son. Ordained in 1808, he served briefly at parishes in Surrey and Staffordshire before, two years later, becoming curate at Milford and Hordle, hard by Mrs Wall's new residence at Everton. In 1815, at an early stage in the Schism and perhaps due to his mounting opposition to the existence of a national religious establishment, he began to be drawn into its inner circles, eventually becoming recognized as the most able scholar of the party.[80] When Evans's new opinions became apparent, his incumbent quickly gave him a six-month notice to quit; he then decided (against his father's wishes) to pursue his vocation outside the Church of England. This decision to secede was based on three objections, all by now familiar: the Church's civil connection, its baptism of infants, and its absence of discipline.[81]

Evans then set about building a chapel at Milford and establishing a local congregation.[82] In January 1816, as the Schism

[78] See Carter, 'George Baring'. [79] See ibid.

[80] See Hole, *A Manual of English Church History*, 391. Evans was described by Sabine Baring-Gould as a man of 'education and talent', but possessing 'peculiar views'. See Baring-Gould, *The Church Revival*, 96.

[81] Evans, *Memoir of James Harington Evans*, 29. See also *A Brief Account of the Revd James Harington Evans, M.A.*, in James Harington Evans, *Three Funeral Sermons* (1850), 2.

[82] The *Salisbury and Winchester Journal*, 22 July 1816, 4.

moved into its second phase, he and his wife moved to Baring's new residence at Durston. Shortly afterwards, in May 1816, they were baptized by immersion at the Octagon Chapel.[83] Evans then launched himself into a round of local evangelism in towns and villages. The seceders encountered a host of difficulties, however, for they had moved so quickly, following the impulses of conscience, that they lacked any clear plan of action and had to hammer one out in conclave together.[84] As the most able theologian of the party, Evans made an important contribution to this process. He also proved a capable preacher, attracting widespread attention including that of Henry Drummond, who was so moved by Evans's natural eloquence that he quickly set about looking for a site in London where a chapel could be built for his exclusive use. During 1818, Drummond presented Evans with a life tenancy in John Street Chapel, Holborn, where he remained until his retirement.[85]

Although developing no formal theological system, Evans advanced particular doctrines which distinguished him—and the Schism—from mainstream evangelicalism. One charge frequently levelled against the seceders was that of antinomianism. In a letter written to his father in December 1816, Evans had denied the accusation. 'You much misunderstand my religious views, if you suppose that to be a Calvinist is with me the one thing needful. Far from it . . . I desire to follow One indeed whom John Calvin followed, but this is all.'[86] Such claims, however sincere, reveal little about Evans's actual doctrinal stance, for it was a common plea in the defensive apologetic of those considered as 'antinomians' that their creed was hewn from the rock of Scripture and not derived from human authority.

Later, Evans came to accept that his preaching had been culpable in ignoring the necessity of seeking holiness and growth in grace. He commented that among the seceders there was 'a baleful system at least partially received, and the consequence of this was, as it must ever be, declension. The work of Christ, as having finished transgression and brought in an everlasting

[83] Evans, *Memoir of James Harington Evans*, 113.

[84] Ibid. 32.

[85] *BM* (1850), 36; Evans, *Memoir of James Harington Evans*, 34. In 1849, John Street Chapel became the spiritual home of Baptist Noel after his secession from the Church of England.

[86] Evans to his father, 2 Dec. 1816, in Evans, *Memoir of James Harington Evans*, 152.

righteousness, was a subject on which our minds seemed to dwell with ceaseless delight.'[87] Dangerously, the seceders came to believe that if they preached these doctrines, 'sanctification must be the necessary result'. They did not realize that although justification was free and unconditional, it is the very means of endearing oneself to the righteousness of Christ. We did not understand, Evans concluded, 'that the Gospel to be really profitable must be wholly, not partially, received', and that 'not one particle of it can ever be systematically omitted, but to the serious injury of the patient himself.'[88]

Another charge frequently levelled against the Western Schismatics was that of sabellianism. Evans, their acknowledged theologian, was prevailed on to publish a declaration setting out the party's new understanding of the Trinity. In his *Dialogues on Important Subjects* (1819), he admitted the existence of 'three divine persons in the one true God', and 'one God, one mediator between God and man', but went on to claim that the origin of Christ's human nature was not coeval with that of man, but *prior* to it.[89] Jesus therefore could not have been the *son of man*, as begotten in the day *man was created*, but merely a son of woman.[90] The appearance of such claims in print greatly increased the publicity and controversy surrounding the Schism, and left Evans and his confederates open to the charge of promoting Trinitarian heresy.[91]

Evans had quarried his Trinitarian views from the writings of the celebrated eighteenth-century hymnologist Isaac Watts, himself well known for advancing unorthodox Trinitarian notions suggestive of both arianism and sabellianism.[92] Though denounced by both friends and acquaintances, Evans continued for a time to hold fast to his new doctrines.[93] Within a few years, however, his opinions shifted once more, displaying the volatility common to so many of the Western Schismatics. By early 1823, after corresponding with the Scottish Congregationalist Ralph Wardlaw,[94] Evans began to return to orthodox Trinitarian and Christological positions, a letter announcing his change of

[87] Evans to his father, 2 Dec. 1816, in Evans, *Memoir of James Harington Evans*, 113.
[88] Quoted ibid. 114.
[89] See James Harington Evans, *A Series of Dialogues on Important Subjects* (1819), 4.
[90] See John Overton, *The Books of Genesis and Daniel Defended* (1820), 218.
[91] Evans, *Memoir of James Harington Evans*, 37.
[92] See ibid. 36, 53.
[93] Ibid. 51; the *Taunton Courier*, 1 Mar. 1820, 7.
[94] Ibid. 38–48.

opinion appearing in the *New Evangelical Magazine* in May of that year.[95] In 1826, he published another work, *Letters to a Friend*, which penitentially retracted his earlier views, which he now regarded as 'subversive of the real deity of the son of God'.[96] No doubt his adherence to the doctrines of high Calvinism also began to wane at around the same time. In 1849, while close to death, he was asked by his wife what instructions he had for her. His instant reply was: 'beware of antinomianism'.[97]

At least temporarily, Evans continued to advance a strict view on believers' baptism. At one point, however, he abandoned even this doctrine, dissolving his connection with John Street Chapel and scattering the congregation. By 1824, he had again changed his mind on baptism and reorganized the John Street body, some of the members remaining baptists, some paedobaptists, and others rejecting both positions in favour of the 'baptism of the Holy Spirit'.[98] One of those who was baptized by immersion at John Street during this time was Robert Chapman, a young solicitor who would later become a sort of Baptist preacher in Barnstaple (aligned with the work of George Müller and Henry Craik at Bristol), and later still a prominent figure in the early Christian Brethren movement.[99]

After the appearance of his *Letters to a Friend*, Evans came at last to rest, and remained firmly within the ranks of Christian orthodoxy to achieve respectability and prominence in the world of evangelical Dissent. In the late 1820s, when Drummond made yet another spiritual volte-face, the two parted company, Evans denouncing Irvingism as a dangerous heresy.[100] Cured by now of the reckless sectarianism which had characterized his early years, he responded with magnanimity and charity when, in 1842, his son, James Joyce Evans, was ordained into the Church of England.[101] Five years later, Evans retired from John Street

[95] See the *New Evangelical Magazine* (May 1823), 145.

[96] James Harington Evans, *Letters to a Friend* (1826), 15, 28.

[97] Evans, *Memoir of James Harington Evans*, 91.

[98] The *New Baptist Magazine* (1826), 274.

[99] See Henry Pickering, *Chief Men of the Christian Brethren Movement*, 2nd edn. (1931), 26–30.

[100] Evans, *Memoir of James Harington Evans*, 75. He later became equally critical of the Plymouth Brethren.

[101] *Al. Cant.*, ii.435; Evans to his son, 26 Sept. 1842, in Evans, *Memoir of James Harington Evans*, 259–61.

Chapel. In early 1849, he wrote to Baptist Noel (who had recently seceded from the Church of England) that although it had been thirty-three years since he had taken a similar step he had 'never seen cause to regret it'.[102] He died on 1 December 1849 and was buried in Highgate cemetery, London,[103] the *Christian Observer* noting dryly (in a phrase coined earlier by Dr Johnson to describe Isaac Watts) that, as a man of education and talent, Evans was to be admired 'in almost everything "except his Nonconformity"'.[104]

Another significant figure in the progress of the Western Schism was George Bevan. Sometime after being ordained in 1810 to the parish of Cobham, Surrey, he was appointed by Thomas Snow curate at Micheldever and East Stratton. After his secession around the end of 1815, he moved to Taunton to reside with George Baring and the others at Walford House. In the following year, he abandoned his work at the Octagon Chapel and moved to London, perhaps in partnership with Evans. In 1818, he published one of the first works by a Western seceder on the nature of the Trinity, *God in Christ*.[105] Quarrying his views from the writings of Archibald McLean and John Gill, Bevan denied that the Father was '*the Godhead*', that Jesus was 'his begotten son', and that the existence of the Holy Spirit could be proven from Scripture.[106] His secession, he claimed, had been based upon an unwillingness to subscribe to a doctrine which was 'degrading to Christ', for although the Anglican formularies claimed that Christ was equal to the Father, they demeaned him at the same time by claiming that he had been 'derived *from* the Father'.[107] In 1819, the year of his death, Bevan published an *apologia* for his new doctrines.[108] He denied ever having uttered the phrase (frequently ascribed to him by his critics), 'believe in the common translation of the Bible, and believe a thousand errors'; this charge had arisen merely 'from misapprehension'. Nor, he claimed defiantly, had any of his pre-

[102] Evans, *Memoir of James Harington Evans*, 385–6.

[103] *BM* (1850), 36.

[104] *CO* (1852), 790.

[105] George Bevan [Anon.], *God in Christ*, in *Two Letters* (1818). For a response see Anon., *Human Deity Developed or, Familiar Remarks on a Pamphlet Entitled 'God in Christ'* (1818).

[106] Bevan, *God in Christ*, letter 1, 1. McLean (1733–1812) was a well-known Scottish Baptist minister at Edinburgh; the high Calvinist Gill (1697–1771) was a popular Baptist minister at Horsley Down, Southwark.

[107] Ibid., letter 2, 41.

[108] George Bevan, *A Ready Reply to a Pamphlet Entitled 'Human Deity Developed or, Familiar Remarks on a Pamphlet Entitled God in Christ'* (1819).

vious doctrinal assertions been proven incorrect.[109] Bevan's denial of these charges did little to redeem his soiled reputation, especially given his unwillingness to refute the doctrine of sabellianism. In April of that year, he wrote to the *christian Observer* protesting against the charge of antinomianism. He disavowed ever having preached, or held, the doctrine of imputed sanctification (or that of the eternal union of Christ and his church of chosen ones, both typical marks of ultra-predestinarianism), and acknowledged the necessity of personal holiness as both a scriptural command and a Christian duty.[110] He also denied that his secession had been influenced by the Dissenting apologist and well-known Unitarian Michaijah Towgood.[111] Any objections to the Church's communion service, or disapproval of its teachings on authority, had been occasioned by his doubts about subscription.[112] None the less, he now admitted that he could not conscientiously affirm the scriptural consistency of the Prayer Book, in particular the form of absolution in the visitation of the sick and the baptismal service, both of which appeared to be opposed to Scripture. Above all, he objected to the notion of Royal Supremacy. 'He appears', commented the *Christian Observer*, 'to have abandoned the Church because his conscience would not allow him to subscribe to an Article which only affirms that ecclesiastics should, equally with others, be subject in *all causes* . . . to the laws of the realm, as administered by its civil governor, and not to any foreign jurisdiction.'[113] Bevan published no subsequent works and, unlike many of his fellow seceders, it appears that he made no attempt either to rejoin the Established Church or to affiliate with one of the Nonconformist bodies. Sadly, no record survives of his final days. He died on 12 December 1819 at Hempstead, presumably still clinging to the doctrines which had prompted his secession from the Church.[114]

The spiritual odysseys of other members of the Schism are less clear. Mrs Wall continued to hold to some of the movement's more extreme teachings, though she remained willing to promote the less controversial aspects of 'personal religion' among the

[109] Ibid. 1–3. [110] *CO* (1819), 271.

[111] Michaijah Towgood (1700–92) the noted Dissenting minister, was best known for his work, *The Dissenting Gentleman's Letters* (1746–8), a classic compendium of Nonconformist arguments.

[112] *CO* (1819), 271. [113] Ibid. 272. [114] *Al. Cant.*, i.253.

English aristocracy. After the fragmentation of the Schism, her theological wanderings and her interest in the 'novelties of doctrine', eventually led her, together with Henry Drummond, to fall under the spell of Edward Irving.[115]

Thomas Read Kemp resigned his seat for Lewes in March 1816, preaching his first sermon at the Octagon Chapel in the following month.[116] During the same year, he officiated, on behalf of the seceders, at St. James's Chapel, Brighton. In 1817, he transferred his ministry to Trinity Chapel, which he had built from his own funds and which became the centre of the movement in the area.[117] For a time, the work at Brighton prospered. In 1823, however, as the Schism began to fragment, Kemp lapsed from his evangelical principles and rushed unreservedly into the gaieties of the world.[118] Between 1826 and 1837, he again sat as Member of Parliament for Lewes, but rarely took part in the debates. During the mid-1820s, he financed architects Charles Busby and Amon Wilde to design the original 'Kemp Town' estate in open country to the east of Brighton. The project proved disastrous, however, and in 1837 Kemp was forced to flee to France to escape his creditors.[119] He died, suddenly, in Paris in December 1844, aged 63.[120]

Thomas Snow, who in 1813 had been ordained vicar of Winterborne Stoke, Wiltshire, was appointed, during the following year, by Sir Thomas Baring incumbent of Micheldever and East Stratton. After his secession in 1815, he too became resident at Walford House outside Taunton, where he propagated a separatist doctrine similar to that advanced earlier by the 'Glasites' as well as by his contemporaries, the 'Walkerites'. It was unscriptural, Snow claimed, for true Christians to unite with the unconverted in any act of worship; while he was willing to preach to the unconverted, he would only unite in full worship and fellowship with

[115] See Baring-Gould, *The Church Revival*, 97. Perhaps because her resources—financial as well as psychological—had been somewhat depleted by the excesses of the Schism, it appears that Mrs Wall played no significant role in the early formation and progress of the Irvingites. It may have been that she was content to pass on the baton of leadership to the wealthier—and more doctrinally extreme—Drummond, now in possession of her former house at Albury.

[116] The *Salisbury and Wiltshire Journal* (28 Apr. 1816), 4.

[117] See Charles Edward Lamb, 'A Brief History of Kemptown', http://www.kemptown.co.uk/history.htm.

[118] *GM* (1845), 2:442.

[119] Lamb, 'A Brief History of Kemptown'.

[120] *DNB*.

recognized believers.[121] According to one close observer, Snow, unlike his fellow seceders, remained free of the charge of sabellianism.[122] Towards the end of 1816, he abandoned the work at Taunton and, under the patronage of Mrs Wall, migrated to Cheltenham, where he rented a house outside the town and built a new chapel on Grosvenor Street.[123] In 1818, he broke into print in response to an attack on the Schism by John Simons[124] (a well-known Evangelical and a former patron), publishing a spirited defence of the Schismatics.[125]

Simons, rector of St. Paul's, Cray, Kent, who had seen something of these events at close quarters, attacked the seceders' instability and doctrinal incoherence. Their principles seemed to him vague and characteristically indeterminate: they had exhibited '*no articles of their creed*, nor any document or definition of doctrine whatever, by which what they hold might be distinctly known'. Their entire system was pervaded by 'wild fancies and false unscriptural reasonings' which had been derived from the earlier teachings of John Hutchinson and Tobias Crisp.[126] Snow emphatically denied these charges, claiming that Simons had 'twisted' many of their doctrines. He dismissed the allegation of imputed sanctification as 'absolute nonsense', and, while describing the doctrine of the union between Christ and his Church as 'vital', he claimed that he could not believe, as did some of the seceders, in the 'absurd' notion of 'an *actual union from eternity between Christ and his church*'.[127]

By 1826, Snow had undergone something of a change in his views. He then published an *apologia* which sheds interesting

[121] Havergal to his mother, 1818, in Crane, *Life of Wm. Havergal*, 17. In 1819, the *CO* (37), claimed that one of the seceders 'has lately "restrained prayer" in public, except only with the approved members of a carefully selected and small community'. Separatists tendencies here are clearly evident.

[122] Crane, *Life of Wm. Havergal*, 17–18.

[123] Steven T. Blake, *Cheltenham's Churches and Chapels, AD 733–1883* (Cheltenham, 1979), 9–10; the *Salisbury and Winchester Journal*, 29 July 1816, 4.

[124] John Simons, *A Letter to a Highly Respected Friend* (1818). See also *Al. Cant.*, v.512.

[125] Thomas Snow, *A Reply to a Letter Written by the Revd John Simons* (1818).

[126] Simons, *A Letter to a Highly Respected Friend*, p. iv, 67, 70. Tobias Crisp (1600–1643), was the third son of Ellis Crisp, the Sheriff of London, and an Anglican clergyman of Puritan leanings. He became an outspoken advocate of antinomianism in 1642, when he entered into a large public debate on the subject in London. John Hutchinson (1674–1737), the author of *Moses' Principia*, had a marked influence upon eighteenth-century High Churchmanship.

[127] Snow, *A Reply to a Letter Written by the Revd John Simons*, 1, 5, 41, 66.

retrospective light on the progress of the Schism. This admitted that his secession had been based upon 'some ill-founded objections against infant baptism', and blamed these erroneous beliefs on the influence of George Bevan, his curate at Micheldever, who had insinuated them at a time when he was in 'a state of distress' and highly vulnerable. Bevan's objections to the Church had been carefully concealed prior to taking up his appointment, and had been all the more insidious because they only emerged piecemeal over time. Although Snow at first objected only to the Anglican baptismal service, he later developed other doubts which convinced him that it would be disingenuous to continue in a communion which did not completely accord with his own emerging beliefs.[128]

Snow was at pains to explain that his secession was the result of conscientious scruples over his subscription to the Anglican formularies, rather than of a collision with any external authority. There had been no disagreement with his ecclesiastical superiors, since he had only met with 'favour and kindness' from his bishop, nor was his departure due to the blandishments of Dissenters, for he scarcely knew any. Indeed, he had possessed 'every comfort' in his situation, and seceded only upon 'the force of conscience, pressed upon [him] by an erroneous apprehension on the subject of baptism and a consideration of the necessity of maintaining my integrity with the Judge of All'. He was, furthermore, highly critical of the repeated misrepresentations of the seceders' views in the press.[129]

Snow then petitioned John Kaye, the Bishop of Bristol, to reinstate him into the Anglican ministry, claiming that he had become thoroughly convinced that his separation 'originated in a misconception', of which he now repented. After full correspondence on the question of readmittance with the Bishop of Winchester—in whose diocese he served during the Schism—he submitted to Kaye 'the confession of his error'.[130] Following further negotiations, which included the publication of his confession at Kaye's insistence, Snow was duly readmitted into the Anglican ministry in which he remained until his retirement in 1860.

[128] Thomas Snow, *Two Letters From the Rt. Revd the Lord Bishop of Bristol, John Kaye, to the Revd Thomas Snow and His Reply to Each* (Blandford, 1826). Quoted in *John Bull*, 24 July 1826, 237.

[129] Ibid.

[130] Ibid.

Snow's return to the Church seems to have been influenced, at least in part, by the professional and financial difficulties he encountered in the years following the Schism.[131] After an extended period of what he now recognized as 'endless uncertainties and confusion', the possibility of returning with his family to the Anglican ministry, as a 'quiet resting-place', seemed increasingly attractive.[132] Reinstatement allowed Snow to make amends for his previous errors in judgement, though his moving in quick succession from one good living to another suggest that, at least in the view of most churchmen, he had little to atone for.[133]

Very little is known about the early life and career of Thomas Cowan. It appears he became curate at St. Thomas's around April 1815. Shortly thereafter, he began harbouring doubts about certain aspects of the Anglican formularies. When news of these opinions (and his clerical 'irregularities') reached the Bishop of Bristol during July 1817, his licence was revoked. Cowan then seceded from the Church. Later that same year, he published a defence of his behaviour which revealed a familiar story. For a considerable time, he too had been uneasy about the catechism and baptismal service.[134] After struggling with his conscience for nearly two years, he had nearly determined some ten months previously to leave the Church, but, as he described it:

> Swayed by some arguments, more especially the idea of curtailing my usefulness, I bowed to the authority of names, and the influence of friends, 'having confidence in the flesh.' Thus have I gone on, uneasy, and yet afraid to move—cordially disliking many things, and yet, *upon the whole*, preferring her *mode* to any I had yet seen.[135]

Matters were precipitated in July 1817 when William Lort Mansel, Kaye's predecessor at Bristol, received a formal complaint from an unnamed High Churchman who had been alarmed by Cowan's conduct while officiating at the 7 a.m. service at St.

[131] One account (*John Bull*, 24 July 1826, 237) claimed that Snow had become an actor at Covent Garden under the name of Hargrave, but this is to confuse him with another actor of a similar name, Robert Snow (1791–1847).

[132] *John Bull*, 24 July 1826, 237.

[133] Snow became, in succession, rector of Sutton-Waldron, Dorset (1833); rector of St. Dunstan-in-the-West, London (1834); and, vicar of Newton Valence, Hampshire (1842), where he served until his retirement in 1860. Ironically, Richard Lloyd, the Evangelical rector of St. Dunstan's during the Schism, had been one of the chief opponents of the Schismatics. See *Al. Cant.*, v.586; MS EP/A/1/3, Bristol City RO.

[134] See Cowan, *A Brief Account*, 7.

[135] Ibid.

Thomas's.[136] As a result of the rubrical irregularities which were detailed in the complaint, Mansel suspended Cowan from preaching within the diocese. Cowan quickly produced a detailed response. In this, he admitted committing a few minor transgressions during the service, but denied the majority of the accusations. He then sent a copy to Mansel, then in residence at Trinity College, Cambridge.[137] Cowan waited anxiously for a reply, but none was forthcoming. On 22 July he wrote again to Mansel, criticizing his silence and hesitancy to reconsider the matter. He then admitted that he had maintained a number of long-standing objections to the Church which, upon reflection, now compelled him to separate from it. While the baptismal service remained his chief complaint, he also took issue with the Church's 'unscriptural' civil connection. Moreover, through his silence Mansel had shown that the Establishment was as opposed to Scripture in practice as it was in theory. Like many seceders before and after him, Cowan expressed dismay at the Church's unwillingness to exert discipline. This was notoriously evident in its admission to Communion of the worldly, the thoughtless, the impious, and the pharisaic; likewise the undiscriminating use of the burial service by the clergy, which, he now admitted, had occasionally led him to omit sections of the rubric when officiating over the remains of unbelievers.[138]

After his baptism by George Baring, Cowan officiated at Gideon Chapel, Newfoundland Street, Bristol, a body which, around 1809 and under the influence of the hyper-Calvinist William Huntington, had separated from Whitefield's Kingswood Tabernacle.[139] In 1819, he acquired Bethesda Chapel, Great George Street, Bristol, an independent Baptist establishment which was later to experience some notoriety under the ministry of George Müller and Henry Craik, two of the early and most influential leaders of the Plymouth Brethren.[140] After this, no trace of him remains.

IV

What caused the Western Schism? Its ideological origins remain somewhat difficult to determine, primarily because of the seced-

[136] See Cowan, *A Brief Account*, 8. [137] Ibid. 8–12, 23.

[138] Ibid. 21, 24, 30. [139] See Caston, *Independency in Bristol*, 155–6.

[140] The *Bristol Mirror*, 17 Febr. 1838. Curiously, Craik and Müller also occupied Gideon Chapel prior to migrating to Bethesda Chapel. See Caston, *Independency in Bristol*, 157.

ers' reluctance to publish full details of their views or to engage in much theological debate. Unlike some later separatist movements in the Church, the Schism does not seem to have been set in motion by the millennial expectations of the Napoleonic wars, and the absence of an overtly apocalyptic dimension distinguishes it to some extent from the Irvingites, to which some of its leading members subsequently gravitated.[141]

Unquestionably, one trigger mechanism was the sharp controversy over the doctrine of baptism launched by the High Church polemicist Richard Mant.[142] Mant's provocative Bampton Lectures in Oxford in 1812 brought the issue of baptismal regeneration into high salience and set off a controversy which spluttered on for decades.[143] Mant had declared baptismal regeneration to be not only the 'doctrine of the Bible', but also the doctrine of the Church of England, asserted in its formularies and taught by 'the generality of the national clergy'. He provocatively rejected Evangelical ideas of conversion, asserting firmly that it was by the sprinkling of baptism that 'we are made Christians, and are born anew of water and of the Holy Spirit'.[144] This, he claimed, was the doctrine of the Prayer Book, of Anglican teachers like the saintly Thomas Wilson, the early eighteenth-century Bishop of Sodor and Man, and of patristic tradition.[145] The Calvinistic doctrine of election and predestination was, in contrast, 'irreconcilable with the doctrine of the church and her apostles'.[146]

The reverberations of this manifesto were considerable, and several Evangelical champions sprang to the party's defence.[147]

[141] Proby, *Annals of the 'Low Church' Party in England*, i.293.

[142] See Ervine, 'Doctrine and Diplomacy', 70–1.

[143] Richard Mant, *An Appeal to the Gospel* (Oxford, 1812). In 1815, an extract of Mant's lectures was published which included the most controversial portions of the work, including the sections on baptismal regeneration and spiritual conversion. See Richard Mant, *Two Tracts* (1815). In 1817, a modified version of his lectures appeared which admitted that baptism must be correctly received in order to be effective.

[144] Mant, *An Appeal to the Gospel*, 332–3.

[145] However, even Thomas Wilson, deeply admired by the Tractarians during the nineteenth century, could not bring himself to use the burial rubric over a baptized parishioner who had died while intoxicated. See C. Cruttwell (ed.), *The Works Of The Right Reverend Father In God Thomas Wilson* (Bath, 1781) i.p. xli.

[146] Mant, *An Appeal to the Gospel*, 120.

[147] Including: John Scott, *An Inquiry Into the Effects of Baptism* (1815); Thomas Biddulph, *Baptism, A Seal of the Christian Covenant* (1816); Hallifield Cosgayne O'Donnoghue, *A Familiar and Practical Exposition of the Thirty-Nine Articles of Religion of the United Church of England and Ireland* (1816).

The ensuing confrontation, both in tone and substance, bore a remarkable resemblance to the debate set off by the celebrated Gorham affair some thirty-five years later. Thomas Biddulph forcefully argued that Mant's doctrine of baptismal regeneration was opposed to Scripture, to the liturgy and Articles of the Church, and to the writings of the Marian Martyrs, the Reformers, and the greatest of the post-Reformation divines. Baptism, he claimed, must be regarded as 'the outward visible sign of an inward spiritual grace', and nothing more.[148] Another Evangelical critic, Hallifield Cosgayne O'Donnoghue, dismissed Mant's claims as 'downright popery' and 'utterly at variance with the doctrines of the Church of England'. While admitting that divine efficacy often accompanied the outward and visible sign of baptism, and was a vital part of the covenant relationship between God and his children, he nevertheless insisted that the saving, inward, and spiritual effects and grace of baptism were not universally granted but were only received, as the Article stated, by those 'that receive baptism rightly'.[149] Not all Evangelicals were convinced, however, by the construction put on the baptismal rubric by their own apologists. As we have seen repeatedly, many were uneasy at the language of the Prayer Book here, which might suggest support for High Church views on baptismal regeneration. Mant's provocative work was no doubt unsettling to those who were dissatisfied with the ambiguities of Anglican theology.

It was no doubt observed that Mant's Bampton Lectures brought him rapid preferment. In 1813, he was appointed domestic chaplain to Charles Manners Sutton, the Archbishop of Canterbury, and, in 1820, he became Bishop of Killaloe. Three years later he was again elevated by becoming Bishop of Down. The *Christian Observer* complained that Mant's lectures, assiduously propagated by the Salop district committee of the SPCK as an authoritative statement of Anglican teaching, had helped provoke the Schism.[150]

[148] Biddulph, *Baptism, A Seal of the Christian Covenant*, preface, 1.

[149] O'Donnoghue, *A Familiar and Practical Exposition of the Thirty-Nine Articles of Religion of the United Church of England and Ireland*, 228–30.

[150] The Salop district committee of the SPCK was responsible for the publication of a work defending Mant and his claims. A request on behalf of the committee to produce an extract of some nature was made to Mant by the Revd Hugh Owen, of Shrewsbury, on 11 October 1813. The work eventually appeared under the title, *Dr Mant's Sermon on Regeneration Vindicated from the Remarks of T. T. Biddulph* (Shrewsbury, 1816). See also Walter Bishop Mant, *Memoirs of the Right Reverend Richard Mant* (Dublin, 1857), 95.

They were certainly cited at some length by one of the chief seceders, Thomas Cowan, who accepted that Mant's claims were forcefully put, but denied their correctness. 'Dr Mant and his coadjutors *have much to say for themselves*', he conceded, being 'argumentatively *right, but* theologically *wrong*'.[151] Mant's argument was clearly the catalyst, but not the reason, which propelled Cowan and his fellow Schismatics not into the Orthodox High Churchmanship which Mant intended his readers to accept, but into secession from a Church which (they believed) retained far too many relics of its popish past, and hence into Protestant Dissent.

The negative side of the Schism is somewhat more easily ascertained than the positive. The *Christian Observer* took a strong stand against the seceders' ecclesiology and theology, and emphasized their instability. In its view, the only distinct principle behind the movement appeared to be irritable contumaciousness; 'disaffection to the established religious order of this country'. The high Calvinism of the seceders did not pass unnoticed and its connection to a separatist ecclesiology were hinted at. Among the obnoxious principles of the Schismatics were the notions that salvation comes through 'a mere dead faith unproductive of works', that repentance is unnecessary, that divine grace is both 'irresistible and indefectible', that election is 'unconditional', that conversion is 'instantaneous', and that sanctification is 'imputed'. Those who propagated these false teachings were subverting the Establishment with 'malignant hostility'.[152]

Much was understandably made of the fact that the members of the Schism were often, doctrinally, at odds with each other and changed their stance with bewildering speed. They seemed to epitomize the idea of private judgement carried to embarrassing and dangerous extremes. Taken collectively, therefore, the Schism was seen not as an expression of the 'communion of saints', but of 'the individuality of saints'. Indeed, one seceder was alleged to have told his flock not to expect that he would hold the same opinions in a month's time, for he was 'continually advancing towards perfection'. Volatility and flux characterized the theology of the seceders, whose views evolved rapidly, and then soon diverged again. They were, an Evangelical critic complained, 'often as much separated from each other as from ourselves', like 'a few

[151] Cowan, *A Brief Account*, 21. [152] *CO* (1819), 34.

frail and crazy barks launched forth into a boundless and tempestuous ocean, without rudder and compass'.[153]

If portrayed as cranks pursuing their own highly individual trajectories, the seceders were also seen to be frequently united in holding forms of ultra-Calvinism, or, rather, ultra-Predestinarianism. They allegedly carried their 'Calvinism' so far as to see the law in such a crude antithesis of the Gospel that they were virtual antinomians, at least theoretically. For a variety of reasons, these allegations are not easily assessed. For one thing, the seceders published little by way of systematic theology, which made it hard to discover their true and complete tenets.[154] For another, besides being regularly in a state of individual mental flux, their views often differed substantially one from another. Some were alleged to have abandoned baptism entirely, like the Quakers; others differed over the most scriptural mode of its administration.

Ingenuously, Thomas Cowan admitted in print that though his views on baptism were close to those of the Particular Baptists around him in Bristol, he could not see his way to seeking believer's baptism at their hands, but would instead seek it from George Baring—even though he was in disagreement with *him* on two 'highly important' points (i.e. the pre-existence of Christ, and the Holy Spirit's exclusion from the covenant), and could not assent fully to being integrated into his group.[155] Thomas Snow, when rebutting charges of antinomianism against the Western Schismatics in Bristol, was careful to state that the dangerous tenets which had been quoted, apparently verbatim, by his critic, 'must have been furnished by persons whose ministry I have never habitually attended'—a disclaimer which suggests his opinions were changing fast, or that others in the circle may truly have held such eccentric views.[156]

There are indeed strong signs of high Calvinism among some of the members of the group. Certainly Thomas Cowan ranked himself among the higher, rather than the lower, Calvinists when he came firmly to accept the idea of particular redemption—the

153 *CO* (1819), 31–7.

154 Simons, *A Letter to a Highly Respected Friend*, 28–30 n.

155 Cowan, *A Brief Account*, 42–4. A note to Cowan from George Baring in late September 1817 appears to have provoked Cowan to published a second edition of his work, omitting the offending portions.

156 Snow, *A Reply to a Letter*, 28.

notion that Christ's sacrifice was offered not for all, but only for the predestined elect—a tenet disavowed by moderate Calvinists who believed in what has been termed 'hypothetical universalism', or the idea that Christ's redeeming work potentially extended to all Christians, though appropriated only by the elect. To hold otherwise, argued Cowan, was to allow that Christ acted in vain in shedding his blood uselessly for many who were not included in the eternal covenant of grace, thus detracting from the sovereignty of God.

In Cowan's case, the disavowal of 'general redemption' encouraged secession, for it seemed to him to be a doctrine officially enunciated in the Anglican liturgy and catechism, which declared that Christ died 'for all mankind'. Furthermore, he found it offensive to celebrate communion using the words of the rubric, which stated that 'the blood of our Lord Jesus Christ is shed for thee', when required to administer to many who were apparently non-elect. At this point, Cowan's high Calvinism led on to separatism, for the corollary of his views pointed towards the idea that only the plainly regenerate should be allowed to partake of the sacrament—a view not sanctioned by the National Church by law established. Why, he asked, should believers and unbelievers be allowed promiscuously to attend the sacrament together? 'What God hath separated, let no man join together.'

Like others before and after him, Cowan also objected to the indiscriminate use of the burial service, parts of which he had long omitted in practice. He was prepared, if need be, to bury those not actively and visibly wicked, but not the thoroughly ungodly. He had the usual qualms about the baptismal rubric, with its implication that an infant was already being made regenerate and brought in a real sense into the Covenant. For Cowan, infant baptism as administered by the Church of England was not scriptural, but based on '*human tradition*, the *antiquity* of which could afford me no satisfaction; as it still had only the authority of *man*, on which to rest'.[157] He thus firmly rejected the appeal by Mant and others to tradition and Christian antiquity. In his view, the corollary of the evangelical doctrine of conversion was adult baptism—believer's baptism, as practised by Baptists and others—which implied separation from the Establishment and its

[157] Cowan, *A Brief Account*, 32.

unscriptural liturgy. Here again, strong Calvinism, with its extremely sharp dichotomy between elect and reprobate, encouraged the separation of sheep from goats in ways not easily compatible with the pastoral universalism of a National Established Church, in which it was assumed that the clergy had an equal responsibility for all the members of a geographic parish.

The charge of antinomianism was frequently levelled at high (or hyper) Evangelical Calvinists, such as Robert Hawker (1753–1827) of Charles, near Plymouth, and his circle, who were a small, but much feared, element in the Evangelical ranks. The extent to which the Western Schismatics deserved the epithet is not entirely clear. One of the most damning allegations of such teaching within the Schism was levelled by Joseph Cottle, who claimed that the perverted teaching of one schismatic, a Mr Arnold,[158] preaching in Exeter, had convinced more than a hundred members a week to secede from the local parish. Arnold was said to have told his congregation:

> Good men preach the Gospel sometimes, but then they preach that blasphemous doctrine of *sanctification*. I say that blasphemous doctrine of *sanctification*, and *repentance*, and *sorrow for sin*! What do they mean by sorrow for sin? Did not *Christ* feel sorrow for sin? What do *they* want with sorrow? There is no such thing in the Scriptures as Godly sorrow! And repentance—what do they mean by repentance? It never means sorrow for sin, but a turning from the *law* to the *Gospel*! Do they mean to take the glory of Christ's sufferings from him? *Believe* and *rejoice* in all that we are called unto![159]

Yet not all seceders took such an antinomian stance. The *Christian Observer*, after scrutinizing Evans's *Dialogues on Important Subjects* (1819), concluded that the charge of antinomianism was not entirely proven, for his teachings had not contained 'an absolute rejection of the practice of holiness'; Evans still regarded good works as evidence of saving grace and election into life.[160] John Simons, however, produced contrary evidence from unpublished utterances of the seceders. These appeared to promote an ultra-Calvinist view of sanctification that encouraged speculative antinomianism by portraying not only Christ's righteousness, but also

[158] Possibly the Revd Henry Arnold, formally vicar of Longstock, Hampshire.
[159] Cottle, *Strictures on the Plymouth Antinomians*, 41–2.
[160] *CO* (1819), 39.

his holiness as imputed to the elect. Like Hawker and other hyper-Calvinists, they denied that the believer was actually made more holy by a progressive work of sanctification in the heart. Any so-called 'good works' produced by the justified sinner were still held to be evil in God's sight, and to insist on their necessity was held to impugn the 'finished work' of Christ's atonement and detract from God's sovereign glory. Sins, even murder, committed by the elect would not be held against them, for they were covered in the mantle of Christ's perfect holiness.[161]

These charges were parried, though not totally denied, by Thomas Snow. The moral law, he claimed, was 'a rule of life' which was written in the hearts of the elect; they rejected evil not because it was commanded by God, but freely and spontaneously out of a new principle of love towards their Saviour.[162] Some of Snow's fellow seceders many well have taken a considerably more extreme position. In any case, there was more than enough here to alarm moderate Evangelicals like Thomas Scott, who insisted on 'growth in grace' as the only true evidence of justification.[163]

The high Calvinist seceders were thus alarming because they pushed the accepted evangelical doctrines of grace to conclusions which could be argued on logic, but which were carefully avoided by the great mass of 'Gospel clergymen'. The seceders were far less threatening on the question of the Trinity, where (as we have seen) some of them fell into sabellianism:[164] in this they put themselves much more clearly out of court and were far more exposed to ridicule. The Trinitarian views of George Baring and James Evans, for instance, cut them off not only from the great mass of Anglicans, but even from some of their own party, thus serving as a complicated diversion from the primary claims of the Schismatics which rested more on the errors contained in the Articles and liturgy, and the dangers of establishment.

VI

The year 1819 was not a good time for clergymen to be seen undermining the established institutions of the nation. A

161 Simons, *A Letter to a Highly Respected Friend*, 37–8.

162 Snow, *A Reply to a Letter*, 18–19.

163 See Vernon John Charlesworth, *Rowland Hill* (1876), 62. Cf. Thomas Scott, *A Treatise on Growth in Grace* (1795); John Scott, *The Life of Thomas Scott* (1822), 200–5.

164 Sabellianism is an alternative title for the Modalist form of Monarchianism, calling into question the integrity of Christ's body, and thus verging towards Docetism.

recurrence of economic depression had produced alarming popular disturbances, including the massacre at Peterloo, which provoked a massive counter-attack by the forces of conservatism united behind the notorious Six Acts. Critics of the Western Schism, particularly Evangelicals, did not hesitate to set what was apparently a minor schism into the alarming context of nation-wide social dislocation.

Though the Schism had involved only a handful of clergymen, it excited a collective Evangelical response of great vigour and fury.[165] Leading figures of the party, including John Bird Sumner, Charles Simeon, Hannah More, Henry Ryder, Daniel Wilson, Thomas Biddulph, Charles Samuel Wilks, William Marsh, and, of course, their periodicals, the *Christian Observer* and the *Christian Guardian*, produced scathing attacks against the seceders which were more acerbic than anything written by High or liberal Churchmen.

In 1815, J. B. Sumner published a treatise entitled *Apostolic Preaching Considered* which accepted a modified view of baptismal regeneration.[166] Significantly, he directed his attack not on High Church theories of baptismal regeneration, as advanced by Mant and by High Church bishops such as Thomas Wilson and Samuel Horsley, but against the 'high doctrine of strictly Calvinistic preaching' which was being advocated by the Western Schismatics. He rejected the extreme Calvinistic denial of baptismal regeneration, while insisting (on the authority of the Elizabethan divines) that the grace of spiritual regeneration could often be separated from the sacrament of baptism.[167]

In Charles Simeon's view the Western Schism presented a grave threat to the promotion of 'vital religion'. In a letter of November 1815 he revealed his anxiety that 'five pious young men', as he described the seceders, were 'running into Huntington's and Dr Hawker's principles' and leaving the Church.[168] Two years later, he lamented before the university that antinomian teachings 'have been professed of late to a great extent; and many have been

[165] George Bugg, *Spiritual Regeneration, Not Necessarily Connected With Baptism* (Kettering, 1816); G. Notorious, *Two Letters* (1816); Biddulph, *Baptism, A Seal of the Christian Covenant.*

[166] John Bird Sumner, *Apostolic Preaching Considered in an Examination of St. Paul's Epistles* (1815).

[167] Ibid., 9th edn., pp. iii–vii.

[168] Quoted in William Carus, *Memoirs of the Life of the Revd Charles Simeon, M.A.*, 3rd edn. (1848), 294.

deceived by them'. The seceders, he complained, 'are so occupied with contemplating what Christ has wrought out *for* them, that they cannot bestow a thought on what He has engaged to work *in* them'.[169] In June 1830 Power Le Poer Trench, the Evangelical Archbishop of Tuam, wrote seeking Simeon's counsel about a local eruption of antinomianism.[170] Simeon responded by recollecting the past influence of the Western Schism whose deluded members:

> under an idea of exalting Christ and His Gospel, maintained doctrines altogether subversive of the Gospel . . . the scope of their tenets was to lull men asleep in sin: and such persons, if they possess a good measure of fluency and confidence, are sure to gain admirers and followers in every place. If they would listen to reason or Scripture, they might be easily made to see the erroneousness of their views: but they are deaf to counsel of any kind; nor will they regard authority: they even make the efforts of others to reclaim them an occasion of augmented zeal in propagating their errors.[171]

Hannah More regarded the seceders in much the same way. In her alarmist and conservative opinion, their views were symptomatic of the turbulent social currents of the day. She waxed eloquent against their restless search for 'alarming novelties' and institutional change, dismissing them as 'low, designing demagogues', 'religious dogmatists', 'factious assailants of the church', and 'adversaries of serious piety'. The Schism was a product of the Jacobin spirit, founded on a form of 'spiritual democracy' which was contemptuous of authority, impatient of subordination, and bent on dictatorship.[172] At the very least the seceders had dangerously divided Churchmen, causing much damage to the moral fabric of the nation:

> It has been the means of exciting a sort of spiritual vanity, of awakening a desire of departing from received opinions, in certain young persons . . . It has increased the alienation of the lower orders from the Church; it has afforded to some who are not favourable to serious piety, a pretence for indiscriminately classifying together men of different views, character, and principles. Among the more respectable, it has

[169] Charles Simeon, *The True Test of Religion in the Soul* (Cambridge, 1817), 18–19.

[170] Trench to Simeon, 25 June 1830, in Carus, *Memoirs of Charles Simeon*, 461–3.

[171] Ibid. 464.

[172] Hannah More, *Moral Sketches of Prevailing Opinions and Manners* (1819), 144–5; 169–91. For a review see *CO* (1819), 668–85.

stirred up a spirit of debate and controversy, by no means friendly to the cause of genuine Christianity.[173]

Might not the seceders' arguments, she warned, be used by infidels and radicals to provide the profane—those unfavourable to 'serious piety'—with an excuse for rejecting spiritual overseers who did not suit their taste?[174]

Ecclesiological rebelliousness of this type seemed to be catching, and More feared that schismatic and antinomian teachings were no longer isolated within the West Country, but were beginning to appear in various provincial towns and villages throughout England.[175] Behind her anxiety, perhaps, lay knowledge of the much publicized progress of plebeian hyper-Calvinism among the followers of William Gadsby and, above all, William Huntington, which had shattered not only a number of moderate Calvinist Nonconformist congregations, but also some Anglican ones, such as Thomas Robinson's at Leicester.[176] Through dissident high Calvinists like those of the Western Schism, it seemed possible that the contagion was about to be transmitted to the Church of England. Would not the 'loose and careless' be confirmed in their impiety, she asked, when they saw their spiritual overseers not only deserting the altars of the Church, but also attacking her publicly, and setting up 'a perpetual conflict' between Christian ministers? Plebeian Anglicans might well conclude that an Establishment which was so frequently assailed, which seemed in such need of continued vindication, and from which there were so many recent deserters, must be an 'erroneous and unsound church', with an uncertain, if not a false, scriptural foundation.[177] As an exponent of 'practical piety' and simple 'heart-felt religion', she urged increased Christian charity and tolerance on all concerned. Rather than becoming overheated about small issues, religious people should focus their attention on those matters in which all 'vital' Christians were in agreement, and avert their gaze from any 'inferior matters' which might not coincide with their own opinions.[178]

[173] More, *Moral Sketches of Prevailing Opinions and Manners*, 169–70.

[174] Ibid. 170. [175] Ibid. 171.

[176] See Edward Thomas Vaughan, *Some Account of Thomas Robinson, M.A.* (1815), 188–97; Peter Hall, *A Memoir of the Revd Thomas Robinson, M.A.* (1837), pp. xxxvi–xxxvii.

[177] More, *Moral Sketches of Prevailing Opinions and Manners*, 178.

[178] Ibid. 189–91.

Henry Ryder was appointed Bishop of Gloucester in 1815, the first Evangelical on the episcopal bench. Not surprisingly, given the geographic proximity of his diocese to the centres of the Schism, he was quick to join the chorus against the seceders.[179] In a sermon delivered prior to his consecration, he characterized the disruption as an event of 'no inconsiderable importance',[180] and admonished his former parishioners to adhere closely to the Church. On arriving in Gloucester he quickly denounced the Schism to his clergy as one of the perversions of which St. Paul had warned the early church, an 'awful wresting of Scripture to the destruction of those who hear it'.[181] Ryder was eager to defend his party's Anglican credentials, and saw no inconsistency in advancing the doctrine of baptismal regeneration, correctly understood, as central to Christian teaching.[182]

At much the same time, Daniel Wilson, the future Bishop of Calcutta and one of the most influential Evangelicals of the day, fearfully denounced the Schism as a 'subversion' of the Church.[183] By 1818, however, he had become far more cheerful, convinced that 'the antinomian abomination' had spent itself, and that the debate surrounding it had actually imparted some lasting benefits. Wilson was confident that the shock of the Schism had produced a tonic effect on the Evangelical clergy and on the great voluntary societies, producing a healthy upsurge of prayer meetings to call down a new spirit of revival in the nation. In both London and Bristol, he remarked, zealous efforts were now being made to excite regard to the subject of 'vital faith'.[184] Wilson's claims may have been no more than rhetoric, though it is also probable that, in the long run, the Schism helped stabilize Evangelicalism by revealing in a lurid light the dangers of antinomianism, sabellianism, and separatism.

[179] Ryder was presented to the parish of Lutterworth in 1801 and to the neighbouring parish of Claybrook in 1805. In 1812, he became dean of Wells. Later, in 1824, he was translated to the see of Lichfield, where he remained until his death in 1836.

[180] Henry Ryder, *A Farewell Sermon* (Lutterworth, 1815), 18.

[181] Henry Ryder, *Charge to the Clergy of Gloucester* (Gloucester, 1816), 16–17.

[182] Ibid. 20.

[183] Quoted from a sermon by Daniel Wilson, *c.*1818; in Josiah Bateman, *The Life of the Right Revd Daniel Wilson, D.D.* (1860), i.89. Wilson was first licensed to St. John's Chapel, Bedford Row in 1808 and remained there until 1824, when he was appointed as vicar of St. Mary's, Islington. In 1832, he became the fifth bishop of Calcutta.

[184] Daniel Wilson, 'State of the Church in 1821', in Bateman, *Life of Daniel Wilson*, i.210.

The episode could be used as an object lesson in the perils of extremism.

Thomas Biddulph was a prominent West Country Evangelical, a prolific writer and the non-resident rector of Durston, Somerset, where George Baring had been curate prior to his secession.[185] Baring's purchase of Walford House, hard on the edge of Durston, together with the establishment of his congregation at the Octagon Chapel, his role in baptizing his fellow seceders, and the party's evangelistic efforts in the surrounding area, naturally made Biddulph anxious lest a portion of his parish be persuaded to follow their former curate into the ranks of 'unorthodox Dissent'.[186] To counter this influence, he employed the capable William Henry Havergal as Baring's successor.[187] He also published a strong rebuttal against the doctrinal claims of Richard Mant in an attempt to distance himself and his party from Mant's High Anglican doctrines, which were being misrepresented by the seceders.[188] Finally, he published an open attack on the 'Baring party', denouncing it and reaffirming the value of the 'fixed' creed and liturgy of the Established Church.[189] He hoped that his work would not excite controversy, but controvert the seceders' notions of eternal justification and imputed sanctification.[190] Biddulph dismissed the hyper-Calvinists' claims that the consciousness of believing is the only evidence necessary or possible to satisfy the soul of its spiritual safety, and, like Scott and others, insisted on real holiness as the evidence of election. He shared the view of Scott's famous treatise that 'growth in grace' was an essential mark of faith, and hotly denied the hypers' claim that sanctification is not a progressive work.

In a lenthy defence of the Church–State connection, Charles Samuel Wilks, the influential editor of the *Christian Observer*, condemned the Western seceders for striving after the goal of 'ideal

[185] Thomas Biddulph was the pluralist incumbent of St. James's, Bristol, and St. John the Baptist, Durston, Somerset, where he kept a curate-in-charge.

[186] Hole, *A Manual of English Church History*, 392.

[187] Havergal had just completed his studies at St. Edmund Hall, Oxford, the bastion of early nineteenth-century Evangelicalism, having been ordained curate on 24 March 1816. He later became well-known as the author of a number of sacred hymns.

[188] Biddulph, *Baptism, A Seal of the Christian Covenant.*

[189] Thomas Biddulph, *Search After Truth* (Bristol, 1818).

[190] The doctrine of eternal justification asserts that God has justified the elect at the beginning of creation.

perfection', for abandoning the 'scriptural doctrines and decent usages of the National Establishment', and for running into the 'awful heresies' of antinomianism and sabellianism. 'Who can tell', he speculated, 'how widely such delusions might have spread, had not the Established Church thrown its prepondering weight into the opposite scale?'[191]

Not all prominent Evangelicals, however, took such a firm stance against the Schismatics. William 'Millennial' Marsh, who was both an ally of Simeon and a friend of Sir Thomas Baring, was one of the few Evangelical leaders to have been taken in by the Schism.[192] As late as January 1817, he responded to Baring's personal appeal by defending the Schismatics against the attacks of their critics. 'Perhaps', he naively suggested, 'they may have dropped expressions which have been misunderstood; or, in their zeal to establish some grand point, they may have quoted texts which were not designed for that purpose.' Marsh pleaded for the exercise of charity: Christians 'ought to be tender of each other's characters', and be prepared to accept differences of opinion on non-essential points, making allowances in cases of unclear or confusing views. He concluded that much of the difference between the Evangelical clergy and the seceders was the result either of misunderstanding, or slanderous reporting.[193] By 1821, however, long after the Schism had become a spent force, Marsh became more critical. Perhaps reflecting his own dilemma, he now characterized the Schism as an 'adversary' which had misled many Evangelicals, especially on the important issue of sanctification. They had gone sadly astray when they claimed not only to be justified in Christ, but to be immediately accounted so completely holy that they had no need to go on receiving out of His fullness.[194]

In 1818, the Religious Tract Society attacked the Schism by republishing a pamphlet by the seventeenth-century West Country presbyterian John Flavel.[195] Like his nineteenth-century counterparts, Flavel wished 'to discharge and clear the free grace

[191] Charles Samuel Wilkes, *Correlative Claims and Duties* (1821), 69.

[192] Marsh was the incumbent of St. Peter's, Colchester at the time of the Schism, a living to which he was presented by Simeon.

[193] Marsh to Sir Thomas Baring, January 1817, in Catherine Marsh, *The Life of the Revd William Marsh* (1867), 116, 118.

[194] Ibid. 119.

[195] John Flavel, *A Blow at the Root* (1818).

of God from those dangerous errors, which fight against it under its own colours; and to prevent the seduction of some that stagger'. Such individuals, he concluded, had 'been engulfed and sucked into those dangerous quicksands of antinomian errors, by separating the spirit from the written Word'.[196]

In his final Episcopal *Charge* as Bishop of Raphoe in 1821, the moderate Evangelical William Magee warned that recent seceders from the Church, such as John Walker and the Western Schismatics, had perverted and denigrated the Anglican formularies. He was particularly aggrieved over their highly partisan attacks upon the Articles, which, in his view:

> are not enslaved to the dogmas of any party in religion. They are not Arminian; they are not Calvinistic; they are scriptural; they are Christian. As the different parties profess to derive their leading tenets from Scripture, so do they profess to find them in the Articles. But these are answerable for the extravagances of no sect . . . Nothing in truth has contributed to give to some of the sects and parties in religion, so much credit and popularity . . . erroneously ascribing to them, as characteristics of their peculiar tenets which belong to our common Christianity.[197]

Evangelical journals were no less vehement in their attacks upon the Schism. The *Christian Guardian* warned Evangelicals that the seceders, or the 'powers of darkness' as they were described, were attempting to 'multiply divisions' and propel the Church into 'disorder and confusion'. Those who wantonly secede from the Church, it concluded, 'are amenable to a higher tribunal for the evil consequences of unnecessary divisions'.[198] The *Christian Observer* took a more defensive line, disparaging the attempts of High Churchmen to tar all Evangelicals with the seceders' separatism, clerical 'irregularities', and high Calvinism. There was no group, it claimed, 'more attached to the principles of the Church of England' than the Evangelicals. There had been nothing in their collective conduct to authorize suspicion. On the contrary, Evangelicals had displayed a zealous Anglican loyalism for the Church of England which other groups would do well to imitate. Although in a few isolated cases this might have bordered on enthusiasm, even that was far better than the 'cold apathy and religious indifference' of many of their critics.[199] Five months later,

[196] Ibid. 3, 7–8.
[197] William Magee, *Charge to the Clergy* (Raphoe, 1822), 32.
[198] *CG* (1816), 108–9; (1818), 349.
[199] *CO* (1818), 12.

the *Christian Observer* seemed even more nervous, admitting that the Schism had become a 'very critical and distressing controversy' which was gaining ground, even though its doctrines appeared 'almost unintelligible' to most Christians.[200] By early 1819, however, this urgency was replaced by a tone of growing relief, as the seceders were seen to be as much separated from one another as they were from the Church. Their ultra-Calvinism, it now seemed clear, was too extreme to attract more than a handful of eccentrics.[201]

VII

Though the Schism moved off into Dissent, Dissenters seldom welcomed this addition to their ranks. In the aftermath of the Schism, a number of West Country Nonconformists joined with their Anglican counterparts in criticizing its principal adherents in strong terms. Dissenters had long feared that such seceders might take after William Huntington and the other hyper-Calvinists not only in advancing extreme doctrines, but in poaching from their congregations.[202] John Ryland, Jr., the Baptist minister of Broadmead Chapel, Bristol, launched the Dissenting counter-attack by claiming that antinomianism was threatening to destroy the universal church. As a moderate Calvinist, he coldly dismissed the Western Schismatics for denying the 'indefinite call of the Gospel' and for explaining away 'the invitations and exhortations of the New Testament'.[203] Even the Irish seceder John Walker considered their doctrines extreme. 'I have been made sick at heart', he wrote, 'by hearing of the blasphemous extravagances of expression and sentiment' into which the seceders have run. 'I should turn away from them as heady and high-minded speculators.'[204] Of even greater interest was the attack by Robert Harkness Carne, a West Country evangelical who himself seceded from the Church in 1820 on conscientious grounds, but found the Western Schismatics far too volatile and heterodox to permit any welcoming gesture in that

[200] Ibid. 382–7. [201] Ibid. (1819), 31–2, 38.

[202] David Bogue and James Bennett, *History of Dissenters, 1688–1808* (1808–12), 4: 392–6.

[203] John Ryland, *Serious Remarks on the Different Representations of the Evangelical Doctrine* (Bristol, 1818), 3.

[204] Quoted in *WE*, ii.251. See also i.173, 260; ii.222, 239, 404, 407, 582.

direction.[205] In his own *apologia*, Carne perceived the Schism in biblical terms, as an exodus out of the house of bondage which had taken a wrong turn in the desert; instead of pressing forward towards the Land of Promise, however it had fallen in the 'wilderness through an evil heart of unbelief' and lapsed into bizarre heterodoxy. He was struck not only that so many unusually talented clergymen should have seceded from the Church, but still more by the way in which they had so often apostatized from the fundamental truths of the Gospel. This phenomenon might well make every 'serious' clergyman wonder whether all conscientious seceders would share a similar fate.[206] Carne emphasized that the downfall of the Western Schismatics did not come from their separation from the Church (of which he approved in principle, 'for this was no more than the Establishment had done in separating from Rome'), but from *pride*; 'inflated with self-conceit' they often saw themselves in almost exclusive possession of the true Gospel and in virtual opposition to all other churches. He was especially shocked by their doctrinal eccentricity; above all their strange Trinitarianism which, in arguing for the pre-existence of the man Christ Jesus, came very near to sabellianism. Seceder and strong Calvinist though he was, he could not stomach Baring's belief that sanctification was so complete at the moment of conversion that it totally inoculated the believer against the eternal effects of sin. Nor could he accept the idea that forgiveness and pardon were unnecessary (since believers were already forgiven and pardoned), that the Lord's Prayer was erroneous, or that confession was gratuitous.[207]

VIII

High Churchmen had their own reasons for attacking the Schism. Suspicious of any form of religious 'enthusiasm', and convinced that Dissent by its very nature encouraged ecclesiastical factiousness and splintering, High Churchmen saw the Schism as the pre-

[205] Robert Harkness Carne, *Reasons for Withdrawing From the National Establishment* (1820). See also *The Proper Deity, and Distinct Personality, Agency, and Worship, of the Holy Spirit, Vindicated, Against the Recent Evils of Messieurs Baring, Bevan, Cowan, etc.* (Exeter, 1818); *A Defense and Explication of the Sinlessness, Immortality, and Incorruptibility of the Humanity of the Son of God* (1829); Grayson Carter, 'Robert Harkness Carne' in *New DNB*; Brockett, *Nonconformity in Exeter*, 210.

[206] Carne, *Reasons for Withdrawing From the National Establishment*, 75–6.

[207] Ibid. pp. v–vi, 79–80, 81–118, 118–27, 127–44.

dictable outcome of the rejection of episcopal authority, and a dangerous distortion of the right of private judgement. Such sentiments were echoed by the polemical West Country High Churchman, Charles Daubeny, Archdeacon of Salisbury, who, in 1818, declared schism to be 'one of the crying sins of the present day', the product of a 'miscalled liberality' which threatened to undermine the life and stability of the Established and apostolic Church.[208] Although the Church of England had itself separated from Rome, this had not been an act of disobedience based on the right of private judgement, but a justifiable parting based on:

> the undoubted right which one independent branch of the Church of Christ has of separating from another branch of the same church, whenever communion with that branch cannot be continued without sin. It was therefore a right exercised . . . in conformity with the deliberate wisdom of our National Church, in its *collective character*, as a spiritual society.[209]

But when separation based on private judgement occurs from an uncorrupted communion, as was the case in secessions from the Church of England, it is the schism condemned by both Scripture and tradition.[210]

Old fashioned 'low and slow' clergyman were more alarmed by the Schismatics' tendency toward fanaticism than by their challenge to apostolicity. Richard Warner,[211] another influential West Country clergyman, was sufficiently aroused to publish four separate works attacking the seceders, principally for advocating dogmas which were inconsistent with Scripture, reason, and tradition.[212] It was the high predestinarianism of the seceders that most incensed him. In rhetorical terms he described Calvinism as an advancing 'black mist . . . blasting every spiritual joy, withering

[208] Daubeny was well known for his schemes for Church extension, his defence of apostolicity and priestly authority, and his opposition to Evangelicals. See Charles Daubeny, *On the Nature, Progress, and Consequences of Schism* (1818), pp. vii, xiii; *A Guide to the Church*, 2nd edn. (Bath, 1804), 1: 41–63; *A Word in Season On the Nature of the Christian Church* (Bath, 1817).

[209] Daubeny, *On the Nature, Progress, and Consequences of Schism*, 17.

[210] Ibid. 18–19.

[211] Warner, incumbent of Great Chalfield, Wiltshire, and Norton-St. Philip, Somerset, had previously been curate of St. James's, Bath. His opposition to Calvinism and to the Evangelical party was well known, and, except for his opposition to Catholic Emancipation in 1829, he maintained a decided loyalty toward the Whigs.

[212] Richard Warner, *Old Church of England Principles Opposed to the 'New Light'* (Bath, 1817); *Considerations on the Doctrines; All the Counsel of God* (Bath, 1817); *The Claims of the Church of England* (Bath, 1819).

every amiable feeling, and poisoning every social and domestic charity'. If this were not halted, it would transform our understanding of God as a loving, benevolent being into one which characterized him as an inexorable tyrant.[213] To stop the spread of this gloomy creed, he urged bishops and examining chaplains simply to refuse to ordain Evangelicals to positions in the Church.[214]

IX

Although there had been individual departures by Evangelical clergymen from the Established Church prior to 1815, the Western Schism was unique in its collective nature. It was regarded as a disruption and not as a series of individual secessions. Its notoriety was compounded by the antinomianism and sabellianism of some of its adherents, by the social prominence of its patrons and several of its leading figures, and by the vehemence expressed by its critics from very different points of the ecclesiastical compass. It brought into high profile the conflict surrounding the identity of the Church of England which was beginning to strain its comprehensiveness, and call into doubt the principle of establishment.

In perspective, then, we can see the Schism as the precursor of the larger and even more disruptive issues which would plague the English Church in the following decades. In its separatism and high Calvinism it prefigured the pronouncements of such Evangelical seceders as Henry Bulteel, J. C. Philpot, and William Tiptaft during the 1830s. The Western Schismatics' reaction to the popish elements in the rubrics and the pronouncements of Richard Mant and his fellow High Churchmen, foreshadowed those raised in the celebrated secession of Baptist Noel in 1848, and in the Gorham affair which occurred at about the same time.

By late 1818 or early 1819, the doctrinal restlessness of the individual seceders began to diminish, or at least to turn in different directions. Although the principles of the Schism continued to spread, its leadership had by now begun to split apart.[215] In December 1818, it was reported that at least one of the seceders' leading converts, T. R. Garnsey, had already abandoned the

213 Warner, *All the Council of God*, 19.

214 Warner, *Old Church of England Principles Opposed to the 'New Light'*, i.pp. vii–viii.

215 Havergal to his mother, 1818, in Crane, *Life of Wm. Havergal*, 18.

'Baring party' and had returned to the Church of England. He was not alone in his return to Evangelical orthodoxy.[216]

In 1832, the Evangelical Robert Cox remarked in retrospect that the Schism had 'perverted, discouraged, and staggered many', and 'caused grief to us all'. It should be regarded, however, as accomplishing relatively little as a corporate body, either in creating a lasting theological influence or in establishing an alternative form of piety to challenge that of the Evangelicals.[217] Within five years of the Schism's outbreak some of the seceders—including Sir Thomas Baring and Thomas Snow—had returned to the Church of England. A few others—including Harriet Wall and Henry Drummond—would soon adhere to Irvingism. Remarkably, only John Mason and James Harington Evans had become—and remained—attached to orthodox Dissent.[218]

Of more lasting importance were the seceders' criticisms of the doctrines and practices of the Established Church, for these, when separated from their doctrinal eccentricities, reflected some of the concerns quietly expressed by more moderate Evangelicals, but normally suppressed or held in check by ingrained loyalty to the Establishment, its liturgy, and its Articles. Its significance lay less in the provision of any corporate alternative to the Church than in the doubts which it raised. It was more a negative than a positive influence. As we have seen, the doubts entertained by the seceders were not new, but in 1815–19, they gained considerable publicity in the 'Gospel world' because of their dramatically collective character. The Western Schismatics and their critique of the Church were soon to be echoed by louder voices, as we will see in following chapters.

[216] Havergal to Tebbs, December 1818, ibid. Garnsey had been an Evangelical prior to his association with the schismatics. He was afterwards ordained in the Church of England and made an officer of the CMS, where he was accepted for service in Sierra Leone. See also ibid. 28–9.

[217] Robert Cox, *Secession Considered* (1832), 21.

[218] See Baring-Gould, *The Church Revival*, 97.

5

English Millennialism: The English Prophetic Movement and the Albury 'Apostles'

It has been increasingly recognized that the late 1820s and early 1830s were a period of controversy and fragmentation in English Evangelicalism.[1] As Sir James Stephen lamented in 1845: 'Oh where are the people who are at once really religious, and really cultivated in heart and in understanding? . . . The people with whom we could associate as our fathers used to associate with each other. No "Clapham Sect" nowadays.'[2] On one side of this divide were the old moderates represented by the remnants of Clapham and their organ, the *Christian Observer*: eirenical in their theology, fearful of enthusiasm and emotionalism, given over largely to campaigns for moral and social reform and to optimistic missionary endeavours at home and abroad. On the other side were a small number of sterner groups: younger, deeply pessimistic about the 'signs of the times', seized by millennial expectation and a desire to return to pure, radical 'apostolic' practices, some of them emphasizing the role of fresh, direct religious experience of the type described in the Acts of the Apostles—even the imminent return of the 'gifts' of the Spirit recorded there. Those in the second broad category did not all think alike; indeed, there was restless movement among them, and a criss-crossing of groupings and influences. This pessimism tore a number of prominent

[1] See David Newsome, *The Parting of Friends* (1966), 19; N. Cohn, *The Pursuit of the Millennium*, 3rd edn. (1970); E. R. Sandeen, *The Roots of Fundamentalism* (Chicago, 1970); Doreen Rosman, *Evangelicals and Culture* (1984), 24–37; Iain H. Murray, *The Puritan Hope*, 3rd edn. (Edinburgh, 1984), 185–206; D. N. Hempton, 'Evangelicalism and Eschatology', in *JEH* (1980), 179–94; Sheridan Gilley, 'Newman and Prophecy', in *Journal of the United Reformed Church Historical Society* (1985), 160–88; T. C. F. Stunt, '"Trying the Spirits": The Case of the Gloucestershire Clergyman', in *JEH* (1988), 95–105; 'Geneva and British Evangelicals in the Early Nineteenth Century', in *JEH* (1981), 35–46; J. F. C. Harrison, *The Second Coming* (1979); D. W. Bebbington, *Evangelicalism in Modern Britain* (1989), 75–104.

[2] C. E. Stephen, *Sir James Stephen* (Gloucester, 1906), 87.

Evangelicals, lay and clerical, away from the mother Church of England into new religious bodies.[3]

Some form of millennial expectation has always existed in the Church of England, and indeed in the wider Christian tradition, though its strength has ebbed and flowed. It was not, initially, a theme uppermost in the minds of the early Evangelicals, despite some excited hopes in the 1740s that the coincidental awakening in Wales, England, Scotland, and North America might presage the *parousia*. During much of the eighteenth century, 'vital Christianity' was largely absorbed with the work of evangelism and not given over to a great deal of speculation on 'latter things'.[4] The comparative political stability in Britain—and on the Continent—did not encourage the sense of an imminent collapse of the existing order. On the whole, the spirit of evangelicalism at the end of the eighteenth century was confident. The evangelistic 'means' needed to bring about the regeneration of the nation seemed to be obvious, and to be achieving the required result without the need for any apocalyptic intervention by God. Even in the early 1820s, the leaders of the movement could proclaim with some assurance and self-congratulation that, while much remained to be done, much had been accomplished.

At the same time, several recent political and religious undercurrents had begun profoundly to affect Evangelical thinking. The vast upheavals of the French Revolutionary era and the Napoleonic wars revealed that the world was in flux, and provoked a feeling that the tribulations of the present might be the prologue to a new age previously unimagined. The social changes accompanying the recent years of industrialization created deep unease. Doubts arose about existing methods of spreading the Gospel.[5] Despite the work of the Bible Society and other evangelistic agencies, Christianity appeared to be moving into a period of relative decline, especially in the Church of England. Although evangelical Dissent was fast increasing, the Establishment appeared to some as unwilling—or unable—to respond to the spiritual

[3] See Appendix, 1. This heightened interest in the study of prophecy was illustrated by the publication of over one hundred books and at least ten periodicals on the subject in England alone between 1800 and 1840. See Harold H. Rowdon, *The Origins of the Brethren* (1967), 12.

[4] Murray, *The Puritan Hope*, 187.

[5] Bebbington, *Evangelicalism in Modern Britain*, 76–7.

destitution of the great cities where populations were growing fast and vice and godlessness remained largely unchecked. During the late 1820s, the Protestant Constitution came under siege: the repeal of the Test and Corporation Acts appeared imminent; even more worrying to Tory Evangelicals, the clamour for Catholic Emancipation increased, making the passage of some measure of relief increasingly likely. The sense of unease encouraged a heightened interest in extreme forms of Calvinism and a dissatisfaction with the simple, 'heart-religion' of a Hannah More, a Charles Simeon, or a William Wilberforce. Many Evangelicals came to believe that a more dogmatic, systematic, and speculative theology was necessary, if the solvent acids of liberalism were to be resisted.

I

In this climate of anxiety, the expectation of the personal return of Christ to earth to establish His millennial kingdom gripped many minds. Millennial speculation was no longer largely confined to a popular apocalyptic subculture inhabited by enthusiasts like Richard Brothers, James Bicheno, or Joanna Southcott: it became the subject of intense study by well-educated clergymen like Edward Bickersteth, rector of Walton in Hertfordshire, a wealthy banker and MP like Henry Drummond, or a scholar like G. S. Faber.[6] In 1829 it acquired a mouthpiece in the *Morning Watch*, financed by Drummond, which was followed by other millennial publications such as the *Christian Herald*, the *Watchman*, and the *Expositor of Prophecy*.

For the most part, this millennial fervour was contained within the Established Church. Yet there were latent tendencies within the prophetic movement which could easily carry its devotees into outright secession. In a significant study of the prophetic mind in this period—*Prophets and Millennialists* (1978)—W. H. Oliver has analysed the important division between pre- and post-millennialists; that is, between those, like Drummond and Edward Irving, who expected the personal advent of Christ and the bodily resurrection of the Saints to precede the millennium (the period of one thousand years mentioned in Revelation 20: 2–7 as the time of the reign of Christ and the saints over the earth), and those more doctrinally moderate Evangelicals who held that the mil-

[6] Hempton, 'Evangelicalism and Eschatology', 181–2.

lennium would be inaugurated by a spiritual intervention of Christ in the power of His Spirit, not by a bodily advent which would follow the millennium.[7]

It is difficult to calculate precisely how many Evangelicals fell into each camp. Prior to the late 1820s most Evangelicals were probably post-millennialists, as evidenced by the confidence of their movement, shown in their great voluntary societies and missionary efforts, and by their many campaigns such as that for the abolition of the slave trade. This soon began to change, however. By 1845 one Anglican clergyman estimated the number of clerical pre-millennialists in the Church at around seven hundred.[8] In 1851 Edward Bishop Elliott, author of the influential pre-millennial work *Horae Apocalypticae*, could look back with amazement on the change which had occurred during the previous seven years. 'In the year 1844', he wrote, 'the date of the first publication of my own work on the Apocalypse, so rapid had been the progress of these views in England, that instead of its appearing as a thing strange and half-heretical to hold them, as when Irving published his translation of Ben Ezra, the leaven had evidently now deeply penetrated the religious mind.'[9] Four years on, the *British and Foreign Evangelical Review* estimated that more than half of the Evangelicals now favoured pre-millennialist views.[10] In spite of this clear trend, however, many prominent Evangelicals (including Hugh McNeile, William Marsh, and Edward Bickersteth) were highly fluid in their thinking on the subject; as the pronouncements of the English prophetic movement grew more extreme, and as outbreaks of the 'gifts' were alleged by some of its adherents, they stepped back from the extreme pre-millennialist position.

Seen not in exegetical but in psychological terms, this important dichotomy in the prophetic tradition was essentially between pessimists and optimists. The files of the *Morning Watch*, and other pre-millennialist journals, suggest that its contributors were not

[7] W. H. Oliver, *Prophets and Millennialists* (Auckland and Oxford, 1978). See also Gilley, 'Newman and Prophecy'. The middle ground of the debate was held by the a-millennialists: those who believed that the millennial reign of Christ was the age of the church, from the Resurrection of Christ to his Advent. The figure one thousand (as in one thousand years) was taken to be symbolic, not an actual length of time.

[8] This was Mourant Brock. See Murray, *The Puritan Hope*, 197.

[9] Edward Bishop Elliott, *Horae Apocalypticae*, 4th edn. (1851) iv.522.

[10] Sandeen, *The Roots of Fundamentalism*, 40.

only pessimistic about the 'signs of the times' in the wider world of affairs, but pessimistic about the state of the Evangelical movement itself. They had a very strong suspicion that the sometimes frenetic activism of many Evangelical leaders, obsessed by the use of human 'means'—such as Bible Societies, missionary campaigns, parliamentary lobbying—was useless and had been at the expense of the close study of Scripture and the interior life of prayer which were the marks of true piety. Much Evangelical activity represented no more than the intrusion of the 'spirit of trade'—of shopkeepers, merchants, and the like—into the world of 'serious religion'. 'The Religious World', according to one correspondent:

> has taken it into its head that it is going to convert the heathen world, Jews, Infidels, and Papists, by means of books, tracts, and missionaries. It has been labouring at this work for above a quarter of a century; and annually prophesies, at all the annual meetings of all its societies, and of all their provincial auxiliaries, its positive certainty of so doing, provided only the people will give them money enough; and that in the mean time, the world will get better and better every day. The Students of Prophecy have got a very perplexing mode of consulting the Word of God as to future events, rather than speakers on platforms; and they have therein found that the world is not to be converted by any such means.[11]

Edward Irving reinforced this view by announcing, as early as 1823, that he had now come to discard 'that error under which almost the whole of the church is lying, that the present world is to be converted unto the Lord, and so slide by natural inclination into the church—the present reign of Satan hastening, of its own accord, into the millennial reign of Christ'.[12] Instead, he had now come to accept the idea of a dispensation drawing towards its close, together with its natural consequence—that is, of an altogether glorious and overwhelming revolution in which all the dead churches, kingdoms, and fashions of this world would be finally destroyed.

By contrast, the optimistic post-millennialists were not unduly alarmed by the 'signs of the times' provided by wars and social upheavals, for they saw these as opening up the way to further missionary triumphs. Social and political change often broke

[11] The *Morning Watch* (1830), p. ii, 215.

[12] See Mrs Oliphant, *The Life of Edward Irving*, 6th edn. (*c*.1900), 92.

down traditional and customary barriers to the free flow of the Gospel, providing an opportunity for energetic missionizing. On the other hand the pessimistic pre-millennialists saw in the world about them the gathering darkness of catastrophe: they awaited the transformation of the earth by a miraculous, divine intervention—the mass conversion of the Jews, and the descent of the Messiah himself from the heavens to judge and recreate. As Francis Newman, who had for a time fallen under the deep spell of the prophetic movement, put it succinctly in his well-known autobiographical tale, *Phases of Faith*: 'Those who stick closest to the Scripture do not shrink from saying, that "it is not worth while trying to mend the world", and stigmatize as "political and worldly" such as pursue an opposite course.'[13] The implication was clear: Evangelicalism was failing and would never achieve its self-appointed task of restoring the divine will to earth. A major split in the 'Gospel world', beginning in the late 1820s, was that between the optimistic post-millennialists, safely anchored in the present and inspired by a vision of the millennium which was an ameliorated continuation of the existing world, and those pre-millennialists whose despair of contemporary society encouraged them to posit an almost complete caesura between the present and a transfigured future.[14]

The pre-millennial case had important implications for Evangelical views of the Church of England and its establishment. There were many deeply establishmentarian Evangelical pre-millennialists—Edward Bickersteth and Lord Shaftesbury, for example—and many compromise positions between pre- and post-millennialism. Of the seven hundred Evangelical clergy labelled pre-millennialists in 1845, the huge majority did not secede, but remained safely within the Established Church.[15] Many pre-millennialist clerics saw their task as calling the Church to a sense of her destiny, alerting the nation to the fate that awaited it, and preparing believers for the Apocalypse to come. Yet their pessimism about the future, and their distrust of the efficacy of institutional solutions to the evils of the present world, could lead also to a low (sometimes *very* low) view of visible churches. The

[13] Francis William Newman, *Phases of Faith*, 6th edn. (1860), 136.

[14] Oliver, *Prophets and Millennialists*, 83.

[15] See Le Roy E. Froom, *The Prophetic Faith of Our Fathers* (Washington, 1946–54), iii.706.

existing churches were often seen as institutions without a future. They belonged to a 'dispensation' that had failed. From this gloomy premiss it was not difficult to conclude that the churches of the present day should be abandoned, like sinking hulks. The elect, the righteous remnant, should draw apart, to prepare for the new dispensation which was shortly to be ushered in. The Christian should live in a state of expectancy waiting for the imminent Second Coming.

One of the best known of such groups was the one which had evolved from the Albury conferences on prophecy inaugurated in 1826, and was held annually for the next five years. These gatherings were held at Albury Park, between Guildford and Dorking, the spacious country home of the banker and MP, Henry Drummond, whom we have already encountered as an active member of the Western Schism.[16] The theologically erratic Drummond had by now gone over to pre-millennialist pessimism. He was a high Tory deeply disturbed by the Reform Bill crisis, and still more by the 'apostasy' of Protestant England in conceding Catholic Emancipation in 1829, a move which, in his view, had virtually separated Church and State.[17]

Much water, however, had passed under the bridge since the Western Schism. By the early 1820s, most of the Western Seceders had returned, at least for a time, to some degree of Anglican conformity. In early 1822, Drummond attended a service at Percy Chapel in London, where he heard the eloquent preaching of the young Irish Evangelical Hugh McNeile. He responded characteristically, immediately offering him the vacant living of Albury adjoining his country estate.[18] McNeile must have been pleased to have been the recipient of such a magnanimous offer, for Drummond was one of the most influential (albeit oddest) lay figures in the Evangelical world.[19] Intellectually powerful, he was also per-

[16] Drummond's social and economic thought has been well covered in Boyd Hilton, *The Age of Atonement* (Oxford, 1988), especially 40–8.

[17] Four years earlier, Drummond's views on Catholic Emancipation were revealed to a friend: 'What madness it is to think that the miseries of the Irish people will be alleviated by emancipation. Carry over there the English Poor Laws . . . and you will do more to give happiness to the many than all the toleration that can be devised.' Quoted in H. Bolitho and D. Peel, *The Drummonds of Charing Cross* (1967), 138.

[18] *DNB*. McNeile became rector of Albury in July or August 1822. MS PSH/ALB/2/2, Surrey Record Centre.

[19] Rowland Davenport, *Albury Apostles*, 2nd edn. (1973); Robert Lee Lively, Jr., 'The Catholic Apostolic Church and the Church of Jesus Christ of Latter Day Saints: A Com-

sonally engaging and generous to a fault. At the same time he managed, with aristocratic idiosyncrasy, to inspire controversy wherever he landed.

There is no shortage of contemporary comment on Drummond's unusual and colourful personality. His ally Edward Irving admitted his 'propensity to wit and argument'.[20] Thomas Carlyle, who came to know him well, left at least two vivid accounts of the eccentric politician. In August 1831, after being introduced to Drummond for the first time, he wrote to his wife that Drummond 'proved to be a very striking man. Taller and leaner than I, but erect as a plummet, with a high-carried, quick, penetrating head, some five-and-forty years of age, a singular mixture of all things—of the saint, the wit, the philosopher—swimming, if I mistake not, in an element of dandyism.'[21] Some years later, reminiscing on the tragic fate of his friend Irving, Carlyle was less charitable in his assessment:

> He [Irving] talked to me of Henry Drummond as of a fine, a great, evangelical, yet courtly and indeed universal gentlemen, whom prophetic studies had brought to him . . . There had been big 'prophetic conferences' etc. held at Drummond's house, who continued ever after an ardent Irvingite, and rose, by degrees, in the 'Tongues' business, to be hierophant, and chief over Irving himself. He was far the richest of the sect, and alone belonged to aristocratic circles, abundant in speculation as well as in money; a sharp, elastic, haughty kind of man; had considerable ardour, disorderly force of intellect and character, and especially an insatiable love of shining and figuring. In a different element I had afterwards plentiful knowledge of Henry Drummond, and if I got no good of him got also no mischief, which might have been extremely possible . . . He, without unkindness of intention, did my poor Irving a great deal of ill.[22]

Drummond was recognized to be an extraordinary amalgam of the religious enthusiast with the ultra-conservative: his son-in-law, Lord Lovaine, described him as 'a real old Tory', with an

parative Study of Two Minority Millenarian Groups in Nineteenth Century England', D.Phil. thesis (Oxford, 1977); Stunt, 'Geneva and British Evangelicals', 35–46.

[20] Northumberland MSS, Drummond Papers, Alnwick Castle, C/9/18, letter from Irving to Drummond, 4 May 1833.

[21] Andrew Landale Drummond, *Edward Irving and His Circle* (1938), 126.

[22] James Anthony Froude (ed.), *Reminiscences by Thomas Carlyle* (1881), i.297–8, 312.

'unswerving fidelity to the Crown and to the constitution'.[23] He retained little confidence in man's ability for self-improvement. As Drummond once wrote to the secretary of the Peace Society, 'of the first two men born into the world one killed the other; and in this way human nature has manifested itself ever since, and ever will, unless it undergoes a "miraculous transformation".'[24] At times, Drummond could be equally pessimistic about the Church of England, though he 'was always ready to defend the purity and catholicity of her doctrines, and to support her as the national symbol of the recognition by this country of the duty and service she owes to God'.[25]

The third and last Henry Drummond was born at the Grange at Northington, Hampshire, on 5 December 1786, the eldest son of Henry Drummond and grandson of Henry Drummond, both associated with the family's London bank.[26] The youngest Henry was well-connected politically through his mother, Anne, the daughter of Pitt's friend and Scottish ally, Henry Dundas, who was created Viscount Melville in December 1802. On 4 July 1794, the second Henry Drummond died, aged 32, of a strange and incurable illness.[27] His wife, Drummond's mother, was left to survive on a modest legacy. In need of capital in order to pay off substantial debts incurred by her husband and father-in-law (who died a few months after his son), in 1795 she rented the Grange to the Prince of Wales for £900 a year. In December 1798, she married a James Strange and, four years later, abandoned England for India,[28] placing Henry (at Harrow since 1793, where

[23] Lord Lovaine (ed.), *Speeches in Parliament and Some Miscellaneous Pamphlets of the Late Henry Drummond, Esq.* (1860), i. p. vi.

[24] Quoted in Bolitho and Peel, *The Drummonds of Charing Cross*, 137.

[25] Lovaine, *Speeches in Parliament and Some Miscellaneous Pamphlets of the Late Henry Drummond, Esq.*, i. pp. vi–vii.

[26] For further details on Drummond see *GM* (April 1860), 413–14; Davenport, *Albury Apostles*, 15–20; J. Agnew and R. Palmer, 'Report on the Papers of Henry Drummond of Albury (1786–1860) and Members of his Family (1670–1865)', in *Royal Commission on Historic Manuscripts* (1977); G. L. Standring, *Albury and the Catholic Apostolic Church* (Albury, 1985), 33–4; Grayson Carter, 'Henry Drummond', in *BDE*, i.326–7. The Drummond Bank was patronized by a number of prominent individuals, including George III, the Prince of Wales, Spencer Perceval, and Sir Robert Peel. Earlier, the Bank had strong Jacobite leanings. See Lovaine, *Speeches in Parliament and Some Miscellaneous Pamphlets of the Late Henry Drummond, Esq.*, i. p. iv; R. G. Baird, 'Some Reminiscences of Drummond's Bank', in *Three Banks Review* (Dec. 1950), 35–41.

[27] Bolitho and Peel, *The Drummonds of Charing Cross*, 130–1.

[28] Ibid. 132–5.

he was a contemporary of Byron and Peel, and now about to go up to Christ Church, Oxford), into the care of his famous maternal grandfather, through whom he obtained access to the inner circles of the Tory party and became a favourite of Pitt.[29]

Despite his mother's precarious financial state, Drummond's 'situation', according to his grandfather's executors, was 'very good on his coming of age', as he had inherited a substantial ownership in the family bank.[30] In 1807, after returning from a tour of Russia, he married his cousin, Lady Henrietta Hay, eldest daughter of the ninth Earl of Kinnoul.[31] Unaffected by either Oxford scholarship or the world of commerce, Drummond instead became intrigued by politics: in 1810, at the age of 23, he entered Parliament for the first time as representative for Plympton Earls.[32] Two years layer, he was made a partner at the Drummond Bank, although it appears that his involvement remained minimal and eventually he was forced out by the other partners.[33] In 1818, in the midst of the Western Schism, Drummond purchased (from Harriet Wall, also a prominent figure in the Western Schism) Albury Park, a large estate in the Surrey countryside, where he engaged Pugin to convert the house to his emerging Gothic taste, and where he resided until his death in 1860.[34] Despite a good deal of eccentricity in politics as well as religion, Drummond commanded respect, and left his mark on his age in conventional as well as unconventional ways—not least by founding the Drummond Chair in political economy at Oxford in 1825.[35]

It appears from a comment made in mid-life that Drummond embraced the teachings of 'serious religion' at a very early age. 'There was never a time', he claimed, 'when I did otherwise than

[29] *DNB*.

[30] Bolitho and Peel, *The Drummonds of Charing Cross*, 132.

[31] Ibid. 136; *GM* (1860), 413–14. In 1845, his daughter Louisa (1813–90) married Algernon George Percy, sixth Duke of Northumberland.

[32] Gerrit P. Judd (ed.), *Members of Parliament 1734–1832*, 2nd edn. (Hamden, Conn., 1972), 178. Drummond served as MP for Plympton Earl between 1810 and 1812, and for West Surrey between 1847 and 1860.

[33] In 1844, he was compelled to withdraw as titular head in return for a consideration of £10,000 a year for life, and a capital sum of £50,000 to be paid to his estate on his death. See Bolitho and Peel, *The Drummonds of Charing Cross*, 136; Retta T. L. Casbard, MS 'Henry Drummond of Albury' (n.d.), Albury Historical Society, 13.

[34] Bolitho and Peel, *The Drummonds of Charing Cross*, 136–8.

[35] Hilton, *The Age of Atonement*, 42–8.

believe every word of the Bible, in its plain literal meaning.'[36] As we have seen, he was taken in (albeit temporarily) by the high Calvinistic and Sabellian speculations of the Western Seceders.[37] In March 1816, very likely under the influence of the Schism, he became 'satiated with the empty frivolities of the fashionable world, and, pressed by the address of our Lord to the rich young man',[38] he broke up his hunting establishment and sold the Grange.[39] He then departed on an extended tour of the Holy Land. En route, however, and providentially, as he came to regard it, a storm forced their ship into port at Genoa, and his wife urged abandonment of the journey. Having previously learned of the activity of the Scottish evangelical Robert Haldane, Drummond then travelled to Geneva where he quickly offered his assistance to the local religious revival.[40]

Following the reopening of the Continent to British travellers after the defeat of Napoleon, Evangelicals had been understandably attracted to Geneva, where a religious revival was underway.[41] Haldane, who had launched extensive missionary work in his native Scotland, had come to Geneva during the previous year to work for the conversion of students at the university.[42] Never far from controversy, he quickly became embroiled in a local dispute over state intrusion into the doctrines and affairs of the established church,[43] encouraging the evangelical clergy of Geneva openly to resist the civil authorities.[44] In June 1817, when Haldane was preparing to return to Britain, Drummond agreed to carry on the work, throwing his considerable energy into a

[36] Davenport, *Albury Apostles*, 14. [37] See Chapter 4.

[38] Alexander Haldane, *Memories of the Lives of Robert Haldane of Airthey, and of His Brother, James Alexander Haldane* (1852), 446. This account was later incorporated into Drummond's entry in the *DNB.*

[39] The Grange at Northington, Hampshire, a magnificent neoclassical house to which Drummond, under the direction of the architect William Wilkins, had made substantial improvements between 1804 and 1809. On 25 March 1816 Drummond sold the house to Alexander Baring, first Baron Ashburton, financier and statesman, and second son of Sir Francis Baring, founder of the Baring Bank. See MS 11M52, Hampshire RO; the *Hampshire Magazine* (Dec. 1960), 19–20; (Oct. 1974), 52–4; (Apr. 1983), 50–4.

[40] See James I. Good, *History of the Swiss Reformed Church Since the Reformation* (Philadelphia, 1913), 375–9; Froom, *The Prophetic Faith of Our Fathers*, iv.436.

[41] See Stunt, 'Geneva and British Evangelicals', 35–46; K. J. Stewart, 'Restoring the Reformation: British Evangelicalism and the "Réveil" at Geneva 1816–1849', Ph.D. thesis (Edinburgh, 1992).

[42] See E. H. Broadbent, *The Pilgrim Church*, 3rd edn. (1945), 302; Stunt, 'Geneva and British Evangelicals', 35–46.

[43] *CO* (1826), 693–709. [44] *DNB.*

cause that he believed would restore the city of Calvin to its former orthodoxy and spiritual glory.[45] His campaign, bolstered by his great wealth and sharpened by dogmatic zeal, ensured that his efforts would not go unnoticed by the local authorities. Perhaps predictably, Drummond was soon summoned to appear before the Council of State to explain his disruptive behaviour. Facing possible arrest and imprisonment, he quickly fled into France, continuing his campaign for a time from across the border.[46] The subsequent secession of the Genevan evangelicals from the state church, as David Bebbington has suggested, may have prepared Drummond and others ultimately to contemplate a similar step. The pure milk of high Calvinism became for Drummond, and like-minded Evangelicals, the ideal of a primitive, apostolic Christianity.[47] In his hands, as in those of John Walker, the Western Seceders, John Nelson Darby, Henry Bulteel, and many others, high Calvinist asceticism and its rigorous distinction between the world of nature and that of grace, encouraged separatism. 'I saw also in the history of the church', declared a speaker expressing Drummond's own views, 'that in proportion she became Arminian she relapsed into the world, and that in proportion she became Calvinistic she came out of the world.'[48] In subsequent years Geneva remained embroiled in religious ferment, and attracted the attention of both the early Plymouth Brethren (including no less a personage than John Nelson Darby) and the Catholic Apostolic Church.[49]

After some months in the midst of the Swiss controversy Drummond returned to England. In 1819, he joined forces with Haldane and Sir Thomas Baring in founding the Continental Society—a pan-evangelical organization established to 'reform both the Socinian tendencies of the Protestant denominations and those suffering under popish Christianity' in Europe.[50] Baring was

[45] Haldane, *Memories of Robert and James Alexander Haldane*, 446, 450.

[46] Ibid. 448.

[47] Bebbington, *Evangelicalism in Modern Britain*, 77.

[48] Henry Drummond, *Dialogues on Prophecy* (1828–9), i.212.

[49] See Tim Grass, 'The Church's Ruin and Restoration: The Development of Ecclesiology in the Plymouth Brethren and the Catholic Apostolic Church, *c*.1825–*c*.1866', Ph.D. thesis (King's College, London, 1997), 39–40.

[50] See *First Report of the Continental Society For the Diffusion of Religious Knowledge* (1819), 5–6; Haldane, *Memories of Robert and James Alexander Haldane*, 463. The Society was later renamed the European Missionary Society; it eventually merged into the Foreign Aid Society.

elected as the Society's first President with Drummond assisting, first as a member of its Central Committee, and later as a Vice-President.[51] Drummond was also responsible, through his considerable donations, for ensuring the Society's financial well-being—a cause which led to the enlistment of a number of his former associates from the Western Schism, including (besides Sir Thomas Baring) George Baring, James Harington Evans, and Thomas Snow. It also attracted the support of other well-known Evangelicals, including James Alexander Haldane, William Marsh, Robert Harry Inglis, Rowland Hill, Charles Simeon, Thomas Kelly, Hugh McNeile, William Wilberforce, and the Baptist Dr Ryland.[52] So influential was Drummond in the Society's affairs that he eventually secured places on its Central Committee for his friends, and soon-to-be fellow 'apostles' in the Catholic Apostolic Church, Edward Irving and Spencer Perceval, the son of the assassinated Evangelical Prime Minister.[53] He also appears to have imparted some of his separatism and pre-millennialist pessimism to the Society. In 1830, the following resolution, moved by Drummond, was carried at the Society's annual gathering: 'This meeting, impressed with the thought that the day of labour is far spent, and must soon close . . . do recognize the great duty and privilege of raising the cry throughout apostate Christendom, "Come out of her, my people, that ye not be partakers of her sins, and that ye receive not of her plagues." '[54]

Alarmed by the wild speculation in Latin American mining shares, in late 1825 Drummond began (in his words), 'to direct attention to the events connected with the close of the Christian dispensation'.[55] The insecurities of the commercial and financial world intensified his growing pessimism about the state of the world. In the following year he was drawn into the consideration of unfulfilled prophecy through Lewis Way, a wealthy London lawyer turned Anglican clergyman who, under pre-millennialist inspiration, had seceded from the Church of England and formed

[51] Baring continued as President until 1827 when, although continuing to provide generous financial support, he mysteriously withdrew from the Society. See *Nineteenth Report of the Continental Society*, 93; Froom, *The Prophetic Faith of Our Fathers*, iv.435–40.

[52] See *Fourth Report of the Continental Society* (1822).

[53] In 1825 and 1826 respectively.

[54] See *Proceedings of the Continental Society . . . Twelfth Year, 1829–1830* (1830), 3.

[55] Henry Drummond, *Abstract Principles of Revealed Religion* (1845), iii.

an independent Christian body in Paris.[56] This transformation in Drummond's religious thinking marked not only his introduction into the early stages of the English prophetic movement, but also his final rejection of mainstream Claphamite Evangelicalism. As he later explained, he had already come to believe that all religious systems:

> were perceived more or less to pervert or to overlook some important points; but it was not until the year 1826, when Mr Lewis Way informed me that the majority of what was called the religious world disbelieved that the Jews were to be restored to their own land, and that the Lord Jesus Christ was to return and reign in person on this earth, that I had the remotest idea of the mass of infidelity which lurked under the guise of what was called evangelical religion.[57]

As a high 'Church and State' Tory, Drummond's adherence to the English prophetic movement was inspired in no small measure, like that of other political conservatives, by the 'constitutional revolution' of 1828–32. He denounced proposals granting concessions to Catholics as an abrogation of Britain's responsibility as a highly favoured Christian nation to oppose the apostasy of Rome, and as a violation of the unity of Church and State.[58] His opposition to religious and political reform reflected his strongly held notions of authority, paternalism, and the maintenance of a strict and hierarchical social order. In 1829 he published anonymously a letter he had written to the King urging him to refuse his assent to the repeal of the Test Act.[59] This was followed, two years later, by the publication of another work highly antagonistic to the Reform Bill.[60] So opposed had Drummond become to the process of reform that he began to see the issue in terms of complete and irretrievable polarization. In an alarmingly agitated diatribe in 1832, he warned all true believers that it is 'no longer a question between Whig and Tory, but between constitution and no constitution, between order and

[56] See John Oakes, 'Lewis Way', in *BDE*, ii.1164.

[57] Davenport, *Albury Apostles*, 14.

[58] Drummond, *Dialogues on Prophecy*, ii.250–68.

[59] Henry Drummond [A Tory of the Old School], 'A Letter to the King Against Repeal of the Test Act by a Tory of the Old School', 1829, in Lovaine, *Speeches in Parliament and Some Miscellaneous Pamphlets of the Late Henry Drummond, Esq.*, ii.39–59.

[60] Henry Drummond, 'Reform Not a New Constitution', 1831, in Lovaine, *Speeches in Parliament and Some Miscellaneous Pamphlets of the Late Henry Drummond, Esq.*, ii.77–118.

anarchy. It is no longer a question between this or that *form* of Christianity, but between Religion and Infidelity, between Christ and Antichrist.'[61]

In many ways Drummond continued to remain an old-fashioned Tory paternalist, emphasizing the need for authority in Church and State and the duty of superiors to protect their dependents in recognition of their social obedience. He strongly expressed traditional notions of social hierarchy, of organic links holding the various layers of the hierarchy together, and of the divinely ordained nature of such a society. But by now he had added to these paternalist views a potentially radical ecclesiastical position in which theology and politics cohered together in what W. H. Oliver has described as the theory of the 'apostate nation': the British were a people which had been chosen by God, but had rejected the spiritual duties which accompanied their elect status, and had wickedly abandoned the divine commission.[62]

An important corollary to the theory of the 'apostate nation' was the notion that normative—and moderate—Evangelicals had lost their spiritual purity and direction: they had apostatized from true Christian faith and devotion. Drummond believed this implicitly. Unlike most pre-millennialists, however, he carried his pessimism to the point of outright secession from the Church of England. As pressure rose to enact political and religious reform—generally favoured by the moderates of the 'Christian Observer school'—conservative, pre-millennialist Evangelicals became convinced that their efforts to extend the Revival were under siege; concessions to the forces of liberalism were beginning to destroy the religious purity of the nation. 'The Evangelicals in Britain,' Drummond declared in 1828, 'assuming that their Bible and Missionary Societies are going to convert the world, can never believe that the Churches of England and Scotland, and this Pharisaic and Infidel nation, will, because she has been most highly honoured, be the first to feel the weighty hand of the Lord's vengeance.'[63] They would soon discover their mistake. Britain had been displaced from God's favour because her Church had succumbed to the world. While 'this land has been more favoured

[61] The *Morning Watch* (1832), 237.

[62] Oliver, *Prophets and Millennialists*, 108.

[63] Henry Drummond, *A Defence of the Students of Prophecy* (1828), 50.

than any spot on the whole earth with the number of preachers of God's Word', and while it has been 'selected by Jehovah to be His witness against the popish Apostasy', it had squandered its talents and would soon be called to judgement. The '*peril* of the *last days*', as he described it, would not be caused by the openly profane, but by serious-minded professed Christians—often professed Evangelicals—'those who are lovers of their own institutions, and of wealth; boasters of their charitable, and missionary exploits; lovers of expediency rather than of principle; laying false accusations; speaking against the plain letter of God's Word; and yet having the form, circumstance, and profession of godliness'.[64]

Drummond also attacked the Evangelicals for denying the doctrine of justification by faith alone, as it was taught by the Protestant Reformers; 'calling the expression of Luther in his Commentary on the Epistle to the Galatians, and cited by Mr Irving in his sermons on the Last Days, as antinomian'.[65] Their adulteration of the full Gospel of predestination failed to offer the comfort to believers which was a main purpose of God's revealed Word. These same Evangelical clergy:

> preach justification by faith only . . . in words; but observe how it turns out in fact. They will not allow the poor sinner to take immediate assurance of his salvation, but expect of him a probation of doubt and uncertainty, of difficulty and perplexity, before they will permit him to have confidence before God . . . The people . . . as permitteth not assurance of faith from the very first and onwards, are put upon the rock and torture of inward uncertainty and fear, and led to count and rest upon the number of their inward spiritualities . . . the state of the Christian church . . . is exceedingly to be deplored . . . I warn all men to give no heed to such unsafe, uncertain, and false teaching; but to receive, through faith, the grace of God, which hath appeared unto you, bringing salvation.[66]

Nor was Drummond alone in expressing such concerns. Irving too saw the future in the darkest prospect. As early as 1825, he informed the members of the Continental Society that the English Church was far from being on the threshold of a new era of blessing, and was about to enter 'a series of thick-coming judgments and fearful perplexities' foreshadowing Christ's imminent

[64] Ibid. 115–16. [65] The *Morning Watch* (1829), 266. [66] Ibid. 644.

advent.[67] The present Gentile (New Testament) dispensation, he warned, was about to burst forth with great vitality and fill the earth with the millennial blessedness, after which the Lord would return. Post-millennial Evangelicals who believed that Christ's return would occur at some indefinite point in time, had been deluded by a false theology which deprived Christians of comfort and spiritual power:

When the great scriptural doctrine of Christ's second advent is thus removed to an indefinite distance of future time, not only is its present influence in keeping alive and awake all the fruits of the Spirit, wholly lost; but also most insufficient, and I may say, false views of the doctrine of a future state are introduced, which are attended with the most prejudicial effects upon the soul.[68]

Believers should therefore live as if Christ might return at any moment. Such a situation would endow the church (or at least its righteous remnant) with boldness and zeal to proclaim and live out its message with a new hope: the advent hope.

Having rejected mainstream Evangelicalism, some more radical pre-millennialists soon determined that a new mouthpiece was required for their movement. This came out under the title the *Morning Watch.* Financed by Drummond and edited by another Evangelical seceder, John Tudor (who in 1835 was called as an 'apostle' in the Catholic Apostolic Church), this short-lived (1829–33) quarterly was unequivocal in its condemnations of the liberalizing tendencies of the Evangelical movement and the Established Church to which it adhered. While intended to advance the views of the English prophetic movement at large, it was instead dominated by Irving's and Drummond's opposition to religious and social liberalism. In the first volume, Irving, by now embittered by the increasingly strident attacks of the Evangelicals, criticized the 'Gospel party' in no uncertain terms:

I would rather go and preach the Gospel to the most untutored of the people, to a company of wretched women in the prison, or to the sweepings of the streets, which are gathered into asylums for the night, than preach it to a congregation of men resting on their experiences and their

[67] Murray, *The Puritan Hope*, 189.

[68] Edward Irving [Juan Josafat Ben-Ezra], *The Coming of Messiah in Glory and Majesty* (1827). i. p. liv.

evidences: and therefore I hold it to be well spoken by our Lord, that these proselytes 'are more the children of hell than before' . . . they are further from the kingdom of heaven: according as it is written, 'The publicans and harlots enter into the kingdom of heaven before you.' These are solemn and awful truths which I utter; but the time is uncertain, and admitteth not of delay: the judgements are near. 'Behold, he standeth at the door.'[69]

In the same volume, Drummond rounded on the Evangelical press and clergy, and denounced their adherence to moderate forms of Calvinism. The *Christian Observer*, he argued, with its low, utilitarian tone, had sold out to the liberal obsession with change, 'reform', and 'improvement', much of which was inspired by the spirit of shopkeeping Nonconformity: 'The increasing zeal for popular instruction is mistaken for the actual progress of improvement . . . There is . . . much of ill-supported pretense, much secret infidelity, more of negligence and indifference, and a still greater abundance of sectarian pride, mixed up with all the low cunning and base rancour which the spirit of schism can inspire.'[70] In high Tory rhetoric the editors of the *Christian Observer* were denounced for favouring such schemes as the founding of the non-sectarian University of London and its liberal system of education; they were seen as being in tune with the radical, demagogic Whiggery of Lord Brougham. Evangelical clergymen, for their part, were lashed for their appalling blindness to the plain meaning of God's Word:

The Evangelical clergy have been telling the people that the Lord Jesus was not to return to this earth until after the whole world was converted; that Bibles, and tracts, and missionaries, were to convert it: they have denied that the Christian dispensation was to close in judgments, as did the Jewish; and they are utterly unable to see the finger of God in any one of the transactions now passing in Europe. The priesthood of Britain, as were the priesthood of Jerusalem, are drunk, not with wine, but with delusion; they have a moral incapacity to believe God's Word; they say that *earth* means *heaven*; that the *age to come* means *age that is past*; that the *throne of David* means *Englishmen's hearts*; that *Jews returning to their own land* means *Christians going to heaven*; with a thousand other dishonest perversions, which are proofs indisputable of disbelief—that is, of infidelity—in the plain meaning of plain words.[71]

[69] The *Morning Watch* (1829), 652–3. [70] Ibid. 244. [71] *CO* (1831), 745.

The capital charge against the *Christian Observer* however was that it had become 'deeply imbued with liberalism, which is but a modified infidelity', and thus had 'leaned much more to the infidel than to the High Church party in the country'.[72] The more conservative *Record*, on the other hand, was praised by the ultra pre-millennialists for standing firm against the rise of liberalism and infidelity, and for faithfully upholding the true principles of a Christian state and society.[73] There was thus a strong strain of enraged Toryism in this wing of the prophetic movement, fearful and reactionary. Political outrage and disillusionment fuelled the millennial sense of impending doom.

Broadsides like these must have gone some considerable way in furthering the estrangement between Albury and Clapham. Without mainstream interest, however, the prophetic movement began to be cut off from its primary source of new recruits, and each new attack in the pages of the *Christian Observer* contributed to its further isolation, increasingly detaching it from its Anglican roots and separating it from the wider Evangelical world.

II

Drummond's ecclesiology was curious and eclectic. It combined a strictly hierarchical view of social order, high Toryism, a determined Protestantism, a High Church view of the liturgy, and a belief in the pre-millennial advent of Christ. Hierarchy was a mark of an ordered society, so also was it a characteristic of the apostolic church. As the Church was part of the divinely given order, so its welfare should be the first object of the Christian king.[74] Indeed it was impossible to imagine a State existing 'without a religion of some sort being united to it'. The ordained clergyman, far from being dispensable (as was argued by some high Calvinist seceders), was elevated by Drummond as the 'one who has a right to speak with authority in the name of his Master'.[75] The catholic estimates of baptism and the Eucharist were seen by him as nearer the truth than the notion that these sacraments 'are mere signs, as held by all the Dissenters, and by most of the Church of England Evangelicals'.[76] Drummond also

[72] The *Morning Watch* (1832), 235–6. [73] Ibid. 234–7.

[74] Oliver, *Prophets and Millennialists*, 112.

[75] Henry Drummond, *Social Duties on Christian Principles* (1830), 155, 121.

[76] Drummond, *A Defence of the Students of Prophecy*, 57–8.

expressed approval of the liturgical calendar: 'the various anniversaries which were instituted by the first Christians, in commemoration of the different important events'.[77] By 1828, he urged that 'the popish practice of praying from a liturgy . . . without preaching, is nearer being a proper ceremonial for God's house, than making it a mere preaching house without prayer, as it is generally considered now.'[78] Already he foreshadowed the hierarchy of the Catholic Apostolic Church in speaking of 'ministers', 'pastors', 'bishops', and 'angels' and their functions. The timing of Drummond's pronouncements on this theme clearly document that the subsequent movement of the Catholic Apostolic Church into hierarchy and high ritualism was not an attempt to mimic Tractarianism, but an important parallel movement.[79] This development is not without a certain irony when we consider the ardent anti-popery often characteristic of elements of the English prophetic movement. The two movements differed, however, in several other important respects. Tractarians saw the true church lurking behind the corrupt Establishment, while Drummond saw it in the post-adventist church of the millennium and in the contemporary remnant which would be its nucleus. Tractarians saw salvation occurring in a church which was in, but not of, the world, while Drummond saw the church and the world as always interpenetrating. Tractarians also placed the invisible and visible church in a much closer relationship than Drummond and his followers, who, like other Evangelicals, saw the two as more distinct, often competing, bodies.[80]

Much of this teaching was set out in Drummond's influential three-volume work, *Dialogues on Prophecy* (1828–9), which also contained his views on the Church–State connection.[81] 'The Church must rise; the State and she are no longer one' was a statement repeatedly asserted.[82] The Church should be thought of as a perfect society and not dependent on the State for its continuance or prosperity. The establishment and endowment of the Church

[77] Drummond, *Dialogues on Prophecy*, i.349.

[78] Drummond, *A Defence of the Students of Prophecy*, 58.

[79] See Oliver, *Prophets and Millennialists*, 112. For a full discussion of the liturgy of the Catholic Apostolic Church see Kenneth W. Stevenson, 'The Catholic Apostolic Eucharist', Ph.D. thesis (Southampton, 1975).

[80] Oliver, *Prophets and Millennialists*, 112–13, 118.

[81] Henry Drummond, *Discourses on the True Definition of the Church* (1858).

[82] Drummond, *Dialogues on Prophecy*, iii.463.

of England 'is not an act on its part, but on the part of the kingdom who [sic] establishes it; the kingdom comes into the Church, but the Church does not go forth to take the kingdom.'[83] In this relationship, all the benefits are conferred upon the Church and all the obligations upon the State. It is, in effect, a relationship between the State and two churches: at the centre is the invisible church of the elect, and surrounding it is the visible Church of England. The State stands guard over both.[84]

While in some ways Drummond's ecclesiology resembled that expressed by John Walker and a number of other seceders, it also differed in at least two important aspects: its high Toryism and its determined adherence to Erastianism. Drummond believed that he had found in the remnant of God's true people in Britain not only true religion, but also true politics. This remnant 'reverence the vicegerent of the only King of kings'; they:

> will be found to have a place in that kingdom in this earth, which shall be under One absolute autocrat; with a Church and State inseparably united; with a Priest on a throne; where there shall be no toleration, no republicanism, no liberalism; and where those who say that the people are the only source of legitimate power, shall be held accursed; while many who have been worshipping idols set up in their own hearts, and refusing to have this Man rule over them, and trying by societies to establish a millennium without him, shall be cast out.[85]

III

The details of Edward Irving's ministry and complex pre-millennialism are far better known and can be briefly summarized.[86] In 1822, after being ordained into the Scottish Kirk, he had moved to London to take charge of the chapel in Hatton Garden. As one biographer put it, 'Byron scarcely leapt into fame with more suddenness than Irving.' Tall and handsome, authoritarian, and with a powerful gift for oratory, he possessed an intense pulpit passion which attracted large and wealthy congre-

[83] Ibid. ii.240. [84] Oliver, *Prophets and Millennialists*, 115.

[85] Drummond, *Social Duties on Christian Principles*, 160–1.

[86] See *DNB*; Oliphant, *Life of Edward Irving*; Washington Wilks, *Edward Irving: An Ecclesiastical and Literary Biography* (1854); Drummond, *Edward Irving and His Circle*; James Fleming, *The Life and Writings of the Revd Edward Irving, M.A.* (1923); H. C. Whitley, *Blinded Eagle* (1955); C. Gordon Strachan, *The Pentecostal Theology of Edward Irving* (1973); George C. Cameron, *The Scots Kirk in London* (Oxford, 1979), 107–10; Standring, *Albury and the Catholic Apostolic Church*, 52–4.

gations.[87] Yet, despite Irving's considerable natural talent, all was not well. Thomas De Quincey, who regarded him as 'unquestionably, by many, many degrees, the greatest orator of our times', noted with alarm his melancholy and predicted that he would end his days in an lunatic asylum.[88] Henry Brougham, a harsh judge of religious figures, confided to Zachary Macaulay that he had heard Irving 'with no admiration', and had read him 'with very much less'. Though he 'shows very considerable powers', he is 'so long—so affected, and often so extravagant, and his taste is so very bad, and his doctrine (his new kind of purgatory for instance) so odd—that I cool down to temperate, if not below'.[89] Though temperamentally more disposed to Irving's evangelicalism, Macaulay too was unimpressed. In a letter to Hannah More, he ridiculed Irving for his 'miserable taste' and his 'uncouthness and rudeness'.[90] In some ways, Irving was temperamentally unsuited to public life, his sudden rise to fame reinforcing his own sense of prophetic status and authority fanned by his large entourage of flatterers and fanatics—including Drummond, who had an extraordinary capacity to spot new religious talent and associate with it.

The first encounter between the two men had occurred in November 1825, while Drummond was chairing a meeting at J. H. Evans's John Street Baptist Chapel.[91] At first, Irving was unimpressed by Drummond and quickly dismissed the eccentric politician as shallow and superficial. 'Henry Drummond was in the chair,' he remarked, 'he is in all chairs—I fear for him. His words are more witty than spiritual; his manner is *spiritual*, not grave.'[92] Unperturbed by Irving's initial coolness, Drummond aggressively pursued the popular evangelist, especially after he began preaching on the 'Second Advent' during the following month.[93] Before long, according to Carlyle, Irving's earlier reservations about Drummond begin to yield, and their occasional encounters soon developed into a close association, strengthened

[87] Stewart J. Brown, *Thomas Chalmers and the Godly Commonwealth in Scotland* (Oxford, 1982), 214. Fleming, *Life of Edward Irving.*

[88] Quoted in A. J. A. Symons, *Essays and Biographies* (1969), 63–4.

[89] Brougham to Macaulay, 1823, quoted in Margaret Jean Holland (ed.), *Life and Letters of Zachary Macaulay* (1900), 389.

[90] Macaulay to More, 8 Sept. 1823, quoted ibid. 390.

[91] Built for Evans by Drummond in the aftermath of the Western Schism.

[92] Entry of 21 Nov. 1825, in Oliphant, *Life of Edward Irving*, 176.

[93] Drummond, *Edward Irving and His Circle*, 127; Murray, *The Puritan Hope*, 189.

by their mutual involvement in the Continental Society.[94] In the following year Drummond was instrumental in introducing Irving to the theological works of the Chilean Jesuit, Lacunza—an event of considerable significance to the progress of the English prophetic movement.[95]

Lacunza's notable apocalyptic work, *The Coming of the Messiah in Glory and Majesty*, had an extraordinary impact on the religious world, Protestant as well as Catholic, English as well as European.[96] By reading it, Irving's interest in the study of biblical prophecy was deepened considerably.[97] He was, in fact, so impressed by Lacunza's work that, despite his lack of fluent Spanish, he quickly resolved to pursue the subject in depth and translate Lacunza's essay into English. This he did, bringing it successfully to publication in 1827.[98]

In tandem with Irving's interest in the area of unfulfilled biblical prophecy was his growing opposition to the political and religious reforms of the day. During the debate over the repeal of the Test and Corporation Acts, he joined Drummond in writing an impassioned plea to the King, urging him not to assent to any plan which would undermine the cause of national Christianity.[99] The passage of such an act, he argued, would open offices of trust, magistracy, judgment, and legislation to men 'who profess no faith in God, nor in the Lord Jesus Christ, by whom Kings reign, and princes decree justice'. Irving became so alarmed by the prospect of repeal that he went on to claim that the King, by granting his assent, would 'sign away the charter of his kingdom' as a Christian nation.[100]

In 1829, moved by the even more threatening attack on the

[94] Wilks, *Edward Irving*, 186.

[95] Lacunza left for Italy when the Jesuits were expelled from Chile in 1767. His work on prophecy was circulated in manuscript form under the pen name Juan Josafat Ben-Ezra, and was only published after his death. Irving read a Spanish copy of the published work. See Lively, 'The Catholic Apostolic Church', 61.

[96] Juan Josafat Ben-Ezra [Manuel Lacunza Y Diaz], *Venida del Mesias en gloria y majestad* (Mexico, 1825).

[97] As well as through recent contact with Samuel Taylor Coleridge and James Hatley Frere. See. Oliphant, *Life of Edward Irving*, 104–5; Oliver, *Prophets and Millennialists*, 99, 106–7; Sandeen, *The Roots of Fundamentalism*, 16.

[98] Irving [Ezra], *The Coming of Messiah in Glory and Majesty*.

[99] Edward Irving, *A Letter to the King, On the Repeal of the Test and Corporation Laws* (1828).

[100] Ibid. 3–4.

established order represented by Catholic Emancipation, Irving published a lengthy account of the relationship between Church and State.[101] Once again, he saw political change as an irreparable breach in the old British constitution, all but destroying its standing as a Christian nation. He called desperately for action by the monarch to bring about the divine appointment of those 'lieutenants of God' (as he referred to Anglican politicians), who reigned in order not merely to uphold civil policy, but to maintain true religion, and to suppress idolatry and superstition. Though these 'lieutenants' were to 'keep to that place and might not usurp anything that pertains . . . to the offices that are merely ecclesiastical . . . or any part of the power of the spiritual keys, which our Master gave to the apostles, and to their true successors', Irving's expectations for them were very high. In his view, the magistrate:

> Hath authority, and it is his duty to take order, that unity and peace be preserved in the Church; that the truth of God be kept pure and entire; that all blasphemies and heresies be suppressed; all corruptions and abuses in worship and discipline prevented or reformed; and all the ordinances of God duly settled and ministered, and observed.[102]

He dismissed as sheer heresy the notion of 'the modern innovations of schismatics and politicians' that the magistrate obtains his power from the people, and not from God. So too he objected to any call for the disestablishment of the Church. The mischief of liberal innovations was that 'they look upon the people as if they were not Christ's' and 'upon Christ as if he were not the Prince of the kings of the earth', and 'thus they are guilty of the most deadly schism, in separating the government of nations from the government of Christ'.[103] The connection between Church and State, he concluded:

> is necessary for the well being of both . . . a mutual acknowledgment . . . of the common stem out of which they grow. For the State to establish the Church, is an act of homage unto Christ; for the Church to be Established, and to help the State with its instruction, prayer, and faith,

[101] Edward Irving, *The Church and State Responsible to Christ, And to One Another* (1829). See also *The Last Days* (1828) in which Irving called for a revival of the Puritan doctrine of a covenant people bound to Christ and submitted to His authority in all things.

[102] Ibid. v.

[103] Ibid. vi.

is an act of dutifulness unto the magistrate, and unto Christ whom he represents. It is not, therefore, a matter of convenience nor of expediency, but a matter of absolute and peremptory duty.[104]

IV

Irving's speculative interest in unfulfilled biblical prophecy was advanced through his involvement in the London Society for Promoting Christianity Amongst the Jews.[105] The Jew Society, as it became known, had been founded primarily by Protestant Dissenters in 1809; six years later, however, it became an exclusively Anglican institution. Despite the provision that membership be restricted to members of the Church of England,[106] both Sir Thomas Baring (who was elected President in 1815) and Henry Drummond (who was elected Vice-President in 1823) continued to adhere to the Jew Society after the outbreak of the Western Schism.[107]

Preaching to the Society in May 1826, Hugh McNeile drew the parallel between the interests of the prophetic movement and those connected with the conversion of the Jews.[108] During the following summer, Lewis Way and Irving, together with James Hatley Frere, the prominent writer on prophecy, formed the Society for the Investigation of Prophecy which began occasionally to meet in London to study the issue of the immediate fulfillment of prophecy.[109] To these gatherings Way invited numerous members of the Jew Society, including Drummond. Finding London too noisy and distracting for the quiet, speculative study required, the meetings were soon transferred—at Drummond's suggestion—to his spacious country home at Albury, where the relationship between unfulfilled prophecy and the restoration of the Jews to their homeland was hotly debated. To advance the

[104] Ibid. 567.

[105] H. H. Norris, *The Origin, Progress and Existing Circumstances of the London Society for Promoting Christianity Amongst the Jews* (1825); W. T. Gindey, *The History of the London Society for Promoting Christianity amongst the Jews* (1908); Sandeen, *The Roots of Fundamentalism*, 9–12; Wilks, *Edward Irving*, 187. See also 'The Christian Dispensation Miraculous', in the *Jewish Expositor* (Feb. 1831).

[106] See Ford K. Brown, *Fathers of the Victorians* (Cambridge, 1961), 342.

[107] See Sarah Kochav, 'Britain and the Holy Land: Prophecy, the Evangelical Movement, and the Conversion and Restoration of the Jews 1790–1845', D.Phil. thesis (Oxford, 1989), 63, 70, 160; Brown, *Fathers of the Victorians*, 356, 360; Oliphant, *Life of Edward Irving*, 372–3; Froom, *The Prophetic Faith of Our Fathers*, iii.416, 428.

[108] Hugh McNeile, *A Sermon* (1826).

[109] See Lively, 'The Catholic Apostolic Church', 49.

investigation, Way suggested that Drummond convene a formal conference to study the subject of prophecy in greater depth.[110] Never one to hesitate in matters of religion or politics, Drummond immediately set about organizing the first of the so-called Albury conferences, which was held during November 1826.[111]

Drummond intended the first conference to be a pan-evangelical affair involving both clergy and laymen. Invitations were sent to many prominent evangelicals throughout England, Scotland, and Ireland, with attendance varying at any one time between forty to forty-four. The conference was remarkably diverse. It included Anglicans, Independents, Presbyterians, Methodists, and Moravians, drawn from widely differing professions. Clergy outnumbered laity two to one, and Anglicans formed about two-thirds of those present.[112] Those attending included (in addition to Drummond and Irving) William Cuninghame, the author of prophetic works, Alexander Haldane, the editor of the *Record*; Lord Manville (later sixth Duke of Manchester), William Marsh, the incumbent of St. Peter's, Colchester and associate of Charles Simeon, Daniel Wilson, the future Bishop of Calcutta, and Joseph Wolff, the itinerant traveller and evangelist. Hugh McNeile, in his capacity as rector of Albury, chaired the conference.[113] Both William Wilberforce and Thomas Chalmers received invitations, but declined (or were unable) to attend.[114]

The first Albury conference lasted eight days. It had a demanding agenda. At eight in the morning the group assembled to listen to a discussion paper, taking notes but making no comments; at nine, breakfast was served; at eleven, each in turn then offered his views on the subject opened earlier in the day while the rest took notes. No appeal, save to the text of Scripture, was allowed: doubtful interpretations were referred to Joseph Wolff, the learned Hebraist. After four to five hours, dinner was served. At seven, the subject was resumed, and a general discussion of the difficulties permitted; at eleven, hymns and prayers were organized.[115]

110 Edward Miller, *The History and Doctrines of Irvingism* (1878), i.36.

111 Ibid. i.36–7; Davenport, *Albury Apostles*, 21–8.

112 See Columba Flegg, *'Gathered Under Apostles'* (Oxford, 1992), 36; Drummond, *Edward Irving and His Circle*, 133; Davenport, *Albury Apostles*, 22–3.

113 For a complete list of those attending see Flegg, *'Gathered Under Apostles'*, 37–8.

114 Miller, *The History and Doctrines of Irvingism*, i.44.

115 See Symons, *Essays and Biographies*, 62.

During the course of the first conference, seven principal topics were examined.[116] Extensive notes of the discussions were kept by Drummond as secretary, and published by Irving in his *Preliminary Discourse to the Work of Ben Ezra* (1827). Drummond also produced an account of the proceedings of the conference, in which he listed six major points of biblical chronology on which there had been complete unanimity:

1. That the present Christian dispensation is to be 'terminated by judgments' ending in the destruction of the visible church and polity.
2. That during the time of these judgments, the Jews will be restored to the Holy Land.
3. These judgments will fall primarily, if not exclusively, upon Christendom, especially on 'that part of the Church of God which has been most highly favoured, and is therefore most deeply responsible' (e.g. Protestant Evangelicals).
4. The termination of these judgments is to be succeeded by the Millennium, 'a period of universal blessedness'.
5. The second advent of the Messiah will either precede, or take place at, the commencement of the Millennium.
6. That a great period of 1260 years commenced in the reign of Justinian, and terminated at the French Revolution; and that the vials of the Apocalypse began then to be poured out.[117]

Though Drummond gave a favourable account of the proceedings, disagreements within the prophetic 'parliament' quickly began to surface. By mid-1827, for example, Drummond reported that 'some of the people [who had attended] last year had not been very faithful' to the teachings of the movement, and he consulted with Irving in order carefully to organize the invitations to the second conference.[118] These differences continued to multiply as the declarations of subsequent conferences became less restrained;

[116] Including the doctrine of the Holy Spirit concerning the time of the Gentiles; the duties of Christian ministers and laymen connected with this; the present and future condition of the Jews, and the Christian duty towards them; the prophetic visions and numbers of Daniel and the Apocalypse; the doctrine concerning the future advent of Christ, and the duties of the church and world arising from it. See Edward Miller, *The History and Doctrines of Irvingism*, i.37–8.

[117] Drummond, *Dialogues on Prophecy*, iii. pp. ii–iii. This provided a record of the first four Albury conferences.

[118] Davenport, *Albury Apostles*, 25.

before long, the divisions within the English prophetic movement were so great as to open up a major three-way schism.[119]

Five separate Albury conferences were held between 1826 and 1830.[120] During the second conference, attendance reached its highest level, while in each subsequent year, as the prophetic speculations became more and more extreme, and perhaps as London's fashionable society began to lose interest in the issue of biblical prophecy, numbers steadily declined. But then, in the spring of 1830, reports reached London of the outbreak of miraculous healings and other related spiritual phenomena in the west of Scotland. To consider these sensational reports the final conference was delayed until July, in response to an emergency summons.[121] After the fifth conference, Drummond and Irving determined that the conferences had outlived their purpose, and that the debate over biblical prophecy should now centre on the National Scots Church, Regent Square, where Irving served as minister.[122]

V

Tragically, while Irving was plunging into prophetic speculation he was also being drawn into another even more dangerous exegetical mire, that of Trinitarian theology. His alleged deviation from orthodoxy on this sensitive topic eventually resulted in his deposition from the ministry of the Church of Scotland.[123] The causes of this breach were complex and problematic, extending over several years. The catalyst for the break seems to have lain in a sermon Irving preached before a society concerned with the distribution of Gospel tracts in 1827. According to Irving's

[119] In 1832, McNeile attempted to differentiate the three distinct positions in terms of divergent views of the 'gifts': 1. The 'gifts' had been bestowed upon the primitive church only because its infant state required extraordinary assistance; however, as it grew and gained comparative security, God weaned the church by degree from such 'miraculous' aids. 2. Both the *manifestations* and the *characteristics* of the Spirit are the inheritance of the church. There can be no church without the Holy Ghost dwelling within it. 3. There is, at this time, a visible revival of at least two of the 'miraculous gifts'—speaking in tongues, and prophesying. See Hugh McNeile, *Miracles and Spiritual Gifts* (1832), pp. x–xi.

[120] See Whitley, *Blinded Eagle*, 41.

[121] Davenport, *Albury Apostles*, 27.

[122] This lofty Gothic structure, designed by William Tite, had been built for the Presbyterians between 1824 and 1825.

[123] Strachan, *The Pentecostal Theology of Edward Irving*, 13.

biographer, Mrs Oliphant, some of those present believed that, during this address, he claimed that the human nature of Christ was 'identical with all human nature'.[124] This accusation was immediately picked up by one Henry Cole, who undertook publicly to expose Irving's heresy. After an evening service at Irving's church, Cole confronted the exhausted preacher and accused him of maintaining unorthodox views on Christology. Receiving what he considered an unsatisfactory reply, he published a scathing attack on Irving, accusing him of promoting false and dangerous teachings on the Trinity.[125]

Characteristically, Irving ignored Cole's accusations. Given his accuser's dogged persistence, however, this tactic did little good. To make matters worse, during a tour of Scotland in the following year Irving called upon John Macleod Campbell, who was himself about to be tried by the Kirk on charges of heresy.[126] Reports of this meeting soon began to circulate within Scotland's tight-knit religious community, feeding the growing sense of suspicion about Irving's theological 'soundness'. By the time his sermons on the Trinity were finally published in late 1828,[127] polite whispers had been transformed into open speculation.[128] Irving's publication of a work on the nature of Christ, two years later, did little to redeem his tarnished reputation.[129]

Although enthusiastically defended in print by Drummond, Irving quickly found himself embroiled in a controversy within his own spiritual constituency. In December 1830 the Scots Presbytery of London (under whose jurisdiction Irving, as minister of the National Scots Church, served) initiated action against him on the ground that he taught that Christ had been a sinner. Irving responded by simply withdrawing himself and his church from

[124] Oliphant, *Life of Edward Irving*, 220–1.

[125] Henry Cole, *A Letter to the Revd Edward Irving* (1827).

[126] Brown, *Thomas Chalmers*, 214–15.

[127] Edward Irving, 'Sermons, Lectures and Occasional Discourses', in *The Doctrine of the Incarnation Opened in Six Sermons* (1828).

[128] See James Alexander Haldane, *A Refutation of the Heretical Doctrine Promulgated by the Revd Edward Irving* (Edinburgh, 1828); Henry Drummond [Layman], *Candid Examination of the Controversy Between Messrs Irving, A. Thomson, and J. Haldane* (1829); James Alexander Haldane, *Answer to Mr Henry Drummond's Defence of the Heretical Doctrine Promulgated by Mr Irving* (Edinburgh, 1830); Henry Drummond [Layman], *Supplement to the Candid Examination of the Controversy* (1830); James Alexander Haldane, *Reply to Mr Henry Drummond's Supplement to the Candid Examination* (Edinburgh, 1830).

[129] Edward Irving, *The Orthodox and Catholic Doctrine of Our Lord's Human Nature* (1830).

the jurisdiction of the London Presbytery, and the case died a quiet death.

Outbreaks of the 'miraculous gifts' then began to occur, first at Rosneath, Dumbartonshire, then at a private residence in London (discussed below), and finally, on 30 October 1831, within the vestry at Regent Square.[130] On the following Sunday—and with Irving's tacit approval—outbursts of tongues and prophecy repeatedly interrupted public worship. When Irving refused to suppress these 'gifts' at the insistence of the trustees, a split quickly developed in the congregation.

A formal complaint against Irving was then filed by the trustees with the Presbytery of London. The Presbytery responded by offering to proceed against Irving if, in turn, the trustees would once again submit to the authority of the Presbytery and concur in its previous condemnation of Irving on Trinitarian grounds. This scheme was warmly received by the trustees, who were now anxious to rid themselves of both Irving and the alarmingly 'enthusiastic' pentecostalism now burgeoning in Regent Square.

Irving's trial before the London Presbytery opened in late April 1832. He was quickly condemned and locked out of his church. The General Assembly of the Church of Scotland then took action against him on the grounds of Christological heresy, and, in the following March, he was found guilty by the Presbytery of Annan and deposed from the ministry of the Kirk.[131] He then gathered the remainder of his followers, which now numbered about eight-hundred, into a new body, which would later become known as the Catholic Apostolic Church.[132]

At first Irving's followers were compelled to gather in a small, dilapidated room in Gray's Inn Road, occupied at other times of the week by none other than the dreaded Socialist Robert Owen.[133] After months of humiliating cohabitation, Irving secured a house in Newman Street with a picture gallery large enough to assemble his entire following. The room was fitted up with pews and galleries in traditional form, though at the front he built a large platform capable of containing some fifty people. On its various levels were seats for (in descending order) the six 'elders'

[130] Strachan, *The Pentecostal Theology of Edward Irving*, 13.
[131] Ibid. 14. [132] *DNB*. [133] Oliphant, *Life of Edward Irving*, 369.

and the 'angel', the seven 'prophets', and the seven 'deacons'. The 'angel', or chief pastor (Irving, who had been ordained to the position on 5 April 1833), ordered the service, while the preaching and expounding was generally performed by the 'elders' in order. The 'prophets' spoke as utterances came upon them.[134] At a prayer meeting held at Albury on 7 November 1832, as Irving was praying for an outpouring of the Holy Spirit, there came a word of prophecy announcing that God had called John Bate Cardale as the first 'apostle' in the church and to convey the sacrament of holy unction. Drummond spoke at the meeting with great power through the Spirit, addressing Cardale with the exclamation 'convey it, convey it, for art not thou an apostle of the Lord?'[135] On 25 September 1833, Drummond was also called as an 'apostle' in the new body.[136] Before long, separate but dependent congregations were being formed by two evangelical clerical seceders from the Church of England: the Irishman Nicholas Armstrong, and Henry John Owen of Park Chapel, Chelsea.[137] Yet another body was organized by J. L. Miller, minister of Bishopsgate Independent Chapel.[138] Tragically, Irving did not survive to act out the final scene of this remarkable drama, dying of consumption in December 1834.[139] Whether he continued in his assurance that the 'gifts' had truly returned remains an open question.[140] After his death, the administrative centre of the Catholic Apostolic Church was quickly transferred from London to Albury, where Drummond financed the construction of a new cathedral and chapter house for its exclusive use. To Cardale fell the task of developing the new church's liturgical and devotional life by creative borrowing from ancient liturgies (mostly Orthodox), blending the 'Catholic' and 'Apostolic' strains in the new body.[141]

[134] Ibid. 381–2; Standring, *Albury and the Catholic Apostolic Church*, 26.

[135] Ibid. 24.

[136] Ibid. 11. Drummond (*Edward Irving and His Circle*, 232), wrongly begins Drummond's 'apostleship' in 1832. Ordination was vested solely in the 'apostles'; however, as the last 'apostle' died in 1901, the perpetuation of the ministry of the church became impossible.

[137] See Drummond, *Edward Irving and His Circle*, 231; Oliphant, *Life of Edward Irving*, 371; *Fraser's Magazine* (1837), 196. Armstrong was called as an 'apostle' on 18 Jan. 1834.

[138] Drummond, *Edward Irving and His Circle*, 231.

[139] Strachan, *The Pentecostal Theology of Edward Irving*, 14.

[140] Lively, 'The Catholic Apostolic Church', 74–7, offers a discussion on this point.

[141] See J. Lancaster, 'John Bate Cardale, Pillar of Apostles: A Quest for Catholicity', B.Phil. thesis (St. Andrews, 1978); T. C. F. Stunt, 'John Bate Cardale', in *New DNB*; John Bate Cardale, *Readings Upon the Liturgy and Other Divine Offices of the Church* (1848–78).

VI

Divisions on the issue of prophecy and the return of the miraculous 'gifts' created one of the most bitter and far-reaching conflicts affecting the Anglican Evangelical clergy during the late 1820s and early 1830s, sharply changing the ethos of the party.[142] Prominent figures offered differing interpretations of the controversy. Edward Bickersteth, one of the most respected English Evangelicals of his generation and a major figure in the prophetic movement, took a moderate position on the question of the return of the 'gifts'.[143] Early in his ministry he had accepted the standard post-millennialist line, looking forward to the gradual conversion of the world by the spread of missions and a larger blessing of the ordinary means of grace.[144] His gradual shift to a pre-millennialist position no doubt paralleled that of many other Evangelicals. In about 1814 he became interested in the conversion of the Jews, possibly through the influence of the Scottish layman William Cuninghame of Lainshaw.[145] His first work on prophecy, which advanced a post-millennialist position, was published in 1824.[146] Four years later, deeply shaken by the imminent passage of Catholic Emancipation, he remarked that 'we have displeased God, and may expect tokens of his displeasure.' In 1830, horrified by the Bristol riots, he concluded that 'the Lord is shaking these kingdoms.'[147] His certitude about the continuous improvement of the world was rapidly diminishing. At the same time, he remained anxious lest the issue of prophecy should begin to dominate the minds of immature and impressionable believers. As he wrote while travelling in England in March 1828: 'I find the prophetic question doing injury to some. Men get full of their own views, and press them as all-essential, and speak as positively as if futurity were as open to them as what is past; and then others publicly speak against them; and so the dividing spirit of the age increases and spreads.'[148] Three years later, writing to his wife

[142] See W. J. C. Ervine, 'Doctrine and Diplomacy: Some Aspects of the Life and Thought of the Anglican Evangelical Clergy, 1797–1837', Ph.D. thesis (Cambridge, 1979), 277.

[143] T. R. Birks (ed.), *Memoir of the Revd Edward Bickersteth, Late Rector of Watton, Herts.*, 2nd edn. (1852), ii.44.

[144] Ibid. i.42.

[145] Oliver, *Prophets and Millennialists*, 90.

[146] Edward Bickersteth, *Practical Remarks on Prophecies* (1824).

[147] Birks, *Memoir of Edward Bickersteth*, i.421; ii.17.

[148] Ibid. i.420–1.

from the Midlands about the subject of missions, Bickersteth expressed similar anxiety: 'Things are in a most dead and cold state here . . . The good men are all afloat on prophesying and the immediate work of the Lord is disregarded for the uncertain future. These things ought not to be so. But I think any one who has known this place for the last seven or eight years might have foreboded all we now see.'[149]

Bickersteth's own personal views were nevertheless moving closer to pre-millennialism. When the outbreak of 'tongues' occurred in Irving's Regent Square congregation, he attended a service to witness the spectacle for himself. 'It did not appear to me', he regretfully remarked, 'as a real work of the Spirit. I was depressed by it, as a delusion on the minds of eminent Christians.'[150] In August of that year he preached four sermons on the subject of prophecy which were quickly published; with some precision, these document his move to a pre-millennialist position.[151] Later, the fourth edition of his *Practical Remarks on Prophecy* (1835), was revised in favour of the pre-millennialist argument. Other publications followed, written in an attempt to 'quiet the minds of those Christians who were in danger of forsaking plain and immediate duties for the path of thorny and doubtful speculation'.[152] Despite his prominence in many areas of Evangelical endeavour, Bickersteth remained on the fringes of the prophetic movement. Though still fearful of the political future, he did not entirely abandon his sense of spiritual optimism or his long-standing interest in foreign missions. In this way, he was representative of most Evangelical pre-millennialists.

As the course of the prophetic movement became increasingly eccentric, Hugh McNeile, too, found himself precariously placed between his loyalty to his patron and his doubts over the direction of Drummond's theology. In two earlier publications, *The Times of the Gentiles* (1828) and *Popular Lectures on the Prophecies Relative to the Jewish Nation* (delivered, 1827; published, 1830), McNeile had

[149] Ibid. ii.43.

[150] Edward Bickersteth, journal entry for 1 Apr. 1832, ibid. ii.27.

[151] Edward Bickersteth, *Preparedness for the Day of Christ Urged on all Christians* (1833).

[152] Birks, *Memoir of Edward Bickersteth*, ii.43. Edward Bickersteth, *Practical Remarks on the Prophecies* (1824); 'Practical Remarks on the Prophecies', in *A Scripture Help*, 12th edn. (1825); 'The Coming of Christ', in *The Book of Private Devotions* (1839).

adopted a line close to the arguments of the Albury set, of which he was a member. It appears also that he continued to chair the Albury conferences until their discontinuance in 1830. Nevertheless, doubts remained. Towards the end of 1830, McNeile began to oppose Drummond's efforts to organize private prayer meetings at Albury, for McNeile would not suffer laymen to pray publicly in his presence.[153] When he expressed unease over the direction of the prophetic movement, Drummond urged him to seek personal experience of the 'gifts' and judge them for himself. Though McNeile at first concurred, over time this merely added to his growing sense of disquiet. So too did Drummond's prayer meetings at his home, which McNeile attended reluctantly. When a woman spoke in an unknown tongue on one occasion, McNeile quickly objected: it was not of God, he insisted, for it contradicted the biblical injunction against women teaching in church.[154] For a time, at least, McNeile maintained in public the Albury 'party line' on the question of 'gifts'. In March 1831, for example, he wrote to the *Christian Observer* defending their reappearance. 'The miraculous gifts of healing and speaking in unknown tongues', he claimed, 'are a regular part of the Christian dispensation, and . . . nothing but our want of faith prevents our using them.' Any position contradicting this would 'render the Epistles useless to us.' But he introduced a note of caution. Although the 'gifts' have been in the church 'in some measure . . . neither the one nor the other are or have been in the church according to the full dimensions of the Apostolical description'.[155] Before long, McNeile began to develop serious doubts about this too, and said so publicly. Drummond was then compelled to comment on the growing rift with his friend: 'We merely stand as representatives of two classes of an opinion, each thinks he is right and the appearance of The Lord Jesus Christ will alone determine who is.'[156] Before long, Drummond's decision to secede once again from the Church dealt a fatal blow to their relationship.

[153] Davenport, *Albury Apostles*, 70. See also Casbard, 'Henry Drummond of Albury', 7. Mrs Harriet Wall had organized similar meetings in the same house during the early phase of the Western Schism. See Chapter 4.

[154] Ibid. He equated Drummond's home with the church.

[155] *CO* (Mar. 1831), 154.

[156] Quoted in Casbard, 'Henry Drummond of Albury', 8.

Later, Drummond explained the circumstances surrounding his second secession. In March 1832, shortly before the expulsion of Irving from Regent Square, Drummond had visited London in a determined state of mind:

The situation was not one which admitted of half-measures; if I believed that the Holy Ghost was now speaking in the church, I must also believe that all who openly rejected Him were in fatal error. I had been in treaty for the purchase of a pew in Trinity Church, Chelsea; but finding that the minister there preached against the work of the Holy Spirit, I withdrew from it. I then saw the use, or rather the necessity, of the voice of the Spirit, and the Lord's object in sending it—namely, for the building up of a church in holiness, in order to be prepared to meet Him whose speedy appearance we had all at Albury unanimously professed to accept.[157]

The obvious course was to unite with Irving and his cause at Regent Square. Perhaps because he considered the Presbyterian Irving's claims to the apostolic ministry to be invalid, or perhaps because of his own independent nature, Drummond rejected this idea, albeit temporarily. Before returning to Albury in July 1832, he wrote to McNeile (now preaching publicly at Albury against the 'gifts') to tell him how much he regretted that it was impossible for him to remain in the Church of England 'if he [McNeile] persisted in preaching against the work of the Lord and against all who believed in it'. Though Drummond 'valued the ordinances of a Christian Church', and was aware of the spiritual danger he incurred in abstaining himself from them, he could not attend a place of worship where 'the work of the Holy Spirit [was being] attacked'.[158] Their exchanges were marked by a sense of 'kindness and courtesy', but the breach between the two was complete. Some twenty members of the Albury congregation were persuaded to secede with Drummond, to meet at his home on Sundays, and to pray for the gifts of the Spirit.[159] They continued to use the Anglican liturgy, but with special prayers added.[160] On 29 July 1831, Drummond was called as a 'pastor' to the group. Before long, faced with an increasing number of adherents drawn from both Anglican and Methodist circles, the group began to pray for a sympathetic priest who would relieve them from their

[157] Davenport, *Albury Apostles*, 71. [158] Ibid. 72. [159] Ibid.

[160] Standring, *Albury and the Catholic Apostolic Church*, 34.

virtual self-excommunication from the sacrament of holy communion. These prayers were answered on 26 December 1832, when it was revealed, prophetically, that Drummond was to be ordained by Cardale (the first 'apostle') as an 'angel', or 'bishop'.[161] In this way, the blossoming Catholic Apostolic Church was first given episcopal organization at Albury, albeit without apostolic succession.

Some time during 1832, McNeile abandoned the English prophetic movement altogether. This break was finalized with the publication of a volume of impassioned letters to his friend Spencer Perceval, urging him not to secede from the Establishment.[162] Having been so close to the movement in its early phase, he reckoned himself highly qualified to pronounce judgement on it. Of Drummond and Irving, he warned that these were men whose teachings had 'perverted religion':

> Filled with admiration of the predicted holiness and beauty of the *perfected* Church of Christ, at the second advent of her Lord, and looking at this truth alone, to the neglect of present duties arising out of other portions of holy Scripture [they] have become impatient of human infirmity, and determined to have a holy company even now. Forgetful of what manner of spirit they are themselves, they have hastily seceded from the militant and imperfect Church in which they were baptized, gone into diverse excesses of extravagant excitement, and denounced all who will not go with them.[163]

After his resignation from Albury in June 1834,[164] McNeile went on to enjoy a distinguished career in the Church. As perpetual curate at St. Jude's, Liverpool, he became a figure of national importance as champion of militant Protestantism and (as we have seen) as a vociferous defender of the Anglican Establishment.[165] In 1845, the Archbishop of Canterbury conferred upon him a stall at Chester Cathedral, where he became a canon residentiary in 1860. Eight years later he was appointed Dean of Ripon.

[161] Ibid. 26, 33–4; Davenport, *Albury Apostles*, 80.

[162] Hugh McNeile, *Letters to a Friend* (1834). These were written in 1833; Perceval was called as an 'apostle' on 14 Dec. 1833.

[163] Ibid., pp. ix–x.

[164] MSS PSH/ALB/2/2; PSH/ALB/3/1, Surrey Record Centre.

[165] See Chapter 1.

Another well-known Evangelical whose interest in the conversion of the Jews coincided with his interest in the study of prophecy was William Marsh.[166] In 1829, possibly uneasy over some aspect of the Albury conferences, he convened his own annual gatherings at his home in Colchester, attracting clergy and laymen from all parts of the country. Similar meetings for the study of prophecy, probably under Marsh's initiative, were held in Oxford, Plymouth, and Bristol.[167] When Marsh took up the incumbency of St. Thomas's, Birmingham, later that same year, he acquired the famous sobriquet 'Millennial Marsh'. His commitment to the English prophetic movement, however, was relatively short-lived. By 1834, his alarm at the wayward odysseys of Drummond and Irving turned into hostility, and he began to condemn the miraculous appearance of the 'gifts' as a 'plausible delusion'.[168] Eventually, he published his own views which pursued a moderate line between the various extremes.[169]

Among the most unyielding Evangelical opponents of the Irving circle was Baptist Noel, the influential minister of St. John's Chapel, Bedford Row, London. Noel remained a keen post-millennialist, despite the contrary position taken by his elder brother, Gerard, well-known in the 'Gospel world' as an ardent pre-millennialist. A Whiggish reformer and protagonist of city missions, Noel worked intensively for the improvement of society as it existed. His encounter with the prophetic movement in its extreme form was accentuated in the spring of 1831 by his clash with John Bate Cardale, a long-standing member of St. John's and a prominent London lawyer, with offices across Bedford Row from the chapel.[170]

In about 1830, Cardale developed a keen interest in the study of prophecy which took him, in September of that year, to Scotland to examine the reports of an outbreak of tongues.[171] He returned convinced of their authenticity. He then opened his home for weekly prayer meetings, where an 'outpouring of the spirit' could occur, and in April 1831 his wife began speaking in

[166] C. Marsh, *The Life of the Revd William Marsh*, 6th edn. (1867), 91.

[167] Ibid. 139. [168] Ibid. 184–5.

[169] William Marsh, *A Few Plain Thoughts on Prophecy* (Colchester, 1840); *Passages from Letters by a Clergyman on Jewish, Prophetical and Scriptural Subjects* (1845).

[170] See Stunt, 'John Bate Cardale'.

[171] A detailed account of the case of Miss Fancourt appeared in the *CO* (Nov. 1830), 708–18.

tongues.[172] Noel was quickly summoned to sanction the 'miracle', but declined the offer and instead began to denounce the utterances from his pulpit.[173] Soon afterwards, he published a thinly veiled attack on Irving, denouncing both pre-millennialism and predictions of Christ's imminent advent.[174]

Noel was not alone among prominent Evangelicals in condemning the Albury circle.[175] Charles Simeon was equally anxious to distance himself and his party from the excesses of Irvingism. The brunt of his attack fell—like so many previous attacks on Evangelical seceders—on the doctrinal volatility of those infected by the 'prophetic fever'. In Simeon's opinion, the speculators were 'brain-sick enthusiasts' intent on diverting Christians away from more important biblical truths and from the propagation of 'vital religion'.[176] 'I do not say they are not holy men,' he remarked in one of his famous Cambridge conversation parties, 'but I say that none of them have grown in religion since they entered upon these views; nay, that just in proportion as they have followed these millenarian views, they have been losing the lowly, subdued humility and tenderness of spirit which they had before.'[177] In February 1830, he complained that the millennial craze was one 'in which no two of its advocates agree, and which, as adding to the honour of God, or the happiness of the redeemed, does not weigh so much as the mere dust upon the balance'. It fills believers 'only with vain conceits, intoxicates the imagination, alienates the brethren from each other, and, *by being unduly urged upon the minds of humble Christians*, is doing the devil's work by wholesale'.[178] Later, he added:

My complaint is, not that they study prophecy, to whatever it may relate; but, that they give it an undue measure of their attention, (making all the wonders of redemption itself almost secondary to their views of Christ's personal reign on earth), and that they press this their favourite

[172] Standring, *Albury and the Catholic Apostolic Church*, 24; *DNB*.

[173] Ibid. W. H. B. Proby, *Annals of the 'Low Church' Party in England* (1888) i.337.

[174] B. W. Noel, *Remarks on the Revival of Miraculous Powers in the Church* (1831). See also Thomas Boys, *The Suppressed Evidence* (1832).

[175] See also Anon., *Modern Fanaticism Unveiled* (1831); Anon., *Try the Spirits* (1831).

[176] Proby, *Annals of the 'Low Church' Party in England*, i.338.

[177] Abner William Brown, *Recollections of the Conversation Parties of the Revd Charles Simeon, M.A.* (1863), 316.

[178] Letter of 19 Feb. 1830, in William Carus, *Memoirs of the Life of the Revd Charles Simeon, M.A.*, 3rd edn. (1848), 460.

subject with an undue zeal upon the attention of the religious public; making (as Mr D. has done) a love to all the great principles of the Gospel no better than *idolatry* in comparison of it, and *declaring the reception of their views essential to the salvation of the soul.*[179]

The *Christian Observer*, seldom reticent in pronouncing magisterially on events affecting the Evangelical party, initially showed cautious sympathy towards the aims of the prophetic movement. In 1829, it described Irving in terms of guarded respect. 'Mr Irving', it remarked, 'is no trimmer and his talents are equal to his courage: so that where he is right, he is nobly right; and where he is wrong, proportionably wrong. He gives no quarter to any man of any party; he graduates only for the extremes of heat and cold, frost and fever; all measure, all qualification he instinctively rejects.'[180] Such qualified praise was soon swept away by the sudden appearance of the 'gifts', the *Christian Observer* recognizing that these might bring the hard-won respectability of the Evangelical party into disrepute and reawaken fears of the 'enthusiasm' concealed beneath the surface of its Anglican profession. The 'spirit of fanaticism has been busily at work', it now complained. 'Dreams, miracles, and the most absurd pretenses to the gift of tongues, have been urged . . . to prove doctrines most mischievous, extravagant, and unscriptural.'[181] Could any believer in his right mind accept that this 'compound of fraud and folly' had truly been produced by the work of the Divine Spirit?[182]

VII

The overall impact of the English prophetic movement upon the larger arena of nineteenth-century Anglican Evangelicalism is difficult to assess. Drummond and Irving were not alone in seeing decay and degeneracy in the Christian religion, even in the Evangelical movement by whose spirituality they had been nurtured. Yet, in their quest for a return to the purity of the apostolic dispensation, they travelled even further than most other Evangelical seceders. Groups like the 'Sandemanians', the 'Walkerites', the Western Schismatics, the Gospel Standard Baptists, and the Free Church of England, were all content with their different 'apostolic' models for the church, which in their view offered a return

[179] Letter of 17 Sept. 1830, in carus, *Memoirs of the life of the Revd Charles Simeon*, M.A., 460n. [180] *CO* (1829), 289. [181] Ibid. (1830), 708. [182] Ibid. 782.

to the pristine world of the Acts of the Apostles. Drummond and Irving, on the other hand, made a virtual *tabula rasa* of the past. The Christian dispensation had failed; a totally new one lay ahead whose mission was to be fulfilled through the Catholic Apostolic Church. As Drummond advised a clergyman in July 1831, it was 'the sign' of Christ's second coming that the Bible Society was 'breaking up', and thus it was his duty to destroy rather than to purify and reform it.[183] Those who had been divinely entrusted with the duty of protecting the purity of the Church's teaching had failed utterly; God had rejected the dispensation of the Gentiles and was ushering in a new Christian era. The emergence of the 'gifts' in this new advent merely served to confirm the glorious restoration of God's church to the fullness of its apostolic purity and power.[184]

While a considerable number of Evangelicals eventually came to accept the pre-millennialist argument, only a handful fully embraced the 'gifts' as genuine phenomena;[185] even fewer joined Drummond and Cardale in seceding from the Established Church and in affiliating with the English prophetic movement. In the event, no more than six Evangelical clergymen abandoned the Church of England for the Catholic Apostolic Church: Nicholas Armstrong, Henry Bulteel, Edward Hardman, Timothy Matthews, Robert Norton, and Henry John Owen.[186] Moreover, in spite of the accession of a few wealthy and influential laymen into the upper echelons of the new body, and of those who followed Irving on his expulsion from Regent Square and Drummond on his secession from Albury, the English prophetic movement proved unable to engineer a major lay disruption from the ranks of the English or Scottish Establishments. Why was this?

The most obvious reason was the perceived extremism and heterodoxy of the English prophetic movement. While many Evangelicals accepted the Irvingites' pre-millennialist assumptions, the overwhelming majority could not countenance the supposed return of the 'gifts', or the formation of a new church which

[183] See Roger H. Martin, *Evangelicals United: Ecumenical Stirrings in Pre-Victorian Britain, 1795–1830* (1983), 137.

[184] Miller, *The History and Doctrines of Irvingism*, ii.21–2.

[185] Hempton, 'Evangelicals and Eschatology', 193.

[186] See Appendix. Bulteel's tenure in the Catholic Apostolic Church was brief.

claimed universal apostolic jurisdiction over all of Christendom. This factor proved the major stumbling block, preventing a large secession of Evangelicals into the ranks of the Catholic Apostolic Church.

Secondly, the esoteric and eclectically 'High Church' and 'Catholic' practices of the Catholic Apostolic Church were a major deterrent, preventing any significant secession of conservative 'Recordites' (much the most likely source of Evangelical recruits) out of the Church of England. For though they shared Drummond's and Irving's deep fear of liberalism, the 'Recordites' perceived themselves as vehement upholders of Protestantism and the opponents of all that smelt of popery. As it rapidly developed, the Catholic Apostolic Church looked altogether too eccentric a body—with its blend of Eastern Orthodox, Roman Catholic, charismatic, and millennial ingredients—to encourage large numbers of vehemently Protestant Evangelicals to secede from the Church, however attractive their conservative politics might appear.

A third factor was that, for all his eloquence, Irving was temperamentally unsuited to lead a major religious movement, while Drummond was dismissed by most Evangelicals as a wealthy extremist with bizarre political and social views, and a dubious doctrinal past linking him to the odd heterodoxy of the Western Schism.

The appeal of the Catholic Apostolics was also limited by internal controversy and schism, as well as by the inability (or unwillingness) of the movement to secure its own permanence. Drummond and a number of the 'apostles' rounded on Irving shortly before his death, not because they rejected the thrust of his teachings or because they disputed his divine call to the position of 'angel' in their new body, but because they fell out over the exercise of their newly appointed 'apostolic' authority. It became a question of *who* had been divinely appointed to lead the church, Irving or the 'apostles'?[187] This issue was not easily dealt with until resolved by Irving's premature demise. Then, during the summer of 1855 (and following the death of three of the 'apostles'), the delicate question of apostolic succession was raised.

[187] See Davenport, *Albury Apostles*, 89–90.

Should new 'apostles' be appointed to take their place? Other, rival, millennialist groups had followed this course. As a result, both Adventism and Mormonism have survived to this day, in part because they developed an ecclesiological system which could be perpetuated.[188] After considerable debate among the surviving 'apostles' at Albury, however, it was decided that Scripture provided no precedent or authority for appointing new 'apostles', and the matter was closed.[189] Not all Catholic Apostolics concurred. In 1860, Heinrich Geyer ('angel-prophet' in Berlin) prophetically called two 'angels' to the office of 'apostle', though this was quickly rejected by the 'apostolic college' at Albury. In the following year, he called Rudolf Rosochacki, an 'elder' of the congregation at Königsberg, to be an 'apostle', an act which was recognized by Frederich Schwartz ('angel' at Hamburg) and supported by his congregation, although rejected by the 'college'. Geyer, Rosochacki, and Schwartz were then suspended from office and (in 1863) excommunicated from the Church, setting in motion the so-called 'Hamburg schism'. Additional apostles were then called by the German body (now styling itself 'the German Christian Apostolic Mission'), severing the already strained relations between Albury and Hamburg.[190]

As a result, the Catholic Apostolic Church was unable to attract the level of clerical and lay support its leaders had expected from the ranks of the English and Scottish Establishments. But these explanations do not account for the fact that the Catholic Apostolic Church drew sizeable congregations of ordinary laymen and women to its seven London churches, as well as to its churches meeting elsewhere in Britain, Europe, and overseas during the mid-nineteenth century.[191] Why was this?

No doubt many of those who initially filled the pews of the new church were Evangelicals who came out of curiosity; when satisfied, they either remained or moved on. Of the latter, some returned to the Established Church, while not a few were drawn by the 'apostolic' claims of a rival millennial body, the Christian

[188] Flegg, *'Gathered Under Apostles'*, 438. [189] Ibid. 88.

[190] See ibid. 87–90; Standring, *Albury and the Catholic Apostolic Church*, 45–6.

[191] According to the religious census of 1851, the Catholic Apostolics had 30 congregations in England and Wales with nearly 6,000 communicants. See Horace Mann, *Report on the Religious Worship in England and Wales* (1851).

Brethren.[192] It is also likely that a number of early converts to the Catholic Apostolic Church were drawn from evangelical Dissent; a few might have even been quarried from Roman Catholicism. It is not impossible that the new church also had some proselytizing success amongst the non-churchgoing public, attracting those who could not be lured into the more sedate and less colourful services of the Established Church. Though at least one attempt to draw a social and denominational profile of the early converts to the Catholic Apostolic Church has been undertaken,[193] a number of important questions relating to the nature of its early membership remain unanswered.

Despite its limited success, the English prophetic movement was important, particularly because it contributed to the general unease of the English religious scene during the late 1820s and early 1830s. Benjamin Wills Newton, a first-hand witness of the destabilizing influence of Irvingism on Oxford's fragile religious climate, later claimed (referring to his friend Bulteel's involvement with Irving and his circle) that 'Newmanism would never be the success it is if it hadn't been for that flood of Irvingism.'[194] And when the repercussions of the Albury 'apostles' upon the wider circle of Anglican Evangelicalism are considered—especially in Ireland and the West Country of England, a theme to be addressed in the following chapter—it seems likely that the movement also served as a catalyst for further secessions and outbreaks of millennial extremism. The legacy of Drummond and Irving extended far beyond the events at Albury.

[192] For a comparison of the Catholic Apostolic Church and the Plymouth Brethren see T. C. F. Stunt, 'Irvingite Pentecostalism and the Early Brethren', in the *Journal of the Christian Brethren Research Fellowship* (Dec. 1965).

[193] See Lively, 'The Catholic Apostolic Church'.

[194] See Fry, 234. See also n. 359 of Chapter 7.

6

Irish Millennialism: The Irish Prophetic Movement and the Origins of the Plymouth Brethren

While the English prophetic movement coalesced around Henry Drummond and Edward Irving, a similar outburst of millennial speculation occurred among Dublin's influential, but unsettled, Evangelical community.[1] As the prospect of Catholic Emancipation drew ever nearer, Ireland experienced a sense of political unease even greater than that occurring simultaneously in England. Although it had long remained an 'open question' in the Cabinet, Catholic Relief Bills passed through the Commons in 1822 and—in a more far-reaching form—in 1825, only to be defeated in the Lords. Lord Liverpool's retirement in 1827, and his replacement by the 'Protestant' Canning, illustrated, however, that government neutrality on the issue was not likely to continue.[2] In 1823, alarm was intensified by news that Daniel O'Connell had formed the militant Catholic Association. The future of the Protestant ascendancy in Ireland seemed dark. In this precarious situation it was hardly surprising that millennialism, with its attempt to equate the Roman Church with the 'man of sin' in prophecy, should gain an especial foothold in Ireland. As David Hempton has observed, it is striking to note the number of prophetical writers who were educated at Trinity College, Dublin, or who had strong Irish

[1] Scholars have recently begun to recognize the growing influence of the Evangelical party in the Church of Ireland during the early to mid-nineteenth century. See Alan Acheson, 'The Evangelicals in the Church of Ireland, 1784–1859', Ph.D. thesis (Queen's University, Belfast, 1967), 77; *A History of the Church of Ireland 1691–1996* (Dublin, 1997), 120–1, 126–7, 155–60. See also James and Freeman Wills, *The Irish Nation: Its History and Biography* (1875), iv.536.

[2] See Norman Gash, *Aristocracy and People*, 3rd edn. (1983), 125–8, 137–42; Thomas Bartlett, *The Fall and Rise of the Irish Nation: The Catholic Question, 1690–1830* (Savage, Md., 1992), 327–42.

connections.[3] The expectation of imminent nationalistic Catholic rebellion drove many devout Protestants to an unusually close study of the 'signs of the times'.

In this unsettled atmosphere, still being stirred by John Walker's extreme Calvinistic and separatist teachings and by Thomas Kelly's saintly appeal, a new religious party appeared on the scene, dedicated like theirs to restoring Christianity to its 'apostolic' purity and doctrinal orthodoxy. Although the origins of the Brethren movement were rooted in the Established Church, its followers came to reject the doctrinal moderation of the Evangelical consensus: more than twenty English and Irish Evangelical clergy seceded into the Brethren during its formative years, in addition to a large body of talented—and often wealthy—lay men and women.[4] These seceders adopted a cluster of the more radical 'Gospel teachings' then in circulation, modifying them in eclectic fashion to suit their own purposes in what became the Brethren's own unique formulation of Christian doctrine and experience.[5]

I

The seedbed of the Brethren movement was the same unsettled Irish Evangelical environment which, a few years earlier, had produced such bodies as the 'Walkerites' and 'Kellyites'. During the 1790s, a number of small and apparently unconnected religious

[3] David Hempton, 'Evangelicals and Eschatology', in *JEH* (1980), 184–5.

[4] See Appendix, 1.

[5] This chapter builds upon the increasingly substantial corpus of scholarship on the Brethren. See Napoleon Noel, *The History of the Brethren* (Denver, 1836); *Plymouth Brethrenism: Its Ecclesiastical and Doctrinal Teachings; With a Sketch of its History*, 2nd edn. (1874); James Grant, *The Plymouth Brethren: Their Histories and Heresies* (1875); George T. Stokes, 'John Nelson Darby', in the *Contemporary Review* (Oct. 1885), 537–52; William Blair Neatby, *A History of the Plymouth Brethren* (1901); Thomas Stewart Veitch, *The Story of the Brethren Movement* (*c.*1920); Henry Pickering, *Chief Men Among the Brethren*, 2nd edn. (1931); David J. Beattie, *Brethren: The Story of a Great Recovery* (Kilmarnock, 1940); C. B. Bass, 'The Doctrine of the Church in the Theology of J. N. Darby', Ph.D. thesis (Edinburgh, 1952); Peter L. Embley, 'The Origins and Early Development of the Plymouth Brethren', Ph.D. thesis (Cambridge, 1966); Peter L. Embley, 'The Early Development of the Plymouth Brethren', in Bryan R. Wilson (ed.), *Patterns of Sectarianism* (1967), 213–43; Harold H. Rowdon, *The Origins of the Brethren* (1967); F. Roy Coad, *A History of the Brethren Movement*, 2nd edn. (Exeter, 1968); Robert Baylis, *My People* (Wheaton, Ill., 1995); James Patrick Callaghan, *Primitivist Piety: The Ecclesiology of the Early Plymouth Brethren* (Lanham, Md., 1996); Tim Grass, 'The Church's Ruin and Restoration: The Development of Ecclesiology in the Plymouth Brethren and the Catholic Apostolic Church, *c.*1825–*c.*1866', Ph.D. thesis (King's College, London, 1997).

gatherings were being convened in middle and upper-middle class homes in Dublin and elsewhere. As early as 1794, Alderman Hutton opened his home in Luson Street, Dublin, one evening a week, 'wishing to afford the fashionable folk in the south portion of the city an opportunity of hearing the Gospel'. Thomas Kelly performed the clerical duties for this body, and even John Law, the Bishop of Elphin, lent it his support and sometimes his attendance.[6] Around the same time, Wilmott House, a large family home outside Dublin, was opened to preachers from the Established Church, the Methodists, the Moravians, and other evangelical bodies.[7] The Scottish evangelical James Alexander Haldane, who visited Dublin in 1804, was a first-hand witness to this Evangelical effervescence. In his memoir we find mention of several small religious gatherings meeting at this time throughout the city, closed to those not sharing their particular views and receiving the Lord's Supper at an hour when it was not publicly administered in the parish churches. Impressed by the effectiveness of this development, Haldane exported it back to Scotland where he undertook to establish a similar movement.[8]

Throughout the 1820s, these so-called 'drawing-room meetings' enjoyed widespread popularity among many 'serious-minded' folk in and around Dublin. Influenced perhaps by Walker's separatist teachings, disillusioned with the political Protestantism of the day, or opposed to the sacrilegious use of holy communion as a mere test for office-bearers, these Evangelical seekers were drawn in surprising numbers to the less structured atmosphere of the Irish 'house meeting'.[9] One such gathering was described by the Quaker, Joseph John Gurney. Invited to dine at the fashionable home of the Dublin lawyer John Henry North, Gurney was surprised when a postprandial sermon was preached, after which the entire company dropped to its knees to pray. A similar meeting was organized in Dublin by William Russell (grandfather of the famous Crimean War correspondent), together with Thomas Parnell, an evangelist known for his widespread distribution of

[6] *EM* (Feb. 1856), 64. This gathering eventually led to the founding of a chapel in York Street, Dublin.

[7] A. Seymour, *The Life and Times of Selina Countess of Huntingdon* (1839), ii.215–16.

[8] Alexander Haldane, *Memoirs of the Lives of Robert Haldane of Airthrey, and of His Brother James Alexander Haldane* (1852), 235, 342.

[9] Stokes, 'John Nelson Darby', 542; Neatby, *A History of the Plymouth Brethren*, 1–24.

religious tracts.[10] Yet another coalesced around Richard Pope, to which, in 1828, Anthony Norris Groves (a West Country dentist turned missionary) was invited to preach.[11] Two years earlier, Groves had travelled to Dublin in order to study at Trinity College in preparation for ordination in the Church of England. There, after a brief exposure to the city's unsettled spiritual atmosphere, his view of ministry was radically transformed. Groves came to accept that believers were free to 'break bread' together and, according to apostolic tradition, should do so each Sunday.[12] With little or no hesitation, he began to encourage others in Dublin to act likewise. 'This, I doubt not, is the mind of God concerning us,' he announced to his friends towards the end of 1828, 'that we should come together in all simplicity as disciples, not waiting on any pulpit or minister, but trusting that the Lord would edify us together, by ministering as He pleases and saw good from the midst of ourselves.'[13] Groves thus became one of the first to articulate early Brethren doctrines, and initiate their practices.

Small groups like these, which gathered for the 'breaking of bread', Bible readings and prayer, and eschewing card playing and other such 'worldly' amusements, became an important feature of 'respectable' Dublin society during the 1820s.[14] To be sure, their proliferation owed something to the revival of family worship among both English and Irish Evangelicals which had brought personal religion out of the Church and into the home during the early nineteenth century.[15] At the same time, the 'signs of the times', combined with the restless idealism of this small-group piety, led a number of Irish Evangelicals to begin to look beyond the confines of their own religious Establishment for spiritual nourishment and expression. The dissatisfaction of Dublin Evangelicals with the state of their own Church, their fears for the future of the Protestant ascendancy in Ireland, and their yearning for voluntary association in religious activities outside the Church, were caused in part by a conviction that the structures of

[10] J. B. Atkins, *Life of Sir William Howard Russell* (1911), i.6–7. 'Tract' Parnell was the elder brother of C. S. Parnell's grandfather.

[11] Ibid. i.220.

[12] See Mrs Anthony N. Groves (ed.), *Memoir of the Late Anthony Norris Groves* (1856) 39.

[13] See Anon., *Interesting Reminiscences of the Early History of 'Brethren'*, with letter from J. G. Bellett (n.d.), 5.

[14] Joseph Bevan Braithwaite, *Memoirs of Joseph John Gurney* (Norwich, 1855), i.326–7.

[15] See Christopher Tolley, *Domestic Biography* (Oxford, 1997).

the Established religion were rigid and immobile, hindering evangelism, and preventing the formation of new congregations where needed. There was also anxiety at the exclusion of the Evangelical clergy from many Irish parishes, or even entire dioceses. This informal Evangelical network—prosperous, lay-dominated, gathered into coteries outside the control of the Anglican hierarchy, and often bitterly critical of the worldliness of the Irish Church—were a propitious environment for separatism. The Irish Evangelicals became the seedbed of the Brethren.

Several local gatherings meeting in and around Dublin were particularly important in the emerging Brethren movement. John Parnell, a figure of considerable prominence in the early Brethren, wrote late in life that in about 1825 he began to meet in Dublin to 'break bread' with a number of local Evangelicals, including William Stokes and a Scripture reader named Patterson, though this date may be somewhat premature.[16] More certain is that by November 1829, a gathering had been organized at 9 Fitzwilliam Square, the home of Francis Hutchinson, son of the Archdeacon of Killala. According to the Brethren historian Henry Pickering, considerable interest was awakened as a consequence of this meeting, and those who ventured to it were struck by the sight of hundreds of people coming together to worship without a clergyman, yet there was no confusion, but 'all things were done decently and in order'.[17] Held on Sunday morning, but not at a time which conflicted with Anglican services (since many of those present also attended their parish church), the meeting quickly proved so popular that larger premises were required. In May 1830, therefore, the focus of Dublin's 'drawing-room meetings' shifted to a large auction room in Aungier Street, hired by Parnell to serve the needs of the growing constituency.

Beyond the requirement for larger premises, the move to Aungier Street may have been set in motion by the desire of some participants to consolidate as many of the smaller, local meetings as possible, and to raise the public profile of the emerging movement in and around Dublin. Both Hutchinson and John Gifford Bellett (and perhaps others) were reluctant to make the move to Aungier Street, fearing that those in attendance would adopt

[16] See Embley, 'The Origins and Early Development of the Plymouth Brethren', 56.
[17] Pickering, *Chief Men Among the Brethren*, 57–8.

publicly the status and position of a church—a significant transformation which, they feared, would compromise the movement's pan-evangelical nature and its attractiveness. Another reason behind the move may have been social concerns, in that Aungier Street was regarded as more accommodating to those from the city's 'lower orders' who felt out of place in the fashionable confines of Fitzwilliam Square.[18] In any case, the establishment of the Aungier Street meeting proved to be something of a turning point in the history of Dublin's disparate 'drawing-room meetings', uniting a number of them under one banner, adding to their numbers, increasing their local publicity, and providing them with something approaching an organizational structure. Several individuals who were soon to play a critical role in the life and expansion of the early Brethren—including Edward Cronin, Parnell, and Stokes—formed the nucleus of the leadership at Aungier Street, and provided much of its financial backing.

From various accounts, it seems likely that most (if not all) of these early gatherings in and around Dublin adopted a pre-arranged order of worship.[19] At Fitzwilliam Square, for example, in addition to hosting the meetings, Hutchinson also prescribed their order. This included the 'breaking of bread', prayers, singing, and teaching.[20] At Aungier Street, Cronin recalled, 'we felt free up to this time and long afterwards to make arrangements among ourselves as to who should distribute the bread and wine, and take other ministries in the Assembly,' being unwilling to leave such important tasks to the impulse of the Spirit.[21] Cronin's account is supported by the suggestion of James Butler Stoney, a 1834 convert to the Aungier Street meeting, who attested that 'Stokes used to read regularly some portion of Scripture every Lord's day.'[22] This pre-arranged order, or plan of worship, which had perhaps been influenced by the practice of the 'Kellyites', continued to evolve within the Dublin gatherings. Eventually, in most Brethren assemblies it was abandoned in favour of services which were left largely unstructured to allow more direct access to the prompting of the Spirit. Why this change occurred is not

[18] See Embley, 'The Origins and Early Development of the Plymouth Brethren', 59.

[19] See Anon., *Interesting Reminiscences*, 7. For a more thorough discussion of the issue of Church order see Rowdon, *The Origins of the Brethren*, 227–30.

[20] See Embley, 'The Origins and Early Development of the Plymouth Brethren', 60.

[21] Ibid. [22] Ibid.

entirely certain. Some of those involved in the formation of the early Brethren may have regarded the adoption of a more open form of worship as reflecting true scriptural discernment.[23] Others may have desired to attract members of Protestant Dissent, which tended to be more democratic in nature, or to incorporate some of the traditions of their early Quaker upbringing.[24]

Before their amalgamation into the so-called 'meeting of the discontented' at Aungier Street, none of the smaller gatherings in and around Dublin could be clearly identified as holding pre-eminence over the others.[25] None were known by the title 'Brethren', nor could any be described as a distinct or separate church. Each served its unique function within its own small constituency. At the same time, those associated with the emerging movement had much in common. They concurred on many points of doctrine. Most had been raised within Anglican Evangelicalism, and many shared an interest in the prophetic 'signs of the times'. Some were old friends, or had been associated in a previous religious enterprise. Several had long-standing connections with the West of England,[26] and many had been educated at Trinity College, Dublin. Moreover, as in Irvingism, many were well-to-do—'refugees from the aristocracy' as they were sometimes called—disenchanted with the Established Church, but repelled by the lower social standing attached to Protestant Dissent, and by its inherent democracy. More attractive was the mixture of strong, often autocratic, leadership, and an environment receptive to new expressions of ultra-Evangelical doctrine and devotion.

II

A further influence in the history of the early Brethren was one of those devout, wealthy, formidable, aristocratic women who have often made their mark on Evangelical history, Theodosia Powerscourt. Like many of her fashionable contemporaries, Lady Powerscourt had fallen under the spell of 'serious religion', perhaps (like her husband and brother-in-law) through the

[23] See Rowdon, *The Origins of the Brethren*, 228.

[24] See Embley, 'The Origins and Early Development of the Early Brethren', 84; Neatby, *A History of the Plymouth Brethren*, 35–6.

[25] See Mrs Hamilton Madden [An Old Pensioner], *Personal Recollections of Robert Daly* (Dublin, 1872), 23.

[26] G. H. Long, *Anthony Norris Groves, Saint and Pioneer* (1939).

influence of Robert Daly, the Evangelical Rector of Powerscourt and future Bishop of Cashel.[27] She was the widowed second wife of Richard Wingfield, fifth Viscount Powerscourt,[28] the daughter of the Hon. Hugh Howard, and the niece of William Howard, the third Earl of Wicklow.[29] In about 1826, Lady Powerscourt developed an intense interest in the study of unfulfilled biblical prophecy and in the reappearance of the miraculous 'gifts', or powers of the Spirit. She very likely attended Edward Irving's congregation at Regent's Square during one of her visits to London and, although out of step with his odd Trinitarian notions, she entered enthusiastically into the burgeoning English prophetic movement which aimed to arouse an adventist concern in 'Gospel circles'.

While some reports place Lady Powerscourt in London during 1826, it is not certain whether she attended the first Albury conference.[30] What is clear is that, under the inspiration of Irving and Drummond, her enthusiasm for the subject of unfulfilled prophecy led eventually to the organization of her own conferences at Powerscourt House, her magnificent country estate near Bray, County Wicklow, and thus to the commencement of the Irish prophetic movement itself. Why these conferences were organized at a time when their Albury equivalents were no longer deemed necessary remains an open question. Likewise, some of the basic details of the Powerscourt conferences. When, for example, did they begin and end? And what role did they play within the nascent Irish prophetic movement?

It is not entirely clear why Lady Powerscourt (and others) set out to organize prophetic gatherings in Ireland when the Albury

[27] See Acheson, *A History of the Church of Ireland*, 126.

[28] Powerscourt was described as 'an Irish nobleman deeply interested in the spiritual welfare of his countrymen'. See W. D. Killen, *The Ecclesiastical History of Ireland* (1875), ii.418.

[29] See *Burke's Peerage and Baronetage*, 10th edn. (1980), 2173; Mervyn Edward, seventh Viscount Powerscourt, *Muniments of the Ancient Saron Family of Wingfield* (1894), 44; *Letters and Papers by the Late Theodosia A. Viscountess Powerscourt*, ed. Robert Daly (Dublin, 1838); Viscount Powerscourt, *A Description and History of Powerscourt* (1903). Her stepson, the Hon. and Revd W. Wingfield, married the daughter of Thomas Kelly. See *EM* (Feb. 1856), 69.

[30] See Mrs Hamilton Madden, *Memoir of the Late Right Revd Robert Daly* (1875), 149–50; Stokes, 'John Nelson Darby', 543; Pickering, *Chief Men Among the Brethren*, 20; Rowdon, *The Origins of the Brethren*, 86. See also James Hews Bransby, *Evans' Sketch of the Various Denominations of the Christian World*, 18th edn. (1841), 288–9; Andrew Landale Drummond, *Edward Irving and His Circle* (1938), 133; Edward Miller, *The History and Doctrines of Irvingism* (1878), i.37–47; E. R. Sandeen, *The Roots of Fundamentalism* (Chicago, 1970), 34–5.

counterparts were being discontinued. They may have believed that a number of important issues remained unresolved, or that the local political and ecclesiastical circumstances in Ireland required special consideration. By this time, moreover, they may also have believed that the emerging doctrinal differences between the English and Irish prophetic movements necessitated further debate during which pre-millennial eschatology could be advanced within a dispensational framework.

There has also been considerable confusion surrounding the question of dates. For example, Mrs Madden, Robert Daly's biographer, incorrectly claimed that the conferences began in 1827,[31] while L. E. Froom, the Adventist historian, has argued that they commenced in 1830.[32] Equally confusing, Brethren historians have been unable to agree on when the conferences ended: one has suggested 1833 (perhaps because this marks Daly's withdrawal from the movement), while at least one other has argued for 1838.[33]

Probably the most reliable evidence on the question of dates comes from the *Christian Herald*, the mouthpiece of the Irish prophetic movement. Published in Dublin between 1830 and 1835, and edited by the Evangelical clergyman E. N. Hoare, the *Christian Herald* provided detailed reports of the first two conferences.[34] Unfortunately, the journal made no mention of the subsequent sessions, perhaps because they were no longer held in the opulent surroundings of Powerscourt House (they had become increasingly private gatherings, assembling in a more secluded milieu of Dublin), or because the extremism of the later conferences ran counter to the more moderate views of its editor.[35]

From this source it can be ascertained with some confidence that the initial Irish prophetic conference was held at Powerscourt House between 4 and 7 October 1831 under the guidance of her

[31] See Madden, *Memoir of Robert Daly*, 150–1.

[32] Le Roy Edwin Froom, *The Prophetic Faith of Our Fathers* (Washington, 1946–54), 422, 1,223 n.

[33] See Stokes, 'John Nelson Darby', 543; Neatby, *A History of the Plymouth Brethren*, 39. See also Benjamin Wills Newton and Henry Borlase, *Answers to the Questions Considered at a Meeting*, 2nd edn. (1847), p. i.

[34] See the *Christian Herald* (Dec. 1831), 287; (Dec. 1832), 290.

[35] See *CW* xx.20 n. The editor ceased publication of the *Christian Herald* at the end of 1835, so dissatisfied had he become with the rupture of the prophetic movement into two opposing camps. See the *Christian Herald* (1835), 218.

Ladyship's trusted confidant, Robert Daly.[36] To the first of these pan-evangelical gatherings Lady Powerscourt invited a number of churchmen and Dissenters from both Britain and Ireland, of which thirty-five clergy, fifteen laymen, and about twenty ladies attended—eager to be engaged in Adventist study and speculation while being entertained in the grand style.[37] As at Albury, the conferences focused on the study of unfulilled biblical prophecy. After an opening prayer, the subjects for conversation were announced by Daly. Each gentleman who felt so disposed discoursed on the subject brought forward; the women did not speak. Significantly, there was no discussion, but each spoke his sentiments in turn.[38] While, inevitably, there was some variety of opinion among the participants, overall it seems that the first Powerscourt conference was held in a spirit free from serious rancour or divisiveness.

The second conference, organized along similar lines, was held at Powerscourt House between 24 and 28 September 1832. By this time, however, divisions had began to emerge within the Irish prophetic movement, its atmosphere deteriorating into open conflict.[39] Though Daly, the acknowledged leader of the 'moderates', attempted to avoid public debate on highly divisive points, strong pre-millennialist and separatist tendencies often simmered just below (and sometimes above) the surface. The sessions, for example, dwelt increasingly upon the expectation of Christ's expeditious return to earth, the preceding—or accompanying—restoration of the miraculous 'gifts', and the question of separation from the Established Church.[40] Consequently, Daly was compelled publicly to rebuke several of the more provocative speakers, referring openly to the 'great differences of opinion upon which appear to be fundamental points of doctrine'. He foresaw such divisions arising in the Evangelical world—'those',

[36] The *Christian Herald* (Dec. 1831), 287; Newton and Borlase, *Answers to the Questions Considered at a Meeting*, p. i; *Letters of John Nelson Darby*, ed. J. A. Trench (1886), i.6; Froom, *The Prophetic Faith of Our Fathers*, iii.584–5, iv.1223–4. Powerscourt was one of the largest and most influential parishes in the Church of Ireland, comprising some 2,000 Protestants. See D. H. Atkinson, *The Church of Ireland* (New Haven, 1971), 133.

[37] See the *Christian Herald* (Dec. 1831), 287; Madden, *Memoir of Robert Daly*, 150; Iain H. Murray, *The Puritan Hope*, 3rd edn. (Edinburgh, 1984), 199. Darby, Bellett, Newton, Percy Hall, Henry Craik, and George Müller (all early adherents of the Brethren) attended one or more of the Powerscourt conferences.

[38] The *Christian Herald* (Dec. 1831), 287.

[39] Ibid. 290.

[40] See Madden, *Memoir of Robert Daly*, 150.

as he put it, 'being separated upon the earth who I hope are joined together in the Lord'—that he professed no desire to remain alive 'to witness all the evil, the separation, and the variety of errors with which it seems as if the Lord is beginning to allow the Church to be tried even now'. Of the conflicts which had disrupted the final session, he concluded gloomily: 'I certainly felt this evening a more awful sense of coming evil then I ever did before.'[41] Lady Powerscourt too was torn between competing interests: on the one hand, her loyalty towards Daly and the Established Church; on the other hand, her fascination with the (sometimes contradictory) doctrines advanced by the 'extremists' in the movement, such as John Nelson Darby. She had, in fact, become so emotionally distraught over the question of her loyalty to the Church that she confessed to having spent the night after the final session in tears.[42] Likewise Peter Roe, the influential Evangelical incumbent of Kilkenny, who confided to his diary that the conference had been, on the whole, 'unprofitable'. Many of the subjects had been difficult to understand, 'the most extravagant assertions' had been made, and 'dogmas quite opposed to each other' had been 'maintained with the greatest pertinacity'. Perhaps most annoying of all, 'the duty of seeking for miraculous gifts' had been 'strongly insisted upon! Oh!', he concluded, 'What a fool is man!'[43]

Rumours about these divisions soon began to circulate within the close-knit Irish Evangelical community. In October 1832, Darby, formerly curate of the nearby parish of Calary and the emerging leader of the 'extremists' within the Irish prophetic movement, made cryptic references to the 'Spirit' at Powerscourt—probably an allusion to the preoccupation of the assembly with charismatic themes and strict separatism.[44] He wrote to the *Christian Herald* denying that the recent conference had lapsed into theological extremism or open dissension. Concerned about divisions in the English prophetic movement, as well as the way in which Albury had become absorbed with the return of the miraculous 'gifts' of the Spirit, Darby went out of his way to emphasize that at Powerscourt he had only witnessed one scene of disagreement—a reference to an argument over the 'gifts'—

[41] Ibid. 153–4. [42] *Letters of John Nelson Darby*, ed. Trench, i.156.

[43] Samuel Madden, *Memoir of the Life of the Late Peter Roe* (Dublin, 1842), 445.

[44] See *Letters of John Nelson Darby*, ed. Trench i.9.

and little had been said on the subject. 'While the principles were calmly inquired into by a few', Darby added, rather evasively, this had not disrupted the session. In fact, this aspect of the meeting had been 'the most practically profitable' of all, for it allowed scriptural evidence to be marshalled against the theological errors now current in the 'Gospel world'.[45] Far from calming anxieties, Darby's remarks led to heightened tensions between the 'moderates' and 'extremists' in the Irish prophetic movement, and advanced the perception of some that he opposed traditional Evangelical doctrines.

From all appearances, the third Powerscourt conference, held between 23 and 28 September 1833, gave vent to even greater controversy.[46] The diary of Henry Craik provides some detail of the various discussions, which seem to have been well advanced in their concentration on dispensational themes (discussed below).[47] Much time was also spent in discussion of separatism and in denunciations of Erastianism, in which those present seemed unable to unite on anything except their criticism of the Established Church. As Benjamin Wills Newton, one of the foremost personalities among the early Brethren, later commented: 'I went, and never was more disappointed. An amazing lack of both intelligent understanding and of devotedness.' At the conclusion of the conference, Lady Powerscourt organized the so-called 'garden-house communion' for those 'differently minded from the rest'. '*Well*', Newton exclaimed, '*even we seven were all agreed as to the necessity of separation, but as to doctrine—no two of us were agreed!*'[48] In evidence at Powerscourt were so 'many erroneous doctrines and unfit persons' that Newton wished he had remained at home. In fact, he could recognize factors which, during the previous year, had compelled him to secede from the Church of England as much in evidence within the Irish prophetic movement.[49] Particularly provocative was Darby's attempt to stifle opinion, Newton complaining bitterly that the conference had been organized in such a way as to 'control' private judgement.[50] So dogmatic were Darby's opinions, so dominant his personality, so divisive the gathering, and so irreparably fragmented the Irish prophetic move-

[45] The *Christian Herald* (Dec. 1832), 290.

[46] See *Passages from the Diary and Letters of Henry Craik* ed. W. E. Tayler (Bristol, 1866), 166.

[47] See ibid. 168–9.

[48] See Fry, 261, 282, 302.

[49] Ibid. 302.

[50] Ibid. 283.

ment, that Newton later described the 1833 conference as 'really the commencement of Brethrenism'.[51]

These controversies quickly isolated the Powerscourt conferences from mainstream Irish and English Evangelicalism, from the 'moderates' within the Irish prophetic movement, and from the English prophetic movement. Most 'Gospel clergymen' at this time remained well outside the pre-millennialist camp, and firmly attached to the Established Church; relatively few shared the intense enthusiasm for speculation about unfulfilled prophecy and Christ's imminent return shown by Darby and his like. Even fewer accepted Darby's stern separatist teachings. Robert Daly became so alarmed at the possibility of secessions in his parish, that following the second conference he (like Hugh McNeile, his counterpart at Albury) withdrew from participation in the prophetic movement altogether.[52]

In spite of their close and long association, Lady Powerscourt ignored Daly's warnings and continued to be drawn deeper into the advanced camp of the prophetic movement. No doubt the magnetic Darby exercised a strong influence over the development of her views. So too did George Müller, a German immigrant who had become a Baptist minister of sorts in the West of England, and who was later to be known as the founder of the celebrated Ashley Down Orphanage near Bristol.[53] Müller had travelled to Ireland to attend the third conference, where his hostility to all religious tests and subscriptions, as well as his desire to unify believers in some kind of 'apostolic union', held great sway with her Ladyship. She invited him to stay on at Powerscourt in order to establish a regular meeting for worship and the 'breaking of bread', which would be open to all believers. Before long, Müller seems to have severed his ties with his Baptist congregation and amalgamated the Powerscourt gathering with the Aungier Street meeting, to form what might be considered the first recognizable body of the Brethren.[54]

The establishment of this regular gathering for worship at Powerscourt marked the end of Lady Powerscourt's association

[51] Ibid. 302. [52] See Madden, *Memoir of Robert Daly*, 151.

[53] E. H. Broadbent, *The Pilgrim Church*, 3rd edn. (1945), 360–8.

[54] One Brethren historian has claimed that Müller had become leader of 'the English Separatist movement', a West Country communion which, in a number of ways, held teachings in common with both the 'Walkerites' and the early Brethren. See Stokes, 'John Nelson Darby', 544.

with the Church of Ireland. Her secession was a painful blow to Daly and the other 'moderates', who had prayed that she might remain within the Establishment.[55] To Irish Evangelicalism as a whole, moreover, her secession was of considerable significance, for although Daly was able to retain the majority of his congregation within the Church, Lady Powerscourt's secession encouraged several leading Irish Evangelical families to abandon it in favour of the emerging Brethren.[56] Despite this public rupture, it appears that she remained on warm personal terms with Daly until her premature death in 1836. At her funeral, Daly referred to Lady Powerscourt's secession in kindly terms, seeing it as activated by a desire for holiness and perfect purity, and not by malice or vindictiveness.[57] He then undertook to edit her various letters and papers, bringing them to publication in 1838.[58] Had she lived longer, Lady Powerscourt might well have exercised an even greater influence upon the early Brethren, following in the footsteps of other noted aristocratic Evangelical 'mothers in Israel', like Lady Glenorchy, the Countess of Huntingdon, and Lady Barham. She might also have made an important second marriage; rumours linking her and Darby romantically have been a regular feature of Brethren folklore and historiography for many years.[59] Her death at the age of thirty-six, however, cut short her contribution to the Irish prophetic movement, and within Brethrenism she is now remembered primarily for inviting Edward Irving to Powerscourt during his visit to Ireland in September 1830 (when she introduced him to a number of influential Irish Evangelicals), and for hosting and organizing the initial Irish prophetic conferences.[60]

Few details of the final three (1834–6) Irish prophetic conferences have survived. In late 1833, in part because family members disapproved of her activities (in particular her recent secession from the Church), Lady Powerscourt moved out of Powerscourt House into a smaller residence on the estate. The final confer-

[55] See Madden, *Personal Recollections of the Right Revd Robert Daly, D.D.*, 23.
[56] Walter Alison Phillips, *History of the Church of Ireland* (Oxford, 1933), iii.352.
[57] Madden, *Memoir of Robert Daly*, 157–8.
[58] *Letters and Papers by the Late Theodosia A. Viscountess Powerscourt*, ed. Daly.
[59] See T. C. F. Stunt, 'John Nelson Darby', in *New DNB*.
[60] Mrs Oliphant, *The Life of Edward Irving*, 6th edn. (*c.*1900), 299–302.

ences were then moved from Powerscourt to Dublin.[61] The proceedings, which were smaller and more exclusively Brethren in nature, and largely given over to pre-millennialist conjecture, remained under the firm domination of Darby. A brief account of one of the final conferences by James Butler Stoney, suggests that Darby exercised a tight grip on the proceedings.[62] According to Stoney, John Synge, of Glanmore Castle, County Wicklow, occupied the chair (as he had since Daly's departure), calling on each to speak in turn on a given subject: Darby reserved the right to speak last, which provided him with the opportunity to correct all previous errors and advance his own interpretation of the theme. George Wigram sat next to him; prominent also at the conferences were Captain Percy Francis Hall and Bellett—all leading personalities in the emerging Brethren movement.[63]

Despite the withdrawal of the 'moderates' from the Irish prophetic movement, tensions remained. In each succeeding year the early Brethren (as the 'drawing-room meetings' and the Irish prophetic movement must now be regarded), fell increasingly under Darby's dogmatic control, to move further beyond the orbit of the Established Church and to adopt more dispensational doctrines. These new teachings alienated many in millennial circles. Evidence of such tensions can be found in Newton's account of a rival prophetic conference held at the Mechanics' Institute, Plymouth, during September 1834.[64] This was organized by several West Country leaders of the early Brethren—including Newton, James Lampden Harris, and Henry Borlase. Though eager to discuss prophetic themes like those being advanced at the Powerscourt conference, the three appear to have been firmly opposed to Darby's assumption of leadership, and thus unwilling

[61] This may have been the result of strained relations between Lady Powerscourt and her stepson (and heir to the title), who had not only come of age, but was opposed to her recent secession and to aspects of the emerging Brethren movement. See Coad, *A History of the Brethren Movement*, 109–10; Embley, 'The Origins and Early Development of the Plymouth Brethren', 88.

[62] Neatby's attempt to connect Stoney's account to the 1838 conference is inaccurate. See Neatby, *A History of the Plymouth Brethren*, 39.

[63] It was also claimed that a number of Anglican clergy and some Irvingites attended this conference, but this too seems unlikely. Synge has been described as 'a solitary man', who remained close to the Brethren, but continued to attend the Established Church. See T. C. F. Stunt, 'John Synge and the Early Brethren', in the *Christian Brethren Research Fellowship Journal* (1976), 39–62.

[64] See Newton and Borlase, *Answers to the Questions Considered at a Meeting.*

to travel to Ireland. Predictably, Darby reacted unfavorably to this direct challenge to his leadership, and the Plymouth conference contributed to a growing sense of estrangement between himself and Newton. More importantly, it helped set the stage for what would later become the movement's first major internal schism.

III

Perhaps the most salient feature of the Irish prophetic conferences was the dominance and theological dogmatism of John Nelson Darby. Though often regarded as the founder of the Brethren, at the time of the first Powerscourt conference he was a relatively young and inexperienced Irish Evangelical clergyman. In spite of his unpretentious credentials, Darby quickly rose to a position of influence within the embryonic Brethren movement, which from an early date tended to reflect his doctrinal views and fall under the spell of his magnetic personality. Like Wesley a century earlier, he transformed a fledgling spiritual movement into something like an international denomination. By the time of Darby's death in 1882, over forty volumes of his published works and letters, together with some fifteen hundred worldwide Brethren assemblies, testified to his strength of personality, his organizing skills, and his powerful attraction as a theologian, confessor, writer, preacher, and religious leader.[65]

Darby was the sixth son (and eighth child) of John Darby, a prosperous merchant, of Markly, Warbleton, Sussex, and of 9 Great George Street, Westminster, and his wife, Anne, daughter of Samuel Vaughan, a wealthy London merchant. He was born in London on 18 November 1800.[66] His second name of Nelson celebrated the arrival in England in the month of his birth of the great admiral under whom his uncle, Sir Henry D'Esterre Darby, served with distinction at the Battle of the Nile in 1798.[67] The family's Irish connections can be traced back to the sixteenth century when his relation, John Darby, served under the Earl of Sussex as Captain of Horse in his Irish campaigns.[68] After Westminster School, where he was a contemporary of Baptist Noel, Darby entered Trinity College, Dublin, as a fellow commoner, graduating in 1819 with great distinction as a classics gold

[65] Coad, *A History of the Brethren Movement*, 106.

[66] See Stunt, 'John Nelson Darby'. [67] Ibid.

[68] See Max S. Weremchuk, *John Nelson Darby* (Neptune, NJ, 1992), 19.

medallist.[69] He was admitted (also with Noel) to Lincoln's Inn in November 1819; to King's Inn, Dublin, during Hilary 1822; and to the Irish Bar in January 1822.[70]

During his legal studies in 1820 or 1821, Darby passed through some kind of religious conversion.[71] Against his father's wishes, he then abandoned the law in order to prepare for a career in the Church. He was ordained in August 1825 to serve as curate in the parish of Calary, near Enniskerry, County Wicklow.[72] In December of the following year he was injured in a riding accident. While convalescing at the home of his sister, Susannah Pennefather, he underwent something akin to a second spiritual conversion, experiencing (as he later refer to it) a 'deliverance from bondage' and a powerful sense of the reality of his 'union with Christ'.[73]

Meanwhile, the pattern of Darby's ecclesiology—which shaped both his own theology and the character of the early Brethren movement—began to emerge. The impetus was in part a negative one: he objected to the pervasive Erastianism of the Church of Ireland and to its ministerial hierarchy, both of which he regarded as unscriptural, and he deplored the Church's secularity and its apparent indifference to the leading of the Spirit. Nor was he alone here, for in this he articulated deep-seated worries in the Evangelical milieu. By way of reaction, this negative assessment of the state of Anglicanism prepared the way for a new openness to alternative, more radical, forms of ecclesiology, which to Darby and some of his circle seemed to offer a more spiritual model than those provided by a moribund Anglican Establishment.[74]

The rapid development of Darby's anti-Erastianism can be traced to two events which occurred shortly after his ordination.

[69] See G. F. Russell and Alan H. Stenning, *The Westminster School Register From 1764 to 1883* (1892), 60; *Al. Dub.*

[70] See *The Records of the Honorable Society of Lincoln's Inn* (1896); Edward Keane, P. Beryl Phair, and Thomas U. Sadleir (eds.), *King's Inn Admission Papers 1607–1867* (Dublin, 1982), 120.

[71] Weremchuk, *John Nelson Darby*, 33–4.

[72] He was ordained deacon on 7 August 1825, by William Bissett, Bishop of Raphoe, and priest on 19 February 1826, by William Magee, Archbishop of Dublin. See Stunt, 'John Nelson Darby'.

[73] The Pennefathers lived at Temple Carig, Delgany, Co. Wicklow, and at 20 Fitzwilliam Square, Dublin.

[74] Grant, *The Plymouth Brethren*, 5.

During the mid-1820s, William Magee, the Archbishop of Dublin, like many of the Irish clergy, became alarmed over the possibility that the Tory government of Lord Liverpool might enact some measure of Catholic Emancipation.[75] In his episcopal charge of 1826, Magee dismissed with contempt the notion that a religious establishment possessed any interest distinct from the State as 'a sort of incorporated craft, seeking its own ends through the power of its temporal associate'.[76] He decried the claim that religion was a concern only between the individual and his God, over which the civil magistrate had no control. Starting from the axiom that sovereignty in any state was indivisible, Magee asserted that the sovereign could never support a system that maintained 'a spiritual supremacy independent of civil government', for he could admit no authority above his own. He also rounded on Roman Catholic apologists who attempted to distinguish between the spiritual and the temporal in the case of sovereign power.[77] On 1 February 1827, in an excited atmosphere, a number of clergy from the diocese of Dublin, fearful of constitutional change, met to petition the House of Commons for protection against the 'hostility and calumny with which they and their religion have been, for a length of time, systematically assailed'.[78]

The bold Erastian claims contained in Magee's episcopal charge outraged Darby, who believed that the archbishop had failed to address the historical origins and political traditions of Anglicanism, and had opened the door for unwarranted State intrusion. Darby considered the supremacy of Christ and His church to be a spiritual supremacy independent of the civil government, as exemplified by Jesus' assertion before Pilate that His kingdom was not of this world.[79] Perhaps even more unsettling was the discovery that many of his closest Evangelical allies had been signatories to the parliamentary appeal. 'I could weep',

[75] See Joseph Liechty, 'Irish Evangelicalism, Trinity College Dublin, and the Mission of the Church of Ireland at the End of the Eighteenth Century', Ph.D. thesis (Maynooth, 1987), 250–312; Acheson, *A History of the Church of Ireland*, 67–8, 136–7, 150, 156–7.

[76] William Magee, *A Charge Delivered at His Triennial and Metropolitan Visitation* (Dublin, 1827), 4.

[77] Ibid. 29–30.

[78] *Ecclesiastical Intelligence* (Mar. 1827), 242; Weremchuk, *John Nelson Darby*, 45, 212–13.

[79] Darby, 'Considerations Addressed to the Archbishop of Dublin' (1827), in *CW* i.8–9.

Darby lamented, 'at men whom I love and respect having unwittingly put their hands to this Petition.'[80]

Darby also took strong exception to Magee's decision, in 1826, to require all new converts from Roman Catholicism to take the oaths of allegiance and supremacy to the English sovereign.[81] This demand produced great unrest among those who (like Darby) were deeply involved in the Irish Home Mission, an evangelistic work which was then allegedly gaining some six to eight hundred new converts from Rome each week within the diocese of Dublin.[82] Here, in disturbing fashion, and with regrettable consequences, the Erastianism of the Irish Evangelical party collided head-on with its commitment to evangelism and its desire to initiate (albeit three centuries after its English and Continental counterparts) a true Protestant Reformation in Ireland.

Darby's objections to this new requirement were mainly pragmatic. In Magee's demand that all converts to Protestantism should substitute an allegiance to the Crown in place of their former allegiance to the Pope, he saw the Church as confusing the issue of spiritual conversion with that of English political domination of Ireland. Perhaps predictably, for the Ulster-born Magee (and no doubt for most Evangelical clergy) the two issues could not be separated; for Darby, however, and for the majority of Irish Catholics, the substitution of the despotic authority of the English Crown for that of the Pope was highly provocative. As he complained bitterly, the evangelistic work of the Home Mission 'instantly ceased'.[83] The Reformation of Catholic Ireland now seemed suddenly to lie beyond the grasp of the Established Church.

Taken collectively, these shifts in the nature of Anglicanism convinced Darby that the Irish Establishment had been reduced to little more than a branch of the civil service. Even more disturbing, perhaps, was the realization that he would receive little assistance in combating Erastianism from his fellow Evangelicals, who exhibited scant interest in reforming the institutional life of the

[80] Ibid. i.14.

[81] Darby, *Disendowment—Disestablishment* (1869), in *CW* xx.288.

[82] Ibid.; Darby, 'Considerations Addressed to the Archbishop of Dublin', *CW* i.1. See also 'Thoughts on the Present Position of the Home Mission' (1833), in *CW* i.53–67.

[83] Darby, 'Considerations Addressed to the Archbishop of Dublin', *CW* i.1.

Church or the abuses arising from its civil connection.[84] Convinced that he must act unilaterally, Darby penned a modest essay under the title, 'Considerations Addressed to the Archbishop of Dublin and the Clergy Who Signed the Petition to the House of Commons for Protection' (1827), which he circulated privately among the local clergy. Its aim was to help defend the Irish Church from unscriptural and unwarranted state intrusion, and preserve its apostolic constitution. Curiously, as Peter Embley has pointed out, Darby's essay—and the doctrines it advanced—bore a striking resemblance to a work by the Scottish seceder John Glas, published exactly a century earlier: *The Testimony of the King of Martyrs Concerning his Kingdom* (1727).[85]

After objecting to Magee's Erastian tendencies, Darby offered his own definition of the true church: it was a congregation of souls redeemed out of the world by God, manifest in the flesh, and knit together by the band of their common faith. As a consequence of its divine heritage, its interests and polity were heavenly, and not worldly.[86] When encumbered by the trammels of State control, however, the Church was unable actively to exercise its missionary function, for its clergy were confined within the bounds of the secular social order whose interests they were obliged to uphold and defend.[87] Tragically, this had become the case in Ireland. Rather than encouraging Roman Catholics to convert to Protestantism, Magee's imposition of the oaths of supremacy had made 'the admission into the Establishment a necessary condition' of salvation and redemption. This action was analogous to the policies which had long ago created such difficulties at Antioch over the admission of the Gentiles to the primitive church, setting a stumbling block in the path of weak believers.[88]

With the threat of Catholic Emancipation now uppermost in the minds of the Irish clergy, Darby's tract was largely ignored by those he most desired to influence. Robert Daly, for one, dismissed it out of hand, suggesting that Darby should abandon the Church in favour of Protestant Dissent. To this, Darby replied with characteristic firmness. 'No; you have got into the wrong, and you want

[84] Stokes, 'John Nelson Darby', 540.

[85] See Embley, 'The Early Development of the Plymouth Brethren', 215n.

[86] Darby, 'Considerations Addressed to the Archbishop of Dublin', *CW* i.5.

[87] Ibid. 11–12. [88] Ibid. 18.

to put me there—but that you will not do.'[89] Hoping that a wider public appeal might succeed where quiet effort had failed, Darby then revised the tract and had it published under the title, *Considerations on the Nature and Unity of the Church of Christ* (1828).[90] Although it showed numerous signs of incipient separatism, the work expressed no clear admonition to secede from the Established Church, whose numerous shortcomings Darby carefully avoided. By this time, at least in the view of one Brethren historian, Darby could still be regarded as 'a very exact churchman', who took his stand at a point where Evangelicalism and Anglo-Catholicism often met during this intense period of political disruption—a determined opposition to Erastianism.[91]

Darby's matured ecclesiology came to reject the principle of a national church in favour of an elect, 'gathered' body, defined as the sum total of true believers in any locality.[92] There was to be no separate ministry for administering the sacraments or for preaching, since no evidence for the selection of ministers could be found in Scripture.[93] Moreover, membership in the church must not be regulated by parochial boundaries—'a confusion established by man'[94]—for the call of the elect into fellowship and the universal priesthood was divine, not earthly.[95] In each of these instances, however, Darby often resisted moving beyond the theoretical. A number of his teachings thus remained unsubstantiated, and even contradictory. Why was this? Perhaps he believed that the imminence of the Advent rendered detailed formulation unnecessary?[96] When Christ failed to return during the mid-1840s, however, as Darby—and others—had expected, his difficulties in formulating a clear and workable ecclesiology compounded the internal strife which was to dog much of the history of the early Brethren.

Shortly after the publication of Darby's tract, rumours began to circulate that he might be on the verge of seceding from the

[89] Ibid. 1. [90] In *CW* i. 21.

[91] Turner, *John Nelson Darby*, 14.

[92] See Darby, 'On the Formation of Churches' (1840), in *CW* i.138–55.

[93] Ibid. 148–9; Darby, 'The Notion of a Clergyman' (*c.*1834), in *CW* i.36–51.

[94] Darby, 'A Glance at Various Ecclesiastical Principles' (n.d.), in *CW* iv.22; 'Parochial Arrangements Destructive of Order in the Church' (1834), in *CW* i.80–91.

[95] Darby, 'Who is a Priest and What is a Priest?' (n.d.), in *CW* x.209–14; 'Disendowment—Disestablishment', xx.288–91; 'What is the Church?' (1849), in *CW* iii.358–92; 'The Church—What is It?' (1887), in *CW* xii.372–83.

[96] Darby, 'Studies on the Book of Daniel' (n.d.), in *CW* v.204.

Church. Later that same year, he simply resigned from his curacy without formally seceding, while continuing to wear his clerical robes and engaging in both Anglican and non-Anglican ministry.[97] When a puzzled Robert Daly inquired of him: 'Well, John, have you left us: what church have you joined?', he received a characteristic reply: 'None whatever; I have nothing to do with the Dissenters, and am as yet my own church.' Darby made it clear to one and all that he had neither resigned his holy orders nor abandoned the practical care of souls. Like Wesley a century earlier, he had taken the world as his parish.[98] Initially, it appears that Darby was reluctant to join those, like Groves and Bellett, who began 'breaking bread' informally, either in Dublin or in Plymouth.[99] As we will see, however, it was not long before he began to enter enthusiastically into such practices. After resigning from his curacy much of his time was occupied in ministering to the embryonic religious gatherings in and around Dublin, at least one of which was known as the 'Separatists'—an ascribed title they shared with Walker's connexion though it remains doubtful whether any ties, formal or informal, developed (or were established) between the two movements.[100]

The question of whether Darby ever formally seceded from the Church (and, if so, when) remains unanswered. His rather anomalous relationship with the Irish Establishment seems to have continued until 1832, when the introduction of a new system of education brought about something close to a complete rupture between the two.[101] A salient feature of the proposed measure involved Anglican co-operation with Roman Catholicism. Darby was so outraged by this that he published a scathing attack on Richard Whately, the liberal Archbishop of Dublin and one of the scheme's principal proponents, which characterized the plan as 'an unholy marriage between infidelity and popery', and accused Whately of advancing the heretical doctrine of sabellianism.[102] Receiving no satisfaction in the matter, he then abandoned all contact with the Church. Later comments shed some retrospec-

[97] See Stunt, 'John Nelson Darby'.

[98] Turner, *John Nelson Darby*, 17–18, 21.

[99] See Stunt, 'John Nelson Darby'.

[100] See Miller, *The History and Doctrines of Irvingism*, ii.203; Stokes, 'John Nelson Darby', 544.

[101] See Darby, 'A Letter on a Serious Question Connected with the Irish Education Measures of 1832' (1832), in *CW* xxxii.306–13.

[102] Ibid. 306–7.

tive light on Darby's thinking during this period, especially a letter to the Revd James Kelly which contains some thoughts on the Established Church:

I find no such thing as a national church in Scripture. Is the Church of England—was it ever—God's assembly in England? I say, then, that her constitution is worldly, because she contemplates by her constitution—it is her boast—the population, not the saints. The man who would say that the Church of England is a gathering of saints must be a very odd man, or a very bold one. All the parishioners are bound to attend, by her principles. It was not the details of the sacramental and priestly system which drove me from the Establishment, deadly as they are in their nature. It was that I was looking for the body of Christ (which was not there, but perhaps in all the parish not one converted person); and collaterally, *because I believed in a divinely appointed ministry*. If Paul had come, he could not have preached (he had never been ordained); if a wicked ordained man, he had his title and must be recognized as a minister; the truest minister of Christ unordained could not. *It was a system contrary to what I found in Scripture.*[103]

Though for some time Darby continued to regard the Established Church as an effective prophylactic against popery, the rise of the Oxford Movement convinced him that Anglicanism had become for many the road *to* Rome instead of the road *from* Rome.[104] Despite these various protestations, there is no evidence that Darby ever renounced his Anglican orders or formally seceded. In April 1832, the Plymouth papers were still referring to him as 'the Revd Mr Darby'.[105] In the following year, Darby admitted that he was still 'no enemy to episcopacy abstractedly, if it be real and done from the Lord'.[106] During 1834 Bellett claimed that he had by now become '*all but detached* from the Church of England'.[107] What is more certain is that, by the mid-1830s, Darby seems to have regarded himself as being outside the Established Church. Towards the end of his life, he wrote that beyond everything else it had been the Church's disunity and lack of discipline, combined with his own emerging doctrine of separatism, that had

[103] Turner, *John Nelson Darby*, 18.
[104] Darby, 'The Notion of a Clergyman', *CW* i.36–51.
[105] Embley, 'The Origins and Early Development of the Plymouth Brethren', 66.
[106] *Letters of John Nelson Darby*, ed. J. A. Trench, i.17.
[107] See Embley, 'The Origins and Early Development of the Plymouth Brethren', 66 (italics added).

driven him from its ranks: if churchmen wished to have blasphemers at the Lord's table, he concluded, simply but characteristically, 'they will not have me'.[108]

IV

If the ecclesiological precepts of Darby and other early Brethren had been influenced by disquiet at the growing secularity of the Irish Church, by annoyance at the high-handedness of various diocesan bishops, and by alarm at the prospect of government by Whig sceptics or infidels, it was also influenced by some similar independent religious movements already active in English and Irish Evangelicalism. These included, most prominently, the 'Walkerites', the 'Kellyites', and the English prophetic movement.

Although the 'Walkerites' had always maintained the desire to attract new converts, they in fact converted relatively few clergy or laymen from either Church or chapel. More successful were their attempts to diffuse their provocative teachings into the restless waters of Irish Evangelicalism, where they attracted some attention by their high Calvinism, their rejection of the idea of ordination and an appointed ministry, and (most notably) by their militant and exclusivist doctrine of separatism which barred all but their own members from shared fellowship. So strict were the Walkerites in their determination to withdraw from spiritual contact with the world that they even refused to sing hymns or pray with those outside their own narrow spiritual connexion; such promiscuous association with the ungodly was for them an abomination to the Lord. A number of these 'Walkerite' teachings had close parallels with the doctrinal system of the early Brethrenism, especially their separatism which became the hallmark of the 'Darbyite' wing of the movement.[109]

A second influence upon the ecclesiological development of the early Brethren can be traced to the 'Kellyites'. Though Kelly was a moderate Calvinist, rejecting Walker's strong predestinarianism, strict separatism, and practice of closed worship, he nevertheless shared Walker's fervent anti-Erastianism, and his rejection of ordination and a separate ministry. In particular, it appears that Kelly provided the inspiration for the Brethren's early adoption of

[108] Darby, *On Ecclesiastical Independency* (1880), in *CW* xiv.303.
[109] See James Godkin, *Ireland and Her Churches* (1867), 209.

a pre-arranged plan setting forth the names of those who would speak at worship services, for such an arrangement (which seems to have been standardized very early within many of the Brethren assemblies) appears in no other Irish religious movement of the period.[110] Moreover, the social catchment area of the 'Kellyites' was the fashionable milieu in and around Dublin's Fitzwilliam Square—the very circles from which, a few years later, the early Brethren drew many of its most prominent middle and upper-class adherents.[111] Uptown Dublin, and its vibrant Evangelical community, served as the seedbed of both movements.

The Brethren historian, William Neatby, is correct in the strictest sense in seeing no direct, linear descent of the early Brethren from either the 'Walkerites' or the 'Kellyites'.[112] Darby had powerful views of his own: he was a creative religious leader rather than a follower. All the same it must be recognized that, in the years which preceded the emergence of the Brethren, Dublin's unsettled Evangelical community had been mesmerized by Walker's dynamic and powerful personality and by Kelly's rejection of denominational religion. The 'serious' and often intimate world of Dublin Evangelicalism was marked by intense debates, close personal relationships, and contact with the *alma mater* of so many ultra-Evangelicals, Trinity College. It seems most unlikely, therefore, that the early Brethren, many of whom had grown up in the shadow of Walker and Kelly, had not garnered at least some of their doctrinal inspiration from these seceders' highly publicized campaigns to restore the 'brotherhood' of the apostolic era, or imbibed at least a portion of their unusual ecclesiology. In the absence of firmer evidence, this element in the spiritual genealogy of early Brethrenism must admittedly remain speculative, but the parallels between these various contemporary 'apostolic' movements—the 'Walkerites', the 'Kellyites', and the early Brethren—should not be ignored.

Another source of inspiration can be traced to the English prophetic movement, which was in its zenith during the late 1820s

[110] See S. P. Tregelles, *Three Letters to the Author of a Retrospect of Events That Have Taken Place Among the Brethren*, 2nd edn. (1894), 8, 11–13.

[111] The teachings of the early Brethren also held some points in common with the leaders of the Western Schism—a point not lost on a number of contemporary observers. See Miller, *The History and Doctrines of Irvingism*, ii.203; *Plymouth Brethrenism*, 5; 'The Plymouth Brethren', in *ER* (May 1839), 572; the *Inquirer* (Oct. 1839).

[112] See Neatby, *A History of the Plymouth Brethren*, 28.

and early 1830s.[113] Though in some ways Darby's ecclesiology resembled that of the Irvingites, it contained several important differences. Most especially, he opposed the close association of the visible and invisible church so prominent in Irvingism. The 'true' church was not visible and worldly, he argued, but invisible and spiritual: a mystery of which only Paul speaks; Christ's mystical body will be completed only at the 'rapture'. Those converted before Christ's first coming, or after his second, are not part of the true church: 'the assertion that his mystical body is the universal family of the redeemed is unscriptural; all the declaration is founded on this gross and unscriptural error, that all the saved belong to the church.'[114] The church, therefore, is in ruins, the Advent still impending. Its redemption is not God's immediate intention. Believers should strive to escape from its certain downfall and await Jesus' imminent arrival.[115] 'I believe from Scripture that the ruin is without remedy,' Darby proclaimed, 'that the professing church will be cut off.'[116] It belonged to a failed dispensation, and God's method is not to restore a dispensation, but to usher in a new one. Thus, the next great event in history will not be a reformation or revival of the church, but Christ's Advent. Consequently, attempts to 'restore' the church with an elaborate fourfold 'order' of ministry based on 'apostles', 'angels', 'priests', and 'deacons', to expect the conversion of the Jews, or to embark on bold missionary expeditions, were delusions, or misinterpretations, of the divine plan.[117]

V

More significant was the influence of the English prophetic movement on the formulation of Brethren eschatology. Both Anthony Norris Groves and Henry Craik were reading Irving as early as 1826, and it seems unlikely that they were alone among the early Brethren.[118] As mentioned earlier, it appears that Lady Powerscourt visited England during the same year, making contact with

[113] See Henry Groves, *Darbyism: Its Rise and Development* (1866); Embley, 'The Origins and Early Development of the Plymouth Brethren', 89–94.

[114] See Darby, 'Brief Remarks on the Work of the Revd David Brown' (n.d.), in *CW* xi.346–7.

[115] Murray, *The Puritan Hope*, 200.

[116] Darby, 'What the Christian Has Amid the Ruin of the Church' (n.d.), in *CW* xiv.275.

[117] Murray, *The Puritan Hope*, 201.

[118] Coad, *A History of the Brethren Movement*, 19.

the leaders of the English prophetic movement, and very likely imbibing portions of their teaching.[119] In the following year, Irving published a translation of the famous apocalyptic work, *The Coming of the Messiah in Glory and Majesty*, by the Jesuit Lacunza, which was probably read by Darby and others among the early Brethren.[120] In September 1830, Irving gave a series of lectures on prophecy at the Rotunda in Dublin,[121] which stirred popular feeling and made an abiding impression upon the Irish religious scene.[122] There were Irvingites present at some of the early Powerscourt conferences, though it seems that they were increasingly isolated as Irving slipped deeper into Christological disarray, and as the proceedings became more extreme.[123] Several of the early Brethren converted to Irvingism, including Edward Hardman, a former Anglican curate from Westport.[124] A number of others, though unwilling to abandon Brethrenism, were nevertheless attracted by the Irvingites' emphasis on charismatic experience. Captain Hall, for example, an important influence among the early Brethren, 'became quite fascinated by Irvingism', praying in earnest 'that the same gifts might be bestowed upon Christians at Plymouth'.[125]

Despite these points of contact, as the Irish prophetic movement fell increasingly under Darby's dogmatic leadership, and as its English counterpart began to evolve in its own specific direction, tensions began to emerge between these two closely related, but nevertheless distinct, millennial movements. During the early 1830s, for example, when Hall invited Irving to travel to Plymouth, Irving refused, denouncing the place as a 'slough of love'.[126] When Hall travelled to London instead, Irving made it clear that he rejected the distinction between the Church and the World as

[119] The first (of many) references to the Second Advent began to appear in her correspondence during May 1826. See *Letters and Papers by the Late Theodosia A. Viscountess Powerscourt*, ed. Daly, 31; Fry, 237.

[120] See Edward Irving [Juan Josafat Ben-Ezra], *The Coming of Messiah in Glory and Majesty* (1827).

[121] See the *Christian Herald* (1830), 176; Columba Graham Flegg, *'Gathered Under Apostles': A Study of the Catholic Apostolic Church* (Oxford, 1992), 435.

[122] Though it appears that Darby was absent in England at the time. See *HD* 7a, 28 May 1830; 7b, 31 May 1830, and 29a, 9 December 1830; the *Christian Herald* (1830), 176; Fry, 235.

[123] See Embley, 'The Origins and Early Development of the Plymouth Brethren', 90.

[124] See *Letters of John Nelson Darby*, ed. Trench, i.27.

[125] Fry, 256.

[126] Ibid. 257.

separate bodies, and condemned Hall for resigning his commission. He took exception to Hall's belief that a Christian had no right to exercise temporal power, such as serving as a local magistrate. When Hall protested, Irving silenced him: 'Sir I forbid you saying any more of such things; I will not have the ears of my family listen to it.' Hall quickly withdrew, entirely cured of Irvingism.[127] Another prominent critic of Irvingism to emerge from the early Brethren was Benjamin Newton. At the time of his conversion to 'serious religion' in 1827, Newton set aside many aspects of his Quaker upbringing, especially its emphasis on the 'inner light'. He now believed that religious experience, in contrast to a strict biblicism, often led believers into theological heterodoxy.[128] Thus, after investigating the authenticity of the 'gifts' for himself, and after witnessing their destructive effects on some of those around him, Newton became highly critical of both Irving and the English prophetic movement. 'I was at the meeting when the healing took place,' he wrote, 'and heard the prayer, and felt the influence.' I felt as if I was 'paralyzed after it. I couldn't take the Bible, couldn't pray.' This 'prophetic' activity, he concluded, was 'of the devil and not of God'.[129] When his friend Henry Bulteel began 'healing' members of his Oxford congregation, and moved on into bizarre forms of speculative theology (all based on religious experience), Newton railed publicly against Irvingism, travelling to different parts of the West Country where the movement was gaining converts. He, in turn, was 'solemnly cursed' by the Irvingites in public.[130] Finally, in April 1835, Newton wrote a scathing attack on the Catholic Apostolic gathering in Newman Street for the Brethren quarterly, the *Christian Witness*.[131]

The evolution of Darby's eschatology, which in some ways resembles that of the English prophetic movement, and in other ways rejects several of its most salient features, is not easy to trace. Darby's letters from the late 1820s reveal some development in his

[127] Ibid. 256.

[128] The author is indebted to Jonathan Burnham for this insight into Newton's background.

[129] Ibid. 133–4.

[130] Ibid. 142. Bulteel's flirtation with Irvingism is discussed in Chapter 7.

[131] B. W. Newton, 'Doctrines of the Church in Newman Street', in the *Christian Witness* (April 1835).

prophetic views, though the exact nature of this change remains uncertain.[132] In early 1828, when Bellett wrote informing Darby that his views on prophecy had been 'greatly enlarged' through contact with the English prophetic movement, Darby replied that his own views on the subject had already 'travelled rapidly' in a similar direction.[133] His *Considerations on the Nature and Unity of the Church of Christ*, published later the same year, refers to several eschatological themes, but only in the most general terms.[134] During the following year, he responded publicly to a number of recent works on prophecy, in the process distancing himself from the English prophetic movement.[135] Although Darby referred to a sermon by Irving as 'deeply interesting and, I think, profitable and timely',[136] he denounced Irvingism for its numerous contradictions and inaccurate interpretations of Scripture.[137] Equally defective (in his view) was the *Morning Watch*, the mouthpiece of the English prophetic movement, which he criticized as partisan and untruthful.[138] In the same work Darby inquired whether a lay person was free to preach the Gospel?—an ecclesiological point on which the increasingly sharp distinction between the two movements was readily apparent.[139] When the supposed outbreak of the 'gifts' occurred in Scotland in early 1830, Darby responded with caution, writing little on the subject. According to Newton, he was eventually persuaded to investigate the phenomenon at first hand, returning unconvinced of its authenticity.[140] A few years later, Darby (like Newton) published a pamphlet highly critical of the Catholic Apostolic gathering in Newman Street.[141] Despite his emerging opposition to the teachings of the English prophetic movement, Darby remained deeply interested in the subject of prophecy. Moreover, despite his own characteristic certitude in matters of Christian doctrine, he continued to read extensively, and remarkably widely, in the field of eschatology, drawing on a

[132] See *Letters of John Nelson Darby*, ed. Trench, i.344; iii.298.

[133] See Neatby, *A History of the Plymouth Brethren*, 12.

[134] Darby, *Considerations on the Nature and Unity of the Church of Christ* (1828), in *CW* i.34, 41, 44, 45.

[135] See Darby, 'Reflections upon the Prophetic Inquiry and the Views Advanced in it' (1829), in *CW* ii.1–31.

[136] Ibid. 19. [137] Ibid. 26. [138] Ibid. 20–1. [139] Ibid. 31.

[140] See Fry, 208, 236–7.

[141] Darby, 'A Letter to a Clergyman on the Claims and Doctrines of Newman Street' (n.d.), in *CW* iv.24–51.

variety of traditions. Samuel Tregelles, for example, who first came into contact with Darby around 1835, recalled that, at the time, Darby repeatedly pushed onto others the prophetic views and writings of the French Dominican Bernard Lambert, those of the French Jansenist Pierre-Jean Agier, and those of the German Protestant Hermann Olshausen.[142]

Over time, Darby set out to formulate his own intricate millennial system. It divided the second coming of Christ into two distinct and separate parts: His secret Advent (or 'rapture') in which the saints will be instantly removed from the earth, thus sparing them the pain of the seven-year tribulation;[143] and His coming in splendour in the presence of the saints to rule over the earth after the tribulation.[144] This serial interpretation of unfulfilled prophecy has been given the label 'dispensationalism', in that it divides biblical history into well-defined time periods, or dispensations, into which God reveals a particular purpose to be accomplished in that period, and to which men respond in faith or unbelief.[145]

One of the salient features of dispensational theology, with its inherent pessimism regarding established religion, was the prediction of the rise of modernism, secularism, and apostate religious structures.[146] Another was its radical distinction between the Jewish and Gentile dispensations—'the hinge', as Darby referred to it, 'upon which the subject and the understanding of Scripture turns.'[147] As Harold Rowdon and others have rightly observed, the distinction between these two dispensations forms the basis for Darby's understanding of both ecclesiology and eschatology.[148] In this perspective, during the present—Gentile, or church—dispensation, the power of the Kingdom of God is unseen on earth. The Church, therefore, should focus on things heavenly, not

[142] See T. C. F. Stunt, '*A Bibliographic History of Dispensationalism* by Arnold Ehlert—a review', in the *Christian Brethren Research Fellowship Journal* (1968), 24.

[143] Darby initially held to a three and a-half year (1,260 days) tribulation; only later did he accept a seven-year tribulation.

[144] See D. W. Bebbington, *Evangelicalism in Modern Britain* (1989), 86.

[145] See Sinclair B. Ferguson and David F. Wright (eds.), *New Dictionary of Theology* (Leicester, 1988), 200.

[146] See Ray S. Anderson, 'Fundamentalism', in Alister E. McGrath (ed.), *The Blackwell Encyclopedia of Modern Christian Thought* (Oxford, 1995), 221.

[147] See Darby, 'Reflections upon the Prophetic Inquiry and the Views Advanced in it', in *CW* ii.18.

[148] See Rowdon, *The Origins of the Brethren*, 51.

temporal,[149] for it will soon (through the 'rapture') be 'removed' from the earth. Subsequently, the focus of God's attentions will return to the nation of Israel, whose hopes are earthly.[150]

Since its formulation, the worldwide influence of dispensationalism has been immense. Among those who absorbed Darby's teaching was Henry Moorhouse, a Brethren evangelist, who, in turn, influenced the American Dwight L. Moody, probably the most esteemed evangelist of the late nineteenth century. Still more momentous has been the impact of Darby's teachings on Cyrus I. Scofield, whose popular *Reference Bible* (1909) has ensured the acceptance of 'Darbyite' pre-millennialism throughout much of the evangelical world, especially in the fertile soil of the American revivalist movement where the literal interpretation of Scripture, combined with a strong emphasis on pre-millennial eschatology, has long prevailed.[151]

Given its dispensational structure, and given the historical complexities out of which it emerged, scholars have not found it easy to explain or categorize Darby's eschatology. The Scottish Calvinist historian and publisher, Iain Murray, for example, has argued that all the salient features of Darby's complex pre-millennialist scheme can also be found in the teachings of Irving and the English prophetic movement. These include the expectation of impending judgements upon Christendom, the imminence of Christ's Advent, and Christ's consequent millennial reign on earth.[152] The English Orthodox writer, Columba Flegg, however, in his close study of the Catholic Apostolic Church, argues instead that the two eschatologies are more notable for their points of disagreement.[153] For example, the Brethren adopted a 'futurist' view of the apocalypse, attacking in particular the interpretation of prophetic 'days' as 'years' which was so central to the 'historicists'

[149] See Darby, 'The Dispensation of the Kingdom of Heaven—Matt. XIII', in the *Christian Witness* (1834), 129–30.

[150] See Jonathan David Burnham, 'The Controversial Relationship between Benjamin Wills Newton and John Nelson Darby', D.Phil. thesis (Oxford, 2000), 128–33.

[151] See Murray, *The Puritan Hope*, 198. Darby's expository writings, of which the *Synopsis of the Books of the Bible* is the best known, enjoyed a wide readership on both sides of the Atlantic, while his translations of the Bible into English, French, and German were respected for their literal accuracy. See Stunt, 'John Nelson Darby'. Over 3 million copies of the *Scofield Reference Bible* have been sold throughout the world since 1909; a second edition was published in 1917; in 1967, the *New Scofield Reference Bible* was published.

[152] See Murray, *The Puritan Hope*, 200.

[153] See Flegg, *'Gathered Under Apostles'*, 436.

who dominated the English prophetic movement.[154] Nor can Darby's concept of a *secret* 'rapture' (which quickly became one of the hallmarks of Brethren eschatology), an event which preceded all fulfillment of apocalyptic prophecy, be found in the teachings of Irving or any member of the Catholic Apostolics.[155]

As his dispensational system coalesced, Darby concluded that the miraculous 'gifts', which had been given to the original apostles to exalt Christ and to advance his kingdom, were no longer available and should not be expected in the present dispensation.[156] But what *could* believers expect and look for? Could they hope for revival prior to Christ's return? Such questions, now being raised within an atmosphere of increasing millennial hope, required answers. During the 1830s, Darby's thinking on such issues, and a host of related themes, continued to evolve. Evidence of this development can be found in his eleven 'prophetical' lectures, delivered at Geneva during 1840, where he argued that believers should not permit themselves 'to hope for a continued progress of good', but 'expect a progress of evil'. In fact, 'the hope of the earth being filled with the knowledge of the Lord before the exercise of His judgment, and the consummation of this judgment on earth, is delusive.' Contemporary Christendom, he concluded, had 'become completely corrupted; the dispensation of the Gentiles has been found unfaithful'. Can it again be restored? 'No: impossible. As the Jewish dispensation was cut off, so the Christian dispensation will be also.'[157]

As Murray has pointed out, Darby's teaching denounced as presumption the expectation that Christianity will claim vast numbers of new converts from all corners of the earth. Believers were not to look to the fulfillment of God's kingdom by spiritual

[154] Futurists believe that none of the prophecies of the 'last days' have been fulfilled in the history of the church, and they expect them all to come to pass within a short period of time just prior to the return of Christ. All the great events prophesied in the Bible still await fulfillment. Historicists believe that the prophetic Scriptures, especially those found in Daniel and Revelation, present the entire history of the church in symbolic form. Thus, they look into the church's past and present to find prophetic fulfillments and to see where they are in God's timetable. See Timothy P. Weber, *Living in the Shadow of the Second Coming* (Oxford, 1979), 9–11.

[155] Flegg, *'Gathered Under Apostles'*, 436. Darby believed that the prophecies contained in Scripture would be fulfilled only after the rapture. No prophetic event would precede this, including the seven-year tribulation.

[156] The *Christian Witness* (1840), 254.

[157] Darby, 'Progress of Evil on the Earth' (1840), in *CW* ii.310–11, 320–1.

labour on earth, but to Christ's imminent Advent. Seen in psychological terms, Darby's teaching appears deeply pessimistic. After all, Irish and English Evangelicals had been labouring at home and overseas for many years, evangelizing the heathen and working to transform social conditions, and with some success. Was all this now to be abandoned? Was there *no* hope for the present dispensation? Yes, Darby countered, there *was* hope: not the hope of the Puritans and Evangelicals, which expected the spread of the Gospel on earth *and* Christ's glorious appearance, but the hope of His Second Advent only.[158]

Darby's pre-millennialist teaching encouraged profound changes in the outlook of Evangelical thought, as had Irvingism. It was, for the most part, highly pessimistic; it discouraged believers from becoming too involved in the quotidian of science, politics, and business; it dismissed overseas missions, and it minimized the importance of the visible church. Most important for this study, it encouraged secession by advancing the idea that the Established Church was an irremediably fallen body which had no future and could be safely ignored. As Darby wrote in 1833, 'I do feel that the ignorance and narrowness of the Church of England will be what will be judged for all this, and the judgment is at hand, lingereth not. The Lord have mercy on many in it—dear saints.'[159] Of Ireland, then in the grip of nationalistic and political turmoil, he predicted that 'there will be an entirely new state of things in a year or two. The country will, I doubt not, be practically separated from England, probably entirely.'[160] A year or two later, he predicted the imminent downfall of the English Church, now apparently reeling under the two-pronged onslaught of liberalism and Roman Catholicism. 'I have no doubt at all', he wrote, 'that the present arrangements (ecclesiastical I mean) of the country, will not last a year, and that the result of the arrangements which will follow, will be to put the country under the direct dominion of infidelity and popery, and of the Pope or Primate of Rome.'[161] Ten years later, despite the survival (even revival, albeit Catholic) of the Church of England, his tune had not changed. Increasingly pessimistic about the spiritual state of the Church of England, Darby considered the possibility of redirecting the focus

[158] Murray, *The Puritan Hope*, 202.
[159] *Letters of John Nelson Darby*, ed. Trench, i.19.
[160] Ibid. 23.
[161] The *Christian Witness* (1834), 28.

of his public teaching. 'I am deeply convinced', he wrote, 'that the [Brethren] testimony is urgently demanded in England, and I think that I must return to work there, that at least a testimony may be borne by the grace of God, before Puseyism possess the country, and whilst religious liberty remains to us, which I do not think will last too long.'[162]

Given the rise of Darby's dispensationalist teachings, with its pre-millennialist pessimism, it is perhaps of little surprise to discover that he came to denounce the English prophetic movement's increasing infatuation with the miraculous 'gifts'. All such manifestations of the Spirit, he now believed, had disappeared with the apostolic age and would only return at Christ's Advent.[163] At the same time, and despite his unveiled condemnation of Irving's Christological heresies,[164] the two men continued to hold in common a number of doctrines. Both advanced certain 'Catholic' teachings deemed unacceptable by some of their more Protestant-inclined sympathizers. Both held to paedobaptism. Both saw the church as a universal, apostolic, and prophetic body. Both were inclined towards asceticism. In a critique of Newman's *Apologia Pro Vita Sua*, Darby even admitted that, at one stage, while looking for the ideal church and 'governed by a morbid imagination', he had thought much of Rome and its professed sanctity, catholicity, and antiquity.[165] In retrospect, he saw himself as a kind of Tractarian even before the onset of the Oxford Movement:

I know the system. I knew it and walked in it years before Dr Newman . . . thought of the subject; and when Dr Pusey was not heard of. I fasted in Lent so as to be weak in body at the end of it; ate no meat on week-days—nothing till evening on Wednesdays, Fridays, and Saturdays, then a little bread or nothing; observed strictly the weekly fasts, too. I went to my clergyman always if I wished to take the sacrament, that he might judge of the matter. I held apostolic succession fully, and the channels of grace to be there only. I held thus Luther and Calvin and their followers to be outside . . . I searched with earnest diligence into the evidences of apostolic succession in England, and just saved their validity for myself and my conscience. The union of Church and State I held

[162] *Letters of John Nelson Darby*, ed. Trench, i.66.

[163] See Darby, 'Remarks on a Tract Circulated by the Irvingites Entitled, "A Word of Instruction"' (n.d.), in *CW* xv.1–15; 'On Ministry: Its Nature, Source, Power and Responsibility' (n.d.), in *CW* i.215–16.

[164] See Darby, 'The Dispensation of the Fullness of Times' (1850), in *CW* xiii.152.

[165] Darby, *Analysis of Dr Newman's* Apologia Pro Vita Sua (1866), in *CW* xviii.145–6.

to be Babylonish, that the church ought to govern itself, and that she was in bondage but was the church.[166]

Elsewhere, providing another glimpse into his early asceticism, Darby wrote: 'I said, if I fast three days I can fast four, and if four, five, and if five, better six, and if six, better seven.'[167]

Why Darby moved away from such a regimen remains uncertain. His early spiritual transformation, during his convalescence after the riding accident in late 1826, seems to have encouraged his interest in asceticism. While serving as curate at Calary, for instance, he made his home in a peasant's hut high on a lofty upland a thousand feet above the sea: here he lived the life of an ancient anchorite, wearing clothes of the meanest kind and so neglecting his personal appearance that he often resembled a common beggar.[168] Francis Newman, then living nearby at the Pennefathers', sharply described Darby at this stage of his life: 'a fallen cheek, a bloodshot eye, crippled limbs resting on crutches, a seldom shaved beard, a shabby suit of clothes and a generally neglected person, drew at first pity, with wonder to see such a figure in a drawing-room.'[169] Darby laboured with burning intensity, striving to instil a sense of the impending Advent in his rural and impoverished Irish flock. His resemblance to the model of the 'holy man' in Roman spirituality even led his Roman Catholic neighbours to speculate whether one of the old Irish saints had been resurrected in their midst.[170] No doubt Irving and some of the early leaders within the Catholic Apostolic Church would have found much of this to their liking.

So too did several of the early Brethren. Lady Powerscourt herself, though remaining a *grande dame*, maintained her own mountain retreat high above Powerscourt House, to which she would escape to pray and meditate. John Parnell, the second Lord Congleton, in spite of a personal fortune of some £1,200 a year, took a modest house in Teignmouth at an annual rent of £12, furnished it with wooden chairs, a plain deal table, steel forks, and pewter teaspoons. The table, 'by concession to the housemaid', was afterwards stained because of the trouble it gave in constant

166 Ibid. 156.
167 Darby, 'Substance of a Reading on Ephesians' (n.d.), in *CW* xxvii.92.
168 Stokes, 'John Nelson Darby', 544.
169 Francis William Newman, *Phases of Faith*, 6th edn. (1860), 17.
170 Stokes, 'John Nelson Darby', 544.

scouring to keep it clean.[171] He also dispensed with all carpets. Indeed the whole subject of carpets seems to have become the mark of pure apostolic spirituality within the early Brethren, as other adherents eagerly followed Parnell's example.[172] After his conversion to 'serious religion', A. N. Groves abandoned his dental practice in Exeter, worth over £1,000 a year, in order to study for the mission field.[173] His single-minded devotion to spiritual matters influenced many within the early movement, especially Craik and Müller.[174] After marrying Groves's sister, Müller began to share his suspicion of 'human direction' in 'the things of God'. He then refused to accept a regular salary, relinquished all attempts to save money, and accepted literally the command to 'sell your possessions, and give alms' (Luke 12:33).[175] Another adherent to the early Brethren, Sir Alexander Campbell, insisted that his domestic servants dine at table with him. On one occasion, when he was late in arriving, he found that the servants had already set to work consuming the dinner themselves. They explained to their surprised employer that, as he was so slow in arriving, they had better commence without him lest the food grow cold.[176] The adoption of such attitudes by some members of the early Brethren can perhaps in part be attributed to their acceptance (at least initially) of a highly realized eschatology. Drawn from the communitarianism found in the Acts of the Apostles, the eschatological ethic of the early movement (prior to its acceptance of Darby's dispensational scheme) naturally found expression in both asceticism and a heightened expectation that the *parousia* was at hand. Examples of similar rigorism can be found today in Pentecostal communalism.

Why Darby, along with others in the movement, gradually abandoned such practices remains an open question. Perhaps it was due to health reasons. Perhaps it was related to a desire to widen the social catchment area of Brethrenism, attracting those to whom ascetic and communal spirituality did not come easily.

[171] See Henry Groves, *Memoir of Lord Congleton* (1884), 62. He eventually died while lying on a small iron camp bed. See ibid. 29.

[172] Neatby, *A History of the Plymouth Brethren*, 41.

[173] See Coad, *A History of the Brethren Movement*, 15–25.

[174] As exemplified in his first publication. See A. N. Groves, *Christian Devotedness* (1825).

[175] See Neatby, *A History of the Plymouth Brethren*, 54; Rowdon, *The Origins of the Brethren*, 117.

[176] Neatby, *A History of the Plymouth Brethren*, 41–2.

It may have arisen as the result of opposition to the historicism of the English prophetic movement; the development of Darby's dispensational system, with its future eschatology, seems to have rendered such austerities less urgent. In any case, by 1845, if not earlier, it appears that Darby had abandoned the sterner forms of Christian self-denial. As he admitted to a rather surprised William Kelly while the two dined together, 'it is my habit to have a small hot joint on Saturday, cold on Lord's Day, cold on Monday, on Tuesday, on Wednesday, and on Thursday. On Friday I am not sorry to have a bit of chop or steak; then the round begins again.'[177] Darby, Kelly concluded, now had 'not a whit of asceticism, but liberty and his heart bent on pleasing the Lord as to necessary food'.[178]

VI

One of the most significant developments in the early history of Brethrenism was its export from Ireland to England. Here, while the movement first took root at Oxford, it quickly branched out through the peripatetic activity of a handful of young adherents to two important West Country locations: Bristol and Plymouth. As in Ireland, small groups, unconnected and unaware of each another, but with similar concerns and objections to the Established Church, began meeting in various parts of England at about the same time. In about 1831, for example, Bellett was staying with friends in rural Somerset where he was asked by his hosts to give an account of the early Brethren movement. Present that evening was the daughter of a local clergyman, who, after hearing Bellett's remarks, exclaimed with surprise that the tenets of the early Brethren were precisely those which she had recently developed on her own, and which, until now, she believed were held by no one else. Also present were her mother and a local couple, and they too revealed that they had been meeting in the simplicity of the Brethren's ways for some time, worshipping and 'breaking bread' in private, unaware of like-minded souls in either England or Ireland.[179]

The connection between Oxford and the early Brethren is of some importance in that it not only established a number of

[177] Quoted in W. G. Turner, *John Nelson Darby* (1901), 44. [178] Ibid.
[179] Neatby, *A History of the Plymouth Brethren*, 25.

relationships which served the movement in significant ways, but it also, through doctrinal extremism and its encouragement of secession, added to the spiritual unrest and theological volatility already recognizable in Oxford Evangelicalism.[180] This contributed, by way of reaction, to the outbreak and progress of the Oxford Movement. The initial link between Oxford and early Brethrenism was forged by Darby's relationship with two influential Oxford Evangelicals, Joseph Charles Philpot and Francis Newman.

Philpot had enjoyed considerable success at Oxford, gaining a coveted First in classics in 1824, followed by election to a fellowship at Worcester. In early 1826 he became private tutor to the sons of Edward Pennefather at Temple Carig, Delgany, County Wicklow. Pennefather, a leading Irish jurist who was later to become Lord Chief Justice of Ireland and a Privy Councillor, was married to Darby's elder sister, Susannah. Moreover, Darby had already established himself as the spiritual master of the Pennefather household, which deferred to him on all matters theological and doctrinal.[181] While resident at the Pennefathers', and through Darby's influence, Philpot underwent a classic evangelical conversion experience. Here in Ireland, Philpot was also able to witness at first hand the intense spiritual atmosphere created by the recent success of the 'Walkerites' and 'Kellyites', as well as the highly charged debates over Catholic Emancipation and the Home Mission which had produced such a determined anti-Erastian response from Darby and other Irish Evangelicals. Philpot's premature return to Oxford in 1827, where he played a prominent role within local Evangelical circles, ensured that these ideas would enjoy prominence in another important centre of spiritual volatility, where strong anti-Erastian sentiment was soon to coalesce with apostolic fervour in the launch of Tractarianism.

Francis Newman, the younger brother of the celebrated John Henry, had also enjoyed an academic career of some distinction at Oxford, taking a double First in mathematics and classics in 1826, and being elected soon afterwards to a fellowship at Balliol.

[180] See Chapter 7.

[181] Darby was then residing at the Pennefathers' in Delgany and Dublin, recovering from an injury to his leg. See Stunt, 'John Nelson Darby'; Turner, *John Nelson Darby*, 27; Sandeen, *The Roots of Fundamentalism*, 32.

In the following year he succeeded Philpot as tutor at the Pennefathers'—another capable, but highly impressionable, young man plunged into an intense spiritual atmosphere.[182] Given the extent of his influence over Philpot, it is not surprising that Darby quickly gained sway over his new acquaintance. In Darby, Newman came to see a man defiantly putting into practice the principles to which others gave only nominal assent.[183] Though at first put off by Darby's extremism and eccentricities, Newman quickly fell under the spell of his sharply formed theology, his forceful separatism, and his relentless logic. Darby's personal magnetism was intensified by the 'unflinching consistency' of his principles, whose simple coherence could well impress those disturbed by the intellectual and spiritual confusion of the religious world at this critical juncture. For all his academic accomplishments, Darby dismissed human learning and accepted, with intense literalness, the words of the New Testament which he saw as a clear guide for the issues of the day. When Darby was asked by Newman, 'but do you really think that *no* part of the New Testament may have been temporary in its object?', Darby gave an emphatic *no*: all was to be judged by the scriptural Word. 'For the first time', wrote Newman, 'I saw a man earnestly turning into reality the principles which others confessed with their lips only.'[184] By his extraordinary blend of tenderness and inflexible certitude Darby displayed (in a remarkable resemblance to Newman's brother John Henry, albeit with a determined Protestant slant) 'a wonderful power of bending other minds to his own, and even stamping upon them the tones of his voice and all sorts of slavish imitation'. Seen in psychological terms, Darby became a kind of substitute for Newman's older brother, a representative figure of authority and power. Before long, Newman began to defer to Darby, asking him what he would say about this or that, and (but for occasional weaknesses which warned him of Darby's infallibility) would almost have accepted him as an apostle commissioned to reveal the very mind of God.[185]

Under Darby's influence, Newman came to reject all human creeds, all articles of faith, and all councils and synods, and to make Scripture alone his source of revelation and truth.[186] In late

[182] Stokes, 'John Nelson Darby', 545–6.
[183] Newman, *Phases of Faith*, 17–18.
[184] Ibid. 18–19.
[185] Ibid. 20–1.
[186] Stokes, 'John Nelson Darby', 546, 549.

1827, he wrote to his Oxford friend, C. P. Golightly, about the impact of Darby's emerging pre-millennialism upon his own thinking:

How strong is the contest when I turn to the new friends God has given me! They in turn exhibit the Gospel in its *simplicity* . . . One thing I see; that I have of late been led astray by the false dream that God intended this world to be otherwise than a scene of suffering: an error which obscured my view of the true nature of Christ's Kingdom, and led me to pay to passing political events ten times the attention they deserved.[187]

At much the same time, Newman met Anthony Norris Groves, whose piety and spiritual devotion inflamed him with the greatest admiration. Newman concluded immediately that this was another man whom he should 'rejoice to aid or serve'.[188]

When Francis Newman returned to Oxford in late 1828, he quickly invited Darby to visit the university. Keen to extend his influence, Darby made the first of several visits to Oxford in May 1830.[189] On arrival, he immediately assumed the place of father-confessor to a host of impressionable undergraduates, who accepted him as if he were a known and long-trusted friend. His insight into human character and his striking mixture of tenderness and austerity gave him (again, like John Henry Newman) a remarkable psychological ascendancy over his followers, who flocked to him for secret closetings. Francis Newman quickly began to envision the prospect of so considerable a movement of mind as might lead many in Oxford in the same direction that he himself had travelled: in no other manner, he concluded, could a new, pure, and truly effective spiritual movement be launched and sustained.[190]

As it so happened, the timing of Darby's initial visit to Oxford could hardly have been more propitious, for (as in Ireland) many serious-minded young men were experiencing an increased sense of anxiety over the Church's growing secularization.[191] Questions over the revival of the Establishment's flagging spirituality were frequently raised by Evangelicals, as well as by those with more

[187] Quoted in R. W. Greaves, 'Golightly to Newman, 1824–45', in *JEH* (1958), 210.

[188] Newman, *Phases of Faith*, 24.

[189] Ibid. 28. See also *HD* 7a, 28 May 1830; 7b, 31 May 1830, and 29a, 9 Dec. 1830; Fry, 235.

[190] Newman, *Phases of Faith*, 28.

[191] See Chapter 7.

Catholic leanings. Moreover, the 'constitutional revolution' of 1828–32 was by then well under way, provoking anguished concern in Oxford about the consequences for Church and State. Primitive, yet evangelical, alternatives to the 'apostolic' questions now beginning to be raised by the emerging leaders of the Oxford Movement were urgently required. Darby and his followers were all too willing to suggest such alternatives, and their efforts in offering a Protestant response to John Henry Newman's influential ministry at St. Mary's—and later to the *Tracts* themselves—did not go unrewarded. One of the first of these suggestions came in the form of an anonymous attack by Darby upon Edward Burton, the Regius Professor of Divinity, who had himself published a recent attack upon Henry Bulteel, the high Calvinist curate of St. Ebbe's.[192] Too astute to defend Bulteel's *outré* antinomianism in print, Darby instead simply dismissed Burton's claims and advanced his own notions of Calvinistic dogma. Thus did Darby make clear to opponents and supporters alike his assumption of leadership (even among the Oxford Evangelicals), and his determination to set an independent doctrinal course for the early Brethren free of wild antinomian speculation.

VII

The advance of the Brethren into the West of England was made possible through the involvement of a number of like-minded, talented, and decidedly committed individuals. Among them was George Müller, Groves's brother-in-law,[193] who had introduced a number of innovations into his early ministry in Bristol.[194] He established a weekly communion service and abandoned pew rents. He also adopted an open ministry in some meetings, allowing any member of the body to exhort or teach the rest.[195] These innovations, also being implemented within some of the 'drawing-room meetings' in Dublin, eventually became standard practice among the Brethren in the West of

[192] J. N. Darby [Oudies], *The Doctrine of the Church of England at the Time of the Reformation* (Oxford, 1831). For further details of Bulteel's University Sermon see Chapter 7.

[193] See George Müller, *A Narrative of Some of the Lord's Dealings With George Müller* (Bristol, 1837); R. Morris, *Faith, Prayer, and Work* (1866); Frederick G. Warne, *George Müller* (1898).; Arthur T. Pierson, *George Müller of Bristol* (1899); Edward Kennaway Groves, *George Müller and His Successors* (Bristol, 1906); William Henry Harding, *The Life of George Müller* (1914).

[194] See Embley, 'The Origins and Early Development of the Plymouth Brethren', 81–2.

[195] Neatby, *A History of the Plymouth Brethren*, 54.

England. Through the work of Müller and his close associate Henry Craik, the Brethren extended their influence in and around the city of Bristol.

Benjamin Newton was a native of Plymouth and, since 1824, a member (later fellow) of Exeter College, Oxford, where he was tutored privately by Francis Newman.[196] Although raised a Quaker, Newton was converted to 'serious religion' in large part through the influence of Henry Bulteel, also a native of Plymouth, a fellow of Exeter College since 1823, and a determined high Calvinist.[197] It was Bulteel who was responsible for introducing Newton to the ministry of the celebrated hyper-Calvinist, Robert Hawker of the parish of Charles, near Plymouth,[198] which deepened his commitment to 'ultra' Evangelicalism.[199] At much the same time, Newton also became acquainted with John Hill, the Evangelical Vice-Principal at St. Edmund Hall. So unfavourably were the Calvinistic doctrines of Bulteel and Hill then regarded in Oxford, that Newton was ostracized from much of university life and compelled to abandon all hope of college preferment. When Francis Newman returned to Oxford from Ireland in 1828 he raised the subject of unfulfilled prophecy, which he had heard discussed by Darby and various Irish Evangelicals. Newton was so captivated by the issue that he convened a series of meetings in his rooms at Exeter, where the issue of unfulfilled prophecy was discussed at length.[200]

Bulteel also introduced Newton to George Vicesimus Wigram, then an undergraduate at Queen's, son of a wealthy merchant from London and Wexford, and the younger brother of Sir James Wigram, the Vice-Chancellor of the university, and Joseph Cotton Wigram, the future Bishop of Rochester.[201] Wigram had early on embarked on a military career: in 1824, however, he passed through a spiritual crisis which caused him to abandon all thought

[196] See Burnham, 'The Controversial Relationship between Benjamin Wills Newton and John Nelson Darby', 46–78.

[197] Ibid.; see also Chapter 7.

[198] Rowdon, *The Origins of the Brethren*, 61, 63. Bransby, *Evans' Sketch of the Various Denominations of the Christian World*, 305.

[199] Fry, 99. See also 137–8.

[200] Ibid. 62–3.

[201] Ibid. His father, Sir Robert Wigram, was a merchant and shipbuilder in London and Wexford, and later became MP for Fowey and Wexford. See *DNB*; Pickering, *Chief Men Among the Brethren*, 41–2.

of a life in the army. Two years later, he enrolled at Oxford intent on taking holy orders in the Church of England. Through contact with Newton and Harris, he came to accept some of the radical ideas then percolating in and around the Oxford Evangelical milieu. According to one contemporary account, so transformed were Wigram's views that, during his student days, he even began to receive communion in a small group setting, without the benefit of clergy—an activity which, if discovered by the authorities, might well have led to his being sent down from the university.[202]

During 1829, Newton deepened his friendship with Harris, who had preceded him as a fellow of Exeter. Like his cousin Bulteel, Harris was both a native of Plymouth and an Etonian. Married to the daughter of the prominent Evangelical Legh Richmond, he had been ordained in 1816; ten years later, he had been presented to the perpetual curacy of Plymstock, a village on the outskirts of Plymouth.[203] In 1829, when Harris visited Oxford to cast his vote in the celebrated parliamentary election following the passage of Catholic Emancipation, he was met by Newton and introduced to his Evangelical circle. At St. Edmund Hall, he was introduced to the well-known Evangelical William 'Millennial' Marsh, also in Oxford to vote in the election, and the two spent some time together discussing the issue of unfulfilled prophecy.[204]

This trio—Wigram, Newton, and Harris—quickly coalesced into what was to become the driving force behind the establishment of the Brethren in and around Plymouth—the most significant point on the denomination's geographical and spiritual compass. In 1830, Wigram (who was apparently refused ordination by Bishop Blomfield of London as the result of his Evangelical convictions) moved to Plymouth where he devoted himself to writing biblical study texts.[205] In the following year, he established Monday evening lectures at the disused Providence Chapel, one of several contemporaneous ecclesiastical experiments arising

[202] Anon., *Interesting Reminiscences*, 15.

[203] Charles William Boase, *Register of Exeter College, Oxford* (Oxford, 1879), 121.

[204] Rowdon, *The Origins of the Brethren*, 64.

[205] See ibid. 74. For an example of Wigram's scholarly work see *The Englishman's Greek Concordance to the New Testament* (1839).

largely from the recent secessions at Oxford.[206] As Harold Rowdon has explained, it was apparently on Wigram's initiative that his group began to celebrate the Lord's Supper at the chapel, at first privately with some half dozen who met in the vestry on a Sunday evening, and then more publicly—to the astonishment of both Darby and Newton—in the chapel itself.[207] Though a number of local Evangelical clergy participated in the private administration of communion,[208] when the practice became public the 'Gospel clergy' were nowhere to be found.[209]

Newton had been greatly moved by Bulteel's celebrated University Sermon of February 1831, which promoted high Calvinistic doctrines in a provocative manner, later describing the occasion as 'the turning point of all my life'.[210] He had also been influenced, by abraction, by Bulteel's highly unsettled spiritual course in the months following his secession from the Church. A further thread in the tapestry of his theological development came through contact with the Evangelical William Lambert, author of *A Call to the Converted* (1831)—a work so provocative in its attack upon the Church that Charles Sumner, the Evangelical Bishop of Winchester and Visitor of Corpus Christi College, Oxford, initiated proceedings against Lambert, attempting to deprive him of his College fellowship.[211] Newton now abandoned his plans to be ordained, resigned his fellowship at Exeter, and seceded.[212] In March 1832, he married Hannah Abbot of Plymouth, and immersed himself in the work of the early Brethren in and around south Devon.[213] Newton's doctrinal moderation was destined to raise tensions in the movement, however, and it was not long before his relationship with Darby began to deteriorate, especially after Newton's role in organizing the prophetic conference in Plymouth in 1834.[214]

James L. Harris continued to serve as perpetual curate at

[206] See Fry, 256. In January 1832, when public worship began at Providence Chapel, William Tiptaft's chapel was being built at Abingdon, Henry Bulteel's at Oxford, and William Morshead's at Bath. See Chapter 7; also Embley, 'The Origins and Early Development of the Plymouth Brethren', 77.

[207] Rowdon, *The Origins of the Brethren*, 76. [208] Ibid. [209] Fry, 256.

[210] Ibid. 100, 132. [211] See ibid. 279. [212] See ibid. 43, 250.

[213] The *Royal Devonport Telegraph and Plymouth Chronicle*, 24 Mar. 1832. The officiating minister was J. L. Harris.

[214] See Burnham, 'The Controversial Relationship between Benjamin Wills Newton and John Nelson Darby', 149–52, 157–8.

Plymstock until September 1832, when he too seceded from the Church. In this critical year of the Reform Bill, he published two works which disclosed what were by now standard objections to the Established Church: opposition to indiscriminate infant baptism, to aspects of the baptismal service itself, and to other passages in the Prayer Book; and opposition to continued State control over canon law which, he now believed, subverted all effective ecclesiastical discipline.[215] For him the true church was a 'congregation of faithful men' and an 'assembly of believers united in fellowship', which excluded those who had made a merely nominal profession of faith. Such a church was so unlike any assembly of non-believers that the world could easily recognize its distinctiveness.[216] After his secession, Harris went on to play a significant role in the development of the early Brethren in and around Plymouth. In the religious census of 1851, he is listed as 'occasionally ministering' at a room in How Lane, in Plymstock, described as 'part of an out-house in a farmyard, at present used only for preaching' and attracting an average Sunday congregation of between fifty and eighty.[217]

During his first visit to Oxford in 1830, Darby had been encouraged by Newton to visit Plymouth, where his ministry could be extended to other like-minded believers gathering in similar fashion to the Brethren in their 'drawing-room meetings'.[218] Darby soon became closely identified with the work in the area. 'Plymouth', he wrote in April 1832, 'has altered the face of Christianity to me, from finding brethren, and they acting together.'[219] Amid the confusion surrounding the contemporary 'Gospel world', Darby witnessed at Plymouth the emergence of a true 'apostolic' movement which he believe could transform the spiritual life of England. He later described his visit:

[215] J. L. Harris, *Address to the Parishioners of Plymstock* (Plymouth, 1832); *What is a Church? Or, Reasons for Withdrawing from the Ministry of the Establishment* (Plymouth, 1832). For a moderate Evangelical response see Robert Cox, *Secession Considered* (1832); T. H. Ley [A Clergyman], *A Letter to the Late Perpetual Curate of Plymstock* (Devonport, 1832).

[216] Harris, *What is a Church?*, 4.

[217] See Michael J. L. Wickes (ed.), *Devon in the Religious Census of 1851* (Appledore, 1990), 70.

[218] See Stunt, 'John Nelson Darby'. James Grant claimed incorrectly that Darby first visited Plymouth in 1832 or 1833. See Grant, *The Plymouth Brethren*, 8.

[219] *Letters of John Nelson Darby*, ed. Trench, iii.230, 271.

By invitation I went to Plymouth to preach. My habit was to preach wherever people wished, whether in buildings or in private houses. More than once, even with ministers of the National Church, we have broken bread on Monday evening after meetings for Christian edification, where each was free to read, to speak, to pray, or to give out a hymn. Some months afterwards we began to do so on Sunday morning, making use of the same liberty, only adding the Lord's supper, which we had, and still have, the practice of taking every Sunday. Occasionally it has been partaken of more often. About that time also some began to do the same in London.[220]

By now Plymouth had become notorious in the 'Gospel world' as the centre of extreme Calvinistic theology, thanks to the presence of Robert Hawker, deemed by alarmed Evangelicals to be 'the great patron and apostle of antinomianism'.[221] Through his many publications and his work with two influential religious societies,[222] Hawker was at the centre of a hyper-Calvinist network which extended far and wide, especially within the West Country, where (according to at least one contemporary account) it made 'alarming progress' during the 1820s.[223] When Darby travelled to Plymouth for the first time, he thus alighted in a place which was, in many respects, already well disposed to ultra-Evangelicalism.

Very soon after his arrival in Plymouth, Darby made the acquaintance of Captain Hall (son of the late Charles Henry Hall, former Dean of Christ Church and Regius Professor of Divinity at Oxford, later Dean of Durham), a former naval officer who had resigned from his commission as a matter of conscience and was now engaged in advancing 'Gospel principles' in and around Plymouth through an extensive work of itinerant preaching.[224] Through Darby, Hall was introduced to Wigram, Harris, and other like-minded local evangelicals. Hall now began to play an important role in the embryonic Brethren movement, contributing substantially to its early growth in and around south Devon.[225] This addition to the movement stiffened its anti-

[220] Ibid. iii.301–2.

[221] Joseph Cottle, *Strictures on the Plymouth Antinomians*, 2nd edn. (1824), 4, 11.

[222] See Grayson Carter, 'Robert Hawker', in *New DNB*.

[223] See Cottle, *Strictures on the Plymouth Antinomians*, 45.

[224] See Pickering, *Chief Men Among the Brethren*, 20.

[225] Despite the reluctance of the early Brethren to recognize their gatherings as 'churches' or to return census information to the government, they were (to some degree)

Erastianism, for Hall opposed all submission to earthly rulers and even the notion of Christians serving as local magistrates.[226]

The final addition to the Plymouth coterie was Henry Borlase, a Cornishman and a Cambridge man, who in August 1830 had been ordained to the curacy of St. Keyne, Cornwall, where he remained until his secession two years later.[227] His *Reasons for Withdrawing from the Ministry of the Church of England* (1833), another typical Evangelical *apologia* for secession, advanced pre-millennialist tendencies and denounced the Church for its open apostasy.[228] Like a number of other Evangelical seceders he lambasted both infant baptism and the communion service, and laid out a narrow 'gathered' ecclesiology.[229] Borlase reinforced these sentiments in the pages of the *Christian Witness* (which he edited), advancing the standard Brethren doctrine of separatism: as the Church was in ruins, it was no sin for Christians to separate from it; separation was in fact the only course open to true believers. Indeed, Anglicanism had itself been established on the same principle during the sixteenth century. Borlase also predicted, disparagingly, that there would be a gradual movement toward external union of the visible churches—a claim which foreshadowed the rise of modern ecumenicism.[230] He continued as editor of the *Christian Witness* until the summer of 1834, when he fell ill. He died in November 1835.[231] Two years after his death, a second edition of his *apologia* was reprinted, with additions, by three of his friends.[232]

represented in the religious census of 1851. In and around Plymouth 10 places of worship, described as 'isolated congregations', were listed; in the county of Devon 36 places of worship with 4,418 in attendance were listed; and in England and Wales as a whole, 132 chapels with 18,529 sittings were listed. See Bruce Coleman, 'The Nineteenth Century: Nonconformity', in Nicholas Orme (ed.), *Unity and Variety: A History of the Church in Devon and Cornwall* (Exeter, 1991), 148; Wickes (ed.), *Devon in the Religious Census of 1851*; Horace Mann, *Report on the Religious Worship in England and Wales* (1851).

226 See Pickering, *Chief Men Among the Brethren*, 20; Rowdon, *The Origins of the Brethren*, 75, 78, 80.

227 See *DNB.*

228 Henry Borlase, *Reasons for Withdrawing from the Ministry of the Church of England* (Plymouth, 1833), 32.

229 See E. Crossley and A. Andrews, *Extracts from the Writings of the late Henry Borlase on subjects connected with the Present State of the Church* (1892), 8–9, 13, 33.

230 See Henry Borlase, 'Separation from Apostasy not Schism', in the *Christian Witness* (1834), 339, 354, 356.

231 See Embley, 'The Origins and Early Development of the Plymouth Brethren', 76.

232 See *Papers by the Late Henry Borlase, Connected with the Present State of the Church* (1836).

VIII

The Brethren had now coalesced into a separate and identifiable religious movement (if not a denomination) functioning in three principal locations: Dublin, Bristol, and Plymouth. During this period a cluster of doctrinal positions, though still evolving, became increasingly associated with the new body. Perhaps most distinctive was its teaching on the church and ministry.[233] The Brethren rejected apostolic succession, the historic creeds, and the principle of paedobaptism (although Darby and a few others continued to adhere to it, apparently without serious objection from others).[234] They also repudiated any form of fixed ministry or formal ministerial training, the maintenance of private pews, the practice of preaching to the non-elect, the employment of ministers, the specifying of any type of monetary contribution, congregational voting on doctrinal matters, and the imposition of any confession as a test of communion.[235] More positively, the Brethren pushed to radical lengths the 'priesthood of all believers', calling every member to an equal share in its ministry and leadership (at least in theory). No humanly appointed minister was therefore required, since they regarded themselves as meeting together under Divine presidency, in fulfillment of Jesus' promise in Matthew 18: 20, 'For where two or three are gathered in my name, there I am in the midst of them.' Moreover, the Brethren maintained that each believer was capable of receiving inspiration directly from the Spirit, for every Christian had been called to the priesthood—a point of similarity between the early Brethren and the Society of Friends.[236]

A further characteristic doctrine of the new movement was separatism. For a number of the early Brethren separation from the non-elect (or from those who differed from 'true' believers by accepting some false teaching) was not equal to the sin of 'schism', but instead a Christian imperative founded on Scripture. As

[233] See T. C. F. Stunt, 'Two Nineteenth Century Movements', in the *Evangelical Quarterly* (1965), 221.

[234] See *ER* (May 1839), 577–8; *Plymouth Brethrenism*, 8 n; Rowdon, *The Origins of the Brethren*, 271–2.

[235] *ER* (May 1839), 576–7.

[236] Ibid. ii.202. See also T. C. F. Stunt, 'Early Brethren and the Society of Friends', in *Christian Brethren Research Fellowship Occasional Paper*, No. 3, 1970.

Darby asked the readers of the *Christian Witness*, in reference to both the Established Church and the Dissenting bodies:

> Does anyone doubt they are seeking worldly power as others to keep it? The path of the saints is most simple; their portion is heavenly; to be not of the world, as Christ is not of the world; to be clear from all their plans . . . If the saint knows *his* intrinsically, his path is very clear, to wit the spirit of separation from the world, through the knowledge of death, and power, and glory, and coming of the Lord Jesus Christ . . . and hence growing positive separation from them all.[237]

The early Brethren thus regarded themselves as something akin to an 'apostolic' assembly, holding exclusive possession of the Spirit.[238] And what was there in Britain, or elsewhere, to challenge this assumption by offering a purer, more scriptural alternative? Archbishop Magee's episcopal charge of 1826, and a series of Erastian acts of Parliament, had proved conclusively that the Established Church was not the true body of Christ, but an irredeemably corrupt and secularized institution founded by man. This was no Church of the apostles. Nor was the Church redeemed by the presence of an allegedly 'righteous' remnant of faithful Evangelicals within its ranks, for their unwillingness to resist the intrusions of Erastianism proved their complicity in the corruption of the body to which they belonged.[239]

Defending the related practice of believers meeting together in private to 'break bread', Darby denied that this was any form of apostasy, but 'schism only from what is worldly, which is a Christian's duty'. In referring to their gatherings, the early Brethren remained reluctant to employ the term 'church' or 'denomination'. Christians should meet together, Darby claimed, 'not leaning upon ministry or assuming anything, or pretending to set up churches, but simply . . . as individuals, merely separating from present evil'.[240] Yet, for all the strength of Darby's rhetoric it is

[237] The *Christian Witness* (1834), 29.

[238] Thomas Croskery, *Plymouth-Brethrenism: A Refutation of its Principles and Doctrines* (1879), pp. vii–viii.

[239] Stokes, 'John Nelson Darby', 540.

[240] As Captain Hall wrote, 'there may be a thousand collective bodies of Christians in a place, and yet if they are not formed so as to be able to obey, the Lord Jesus cannot rule them, and he therefore cannot recognize them as churches, and the Christians belonging to them are only associates in disobedience.' The continuation of such apostate bodies was seen as no proof of their orthodoxy, but of God's Providence and mercy. See the *Christian Witness* (1834), 70–1, 337.

clear that the members of the early Plymouth assembly (and perhaps those of a number of other related local gatherings) did not in fact practice strict separatism; they had no qualms about sharing communion with those outside its ranks, including clergy and laity from the Established Church. Only later, under Darby's determined inspiration, did a portion of the Brethren become 'strict' or 'exclusive'.[241]

There was, in fact, serious debate within the early Brethren over the doctrine of separatism. Despite remaining a member of the Church of England, John Synge served as a much-respected leader within the 'inner circle' of the early Brethren.[242] In 1831, he published a reply to William Lambert's *A Call to the Converted*, which had raised a number of salient points in favour of strict separatism.[243] Synge opposed Lambert's call for secession from the Church in favour of a 'gathered' body of believers. '"A Church so strictly spiritual" as our friend speaks of is not so easily attainable', he warned. Like Wesley half a century earlier, he encouraged believers to 'keep to the Church', while assembling 'as often as circumstances will allow, in some convenient place', not to 'break bread' together, but to meditate and pray, to study the prophetic Scriptures, and interpret the complexities of Christian doctrine.[244]

A more serious challenge to the doctrine of separatism was launched in March 1836 by Anthony Groves, then about to return overseas to convert the heathen. Groves had been absent from 1829 to 1834, serving on the mission field. Since his return, he had travelled extensively among the Brethren in Bristol, Plymouth, Dublin, and elsewhere, during which time he became deeply disturbed about the transformation in the nature of the movement. Consequently, he wrote to Darby challenging the doctrine of separatism and commenting on the harm which it was inflicting upon Brethrenism:

[241] The author is indebted to Jonathan Burnham for this insight into the early life of the Brethren. For more details of the division between 'open' and 'exclusive' Brethren see Roger N. Shuff, 'Open to Closed: The Growth of Exclusivism Among Brethren in Britain, 1848–1953', in the *Brethren Archivists and Historians Network Review* (Autumn 1997), 10–23.

[242] See T. C. F. Stunt, 'John Synge and the Early Brethren', 39–62.

[243] John Synge, *Observations on A Call to the Converted* (Teignmouth, 1831).

[244] Ibid. 4, 11–12.

Was not the principle we laid down as to separation from all existing bodies at the outset, this: that we felt ourselves bound to separate from all individuals and systems, *so far* as they required us to do what our consciences would not allow, or restrained us from doing what our consciences required, and no further? And were we not as free to join and act with any individual, or body of individuals, as they were free *not* to require us to do what our consciences did *not* allow, or prevent our doing what they did? And in this freedom did we not feel brethren should *not* force liberty on those who were bound, nor withhold freedom from those who were free?[245]

At the heart of this comment lies Groves's fear that Darby, in his determination to separate from the Church, had set about creating a narrow and constrictive religious sect. The generous and missionary-minded Groves fretted at the negativism of the early Brethren, and their proneness to find fault in other churches:

Some will not have me hold communion with the Scots, because their views are not satisfactory about the Lord's Supper; others with you, because of your views about baptism; others with the Church . . . because of her thoughts about ministry. I receive them all, and join with them . . . Nor shall I ever feel separation from the good for the sake of the evil, to be my way of witnessing against it, till I see infinitely clearer than I do now, that it is God's.[246]

Groves also predicted that Darby's extremism would lead to the movement being dismissed by many as disputatious, narrow-minded, schismatic, and doctrinaire. If it travelled a step or two further, it would begin to exhibit the same evils as the system from which it professed to have separated, for its basis of union was daily becoming one of formal doctrine and opinion rather than life and love. It would be known by its denials instead of its assertions: more by what it witnessed against than what it witnessed for: it would be an introverted, self-regarding sect like the 'Glasites', the 'Walkerites', the Gospel Standard Baptists, and the Catholic Apostolics.[247]

Groves's appeal fell on deaf ears. Darby would not be moved. Groves continued to oppose Darby's separatism and his pre-

[245] 10 Mar. 1836, quoted in Groves, *Memoir of Anthony Norris Groves*, 533–4.

[246] Ibid. 535–6.

[247] Groves to Darby, 10 Mar. 1836, in Groves, *Darbyism: Its Rise and Development*, 9.

millennial pessimism, devoting his life largely to the cause of Indian missions. In ecclesiological terms, he was saddened that a movement of small, informal assemblies, 'without connexion' with one another, and 'dependent upon the energy of individuals', had developed into a 'centralized organization'. The Brethren's original principle of communion had been the possession of the common life of the family of God, and this was largely unchanged. Groves concluded (perhaps reflecting his growing antipathy of Darby) that the rise of separatism had allowed the most 'narrow-minded and bigoted' to rule over the others, primarily because their consciences would not yield to rival opinion. Into this position, he concluded, some local Brethren assemblies had already rapidly degenerated.[248]

In 1846, another voice was raised from within the movement opposing the doctrine of separatism. In that year, Charles Hargrove, although himself a seceder from the Church, announced his willingness to participate in the organization of the Evangelical Alliance. As he explained to the participants, many of whom were no doubt shocked to find a member of the Brethren among them:

> I feel just as much in communion with them as ever; but I do not feel myself so exclusively in communion with the Plymouth Brethren, as not to be just as much in communion with any Brother in this room. Furthermore, anything God has given me to minister, I feel as free to minister in another place, as in any building of the Plymouth Brethren . . . When I heard of this Alliance, my whole heart went out; and when I see the Basis, I see, permit me to say, (I hope I do not offend) that the grand principle of this Alliance is the principle of the Plymouth Brethren. It is the identical principle.[249]

These examples of continued ecclesiastical moderation within Brethrenism not only provide an interesting glimpse into the doctrinal diversity characterizing the early movement, but also foreshadow the deep divisions which would soon divide it over the so-called 'Bethesda Question'.[250] Darby, however, continued to

[248] Ibid. 10–11.

[249] See *The Evangelical Alliance: Proceedings of the Conference held at Freemasons' Hall, London from Aug. 19th to September 2nd 1846* (1847), 149. The author is indebted to T. C. F. Stunt for this quotation. For further details on Hargrove see Joseph D'Arcy Sirr, *A Memoir of the Honourable and Most Reverend Power Le Poer Trench* (Dublin, 1845), 218–20.

[250] See Coad, *A History of the Brethren Movement*, 157–64.

dismiss all warnings of impending schism. By the mid-1840s, if not much earlier, he had moved far beyond the influence of others, even that of his closest allies within his own movement. He had established something akin to a strict hierarchy of authority within the Brethren. In the succeeding years, the doctrine of separatism led to endless internal strife, disputes, and schisms, in part because of Darby's assumption of authority, but also because he had failed to work out the practical implications of separatism when applied to the administration of a enlarging communion.[251] These developments overshadowed much of the creative contribution made by Brethrenism to the advancement of Christianity, not only in Britain but throughout the world.

IX

The impact of Brethrenism on the Anglican Evangelical movement was far-reaching. In the secession of more than twenty Evangelical clergy, together with a number of gifted—and often wealthy and influential—lay men and women, Brethrenism represented perhaps the most significant internal disruption which confronted the 'Gospel party' during the entire nineteenth century. Moreover, it is likely that the progress of Brethrenism was yet another factor in unsettling 'serious religion' during a period of fracture from within and challenge from without, when both liberalism and Tractarianism were in the ascendant. It also diminished the Evangelicals' ability successfully to rebut the antinomian tendencies of other 'ultras' from within its own ranks, especially in and around the West Country where the influence of Brethrenism was most pronounced.

A similar assessment can be made regarding the impact of Brethren doctrines on Anglican Evangelicalism. Though most Evangelicals remained unimpressed by Darby's strict separatism, high Calvinism, and unique dispensational doctrines (including his notion of a secret 'rapture' preceding the tribulation), the ecclesiological precepts of the early Brethren continue to exert a significant influence on Anglican Evangelicalism to this day. This is particularly true in regards to the movement's emphasis on the role of the laity and the 'priesthood of all believers', and its

[251] See Darby, 'On the Apostasy: What is Succession a Succession of?' (1840), in *CW* i.112–23; 'The Apostasy of the Successive Dispensations' (1836), in *CW* i.124–30; Henry Borlase, 'Separation from Apostasy not Schism', in the *Christian Witness* (1834), 174–91.

rejection of an ordained ministry (which has contributed to the ongoing debate in Evangelical circles over the introduction of 'lay presidency' and the continued use of clerical robes). Moreover, though much of the history of Brethrenism has been characterized by denominational fragmentation and controversy, the influence of the movement on the larger history of British and Irish Protestantism is now beginning to be appreciated.[252] Nor has its influence been confined to Britain and Ireland: while estimates of a movement comprised of anonymous bodies (many holding strong separatist tendencies) are notoriously difficult, Brethrenism is today a worldwide movement with a following estimated at over a million, with particular strength in North America, Latin America (especially Argentina), Zaïre, Zambia, Southern India, Singapore, and New Zealand.[253]

[252] See Bass, 'The Doctrine of the Church in the Theology of J. N. Darby'; Embley, 'The Origins and Early Development of the Plymouth Brethren'; Embley, 'The Early Development of the Plymouth Brethren'; Rowdon, *The Origins of the Brethren*; Coad, *A History of the Brethren Movement*; Baylis, *My People*; Callaghan, *Primitivist Piety*; Grass, 'The Church's Ruin and Restoration'.

[253] See Peter William Brierly and Patrick J. Johnstone (eds.), *World Churches Handbook* (1997).

7

The Oxford Seceders

Though Oxford, as the home of Wesley's famous Holy Club, is regarded as the cradle of the Evangelical Revival, Cambridge is generally credited with the nurture of the movement's celebrated second generation, the alma mater of well-known leaders such as Henry Venn, Joseph Milner, Rowland Hill, Isaac Milner, John Venn, William Wilberforce, Legh Richmond, and, above all, Charles Simeon.[1] During the 1820s, however, the spiritual and intellectual focus of the Revival began to shift back to Oxford, to which, significantly, a number of the sons of the Clapham Sect (and other Evangelical families) were sent to be educated.[2] Wilberforce sent his three younger sons to Oxford primarily because he had become disillusioned with the low state of Cambridge society (which seemed to be borne out by the disastrous career of his eldest son William at Trinity) and the lack of discipline and regularity in college life. He had been favourably impressed by Edward Hawkins, tutor (later Provost) of Oriel College, to whom he entrusted his sons.[3] For similar reasons, Hannah More also transferred her loyalties to Oxford at about the same time. In 1818 she wrote anxiously to her friend Marianne Thornton about the 'contagious atmosphere' of Cambridge society which awaited young Henry Thornton who was about to

[1] See V. H. H. Green, *Religion at Oxford and Cambridge* (1964), 222–54; William Carus, *Memoirs of the Life of the Revd Charles Simeon, M.A.* (1847); Charles Smyth, *Simeon and Church Order* (Cambridge, 1940); Hugh Evans Hopkins, *Charles Simeon of Cambridge* (1977).

[2] With some notable exceptions, including Francis Close, George Cornelius Gorham, Thomas Macaulay, Baptist Noel, and Henry Thornton.

[3] David Newsome, *The Parting of Friends* (1966), 57–62. Robert Wilberforce matriculated in 1820, Samuel in 1823; and Henry in 1826. Other Evangelical 'sons' at Oxford at the time included William Gladstone (Christ Church, 1828); Henry Manning (Balliol, 1827); and the Ryders: Dudley (Christ Church, 1818), Henry, George, Thomas, and Richard (Oriel, 1821, 1828, 1833, and 1840 respectively), and William (Exeter, 1831).

go up to Trinity, adding, 'I am much changed with respect to the two universities. I used greatly to prefer Cambridge, but this summer I have had so much intercourse with men of talents and piety from Oxford that I believe not only that the general discipline there is much stricter but in two or three Colleges religion is in more esteem.'[4]

Conservative, orthodox, and suspicious of reform, Oxford was slowly awakening from a long period of spiritual and intellectual lethargy, evidenced by the reintroduction of the teaching of Aristotle and Butler, and the study of logic.[5] The university was a bastion of the Protestant constitution in Church and State, a pillar of the Establishment in the broadest sense, and a privileged oracle of the *ancien régime*, looking to the State to maintain its exclusive rights. Once again its professors lectured and its students were expected to work and, increasingly, to be examined.[6] In matters of religion, it was much the same. The Anglican monopoly was fiercely defended on all fronts, subscription to the Articles was twice required (at matriculation and upon taking a degree), and Dissent was stridently opposed.[7]

The intense political and religious excitement at Oxford accompanying the Reform Bill crisis and the 'constitutional revolution' of 1828–32 gave rise to what has often been characterized as a golden age, enlivened by political intrigue, spiritual richness, and uncertainty. It was a time for the cult of personality and intense hero-worship, passionate friendships, and fierce enmities.[8] The atmosphere was perhaps best captured by Dean Church, whose impression as an undergraduate and young don was of an Oxford which resembled Florence in the age of Savonarola, with its nicknames, 'Puseyites', and 'Neomaniacs', and 'High and Dry', counterparts to the *Piagnoni* and *Arrabbiati*. Like a Renaissance city-state, Oxford teemed with polemical vitality. It was:

as proud and jealous of its own ways as Athens or Florence; and like them had its quaint fashions of polity; its democratic Convocation

[4] E. M. Forster, *Marianne Thornton* (1956), 78.

[5] Henry Nettleship (ed.), *Essays by the Late Mark Pattison* (Oxford, 1889), i.462–6.

[6] W. R. Ward, *Victorian Oxford* (1965), pp. xiii–20.

[7] For a detailed description of this period see M. G. Brock and M. C. Curthoys (eds), *The History of the University of Oxford: Nineteenth Century Oxford* (Oxford, 1997).

[8] Newsome, *The Parting of Friends*, 63.

and its oligarchy; its social ranks; its discipline, severe in theory and usually lax in fact; its self-governed bodies and corporations within itself; its faculties and colleges, like the guilds and 'arts' of Florence; its internal rivalries and discords; its 'sects' and factions. Like these, too, it professed a special recognition of the supremacy of religion; it claimed to be the home of worship and religious training . . . to be eminently the guardian of 'true religion and sound learning'; and therefore it was eminently the place where religion should be recalled to its purity and strength, and also the place where there ought to be the most vigilant jealousy against the perversions and corruptions of religion.[9]

Of the diverse manifestations of this effervescence, the Oxford Movement is the most obvious and the best chronicled. Yet those at the other end of the Anglican spectrum, the Oxford Evangelicals, were also experiencing conflicts, both external and internal, which exerted an influence upon Evangelicalism at large, upon the Oxford Movement, and upon the course of religious debate within England during the nineteenth century.

Although overshadowed in Oxford by High Churchmanship,[10] Evangelicalism nevertheless made its presence felt in the university during the 1820s. While some observers have claimed that Evangelicalism was then the 'dominant' religious force in Oxford,[11] and others have seen it as relatively insignificant,[12] the true strength of the movement in Oxford during the 1820s

[9] R. W. Church, *The Oxford Movement*, 3rd edn. (1892), 160–1.

[10] Tension between the two schools had long existed. See Nehemiah Curnock (ed.), *The Journal of the Revd John Wesley* (1938), i.5; Green, *Religion at Oxford and Cambridge*, 202–3; Peter Nockles, *The Oxford Movement in Context* (Cambridge, 1994).

[11] See W. Tuckwell, *Reminiscences of Oxford* (1900), 227. As Benjamin Wills Newton later reminisced, 'at that time Evangelicals had all the power, as may be seen by the ease with which Newman was turned out of the secretaryship of the C.M.S. Oxford branch. It was my doing, ostensibly, and I had only just taken [my] B.A. degree, and therefore was not comparable to Newman in position and influence.' See Fry, 136.

[12] Vivian Green has argued that by the 1830s Evangelicalism had become a matter of theological sympathies rather than a distinctive party, and that there is little to suggest that it offered a lead in the heated religious atmosphere of the time. David Newsome suggests that Oxford was overwhelmingly weighted on the side of the opposite tradition. Thomas Mozley commented on the very low status of Evangelicalism in the university during the 1820s; it 'could not show a single man who combined scholarship, intellect, and address in a considerable degree'. See Green, *Religion at Oxford and Cambridge*, 215–16; Newsome, *The Parting of Friends*, 8, 57; Thomas Mozley, *Reminiscences Chiefly of Oriel College and the Oxford Movement* (1882), i.23–4, 98.

probably lies somewhere in between.[13] Nowhere was the influence of Evangelicalism, whether extreme or moderate, more obvious than at St. Edmund Hall, which was recognized as the centre of the movement within the university,[14] a reputation gained by a continuous succession of Evangelical Vice-Principals between 1783 and 1851.[15] During the 1820s, it was joined by Wadham, especially after the election of Benjamin Parsons Symons as Sub-Warden, who secured the election of several Evangelical fellows in his forty-year tenure of office;[16] Worcester, largely through the influence of Richard Cotton, who became Provost in 1839;[17] and Exeter, which, through its close West Country connections, had links with the high Calvinism of that region—most notably through the election of four well-known West Country Evangelicals as fellows between 1800 and 1826.[18] At least one of these Exeter fellows, Henry Bellenden Bulteel, though an old Etonian,

[13] Peter Nockles has argued that although less significant than at Cambridge, Evangelicalism 'nevertheless retained adherents among a minority' at Oxford. See Peter Nockles, '"Lost Causes and . . . Impossible Loyalties": The Oxford Movement and the University', in Brock and Curthoys (eds.), *The History of the University of Oxford*, 198. W. R. Ward has claimed that the influence of the Oxford Evangelicals increased during the 1820s. See Ward, *Victorian Oxford* (75). For more information on Oxford Evangelicalism see A. C. Downer, *A Century of Evangelical Religion in Oxford* (1938); J. S. Reynolds, *The Evangelicals at Oxford 1735–1871*, 2nd edn. (Appleford, 1975).

[14] Mozley, *Reminiscences*, i.23, 241–6; Richard Hill, *Pietas Oxoniensis* (1768); Thomas Nowell, *An Answer to a Pamphlet, Entitled Pietas Oxoniensis* (Oxford, 1768).

[15] Including Isaac Crouch, Daniel Wilson, and John Hill. See William E. Gladstone, *Gleanings of Past Years* (1879), vii.211–12; W. Tuckwell, *Pre-Tractarian Oxford* (1909), 8; Mozley, *Reminiscences*, i.242; Reynolds, *The Evangelicals at Oxford*, 58–76.

[16] Sub-Warden in 1823; Warden in 1831, a position he retained for forty years, during which time he secured the election of a number of Evangelicals as college fellows and established the college's reputation as the centre of Evangelicalism in the university after 1830. He is said to have arranged evening prayers at a time which prevented undergraduates from hearing Newman preach at St. Mary's. See Reynolds, *The Evangelicals at Oxford*, 93–4, 102–3, 166, 169, 184–5; Green, *Religion at Oxford and Cambridge*, 215–16.

[17] Cotton was elected fellow in 1816, Provost in 1839, and Vice-Chancellor in 1852. He was the brother-in-law of Edward Pusey and one of the promoters of the Martyrs' Memorial in 1841. See John William Burgon, *Lives of Twelve Good Men* (1888), ii.71–92; Lilian M. Quiller Couch, *Reminiscences of Oxford* (Oxford, 1892), 208; Green, *Religion at Oxford and Cambridge*, 215; Ward, *Victorian Oxford*, 122–3, 138; Reynolds, *The Evangelicals at Oxford*, 162, 165, 173–4, 180, 186.

[18] John David Macbride (1800–5; Principal of Magdalen Hall, 1813–68), Henry Bellenden Bulteel (1823–9), James Lampen Harris (1815–29), and Benjamin Wills Newton (1826–32). All except Macbride soon seceded from the Church. By 1837, Exeter had fallen heavily under the spell of Tractarianism. See W. K. Stride, *Exeter College* (1900), 134, 166; Reynolds, *The Evangelicals at Oxford*, 70, 97, 176; John Morley, *The Life of William Ewart Gladstone* (1905), i.54–5; Newsome, *The Parting of Friends*, 196.

was also an attender at the hyper-Calvinist preaching of Robert Hawker at St. Charles the Martyr, Plymouth.[19] Beyond these strongholds, there was a recognizable Evangelical presence at a number of other Colleges during the 1820s, including Oriel, with the zealous Culling Eardley Smith, and Magdalen, with the mercurial Richard Waldo Sibthorp.[20]

Outside the university, the Evangelicals' spiritual centre, according to Gladstone, was located in the parish of St. Ebbe's, where Bulteel officiated as perpetual curate.[21] Bulteel was born on 14 September 1800 at Plymstock, Devon, the fourth of ten children of Thomas Hillersdon Bulteel and his wife Anne, daughter of Christopher Harris of Radford, Plymstock.[22] Despite having one eye knocked out by a cricket ball while at Eton, he became one of 'the most rollicking and rowdy' Oxford undergraduates of his generation, with a well-earned reputation as 'a rather wild young man'.[23] In 1820, during the trial of Queen Caroline, Bulteel 'sallied forth and knocked down the first man he met and questioned', provoking an extensive 'town–gown' riot.[24] Two years later, he exhibited his sporting prowess on the Isis as stroke in the winning Brasenose boat, the undergraduates crying out 'Bravo Bulteel' from the banks of the river.[25] After matriculating at Brasenose in 1818, Bulteel was elected a fellow of Exeter College on 30 June 1823.[26] During 1824, he attended the theology lectures given by Charles Lloyd, the Regius Professor of Divinity,[27] and

[19] See Fry, 99, 137–8.

[20] Culling Eardley Smith matriculated in 1823, and was later known as a champion of ultra-Protestantism in the West Country and an outspoken critic of Bishop Phillpotts. See *Al. Ox.*, iv.1311. Sibthorp matriculated at University College in 1809, migrating as a scholar to Magdalen in the following year, where he later became a fellow; later still, he achieved a certain notoriety as evening lecturer at St. John's, Bedford Row, under Baptist Noel, as well as for seceding—twice—to Roman Catholicism. See *Al. Ox.*, iv.1295; J. Fowler, *Richard Waldo Sibthorp: A Biography* (1880); Christopher Sykes, *Two Studies in Virtue* (1953); R. D. Middleton, *Magdalen Studies* (1936), 195–228. In Michaelmas 1828, Gladstone recorded that 'a new party of hearers apparently of Mr Bulteel at St. Ebbe's' had also developed at Christ Church. See entry of 15 Nov. 1828, in *The Gladstone Diaries*, ed. M. R. D. Foot and H. C. G. Matthew, (Oxford 1968–90), i.211

[21] See W. E. Gladstone, 'The Evangelical Movement', in *QR* (July 1879), 8.

[22] *DNB*; T. C. F. Stunt, 'Henry Bulteel' in *New DNB*.

[23] Fry, 99, 115, 137. [24] Ibid. 98, 115.

[25] Ibid. 137; *Eton School List*; John Buchan, *Brasenose College* (1898), 97. See also Downer, *A Century of Evangelical Religion in Oxford*, 12; Stride, *Exeter College*, 166–7.

[26] *DNB*; *Al. Ox.*; Charles William Boase, *Register of Exeter College* (Oxford, 1879), 124.

[27] MSS Oxford Diocesan Papers c. 222, Oxford County RO.

that summer (with John Henry Newman) was ordained by Edward Legge, the Bishop of Oxford, perhaps to take up a rural curacy somewhere in the West Country.[28] Soon afterwards, through reading a religious novel, he was converted to Evangelical Christianity, although he had not yet imbibed the high Calvinistic doctrines for which he was later notorious.[29] In December 1826, he became perpetual curate of St. Ebbe's, where he preached conventional Evangelical doctrines, quickly establishing himself as one of the most popular preachers in Oxford.[30] In January 1829, having previously been influenced by Robert Hawker's hyper-Calvinism, he became tutor and bursar at Exeter (where he taught mostly Greek), his extreme religious views provoking some disquiet in the Common Room.[31] On 6 October 1829 Bulteel resigned his college fellowship and married Eleanor Sadler, a pastry cook and daughter of a High Street merchant.[32]

In the years preceding Bulteel's appointment at St. Ebbe's, 'serious religion' in Oxford had reflected the moderate tone of mainstream Evangelical piety: firmly attached to the Church and to 'regular' patterns of worship and evangelism, careful to avoid over-cordial relationships with orthodox Dissent which might compromise the authority of the Establishment, and mild in its Calvinism. By its moderation and regularity the movement attracted a number of influential Oxford undergraduates, though many of these would soon abandon 'serious religion' for Tractarianism, or even Rome itself. At this period, however, Evangelicalism in Oxford, as elsewhere, began to undergo profound changes.[33] There was a marked break in continuity as the great leaders of its celebrated second generation were quickly passing from the scene, and the party was unable to win those who

[28] This is suggested in Fry, 115, 137. Alternatively, Bulteel may have been ordained in his capacity as a fellow of Exeter College.

[29] See ibid. 99, 115; MS Topographical Oxfordshire, c. 250, Bod; MSS Oxford Diocesan Papers, c. 222, Oxford County RO; Fry 115, 137.

[30] See Gladstone, *Gleanings of Past Years*, v.29; Newman to anon., 14 Mar. 1830, in *Letters and Correspondence of John Henry Newman*, ed. Anne Mozley (1891), i.226. For an explanation of the circumstances surrounding Bulteel's appointment to St. Ebbe's see Fry, 99–100, 138.

[31] Fry, 76, 95, 98–9.

[32] Eleanor Sadler was the daughter of Thomas Blakeney Sadler and niece of James Sadler, the pioneer balloonist. See *HD*, 64b, 6 Oct. 1829, Bod; *DNB*; Stunt, 'Henry Bulteel'; Boase, *Register of Exeter College*, 124, 216. One source incorrectly records the date as 10 Oct. 1829. See MS Topographical Oxfordshire, d 165, 334, Bod.

[33] Mozley, *Reminiscences* (i.107) claimed that the Evangelical party was then undergoing 'a rapid decomposition'.

should have been their natural successors: the sons of Wilberforce and Ryder, Gladstone, Manning, Newman, and others. To make matters worse, this transition occurred at the precise moment when the tensions between Church and State, and between conservatives and liberals, was heating up. Evangelicals spoke with a divided voice on the emotive political issues of the day. A distinct cleavage opened up between the mildly reformist 'Claphamites', whose views were expressed in the *Christian Observer*, and the more fiercely Tory and anti-Catholic 'Recordites'. The repeal of the Test and Corporation Acts, the passage of Catholic Emancipation (and the subsequent parliamentary election contest in Oxford between Robert Harry Inglis and Robert Peel), the enactment of the Great Reform Bill, and the debate over mandatory subscription at the university, split and demoralized the Evangelicals, thus rendering them incapable of taking a lead.[34] As David Newsome has argued, the situation cried out for effective leadership so that any party which championed the cause of the Church against liberalism and secular intrusion with sufficient militancy would be likely to attract large numbers—especially of the young men ardent for a crusade—to fight under its banner.[35]

The constitutional crisis of 1828–32 accentuated a process of fragmentation in the Evangelical camp which had already become visible in the mid-1820s in the sharp internal controversy over the circulation of the Apocrypha with the Scriptures, which divided the Bible Society.[36] The moderate Clapham-Cambridge

[34] Subscription was a particularly emotive issue with the *CO*, which objected to any requirement which profaned sacred things and encouraged 'bigotry, popery, and intolerance'. It could not accept the belief (championed by Bishop Phillpotts and others) that the youth subscribes first, and learns to understand what he has subscribed afterwards. Culling Eardley Smith, who had subscribed to the Articles upon matriculating at Oriel, refused to subscribe a second time and left Oxford without a degree. How effective subscription was in promoting religious practice remains an open question. Francis Newman remarked that, despite compulsory subscription, not one in five Oxford undergraduates 'seemed to have any religious convictions at all: the elder residents seldom or never showed sympathy with the doctrines that pervade that formula.' See *CO* (1831), 614–15; (1832), 88; (1833), p. iii, 323; (1834), 258, 323; (1835), 520; Ward, *Victorian Oxford*, 202; Francis William Newman, *Phases of Faith*, 6th edn. (1860), 2.

[35] Newsome, *The Parting of Friends*, 10.

[36] This fragmentation was perhaps first discussed by Haddon Willmer and later by David Newsome. See Haddon Willmer, MS 'Evangelicalism 1785–1835', unpub. Hulsean Prize Essay, 1962, Cambridge University Library, 75–6; David Newsome, 'Justification and Sanctification: Newman and the Evangelicals', in the *Journal of Theological Studies* (Apr. 1964), 34.

consensus which had dominated Evangelicalism since the 1790s now showed signs of disintegration. There was dissatisfaction with the degree of accommodation to the polite 'world' shown by those such as the Clapham group and Charles Simeon. The more rigorist *Record*, taken over in 1828 by the Scots barrister Alexander Haldane, offered a sterner, more dogmatic Protestantism, which set its face hard against liberalism and compromise. As we have seen, millennial excitements, always simmering below the surface, broke out in dramatic forms, most notably in Irvingism and the Christian Brethren. As a result, the Evangelical movement began to fragment into four more or less distinct—and increasingly separate—camps during the late 1820s: the old moderates of the '*Christian Observer* school',[37] the strongly anti-Catholic (and anti-liberal) 'Recordites',[38] the small band of hyper-Calvinists some of them later associated with the Strict Baptist journal the *Gospel Standard*,[39] and the millennialists whose extreme notions were advanced in the *Morning Watch*.[40] Thus, the labours of Wilberforce, Hannah More, and others to establish a moderate Evangelical consensus and to transform 'serious religion' into the attractive and respectable faith of the middle and upper classes; Simeon's tireless efforts to ensure the adherence of Evangelicals to clerical 'regularity' and loyalty to the National Church; and the considerable, but often overlooked, kinship between Evangelicals and High Churchmen in pre-Tractarian England; were now being challenged by fragmentation and extremism within the ranks of the Evangelical party itself.

I

The effect of these upheavals in Church and State, and within Evangelicalism itself, were soon evident in Oxford. Thomas Mozley sadly chronicled the secession in 1829 of a dozen or so young Oxford men from the Church, possibly as the result of Catholic Emancipation; all of these unidentified seceders appar-

[37] Including John Bird and Charles Richard Sumner, Baptist Noel, and Daniel Wilson. The *Christian Observer* had been published since 1802.

[38] Including Hugh McNeile, Hugh Stowell, and Francis Close. The *Record* was first published in January 1828.

[39] Including J. C. Philpot and William Tiptaft. The *Gospel Standard* was first published in 1835.

[40] Including Henry Drummond and Edward Irving. The *Morning Watch* was first published in 1829.

ently agreed that the Church had become incurably corrupt.[41] On 11 December of that year, Newman wrote to John Hill, the Evangelical Vice-Principal of St. Edmund Hall, complaining that two provocative sermons (recently preached at St. Ebbe's by Bulteel and Sibthorp) had not, as had been publicly alleged, been authorized by the Oxford Association of the Church Missionary Society.[42] At about this time Gladstone observed the emergence of 'a score or two of young men . . . nestled together in St. Edmund Hall', who 'belonged to a school of ultra-Calvinism, which lay far in advance of the ordinary Evangelical tenets'.[43] Reminiscing in old age, Benjamin Wills Newton, a former undergraduate and fellow at Exeter, described how two opposing camps had emerged within Oxford Evangelicalism during the early 1830s, one centred around the high Calvinist Bulteel and the other around the Arminian Sibthorp.[44] Newton himself fell in with the Bulteel set, though, like some others, he later fell out with them over their drift into hyper-Calvinism. As a result, he said, '*I broke my connexion with that circle.* I remember that on one occasion at a dinner-table they were discussing the certainty of Wesley being damned.'[45] By September 1833, these tensions were attracting the attention of the Evangelicals' most ardent critics, Hurrell Froude predicting that soon they 'would all be pulling different ways with mare's-nests of their own'.[46] Nor were the Oxford Evangelicals immune from the influences of the 'prophetic fever' which had already infected Albury, Powerscourt, and much of London.[47] Even John Henry Newman, by this time less sympathetic with 'Gospel teachings', got caught up in prophetic speculation. In 1826 he produced the first of his two essays on miracles,[48] and during the Michaelmas term of 1829 he met twice a week with a number of other Oriel men to discuss the issue of prophecy. Was Napoleon or was the pope the antichrist? 'It was everywhere held

[41] Mozley, *Reminiscences*, i.175–6.

[42] *Letters and Correspondence of John Henry Newman*, ed. Mozley, i.215–16; entry of 11 Dec. 1829, *The Letters and Diaries of John Henry Newman*, ed. Ian Ker and Thomas Gornall (SJ) (Oxford, 1979), ii.178.

[43] Gladstone, *Gleanings of Past Years*, vii.211–12.

[44] See Fry, 236. [45] See ibid. 135.

[46] *Letters and Correspondence of John Henry Newman*, ed. Mozley, i.455.

[47] See Fry, 135; W. H. Oliver, *Prophets and Millennialists* (Auckland and Oxford, 1978), 142–9.

[48] J. H. Newman, *Two Essays on Scriptural Miracles and On Ecclesiastical*, 2nd edn. (1870).

to be of vital importance to have a right understanding of this question.'[49]

Yet another catalyst was soon introduced into this unsettled and volatile atmosphere. In mid-1830, the Irish millennialist Evangelical John Nelson Darby visited Oxford.[50] Thanks to propaganda by his admirer Francis Newman, Darby's arrival had been keenly anticipated by local Evangelicals.[51] As we have seen, so successful was Darby in provoking and agitating the local religious scene that at least three prominent Oxford Evangelicals—James Harris, Benjamin Wills Newton, and George Wigram—soon abandoned Anglicanism for the greener religious pastures of the West Country and enlisted in its embryonic Christian Brethren movement.

The parish of St. Ebbe's was most agitated by the changes now sweeping through 'serious religion'. Shortly after being appointed curate of St. Ebbe's, and inspired by his Hawkerite leanings and characteristic impetuosity, Bulteel began to advance antinomian views.[52] Thomas Byrth, the Evangelical curate at St. Clement's, Oxford, wrote disapprovingly on 5 February 1827, that Bulteel 'has created a most powerful sensation here, by preaching ultra-Calvinism, and circulating Dr Hawker's tracts'.[53] Some insight into Bulteel's conversion not merely to the 'doctrines of grace', but to the more extreme forms of high Calvinism, is given by Benjamin Wills Newton:

> one day I had breakfast with him [Bulteel] and found he read Scott's Bible every morning. I said, what do you think about Baptismal Regeneration? 'I am doubting about it' [he replied] . . . He lived near Plymouth, and while at his home [during March 1827] he came to me, and

[49] Mozley, *Reminiscences*, i.176; J. H. Newman, *Apologia Pro Vita Sua* (1879), 23, and Appendix; Tiptaft to anon., 16 Nov. 1831, in J. H. Philpot, *The Seceders*, 2nd edn. (1931), i.50.

[50] See Newman, *Phases of Faith*, 28. John Hill's diary places Darby in Oxford between May and Dec. 1830. See *HD*, 7a, 28 May 1830, 7b, 31 May 1830, and 29a, 9 Dec. 1830.

[51] See Fry, 235.

[52] See Charles Hole, *The Life of the Reverend and Venerable William Whitmarsh Phelps, M.A.* (1871), ii.110 n. William Hanbury was rector of St. Ebbe's (he also held the living of Great Harborough, Warwickshire). In 1815, he left Oxford and shortly afterwards became incurably insane. See MSS Oxford Diocesan Papers c. 428, fol. 38; b. 14, fol. 35v, Oxford County RO. As Hanbury could not be deprived, the parish was served by a succession of curates, appointed by the Bishop on the vestry's (or their predecessor's) recommendation. This situation continued until 1868. See MSS d d., Parish Oxford St. Ebbe's, e, I, s a 1816; d, I, s a 1825, Oxford County RO. Curates at St. Ebbe's were relatively poorly paid: in 1818, he received only £70 a year plus surplice fees of £10. See MSS Oxford Diocesan Papers b. 14, fol. 38, Oxford County RO.

[53] G. R. Moncreiff, *Remains of Thomas Byrth, D.D., F.A.S.* (1851), 101.

asked me to go with him and hear Dr Hawker. 'Dr Hawker! I said. I wouldn't go to hear a Calvinist!' But I did, however. There was a lady present who saw us and lifted up her heart in prayer that the sermon might be a blessing.'[54]

And so it was. While Newton shortly afterwards returned to Oxford, Bulteel remained for ten days longer in Dr Hawker's company.[55] When he finally returned to the university, it was clear to friends and opponents alike that a remarkable transformation of his views and personality had taken place within the space of three months. His sermons had a new fire and a sharp, dogmatic cutting edge. Some seventy-four young men were soon converted under his preaching.[56] Bulteel now drew such large congregations at St. Ebbe's (principally undergraduates and new residents in the parish), that plans were drawn up to build a substantial gallery above the north aisle of the church.[57]

This shift in Bulteel's views prompted the churchwardens at St. Ebbe's, William Albutt and John Chaundry, to write to Charles Lloyd, Bishop of Oxford (allegedly on behalf of the parishioners) protesting against his doctrinal eccentricities, his failure to maintain discipline, and his assumption of the right to appoint one of the churchwardens.[58] The charge that Bulteel failed to maintain discipline was based upon four principal claims:

1. That he deprived parishioners of their pews in order to accommodate favourable members of the university, Dissenters, and those who lived outside the parish (he was said to have filled the reading desk with undergraduates).
2. That he allowed 'quarrelling, swearing, and indecencies of several kinds' to take place during a recent vestry meeting.
3. That he used extempore prayer and expositions of Scripture during many vestry meetings.
4. That he encouraged a local chimney sweep to pray extempore in the Sunday school.[59]

After summoning Bulteel for an explanation, Lloyd penned a lengthy reply to the churchwardens stating his unwillingness to

[54] Fry, 137. [55] Ibid. 99. [56] Ibid. 138.

[57] See MSS Oxford Diocesan Papers, c. 435, 503; c. 2170, no. 9, Oxford County RO.

[58] MSS Records of Oxford City Parishes, d d., Parish Oxford St. Ebbe's, b, I, 25–8, Oxford County RO.

[59] Ibid.

rule on matters of doctrine, allowing 'it to the character of every clergyman to believe that he has not opposed the Articles and formularies of his church'. Only when these charges were substantiated by definite and positive proof would he be persuaded to act. Bulteel appears to have assured Lloyd that all such 'irregularities' had occurred without his approval—a claim backed up in a petition presented to Lloyd by a group of Bulteel's supporters, all said to be parishioners in good standing. Upon investigation, however, Lloyd discovered that among the petitioners were a number of Dissenters, Dissenting ministers, and even, apparently, some of the most abandoned prostitutes and wastrels in Oxford. This revelation did little to advance Bulteel's already compromised status in the diocese, though he was left uninhibited by his diocesan and allowed to remain at St. Ebbe's.[60]

The tension between Bulteel and his churchwardens continued to simmer for some time. In early May 1828, Albutt, Bulteel's chief opponent, petitioned the Hebdomadal Board to prohibit undergraduates from attending services at parish churches, 'on the plea that they prevent the parishioners from coming'. When Richard Jenkyns, the Vice-Chancellor, read out the petition at a meeting of the heads of houses, 'many violent things were said by several against Bulteel'.[61] 'Heterodox—insane' was how George Thompson, the principal of St. Edmund Hall, characterized him.[62] On 11 May, on Jenkyns's authority, Albutt attempted to prevent members of the university from attending St. Ebbe's, and took the

[60] Ibid. The bishop also refused to rule on the question of whether Bulteel had the right to appoint one of the churchwardens; however, when Bulteel appeared before the archdeacon's visitation at St. Mary's in June 1828, his plea on this question was denied. William Baker has argued that Lloyd's inaction in this matter was not merely the result of innate conservatism. Rather, throughout 1828 and 1829, his attention was divided between his university duties and the pressing demands of parliamentary politics, which included such momentous issues as the repeal of the Test and Corporation Acts, and Catholic Emancipation. See William J. Baker, *Beyond Port and Prejudice, Charles Lloyd of Oxford, 1784–1829* (Orono, Me., 1981), 168. Of no small consequence, Lloyd was seriously ill during May 1829 (when Bulteel's case was being debated by the Hebdomadal Board), dying on the 31st.

[61] *HD*, 67/6, 115b, 5 May 1828.

[62] Hill received this account of the meeting directly from Thompson. Afterwards, Hill called on Bulteel and together the two prayed over the matter. Bulteel 'goes on in simple faith', he wrote. See *HD*, 115b, 5 May 1828, 116b, 9 May 1828. Hill also refers to a petition with 146 names attached, a copy of which was sent to the bishop and another to the vice-chancellor, on the subject of the charges against Bulteel. It remains uncertain whether this petition favoured—or opposed—Bulteel, or if it was the same petition mentioned earlier by Lloyd.

names of those who tried to gain entry. This was a step too far. When Bulteel called upon the Vice-Chancellor the following day to protest, he found Jenkyns repentant, admitting that he had been unwise in authorizing Albutt to act in such a manner.[63] Jenkyns's prompt volte-face reveals something of the unsettled atmosphere within the university, for, on revealing to the Hebdomadal Board what had occurred at St. Ebbe's he was reprimanded by several of the more liberal heads, especially Whately, of St. Alban Hall, and Shuttleworth, of New College, who resented what seemed an unwarranted restriction on the religious liberty of members of the university.[64] The chastened Jenkyns even refused to receive Albutt when he next called or accept his list of offending undergraduates.[65] This crude attempt to stifle Bulteel's popularity among undergraduates thus proved counterproductive (as is often the case with prohibitions of the kind), giving him useful publicity as a martyr to the vindictiveness of gerontocratic heads of house. As Newton later recalled proudly, 'it was a wonderful movement: it roused and even terrified the university, and the authorities tried to put it down, forbidding attendance at St. Ebbe's church, and ordering the names to be taken of those who persisted. My name was the first!'[66]

Given such opposition—and its attendant fame—it is not surprising that Bulteel became increasingly provocative in his pronouncements. He opened his pulpit to the flamboyant John Nelson Darby, who stirred up the congregation with his theory of a new Jerusalem with its dangerously separatist implications.[67] In early 1831, Bulteel even contemplated seceding from the Church, only to be dissuaded by Newton.[68] St. Ebbe's thus became a fiery Evangelical counterpart to the seductive, but far more tranquil St. Mary's, where John Henry Newman served as vicar from March 1828. And Bulteel did not disappoint his large and enthusiastic congregations. His passion and intensity were intoxicating. Gladstone, who periodically sat under his preaching while an under-

[63] *HD*, 117b, 12 May 1828. [64] See Fry, 135.

[65] Ibid. Hill responded to this victory in characteristic fashion, writing 'God has mercifully turned the counsel of the opponents of the gospel into foolishment.'

[66] Fry, 135.

[67] On 9 December 1830 he preached at St. Ebbe's from Romans 11: 22, a significant text on the world's rejection of the gentile church, which had potentially separatist implications, as he undoubtedly pointed out. See *HD*, 67/8, 29a, 9 Dec. 1830.

[68] See Fry, 100, 104.

graduate at Christ Church, described how 'the flame', at St. Ebbe's, 'was at white heat'.[69] J. C. Philpot, high Calvinist fellow of Worcester, summarized the impact of Bulteel's extraordinary character on Oxford:

> Bulteel had for some years embraced the doctrines of grace, and preached them with much fervour of mind and strength of expression. This was a new sound at the learned university, and a thing almost unheard of, that a fellow and tutor of one of the colleges . . . should embrace so thoroughly and above all proclaim so boldly, the obnoxious doctrines of the Calvinistic creed. His church was crowded with hearers, and among them were seen many of the university students, and now and then a master of arts, myself being one of them, some of whom became his attached and regular hearers.[70]

II

The tension excited by Bulteel's highly charged ministry reached a climax in early 1831. On 2 February, John Hill confided to his diary that he spent 'a good part of the morning with Bulteel, hearing him read his [University] Sermon for the next Sunday at St. Mary's and conversing on it'.[71] Hill agreed to preach on the same text (1 Corinthians 2:12) that same Sunday at Hampton Gay, outside Oxford. This concerted action suggests that Oxford Evangelicals were now attempting to advance a party line, perhaps in an attempt to counter the ascendancy of liberalism and Catholicism within Oxford theology.[72] Certainly this seems to have been the expectation within the university, for the atmosphere which greeted Bulteel as he ascended the pulpit at St. Mary's on 6 February was nothing short of electric: according to contemporaries, no larger audience had ever assembled at the university church in modern times.[73] Nor was the gathering of sensation-seekers to be

[69] Gladstone, 'The Evangelical Movement', 8. For a thorough examination of Gladstone's religious development see: David W. Bebbington, *William Ewart Gladstone: Faith and Politics in Victorian Britain* (Grand Rapids, Mich., 1993); Peter J. Jagger, *Gladstone: The Making of a Christian Politician* (Allison Park, Pa., 1991).

[70] J. C. Philpot, *William Tiptaft*, 3rd edn. (Leicester, 1972), 43.

[71] *HD*, 67/8, 33b, 2 Feb. 1831. In preaching the University Sermon, Bulteel was performing a duty which fell in rotation upon every resident MA in holy orders. See the *Oxford University, City, and County Herald*, 5 Feb. 1831.

[72] *HD*, 67/8, 33b, 6 Feb. 1831. Hill goes on to state 'In this text Bulteel preached an admirably faithful and spiritual sermon this afternoon at St. Mary's.'

[73] See Edward Burton, *Remarks Upon a Sermon* (Oxford, 1831), 3; G. V. Cox, *Recollections of Oxford* (1868), 244.

disappointed. In a lengthy and emotional diatribe Bulteel advanced, without inhibition, his strong views concerning free grace and the evils which had recently desolated the Established Church. The most provocative of his statements was a flagrantly antinomian declaration in which he proclaimed the punishment and guilt of sin to have been removed from believers, because their transgressions had been completely hidden from the sight of God; consequently, they were not only free from sin but actually unable to sin.[74] This was followed by a Jeremiad against the Anglican clergy, who were dismissed as men of pleasure, indulging in such vices as the theatre, dances, balls, card-playing, horse-racing, and hunting; as habitual gamblers, drunkards, misers, gluttons, fornicators, adulterers, or worse.[75] In particular, Bulteel indicted heads of house for their lax and indiscriminate provision of testimonials for profligate undergraduates seeking ordination—a charge which, although reluctantly acknowledged by some,[76] was destined to annoy more. Bulteel claimed that these testimonials, attesting that a young man has behaved himself:

Honestly, *piously*, and *soberly* . . . have been given to men notorious for nothing so much in their day as profaneness, debauchery, and all kinds of riotous living; and on the other hand I also know for a certainty, that these testimonials have been withheld from piety, honesty, and sobriety, for no other reason than that they have happened to be accompanied with a profession of the grace Articles of the Church of England.[77]

The reaction of both town and gown to Bulteel's sermon was one of intense excitement. The *Oxford Herald*, describing the event as having been 'so much talked of and [its claims] so much exaggerated', printed a lengthy extract of the sermon on its front page.[78] Another commentator noted that the text was 'watched with extreme interest by all sections of the church.'[79] Benjamin Wills Newton, then a fellow at Exeter, willingly walked in proces-

[74] Henry Bulteel, *A Sermon on 1 Cor 2: 12* (Oxford, 1831), 17, 24–5.

[75] Ibid. 45–6.

[76] Cox, *Recollections of Oxford*, 244. The rector of Exeter College allegedly remarked afterwards: 'Well, I must say I quailed, for indeed it is true: you all know that we do have young men brought to be qualified for ordination, and we have to sign the papers declaring that they are called by the Holy Ghost, some of them ungodly young men.' See Harold H. Rowdon, *The Origins of the Brethren 1825–50* (1967), 67.

[77] Bulteel, *A Sermon on 1 Cor 2: 12*, 46–7.

[78] The *Oxford University, City, and County Herald*, 19 Feb. 1831.

[79] James Moore, *Pictorial and Historical Gossiping Guide to Oxford* (Oxford, 1882), 19.

sion with Bulteel to the university church, knowing full well that doing so 'would ruin me in my university prospects and career'. During a college meeting, at which the sermon was discussed, Newton observed that 'some were highly indignant, but the head of my college said (I was sitting opposite to him and he looked at me as he said it) "I trembled as I heard that [Bulteel's charge regarding testimonials], gentlemen: we know it is true."'[80] Young Gladstone, already bewildered by reading Erskine of Linlathen's *The Brazen Serpent* a few days earlier, responded to Bulteel's sermon with a mixture of emotions, perhaps reflecting the confusion experienced by other young and impressionable Oxford Evangelicals. In his diary he recorded:

> a long letter home, giving an account of Bulteel's extraordinary sermon. It must rouse many and various feelings. God grant it may all work for good. May my proud heart never lose one jot of the truth of God through its prejudices and passions, and may all their strongholds be cast down, and may there be an absorption of my will in the will of God and a perfect prostration of my soul before Him, through the one and only Mediator. But after having heard the remarkable sermon of this remarkable man, I cannot but still remember the words of St. Paul (in reference to the extent of redemption) 'For as by the disobedience of one *the many* were made sinners, so also by the obedience of one shall *the many* be made righteous'.[81]

Bulteel's sermon was published on 15 February and quickly ran through a number of editions (the sixth containing a new preface and a sequel in which Bulteel defended his recent preaching tour, discussed below, and his high Calvinistic doctrines).[82] To lead their counter-attack, Bulteel's critics quickly moved to enlist no less a personage than Dr Edward Burton, the Regius Professor of Divinity and Canon of Christ Church. Temperamentally unsuited to the cut and thrust of religious polemic, Burton made a feeble attempt to counter Bulteel's charges by accusing him of confusing justification with salvation, and by claiming that the basis of English Reformed theology was inherently Lutheran and not Calvinist. The results were disappointing. Bulteel's critics acknow-

[80] Fry, 132.

[81] Entry of 6 Feb. 1831, in *The Gladstone Diaries*, ed. Foot and Matthew, i.343. Two days later, Gladstone wrote an anonymous letter to Bulteel.

[82] Ibid. i.344.

ledged, both privately and publicly, that Burton's effort had accomplished little in aid of their cause.[83]

As the public controversy escalated, a flurry of private letters and public pamphlets by well-known churchmen of varying doctrinal persuasions began to appear. Edward Copleston, the High Church Bishop of Llandaff, denounced Bulteel's sermon as 'a sad affair' and Bulteel himself as 'incurably enthusiastic'.[84] The more progressive Edward Hawkins, Copleston's successor as Provost at Oriel, delivered a lengthy sermon in Oriel College chapel in which he denounced antinomianism as 'a fundamental and fatal error' and accused Bulteel of abandoning the pursuit of holiness and encouraging spiritual indolence. He urged his undergraduate audience to confront such error wherever it arose.[85] Hawkins quickly had his sermon published, encouraged by Blanco White that it 'would do more good than any direct answer to Bulteel'.[86] Several other, lesser-known Anglican controversialists also entered the fray, publishing tracts which were guaranteed to prolong the controversy and raise Bulteel's standing among his admirers, but do little to counter his extreme teachings.[87]

Perhaps reflecting the current disarray amongst the adherents of their own party, the Evangelicals were unable to present a united response to Bulteel. Daniel Wilson, soon to be elevated to the See of Calcutta, was scathing in his criticism, seeing 'the very essence of antinomianism' concealed in Bulteel's homily, though he admitted that Burton's response was, if anything, even 'more deadening and fatal' to the cause of true religion.[88] Likewise the *Christian Observer*, which compared Bulteel with the dreaded hyper-Calvinist William Huntington, and the eccentric George Baring, and expressed alarm lest such distortions of the Gospel spread

[83] Burton, *Remarks Upon a Sermon*, 12, 21, 23–4. For a response to this see Henry Bulteel, *A Reply to Dr Burton's Remarks* (Oxford, 1831). Gladstone remarked after reading Burton's pamphlet: 'I much like some [points] and am much grieved at others.' See entry of 18 Feb. 1831, in *The Gladstone Diaries*, ed. Foot and Matthew, i.345. Other critics were less kind. See *The British Critic*, 1831, 454–61; William Josiah Irons [Oxoniensis], *Strictures on the Revd Mr Bulteel's Sermon and on the Revd Dr Burton's Remarks* (Oxford, 1831), 3; Peter Hall, *Congregational Reform* (1835), 212; Cox, *Recollections of Oxford*, 244.

[84] MS Oriel College Letters no. 389.

[85] Edward Hawkins, *A Sermon Upon the Way of Salvation* (Oxford, 1831), 7–8.

[86] MS Oriel College Letters no. 90.

[87] See J. R. Barber, *A Letter to the Revd H. B. Bulteel* (1831); Irons, *Strictures on the Revd Mr Bulteel's Sermon;* Edward Burton, *One Reason for Not Entering Into Controversy With An Anonymous Author of Strictures* (Oxford, 1831); Philippus Anti-Osiander, *A Friendly Letter* (Oxford, 1831).

[88] Daniel Wilson, *The Character of the Good Man* (1831), 32 n, 69.

further within Evangelical circles.[89] On the other hand, John Nelson Darby, who had been present at St. Mary's,[90] publicly defended Bulteel and his Calvinistic doctrines, and rejected Burton's claims regarding the Lutheran origins of the Articles.[91] From within the university, J. C. Philpot, who shared many of Bulteel's views, described the sermon as 'a bold and faithful discourse, distinctly and clearly advocating the full Gospel of grace'.[92] Nor were all his supporters clerics. In May 1831, when debate over the Reform Bill was raging in Parliament and throughout the shires, Bulteel received an invitation from the (now) deeply conservative, pessimistic, and pre-millennialist Henry Drummond to address a gathering of the Continental Society at St. Clement Danes, London. Founded by strong Evangelicals like Robert Haldane, the Western Schismatic Thomas Baring, and Drummond himself, the Society had been established to extend evangelical Protestantism across the Channel and counter the liberal 'neologism' which had infiltrated many churches. In inviting Bulteel, however, Drummond got more than he had bargained for. Bulteel assured the Society that it now had no prospect whatsoever of converting Europe to Protestantism. He astonished his hearers by unfolding a narrowly separatist ecclesiology which seemed to discountenance energetic evangelism to the unconverted. Worse, he spiced his sermon with statements that could be, and were, seen as antinomian; God, he claimed, 'does not behold sin' in his believers.[93]

The Bulteel affair not only widened a long-standing tension between the Oxford Evangelicals and their critics in the university, but exposed some of the fractures opening up within the Evangelical world itself. The strain of high Calvinism which had largely been marginalized among the more obscure of the 'Gospel clergy' now emerged in the citadel of the Anglican Church, and in a provocative and energetic form which ensured high visibility. Moreover, Bulteel's appearance before the members of the Continental Society brought together, albeit temporarily, two distinct

[89] *CO* (1831), 300, 392–4, 688.

[90] Fry, 239–40; F. Roy Coad, *A History of the Brethren Movement* (Exeter, 1968), 63.

[91] John Nelson Darby [Oudies], *The Doctrine of the Church of England at the Time of the Reformation* (Oxford, 1831).

[92] J.C. Philpot, *The Seceders*, i.57.

[93] Henry Bulteel, 'Sermon for the Continental Society', 10 May 1831, in the *Preacher* (1830–5), ii.162–74.

points of the conservative Evangelical compass—the Oxford Evangelicals and the Albury circle—at a critical moment. This contact may also have provided Bulteel with his first introduction to Edward Irving, who would soon come to have a marked influence on his own doctrinal position.

III

In May 1831, Bulteel invited William Tiptaft, the Evangelical vicar of the nearby village of Sutton Courtenay, to join him on a preaching tour of the West Country, 'not confining themselves to Church of England places of worship, but to proclaim the Gospel wherever the door might be opened in chapels, rooms, private houses, or the open air'.[94] The reasons for such a tour at this particular moment remain uncertain. Perhaps Bulteel saw it as a means of escape from the unrelenting pressure in Oxford produced by his University Sermon? Alternatively, he may have regarded it as a provocative means of advancing his views in his home county of Devon, and countering the aggressive High Church Arminianism of the new diocesan bishop, Henry Phillpotts. It may have been a simple act of defiance. Benjamin Wills Newton later suggested that Bulteel was then attempting to break 'every rule of the Church of England that he could', witnessing against 'the whoredoms of the English Aholibah!' which he had denounced in his University Sermon.[95] At all events, it is clear that Bulteel had now come firmly to reject the 'enormous abuses, wicked government, and unscriptural system of the National Church'. He considered himself to have crossed a Rubicon in his Anglican career. He expected never again to preach within the walls of St. Ebbe's, for he was certain that on hearing of his 'irregular' proceedings in the West Country, the Bishop of Oxford would swiftly deprive him of his curacy. None the less, he did not doubt that his behaviour was both scriptural and apostolic. If he were deprived, his punishment would be a reflection not of his own turpitude, but of the deep moral corruption of the English Church to which he belonged.[96]

[94] J.C. Philpot, *William Tiptaft*, 44. Their tour received extensive coverage in both Oxford and West Country papers. See the *Oxford University, City, and County Herald*, 30 July 1831; *Woolmer's Exeter Gazette*, July 1830.

[95] See Fry, 102, 105.

[96] Bulteel, *A Sermon on 1 Cor 2: 12*, 6th edn. (1831), 55.

Tiptaft was equally confident that their preaching tour was justified, and that it would signal a return to apostolic purity and vigour. 'We shall preach in churches, chapels, barns, rooms, or in the open air', he proclaimed, and we shall 'give great offence. But it is a glorious work to preach the everlasting Gospel. It is the very purpose for which I was ordained.'[97] During the course of their travels, he observed:

> Very many, both rich and poor, wondered how we dared preach everywhere and anywhere, and they wanted to know what our diocesans will say. I have heard nothing from mine, although I am sure he knows of it. Bulteel . . . I do not think . . . has heard from his bishop. We are both indifferent to how our diocesans may act. If they turn us out of the Church of England, we shall see our way clear; for we both think that if a mother ever had a daughter, our Established Church is one of Rome's. Bulteel can easily be removed; but they will find difficulty in removing me, as I am an incumbent. I think they will be afraid in interfering with Bulteel, as his name is so well-known, and the poor Establishment is tottering to its very basis.[98]

Despite these anxieties, on their two-month journey throughout Somerset and Devon Bulteel and Tiptaft glowed with an evangelistic fervour reminiscent of a Wesley, a Whitefield, or a Rowland Hill, and were greeted by scenes of triumph and turbulence characteristic of the eighteenth-century Revival. They delighted in the catalytic effect which their preaching had in the parishes upon which they descended. It was a source of great satisfaction to Tiptaft that their arrival divided congregations and parishes, embroiled clergymen friendly to their cause in altercations with the ecclesiastical authorities, and stirred up the public. These scenes of excitement, it seemed, were almost redolent of the Acts of the Apostles. As Tiptaft wrote on 11 June 1831:

> We . . . have almost every evening . . . been preaching . . . in church, chapel, or the open air. We have, almost in every instance, asked for the Church, and if refused, preached in the chapel or open air . . . I need not say that our conduct excited surprise. We have many hearers. The places of worship are generally much crowded; people come from far to hear us, and invite us to come and preach to them . . . Many think we have no right to preach in Dissenting chapels; but it is not forbidden, either by the canons or the Word of God, for the latter is altogether in

[97] J.C. Philpot, *William Tiptaft*, 45.

[98] Ibid. 51.

our favour. I believe the Lord is with us, and makes us instruments in exciting a great inquiry into spiritual things . . . We bring, I am glad to say, a reproach upon all that receive us, particularly those who open their churches to us after having preached in the chapels in the neighbourhood. Some say we are mad; some, that we are beside ourselves; some cry out, 'My Lord Bishop, restrain them', and some wish us God speed; but the generality wonder at our conduct. We are both willing to be turned out of the Establishment for preaching the Gospel . . . Many seemed opposed to us at first, who afterwards support us, acknowledging they cannot say a word against us, for the work may be of God.[99]

Not surprisingly, their mission generated regional as well as national publicity.[100] It also aroused the wrath of many of the local clergy, who repeatedly attempted to silence the two itinerants. When they preached in and around Plymouth, the heartland of the hyper-Calvinists, Tiptaft observed with pleasure 'the great annoyance of the Church clergy', who not only demanded action from the Bishop of Exeter but contemplated setting the two evangelists in the stocks.[101] During their second night in Exeter a constable and a magistrate warned them that they were committing a breach of the peace. They refused to obey any authority, however, except that which was in writing, or unless they were removed by force.[102] The constable and magistrate, in turn, dared not inhibit them for fear of the crowds.[103]

The recently consecrated Bishop of Exeter was the formidable High Churchman Henry Phillpotts, whose application of episcopal discipline was probably unmatched by any of his contemporaries on the Bench. Of all bishops he was the least likely to overlook the 'invasion' of his diocese by ordained clergymen intent on itinerancy and disruption. And sure enough, such a challenge to the provocative pair soon developed. One aggrieved incumbent who sought counsel on the possibility of legal prosecution received a confident reply from the rising ecclesiastical lawyer Stephen Lushington, who advised: 'the conduct imputed to these gentlemen is clearly a gross violation of the ecclesiastical

[99] Ibid. 46–7. In a letter of 27 July 1831, Tiptaft wrote that during one part of the tour they preached in the open air fifteen nights out of eighteen. See ibid. 49.

[100] See *Jackson's Oxford Journal*, 13 Aug. 1831.

[101] J.C. Philpot, *William Tiptaft*, 49.

[102] The *Oxford University, City, and County Herald*, 30 July 1831.

[103] J.C. Philpot, *William Tiptaft*, 50.

law, and if proved, must be followed by punishment.'[104] Phillpotts, exhibiting his customary adroitness and keen capacity for ecclesiastical law, urged the churchwardens to prosecute, but warned that they would 'do well to call a vestry, and to receive the authority of that vestry, *in order to indemnify themselves, and to justify a rate for the expenses of the suit*'. These expenses, he shrewdly added, would 'be awarded against the offenders, if they be convicted'.[105] It appears that Phillpotts then took matters into his own hands, pressing for the case to be pursued in the courts,[106] but as the particular churchwardens in question refused to sanction such a scheme the matter came to nothing.[107] Back in Oxford, Richard Bagot was more successful. When reports of Bulteel's clerical 'irregularity' reached his ears, he resolved to allow no further breaches of ecclesiastical order by unbeneficed curates licensed in his diocese.

IV

During his three month absence, Bulteel had entrusted St. Ebbe's to the care of the Hon. and Revd Lancelot Brenton of Oriel, another of the Oxford 'ultras'.[108] To support Brenton, he engaged a number of local Evangelicals, including John Hill, G. W. Phillips, and Nicholas Armstrong (who was unlicensed by the bishop) to preach when Brenton was unavailable.[109] Tiptaft returned to Sutton Courtenay on 15 July.[110] On the following day, Bagot wrote to Bulteel warning that 'various communications' had been made to him of their recent itinerations which were in violation of canon law. Bulteel replied from Devon on 21 July that 'the information received by you respecting me is perfectly correct.' He freely admitted preaching in Dissenting meeting houses and in the open air, adding 'I have not the slightest wish to conceal or excuse what I have done, as the Word of God is entirely on my side, and I see nothing against the practice in any of the canons of the Church of England.'[111] Bulteel received no further communica-

[104] Bulteel, *A Sermon on 1 Cor 2: 12*, 6th edn., 61.

[105] Ibid.

[106] *Non* (19 Apr. 1848), 268–9.

[107] James Shore, *The Case of the Revd James Shore, M.A., by Himself* (1849), 23.

[108] MS Register of Baptisms, Funerals, and Marriages, St. Ebbe's parish, Oxford County RO.

[109] *HD*, 67/8, 41a–51b, 19, 26 May 1831; 2, 4, 9, 12, 16, 23, 30 June 1831; 14, 21, 28 July 1831 On 4 June, Armstrong was informed by the churchwardens that he would not be allowed to preach St. Ebbe's again without a licence.

[110] J.C. Philpot, *William Tiptaft*, 49.

[111] Bulteel, *A Sermon on 1 Cor 2: 12*, 6th edn., 62.

tion from Bagot during the remainder of his tour, and he returned to Oxford on 30 July.[112] On 5 August 1831, however, Bagot revoked his licence to officiate in the diocese of Oxford.[113]

Bulteel regarded the withdrawal of his licence as an irrelevance, for he now held himself to be in miserable bondage to an evil religious Establishment.[114] None the less, after receiving a writ of ejectment from his curacy, he complained that 'no notice whatever has been taken of Mr Tiptaft's proceedings', adding, 'what then can we think of the government of that Church, which makes that which is sin in the curate, to be no sin in the vicar or rector? And what Scripture can be found to warrant the continuance of a race of men in the Church, whose *duty* compels them to become hinderers of the freest preaching of the Gospel of Christ?'[115] For all Bulteel's contumaciousness, he was not entirely without support from within the university, gaining some sympathy as a martyr to High Church bigotry. John Hill, for one, poured out his emotions into his diary. 'Deeply grieved this day—Bulteel has received notice from the bishop of the withdrawal of his licence as curate of St. Ebbe's. Thus Oxford is destitute of a single faithful preacher in any church among a population of 20,000.'[116] In a comment which revealed the extent to which the cause of 'serious religion' had recently been split apart, Hill mused that no alternative to Bulteel's dynamic ministry could be found even among the local 'Gospel clergy': 'On my return home found my dear family in distress. The sermons they have heard today at St. Peter's most lamentably deficient and erroneous. Many of Bulteel's hearers are scattered in different directions, weeping over the famine of God's Word. Such are the first fruits of his lamentable secession (for such it virtually is)—O God—say, let there be light, and there shall be light.'[117] More surprisingly, Hurrell Froude, the arch-opponent of Evangelicalism, went around for days muttering with a rueful countenance, and could only say

[112] Ibid.; *HD*, 67/8, 52a, 31 July 1831.

[113] Bulteel, *A Sermon on 1 Cor 2: 12*, 6th edn., 63. Four days later, Bagot signed and sealed the two parts of the revocation. See MSS Oxford Diocesan Papers d. 109, fol. 26, Oxford County RO; *Jackson's Oxford Journal*, 20 Aug. 1831; The *Oxford University, City, and County Herald*, 20 Aug. 1831.

[114] Henry Bulteel, *An Address Delivered on the Opening of a Free Episcopal Church* (Oxford, 1844), 14.

[115] Bulteel, *A Sermon on 1 Cor 2: 12*, 6th edn., 63.

[116] *HD*, 67/8, 54b, 10 Aug. 1831.

[117] Ibid. 67/8, 4 Sept. 1831.

'poor Bulteel!'; he was convinced that the errant Calvinist had shown exemplary spiritual humility by marrying the sister of a local pastry-cook to chasten his earthly affections and to show how Christians ought to live.[118] Simultaneously, Froude engaged in a conspiracy with John Henry Newman to secure the pulpit at St. Ebbe's for James Mozley and the High Church party.[119] Gladstone too was struck with regret. 'Poor Bulteel has lost his church for preaching in the open air', he confided to his diary, 'pity that he should have acted so: and pity that it should be found necessary to make such an example of a man of God. May He overrule all to the glory of his name.'[120]

Bulteel was eager to provoke a further crisis and capitalize on such local sympathies. On the Sunday morning following the revocation of his licence he appeared at the vestry at St. Ebbe's at the beginning of the service and in the presence of the church-wardens and officiating minister, to protest at his recent treatment. He announced that divine service would be held that evening in his garden on Pembroke Street.[121] When the appointed hour arrived, over a thousand curious supporters crowded into Bulteel's house and garden (and the gardens and windows of his neighbours) to be told that, in their West Country preaching tour, he and Tiptaft had 'merely followed the plain command of the Lord', had done nothing contrary to the Word of God, and had not violated canon law. Episcopal censure was brushed aside by an appeal to the higher call of evangelistic necessity: it was the duty of a bishop to promote by all means in his power the preaching of the Gospel, not to prevent it.[122] Thus, the revocation of his ministerial licence was an 'iniquitous and tyrannical proceeding', which

[118] Nor was Froude's faith in Bulteel shaken when it turned out that she was still young, accomplished, rather good-looking, not at all dowdy, and had a private fortune of her own. See Mozley, *Reminiscences*, i.228. Froude's later views of Bulteel were less charitable. See Richard Hurrell Froude, *Remains* (1838–9), i.252.

[119] See *Letters and Correspondence of John Henry Newman*, ed. Mozley 1:245; entry of 10 Aug. 1831, in *The Letters and Diaries of John Henry Newman*, ed. Ker and Gornall, ii.347.

[120] Entry of 14 Aug. 1831, in *The Gladstone Diaries*, ed. Foot and Matthew, i.374.

[121] The *Oxford University, City, and County Herald*, 20 Aug. 1831; *Jackson's Oxford Journal*, 20 Aug. 1831; James Charles Stafford, *An Earnest Persuasive to Unity* (Oxford, 1840), 28–9. Bulteel was succeeded at St. Ebbe's by the well-known Evangelical William Weldon Champneys (1807–75), who founded National Schools in the parish and regularly visited his parishioners, especially during the cholera epidemic of 1832. See MSS Records of Oxford City Parishes, d d, Parish Oxford St. Ebbe's, c, 17, Oxford County RO.

[122] Moore, *Pictorial and Historical Gossiping Guide to Oxford*, 15.

true believers would recognize as the 'act of an officer of the Church antichrist'.[123] Bulteel then dramatically tore up the prohibition from Bagot forbidding him from officiating in the diocese.[124] Such theatricals, however popular among Bulteel's local followers, did little to impress his more intelligent sympathizers, though he continued to attract substantial congregations to his services, including a number of undergraduates, for several months. As Gladstone noted in his diary, 'heard Bulteel's service from a window in Mrs Albutt's house—congregation large and very attentive—some of his sermon interested [me]—but there seemed to be a soreness of spirit in him.'[125] Bulteel later softened his rhetoric somewhat, suggesting that Bagot had not been a *willing* agent but had been compelled by the pressure of others, in Oxford and elsewhere, until almost obliged to act in self-defence.[126]

Bulteel then turned his mind to the question of his continued relationship with what he now castigated as the 'Church antichrist'. Styling himself 'the outcast minister of Christ', he concluded that he might yet remain in the Church of England to protest against her iniquities, since the root of the problem lay within her evil constitution.[127] His relationship with the Church as by law established, however, was destined to be short-lived, and he formally seceded during the autumn of 1831.[128]

V

In the months following the revocation of his licence, Bulteel embarked upon a highly erratic and unsettled spiritual course. Some of his time was spent preaching for Tiptaft at Sutton Courtenay, or in the open air at Abingdon, where he attracted large congregations.[129] In September 1831, an unidentified clergyman passing through Oxford invited Bulteel to accompany him to London, where they would speak with Edward Irving. While

[123] The *Oxford University, City, and County Herald*, 20 Aug. 1831. Soon afterwards, Bulteel was attacked in print by a former admirer. See ibid. 27 Aug. 1831.

[124] James Moore, *Earlier and Later Nonconformity in Oxford* (Oxford, 1875), 14–15.

[125] Entry of 25 Sept. 1831, in *The Gladstone Diaries*, ed. Foot and Matthew, i.384.

[126] Bulteel, *A Sermon on 1 Cor 2: 12*, 6th edn., 3, 60.

[127] Bulteel, *An Address Delivered on the Opening of a Free Episcopal Church*, 14.

[128] Cox, *Recollections of Oxford*, 248.

[129] Which numbered between two and three thousand. See J. C. Philpot, *William Tiptaft*, 52; J. H. Philpot, *The Seceders*, i.60.

meeting with Irving and some of his followers Bulteel spoke out strongly against the clergy who favoured Catholic Emancipation, only to be rebuked rather sharply by one of Irving's female 'prophets', who demanded: 'Is this the way that God's servants speak evil of dignities?' Bulteel quailed at her vehemence, and submitted to her authority.[130] He returned to Oxford a changed man, not only satisfied by the genuineness of the miracles of healing and tongues but (remarkably for an erstwhile high Calvinist) convinced by the doctrine of general redemption.[131] His friend Newton, who had been out of Oxford for a short time, was now shocked to find Bulteel preaching 'forgiveness—only forgiveness'; as he described it, Bulteel 'sought now to preach "in the power", and was haunted by an excited desire for "gifts"'.[132]

Thus transformed, Bulteel fully expected that a similar work would soon break out within his own congregation; and so it did, for allegedly miraculous manifestations soon appeared in Oxford, Bulteel's two young children being the first to receive the gift of tongues.[133] Their father was quick to relate these powerful 'gifts of the Spirit' to his own case, treating them as a divine response to his 'having been cast out by one of the chief officers of a carnal church'.[134] During this phase of his ministry, such excitement prevailed among the members of his congregation that several rushed out of their beds one night and baptized one another in the Isis.[135] Nor was such Pentecostal fervour restricted to a tiny coterie of the 'spiritually converted'. As Bulteel candidly revealed to the 'prophet' Robert Baxter (who later defected from Irvingism when his own prophecies remained unfulfilled):

On the last Sunday in last November [1831] I received *the spirit*, since which time he has entered into or exercised powerful influence upon as

[130] Fry, 96, 98, 105–6.

[131] See *HD*, 67/8, 64b, 18 Oct. 1831. One account suggests that Irvingism was being advanced for a time in St. Clement's, Oxford, during 1826. In 1874, a congregation of the Catholic Apostolic Church was gathered in a room behind 114 High Street, but it is doubtful whether any *formal* meeting of that body assembled at Oxford prior to that date. See Alan Crossley, (ed.), 'A History of the County of Oxford: The City of Oxford', in *The Victorian History of the Counties of England* (Oxford, 1979), iv.423–4; Moore, *Earlier and Later Nonconformity in Oxford*, 14.

[132] Fry, 96, 135–6.

[133] See Henry Bulteel, *The Doctrine of the Miraculous Interferences of Jesus*, 2nd edn. (Oxford, 1832), 30–1; J.C. Philpot, *William Tiptaft*, 54.

[134] Bulteel, *The Doctrine of the Miraculous*, 30; Fry, 131.

[135] Ibid. 96.

many as between sixty and seventy of my flock, as I should suppose; the power under the word preached having been so great that I have had on two occasions nearly twenty people carried out of church completely overthrown by it; some under the most powerful convictions of sin, the tears streaming in perfect torrents from their eyes; others so full of joy as to be completely like drunken men, so as to open to me the Word in Acts 2. These men are full of new wine; others clapping their hands together and crying out glory, glory. Four [?] children between the ages of eight and twelve were brought into such a state as would melt the heart of any beholder—their arms stretched out, their eyes overflowing, a supernatural cry for sin, and for mercy, and such wonderful liberty of prayer as is surprising. There never has I think been a meeting since I received the Spirit in which there has not been a wonderful startling of some sort or other.[136]

Though such manifestations of the Spirit would not be treated as unusual in the various congregations of the English prophetic movement (or in modern Pentecostal circles), they were a radical departure from the 'practical' and respectable forms of Christianity advanced by early nineteenth-century Evangelicals, including Bulteel's own 'Gospel contemporaries' at Oxford.

In early 1832, Bulteel published a lengthy defence of his new Pentecostal views. He set forth two possible explanations for the reappearance of the 'gifts': they had always remained in the church, available for the use of believers, but had been ignored; or, they had now reappeared in the church after a long absence.[137] Either possibility seemed consistent with the promises made in Scripture. As evidence of the current revival of the 'gifts', and in the shadow of Oxford's first cholera epidemic (which broke out in 1832 and was especially virulent in the parish of St. Ebbe's),[138] Bulteel cited a number of cases of 'miraculous' healings, several of them in his own congregation: Charlotte Charriere, Mary Sadler (his sister-in-law), Elizabeth Sawdy,[139] a Mr Barnes, and Alice Seary.[140] Each of these had been touched, Bulteel claimed, by a 'supernatural power, put forth by our Lord Jesus Christ in

[136] Bulteel to Baxter, 20 May 1832, in possession of the Revd Iain H. Murray, Edinburgh.

[137] Bulteel, *The Doctrine of the Miraculous*, 30.

[138] See V. Thomas, *Memorials of Malignant Cholera in Oxford* (Oxford, 1855); Crossley, 'A History of the County of Oxford', iv.236–8.

[139] Bulteel, *The Doctrine of the Miraculous*, 30–4; the *Morning Watch* (1832), v.218–21.

[140] Bulteel, *The Doctrine of the Miraculous*, 34–5.

direct answer to the prayer of faith'.[141] His claims were derided, however, by James Mozley, the future Regius Professor of Divinity (then an undergraduate at Oriel), who dismissed the healings as 'nothing very wonderful'. Bulteel, he claimed, effected the cure of Miss Sadler by constant prayer in an adjoining room, 'she being all the time aware of it'. 'Everyone knows', Mozley observed dryly, 'the influence of imagination in such cases.' As to Bulteel, there was little doubt that he was 'partially deranged'. Mozley conceded that these 'absurdities' might possibly 'work some good, as showing the state that men come to when they choose to caste off all restraint. One man who used to be a constant attendant at his church, abuses him now without the smallest hesitation.'[142] John Henry Newman was equally sceptical, dismissing the affair as the product of auto-suggestion. 'Providence', he wrote to a correspondent some years later, 'seemed to "countenance a delusion". Mr B[ulteel] spoke in order to effect the cure . . .'[143]

Bulteel now began to advance a new position on the doctrine of baptism, rejecting the practice of sprinkling.[144] At first he was uncertain about abandoning paedobaptism altogether, and although inclined to baptize his own children, he determined not do so until receiving a plain command from God.[145] More remarkable perhaps than Bulteel's conversion to pre-millennialism and the modification of his views on baptism, was his renunciation of the high Calvinistic doctrines for which he had pleaded so passionately and recently in his University Sermon.[146] In their place he now embraced not merely moderate Arminianism, but universal redemption and pardon—changes which quickly resulted in his ostracism by the Oxford high Calvinists.[147] Benjamin Wills Newton, who had been captivated by Bulteel's ministry while an undergraduate at Exeter College and had been tutored by the then-Evangelical Francis Newman,[148] was so disgusted by Bulteel's

[141] Ibid. 35.

[142] Mozley to his mother, February 1832, in *Letters of the Revd J. B. Mozley, D.D.* (1885), ed. Anne Mozley, 25–6.

[143] Newman to Ward, 12 Oct. 1848, in *The Letters and Diaries of John Henry Newman*, ed. Charles Stephen Dessain (1962), xii.292.

[144] Bulteel, *The Doctrine of the Miraculous*, 38.

[145] Ibid. 38–9.

[146] Anon., *The Unknown Tongues*, 6th edn. (1832), 31.

[147] J.C. Philpot, *William Tiptaft*, 53–4.

[148] See T. C. F. Stunt, 'John Henry Newman and the Evangelicals', in *JEH* (1970), 70; E. R. Sandeen, *The Roots of Fundamentalism* (Chicago, 1970), 30. It was through Newman that Newton developed his interest in the subject of prophecy.

change of view that he abandoned Oxford for Plymouth, never to return.[149] 'Bulteel fell into connexion with Irvingism,' Newton wrote, 'I knew it was injurious. I was myself at one of the meetings and felt a supernatural power over me. I went home and couldn't read my Bible, and I resolved never to be again within that circle. I left Oxford soon after. *These things caused my leaving Oxford*.'[150] Even William Tiptaft now painfully admitted: 'My old friend Bulteel and I can now have no communion. He holds the doctrine of universal pardon, is now distinguished for universal charity, and accuses God's children, who hold the doctrine of particular redemption, as having a bad spirit.'[151] Likewise John Nelson Darby, who wrote on 19 August 1833 to a friend: 'What is poor [Bulteel] doing at Oxford? I love that man, much erred as I think he has. Oh how little we have of the Spirit, to baffle the plans and devices and snares of Satan! . . . But the positive work of the enemy I do think most manifest as Irving's, but where was the energy to keep it out?'[152]

Bulteel's religious volatility continued for some time. In early 1832, he rejected paedobaptism altogether, being baptized by immersion on 12 February by the younger James Hinton at his Baptist chapel in George Street, St. Clement's, Oxford, where he had of late been a regular preacher.[153] Several months later, Bulteel opened a new chapel (known locally as Adullam Chapel) which he had built on Commercial Road (at the bottom of Littlegate, behind Pembroke College and within the boundaries of St. Ebbe's parish) at a cost of around £4,000.[154] Here he propagated his new views before a substantial congregation (quickly labelled as 'Bulteelers'),[155] who travelled in from every part of

[149] Coad, *A History of the Brethren Movement*, 63.

[150] Fry, 96, 135.

[151] J.C. Philpot, *William Tiptaft*, 66.

[152] J. A. Trench, (ed.), *Letters of John Nelson Darby* (1886–8), i.28.

[153] William Palmer, *A Hard Nut to Crack* (Oxford, 1831), 7; James Hinton, *A Nut Cracker* (Oxford, 1832), 6; Bulteel, *The Doctrine of the Miraculous*, 38–9. The younger James Hinton had been ordained in 1825 to serve in the chapel at George Street, founded the previous year by members of New Road Baptist Chapel. See *BMag* (1824), 532; Tim Grass, '"The Restoration of a Congregation of Baptists": Baptists and Irvingism in Oxfordshire', in *BQ* (forthcoming); Moore, *Earlier and Later Nonconformity in Oxford*, 14.

[154] Designed by William Fisher and seating 800, it was, for many years, the largest Nonconformist chapel in Oxford. See Moore, *Pictorial and Historical Gossiping Guide to Oxford*, 15; Crossley, 'A History of the County of Oxford', iv.418. The chapel was registered as a Dissenting meeting-house on 1 June 1832. See MSS Oxford Diocesan Papers c. 645, fol. 201, Oxford County RO.

[155] Cox, *Recollections of Oxford*, 244 n.

Oxfordshire and from a number of adjoining counties to form the largest Nonconformist gathering in Oxford.[156]

These twists and turns of Bulteel's spiritual odyssey produced yet another war of Oxford pamphlets.[157] One of these, written by the learned High Churchman William Palmer of Worcester College, attacked Bulteel for labouring under 'a spirit of delusion and error'.[158] Bulteel's refusal to respond to these charges (his friend James Hinton did so on his behalf), incited Palmer to publish a second vigorous attack encouraging believers to ignore Bulteel's teachings and to refuse him access to their homes until 'he is able to prove that he is not a false prophet'.[159] Not surprisingly Palmer made much of Bulteel's changes of doctrinal opinion, which he thought suggested unusual instability. What could one make of a man who had, in rapid succession, appeared as a Calvinist, an antinomian, a paedobaptist, a Puritan, a seceder, an Arminian, and was now a sort of mongrel Baptist?[160] Next month, might he not be a Quaker, a Socinian, an infidel, or a papist? Could Bulteel provide any security that his creed would not differ next Sunday from what it was now?[161] Palmer was especially scornful of Bulteel for styling himself 'the *only true minister of God in Oxford*', and threatening '*eternal damnation* to all who refused to embrace the very opinions which he himself gave up immediately afterwards'.[162]

The course of Bulteel's religious life continued to be erratic. In the spring of 1833, he severed his connections with the English prophetic movement, provoking a schism from his own congregation.[163] The reasons behind this decision are not clear. According to one source, Bulteel and Irving had agreed between them that the 'prophetic' clergy should confer regularly, but otherwise remain independent—an arrangement which suited Bulteel.[164] Before long, however, Irving and his followers began moving in

[156] Moore, *Earlier and Later Nonconformity in Oxford*, 15; Crossley, 'A History of the County of Oxford', iv.255. In a survey of Baptist chapels in 1835, the *Baptist Magazine* claimed that Bulteel's chapel had 60 members and no less than 800 hearers. See *BMag* (1835), 561.

[157] Palmer, *A Hard Nut to Crack*; Hinton, *A Nut Cracker*, William Palmer, *At Him Again!* (Oxford 1832).

[158] Palmer, *A Hard Nut to Crack*, 10.

[159] Palmer, *At Him Again!*, 4.

[160] Ibid. 6.

[161] Ibid. 6–7.

[162] Ibid. 7.

[163] See Bulteel to Baxter, 16 Apr. 1833, in the possession of the Revd Iain H. Murray, Edinburgh.

[164] Grass, '"The Restoration of a Congregation of Baptists"'.

more catholic directions, developing a hierarchical and highly centralized structure based in London and (eventually) Albury. This Bulteel could not accept, for (especially after his conflict with the Bishop of Oxford) he remained adamantly opposed to any suggestion of an apostleship with universal jurisdiction.[165] Bulteel may also have become concerned over Irving's continued slide into Christological heresy.[166] A further catalyst for his break with the prophetic movement seems to have been the recantation of the former Irvingite 'prophet' Robert Baxter, after his predictions failed to materialize: realizing that he himself had failed to seek divine guidance in determining the validity of the 'gifts', Bulteel now prayed that if they were true the manifestations might increase, if false, that they might cease. The next morning the 'gifted persons' in his congregation were silent.[167] Another factor arose out of Bulteel's realization that since accepting the authenticity of the 'gifts' he had tended to neglect his Bible: in fact, he could not read even two pages of Scripture without falling asleep.[168] A final factor was the deteriorating state of Bulteel's mental equilibrium. Over time, he had discovered that the only way to restore his spiritual health was to distance himself and his flock from the prophetic movement. Writing to Robert Baxter in April 1833, he laid bare his soul, describing how Satan had laboured to destroy him:

for whole nights I have not been able to close my eyes in anything like sound sleep, for he [Satan] has come upon me . . . I cannot tell you the state to which I have at times been seduced by these fierce attacks. My strength seems while under them to be entirely gone . . . I have been sometimes in this condition when about to stand up to preach to the people and yet the Lord has always given me strength to testify against him [Satan], and brought peace into my soul after the delivery of the testimony. These attacks come upon me about every other night, or one night in three, though sometimes they last the whole night and day; my only strength is to be quite still and throw myself upon the Cross of Jesus, for I find I cannot lift myself up to a glorified Christ; I can only lay hold on him in his suffering condition. I hope and trust that this will wear off in a short time, as it brings my nerves into such a state as to resemble

[165] Ibid.

[166] Irving's trial before the London Presbytery commenced in late April 1832. See Chapter 5.

[167] See Grass, '"The Restoration of a Congregation of Baptists"'.

[168] The *Christian Herald* (1833), 127.

the leaves of an aspen ready to be shaken with the least wind. My trials now are great in consequence of the rents in the flock; for several cleave to them, and one of the gifted ones who had been recovered has gone back again and is worse than ever. Damnation and destruction is [*sic*] thundered against me and my flock within a short space of time, and the terror brought upon the minds of the weak ones who see [that] the cheat is very painful to me as well as to them, for I have enough to do to hold myself up, and almost fear at times to go among the people because of the weak state of my nerves.[169]

Though Bulteel's ultra-Protestantism changed its form again and again, it did not disappear altogether. After abandoning the prophetic movement, he came to embrace many of the doctrines which were now being advanced by the emerging Christian Brethren, with which he maintained close personal ties, especially when its focus was transferred from Dublin and Oxford to his home town of Plymouth.[170] He remained a vigorous activist, especially on the issue of establishment. On 31 May 1836, at the conclusion of the anniversary celebration of the Reformation Society in Oxford, he stood on a bench in the middle of the room demanding that the meeting address the issue of disestablishment, only to be informed that the question had nothing to do with the Society.[171] In 1841, he published an attack on the Oxford Movement and upon Anglican subscription to the Articles, which he dismissed as hypocritical.[172] Three years later, in a pan-evangelical spirit, he preached at the opening of a new Congregationalist chapel in Summertown, north Oxford, which had been erected by Protestants to check the spread of Tractarianism.[173] In the same year, he assisted in Exeter with the opening of the second congregation of the Free Church of England, a Protestant body composed of Evangelical seceders from the Church of England.[174]

[169] Bulteel to Baxter, 16 Apr. 1833, in the possession of the Revd Iain H. Murray, Edinburgh. Cf. *HD* 67/9, 64b, 18 May 1833.

[170] See Stunt, 'Henry Bulteel'. How closely tied he was to the movement remains uncertain. About 1840, some of Bulteel's local congregation seceded to form a separate Brethren assembly in a house in Queen's Street, probably because Bulteel was the chapel's only minister. See MS Anon., Miscellaneous Newspaper Cuttings, 26 Nov. 1874, No G. A. Oxon. 4° 271, Bod.

[171] *HD* 67/10, 78b–79, 31 May 1836.

[172] Henry Bulteel, *To All that Love Truth and Consistency* (Oxford, 1841).

[173] William Henry Summers, *History of Congregational Churches* (Newbury, 1905), 256; Crossley, 'A History of the County of Oxford', iv.422. In the following year, Bulteel penned a popular skit against the Tractarians. See Henry Bulteel, *The Oxford Argo* (1845).

[174] See Chapter 9.

In his address, which was quickly published,[175] he claimed that the Articles, canons, and parliamentary enactments which established and regulated the Church of England had brought the Anglican clergy into 'a complete state of bondage'.[176] This was due to the 'original sin' of establishment, which had granted to the State important rights and powers intended by God for his Church.[177] By contrast, in the Free Church of England Bulteel saw a body in healthy competition with the Establishment, which would allow those who were conscientiously attached to episcopal government, yet objected to the abuses of the Church, to separate into a purer form of episcopacy.[178]

Perhaps hoping that the recent Scottish Disruption would have a catalytic effect on the 'serious clergy' in England, Bulteel called on Evangelicals to secede *en masse* from the Establishment and affiliate with the Free Church of England. Until they undertook such a step nothing could help stem the rising torrent of Puseyism, for as long as they remained ensnared in the trammels of a Laodicean State Church Evangelicals could do little to resist it. They were shackled to a liturgy which still countenanced relics of a popish past. Was it not hypocritical to preach against the errors of baptismal regeneration while in the next moment thanking God for regenerating the infant just baptized? Inconsistencies like these damaged the Evangelicals' witness to the world and rendered their testimony 'null and void'. If they were to secede *en masse* from the Establishment and affiliate with this new Episcopal body, their testimony against Tractarianism would acquire a dramatic 'twofold power'.[179] Apostolic succession, if desired, could be secured from the bishops in America.[180] Bulteel suggested Exeter as the ideal headquarters for such a body. The high-handed behaviour of Bishop Phillpotts who had 'deprived more clergymen of their licences', and 'pronounced more ecclesiastical censures' than perhaps all other bishops combined, was the living embodiment of everything incurably wrong in the Church of England. If his determined vendetta against Evangelicals continued, Bulteel predicted, it would drive many other exasperated clergy into the Free Church of England.[181]

Details of Bulteel's subsequent ministry are sketchy, but he

[175] Bulteel, *An Address Delivered on the Opening of a Free Episcopal Church.*
[176] Ibid. 3. [177] Ibid. 14. [178] Ibid. 15–19.
[179] Ibid. 19–20. [180] Ibid. 23–5. [181] Ibid. 26.

seems to have continued to float rather uncertainly from one Calvinistic cause to another. Eventually, he appears to have affiliated with the 'open' faction within the Brethren movement, both in Oxford[182] and later at his native Plymouth,[183] to which he moved after his mother's death in 1849 and where he lived for the remainder of his life.[184] He emerges again in May 1851 when John Hill encountered him at the parish church at Hampton Gay, the two men sitting and talking together for a time.[185] In the religious census of 1851, Bulteel is listed as minister of Ebrington Street ('Calvinistic') Chapel in Plymouth, which had been erected 'about 1840', and residing at 11 Hain Street.[186] Some time after 1862, perhaps in retirement, he began to attend Compton Street ('Christian') Chapel.[187] From February 1865 his health began to decline, and he died at the Crescent, Plymouth, on 28 December 1866.[188]

On the wide and crowded stage of nineteenth-century religious controversy, Henry Bulteel made only a brief appearance under the spotlight before he vanished into the shadows. Yet his role was not a trivial one, for at a critical moment in the nation's foremost seminary and seat of learning he brought into full view some of the new developments that were germinating in English Evangelicalism—resurgent high Calvinism, unease over the Erastian and sacerdotal character of the Establishment, pre-millennial expectation, and the Pentecostal hope of the return of the miraculous 'gifts' of the Acts of the Apostles. Bulteel brought the prophetic movement into high profile at a time when both Evangelicals and

[182] It has been suggested that Darby found sympathizers in Oxford as early as the summer of 1827, but this is probably too early. See Napoleon Noel, *The History of the Brethren* (Denver, 1936), i.22, 24. By 1869, the leader of the Brethren in Oxford was a former minister of Bulteel's chapel. By 1875, there was an assembly of the Brethren meeting in Paradise Square. See Moore, *Earlier and Later Nonconformity in Oxford*, 15; MSS Oxford Diocesan Papers c. 645, fol. 172, Oxford County RO. In March 1877, the Brethren built a chapel at 3 New Inn Hall Street, at a cost of £1,500, which continued in use until 1964. See Crossley, 'A History of the County of Oxford', iv.423; Moore, *Pictorial and Historical Gossiping Guide to Oxford*, 15; *Kelly's Directory of Oxford* (1964), A18.

[183] Henry Pickering, *Chief Men Among the Brethren*, 2nd edn. (London and Glasgow, 1931), 119; Rowdon, *The Origins of the Brethren*, 69.

[184] In 1852 Bulteel's son, having been baptized (against his father's wishes) in the Church of England, married the daughter of James Shore, founder of the Free Church of England. See Stunt, 'Henry Bulteel'; *GM* (Feb. 1867), 258; Michael J. L. Wickes (ed.), *Devon in the Religious Census of 1851* (Appledore, 1990), 74.

[185] *HD* 67/19, 18, 4 May 1851.

[186] See Wickes, *Devon in the Religious Census of 1851*, 74.

[187] Stunt, 'Henry Bulteel'.

[188] *DNB*.

the leaders of the emerging Brethren movement were formulating their own response to the alleged return of the 'gifts'. In the West Country, his preaching tour exacerbated tensions between Evangelicals and Henry Phillpotts which came to a head during the Shore and Gorham cases. It also sowed seeds of high Calvinism and pre-millennialism which would later be harvested by Darby and his followers, as they moulded their local evangelistic efforts into a powerful West Country movement—the Plymouth Brethren.[189] While the controversies surrounding Bulteel were brief, their echoes floated far beyond the cloistered precincts of Oxford.[190]

VI

The secessions of Bulteel's two high Calvinist friends and colleagues, William Tiptaft and Joseph Charles Philpot, contributed greatly to the tensions surrounding Oxford Evangelicalism during the early 1830s.[191] Tiptaft was the third son of James Tiptaft, a wealthy farmer from Braunston, near Oakham, Rutland, and his wife Elizabeth. Born on 16 February 1803, he was educated at Uppingham School and at St. John's College, Cambridge, and ordained in 1826 by George Law, Bishop of Bath and Wells, to

[189] See Rowdon, *The Origins of the Brethren*, 69.

[190] In the 1851 religious census, his former Oxford chapel was referred to as Adullam Particular Baptist Chapel, Willoughby Willey, minister, with an average morning and evening congregation of between five and six hundred. See Kate Tiller (ed.), *Church and Chapel in Oxfordshire 1851* (Oxford, 1987), 77. Within a few years, however, lacking Bulteel's personal force and private means, Willey proved unable to hold the congregation together without an endowment. See MS Anon., Miscellaneous Newspaper Cuttings, 26 Nov. 1874, No G. A. Oxon. 4° 270, Bod. In 1858, the congregation was dissolved; four years later, the chapel was taken over by the Methodist Free Church of Oxford, which moved from Paradise Square. See 'Church Book', 1838–66, s a 1858, New Road Baptist Chapel archives, Oxford; Moore, *Earlier and Later Nonconformity in Oxford*, 16, 30. In 1868, it was purchased by the remnants of the 'Bulteelers' who, under Alexander Macfarlane of Spurgeon's College, Camberwell, had started meetings in the Chequers Sale Room in the High Street (moving, in the following year, to the former Quaker meeting-room in Pusey Lane, St. Giles). In 1869, the renovated chapel was reopened by Charles Spurgeon. See Moore, *Earlier and Later Nonconformity in Oxford*, 14. The congregation was now known as the Tabernacle Baptist Society. See *Webster's Oxford Directory* (Oxford, 1869), 207. It was later described as Particular Baptist and remained so until it was finally closed in 1937. See Crossley, 'A History of the County of Oxford', iv.419; Reynolds, *The Evangelicals at Oxford*, 98–9.

[191] For details of Tiptaft see *Letters of the Late Joseph Charles Philpot*, ed. W. C. Clayton and S. L. Philpot (1871); J.C. Philpot, *William Tiptaft*; Anon., *Reminiscences and Sayings of the late Mr William Tiptaft*, 2nd edn. (Oxford, 1875); Edward C. Starr, *A Baptist Biography* (Rochester, 1976), 23.

serve in the parish of Treborough, Somerset.[192] A few months later, he passed through a classic evangelical conversion experience.[193] In 1828 he became curate of the larger parish of Stogumber, Somerset, and, in February 1829, was presented to the living of Sutton Courtenay, near Abingdon, in the diocese of Salisbury.[194]

While Tiptaft's final sermon at Stogumber (published at the request of the parish) made clear his adherence to the Evangelical 'doctrines of grace', it also revealed that he had yet to imbibe the doctrine of particular election, the characteristic mark of high Calvinism.[195] At Sutton Courtenay, his views changed rapidly. Shortly after his arrival, in May 1829, he attended a clerical meeting at Wallingford where he met Philpot, perpetual curate of Chilsehampton and Stadhampton.[196] During a gathering of the same group in early summer, the two began to converse on doctrinal matters. As Philpot later explained:

> At that time I was further advanced, at least in doctrine and a knowledge of the letter of truth, than he was, being a firm believer in election and the distinguishing doctrines of sovereign grace . . . We therefore soon got on the topic of election, when I at once perceived that he had not been led into the grand truths of the Gospel, and . . . viewed them with a measure both of fear and suspicion.[197]

Despite his conversion experience, Tiptaft yet remained, in his own retrospective view, 'dark, blind, and ignorant'. Gradually, Philpot's arguments took root and Tiptaft embraced the doctrines of particular election and reprobation, or so-called 'double predestination'. He later described this 'second' conversion experience thus:

> How earnestly did I pray that if these despised doctrines were true, that I might receive them; if they were not true, that I might reject them; and the Lord confirmed the doctrine of election to my soul by applying that portion respecting the opening of Lydia's heart. I was convinced of the truth of it, which took place in the latter end of the summer of 1829. Through mercy, I have been enabled to contend for the doctrine ever

192 *Al. Cant.* 193 J.C. Philpot, *William Tiptaft*, 5.

194 Ibid. 4, 8; MS D1/2/32/14 Wiltshire County RO.

195 William Tiptaft, *A Farewell Sermon* (1829).

196 *Letters of the Late Joseph Charles Philpot*, ed. Clayton and Philpot, 19; J.C. Philpot, *William Tiptaft*, 15–16; Anon., *Reminiscences and Sayings of the late Mr William Tiptaft*, 31, 33.

197 J.C. Philpot, *William Tiptaft*, 15.

since, but I know it is a hard doctrine to receive, and feel risings in my own mind against it. It is a blessed doctrine, when fully received in the heart, as the seventeenth Article describes it.[198]

The transformation in Tiptaft's preaching and ministry was so remarkable that his large church was soon thronged with hearers drawn from surrounding parishes. Philpot, who was invited to preach at Sutton Courtenay at this time, later described the scene:

> as we went into the churchyard, it was surprising to see the number of people coming along the various roads, or standing in groups waiting for the service to commence. The church soon became so filled that there was scarcely standing room in the aisles. And of whom was the congregation made up? Almost wholly of poor men and women. Labourers were there in their smock-frocks and week-day clothes almost as if they had just come out of the fields, poor women in the cotton shawls, with a sprinkling of better-dressed people in the pews; but a thorough plain and rustic assembly had gathered together to hear a sermon on the week-day evening—an event which had not probably occurred in that church or neighbourhood since the days of the Puritans.[199]

Despite this parochial success, Tiptaft's personal life and ministry were far from carefree. His acceptance of high Calvinism swiftly led to the breaking-off of his engagement, his fiancée announcing (through her clerical father) that she was unwilling to unite with anyone holding such extreme views.[200] A second controversy arose as the result of Tiptaft's Christmas Day sermon at St. Helen's, Abingdon, in which he advanced a 'new' Gospel, unknown to many in the congregation.

This notorious sermon, delivered before the mayor, the local corporation and a large congregation, was clearly intended to provoke.[201] Christ came, Tiptaft announced triumphantly, to save a *peculiar* people.[202] The 'elect' are indwelt by the Holy Spirit and thus unable to sin, for to them has been imputed God's righteousness.[203] Tiptaft denied the role of human volition in either justification or sanctification: if the Lord required even a single good thought of believers, no man would be saved and all would be damned.[204] His antinomian leanings were unmistakable, and he was quickly censured and ostracized, not least by some of his

[198] Ibid. 5. [199] Ibid. 19. [200] Ibid. 17.

[201] Ibid. 22–5; William Tiptaft, *A Sermon Preached in the Parish Church of St. Helen, Abingdon* (Abingdon, 1830).

[202] Ibid. 8, 10. [203] Ibid. 15, 17. [204] Ibid. 22.

former Evangelical friends, who were alarmed by his 'new and extravagant tenets'. Except for his friends Bulteel and Philpot, who held similar views, the local clergy turned their backs upon him.[205] Tiptaft's friendship with Philpot developed strongly during the winter months of 1830–1 when Philpot slowly recuperated at Sutton Courtenay after a severe illness and nervous breakdown.[206]

One of Tiptaft's most outspoken critics was Joseph Hewlett, the High Church Headmaster of Abingdon Grammar School.[207] On 27 December, Hewlett launched an angry response to Tiptaft's sermon from the same pulpit, refuting the doctrine of particular election with vigour. He then published his sermon.[208] Tiptaft was incensed by what he considered to be a grievous misrepresentation of his teaching. Taking the moral high ground, he dismissed his opponent as 'a wine bibber, a great card-player, and a fox-hunter', and quickly printed his own sermon to justify his position, confidently but perhaps naïvely assuming that local people would side with him once the true details of his sermon had been revealed.[209]

As Tiptaft continued to battle away for his cause at Sutton Courtenay during the winter and spring of 1831, his commitment to the Church of England began to waver. On 14 March 1831 he confessed:

> At this present time my conscience is not very easy about the Church Establishment. I neither like the system nor the forms or ceremonies, particularly the baptismal service and the catechism . . . In the baptismal service we thank God in the surplice for regenerating children, and then put on the black gown, go into the pulpit, and tell them in plain terms that they were not born again. Our liturgy makes every baptized person a member of the true Church . . . And the catechism is so full of errors that I am sure no one with a glimmering of light will teach children it.[210]

Soon after he added: 'I consider the riches of the National Church are a great cause of her corruptions. Take them away, and then who would belong to her? . . . How very different are the ministers of the present day from those in Paul's day'.[211]

[205] *Letters of the Late Joseph Charles Philpot*, ed. Clayton and Philpot, 21.

[206] Ibid. 21–2; J.H. Philpot, *The Seceders*, i.92.

[207] Hewlett's career at Abingdon was described as 'a failure' in the *DNB*.

[208] Joseph Hewlett, *A Sermon Preached at Abingdon* (Abingdon, 1830); Anon., *The Calm Observer* (Abingdon, 1830).

[209] J.C. Philpot, *William Tiptaft*, 24.

[210] Ibid. 36.

[211] Ibid. 44–5.

In July 1831, after his preaching tour with Bulteel, Tiptaft began seriously to consider seceding, especially after Bulteel's licence was revoked by the Bishop of Oxford. By late October he had nearly made up his mind. 'I am harassed in my mind about leaving the Church,' he wrote, 'for I find I cannot hold my living and a good conscience too . . . I believe it to be an unholy system . . . I cannot read the baptismal and burial services . . . What I shall do if I leave it, I know not . . . We must suffer with Christ before we reign with him'.[212] By 10 November his hesitancy had ceased; he wrote a long letter to Thomas Burgess, the Bishop of Salisbury, announcing his resignation from the parish and his secession from the Church.

Tiptaft's letter to Burgess was published on the last day of November 1831, producing a considerable sensation.[213] Three thousand copies of the first edition were sold almost immediately,[214] and eight further editions were soon required, not including the full accounts which appeared in various newspapers, and an edition published surreptitiously by a Southampton bookseller.[215] A series of published replies quickly heightened the controversy.[216]

Tiptaft set before his diocesan fourteen provocative objections to Anglican belief and practice, some of which coincided uncomfortably with those levelled by radicals like John Wade, author of the notorious *Black Book*. He objected to the order of confirmation; to the rubric for King Charles 'the Martyr'; to the optimistic expression, '*our most religious* and gracious King' in the service for Parliament (which he evidently found hard to apply to the reprobate George IV); the practice of 'open communion', in which every baptized person is invited to receive communion; the form for the solemnization of marriage; the service for the 'churching of women'; private patronage; the absence of formal ministerial training and ecclesiastical discipline; the right of bishops to sit in Parliament and their grandiose style of life; and to the oaths, subscriptions, and declarations required at ordination, especially that

212 Tiptaft to anon., 25 Oct. 1831, ibid. 54–5.

213 William Tiptaft, *A Letter Addressed to the Bishop of Salisbury* (Abingdon, 1831).

214 J. C. Philpot, *William Tiptaft*, 64–5.

215 J. H. Philpot, *The Seceders*, i.61.

216 *A Brief Reply to the Reverend Mr Tiptaft's Letter to the Bishop of Salisbury* (by 'a Member of the Church of England') (Reading, 1831); Peter Hall, *A Candid and Respectful Letter to the Revd William Tiptaft* (Salisbury, 1832); Rowland Hill, *A Letter* (Manchester and London, 1835).

relating to the Prayer Book.[217] Nor could he foresee any prospect of improvement as long as the Church's revenues remained immense, providing 'so strong an inducement for ungodly and worldly-minded men to enter the ministry'.[218]

Within two weeks of his secession, Tiptaft used his own money to purchase a small piece of land in Abingdon on which he would construct a new chapel.[219] A Dissenting meeting house in Sutton Courtenay, which could accommodate between three and four hundred hearers, was made available for his use until his new chapel was completed, and he preached twice—without licence—at one of the Anglican churches in Wallingford, where he received appeals from the congregation to become their new incumbent.[220] He also addressed a large crowd at Hosier Street (Baptist) Chapel, Reading, where John Howard Hinton was minister; at the Old (Strict) Baptist Chapel, Devizes, where Roger Hitchcock officiated; and at Zion (Strict) Baptist Chapel, Trowbridge, where the ultra-Calvinist John Warburton, the 'Lancashire Weaver', presided.[221]

Construction of Tiptaft's new chapel was begun immediately (again at his own expense) and it was opened on 25 March 1832, Hitchcock and Warburton preaching to large congregations.[222] Hitchcock was a fellow seceder who had been curate at Figheldean, Wiltshire, before his secession from the Church in 1826. Warburton was a well-known Dissenter of hyper-Calvinist views.[223] Significantly, Tiptaft's new congregation contained relatively few Anglican converts, the majority being drawn from the more Calvinistically minded members of the local Independent chapel.[224] Euphoria at the chapel's opening was, however, marred by the portent of ecclesiastical censure. Bishop Burgess now threatened prosecution on the grounds that Tiptaft still remained in holy orders and as such was culpable for his itinerating and for

[217] Tiptaft, *A Letter Addressed to the Bishop of Salisbury*, 3–8.

[218] Ibid. 9–10.

[219] At a cost of £105.

[220] J.C. Philpot, *William Tiptaft*, 59–60; Summers, *History of Congregational Churches*, 224.

[221] J.C. Philpot, *William Tiptaft*, 64.

[222] Ibid. 65; Anon., *Reminiscences and Sayings of the late Mr William Tiptaft*, 12.

[223] Robert W. Oliver, *The Strict Baptist Chapels of England* (1968), v.57, 65–7; MS D1/9/2/1, Wiltshire County RO; John Warburton, *The Mercies of a Covenant God* (1837).

[224] Summers, *History of Congregational Churches*, 221. The local Congregational minister, William Wilkins, although described as 'a strong Calvinist', was often greeted by his former members with the words: 'oh, sir, you are in the dark! quite in the dark!' Many of these, however, eventually returned to his ministry.

preaching doctrines 'inconsistent with the principles of the Established Church', in direct violation of canon law. If he did not desist, the bishop warned, legal proceedings would be commenced forthwith.[225]

Tiptaft expressed astonishment at the bishop's demand. He disavowed his former membership of the Church, whose jurisdiction he utterly rejected. 'If you still claim me as a minister of your Establishment', he wrote, 'I beg again to renounce my connection with it; and if it be necessary for me to go through any form of dismissal according to the laws of the land, of which I am perfectly ignorant, I am willing to submit to it'.[226] Tiptaft's secession thus raised an important legal issue—the right of a seceding clergyman to take up another form of ministry in the same diocese—which was to gain far greater prominence in the case of James Shore during the 1840s.[227]

On 22 March, Tiptaft was informed by the bishop's secretary that he appeared to have a mistaken idea of the effect of his secession, for this was an act which of itself did not operate as a renunciation of holy orders, nor did it exonerate him from the observance of the ecclesiastical law as it applied to the clergy. In fact, no authority existed which was competent to accept, or give effect to, such a renunciation.[228] Once more Tiptaft offered to undertake any form of dismissal which would formally sever his connections with the Church. If no such form was available, he assured the bishop, he intended to proceed exactly as he had done since his secession, until forced to cease 'by the mighty and alarming power of the ecclesiastical court'.[229]

Apparently alarmed by the publicity which might result, Burgess's secretary quickly replied that his Lordship had no desire to proceed against Tiptaft on account of his religious opinions, but wished merely to prevent his 'violating the law by preaching in unconsecrated places'. None the less, he reiterated that a clergyman could not 'by aid of any authority legally or effectually' renounce his orders or his connection with the Church. Conse-

[225] Burgess to Tiptaft, 14 Mar. 1832, in William Tiptaft, *Two Letters Addressed to the Bishop of Salisbury* (Abingdon, 1832), 7.

[226] Tiptaft to Burgess, 19 Mar. 1832, ibid. 8.

[227] See Chapter 9.

[228] Tiptaft to Burgess, 22 Mar. 1832, in Tiptaft, *Two Letters Addressed to the Bishop of Salisbury*, 13–14.

[229] Tiptaft to Burgess, 27 Mar. 1832, ibid., 15.

quently, Tiptaft was, and would continue to be, 'bound not to offend against the laws of that Church', notwithstanding his alleged secession from it. One of these laws stated that ministers should not preach in unconsecrated places. Since Tiptaft had declared his intention to violate this canon, the bishop would be compelled to enforce its observance by the usual proceedings.[230]

Incensed by the bishop's heavy-handedness, Tiptaft quickly published the entire correspondence, believing that this would expose ecclesiastical despotism in dramatic fashion.[231] It was tactically a good move. It immediately paralysed the bishop's attempt to silence him, and no subsequent correspondence was forthcoming.[232] It also increased public sympathy for Tiptaft's fledgling ministry, many agreeing with his depiction of the bishop's behaviour as autocratic.[233] In June 1832, Tiptaft was baptized by immersion by Hitchcock at his chapel in Devizes.[234] Though from now on he enjoyed a good deal of pastoral success in Abingdon, he became increasingly torn between the claims of local and an itinerant ministry:

> Some think my work is to go from place to place, preaching as I go, but I cannot say so, though I am sometimes inclined to think so. I have repeated invitations to go out to preach, but I scarcely know how to answer, and I cannot get an answer from God to satisfy my mind on these occasions; others . . . condemn me for going away, as I am still so well attended in my own chapel. My hearers think I neglect them, and leave the few sheep in the wilderness; so I am in a strait.[235]

The demand for Tiptaft's preaching was helped by his reputation as a martyr to episcopal power, for he was now an object of much public attention.[236] He clearly enjoyed a local and even national reputation, and it seems that he influenced the departure of at least three other Evangelical clergy. Two of these unidentified secessions occurred in mid-1833; and the third, that of John

[230] Burgess to Tiptaft, 2 Apr. 1832, ibid. 22–3.

[231] Tiptaft, *Two Letters Addressed to the Bishop of Salisbury*.

[232] J. C. Philpot, *William Tiptaft*, 67–9.

[233] Ibid. 73.

[234] J. H. Philpot, *The Seceders*, i.341.

[235] J. C. Philpot, *William Tiptaft*, 83.

[236] The Anglican Peter Hall, for example, claimed that Tiptaft preached in Wiltshire and Somerset during 1835, 'with considerable power and effect'. See Hall, *Congregational Reform*, 212.

Kay, the assistant curate of Cranford, near Kettering, Northamptonshire, the following summer.[237]

Tiptaft remained minister of Abbey Lane Strict Baptist Chapel, Abingdon (as it became known) until his death in 1864.[238] In this he was aided for many years by Kay, who laboured loyally beside him until his own death in 1860. Moreover, a number of other friends and assistants also provided support as Tiptaft exercised a substantial fixed—and itinerant—ministry throughout England. Perhaps most important of these was Philpot, who not only followed Tiptaft's example as a seceder, but remained a trusted associate for the rest of his life, in what his son described as 'a beautiful friendship'.[239]

VII

The secession of Joseph Charles Philpot was as sensational as the departure of his two Evangelical confederates, and in denominational terms more significant. He was the third son of the Reverend Charles Philpot, rector of Ripple, Kent, and later of St. Margaret's-at-Cliffe, Dover, and his wife Maria, only daughter of the Reverend Peter La Fargue, rector of Greatford, near Stamford, Lincolnshire, through which he claimed some Huguenot ancestry. Educated at Merchant Taylors' and St. Paul's, he matriculated at Worcester College, Oxford, on 14 October 1821, as a scholar, and held a fellowship from 1826 to 1835.[240] Soon after arriving at Oxford, he became friendly with Francis and John Henry Newman, and Blanco White, the Spanish theologian and poet.[241]

After taking his BA in the autumn of 1824, Philpot remained in Oxford earning a comfortable living by taking private pupils, in anticipation of a college fellowship.[242] Together with Bulteel, and a number of those soon to launch the Catholic revival in Oxford, he attended the special theology lectures given by Charles

[237] J. C. Philpot, *William Tiptaft*, 84, 90–3.

[238] J. C. Philpot, 'Obituary of William Tiptaft', in *GS* (1864), 306–14.

[239] J. H. Philpot, *The Seceders*, i.1.

[240] Grayson Carter, 'Joseph Charles Philpot', in *New DNB*; *Merchant Taylor's School Register*; *St. Paul's School Register*; *Al. Ox.*; S. F. Paul, *The Story of the Gospel in England* (Ilfracombe, 1948–50), iv.418–32.

[241] J. H. Philpot, *The Seceders*, i.17.

[242] J.C. Philpot to anon., 1869, ibid. 19.

Lloyd.[243] As an old fashioned High Churchman, Lloyd maintained a marked enthusiasm for the study of the Church Fathers, which he believed had been habitually overlooked by generations of Anglican scholars. On becoming Regius Professor, he resigned his lucrative appointment as select preacher at Lincoln's Inn to devote himself entirely to the founding of a new school of theology at the university.[244] His enthusiasm for the Fathers, however, was not shared by Philpot whose churchmanship at this time was conventional and sluggish; in his own retrospective view, at least, he was not at this time 'living an immoral life, but still utterly dead in sin, looking forward to prospects in life . . . and knowing as well as caring absolutely nothing spiritually for the things of God'.[245]

Early in 1826, Philpot was offered the position of private tutor to two of the sons of Edward Pennefather, of Delgany, County Wicklow.[246] Although reluctant to leave Oxford, he was tempted by the offer of a substantial salary.[247] On arriving in Ireland, Philpot still knew (by his own account) 'nothing experimentally of the things of God'; by early 1827, however, after 'a very great trial and affliction', he began to be drawn imperceptibly towards the 'doctrines of grace'.[248] This 'trial' arose as the result of his romantic attachment to one of Pennefather's six daughters. Whether the attraction was mutual remains uncertain: what is certain is that Mr Pennefather wholly disapproved, and that Philpot was required to stifle his passion.[249]

If Philpot's religious conversion was set in motion by romantic disappointment it was consummated through contacts with the local Evangelical clergy, for the Pennefather household was then under the spell of no less a personage than John Nelson Darby, the high Calvinist curate of neighbouring Calary and brother of

[243] Philpot to anon., 1869, ibid. 15–16; Baker, *Beyond Port and Prejudice*, 103. *Letters and Correspondence of John Henry Newman*, ed. Mozley, i.82, 109–10; W. Ince, *The Past History and Present Duties of the Faculty of Theology in Oxford* (Oxford, 1878), 25.

[244] Add MS 40342 fol. 329, British Library.

[245] J. H. Philpot, *The Seceders*, i.16; *Letters of the Late Joseph Charles Philpot*, ed. Clayton and Philpot, 16.

[246] J. H. Philpot, *The Seceders*, i.18–29; S. F. Paul, *Further History of the Gospel Standard Baptists* (Brighton, 1951–66), iii.134–5.

[247] J. H. Philpot, *The Seceders*, i.20. J. C. Philpot was succeeded as private tutor at the Pennefathers' by Francis Newman.

[248] J. C. Philpot, *Secession from the Church of England Defended*, 3rd edn. (1836), 10.

[249] Paul, *Further History of the Gospel Standard Baptists*, iii.135.

Mrs Pennefather.[250] Darby appears to have enjoyed regular access to Delgany. As Francis Newman later explained, Edward Pennefather, despite great learning and high social standing, 'looked to be taught by his juniors, and sat at the feet' of his younger, but captivating, brother-in-law.[251] Philpot, no less well-educated, was equally enthralled by Darby's charm and infectious persuasiveness, especially in light of his highly vulnerable emotional state.

A second influence on the susceptible young Philpot can be traced to the neighbouring village of Powerscourt. In 1826, the year in which Philpot arrived in Ireland, Lady Powerscourt and her Evangelical rector and confidant, Robert Daly (later the energetic Bishop of Cashel), developed an interest in the study of unfulfilled biblical prophecy. As we have seen, in the aftermath of the controversy surrounding the enactment of Catholic Emancipation, this led to the first of the Powerscourt conferences under the spiritual and administrative direction of Daly and Darby, which were devoted to the systematic investigation of prophecy. According to a testimonial signed by Daly, Philpot attended services at Powerscourt parish church regularly between January 1826 and June 1827, which placed him at the very heart of Irish Evangelical activism, political and social alarm, and prophetical speculation.[252]

Later, Philpot described his stay in Ireland as the most significant period of his life.[253] Yet his romantic disappointment became so insupportable that, in the spring of 1827, he abruptly resigned his appointment and fled to Oxford, where in the meantime he had been elected a fellow of Worcester.[254] The transition back into college life was not easy. The change in his personality, behaviour, and views was so marked that he quickly became the butt of Common Room ridicule and censure.[255] Even the mercurial Provost of Worcester, Dr Whittington Landon, began to take offence, warning Philpot that if he stuck to his peculiar religious views, he would be permanently barred from college

[250] J.H. Philpot, *The Seceders*, i.20–1; iii.71.

[251] Francis W. Newman, *Phases of Faith*, 6th edn. (1860), 17.

[252] MSS Oxford Diocesan Papers, c.226, Oxford County RO. It was also signed by Darby and Richard Lynch Cotton, fellow (later Provost) of Worcester College, Oxford.

[253] *Letters of the Late Joseph Charles Philpot*, ed. Clayton and Philpot, 15.

[254] Ibid. 13.

[255] Ibid. 15.

office.[256] Philpot, however, refused to amend his ways. His tutorial career now in ruins, he then turned to parish ministry as his only means of livelihood.

Philpot had no difficulty securing a position in the Church, and was ordained deacon on 1 June 1828 by Charles Lloyd (now Bishop of Oxford), to the perpetual curacy of Chislehampton with Stadhampton, seven miles south of Oxford.[257] For a time he continued to reside in his college rooms, riding back and forth to his parish on horseback. In November 1828, however, he and Henry Biss(e), another fellow of Worcester and Bulteel's predecessor as curate at St. Ebbe's, got into further difficulty with the college authorities for using the Senior Common Room for religious gatherings.[258] Warned yet again by the Provost about his 'enthusiastic' behaviour, Philpot determined to turn his back on Oxford and retired to the more hopeful pastures of Stadhampton, where he took rooms in a farmhouse.[259] By his pastoral energy and sharp, effective preaching, he soon filled the church to overflowing, gathering a congregation from some eighteen neighbouring parishes.[260] The church was soon so full that there was hardly standing, much less sitting room.[261] Philpot was, moreover, a model of evangelistic efficiency. He organized regular prayer meetings, Sunday-school classes for children, and religious lectures for adults; he appointed local visitors to distribute Gospel tracts in the parish; he raised a fund to purchase coal and other necessities for the poor; and he laid in large quantities of flannel and calico to make clothes for those in need.[262] His relations with

[256] J.H. Philpot, *The Seceders*, i.28. Landon was a 'high and dry Tory' who opposed Wellington's suggestions for university reform. Under the patronage of the Duke of Portland, in 1796 he was elected Provost of Worcester; 1802–6, Vice-Chancellor; 1813–38, Dean of Exeter cathedral. He was succeeded as Provost by the Evangelical Richard Cotton. See *GM* (1839), pt. 1, 212; Cox, *Recollections of Oxford*, 187–90.

[257] On the nomination of John Witherton Peers, Evangelical rector of Mordon, Surrey, and incumbent of Stadhampton. Philpot's licence was signed by Lloyd on 31 Oct. See MS Index to the Parishes; MS Clerus Index; Oxford County RO. There is no evidence that Philpot was ever ordained to the priesthood.

[258] *HD* 67/7, 20a, 3 Nov. 1828. Biss(e) was subsequently rejected as a candidate to become college bursar, the Provost moreover refusing to provide a testimonial for his ordination by the Bishop of Salisbury for a curacy at Kennington, Berkshire.

[259] *Letters of the Late Joseph Charles Philpot*, ed. Clayton and Philpot, 556.

[260] J.H. Philpot, *The Seceders*, i.32, iii.303.

[261] Account of Joseph Parry of Allington, Wiltshire. See Paul, *The Story of the Gospel in England*, iv.417–18.

[262] Ibid.; *Letters of the late Joseph Charles Philpot*, ed. Clayton and Philpot, 18.

the local gentry were less successful, however. Expected to lunch each Sunday with the Squire, he quickly abandoned the practice as 'spiritually unprofitable'; predictably, he soon became estranged from more fashionable circles.[263]

In the spring of 1829, Tiptaft was instituted into the nearby parish of Sutton Courtenay. As we have seen, he and Philpot first met at a local Evangelical clerical meeting, organized on the lines of the Elland and Eclectic Societies, whose members gathered monthly for worship and mutual edification. Between November 1830 and February 1831, during his convalescence at Sutton Courtenay, Philpot employed Lancelot Brenton, a close clerical ally of Tiptaft and Bulteel, to officiate at Stadhampton.[264] During the following spring, Philpot travelled to Walmer, Kent, to be near his widowed mother. Here he received a number of invitations to preach at local Dissenting meeting houses, but refused each of them, well knowing that Bulteel's licence had recently been withdrawn by the bishop for similar 'irregularities'.[265] Hearing of Bulteel's proposal to build a new chapel in Oxford, Philpot remarked that if it was founded on true spiritual principles he would be willing to contribute £5, which was all he could afford.[266] When Bulteel's subsequent adherence to Irvingism was met with dismay by his Oxford friends, Philpot suspected that this was only a temporary aberration and cautioned Tiptaft to remain patient and forbearing.[267] Nor was Philpot overly concerned when Tiptaft himself felt driven to leave the Church of England, agreeing warmly with his conviction that where there was no genuine spiritual experience there could be no authentic faith.[268]

At Christmas 1831, Philpot was compelled prematurely to return to Stadhampton when a crisis arose over Brenton's refusal to read the burial service over a local drunkard. In an inflammatory sermon on the promiscuous use of the burial rubric, Brenton announced his intention to secede from the Church.[269] Capricious and unstable, he was the eldest son of the impoverished Evangelical Vice-Admiral Sir Jahleel Brenton, Bt., KCB, well known as a war hero and the intrepid commander of the frigate *Spartan*.

263 Paul, *Further History of the Gospel Standard Baptists*, iii.136.

264 *Letters of the Late Joseph Charles Philpot*, ed. Clayton and Philpot, 22, 24, 33–4.

265 Ibid. 22–5.

266 Ibid. 25–6.

267 J.C. Philpot to anon. (n.d.), ibid. 32.

268 Ibid. 33–4.

269 Ibid. 35; Lancelot Charles Lee Brenton, *A Sermon on Revelations* [*sic*] *XIV: 13*. (Oxford, 1831).

Lancelot Brenton is depicted (perhaps with characteristic exaggeration) in Thomas Mozley's *Reminiscences* as an authoritarian and legalistic enthusiast who endeared himself to nobody outside his own intimate circle.[270] Soon after taking holy orders he had so overtaxed himself in the care of a large parish that he had to return to convalesce in Oriel, where he made a nuisance of himself in the Senior Common Room. 'Wherever he was', Mozley complained, 'he talked and let nobody else talk . . . Indeed it was evident that the poor man was mad'.[271] He himself admitted that he was rather overwrought at this time, a victim of 'secession fever'.[272] After leaving the Church, Brenton sank into near obscurity. During 1832, in partnership with another Oxford seceder, William Morshead, he established a small independent chapel in Bath which later affiliated with the Christian Brethren.[273] He also turned his hand to writing, publishing a translation of the Septuagint, editing a memoir of his celebrated father (whose title he inherited in 1844), and composing a number of minor spiritual works which made little impact outside his small Calvinistic circle.[274]

On his return to Stadhampton, Philpot too was increasingly vexed about the question of remaining within the Church. His unease was heightened by a lengthy conversation with the Baptist minister John Warburton on the subject of the Kingdom of God, and by rebukes taken from local parsons about his close fellowship with Tiptaft and his public denunciations of the local 'fox-hunting clergy'.[275] Soon, Philpot had become so uneasy about the spiritual state of the Church that he refused to send children from his parish for confirmation, dismissing the ceremony as unscriptural.[276]

In the autumn of 1833, yet another local Evangelical cleric

[270] Mozley, *Reminiscences*, ii.114–20. [271] Ibid. ii.118.

[272] See Lancelot Charles Lee Brenton, *Memoir of Vice-Admiral Sir Jahleel Brenton, Baronet, K.C.B.* (1855), p. cxiv.

[273] See Harold H. Rowdon, 'Secession from the Established Church in the Early Nineteenth Century', in *VE* (1964), 84; Peter L. Embley, 'The Origins and Early Development of the Plymouth Brethren', Ph.D. thesis (Cambridge, 1966), 77.

[274] Lancelot Charles Lee Brenton, *The Septuagint Translated into English* (1844); *Memoir of Jahleel Brenton; Reasons for Not Ceasing to Teach and Preach the Lord Jesus Christ* (Bath, 1832); *Diaconia: Or, Thoughts on Ministry* (1852); *Alas, My Brother!* (1854); *The Bible and Prayer Book Versions of the Psalms* (1860); *Thoughts on Self-examination* (1862).

[275] *Letters of the Late Joseph Charles Philpot*, ed. Clayton and Philpot, 36.

[276] Ibid. 37.

seceded from the Church. Thomas Husband, then officiating at Appleford, near Abingdon, had been on intimate terms with both Philpot and Tiptaft for some time and professed the same views of particular election.[277] Like that of Tiptaft's and Brenton's some two years earlier, his secession intensified Philpot's anxiety about remaining in the Church.[278] By October of that year Philpot was warning that his connection with the Establishment would soon be broken, for he was expecting to be put out of his curacy by Richard Bagot, the Bishop of Oxford, as the result of his attitude towards confirmation and his criticism of the local clergy.[279] Bagot, however, was preoccupied with more serious concerns, and Philpot received only a light episcopal rebuke (for his engagement of an assistant without diocesan permission).[280]

Philpot continued at Stadhampton during 1834, dogged by poor health and by doubts about the propriety of remaining in the Establishment.[281] By March 1835, he had become convinced that the errors and corruptions of the Church were so great, particularly those reflected in its occasional services, that he must now withdraw from it.[282] On the 22nd of that month he gave notice of intent in a sermon at Stadhampton. 'You have heard my voice for the last time within these walls,' he told his parishioners, 'for I cannot continue in evil that good may come'. The congregation were staggered: 'the sounds of weeping were heard on every side'.[283] A few days later, with some satisfaction, Philpot described the event to his sister: 'It was as if a thunderbolt had dropped in the congregation . . . The people were much moved. And the next day some met, and said that they could build me a chapel if I would consent to stay. To this, however, I do not feel inclined, though the people wish it much, and say that it should not cost me a farthing'.[284]

As a seceder, Philpot was of course unable to retain his college fellowship. Consequently, he wrote to Dr Landon resigning his

[277] Ibid. After seceding, Husband licensed his house at Appleford and began preaching there, baptizing his numerous followers at a mill dam close to his old church. See J. H. Philpot, *The Seceders*, i.133; J. C. Philpot, *William Tiptaft*, 89.

[278] *Letters of the Late Joseph Charles Philpot*, ed. Clayton and Philpot, 38.

[279] Ibid. 38–9. [280] Ibid. 40: J.H. Philpot, *The Seceders*, i.98.

[281] *Letters of the Late Joseph Charles Philpot*, ed. Clayton and Philpot, 40–5.

[282] J.C. Philpot, *Secession from the Church of England Defended*, p. ii.

[283] *Letters of the Late Joseph Charles Philpot*, ed. Clayton and Philpot, 45.

[284] Ibid. 46.

position and setting out his reasons for seceding in no uncertain terms. He then published his letter, which quickly passed through seventeen editions.[285] In a Jeremiad which echoed Bulteel's earlier condemnation of the Church, Philpot accused the Establishment of possessing a deplorably 'corrupt and worldly system' which he could no longer condone.[286] He lambasted royal supremacy, episcopal luxury and pomp, the abuses of the patronage system by politicians and worldly churchmen, the system of tithes, and the injustice of the ecclesiastical courts: in short, 'all that mass of evil which has sprung out of a worldly and wealthy establishment'. Like Bulteel, he denounced with especial vehemence those Oxford heads of houses who had provided glowing testimonials for profligate undergraduates seeking ordination.[287]

The Evangelical clergy came in for particular censure. For Philpot they were little more than willing tools of a corrupt establishment, exacting tithes from struggling farmers, which they extracted by legal pressure, and extorting burial and other fees from the poor, while riding throughout the countryside in their carriages like country gentry. Extolling the voluntary principle, he claimed that the fiscal exactions of the Church were unscriptural: the New Testament authorized no other payment to ministers but the free and voluntary offerings of spiritual people.[288]

To the sixth edition of his letter, Philpot attached a preface which went even further in its denunciation of the Church and the party to which he had recently belonged. Like many other seceders, he made it clear that he was separating himself not only from the Church of England but also from the ranks of the 'serious clergy' within it. Evangelicals were 'bound up in a system, which, in principle and practice, is opposed to the Word of God, and to the operations of the spirit on the hearts of the elect'. They were either 'ignorant of the nature of Christ's spiritual kingdom and of a true Gospel church', or 'blinded by pride, covetousness, unbelief, [or] love of ease'. He urged former colleagues who remained in the Church that, if they could not follow his example and secede, they should strive to follow the example of saintly predecessors like Toplady, Romaine, Newton, and Hawker (three of

[285] J. C. Philpot, *A Letter to the Provost of Worcester College* (Oxford, 1835); J. W. Peters, *A Few Words on the Sinful Position of the Evangelical Clergy in the Church of England* (1835).

[286] J.C. Philpot, *A Letter to the Provost of Worcester College*, 8.

[287] Ibid. 10–11.

[288] Ibid. 10. See also *GS* (1838), 103–6.

them prominent high Calvinists), who had lived and died in its communion without falling into corruption.[289] At the same time, Philpot distanced himself firmly from political opponents of the Establishment, renouncing any union with 'political Dissenters, radicals, papists, socinians, and infidels', who advanced rationalistic principles and advocated disestablishment by compulsion.[290]

It was the unscriptural nature of establishment—'contrary to the New Testament, and in opposition to the revealed will of God'—which drew Philpot's censure, even more than its place in the exploitative system of Old Corruption.[291] A State Church was incompatible with his separatist vision of God's people as a chosen remnant, who had been gathered out of a 'fallen and apostate world', baptized by immersion, and formed into churches as 'visible societies separate from the ungodly'.[292] On this assumption, where was the scriptural warrant for a Church supported by tithes wrung from the farmer, and by rates levied by the householder? In his view, the hypocrisy produced by a State Church 'destroys every mark of a spiritual dispensation and denies every Gospel doctrine'. There could be no such thing as a truly national and inclusive Church: Scripture declared that God's true people were 'a chosen generation, a royal priesthood, a holy nation, [and] a peculiar people', not a part of the world, but gathered and separated from it.[293] And where was the justification for infant baptism? 'I knew, for instance, that I had never been regenerated in infancy, for I grew up to manhood as ignorant of God as the beasts that perish'.[294]

In his open separatism Philpot resembled other, earlier seceders, especially John Walker, John Nelson Darby, and Henry Bulteel, from whom he may well have quarried his views. In 1858 he advised an American friend:

> As you cannot hear the pure Gospel, and have no confidence in the ministers by whom you are surrounded, I think you do well to be separate from them . . . It must be a very trying path for you to walk in, as it must bring down upon your head much reproach and misrepresentation. But if you are favoured with the testimony of God in your own conscience, and have some manifestations of His presence, it will amply make up for any reproach that may assail you.[295]

[289] Ibid. 6th edn., p. ii. [290] Ibid. p. iii. [291] Ibid. [292] Ibid. pp. iii–iv.
[293] Ibid. pp. iv–v. [294] J. C. Philpot, *Secession from the Church of England Defended*, 10.
[295] J. H. Philpot, *The Seceders*, iii.101.

It did not worry Philpot that his seceding friends and predecessors had been vilified and disowned, and had ended up serving in obscure Dissenting chapels, impoverished, and with few followers. The ecclesiology of high Calvinist separatism could easily come to terms with unpopularity and persecution, for it was axiomatic that the elect were few and that the marks of a true believer included the necessity of suffering for Christ's sake and being hated and rejected by the world.[296]

Philpot's rejection of worldly goods and practices took several interesting twists. He eschewed the customary title of 'Reverend', the wearing of pulpit robes, and ordination by imposition of hands. He rejected the teaching that only clergy could administer the sacraments, claiming that any Church member could undertake this as long as the local body had given its permission.[297] He also sent to auction his valued and extensive theological library, dismissing ministerial training as a waste of time (if not dangerous), for human learning could easily usurp the place of 'divine teaching'.[298]

Set free from his Anglican connections, Philpot was now able to preach in Dissenting meeting houses.[299] The first pulpit he entered in his post-secession ministry was the Strict Baptists' Bethel Chapel, in the village of Allington, Wiltshire.[300] On 2 April 1835 Martha Taman of Stadhampton registered her rooms in the home of Mary Webb as a Dissenting meeting-house, with Philpot as the officiating minister.[301] On 13 September of that year (his thirty-third birthday), he was baptized by immersion by his friend Warburton at Allington Chapel.[302] One account has it that, for a brief time, he became leader of a high Calvinist cause in King Street, Jericho, Oxford, known locally as the 'Hypers', but this seems unlikely.[303] On 24 July 1838, he married Sarah Louisa Keal, eldest daughter of William Tomblin Keal MD of Oakham, an

[296] *Letters of the Late Joseph Charles Philpot*, ed. Clayton and Philpot, 551.

[297] *GS* (1842), 350.

[298] *Letters of the Late Joseph Charles Philpot*, ed. Clayton and Philpot, 51; *GS* (1842), 319.

[299] See A. C. Underwood, *A History of the English Baptists* (1st edn., 1947; repr., 1961), 242–6.

[300] J.H. Philpot, *The Seceders*, iii.11.

[301] MSS Oxford Diocesan Papers, c. 646 fol. 11, Oxford County RO.

[302] *Letters of the Late Joseph Charles Philpot*, ed. Clayton and Philpot, 53; Oliver, *The Strict Baptist Chapels of England*, v.23–4.

[303] Moore, *Earlier and Later Nonconformity in Oxford*, 15.

Anglican seceder and husband of Deborah Ward Tiptaft (William Tiptaft's elder sister), by whom he had four children.[304] Later that same year, he accepted an invitation to become joint minister of Providence Chapel, Oakham, Rutland (opened in 1832 by Dr Keal and known locally as 'The Factory'), and North Street Chapel, Stamford, Lincolnshire (opened by William Tiptaft in 1834), with the idea that he would reside in Stamford with his family and visit Oakham for several days each fortnight.[305] Here he enjoyed considerable success. In the religious census for 1851, 245 attended morning service (plus 42 children); 251 in the afternoon (again plus 42 children); the average attendance during the summer months was 300 in the morning and 320 in the afternoon; the chapel seated 350, and all seatings were free.[306]

In 1836 Philpot became a regular contributor to the *Gospel Standard*, a leading Strict Baptist journal,[307] and he soon began to exercise a considerable influence upon its Calvinistic adherents.[308] Established in Manchester in August 1835 by John Gadsby, the son of the well-known preacher and evangelist William Gadsby, the *Gospel Standard* quickly became one of England's most prominent Calvinistic journals.[309] Early in 1836, Gadsby recruited a travelling packman by the name of John McKenzie (recently excommunicated by the Independents at Preston for holding high Calvinistic doctrines) to serve as co-editor.[310] In about 1840, Philpot joined the two as joint editor.[311] Philpot and McKenzie quickly discovered, however, that they could not restrain Gadsby's theological 'indiscretions' and so were constrained to relieve him of all editorial responsibility.[312] Philpot assumed complete editorial control after McKenzie's death in 1849, a position he retained for the remainder of his life.[313] The journal prospered under his skilled and devoted leadership. At the onset of his

[304] *Letters of the Late Joseph Charles Philpot*, ed. Clayton and Philpot, 90.

[305] Ibid. 92.

[306] Rod W. Ambler (ed.), 'Lincolnshire Returns of the Census of Religious Worship 1851', in *The Lincoln Record Society*, 72 (Lincoln, 1979), 5; *Returns of the Religious Census of 1851 for the County of Rutland*, Microfilm 142, Leicester County RO. At the time of the religious census of 1851, Philpot was living at 14 Rutland Terrace, Stamford, and paying £25 annual rent for the use of North Street Chapel.

[307] For a history of the *GS* see Robert William Oliver, 'The Emergence of a Strict and Particular Baptist Community Among the English Calvinistic Baptists, 1770–1850', Ph.D. thesis (CNAA, 1986), 241–73.

[308] J.H. Philpot, *The Seceders*, ii.18.

[309] Ibid. ii.16–17.

[310] Ibid. ii.17–18.

[311] Ibid. ii.73.

[312] Ibid. ii.30, 59, 71.

[313] Ibid. iii.315.

association with the *Gospel Standard*, only five hundred copies were being printed; by 1841, however, monthly circulation had increased to over seven thousand; by 1857, it had risen to ten thousand; eventually, it exceeded over seventeen thousand, far outstripping any of its rivals.[314]

With a high profile as editor of the *Gospel Standard*, Philpot soon rose to a position of authority in the Strict Baptists, or those Baptists opposed to the open-communion principles of Robert Hall.[315] Not all welcomed this ascendancy, several of his ministerial 'rivals' taking exception to his rising popularity and assumption of leadership. In February 1845, for instance, Frederick Tryon, himself a seceder from the Church of England and now minister of the Strict Baptist chapel at Deeping St. James, Lincolnshire, attacked Philpot from the pulpit of Zoar Chapel, London, charging him with marrying a woman he knew was not a true believer.[316] At first Philpot allowed his defence to be waged by his friend, H. W. Shakespear;[317] but when it became clear that the controversy would not disappear, he issued a brief statement in the *Gospel Standard* admitting many of the charges.[318] By now Tryon had published two additional pamphlets accusing Philpot of implicit antinomianism.[319] Another scathing attack came two years later when William Palmer, the Strict Baptist minister of Chatteris, Cambridgeshire, accused Philpot of tending to 'arrogate exclusive powers and rights' to himself.[320] 'The "old leaven" of Huntingtonianism', he warned, 'has, for the last few years, been silently diffusing itself in many places; and, if not arrested . . . will effect dissensions, separations, and divisions . . . Philpotism is the cuckoo's egg in the sparrow's nest. Only let it be hatched, and it will soon put in a right of claim to the inheritance. It will be the sole occupant of a property never erected nor held in trust for it'.[321]

Among the Gospel Standards (as they are still known), Philpot

[314] Ibid. ii.35; iii.32–3.

[315] See Underwood, *A History of the English Baptists*, 185.

[316] Oliver, 'The Emergence of a Strict and Particular Baptist Community', 262.

[317] H. W. Shakespear, *A Refutation of the Falsehoods contained in Mr Tryon's Letter to J. C. Philpot* (1847); Frederick Tryon, *A Reply to a Letter* (Peterborough, 1847).

[318] *GS* (1847), 318.

[319] Frederick Tryon, *The Single Eye* (1847); *Old Paths and New* (1847).

[320] William Palmer, *A Plain Statement* (1847), 40.

[321] Ibid. 3.

fared much better. As a distinct Calvinistic denomination, this body traces its origins to the mid-nineteenth century when a heated controversy erupted among the Strict Baptists over the denial of the eternal sonship of Christ by some of its ministers.[322] As editor of the *Gospel Standard*, Philpot became the leader of the campaign against what he regarded as a serious departure from orthodox Trinitarian teaching. 'Can we', he asked in 1856, 'contend too earnestly for this faith once delivered to the saints? Can we have any union or communion with those who deny it? What says Holy John? "If there come any unto you, and bring not this doctrine, receive him not into your house, neither bid him God speed; for he that biddeth him God speed is partaker of his evil deeds".'[323] Before long Philpot and others began to promote the idea of formal schism.[324] The first of the Gospel Standard congregations to separate from the other Strict Baptists was that of Zoar Chapel, London, in 1861.[325] A number of others soon followed.[326] In 1861, besides his various editorials in the *Gospel Standard*, Philpot published a defence of the doctrine of eternal sonship.[327] As a consequence of this bitter schism, the Strict Baptists suffered a loss of leadership and morale; never again during the nineteenth century would they regain the strength and momentum they once enjoyed.

Among the Gospel Standards particular recognition has long been given to the witness of several prominent Calvinistic ministers, especially William Gadsby, John Warburton, and John Kershaw.[328] Another influence of some importance (especially upon Philpot) were the writings of the eighteenth-century Calvinist hymn-writer Joseph Hart.[329] Perhaps ironically, given their determined hostility towards the Establishment, the Gospel Standards were for many years particularly indebted to the Church of England for providing a regular flow of seceders

[322] S. F. Paul, *The Seceders* (Letchworth, 1960), iii.42–54.

[323] *GS* (1856), 130; (1859), 88–90; (1860), 186–93, 221, 217–18; (1861), 10–11, 125, 132; *GS*, Wrapper (July 1861).

[324] *GS* (1861), 10–11.

[325] Paul, *The Seceders*, iii.49–52; *Letters of the Late Joseph Charles Philpot*, ed. Clayton and Philpot, 537–40.

[326] Paul, *The Seceders*, iii.52–4.

[327] J.C. Philpot, *The True, and Proper, and Eternal Sonship of the Lord Jesus Christ, the Only-begotten Son of God* (1861).

[328] Paul, *Further History of the Gospel Standard Baptists*, iv. p. i.

[329] See *Letters of the Late Joseph Charles Philpot*, ed. Clayton and Philpot, 13.

into their ministry and diaconate.[330] Most prominent among these was, of course, Philpot himself who, after the death of Gadsby (1844) and Warburton (1857), was regarded as the movement's leading light.

Philpot's ascendancy among the Gospel Standards rested in part on his wide reputation as a pamphleteer;[331] still more as the author of a large number of sermons which appeared in various evangelical journals,[332] of the memoir of his devoted friend William Tiptaft,[333] and of a miscellany of religious tracts.[334] He moved freely among the major Gospel Standard pulpits drawing large congregations. In particular, he was a frequent visitor at William Gadsby's Back Lane Chapel in Manchester; at Eden Street Chapel, Zoar Chapel (Great Alie Street), and Gower Street Chapel, London; and at Zion Chapel, Calne, Wiltshire.[335] For many years, he preached each summer at Allington, a secluded Wiltshire village in the Vale of Pewsey, described by his son as 'a Puritan Little Gidding, a pocket Geneva, where uncompromising Calvinism could be studied in pure culture'.[336] Philpot was also regarded as a spiritual 'father figure' among Gospel Standard ministers, being asked to rule on points of difficult and potentially divisive doctrine and to advise on suitable candidates for vacant pulpits. By the 1850s, he had won an international reputation in the Calvinistic world. A number of his sermons were circulated in America and translated into German and Dutch;[337] in the Netherlands they are still read each Sunday from the pulpits of the *Gereformeerde Gemeende* (i.e. The Reformed Congregations) and deeply admired by the members of the *Nederlandse Hervormde*, organized in the so-called *Gereformeerde Bond*. Little known in his own

[330] Paul, *The Seceders*, iii.302–4.

[331] J.C. Philpot, *Secession from the Church of England Defended.*

[332] Over 450 of Philpot's sermons have been published in various journals, including the *Gospel Ministry*, the *Gospel Pulpit*, the *Gospel Standard*, the *Preachers in Print*, the *Penny Pulpit*, and the *Zoar Chapel Pulpit.* A number of individual sermons—and volumes of sermons—have also been published separately. See K. W. H. Howard, *A Complete Textual Index of the Published Sermons and Pulpit Expositions of Joseph Charles Philpot* (Stamford, 1972).

[333] J. C. Philpot, *Memoir of the Late William Tiptaft* (1867).

[334] Including *What it is That Saves a Soul?* (1837); *The Advance of Popery in This Country* (1869); and a preface to the second edition of John Warburton's *The Mercies of a Covenant God* (1878).

[335] Paul, *Further History of the Gospel Standard Baptists*, i.47; *The Story of the Gospel in England*, iv.431; *The Seceders*, iii.11–13; *Letters of the Late Joseph Charles Philpot*, ed. Clayton and Philpot, 86, 92–3.

[336] J.H. Philpot, *The Seceders*, i.126–7.

[337] Underwood, *A History of the English Baptists*, 243; Paul, *The Seceders*, iii.80–1.

country, Philpot has been the subject of two recent studies in Dutch.[338]

Philpot remained on intimate terms with his old comrade William Tiptaft until the latter's premature death in 1864, but in 1836 he denounced Bulteel as a tragic castaway who had fallen 'into a place where two seas met: the sea of experimental Calvinism and the sea of Arminian Irvingism'.[339] Retiring in 1864 to Croydon, he preached his final sermon at Allington on 8 August 1869. He died on 9 December of that year at home, and was buried a week later at Croydon cemetery.[340]

VIII

Though the series of Oxford secessions—involving Henry Bulteel, William Tiptaft, Joseph Charles Philpot, Lancelot Brenton, and Thomas Husband—were on a relatively small scale, they are recognized as part of a larger movement of disaffected Evangelical clergy into Calvinistic Dissent during the 1830s and 1840s. In a pamphlet exchange in 1836 with Charles Jerram, rector of Witney, Philpot claimed that between forty and fifty Evangelical clergymen, unconnected with each other and in different parts of England, had seceded from the Church during the past four to five years; many more, he prophesied, would soon follow.[341]

As it turned out, the Oxford seceders were too *outré* to attract large numbers of clerical followers. Their strong language in controversy was unattractive. Their denunciation of the Establishment at a time when it was under attack from irreligious radicals and political Dissenters weakened their cause. The seceders were also tarred with charges of antinomianism, though this was an allegation which they vehemently denied. Philpot's son later recalled that next to being called a mystic, nothing exasperated his father more than to be accused of antinomianism, from which he carefully distanced himself.[342] In 1836, he admitted that 'we who hold the doctrines of grace are often called

[338] J. A. Saarberg, *Der pelgrims metgezel* (Houten, 1987); Jon. de Rijke, *Schijn en zijn. Een onderzoek naar de prediking van Joseph Charles Philpot* (Maassluis, 1994).

[339] *Letters of the Late Joseph Charles Philpot*, ed. Clayton and Philpot, 67.

[340] Paul, *The Seceders*, iii.54–5.

[341] Charles Jerram, *Secession From the Church of England Considered* (1836); J.C. Philpot, *Secession from the Church of England Defended*, 7.

[342] J.H. Philpot, *The Seceders*, i.121.

antinomians'; the 'real antinomians', however, are those who 'in a profession of religion are satisfied with defects and errors, and have no trembling anxiety to act in all things according to the will of God'.[343] In the following year, writing from Devonport, Plymouth, he added:

The religion of the place seems to me to be chiefly Bible religion . . . I heard, last Lord's-day evening, John Hawker, a son of the Doctor [Robert Hawker]. If his father were like the son, I would not give a shilling a year for a seat under him . . . Among other things, he said, 'Sin! what is sin? I can't define what sin is! Sin is a principle. The Scriptures says it is a transgression of the Law, and that is all I know about it' . . . I could see, plainer than ever, that dead Calvinism is the best weapon Satan has to harden the hearts and sear the consciences of unhumbled professors. I find almost everywhere the same great mistake—Bible religion substituted for soul religion.[344]

Three years later, Philpot was battling with the same forces. Antinomianism, he wrote to a friend, is 'the hydra of our professing day, the damning sin of Calvinists, as self-righteousness is of Arminians'.[345] Elsewhere he declared that 'God has no antinomians in His family—that is, in the bad sense of the word. He has no loose, licentious, reckless characters who "continue in sin that grace may abound".'[346]

Yet Philpot's hyper-Calvinism still made him suspect as (at the very least) a theoretical antinomian, for elsewhere he contradicted himself by endorsing the teachings of Robert Hawker (describing him as a 'saint'),[347] and the 'immortal' William Huntington, whom he described in a letter of January 1864 as one of his two favourite authors.[348] In 1860, he wrote:

You know very well that my heart has always been much with the real Huntingtonians. I say 'real' because I have no union with the mere nominal followers of Mr Huntington. There is, or rather was, a blessed life, feeling, and savour in those who were partakers of the same grace and spirit as the blessed coalheaver.[349]

[343] J.C. Philpot, *Secession from the Church of England Defended*, 10–11.
[344] *Letters of the Late Joseph Charles Philpot*, ed. Clayton and Philpot, 75.
[345] Ibid. 145. [346] J. C. Philpot, *Early Sermons* (1906), i.6.
[347] J.H. Philpot, *The Seceders*, ii.269.
[348] Ibid., iii.186–7; i.108, 305; ii.131, 170, 240, 282; iii.207–8, 211.
[349] *Letters of the Late Joseph Charles Philpot*, ed. Clayton and Philpot, 294.

Perhaps most damaging of all was Philpot's close association with John Warburton, whose doctrinal antinomianism was influential in hyper-Calvinist circles. It was also impossible to disguise. In a work first published in 1837, the second edition of which contained a preface by Philpot, Warburton had cheerfully accepted the label, admitting, 'I am one of those antinomians. Blessed be God! he has delivered me from that law'.[350]

By abandoning the National Church for pastorates among dissenting denominations like the Strict Baptists, Irvingites, or the Brethren, which were widely perceived to be not only marginal but heterodox, the Oxford seceders ensured that they would not make much direct impact on the English religious world of their day. This would not have worried many of them: it was, after all, the sense of separateness, of being a 'righteous remnant' in a wicked world, which had driven them out. At the same time, their indirect influence was probably considerable. As with earlier schisms—the 'Walkerites', or the Western Schism—the controversies surrounding individual secessions brought into high relief some of the submerged difficulties of Evangelicals within the Established Church. Not only did the seceders draw attention to old problems like the burial and baptismal rubrics, they also gave voice to discontents about a Church–State connection which seemed to hinder evangelism and the propagation of the Gospel. What gave their position particular resonance in the early 1830s was that its critique of establishment as an agency of political corruption and worldliness coincided with that of many radicals, such as John Wade, whose *Black Book, or Corruption Unmasked* (1820–3) came out with additions in 1831, 1832, and 1835, exposing nepotism, pluralism, and worldliness in the Church with a wealth of (often exaggerated) detail. The shock of anti-establishment sermons, like those delivered by Bulteel or Philpot, seemed all the more disturbing, given the panic about the future of the Church which gripped the clergy during the reform crisis. Likewise their high Calvinist pronouncements. Edward Burton, writing to Daniel Wilson in the aftermath of Bulteel's University Sermon, expressed his conviction that 'Mr Bulteel's doctrines have proved deadening and fatal to many an unhappy Christian'.[351]

[350] John Warburton, *The Mercies of a Covenant God*, 2nd edn. (1878), 23.
[351] Burton to Wilson, 10 May 1831, in *CO* (1847), 198.

It is likely too that the Oxford secessions accelerated the disintegration of Anglican Evangelicalism into distinct sub-groupings. The very existence of Bulteelism suggested that all was not well with the party of Wilberforce, Simeon, and Daniel Wilson. Although few clergy made their exit with the Oxford seceders, their propaganda on behalf of a confident, thoroughgoing high Calvinism, and their critique of the compromises and accommodations to 'the world' made by many Evangelical clergy, only served to increase the divisions within the 'Gospel world', especially between those who still followed the moderate *Christian Observer* and those who read the more rigoristic *Record*.

In Oxford itself, the secessions did much to weaken the attraction of Evangelical religion for serious-minded undergraduates. John Hill, at St. Edmund Hall, bemoaned the lack of leadership for the cause in the university and the demoralization which had set in after Bulteel's spectacular departure from the Church of England. On New Year's Day 1832 he confided gloomily to his diary:

> *The state of this place and neighbourhood is humbling.* In the university, little, very little, goes on which betokens any outpouring of the spirit of God. Not one minister fully preaching and living the Gospel in charge of any one of the parishes in Oxford. Bulteel, Tiptaft, Brenton, have deserted the English Church. [William George] Lambert my co-secretary in the Church Missionary Society, has left it and Newton, my co-secretary in the Jews Society, is on the verge of doing the same. I have scarcely a friend left in Oxford who is not altogether like-minded.[352]

In the same year, Daniel Wilson, soon to sail off to Calcutta to take up his new bishopric, expressed concern at the extremism among the youthful elite of the party. Speaking at a large clerical breakfast in London he warned the young men present against taking up new theological notions (as opposed to the good *old* notions of saints like Cecil, Newton, Henry Martyn, and Thomas Scott), and urged them to keep to the Church. Wilson noted with alarm how attachment to the Church was held up as a sign of 'party spirit' among young extremists.[353]

[352] *HD* 67/9, 2b, 3a, 1 Jan. 1832. The Oxford branch of the Jew Society was founded on 12 March 1827, with Hill and Bulteel as co-secretaries. Other early members included Francis Newman, Lancelot Brenton, and J. C. Philpot. See MSS 'Annual Reports of the Oxford and Oxfordshire Auxiliary Society for Promoting Christianity Among the Jews', 3, 7, Bod.

[353] From an account by Henry Wilberforce, in Newsome, *The Parting of Friends*, 13.

It is not unlikely that the notoriety of the Oxford seceders played some part in the rapid rise of the Oxford Movement in the period following Bulteel's University Sermon and secession. As David Newsome has shown in his *Parting of Friends*, the loss to Oxford Evangelicalism of such influential local leaders was a gain to Oxford High Churchmanship. The reforming initiative passed from Evangelicals in favour of the new, revived High Anglicanism of the Tractarians. In this it is difficult not to see the extremism of Bulteel and his allies as a precipitant. Without the intense atmosphere of Oxford Common Rooms the extraordinary odyssey of College fellows like Bulteel and Philpot suggested to some worried churchmen the spectacle of Calvinism (and perhaps of Protestantism itself?) running a natural course towards spiritual anarchy. Here were the unacceptable end-products of evangelical 'enthusiasm', coupled with those of a Calvinist system whose ruthless division of congregations into elect and reprobate appeared to contain the seeds of separatism. The damage caused by the secessions led even some high Calvinists, among them Henry Fowler, minister of Gower Street Chapel, London, and Robert Hawker, to admit that it would have been better for the seceders to have remained in the Church.[354]

Ironically, some of the aims of Bulteelers and Tractarians had strong similarities. Both aimed to resist ungodly Erastianism and rekindle primitive apostolic purity and fervour in the Church; both fostered a rejection of the Anglican *via media* which led their more extreme supporters into secession. The Oxford Evangelical seceders, in fleeing a rich and powerful Establishment for an outcast despised sect, articulated a 'gathered' ecclesiology which John Henry Newman (and some Tractarian ultras) later came to accept: that the true church consists in the body of believers called out of the wicked world; it is a church continually despised and rejected by the powerful and worldly-wise.[355]

Between the Oxford high Calvinists and the Tractarians there was a relationship more close than has perhaps been realized.[356]

[354] See Henry Fowler, *Letters to the Revd H. B. Bulteel* (1831), 11.

[355] Sheridan Gilley, *Newman and his Age* (1990), 234.

[356] This issue is raised in Yngve Brilioth, *The Anglican Revival* (1925); R. W. Greaves, 'Golightly to Newman, 1824–45', in *JEH* (1958), 209–28; John E. Linnan, 'The Evangelical Background of John Henry Newman, 1816–26', Th.D. thesis (Louvain, 1965); Stunt, 'John Henry Newman and the Evangelicals', 65–74.

When Bulteel was appointed curate of St. Ebbe's in 1826, John Henry Newman could still be regarded as an Evangelical, if only marginally. Converted to some form of Calvinism at the age of 15, he retained this position until he was 21, after which, as he later wrote in his *Apologia*, 'it gradually faded away'.[357] It was Evangelicalism in a moderate form that Newman had imbibed: he had 'hung on the lips' of Daniel Wilson at St. John's Chapel, Bedford Row, been delighted with Joseph Milner's *Church History*, and, above all, been deeply influenced by Thomas Scott, whose concern for sanctification and 'resolute opposition to antinomianism' were planted in his youthful mind.[358]

But in the critical years of the reform crisis the extremism of Bulteel, so close at hand in Oxford, came to seem more representative of the true Evangelical spirit to Newman and other Anglicans than the moderation of Scott and his generation. Benjamin Wills Newton later reflected: 'The injury he did to Oxford was very great. *Newmanism and the Tractarian movement would never have been what it was, had it not been for Bulteel's failure.* There had been in his ministry a moral power in Oxford affecting many of those outside its immediate circle: but when he broke down, the power of the enemy was so much the greater.'[359] Nor was Bulteel the only example of high (or hyper) Calvinism which local churchmen had cause to observe. Newman joined the Bible Society in Oxford in 1824 upon taking up his curacy at St. Clement's, and became friendly with James Hinton, the local Baptist minister and friend of Bulteel.[360] On occasion, he met socially with the likes of John Hill and Bulteel.[361] He had a vivid insight into the mind of high Calvinism through his mercurial brother Francis, who, between 1827 and 1828, while tutoring at the Pennefathers' in Ireland, had also fallen under the spell of John Nelson Darby, and, in the belief of a direct communication from the Spirit, had rushed off to Baghdad to convert Islam.[362] In 1830, in a small but

[357] Newman, *Apologia Pro Vita Sua*, 4.

[358] Ibid. 4–5. [359] Fry, 106, 132–3, 234.

[360] *Letters and Correspondence of John Henry Newman*, ed. Mozley, i.84–5.

[361] *HD* 67/6, 22b, 14 Aug. 1826; 56a, 27 Feb. 1827.

[362] Francis apparently assisted his brother in parish work at Littlemore until 1830. See William Robbins, *The Newman Brothers* (1966), 32–3. Francis eventually abandoned orthodox Christianity altogether. This rapid change in his religious views may have seemed, to his brother, as something of an inevitability, given (as he later came to believe) the tendency of Protestantism to encourage continuous schism.

significant *cause célèbre*, Newman was removed as secretary of the Oxford committee of the Church Missionary Society as the result of his attack upon its loose attachment to Church principles and its association with the high Calvinism of the Bulteelers.[363] He was replaced as secretary by none other than Joseph Charles Philpot.[364] For John Henry Newman, the displeasing vision of Bulteel and his Oxford allies seems to have replaced the fragrant memory of Scott and other moderate Evangelicals. Seen in the intense atmosphere of Oxford in the late 1820s and early 1830s, Evangelicalism could be understood as given over to eccentricity, waywardness, and irregularity; it could be plausibly seen as high or hyper in its Calvinism, antinomian in its tendencies, and extremely ambivalent about, if not actively disloyal to, the formularies of the Church of England. Through the writings of the Oxford Movement and its later chroniclers, this unfavourable view of Evangelicalism has been transmitted to posterity. Bulteel and his coadjutors have much to answer for.

[363] For Newman's explanation of this affair see J. H. Newman [A Master of Arts], 'Suggestions Respectfully Offered to Individual Resident Clergymen of the University in Behalf of the Church Missionary Society', in *The Via Media*, 3rd edn. (1877), ii.3–10. For a thorough analysis of this episode see Stunt, 'John Henry Newman and the Evangelicals'; Ward, *Young Mr Newman*, 176–7; *Letters and Correspondence of John Henry Newman*, ed. Mozley, i.223–6, i.215–26; *HD* 67/7, 73a–b, 14 Dec. 1829.

[364] Stunt, 'John Henry Newman and the Evangelicals', 73–4.

8

Evangelicals and Tractarians: Baptist Noel and the Evangelical Response to the Gorham Affair

The 1840s rank as one of the most embattled periods in modern Anglican history. In 1842 Baptist Noel wrote with feeling: 'Our lot is cast in a day of strife . . . In this eternal chaos of opinion or shock of minds, hostile pamphlets fly about us as thick as wintry sleet.'[1] Church leaders were worried about the emergence of more sharply defined parties in the Church and—like W. F. Hook and F. D. Maurice—began to protest about their development,[2] or, like W. J. Conybeare in his celebrated article on 'Church parties' in the *Edinburgh Review*, chronicled their course with fascination.[3] The Evangelical party (if such it can be called) experienced the tension acutely. Tractarianism was then in the ascendant, at least in some cities, and becoming more extreme. The 'Romeward' drift of its advanced elements became increasingly apparent after the crisis over Tract 90 and Newman's withdrawal to Littlemore. Evangelical 'vital religion' seemed to be increasingly under siege, charged with indifference to episcopacy and with propagating spiritual individualism and ecclesiastical anarchy.[4] Evangelicals watched with astonishment as extreme Tractarians denounced the English Reformers, and they observed with sorrow the defection of many of their sons into the new movement.

The 1840s raised a succession of highly disturbing issues: the imprisonment of James Shore in 1844, Newman's secession to Rome in 1845, the Maynooth crisis in the same year, and the long drawn-out Gorham affair. In Scotland the explosive Disruption of

[1] B. W. Noel, *Christian Missions to Heathen Nations* (1842), 296–7.

[2] W. F. Hook, *Letter to the Right Reverend the Lord Bishop of Ripon, on the State of Parties in the Church of England* (1841); F. D. Maurice, *Reasons for Not Joining a Party in the Church of England* (1841).

[3] W. J. Coneybeare, 'Church Parties', in *EdR* (Oct. 1853), 273–342.

[4] Herbert Clegg, 'Evangelicals and Tractarians', in the *Historical Magazine of the Protestant Episcopal Church* (June 1966), 111–53; (Sept. 1966), 237–94; (June 1967), 127–78.

1843 showed a Reformed and Established Church faced by an acute crisis over the issue of lay 'intrusion'. This led Thomas Chalmers, the great exponent of Church establishment, to secede from the Kirk, and provided Evangelicals south of the border with a painful example of the dangers inherent in Erastianism.

In addition to these controversies there was the growing realization of the logistical and pastoral crisis facing the Church as a result of rapid population growth and massive urbanization. The radical demands of Owenism and Chartism forced churchmen to face up to the acute problem of secularization in the cities, and led some to wonder whether the creaking machinery of the Established Church was capable of meeting a critical situation.

In the first three decades of the nineteenth century, pastoral optimism had, on the whole, characterized Evangelicalism. The rapid growth of voluntary societies like the Bible Society, and the extension of bridgeheads at Oxford and Cambridge, seemed to indicate a continuous expansion of influence. Now, as population soared and the extent of urbanization became apparent, it seemed once again that the supply of 'Gospel teaching' lagged far behind the demands created by the 'spiritual destitution' of the cities. To some, new expedients—quasi-regular expedients like street-preaching, or lay-preaching and visitation—seemed called for, as in the days of Whitefield and Wesley. One of those who believed this most emphatically was the Hon. and Revd Baptist Wriothesley Noel, perhaps the most influential 'Gospel clergyman' of his generation. Noel's secession in 1848 was a severe blow to Evangelical hopes, as well as to the Church's defence of its civil connection, producing, as one contemporary exclaimed, nothing less than an 'explosion' in the English religious world.[5]

Noel was one of the acknowledged leaders of the Evangelical party.[6] He was a chaplain to Queen Victoria,[7] a co-founder of the

[5] L. C. L. Brenton, *A Sermon on Revelations XIV: 13* (1849), 37; K. R. Short, 'Baptist Wriothesley Noel', in *BQ* (1963), 389–411; D. W. Bebbington, 'The Life of Baptist Noel: Its Setting and Significance', in *BQ* (1972), 389–411.

[6] John Dix, *Pen and Ink Sketches of Poets, Preachers, and Politicians* (1846), 245. Dix claimed that Noel was so popular that the Royal family ventured to his chapel *incognito* in order to hear him preach.

[7] Noel was appointed chaplain by Melbourne in August 1841 during the final weeks of the Whig ministry, as reward for his opposition to the Corn Laws. See MSS Doc. DE 1797/1 No. 86/2, Leicester County RO.

Evangelical Alliance,[8] the prolific author of scores of religious works which (especially during the 1840s) sold in enormous quantities,[9] a hymn-writer of some accomplishment,[10] and one of the most eminent preachers in London.[11] An anonymous manuscript written in 1844, and providing detailed descriptions of the most prominent London clergy, characterized Noel as 'so well known as to require no comment', and remarked that he was 'uniformly consulted' on all important matters by the Evangelical party.[12] Not surprisingly, his departure from the Church was regarded as the leading ecclesiastical event of the year,[13] causing almost as much sensation as Newman's secession three years earlier.[14] Noel's secession, remarked Daniel Wilson simply, was an 'earthquake'.[15]

Noel was born at Leithmouth, near Edinburgh, on 16 July 1799, into a household which combined Whig politics, Evangelical religion, aristocratic unconventionality, and strong-mindedness in a potent blend.[16] He was the sixteenth child and tenth son of Sir Gerard Noel Noel, Bart., a highly eccentric Whig politician and landowner,[17] and the former Lady Diana Middleton, only child of the Evangelical Admiral Charles Middleton, First Lord of the Admiralty, who had been raised to the peerage by the title of Lord Barham. Diana succeeded to the title upon the death of her father in 1813 and was afterwards known as Lady Barham.[18] Charles

[8] Frederic Boase, *Modern English Biography* (Truro, 1897), 1159.

[9] By 1848, nine of his published works had sold over 108,000 copies, making him one of the most popular religious authors of the Victorian era. See B. W. Noel, *Sermons Preached at the Chapels Royal* (1848), 299.

[10] B. W. Noel, *A Selection of Psalms and Hymns, Adopted Chiefly for Congregational and Social Worship* (1853); *Hymns about Jesus* (n.d.); *Julian's Dictionary of Hymnology* (1892), 809.

[11] See the *Baptist Messenger* (1873), 55. Selina Macaulay, sister of the great historian, waxed lyrically about the effects of Noel's preaching. In 1826, she confided to her journal that after Noel preached at Rothley Temple, the Macaulays' country estate in Leicestershire, 'even Tom praised his sermon'. See MS 'Macaulay Family Papers', Journal of Selina Macaulay, 5 June 1826, Henry E. Huntington Library.

[12] MS Add c.290, 1844, Bod.

[13] The *Baptist Reporter*, Feb. 1849, 45.

[14] C. S. Horne, *Nonconformity in the XIXth Century* (1905), 123; L. E. Elliott-Binns, *Religion in the Victorian Era* (1963), 462.

[15] Josiah Bateman, *The Life of the Right Revd Daniel Wilson, D.D.* (1860), ii.358.

[16] An interesting description of Noel can be found in Henry C. Fish, *Pulpit Eloquence of the Nineteenth Century* (New York, 1857), 541–2.

[17] Sir Gerard (1759–1838) was MP for Maidstone (1784–8), and Rutland (1788–1808, 1814–38). He had a well-deserved reputation for extravagance and eccentricity. See Sidney Noel, *Ernest Noel* (1932).

[18] See Grayson Carter, 'Baptist Wriothesley Noel', in *New DNB*.

Noel, Baptist's elder brother, succeeded to the barony upon his mother's death in 1823 and, in 1841, was created the Earl of Gainsborough.[19]

The influence of Noel's Evangelical mother was especially significant upon his spiritual development and clerical career. Through her wide and influential circle of Evangelical friends and relations, centred at her ancestral home at Barham Court, Teston, Kent, he gained the acquaintance of many leading politicians and religious figures. Her example was of particular importance to his lifelong dedication to the 'Catholic spirit' of pan-evangelical co-operation, for Lady Barham took a view of denominational barriers which was unusually relaxed and eirenical for her time. This attitude was exemplified during the final years of her life by her establishment of 'Lady Barham's Connexion', a Calvinistic body of six chapels and several schools which she organized between 1814 and 1822 on the Gower peninsula of South Wales.[20] It is also very likely that it was through her influence that Noel became a passionate advocate of Christian unity, an attitude which, ironically, as we will see, strongly influenced his secession from the Church. From his eccentric father, Noel acquired a liberal spirit and an affinity to Whig politics that led to his espousal of a variety of reforming causes, and gave him access to circles of political power often closed to Evangelicals.[21]

In 1810, Noel was enrolled at Westminster, and in 1817, as pensioner at Trinity College, Cambridge, where he was a contemporary of Thomas Babington Macaulay.[22] He then settled on a career at the bar, enrolling in 1821 at Lincoln's Inn.[23] Two years later, however, and against the wishes of his family, he abandoned his legal work and entered the ministry of the Church of England, being ordained to serve as curate to William Babington, rector of Cossington, Leicestershire.[24] In 1827, he acquired the lease of St. John's Chapel, Bedford Row, a proprietary chapel of some

[19] Emilia F. Noel (ed.), *Some Letters and Records of the Noel Family* (1910), 25, 28, 32.

[20] Grayson Carter, 'Baroness Barham', in *New DNB*; Iorwerth Hughes Jones, 'Lady Barham in Gower', in *Journal of the Gower Society* (1956); A. N. Jones, *Gower Memories of William Griffiths* (Aberayron, 1957).

[21] Noel was also related to Sir George Grey, the Evangelical Whig MP.

[22] *The Record of Old Westminsters* (1928), ii.693; *Al. Cant.*, iv.557.

[23] *The Records of the Honourable Society of Lincoln's Inn* (1896), ii.93.

[24] In a letter of 23 May 1823, Francis Noel describes the family's unfavourable reaction to his ordination. See Noel Family Papers in the possession of Captain Gerard Noel.

considerable reputation within Evangelical circles, where, over the next twenty-one years, he was to develop a ministry of remarkable scope and influence.[25] Four years later, Noel accompanied Captain William Gordon, the fanatical anti-Catholic, on a mission to Ireland where Gordon announced himself as the Luther, and Noel as the Melanchthon, of a second Reformation.[26]

Though a powerful preacher and evangelist, Noel's wider reputation came with his emergence as a prolific religious author, whose many publications put forward his strong views on a number of contemporary issues. Despite his aristocratic lineage, Noel was neither a high establishmentarian nor a Tory, but a vigorously reformist Whig. In 1828 (the year of the repeal of the Test and Corporation Acts) he published an early tract, *Protestant Unity in Fundamental Doctrines*, which set out his belief that the primary unifying force in the Christian world was not attachment to a particular church or denomination, but to the vital religion of the Bible. In 1844 he stressed again that the unity described in Scripture was no agreement in 'external forms of minor opinions', but a union of hearts in faith, love, and *action*—a belief that led him, not surprisingly, to a militant support for the interdenominational work of the London City Mission.[27] Noel was nothing if not a resolute pan-evangelical. He was scornful of the sternly Anglican Pastoral Aid Society, and a vehement supporter of the London City Mission's use of laymen—many of them Nonconformists—for the mission of evangelizing the great cities.[28] Noel saw co-operation between Dissenters and Anglicans in missionary work as a natural extension of the pan-evangelicalism of the British and Foreign Bible Society. Such attitudes, however, were not embraced by all Evangelicals. In 1839, in supporting the London City Mission, Noel was accused by the conservative *Record* of supporting what was 'in effect a Dissenting Society.' He parried this attack by stressing the Mission's co-operative nature, making it clear that he was far less concerned with its denominational make-up than its effectiveness as an urban agency of conversion.[29] His oppo-

[25] A number of prominent Evangelicals (clergy and lay) were associated with St. John's, including Thomas Scott, Richard Cecil, Daniel Wilson, the Thorntons, William Wilberforce, and Zachary Macaulay.

[26] See Lord Teignmouth, *Reminiscences of Many Years* (Edinburgh, 1878), i.212; ii.220.

[27] B. W. Noel, *The Doctrine of the Word of God Respecting Union Among Christians* (1844), 6–12.

[28] Donald M. Lewis, *Lighten their Darkness* (New York, 1986), 55.

[29] The *Record*, 4 Feb. 1839.

nents, he added, could not '*sketch, much less form*, a church society which could send either lay agents or curates to these perishing creatures'.[30] As this exchange shows, Noel was already regarded by his conservative Evangelical colleagues as closer to Dissent than most of his Evangelical contemporaries. Already he saw the imperatives of evangelism as far higher than those of strict churchmanship.

In politics, Noel distanced himself significantly from the Tory paternalist wing of the Evangelical world. His was a strong meliorist Whiggery; he believed in progress and activism. 'Let others be wedded to the past,' he wrote in 1842, 'we live in the past, the present, and the future.'[31] Nor did he allow his strong belief in human depravity to dampen his belief that much human misery was the result not of the Fall, but of human ignorance and deprivation. 'Poverty, famine, disease, terror, strife, and premature death', he wrote, 'are much more inflicted by ourselves than by the necessity of our condition as men.'[32]

Though Noel attacked Robert Owen and Socialism in conventional terms as anti-Christian, he was intensely interested in the plight of the poor.[33] In 1840, he conducted a public inquiry into the condition of elementary schools in several major cities.[34] He was one of the comparatively few clergymen—among a host of Nonconformist ministers—publicly to attack the Corn Laws as they stood in 1841: his *Plea for the Poor*, which ran through at least twenty-nine editions, urged a low fixed duty on corn instead of the sliding scale, in order to produce a steady price.[35] Unlike many Evangelicals in country parishes, Noel's concern for the 'condition of England question' was based on his first-hand experience of working conditions in the great cities, strengthened by the flow of reports about human misery which came in from the missionaries sponsored by the London City Mission.[36] Though not an avowed exponent of Free Trade, Noel was an advocate of economic liberalism; he was convinced that tariff reduction would do far more than alms-giving to raise the living standards of poor people.

[30] Ibid., 11 Feb. 1839.

[31] Noel, *Christian Missions to Heathen Nations*, 306.

[32] Ibid. 301.

[33] B. W. Noel, 'What is Christianity?', 1840, in *Lectures Against Socialism* (1840).

[34] *DNB.*

[35] B. W. Noel, *A Plea for the Poor, Showing How the Proposed Repeal of the Existing Corn Laws Will Affect the Interests of the Working Classes* (1841).

[36] Ibid. 5.

Such views delighted his Whig friends and won him a chaplaincy to the Queen from the outgoing Whig administration; his arguments were also, allegedly, used by Lord John Russell very effectively in the ensuing election campaign.[37] At the same time, however, they incensed many conservative churchmen and alienated Noel from the increasingly Tory mainstream of Anglican Evangelicalism.[38] It is already possible to see in Noel's stance on social issues some of the attitudes which were later to lead him out of the Established Church. His commitment to economic liberalism was capable of being extended to 'free trade in religion' and hence to Nonconformist voluntaryism. His warm espousal of interdenominational city evangelism already separated him from some of his Evangelical Tory brethren and brought him into close contact with London Dissenters. Noel was a progressive and a pragmatist for whom the immediate alleviation of social—and spiritual—problems counted far more than any adherence to tradition. He distanced himself firmly from the nostalgic politics of high Toryism. 'Let those who read with impassioned fondness the days of the bard and the baron', he wrote in 1842, 'dream on of feudal fealty and chivalrous devotion to the altar and the throne. Thanks be to God', he concluded, 'those days will not return.'[39]

Noel's views on the complex—and highly emotive—question of a national religious establishment, however, took time to evolve. The rise of the disestablishment campaign in the early 1830s led to the first of his numerous publications on the Church's civil connection.[40] At this stage he warmly defended its link to the State on two grounds: its consistent opposition to the 'unbridled licence of fanaticism', and its provision for secular and religious education: claims which bore some resemblance to Thomas Arnold's *Principles of Church Reform*, published during the previous year.[41] But

[37] The *Record*, 7 Mar. 1842.

[38] The *Baptist Messenger* (1873), 55–6; *QR* (1841), 504–5; *CO* (1841), 572. Lord Shrewsbury commented, referring to Noel, that 'one of the most wicked acts of the Whigs was making that canting humbug a Queen's chaplain.' See Edmund Sheridan Purcell, *Life and Letters of A. P. de Lisle* (1900), i.33.

[39] Noel, *Christian Missions to Heathen Nations*, 305.

[40] B. W. Noel, 'An Established Religion' (1837), in *The Important Influence* (1837). Extracted from a sermon of May 1834.

[41] Ibid. 1.

this eulogy of establishment soon gave way to more critical, even contentious, views.

The reasons for this change in Noel's attitude toward the issue of establishment are not easy to determine, but they appear primarily pragmatic in nature. First-hand experience of the industrial city suggested to him that the dead hand of establishment paralysed any serious attempt to meet London's 'spiritual destitution'. The enemy was liberalism and secularism, not Dissent. The enormity of the task was such that it could not be met by the Established Church alone: co-operation with Nonconformity in such organizations as the London City Mission was essential, yet it was being 'repelled at every step' by the religious hierarchy, while the acute need to establish new parishes—or to fortify existing ones—was repeatedly being hindered by insurmountable parliamentary obstacles.[42]

This urgent sense of need led Noel to publish a vigorous letter to Bishop Blomfield of London criticizing the Church's ineffectiveness in meeting the spiritual needs of the metropolis.[43] His *State of the Metropolis Considered* (1835), is a classic—and much neglected—statement of that perception of 'spiritual destitution' in the great cities which electrified many Anglicans in the turbulent 1840s. The argument was pursued with rhetorical passion combined with the attention to statistical detail which was becoming fashionable in the Benthamite era. With anger, Noel pointed out to Blomfield that while England sent out missionaries to Africa and the East, in London 518,000 souls—enough to populate six English counties—'within reach of hundreds of Christian ministers, and thousands of intelligent Christian laymen with wealth and leisure, are almost entirely overlooked!' In Blomfield's diocese there were now parishes in which one clergyman was responsible for 46,000, 68,000, and even 103,000 souls.[44] Noel vividly described the plight of London's poor in Mayhew's world of gin-palaces, prostitution, and mendicants.[45] Significantly, he quoted Thomas Chalmers's *Civic Economy* to support his claim that a

[42] Noel to Nasmith, 8 April 1835, in John Campbell, *Memoirs of David Nasmith* (1844), 303–4.

[43] B. W. Noel, *The State of the Metropolis Considered: In a Letter to the Right Honourable and Right Reverend the Lord Bishop of London*, 2nd edn. (1835).

[44] Ibid. 12, 26.

[45] Henry Mayhew, *London Labour and the London Poor* (1851).

population like this could only be reached by a series of 'aggressive' efforts. If the masses did not come to the Church, the Church must go out to meet them. More Church schools must be erected. The absurd laws still hindering the subdivision of parishes and the easy building of new churches must be repealed. A great army of curates must be mustered to help penetrate the dense, 'unchurched' rookeries of urban England. Even more radical measures were necessary. Noel warmly urged the acceptance of street-preaching—which he saw so clearly sanctioned in the New Testament—as an essential to the Church's mission: 'we must seek for them wherever they are congregated: if we have not buildings within which to gather them, we must preach to them in the open air.'[46] No doubt to the alarm of Blomfield, Noel here commended the example of famous clerical 'irregulars' of the past, such as George Whitefield and Rowland Hill, as well as present-day Dissenting itinerants.[47] Like a Wesley or a Whitefield, Noel pressed home the pragmatic argument from necessity. Were such actions 'irregular'? 'I would answer, that there are times in which an inflexible adherence to rule may become foolish, or criminal.' Would Nelson have won at Copenhagen if he had obeyed the Admiralty rule-book? 'Whitefield would never have ranked among the greatest benefactors of mankind, if he had not dared to be irregular.'[48] In the end, necessity has no law: '*Christ must be preached to perishing sinners*. Before this necessity, all forms, however venerable, all rules, however salutary, must give way.'[49] Noel concluded by urging Blomfield, a rubrical High Churchman, to send out anyone qualified—layman, Methodist, or Congregational missionary—who would save the myriad of souls destitute of the Gospel. 'While we are yielding to our indolence, cherishing our dignity, or punctiliously adhering to modern usage, they are passing into eternity untaught in that excellent knowledge, to obtain which we must, if real Christians, be willing to part with all things.'[50] This was the language of Wesley himself, but applied now not to the Georgian countryside, but to the great Victorian cities. In Noel's view the endowments, rules, and traditions of the Church were subordinate to the 'one thing needful': saving souls. The apparatus of establishment was primarily to be judged by the

[46] Noel, *The State of the Metropolis Considered*, 42–3. [47] Ibid. 46–9.
[48] Ibid. 54–5. [49] Ibid. 70. [50] Ibid. 70, 55.

same standard: pastoral and evangelistic utility. He was already prepared so to judge it; consequently, and over time, he began to see that establishment was not a benefit to the nation's spiritual condition, but often a hindrance.

Noel's proposals met with a mixed response. His statistics were repeatedly cited by Evangelicals in sermons, articles, and lectures, while his pamphlet aroused the attention of evangelical Dissent and did much to facilitate the founding of the pan-evangelical London City Mission, in which he played an important role.[51] On the other hand, the *Christian Observer*, while expressing its admiration of many of his points, could not accept his recommendation of open-air preaching, which was held to be unsuitable to the British climate and temperament: its recent employment by the Irvingites had demonstrated that 'such a plan was not for edification'. The pastoral methods of a Wesley and a Whitefield, however successful and necessary in their day, were no longer patterns for the present time.[52] Some shrewd observers even began to speculate, towards the end of 1835, that Noel had become a 'great deal too liberal for the church' and would not last long within its pale.[53] Such comments prompted Noel to admit publicly that 'the time might come' when he 'may deem it necessary' to secede from the Establishment, though adding quickly that this had not yet occurred, nor did it appear imminent.[54]

In the following year, Noel offered qualified support for Blomfield's church extension campaign,[55] personally contributing £60 to the cause,[56] while stating his conviction that the plan would only succeed if accompanied by pan-evangelical co-operation. Only when all 'ingenuous and unjust' attacks upon Dissent were laid aside would the Church of England regain 'a wholesome and Christ-like ascendancy'.[57] These ideas were firmly rejected by Blomfield, however, who responded by attacking Noel in the House of Lords over his advocacy of pan-evangelical co-operation through the 'promiscuous interchange of pulpits'. Any such

[51] John Matthias Weylland, *These Fifty Years* (1884), 13–15. [52] *CO* (1836), 251–2.
[53] John Dix, *Pulpit Portraits* (Boston, 1854), 75. [54] Ibid. 79.
[55] B. W. Noel, *The Spiritual Claims of the Metropolis* (1836).
[56] Ibid. 21. His brother, Leland, contributed £40. John Henry Newman claimed that the Evangelicals raised £150,000 for Blomfield's campaign. See letter of John Henry Newman to R. H. Froude, 17 Jan. 1836, in *Letters and Correspondence of John Henry Newman*, ed. Anne Mozley (1891), ii.154.
[57] Noel, *The Spiritual Claims of the Metropolis*, 12.

action would demean the principle of a National Church; it would not benefit the Church of England, but would instead transform it into an ecclesiastical 'Noah's ark'.[58]

Over the next few years, Noel became increasingly exasperated over the Establishment's reluctance to promote wholesale church extension. He turned from attempting to goad his diocesan to action, to demanding action from the government. Writing directly to Melbourne in 1839, he set out in detail an account of the effects of the Church's failure to provide spiritual instruction, one of the most serious (in this year of Chartist activity) being increased social unrest.[59] None the less, for all his advocacy of aggressive evangelism and greater pan-evangelical co-operation, Noel could not see his way clear to support the demands of Liberationists to disestablish and disendow the Church, and introduce the voluntary principle. Such action, he argued, would be inapplicable and ineffective, leaving millions ignorant of spiritual truth, free to disturb the country and at liberty to ruin themselves.[60]

Noel denounced the partisans of disestablishment as a small and noisy pressure group unrepresentative of the majority of Dissenters, who were themselves not unfriendly to the Church.[61] Moreover, the Liberationists were highly unlikely to succeed in their campaign, the only tactics open to them being agitation on the church-rate issue, or attempts to influence parliamentary elections through 'harangues on the hustings'. Since few real Christians would participate in such unseemly demagoguery, the disestablishment campaign would be staffed by reprobates: if these eventually prevailed, it would be no victory for Christianity, but a triumph for 'unbridled immorality, for ostentatious irreligion, and for exulting lawlessness amongst all the worst subjects of the land'.[62]

Disestablishment, Noel concluded, would be a disaster. But how could it be stopped? The best reply to the Liberationists was church extension achieved through a huge increase in State funding. If the State wished to preserve the Church it must actively promote the saving of souls and the provision of moral

[58] *CO* (1837), 236. The *CO* concurred with Blomfield.

[59] B. W. Noel, *A Letter to the Right Honourable Lord Viscount Melbourne, on Church Extension* (1839), 21.

[60] Ibid. 20–1. [61] Ibid. 22–3. [62] Ibid. 23.

instruction, which constituted the very *raison d'être* of a National Church. Since the existence of a religious establishment created 'obstacles to the spread of religion by other means', its maintenance therefore involved an obligation on the part of the State to supply the destitute with spiritual instruction.[63]

While rejecting voluntarism and disestablishment, Noel, like many of his prominent Whig friends, eagerly supported the concurrent endowment of evangelical Dissent. 'Common funds should be employed in the service of all', he argued, with each denomination receiving 'similar aid from the state'. This would not be aiding those who opposed the Church, as High Churchmen claimed, but those who were fighting in alliance with the Church against ungodliness and superstition.[64]

Underlying Noel's belief that joint action by Anglicans and Dissenters was the only means to stem the tide of popular infidelity was his heartfelt commitment to Christian unity. His first important work on the subject appeared in 1837 and achieved instant success, running through at least thirty-four editions in its first year alone.[65] Noel encouraged all believers to lay aside thorny points of doctrine (such as infant baptism, church polity, and establishment), and instead focus on points of unity. Churchmen and Dissenters should unite in one profession, and become increasingly 'candid, tolerant, and brotherly', while allowing each believer the right of private judgement.[66]

Though these suggestions were welcomed by many evangelical Nonconformists,[67] they were predictably attacked by High Churchmen as promoting falsehoods which, if carried into practice, would annihilate the distinctively catholic precepts of the Church of England.[68] Noel was accused of advancing views on baptism which were un-Anglican, of bringing the principle of apostolicity into disrespect, of encouraging clerical and lay secession, and of promoting a false liberality that was indistinguishable from Latitudinarianism.[69] Rather than promoting true Christian

[63] Ibid. 26–7. [64] Ibid. 27–9.

[65] B. W. Noel, *The Unity of the Church* (1837). [66] Ibid. 14.

[67] 'Christianus Episcopus', *The Moderator Between the Hon. B. W. Noel and 'Clericus Surriensis'* (1838).

[68] John Courtney [Clericus Surriensis], *An Earnest Protest* (1837), 3, 7; 'M. A.', *A Letter to the Hon and Revd Baptist W. Noel* (1837); J. Hoppus [Schism], *An Examination of the Principles Contained in the Hon B. W. Noel's Tract 'On the Unity of the Church'* (1838).

[69] Ibid. 13, 38.

unity around the core of catholicity, he was labouring to destroy it.[70] Noel was told by a High Churchman that he should secede from the Establishment; then and only then could he attack it with a consistency impossible for him to maintain while he earned his bread as a clergyman in the State Church.[71] No doubt such suggestions began to play on his mind as he began seriously to consider his future.

Noel quickly responded to this criticism—and to the high ecclesiology of the Oxford Tracts, which were still appearing—by publishing a defence of his work on Christian unity.[72] By this time he had perceived the significance of the Oxford Movement and its implicit threat to the principle of Protestant ecumenism, which he had been proclaiming. He soon began a long and restless pursuit of Tractarianism, which he characterized as nothing less than a 'serious offence against Christ'.[73] He rejected the Tract writers' claim that Nonconformists should be excluded from Christian unity, not so much because they dissented from the Establishment (for Tractarians were themselves Nonconformists when in Scotland), but because they dissented from episcopacy.[74] While accepting the scriptural basis for episcopacy (which, when rightly constituted, he considered an excellent form of church government), Noel denied that it was set out in the New Testament as the exclusive form of Christian polity.[75] Unity therefore should rest not on adherence to a single form of polity, but on a consensual acceptance of the primary doctrines of the Gospel: a steady adherence to fundamental truths, with a charitable construction of minor errors.[76]

The 'mischievous' doctrine of baptismal regeneration also came under Noel's repeated attack. As early as 1840 he was admonished by Blomfield for his outspoken criticism of the doctrine.[77] He took up the issue seriously during a six-week period, stretching from 11 December 1842 to 22 January 1843, when he delivered no less than thirteen separate sermons on the subject,

[70] 'A Layman', *Anti-Schism: A Review of the Principles Contained in the Hon. and Revd B. W. Noel's Tract 'The Unity of the Church'* (1838), 3.

[71] Ibid. 12–13.

[72] B. W. Noel, *A Defence of a Tract Entitled, 'The Unity of the Church'* (1837). A later account of Noel's views on Christian unity can be found in John Howe, *Christian Union* (1839).

[73] B. W. Noel, *A Defence of a Tract Entitled, 'The Unity of the Church'*, 6.

[74] Ibid. 4. [75] Ibid. 5. [76] Ibid. 30.

[77] MSS 'Blomfield Papers', 23 f 65, Lambeth Palace Library.

denigrating it as a popish survival and as an unscriptural doctrine which was opposed by the Thirty-Nine Articles.[78] The Church of England, he declared, 'holds no such doctrine'; those 'who are baptized in infancy are *not* regenerate . . . whatever regeneration does accompany baptism, it *precedes* and does not *follow* it'.[79] Evangelicals must therefore stand firm against the imposition of the doctrine of baptismal regeneration by Tractarians. They should not allow themselves to be depressed by High Church propaganda on the issue, and should not consider abandoning the Church as long as it still maintained the fundamental truth of the Gospel in its formularies, while it continued to hold many faithful followers, and while it did not compel them actively to '*maintain falsehood or to commit wrong*'. If, on the other hand, like the Protestant Reformers, some Evangelicals were expelled from the Church, they should not lose heart: they could serve God equally well from within the ranks of Protestant Dissent.[80]

It seems that the secession of Noel's very able (but rather unstable) former evening lecturer, Richard Waldo Sibthorp, to Rome in 1841 accelerated his bitter opposition to the doctrine of baptismal regeneration, as well as to Tractarianism itself.[81] The Tract writers' sole aim, Noel came to believe, was the complete 'unprotestantizing' of the Church of England, for they held the doctrine of justification by faith to be a 'hateful . . . unchristian, and poisonous heresy'.[82] True believers must stand firm against the errors of baptismal regeneration, justification by the reception of the Lord's Supper, the Eucharistic sacrifice, and the elevation of the priesthood, and should especially protest against the universal schism (i.e. popery) of which these doctrines are the source.[83] Noel surprisingly urged members of Parliament to support the petition of the liberal Archbishop of Dublin, Richard Whately, which called for the reinstatement of Convocation,

[78] The *Pulpit*, 42: 423–70; 43: 10–156.

[79] Ibid. 43: 31–2.

[80] The *Church and State Gazette* (2 March 1849).

[81] The *Pulpit*, 43: 48; Roger H. Martin, *Evangelicals United: Ecumenical Stirrings in Pre-Victorian Britain, 1795–1830* (1983), 215: B. W. Noel, *Protestant Thoughts in Rhyme* (1844). Sibthorp was chaplain of Percy Chapel, London, and evening lecturer at St. John's. In 1865 he seceded for the second time to Roman Catholicism; he died in 1879. For further details on Sibthorp see *Al. Ox.*, iv.1295; J. Fowler, *Richard Waldo Sibthorp: A Biography* (1880); R. D. Middleton, *Magdalen Studies* (1936), 195–228; Christopher Sykes, *Two Studies in Virtue* (1953).

[82] The *Pulpit*, 44: 39.

[83] Ibid. 44: 29.

which might set up barriers against the creeping 'Romanism' now infiltrating the Church. This course, he recognized, was not without it dangers, for instead of restoring spiritual unity to the Church it might destroy it; it could just as easily lead to the schism of Evangelicals from the Church, in a manner similar to the convulsions in Scotland which were then producing the great Disruption.[84]

During 1844, Noel published an additional plea for Christian unity and pan-evangelical co-operation;[85] he also issued another public denial that he was about to secede from the Church and (like an English Chalmers) organize a rival episcopal body. However, readers of his scathing condemnation of State intrusion into the affairs of the Scottish Kirk might well have thought otherwise, seeing Noel as a potential leader of an imminent English Disruption.[86] Speculation over the likelihood of a significant group secession in England was aided by an advertisement which brazenly appeared on the front page of the *Record* in February 1844:

> To episcopalians attached to the glorious doctrines of the Reformation—It being in contemplation to form an episcopal church separate from the State, with a revised liturgy, all who are favourable to this object are earnestly requested to communicate, by letter, with B.O., 2, Featherstone Buildings, Holborn, London.[87]

Suggestions that Noel himself had undertaken to organize an Evangelical group secession quickly began to circulate. To make matters worse, an anonymous letter was sent to a number of Evangelical students at an unnamed college, encouraging them to secede from the church and join a 'new Society', described as 'another Episcopal church, not connected with the state', over which newly elected bishops would be placed.[88] In a speech before the annual conference of the London City Mission, Noel denied authorship of either document or any knowledge of the author's identity. He claimed to love the Evangelical clergy and laity more dearly than any other body, as the 'regiment of Christ's army' to

[84] Ibid. 44: 30.

[85] B. W. Noel, *The Doctrine of the Word of God Respecting Union Among Christians*; *CO* (1844), 81.

[86] B. W. Noel, *The Case of the Free Church of Scotland* (1844).

[87] The *Record*, 8 Feb. 1844; the *Christian Remembrancer* (1844), 303.

[88] The *London City Mission Magazine* (1844), 90–1.

which he had been providentially assigned. Nor did he mean to leave the Church to the Tractarians; this would only serve to play into the hands of his opponents and undermine the cause of true religion in the nation.[89]

The outbreak of the Scottish Disruption in 1843 exerted more influence upon Noel's emerging views on the relationship between Church and State than perhaps any other issue: he described the Disruption as nothing less than the 'great religious event of our day.'[90] He saw the cause of spiritual independence as a highly reasonable principle which had apostolic authority behind it: State intrusion, on the other hand, was 'nothing less than tyranny' which hampered the Church by unscriptural constraints and party influence.[91] Noel noted with alarm that as a result of provocative intrusion within the Scottish Establishment between 1734 and 1834, some six hundred evangelical chapels had been constructed, while only sixty-three had been built by the Kirk during the same period.[92] The veto law—or the Church's prerogative to reject unsatisfactory nominations—had produced great spiritual benefits;[93] if abolished, the outcry would soon sweep away the Establishment itself.[94]

The Scottish Disruption placed Noel and the English Evangelicals in a rather delicate position. While they supported the establishment principle, they also recognized that a number of other issues which seemed to be at stake (e.g. the right of private judgement, spiritual liberty, and freedom from civil intrusion) could not be surrendered at any cost. They regretted deeply that religious issues like these had to be contended for in the courts and in Parliament. Yet many English Evangelicals made it clear that if a similarly painful situation were to develop south of the Border, they would be just as willing as their Scottish counterparts to resist State intrusion in order to preserve the Church's spiritual liberty and independence.

Noel offered vociferous support for the Scottish seceders, often in the face of stiff opposition from respected Evangelical

[89] Ibid. The advertisement may have been placed by James Shore, or by his London committee (see Chapter 9), or by Robert Crawford Dillon, a former assistant at St. John's, Bedford Row, who in 1840, after having had his licence revoked by Blomfield over charges of personal immorality, seceded from the church and formed a Reformed English Church in Friar Street, Blackfriars.

[90] Noel, *The Case of the Free Church of Scotland*, 94.

[91] Ibid. 4–5.

[92] Ibid. 11.

[93] Ibid. 20.

[94] Ibid. 33–4.

contemporaries.[95] Two years before, he declared, the ministers of the free churches had been honoured and loved: what had they done since to forfeit that approval? 'They were then ministers of Christ, are they less so now?'[96] Their sacrifice of worldly comforts in order to maintain their principles demanded not condemnation, but universal respect.[97] Under similar circumstances, Noel warned, the English Evangelicals would no doubt be compelled to take the same step. But their condition was now very different. In Scotland, the seceders' ground was that they were required actively to do wrong; here, no clergyman was placed under such compulsion. Secession was therefore unnecessary.[98]

As long as English Evangelicals were permitted to preach the Gospel and fulfil their pastoral obligations, it was incumbent upon them to seek the improvement of the Church from within. The recent proposals for the formation of a Free Episcopal Church were, therefore, altogether premature and hasty. Admittedly, the increasing dissemination of Tractarian errors, occasional acts of 'ecclesiastical despotism', and the absence of a representative assembly such as Convocation through which the Church could drastically reform itself, were great evils, but were there not serious shortcomings in all other religious bodies? And would not a new Free Episcopal Church in England be liable to evils just as great as those which faced the Establishment?[99]

At much the same time, Noel also became embroiled in another Church–State conflict closer to home: the controversy surrounding the proposed increase in the Maynooth grant. It soon became clear that Noel's enthusiasm for concurrent endowment did not extend to providing resources for an Irish Roman seminary. At the heart of his objection lay the belief that the continued State maintenance of the college at Maynooth would permanently strengthen the endowment of Irish—and perhaps English—Roman Catholicism.[100] He angrily pointed out the inconsistency of the proposal, for the State had repeatedly refused to provide support for orthodox Dissent in Britain (it had refused a request

[95] See Hugh McNeile, *Speech* (Edinburgh, 1844), 5; C. Hutcheson, *Tidings from the Mountains* (1845), 52.

[96] Noel, *The Case of the Free Church of Scotland*, 89–90.

[97] Ibid. 90–1. [98] Ibid. 92. [99] Ibid. 92–3.

[100] B. W. Noel, *The Proposed Increase in the Grant to Maynooth* (1845), 10–11; 'The Morning Sermon' (1847), in *Sermons Preached by Eminent Divines* (1847).

by Chalmers for two hundred new Scottish churches), and even for the Established Church of England (Sir Robert Inglis's motion for church extension had been rejected by Peel's government).[101] Since the only rational principle for the establishment of religion was that State funds should be employed for advancing 'public truth', there was no reason for the government to vote additional sums for the diffusion of 'public falsehood'.[102] Rather than support the extension of Irish Romanism, the State should consider the disestablishment and disendowment of the Irish Protestant Church, for even though Parliament would not legislate in favour of true religion, it was certainly bound not to legislate against it; if Parliament concluded that it was imprudent to support the truth alone, let it leave both truth and error unsupported.[103] Noel prophesied that if the State persisted in its plan to enact the Maynooth grant, it would seal the doom of all religious Establishments throughout Britain and Ireland.[104]

The degree of Noel's commitment to the disestablishment of the Church of Ireland remains uncertain.[105] Some parties took him at his word and scrutinized the plan accordingly.[106] One prominent Dissenter, Thomas Price, perhaps speaking for many outside the Church, remarked hopefully that the appearance of such a suggestion from a respected churchman was a significant straw in the wind, promising the future slackening of Anglican Evangelical support for establishment. 'The Church question', he happily predicted, 'is obviously becoming the question of the times.'[107]

Around 1847, Noel began to develop serious personal doubts about remaining a member of the Church of England. That summer, he toured the Continent in order to examine at first hand the results of the 1845 secession in Switzerland and the subsequent formation of the Evangelical Free Church of the canton of Vaud.[108] His inspection convinced him that the Swiss Establishment had become 'hopelessly corrupt': only with difficulty could he disguise his admiration for the seceders and their newly organized body.[109]

[101] Noel, *The Proposed Increase in the Grant to Maynooth*, 38–9. [102] Ibid. 45.
[103] B. W. Noel, *The Catholic Claims Considered* (Dublin, 1845), 15, 25. [104] Ibid. 25.
[105] As suggested in Short, 'Baptist Wriothesley Noel', 56. [106] *CO* (1845), 510.
[107] Thomas Price, *ER* (1845), 312.
[108] B. W. Noel, *Notes of a Tour in Switzerland in the Summer of 1847* (1848), 245–6.
[109] Ibid. 95–108, 127–39.

By mid-November 1848, rumours about Noel's continuation within the Church of England began circulating freely in religious circles in London. On Sunday 19 November a correspondent from *The Times* appeared at St. John's, eager to substantiate the rumours. Despite the chapel being so crowded that it was barely possible to obtain standing room those who came out of curiosity were sorely disappointed, for Noel completely avoided the subject of his future relationship with the Church.[110] Within several days, however, speculation about his secession began to appear in print.[111] During the same week, Noel announced his intentions to the heads of families attending St. John's. Many churchmen must be aware, he began, particularly after reading his tract on the Scottish Disruption, that he had harboured doubts for some time about the propriety of a civil connection of religion. He had struggled against these pressures, had read the best works on both sides of the argument, and had carefully studied the Scriptures. Being in a proprietary chapel, he had at first flattered himself that he had little personally to do with the question, but eventually he came to believe that a man was responsible for the sins of his communion.[112] He had, therefore, concluded that he must leave the Church of England.

Emotional appeals were made by Noel's distressed flock encouraging him to reconsider. It was pointed out that the continued prosperity of St. John's depended on him. Without his continued leadership, nine hundred children would be scattered from schools organized by the chapel, £700–900 a year in collections for various charities would be lost, numerous societies for the relief of the poor would be broken up, and a very large congregation would be scattered.[113] Unmoved by such appeals, Noel responded sternly that duty 'was above and beyond everything'. The question of secession had been so deeply considered that it was now impossible to turn back. At the same time, until his actual departure he would reveal no motive for seceding, nor would he disclose how he had arrived at his decision.[114]

Motivated by a desire to appoint a suitable successor, Noel's intention was to continue at St. John's until the following summer.

[110] *The Times*, 28 Nov. 1848, 5.
[111] *Non*, 22 Nov. 1848, 895.
[112] J. P. Bacon to Dr Patton, 24 Nov. 1848, in the *New York Independent*; *Non*, 7 Feb. 1849, 98–9; the *Baptist Reporter*, Mar. 1849, 122–3.
[113] *Non*, 7 Feb. 1849, 99; 6 Dec. 1848, 928.
[114] Ibid. 99.

On 24 November, however, as news of his secession began to circulate openly around London, Blomfield summoned him for an immediate interview.[115] The bishop's inclination was peremptorily to forbid Noel from officiating within the diocese; however, as Noel firmly refused to submit to such a ban, Blomfield granted him some days to withdraw in grace.[116] On 26 November, during his morning sermon at St. John's, Noel announced his resignation to the congregation, informing them that Blomfield had ruled that he could not continue to preach beyond the following Sunday.[117] Portions of the Evangelical press violently criticized Blomfield for his heavy-handedness in the matter,[118] but Noel characteristically rushed to his defence. The public had been entirely misinformed with respect to the bishop, he wrote to the *Christian Times*. He himself had always experienced forbearance and courtesy from Blomfield, who, in his trying situation, had simply done his duty, showing a personal kindness for which he (Noel) was deeply indebted.[119]

Noel's final appearance at St. John's contained all the excitement and drama accompanying the departure of a distinguished politician. When the chapel's doors were opened, crowds rushed in and took forcible possession of private pews.[120] Those who came expecting a scathing denunciation of the Church, however, were sorely disappointed: Noel's sermon was entirely commonplace, free from any rancour, devoid of any attack on the Church, and containing few references to his secession. Nor did it make any attempt to entice his hearers out of the Church.[121] It soon became clear that Noel had no intention of establishing himself as an English Chalmers. He reiterated that a thorough account of his position would soon be published, and that he would say nothing more on the subject at this time.[122] In seceding, he was following what he believed to be God's will, acting only out of duty, with reluctance, and after considerable delay.[123]

[115] MSS 'Blomfield Papers', 59, ff 209v, Lambeth Palace Library; Herbert S. Skeats and Charles S. Miall, *History of the Free Churches of England, 1688–1891* (1891), 509.

[116] MS *Blomfield Papers*, 59, ff 209v, Lambeth Palace Library; the *Baptist Messenger* (1873), 56; *The Times*, 1 Dec. 1848, 5.

[117] The *Pulpit*, 54: 455.

[118] See the *Christian Times*, 5 Dec. 1848.

[119] Clotworthy Gillmor, *A Reply to the Hon and Revd Baptist Wriothesley Noel's Essay on the Union of Church and State* (1849), 12.

[120] John Dix, *Pulpit Portraits*, 80.

[121] B. W. Noel, *The Substance of Two Sermons* (1848).

[122] The *Pulpit*, 54: 436.

[123] Ibid. 54: 483.

A number of additional complications accompanied Noel's secession. The unanticipated speed of his departure made the task of appointing a suitable successor at St. John's more difficult. The chapel's lease, still held by Daniel Wilson, now Bishop of Calcutta, required renegotiation. Pressure for a public statement continued to mount. Noel's own family even questioned the soundness of his decision.[124] The congregation at St. John's was divided in its response to the situation. Several incensed individuals drew up and circulated a petition to be sent to the Queen, calling for a thorough reform of the canonical defects of the Church, its discipline, its formularies, and its services.[125] Perhaps most threatening of all was the possibility that Noel, like James Shore, might be prosecuted in the ecclesiastical courts if he attempted to preach or officiate outside the confines of the Established Church.[126]

Thomas Dealtry, the Archdeacon of Calcutta, was then in England on furlough and consented to officiate temporarily at St. John's. To help stabilize the chapel's spiritual life, he quickly stepped in and admonished the congregation to hold fast to the Church[127]—a plea which seemed to persuade many to remain at their posts.[128] Shortly thereafter, Noel formally inquired of Blomfield about the likelihood of his being prosecuted for officiating outside the Church, informing him that he now regarded himself to be a Dissenter, that he had so registered before a magistrate, that he had recently preached for Thomas Binney—and had received communion—at the Weigh House Chapel.[129] He remained ready to do 'any other proper and lawful act' which Blomfield might suggest by which he could publicly declare his dissent; however, his Lordship should understand that he had no intention of ceasing to be a minister, nor to preach. If the canon

[124] MS DE 1797/1 No. 102/6, Leicester County RO.

[125] The *Record*, 5 Feb. 1849.

[126] A violation of the 76th canon—the same grounds then being employed by Phillpotts to prosecute James Shore in the ecclesiastical courts. See Chapter 9.

[127] The *Pulpit*, 54: 486. Dealtry (1796–1861) returned to India in the following year and subsequently became Bishop of Madras.

[128] Bateman, *Life of Daniel Wilson*, ii.184, has suggested that only around twenty members of St. John's seceded with Noel. John Dix, *Pulpit Portraits*, 82, characterized it as 'a considerable number'. In either case, it appears that a wholesale secession of the large congregation into evangelical Dissent did not occur.

[129] B. W. Noel, *A Letter to the Bishop of London on the Clergy Relief Bill* (1849), 1; *ER* (1849), 782.

restricting such activity remained in force, he would rather suffer any length of imprisonment for preaching the Gospel than purchase an exemption, either by declaring that he was no minister, or by ceasing to preach.[130] It is not known whether Blomfield ever replied to this appeal.

I

In the final days of 1848, Noel published one of the most detailed and impassioned attacks ever made upon the Church of England and its civil connection, his *Essay on the Union of Church and State.*[131] Despite its wordiness and numerous repetitions, its timing and sensational publicity—aided by Noel's popularity—ensured a complete sell-out of the first edition on the day of publication.[132] Noel clearly intended his *Essay* to be an Evangelical manifesto on the Church and its Established position. It was divided into three parts dealing with the principles of the union of Church and State, the effects of that union, and the most advantageous means of promoting a national religious revival. Its arguments focused on two primary questions: does Scripture sanction the Church's connection with a secular State?, and does it allow clergy to be supported and supervised by the civil powers?[133]

Noel condemned the Church's civil connection as opposed by Scripture, by the constitution, and by utility.[134] An ethically mixed Parliament, composed of men of 'high principle or of no principle', was unfit to rule upon the spiritual affairs of the nation. To entrust such responsibility to this secular body was a dangerous bonding of the church with the world.[135] Noel now regarded the civil maintenance of clergy as a violation of Scripture. He dismissed Royal Supremacy as unprincipled, absurd, and mischievous, and he rounded on the patronage system which trampled down the rights of the churches in the choice of pastors, permitting the ungodly to nominate the ungodly.[136]

Noel also blamed the legally constituted formulae of the

[130] Noel, *A Letter to the Bishop of London on the Clergy Relief Bill*, 1–2.

[131] It appeared during the same month as Macaulay's famous *History of England*, the *Glasgow Post* claiming that 'their respective works have been more extensively read, and . . . more rapidly sold, than those perhaps of any living author.' See the *Baptist Reporter* (1849), 340; the *Church and State Gazette*, 3 Jan. 1849, 3.

[132] 'A Presbyter', *An Examination of the 'Record's' Twelve Articles on Mr Noel's Work* (1849), 10.

[133] B. W. Noel, *Essay on the Union of Church and State* (1848), 10.

[134] Ibid. 13. [135] Ibid. 20, 24. [136] Ibid. 94–5, 180, 239, 250.

Church of England for the continuation of numerous 'unsound' doctrines. Among these was the practice of infant baptism, which he now saw as opposed by Scripture; the doctrine of baptismal regeneration, which he now believed was endorsed by the Prayer Book and required of all the clergy; and the service of holy communion, which vitiated Anglican claims to purity because it allowed reprobates to gain access to the sacrament of communion.[137] Noel not only conceded that Bishop Phillpotts was correct in his interpretation of the sixteenth and twenty-seventh Articles on baptism, but—and even more surprisingly—he blamed the Anglican Reformers for misapprehending the true nature of baptism.[138]

The Church's civil connection, Noel concluded, condemned by reason and religion, by Scripture and experience, was doomed. Why should it be allowed to continue to injure the nation? Its main principles were unsound; worst of all, it grieved and quenched the Spirit.[139] Citing authorities on both side of the issue, Noel predicted that disestablishment would bring great improvement in the spiritual life of the nation, and make England the foremost of all states in godliness and virtue.[140]

II

The appearance of Noel's *Essay* produced a predictable response from the various religious parties of the day. Tractarians and staunch churchmen denounced its disloyalty and 'unsound' ecclesiology. Evangelicals, though often sympathetic to its author and to many of his arguments, objected to his call for disestablishment and to the end of State maintenance of the clergy. Dissenters and Liberationists, most of whom agreed with many (if not all) of Noel's arguments, rejoiced at the capture of such a celebrated and titled seceder to their cause.

The most frantic response came from High Churchmen, especially from their organ, the *Church and State Gazette*, which regarded Noel's praise for Nonconformity as an acceptance of the principles of the regicide fanatics of the Commonwealth.[141] The *Christian Remembrancer* saw Noel's secession in more contemporary

[137] Ibid. 207–8, 439–40, 487. [138] Ibid. 439. [139] Ibid. 627–8.

[140] Ibid. 628–9. In support of establishment were Hooker, Warburton, Chalmers, McNeile, Gladstone, and Birks; opposed were Dick, Graham, Ballantyne, Conder, Wardlaw, Vinet, and Gasparin.

[141] The *Church and State Gazette*, 2 Mar. 1849, 125.

political terms as a great encouragement to Chartist democrats.[142] The *English Churchman* affected to welcome his departure: it would show the remainder of his Evangelical colleagues that their position in the Church was equally untenable and, with luck, encourage them to secede with him *en bloc*, leaving the Church of England to the real Anglicans.[143]

Many Evangelicals were understandably deeply perturbed by the defection of one of their best-known and most talented leaders. Thomas Byrth, the Evangelical rector of Wallasey, Cheshire, responded with 'unmixed grief that so able a champion of truth should have forfeited his vantage ground, and paralysed his future influence for good.'[144] At the same time, there was a certain ambivalence to their reactions: though loyal to the Church they often conceded that it was in dire need of reform, and they were as anxious as Noel about the threat from Tractarianism and the Church's perceived 'Romeward' drift. Two obscure ultra-Protestants were able to fit the episode into the time-honoured mythology of the Jesuit conspiracy, claiming that Noel was in fact a Jesuit in disguise, bent on the internal subversion of the Church of England.[145] Others tried to rebut his criticisms of the Church, like Tilson Marsh (son of William 'Millennial' Marsh), who defended the principle of establishment by Old Testament precedent.[146] The *Record* put on a brave face, and declared magisterially that Noel's secession was 'probably not a subject of regret', but rather diminished the force of this assertion by publishing no less than twelve articles denouncing his unsoundness and defending the Church's civil connection.[147] The *Christian Observer* simply ignored the whole matter, refusing either to mention the occurrence of his secession or issue a review of his *Essay*.

Noel received a number of personal appeals from Evangelicals urging him to reconsider his decision. One, from a friend of his older brother Gerard, expressed deep grief over his secession and stressed the gap which it had left in the front ranks of the Evangelical defence:

[142] The *Christian Remembrancer* (1849), 298. [143] *Non*, 20 Dec. 1848, 966.

[144] G. A. Moncreiff, *Remains of Thomas Byrth* (1851), 167–8.

[145] John Teodor and Dobrogost DeChylinski, *The Misfortunes of B. W. Noel* (1851), 3.

[146] W. Tilson Marsh, *The Church and the State* (1849).

[147] The *Record*, 13 Aug. 1849; 28 Dec. 1848–5 Feb. 1849. See also 'A Presbyter', *An Examination of the 'Record's' Twelve Articles on Mr Noel's Work.*

I have always considered you as the most important member of the Evangelical . . . party, a party of uncalculated importance to stay the plague of ultra-high and Tractarian views and doctrines . . . Your popularity, your birth and high connections make the bishops afraid of you—they dare not silence you as they have done other men . . . God forbid that I should say anything against Dissenters—but what good can *you* do among them? And what can be your motives? . . . Is it because the Church is in bondage to the State? But what church is not in bondage? On this very ground alone . . . I am and will be a churchman . . . Be content . . . with that blessed liberty until He comes, and use the great talents and advantages He has given you in the position He has placed you . . . What you are going to do is just what the Tractarians wish. They always maintain . . . one extreme is sure to lead to Rome and the other to a wandering, unsettled path of Dissent.[148]

On learning of Noel's secession, the prominent Evangelical Edward Bickersteth immediately wrote an impassioned appeal to his old friend, urging reconsideration:

Oh my beloved Noel, how I have been destroyed by your letter to [Daniel] Wilson which he has shown me . . . I sympathize with your conflicts and . . . griefs . . . [however] I firmly believe you are leaving the scriptural for the unscriptural . . . and will . . . lay up many sorrows for yourself and others . . . led by you. I have directed Seely to send you Birks' *Christian State* . . . which has entirely convinced me that opposition to the union of Church and State . . . is anti-christian lawlessness and brings down God's wrath on a country. His answers to Vinet and Wardlaw are, in my views, conclusive.[149]

Bickersteth did not conceal his conviction that he saw Satan at work in Noel's secession. 'Most humbly, most earnestly, most affectionately' he urged Noel to pause and take counsel with his respected elders. Bickersteth had returned late the previous night from York and had been unable to sleep, with thoughts of Noel's secession continually racing through his mind. Pondering on the blow this would inflict upon 'vital religion' and the Evangelical Alliance, he described himself as entirely 'overwhelmed'.[150]

[148] Anon. to Noel, 2 Dec. 1848, MS DE 1797/1, No. 86, Leicestershire RO.

[149] Bickersteth to Noel, 17 Nov. 1848, MS DE 1797/1, No. 87, Leicester County RO. See also A. Vinet, *An Essay on the Profession of Personal Religious Conviction, and Upon the Separation of Church and State, Considered* (1843); Ralph Wardlaw, *National Church Establishments Examined* (1839).

[150] Bickersteth to Noel, 17 Nov. 1848, MS DE 1797/1, No. 87, Leicester County RO.

Elsewhere many Dissenting evangelicals greeted the news with more equanimity.[151] As the *Evangelical Magazine* dryly commented, 'secessions from the Establishment, in our day, have ceased to be matters of notoriety.' It was nevertheless pleased to report the adherence to Nonconformity of one of the leading Evangelicals of the period. The rise of Ritualism, it further advised, had compelled many churchmen to ponder 'the great lessons of the age,' and to look 'with a full and throbbing heart at what is passing around them'. 'Not a few', it hopefully concluded, 'are profoundly exercised as to the path of duty in reference to their ecclesiastical position.'[152] Excited Liberationists described Noel in more triumphant terms: he was the 'great ecclesiastical reformer of the nineteenth century', the 'modern Luther',[153] the 'solitary patriarch',[154] and even 'a martyr' to the cause of religious liberty,[155] although the *Nonconformist*, while acknowledging his secession as a great aid to its campaign,[156] dismissed his *Essay* in rather grudging terms as unoriginal and too impersonal.[157] Other Dissenters expressed bewilderment as to why it had taken Noel so long to abandon the Church. Some disapproved of his anti-paedobaptist leanings: Independents judged them to be provocative and doctrinally objectionable, and considered his entry into the baptismal controversy reckless.[158]

III

After taking leave of St. John's, Noel entered a period of self-imposed retirement. A few engagements were reluctantly agreed to, including a lecture before the YMCA,[159] an additional appearance on behalf of James Shore, and a sermon delivered at the

[151] The *Baptist Reporter*, Feb. 1849, 45.

[152] *EM* (1849), 61.

[153] *Non*, 24 Jan. 1849, 58.

[154] 'A Friend', *Religious Life in the Established Church* (1849), pp. x–xi.

[155] L. C. L. Brenton, 'A Sermon on Revelations XIV:13', 38, in *North British Review* (Nov. 1848–Feb. 1849), 350. See also *EM* (1849), 139; *BMag* (1849), 159.

[156] *Non*, 6 Dec. 1848, 929. See also the *Baptist Reporter*, Feb. 1849, 46.

[157] *Non*, 6 Dec. 1848; 28 Feb. 1849, 94, 157. Others complained that, although the work was very worthwhile, it was far too expensive. See *Non*, 3 Jan. 1849, 4; 10 Jan. 1849, 10; 24 Jan. 1849, 61; 31 Jan. 1849, 81; 7 Feb. 1849, 100.

[158] *BMag* (1849), 778; 'A Dissenter', 'Cautions to Clergymen Seceding from the Episcopal Church', in *BMag* (1850), 109.

[159] B. W. Noel, 'The Church and the World' (1849), in *Lectures Delivered Before the Young Men's Christian Association, 1848–49* (1849).

National Scots Church in Regent Square.[160] He also preached at the Weigh House Chapel,[161] before the London Missionary Society,[162] and, according to one source, was scheduled to preach at the Episcopal chapel in Gray's Inn Lane until Blomfield got word of it and issued a last-minute prohibition against Noel appearing in any pulpit in the diocese.[163]

During this time, public speculation continued to mount over the direction of Noel's future outside the Church. It was predicted that he would lease the Episcopal chapel in Gray's Inn Lane, either as an independent chapel, or in connection with one of the existing Dissenting denominations.[164] In early 1849 James Harington Evans, minister of the nearby John Street Chapel, offered Noel use of his chapel either on Sunday afternoons or on weekday evenings.[165] It was also predicted that he might continue at St. John's and take it out of the jurisdiction of the Church, even though such a move might be resisted by Daniel Wilson (the leaseholder), and Blomfield, who might be provoked into taking action against Noel in the ecclesiastical courts.

Perhaps as the result of the pending Gorham affair, Noel spent much of his time, post-secession, pondering the doctrine of baptism. Concluding that his own baptism had been invalid, he published a lengthy essay which attacked paedobaptism,[166] and submitted himself for rebaptism by immersion—along with thirteen others (many of them fellow seceders from St. John's)—at the nearby John Street Chapel on 9 August 1849.[167] His accompanying sermon denounced infant baptism as an abuse having no sanction in Scripture.[168] This event foreshadowed Noel's entrance into

[160] Clyde Binfield, *George Williams and the YMCA* (1973), 53. See also Boase, *Modern English Biography*, 1159.

[161] *Non*, 9 May 1849, 358.

[162] The *Record*, 17 May 1849.

[163] *Non*, 9 May 1849; 23 May 1849, 398.

[164] Ibid. 15 Aug. 1849, 639.

[165] James Joyce Evans, *Memoir and Remains of the Revd James Harington Evans* (1852), 385, 407.

[166] B. W. Noel, 'Essay on Christian Baptism', in *BMag* (Aug. 1849), 634–9; *EM* (Nov. 1849), 580–5. B. W. Noel, 'The Effects of Infant Baptism', in *BMag* (1849), 677–81, contains a strong argument for insisting on believers' baptism. See also *BMag* (1850), 293–5.

[167] B. W. Noel, 'Address of the Hon. and Revd B. W. Noel on the Occasion of His Baptism at John Street Chapel, August 9, 1849' (1849). The *Nonconformist* claimed that between 2,000 and 2,500 people were in attendance, and that many others were turned away for lack of seating. See *Non*, 15 Aug. 1849, 639.

[168] B. W. Noel, 'Address of the Hon. and Revd B. W. Noel on the Occasion of His Baptism at John Street Chapel, August 9, 1949', in the *Pulpit*, 56, 135–87. Adelphos, 'A Letter to the Hon. and Revd Baptist Noel', in *EM* (Sept. 1849), 476–8; the *British*

the Baptist ministry,[169] the most natural resting place for him and for many of his fellow seceders, whose decision to abandon the Church was often based precisely upon those doctrines about which Baptists were most concerned.[170] Later that same year, Noel was named the new minister at John Street Chapel—an establishment which, in 1818, had been built by another Anglican seceder, Henry Drummond, and had operated under the ministry of yet another seceder, James Harington Evans. Noel was inducted at the chapel in the following spring by James Sherman, Rowland Hill's successor at Surrey Chapel.[171]

Despite his rejection of the principle of establishment, Noel refused to become a partisan of political Dissent. During the 1850s and 1860s, he declined either to join the Liberation Society or to appear on its platform.[172] He was not averse to giving support to overseas causes, however: during the American Civil War he vigorously supported the cause of the North, particularly at the great meeting at the Free Trade Hall, Manchester, in June 1863.[173] Two years later, he published a pamphlet vindicating the conduct of G. W. Gordon, who was executed for participation in the Jamaica outbreak.[174] He was twice President of the Baptist Union, in 1855 and 1867.[175] In 1864, he defended the Evangelical clergy—especially Thomas Scott, Henry Martyn, and Charles Simeon, among others—from an attack by the celebrated Baptist preacher C. H. Spurgeon.[176]

Noel retired from John Street Chapel in 1869. In retirement he resided at Stanmore, Middlesex, preaching on Sunday mornings at the small independent chapel at Edgware.[177] In the evenings,

Banner, 26 Sept. 1849; Benjamin Hanbury, *My Baptized One: Thoughts for Thinking Parents* (1850); Anon., *The Views on Baptism of the Hon. and Revd Baptist W. Noel, M.A.* (Leeds, 1849).

[169] See Arthur Mursell, *Baptist W. Noel: A Tribute and a Memorial* (1873), 7.

[170] Thomas Binney, *The Great Gorham Case* (1850), 108.

[171] John Dix, *Pulpit Portraits*, 81; *BMag* (1850), 296.

[172] See Skeats and Miall, *History of the Free Churches of England*, 510–11. The authors criticize Noel's reluctance to join the Liberation Society, or become involved in the disestablishment campaign, as 'a very illogical and unsound conclusion'.

[173] See B. W. Noel, *Freedom and Slavery in the United States of America* (1863); *DNB*; the *Baptist Messenger* (1873), 56.

[174] See B. W. Noel, *The Case of W. Gordon, Esq.* (1866).

[175] A. C. Underwood, *A History of the English Baptists* (1947), 237–8.

[176] See B. W. Noel, *Letter to the Revd C. H. Spurgeon* (1864).

[177] Boase, *Modern English Biography*, 1159. William Brock, *Memorial Sermon for Baptist W. Noel* (1873).

however, he expressed his continued pan-evangelical convictions by attending services at the local parish church, on Wednesdays assisting the rector at lectures held at the Memorial Institute.[178] He remained healthy and active until shortly before his death on 19 January 1873.[179] Though St. John's, Bedford Row, continued its Evangelical ministry after Noel's secession, it never regained its prominence as a citadel of the 'Gospel party': the glory was departed; the large and influential congregation soon began to disperse and its various charitable institutions were broken up. In November 1856, the roof collapsed and the building was pulled down.[180]

IV

Noel's secession into Protestant Dissent aroused a response among Evangelicals similar to that excited by the secession of John Henry Newman to Rome among High Churchmen, barely three years earlier. Here again was a prominent churchman, the rising hope of his party, who found the *via media* of the Church of England profoundly unsatisfactory. His rejection of the secularizing Erastianism of the religious establishment, though based more on utilitarian than ecclesiological considerations, was in some ways parallel to that already voiced by some Tractarians, which was to find classic expression in Henry Edward Manning's principled exit from Anglicanism three years later.

Noel's departure, however, for all the sensation it caused at the time, led to no group exodus. Apart from several members of the St. John's congregation, only one other Evangelical clergyman appears to have followed Noel's example in abandoning the Church, the comparatively obscure John Dodson, of Cockerham, Lancashire (though he was also impelled by alarm at the progress of the Gorham affair).[181] Why was this? Noel, for all his talents and connections, was seen as something of an outsider by the *Christian Observer* moderates, possibly because of his Whig political leanings. His own refusal to make political capital out of his secession, and his decision to maintain a lower profile on the

[178] *Non*, 29 Jan. 1873, 112.

[179] He was buried in the parish cemetery at Stanmore.

[180] Bateman, *Life of Daniel Wilson*, ii.172; the *Baptist Messenger* (1873), 56.

[181] John Dodson, *Brief Reasons for Leaving the English Establishment* (1849); *Non*, 4 Apr. 1849, 260; 26 Dec. 1849, 1018.

national religious scene, may also have been factors. Moreover, Noel's withdrawal from the Church was an act of personal choice, not the outcome of a tyrannical act by an authoritarian Church or State. He seceded in a year of extraordinary social unrest (1848 was the year of the great Chartist demonstrations in London and a chain of violent Continental revolutions), when the fear of insurrection was acute. This period, most Evangelicals would have concluded, was no time to weaken the established institutions of Church and State: now the prudential arguments for a National Church as a guardian of social order seemed even more convincing than ever.

At the same time, Noel's secession and the publicity given to it contributed to the sense of acute unease which characterized Church–State relations in the mid- to late 1840s. No sooner had one issue arisen to perplex Evangelicals than it was followed by another. Soon after the crisis over Maynooth came that of the Gorham affair. While the impact of the Gorham case on Evangelicalism in general was huge, its influence upon Noel and his decision to secede remains an open question.[182] As early as 1844, an anonymous author, commenting on the growing polarization between Tractarians and Evangelicals, warned that Noel (a particularly embattled opponent of the Oxford Movement) would, with several other prominent Evangelicals, 'openly repudiate all connexion with the Church of England if the High Church principles prevailed'.[183] Surprisingly, during the slow progress of the Gorham case through the courts, Noel made no direct reference to it in any of his numerous publications. In 1848, while brooding over his future in the Church, he came to concur with Phillpotts that the Prayer Book did in fact sanction baptismal regeneration—a conclusion that might have sealed his decision to secede.[184] On the other hand, at the time Noel would have been

[182] Noel's obituarist suggested that his secession was produced by the Gorham affair. See *The Times*, 21 Jan. 1873, 8. This point was later advanced in the *DNB* and in a number of other accounts, including, Horne, *Nonconformity in the XIX Century*, 123–4; Evelyn R. Garratt (ed.), *Life and Personal Recollections of Samuel Garratt* (1908), 220; Lady Norah Bentinck, *My Wanderings and Memories*, 2nd edn. (1924), 94; T. Pinney (ed.), *The Letters of T. B. Macaulay* (1974–81), i.141 n; Lewis, *Lighten their Darkness*, 183. Other accounts, however, have offered alternative reasons. See Elliott-Binns, *Religion in the Victorian Era*, 462; *Non*, 22 Nov. 1848, 895; 6 Dec. 1848, 928.

[183] MS 'The Principal Clergy of London', MS Add c.290, Bod.

[184] Noel, *Essay on the Union of Church and State*, 439–40.

unaware of the final outcome of the Gorham case, since the judgment of the Judicial Committee of the Privy Council was not delivered until some fifteen months after his secession.[185] It is therefore likely that the Gorham crisis was only one of a number of pressures which determined Noel's decision to abandon the ministry of the Church of England.

The case of James Shore (discussed below) was perhaps equally influential. Shore, a seceding clergyman, had been prosecuted by Bishop Phillpotts for seceding from the Church and officiating in a Dissenting chapel, and had been imprisoned. So enthusiastic were Noel's denunciations of Phillpotts's behaviour at a public rally at Exeter Hall, London, that, on 19 April 1848, Blomfield wrote prohibiting him from attending public meetings or from speaking publicly on Shore's behalf. 'Whatever your opinion on Mr Shore's case might be,' the bishop firmly stated, '*that* was not a proper place to express it.'[186] Noel responded by writing to the chairman of Shore's London Committee, explaining what had happened and offering his support to their motion condemning Phillpotts's prosecution of Shore. He objected to all laws exposing clergymen to imprisonment for seceding, for these were contrary to the Toleration Act, unchristian, and unconstitutional, and ought immediately to be repealed.[187] This curb of Noel's free speech by his diocesan, and the claim that clergymen cannot renounce their clerical orders, undoubtedly strengthened his growing sense of resolve to secede from the Church. Although Shore's imprisonment did not occur until some months after Noel's secession, the sensational publicity which surrounded his case—like that of the Gorham case—ensured that its influence upon Noel's decision to seek out 'greener' ecclesiastical pastures was substantial.[188]

V

While Noel's personal crisis was reaching a climax, a far graver issue was emerging which would severely test Evangelical loyalty

[185] Judgment of the Court of Arches, in favour of Phillpotts, was rendered on 2 Aug. 1849. This was appealed by Gorham to the Judicial Committee of the Privy Council and its judgment, made in favour of Gorham, was rendered on 8 Mar. 1850.

[186] MSS 'Blomfield Papers', 59, ff 84v, Lambeth Palace Library.

[187] *Non*, 19 Apr. 1848, 269. Blomfield had also banned George Mortimer, headmaster of the City of London School, from attending the same meeting.

[188] Shore was imprisoned on 9 Mar. 1849.

to the Establishment before a more or less satisfactory resolution could be worked out: the Gorham case. While Noel's was a lonely secession, the Gorham affair seemed to some anxious churchmen, at least for a time, to threaten a mass exodus of Evangelical clergymen from the Church of England in a kind of English version of the Scottish Disruption. The crisis was exacerbated by its coincidence with another Evangelical *cause célèbre*, the secession of James Shore.

The stages of the Gorham affair are well known, and can be briefly summarized.[189] The controversy arose over the refusal of Bishop Phillpotts to institute the Revd George Cornelius Gorham to the living of Bramford Speke, outside Exeter. Gorham was an Evangelical of considerable intellectual ability and a former fellow of Queens' College, Cambridge. Prior to his ordination in 1811, Thomas Draper, the Bishop of Ely, had threatened to disqualify him on the grounds of his 'unsound' views on the doctrine of baptismal regeneration, but when Gorham challenged the bishop, nothing came of it. In 1846, Lord Lyndhurst presented Gorham to the wealthy benefice of St. Just, Penwith, Cornwall, where he was subsequently instituted, without incident, by Bishop Phillpotts.[190]

The relationship between the two men was quickly soured, however, when Gorham placed an advertisement in the *Ecclesiastical Gazette* for a curate who was 'free from all tendency to what is well understood by the term Tractarian error'.[191] The wording of this advertisement was regarded by Phillpotts as not only provocative, but as a sign of possible doctrinal 'unsoundness', and he summoned the prospective curate for an examination in order to determine his catholic orthodoxy. When Gorham was presented by Sir Charles Cottenham, the Lord Chancellor, to the Crown living of Bramford Speke in the following year, Phillpotts hesitated, eventually subjecting Gorham to a gruelling written and oral examination on the doctrine of baptismal regeneration.[192] As a result, Gorham was judged by Phillpotts as unfit to be instituted, by reason of his holding doctrines 'contrary to the true Christian

[189] See Nias, *Gorham and the Bishop of Exeter.*

[190] *DNB.*

[191] G. C. B. Davies, *Henry Phillpotts Bishop of Exeter, 1778–1869* (1954), 231; Nias, *Gorham and the Bishop of Exeter*, 7.

[192] They were held, on and off, from 17 Dec. 1847 until 10 Mar. 1848, and comprised some fifty-two hours of actual examination. See Nias, *Gorham and the Bishop of Exeter*, 11; *DNB.*

faith' and opposed to those contained in the Church's Articles and formularies.[193]

Unwilling to accept the verdict of Bishop Phillpotts, Gorham initiated legal proceedings in the ecclesiastical courts.[194] It was always highly probable that the case, whatever the initial ruling of the Court of Arches, would proceed on final appeal to the Judicial Committee of the Privy Council. The likelihood of an episcopal victory here appeared not only to presage the imposition of the doctrine of baptismal regeneration upon all 'Gospel clergymen', but a split in the Church along Protestant–Catholic lines.[195] It seemed to many that if Phillpotts were upheld, it would mark the end of the tradition of doctrinal inclusiveness which had allowed different parties—Evangelical, Broad, and High Church—to coexist in the same Establishment. To Evangelicals a victory for Phillpotts would have suggested an official disavowal of the doctrine of the Protestant Reformers and the plain, literal construction of the Thirty-Nine Articles which was the basis of their teaching. It would amount to a decisive victory for High Churchmen and Tractarians.

It was feared that the effects of such changes in the nature of the Church would have enormous repercussions, including the likelihood of Evangelicals being refused ordination in a number of dioceses, such as Peterborough where Bishop Marsh had once terrorized Evangelicals with his notorious 'eighty-seven questions', or Bath and Wells where the bishop's examining chaplain had recently rejected at least one Evangelical as the result of his 'unsound' views on the doctrine of baptism.[196] Equally, it might result in Evangelical clergymen being refused installation by High Church bishops, giving *carte blanche* to men like Phillpotts who already boasted of his success in weeding out Evangelicals from his diocese.[197] These fears were heightened at a critical moment by the appearance of a well-publicized sermon delivered at St.

[193] Nias, *Gorham and the Bishop of Exeter*, 44.

[194] Ibid. 45–59.

[195] The case was filed by Gorham in June 1848, with the final appeal of Phillpotts not being settled until around Aug. 1850.

[196] See the *Record*, 14 June 1849.

[197] See ibid., 4 May 1848; 8 Jan. 1849. On 28 Dec. 1848, the *Record* claimed that while Phillpotts had appointed many Tractarians in his diocese, 'a considerable number' of Evangelicals, already serving in Devon and Cornwall, had been rejected by the Bishop 'as unfit to receive institution or license, "by reason", as his Lordship has alleged, "of their holding doctrines contrary to the true Christian faith"'.

Mary's, Totnes, by William Maskell, Phillpotts's domestic chaplain, who condemned the Evangelical party for its 'guilty inconsistency', and admonished its members in the strongest language to follow the example of the two thousand Nonconformists who, under similar circumstances during the reign of Charles II, had been compelled to abandon their positions in the Church.[198] The comments accompanying the account of the sermon in the *Record* indicate that many Evangelicals took it for granted that Maskell was simply parroting Phillpotts's own views on the subject. Consequently, a growing sense of polarization between various Church parties took hold. Evangelicals began to fear that they would be pushed out of the diocese of Exeter and the Church itself by a new, aggressive, and Tractarian-inspired High Churchmanship.[199] It was Phillpotts—far more than Noel and the other seceders—whom many Evangelicals charged with promoting the deadly sin of schism and undermining the foundations of Anglicanism.[200]

Seen in this perspective, the Gorham affair was in part a debate over the imposition of an unacceptable, popish doctrine: as Gorham wrote to a friend, my 'simple object in this contest has been, to resist the attempt to fix a popish sense on our Articles and liturgy—to make a Christian ordinance, (of beautiful simplicity), a superstitious charm.'[201] It was also a debate over the issue of a bishop's right—legal or moral—to demand from ordinands or clergy a double subscription relative to the two offices of baptism (or other points of doctrine): a simple subscription to the offices contained within the formularies, and a subscription to a private, episcopal, construction of that particular doctrine.[202] Did Phillpotts have the right, upon the strength of the thirty-ninth canon, to require not only an honest assent from Gorham to the Articles and Prayer Book, but to demand a further assent to the construction of certain portions of them based on his own private interpretation? If the ecclesiastical courts ruled that he indeed held such a right, it would not be a victory for the simple

[198] This sermon was delivered on 11 Aug. 1848, just nine days after pronouncement of the judgment of the Court of Arches against Gorham. See the *Record*, 28 Aug. 1848.

[199] Garratt, *Life of Samuel Garratt*, 219–20.

[200] R. W. Needham, *The Church and the Synod* (1851), 6.

[201] Gorham to a friend, 15 Jan. 1851, MSS Phillips-Robinson, c.515, 60–2, Bod.

[202] G. S. Faber, *Notes on the Gorham Case*, *c*.1850, MSS Eng. Litt d.142 157–8, Bod. See also *CO* (1849), 648, 822.

exposition of a particular dogma but a virtual end to the Church's comprehensiveness.

VI

The effects of the Gorham case on the Evangelical party and its relationship with the Church of England are difficult to assess. Though several studies have addressed this issue, a number of important questions remain.[203] Were Gorham's views on baptism representative of those held by the majority of the Evangelical clergy? What were Gorham's own views on the case as it progressed through the courts? What level of support did Gorham receive from his own party, and did he consider this to be sufficient? Perhaps most importantly, would the denial of Gorham's appeal by the Judicial Committee of the Privy Council have provoked a major Evangelical schism from the Church of England, similar to that which had recently occurred north of the Border in the Scottish Disruption?

During his prolonged examination by Phillpotts, Gorham consistently defined baptism in terms of the central importance of the doctrine of justification by faith. While assenting to the 'just and favourable' construction of the Articles, he insisted that they must be defined by means of their consistency with Scripture, by their comparison with other passages from the Church's formularies, and by the general view of those by whom the liturgy was reformed and the Articles written.[204] In support of this, he quoted passages from the Articles, concluding: 'Such is the doctrine of the church on the efficacy of both sacraments, and therefore of baptism—where there is no worthy reception, there is no bestowment of grace.' Thus, the Church's declaration on the regeneration of each infant was hypothetical, since no other construction would reconcile the liturgy and the Articles.[205]

As Clyde Ervine and Peter Nockles have shown, though Evangelicals were united in rejecting a mechanical *ex opere operato* theory of regeneration in baptism, they differed among themselves on

[203] Most notably Nias, *Gorham and the Bishop of Exeter*, 134–41; Davies, *Henry Phillpotts Bishop of Exeter, 1778–1869*, 230–63, 370, 390; Peter Toon, *Evangelical Theology, 1833–56* (1979), 86–94; Lewis, *Lighten their Darkness*, 183–7.

[204] Nias, *Gorham and the Bishop of Exeter*, 12–17.

[205] Davies, *Henry Phillpotts Bishop of Exeter, 1778–1869*, 233–4.

the nature of the sacrament and its efficacy.[206] The moderate Evangelical position on regeneration had emerged into full view in the wake of the Western Schism in 1815. Now recalled with alacrity by many of the 'serious clergy', it was led by John Bird Sumner who, in that year, published a treatise *Apostolic Preaching Considered* which accepted a modified view of baptismal regeneration.[207] He directed his attack not on High Church theories of baptismal regeneration, as advanced by Richard Mant in his provocative 1812 Bampton Lectures, and by bishops such as Thomas Wilson, but against the 'high doctrine of strictly Calvinistic preaching' which was being advocated by the Western Schismatics.[208] At the height of the Gorham crisis, Sumner's views were taken up by supporters of the High Church theory of baptismal regeneration. In response, Sumner (now Archbishop of Canterbury) quickly published a revised edition of his work which attempted to establish its Protestant credentials.[209] He rejected the extreme Calvinistic denial of baptismal regeneration, and insisted (claiming to base his theory on the authority of the Elizabethan divines) that the grace of spiritual regeneration could often be separated from the sacrament of baptism.[210] Although he did not accept Gorham's covenant theology, which argued that God bestowed on an infant an antecedent or prevenient grace separate from the rite of baptism itself, he defended the orthodoxy of Gorham's position; after all it had been maintained by some of the Church's 'worthiest members' such as Bullinger and Usher and was a matter about which 'Scripture does not speak definitively'.[211] In 1859, Sumner published another work, *Practical Reflections on Select Passages of the New Testament*, which argued that a mere reception of the sacrament did not confer grace. An individual may be, he complained 'as it is to be feared many are' baptized,

[206] W. J. C. Ervine, 'Doctrine and Diplomacy: Some Aspects of the Life and Thought of the Anglican Evangelical Clergy, 1797 to 1837', Ph.D. thesis (Cambridge, 1979), 72; Peter Nockles, *The Oxford Movement in Context* (Cambridge, 1994), 229–35.

[207] See Chapter 4. J. B. Sumner, *Apostolic Preaching Considered, in an Examination of St. Paul's Epistles* (1815).

[208] Ibid. 7.

[209] J. B. Sumner, *Apostolic Preaching Considered, in an Examination of St. Paul's Epistles*, 9th edn. (1850).

[210] Ibid., 'Preface', pp. iii–vii.

[211] Ibid., 'Preface', p. x; J. B. Sumner, *A Charge Delivered to the Clergy of the Diocese of Chester in 1849* (1849), 13; Nigel Scotland, *The Life and Work of John Bird Sumner* (Leominster, 1995), 87, 118–19.

but not regenerate.[212] Another moderate Evangelical view, also published in the aftermath of the Western Schism, was that of Daniel Wilson, the future Bishop of Calcutta, who agreed with Sumner that regeneration may occur in baptism, but insisted that the spiritual transformation of the soul was 'so much the more important part of the entire work.'[213] A further early contribution to the baptismal debate was that of Henry Ryder, the Bishop of Gloucester (later, Coventry and Lichfield), whose diocesan *Charge* of 1816 argued that regeneration was perfectly consonant with membership of a National Church like the Church of England:

> I would . . . wish generally to restrict that term [regeneration] to the baptismal privileges; and considering them as comprehending, not only an external admission into the visible church . . . not only a covenanted title to the pardon and grace of the Gospel . . . but even a degree of spiritual aid vouchsafed and ready to offer itself to our acceptance, or rejection, at the dawn of reason.[214]

Ryder here took a position beyond that held by Evangelicals like Simeon that the *seeds* of regenerating grace were given to an infant at baptism; consequently, the Church should cultivate these seeds, which had been planted in good works and spiritual graces, until they blossomed into conversion.[215] At the same time, Ryder warned that all baptized individuals should not be regarded as if they had undergone a true spiritual conversion, for baptism was not meant to 'soothe and delude the people into a false peace'.[216] This moderate Evangelical position was reinforced still further by William Goode, the well-known theological writer and sometime editor of the *Christian Observer*, who issued an important series of pamphlets during the Gorham crisis which supported the view that regeneration could occur in baptism, while insisting upon the conditions of faith and repentance for the efficacy of the sacrament (albeit not denying that infants might receive grace through it).[217] He allowed that, in some cases, regeneration and adoption

212 See J. B. Sumner, *Practical Reflections on Select Passages of the New Testament* (1859).
213 Daniel Wilson, *The Doctrine of Regeneration Practically Considered* (1817), 39–41.
214 Henry Ryder, *Charge to the Clergy of Gloucester* (Gloucester, 1816), 20.
215 Ervine, 'Doctrine and Diplomacy', 72.
216 Ryder, *Charge to the Clergy of Gloucester*, 21.
217 Nias, *Gorham and the Bishop of Exeter*, 152.

are 'formally made over, and in that sense given, in and by baptism'.[218] There were some Evangelicals, on the other hand, who appeared to deny any real efficacy to baptism. The *Record*, for example, defined baptism as an ordinance which is not 'for the first importation of grace, but for its increase and confirmation'.[219] While not entirely inconsistent, these differing expressions on baptism led to the Evangelicals being criticized by Nonconformists as holding indefinite views of an important Christian doctrine, and thus unable to take the lead in defending Protestant orthodoxy.[220]

During the course of Gorham's ordeal, it was clear that he was under no illusions as to the difficulty of the task which confronted him. A month before the commencement of his examination, for example, he wrote to his daughter:

> A great trial . . . is at hand for me, and for you all. It is inevitable, I think, that the bishop and I shall disagree on doctrine, and I think he will refuse to institute. My mind is *fully* made up for the crisis. And if he refuses, extensive law processes must follow—ruinous to me—and possibly he will try to eject me from St. Just. Be it so, if it be the will of God.[221]

In spite of the extent of his affliction, Gorham remained optimistic that he would ultimately be vindicated and instituted at Bramford Speke.[222] Perhaps ironically, it was only *after* his appeal was upheld by the Judicial Committee of the Privy Council that he began to abandon hope, for, perhaps worn down by the months of conflict, he began to fear that Phillpotts would find a way to exploit an obscure legal loophole and thus overturn the Privy Council's ruling. 'My institution is very uncertain,' he wrote to his daughter on 4 May 1850. 'I *expected* it to be this, or next week. But all depends on the success of the bishop's quirk about the *non*-jurisdiction of the Judicial Committee of the Privy Council—*if* he succeeds—then I stand condemned by the Articles; and my final *expulsion* from the Church is certain—for alteration is impossible—

[218] William Goode, *A Letter to the Bishop of Exeter* (1850); *The Doctrine of the Church of England as to the Effects of Baptism in the Case of Infants* (1849); *The Case of Archdeacon Wilberforce Compared with that of Mr Gorham* (1854); *CO* (1849), 831.

[219] The *Record*, 10 Sept. 1849.

[220] See Binney, *The Great Gorham Case*, p. vii.

[221] Gorham to his daughter, 17 Nov. 1847, in 'Gorham Letters', MS Eng. Litt d.142 48, Bod.

[222] Gorham to anon., 15 Feb. 1848, in 'Gorham Letters', MS Eng. Litt d.142 55, Bod.

I will', he added, 'under no circumstances avow my belief in the abominable doctrines which it is attempted to enforce.'[223] During this interlude, a number of Gorham's friends and supporters also began to express a similar concern. As his close Evangelical confederate John Rashdall speculated fearfully in his diary, Gorham 'will never be instituted'.[224]

During the long months of battle, Gorham came to resent the reluctance of many Evangelicals publicly or privately to support his position. 'How sad it is', he wrote to Sir Thomas Phillips on 15 January 1851, 'that among the clergy we have so few men of *nerve*, resolution, and wisdom, on the right side of the [baptism] question. I felt myself left all but alone in the great struggle, *until* there seemed to be a first-feel of success.'[225] This was perhaps an overreaction brought about by his emotional state, for Gorham had been the beneficiary of a tireless and influential London Committee which not only underwrote his substantial legal expenses (presenting him with a silver tea service from the balance), but also orchestrated a highly successful campaign which kept his case in the forefront of public attention throughout its long course.[226]

Nevertheless, it must be admitted that Evangelical support for Gorham was not all it might have been. This hesitancy in opposing the decision of the spiritual courts may have reflected the party's natural disinclination to 'appeal unto Caesar', its assurance of the rightness of its cause, its confidence that Providence would look after the outcome, and its weariness at fighting so many serious ecclesiastical 'fires' at the same time.[227] Even more likely, it reflected the complex and confused ecclesiological position in which the various Church–State conflicts had placed the Evangelicals, for their Erastianism naturally encouraged obedience to the decisions of the Privy Council as the highest ecclesiastical authority in the land. When Liberal and High Churchmen at first began to press for the revival of Convocation (ensuring that ecclesiastical disputes be settled by an ecclesiastical body), they received

[223] Gorham to his daughter, 4 May 1850, in 'Gorham Letters', MS Eng. Litt d.142 70, Bod.

[224] 'Diary of John Rashdall', 10 Apr. 1850, MSS Eng. Misc. e.351–60, Bod.

[225] MSS Phillips-Robinson, c.514, 60–62, Bod.

[226] See letter of 19 Jan. 1848, describing the meeting of some 100 Evangelical clergy at Daniel Wilson's in London, in support of his case. MS Eng. Litt d.142 51, Bod; *DNB*.

[227] Garratt, *Life of Samuel Garratt*, 222.

the support of a number of Evangelicals, including Noel. As Tractarianism continued to gain ascendancy, however, many Evangelicals began openly to oppose the idea of a revived Convocation. John Sinclair, the moderate Evangelical Archdeacon of Middlesex, protested that the Church's numerous blessings could well be lost if subjected to the caprice of a national clerical Synod.[228] Likewise James Garbett, the Evangelical Archdeacon of Chichester, who urged that it would be better to persist with the present system, thus preserving the Church from even more internal strife and disruption. But Evangelicals remained divided on the subject.[229] In any case, it was now impossible to ignore the increased influence of the Anglican laity and organize (as High Churchmen advocated) an exclusively clerical Synod.[230] Hugh McNeile, the fiery Evangelical perpetual curate of St. Jude's, Liverpool, also wished to keep spiritual judgements in the hands of the temporal powers, so as to avoid the possibility of adjudication favourable to Tractarians.[231] The *Record*, which encouraged Parliament to continue the plenary exercise of Royal Supremacy as the only means of preserving in the Church the doctrines of the Reformation, steadfastly opposed the revival of Convocation.[232] Surprisingly, the *Christian Observer* expressed approval of Phillpotts's course, for it had brought the question of baptismal regeneration into the open and thus put a stop to attempts by other bishops to enforce their own *private views* as to the standard of doctrine in the Church.[233] But some Evangelicals were deeply perturbed by such talk.[234]

One of the most important questions remaining in the wake of the Gorham affair is whether a decision by the Privy Council upholding Phillpotts's position would have led to a major Evangelical disruption (and exodus) from the Church? The denial of Gorham's appeal would have compelled the Evangelicals to

[228] John Sinclair, *Synodal Action in the Church Unreasonable and Perilous* (1852).

[229] R. W. Needham, the Evangelical incumbent of St. Paul's, Stonehouse, Devon, argued that the revival of Synod would be the best method of preserving the church. See Needham, *The Church and the Synod*.

[230] See James Garbett, *Diocesan Synods and Convocation* (1852).

[231] Hugh McNeile, *The Royal Supremacy Discussed in a Correspondence Between Archdeacon [Robert] Wilberforce and the Revd Hugh McNeile* (1850), 6–44.

[232] The *Record*, 16 Sept., 14 Oct., 15 Nov. 1850; 8 Nov. 1852.

[233] *CO* (1848), 573–4.

[234] See Garratt, *Life of Samuel Garratt*, 221.

choose between one or more distinct options. An appeal to a higher court, especially the House of Lords, was one possibility, although Lord John Russell had advised Gorham against taking such a step as early as January 1848.[235] Another option was to remain within the Church and to continue to labour for the extension of those Reformation principles which had formed the basis of the party.[236] Clearly, many Evangelicals who had determined to remain, no matter what, were busy framing excuses for themselves after the appearance of Sir Herbert Jenner Fust's unfavorable ruling in the Court of Arches in August 1849.[237] One such individual wrote to the *Record* claiming that, had the decision of the Court of Arches occurred forty to fifty years ago, it might have done 'immense mischief' to the Church and the Evangelical party, but not today. The Evangelicals were now too numerous and too well established for that to occur.[238] A third option was mass secession.[239] The *Record* itself was adamant in opposing any suggestion of an Evangelical disruption in the Church: all the Tractarians could gain by a victory, it claimed, would be 'the nominal establishment of an inoperative test', for beside Phillpotts few other bishops would enforce such a policy.[240] Evangelicals were aware that if one or two implacably hostile eccentrics like Marsh and Phillpotts were produced by the episcopate, there were far more bishops who showed no opposition to the ordination (or institution) of Evangelical clergy. After all, things could not be entirely bad when a 'Gospel clergyman' like John Bird Sumner was Archbishop of Canterbury.[241] With one exception, all the letters in the *Record* published on this question were in favour of remaining in the Church.[242] To abandon it in its greatest hour of need was widely regarded as the most serious injury which could possibly be inflicted—mass secession was wholly unnecessary and unjustified; little more than the fulfilment of the Tractarians' deepest ambitions.[243] Edward Bickersteth took up this theme, urging his fellow brethren to remain at their posts 'and help faithful men in it, while there is any hope of remedying so great an evil, in their

[235] Russell to Gorham, 22 Jan. 1848, in MS Eng. Litt. d.307 112, Bod.

[236] 'Another Clergyman', *Is a Decision of the Privy Council a Reason for Secession? A Letter to a Clergyman of the Evangelical School* (1850).

[237] Garratt, *Life of Samuel Garratt*, 221.

[238] The *Record*, 13 Aug. 1849.

[239] See Toon, *Evangelical Theology*, 90.

[240] The *Record*, 13 Aug., 8 Oct. 1849.

[241] Lewis, *Lighten their Darkness*, 183–4.

[242] Ibid. 184.

[243] The *Record*, 17, 24 Sept. 1849.

struggle to withstand error, and uphold the true faith of Christ in our church'.[244] Lord Shaftesbury, who would have been at the forefront of opinion had any such disruption taken place, was even more forthright: 'whoever talks of secession', he wrote, 'is a traitor.'[245]

Not all members of the party shared such a view, however, at least in the early stages of the affair. The *Christian Observer* was so alarmed by Jenner Fust's decision that it declared: 'we believe no such crisis has occurred in our Church for at least two centuries.'[246] While hopeful that the Privy Council would eventually vindicate Gorham, it warned in no uncertain terms that a victory for Phillpotts would likely result in 'as complete a disruption' as that which had recently occurred in Scotland.[247] William Goode, who served for many years as its editor, warned Phillpotts in a separate published letter that the Evangelicals would simply withdraw from the Church if his doctrine of baptism was made authoritative.[248] Phillpotts, no doubt, anticipated this. John Rashdall confirmed Goode's views, claiming that if the decision was not reversed, 'it [might] lead to a great schism'.[249] A letter published by the *Record* warned that 'many Evangelicals and sound churchmen' have decided that they will secede if Jenner Fust is upheld.[250] Even the Nonconformist *Evangelical Magazine* recognized that the decision of the Court of Arches was 'an event of stirring interest to the entire religious community of this country'.[251] It cautioned that the Evangelical clergy 'may not be able to keep their present status', and asked: 'they may be called, for the sake of conscience, to suffer the loss of all things; but can they hesitate, for a moment, if the alternative shall be that they must either quit the Establishment, or teach that baptism is *spiritual regeneration*?'[252]

When the ruling of the Judicial Committee was finally issued, there was much relief in the Evangelical camp. The Broad Churchman J. C. Hare, Archdeacon of Lewis, claimed that it had prevented the secession of 'a very large proportion' of the Evangelical clergy, which would have left the Church in the complete

[244] Ibid. 10 Dec. 1849.
[245] Garratt, *Life of Samuel Garratt*, 221.
[246] *CO* (1849), 809–56.
[247] Ibid., (1850), 72, 140, 289.
[248] Goode, *A Letter to the Bishop of Exeter*, 95–6.
[249] 'Diary of John Rashdall', 2 Aug. 1849, MSS Eng. Misc. e.351–60, Bod.
[250] The *Record*, 24 Sept. 1849.
[251] *EM* (Sept. 1849), 461.
[252] Ibid. 462.

control of the Tractarians.[253] Despite this apparent victory, some Evangelicals remained uncertain of their future in the Church. John Venn, of St. Peter's, Hereford, and son of the famous Evangelical rector of Clapham, was one of those who seriously considered seceding at the time, but was persuaded by his brother to reconsider.[254] Several others, however, were now beyond the point of reconsideration. Unconvinced of the Church's commitment to the Reformation formulae, they seceded *after* the favourable ruling of the Privy Council had been issued, among them Charles Chapman, chaplain of Tresco and Breyer in the Scilly Isles, who denounced baptismal regeneration as 'a monstrous error' which still remains 'unequivocally' set forth as the doctrine of the Church;[255] and T. Tennison Cuffe, incumbent of Colney Heath, Hertfordshire, who expressed similar views.[256]

Despite Gorham's ultimate vindication by the Privy Council, his case left a deep imprint upon English Evangelicalism. It sharpened the party's awareness of its Reformation heritage and underscored its points of divergence with Tractarians.[257] It widened the divide between churchmen and Dissenters, for in securing the Evangelicals for the Church it robbed the Liberationist campaign of valuable potential allies in the cause of disestablishment. Most important of all, the decision of the Judicial Committee, by affirming the Church's comprehensive nature, averted the distinct possibility of a major Evangelical disruption from its ranks. Although some Tractarians did secede as the result of the Gorham affair, they were so few in number that they did not constitute a serious threat to the Church's stability. All the same, if the Church's long-standing tradition of accommodation had been eroded by the ecclesiastical courts, and if sufficient numbers of bishops (like Phillpotts) had taken it upon themselves to insist firmly upon a private construction of the Articles and formularies, it is clear that the Church might not have survived in its historical form. This, of course, is highly speculative, for despite their agitation over the apparent Erastian nature of the final judgment,

[253] J. C. Hare, 'Archdeacon Hare's Letter to the Hon Richard Cavendish' (1850), in *Miscellaneous Pamphlets* (Cambridge, 1855), 4, 95.

[254] John Venn, *Annals of a Clerical Family* (1904), 201 n.

[255] Charles Chapman, 'Address Delivered at his Baptism', in *BMag* (1850), 480.

[256] See T. T. Cuffe, *Reasons for Secession: Or, Objections to Remaining in the Established Church* (1851).

[257] See Lewis, *Lighten their Darkness*, 186, 231.

some old-style High Churchmen like Archdeacon Churton were 'quite content' with it, as was Bishop Samuel Wilberforce, fearing that if Gorham had lost there would have been a enormous popular clamour in his favour.[258] But far larger issues were at stake than the doctrine of baptismal regeneration.[259] The victory for Gorham sent a message to Phillpotts and the episcopate that future attempts to impose a partisan construction of the Anglican formularies were unlikely to be accepted by the courts: the comprehensiveness of the Church was to be maintained. If the case contributed to the exacerbation of party conflict in the Church of England it may be that its long-term effect was, in a curious way, stabilizing, at least for Evangelicals, for after 1850 remarkably few clergymen seceded into Protestant Nonconformity. Perhaps this great crisis, by forcing Evangelicals to take stock of their relationship to the Established Church, had revealed to them the underlying strength of their commitment to it? Perhaps the revelation that the Judicial Committee of the Privy Council—and the Royal Supremacy which lay behind it—remained an important and abiding bulwark against High Church tyranny, was a revelation which pacified many troubled Evangelical consciences? In any case, the period which followed the Gorham crisis, although not entirely devoid of conflict, was characterized by a more eirenic and constructive relationship between the Evangelical party and the Church by law established.

[258] G. I. T. Machin, *Politics and the Churches in Great Britain 1832 to 1868* (Oxford, 1977), 205.

[259] See Needham, *The Church and the Synod*, 3; 'Diary of John Rashdall', 8 Mar. 1850, MSS Eng. Misc. e.351–60, Bod; J. Fowler, *Richard Waldo Sibthorp: A Biography* (1880), 103–4.

9
The Case of the Reverend James Shore

The Evangelical clergymen who seceded from the Church of England into Protestant Dissent during the first half of the nineteenth century often paid a considerable price for their action. By crossing the subtle social boundary between Anglican priesthood and Nonconformist ministry they forfeited status and often, no doubt, income. A number vanished into comparative obscurity as pastors of small chapels, whether as ministers of a major denomination, Strict and Particular Baptists, Christian Brethren, or preachers in some unlabelled and impoverished chapel. If not so severely penalized for their secession as many of their colleagues who went to Rome,[1] particularly those with wives for whom entry into the Roman priesthood was closed, they usually came off the worse in temporal terms for following the dictates of conscience. This, no doubt, they fully anticipated. What was not anticipated, however, was the imposition of a legal penalty for their act of secession. Though Anglican secessions to Rome or Dissent were not infrequent, their legality was apparently seldom, if ever, questioned. Liberal Churchmen like Theophilus Lindsey, who had abandoned the establishment for Unitarianism during the eighteenth century, had set up their chapels with impunity.[2] In 1831, as we have seen, the Evangelical William Tiptaft received a threat from Thomas Burgess, the Bishop of Salisbury, upon seceding from the parish of Sutton Courtenay, Berkshire, but nothing came of it.[3] Those who left the *via media* for Rome were assumed to be acting within the framework of the law when they took up a new ministry as priests of another episcopal confession. Though Anglican bishops deplored such secessions in private or in public, they

[1] See P. A. Adams, 'Converts to the Roman Catholic Church in England, circa 1830–70', B. Litt. thesis (Oxford, 1977).

[2] See Theophilus Lindsey, *The Apologia of Theophilus Lindsey* (1774).

[3] See William Tiptaft, *Two Letters Addressed to the Bishop of Salisbury* (Abingdon, 1832), 7; J. C. Philpot, *William Tiptaft*, 3rd edn. (Leicester, 1972), 67–73.

usually accepted them as *faits accomplis*. Those who departed from the Anglican communion were assumed to be misguided, but not in breach of the law.

This state of affairs was suddenly shattered in 1844, when an obscure Evangelical clergyman by the name of James Shore was imprisoned for attempting to secede from the Church and officiate in his own chapel as a Nonconformist minister.[4] This unprecedented prosecution at the hands of his diocesan was based upon an obscure and long-forgotten canon which appeared to block the path of any clergyman who seceded from the Church and went on to officiate within a body not in communion with it.[5] What gave Shore's case an added dimension of sensationalism was its unfortunate timing. Not only did the affair burst into prominence contemporaneously with the celebrated Gorham case; it also involved the same leading prosecutor, the cantankerous and litigious Bishop of Exeter, Henry Phillpotts.[6] In many Evangelical minds there were clear links between the two cases: both involved 'Gospel clergymen' as the victims of a High Church prelate whose determination to make life difficult for the Evangelical clergy in his diocese was well known.[7] Phillpotts's notoriety as an alleged episcopal tyrant also extended beyond the Evangelical camp. The Broad Churchman W. J. Conybeare held him up for ridicule as an episcopal martinet in the pages of the *Edinburgh Review*.[8] Sydney Smith, a lifelong opponent of persecuting bishops, denounced Phillpotts as a

[4] For an earlier version of this chapter see Grayson Carter, 'The Case of the Reverend James Shore', in *JEH*, 47/3 (1996), 478–504. See also Grayson Carter, 'James Shore', in *New DNB*; John Leach, 'The Revd James Shore of Bridgetown, Totnes', in the *Devon Historian*, 57 (Oct. 1998), 14–19.

[5] Sir John Dodson claimed in April 1845 that Shore's case was the first instance of a clergyman being prosecuted for seceding from the Church of England since the Reformation. See Thomas Thornton (ed.), *Notes of Cases in Ecclesiastical and Maritime Courts* (1843–50), iv.594.

[6] Henry Phillpotts (1778–1869), bishop of Exeter from 1831 to 1869, was a Tory High Churchman of the 'old school'. For details of Philpotts see: 'Dr Phillpotts the Bishop', in *Fraser's Magazine* (Jan. 1831); E. C. S. Gibson, 'Henry Phillpotts', in William Edward Collins (ed.), *Typical English Churchmen: From Parker to Maurice* (1902), 299–323; W. J. Conybeare, 'Bishop Phillpotts', in *EdR* (1852), 59–94; G. C. B. Davies, *Henry Phillpotts Bishop of Exeter, 1778–1869* (1954); John Wolffe, 'Bishop Henry Phillpotts and the Administration of the Diocese of Exeter, 1830–1869', in *Transactions of the Devonshire Association*, 114 (1982), 99–113.

[7] See R. W. Needham, *The Church and the Synod* (1851).

[8] W. J. Conybeare, 'Bishop Phillpotts', 75. For a response to Conybeare's attack upon Phillpotts see Henry Phillpotts, *A Letter to Sir Robert Inglis* (1852).

prime example,[9] and remarked dryly that he had single-handedly proved the existence of apostolic succession, 'there being no other way of accounting for the descent of the bishop of Exeter from Judas Iscariot'.[10]

Though the Shore case has been relegated to an obscure footnote in the ecclesiastical and legal history of the Victorian Church, the story of his secession, subsequent prosecution, imprisonment, and final release was celebrated by contemporaries as an important event in the advancement of religious liberty. It had judicial significance in exposing loopholes in English canon law. It aroused a sharp discussion on the nature of Anglican orders. It illustrated the extent to which the rules of ecclesiastical discipline and order were beginning to be enforced, in contrast to the laxity of earlier decades in which unorthodox theology and clerical 'irregularities' had been frequently ignored. If public interest in the case evaporated within a few years, it nevertheless did a good deal to exacerbate the growing conflict between Church parties in early Victorian England.

Given the contemporary significance of the Shore affair as a *cause célèbre*, the absence of any retrospective historical treatment of it is most surprising. Although briefly alluded to in several nineteenth-century works on English Nonconformity,[11] touched on in a small number of biographical accounts of the period,[12] and in several texts dealing with the obscure thickets of English ecclesiastical law,[13] it has never been examined in depth. The case more-

[9] See Smith to Lady Holland, 25 Nov. 1834, in Nowell C. Smith (ed.), *Selected Letters of Sydney Smith* (Oxford, 1981), 153.

[10] Hesketh Pearson, *The Smith of Smiths*, 5th edn. (1945), 236.

[11] F. S. Merryweather, *History of the Free Church of England* (1873), 66–82; T. E. Thoresby, *The Free Church of England: Its Origin, Constitution, Doctrines, and Objects* (1873), 57; Herbert S. Skeats and Charles S. Miall, *History of the Free Churches of England 1688–1891* (1891), 511–12; Frank Vaughan, *A History of the Free Church of England* (Bath, 1938), 22–5; Allan Brockett, *Nonconformity in Exeter, 1650–1875* (Manchester, 1962), 211–12; A. E. Price, *The Organization of the Free Church of England*, 2nd edn. (1908), 11; A. Elliott Peaston, *The Prayer Book Tradition in the Free Churches* (1964), 70–87. A 2nd edn. of Vaughan's study was published in 1960, and includes a brief chapter on the case, a drawing of Shore, and a photograph of Bridgetown Chapel.

[12] Thomas Archer, *William Ewart Gladstone and his Contemporaries* (1898–9), ii.170; Richard S. Lambert, *The Cobbett of the West* (1939), 132–59, 170–1; Davies, *Henry Phillpotts Bishop of Exeter*, 220–9.

[13] J. E. P. Robertson, *Reports of Cases Argued and Determined in the Ecclesiastical Courts at Doctors' Commons* (1845), 382–99; John Leycester Adolphus and Thomas Flower Ellis, *Queen's Bench Reports* (1848), 640–73; George C. Brodrick and William H. Fremantle, *A Collection of*

over has been entirely overlooked in three recent general studies of Church law in England.[14]

I

The overture to the Shore affair began during the summer of 1832. The Duke of Somerset[15] had recently erected a substantial church structure in the growing hamlet of Bridgetown, Totnes, Devon.[16] Costing some £7,000 it included a reading desk, pulpit, and communion table, and could accommodate some seven hundred worshippers.[17] The duke's intention was that the building be used as an Anglican place of worship. In due course he wrote to Bishop Phillpotts explaining his intentions, and in August 1832 the two met to discuss the situation. Knowing more about the intricate details of these matters than the duke, Phillpotts proposed two options for the building: it could either become a chapel-of-ease within the parish of Berry Pomeroy, in which case the responsibility for providing its services, as well as the consequent right of nominating its curate, would belong to the vicar; or it could become a chapel of a district taken out of the existing parish, and the duke could acquire the patronage upon provision of a suitable endowment.[18] During the course of these negotiations it became clear that the duke was more concerned about retaining the right of patronage for the chapel than about its legal status. Phillpotts, on the other hand, was determined that the chapel's financial stability be guaranteed in order to prevent the subsequent impoverishment of its incumbent. Consequently, he

the Judgments of the Judicial Committee of the Privy Council in Ecclesiastical Cases Related to Doctrine and Discipline (1865), 44–9; Sir Robert Phillimore, *The Ecclesiastical Law of the Church of England* (1873), ii.1,184; C. A. Cripps, *A Practical Treatise on the Law Relating to Church and Clergy*, 6th edn. (1886), 19–20, 42, 580; J. T. Edgerley (ed.), *Ecclesiastical Law* (repr. from Halsbury's *Laws of England*) (1957), 199 n, 186 n, 217 n.

[14] Robert E. Rodes, *Law and Modernization in the Church of England* (Notre Dame, Ind., 1991); S. W. Waddams, *Law, Politics and the Church of England* (Cambridge, 1992); Norman Doe, *Canon Law in the Anglican Communion* (Oxford, 1998).

[15] Edward Adolphus Seymour, the eleventh Duke of Somerset (1775–1855). Little is known about the duke's theological leanings. As a Whig he appeared, in matters of religion as in politics, an advocate of personal freedom and liberty. See *DNB*, xvii.1,253–4.

[16] In the parish of Berry Pomeroy. At the time, the parish contained about 200 families, almost all of which conformed to the Established Church. See Michael Cooke (ed.), 'The Diocese of Exeter in 1821', in *Report of the Devon and Cornwall Record Society* (1960), ii.19.

[17] J. H. Watson, *Year Book of St. John the Evangelist, Bridgetown* (Totnes, 1952).

[18] Maberley to Barnes, 18 Aug. 1832, in Phillpotts, *A Letter to Sir Robert Inglis*, 56; Henry Phillpotts, *The Case of the Revd James Shore*, 4th edn. (1849), 5.

refused to consecrate the building until the duke agreed to establish an adequate endowment. This difference quickly provoked a serious breakdown in relations between the two, for it appears that the duke, having already spent a considerable sum on construction, had not anticipated the need for an endowment or that the building could not be used for Anglican worship without a licence from the bishop.

These differences were finally resolved through a series of complex, protracted, and sometimes acrimonious negotiations. Phillpotts eventually consented to license the building as a chapel-of-ease, providing that the patronage be held by the vicar of Berry Pomeroy and providing that the duke agreed to establish an adequate endowment as soon as possible. When the endowment was forthcoming, the right of appointment would be transferred to the duke and the chapel consecrated.[19] The petition setting out this agreement was prepared by Ralph Barnes, the bishop's secretary, and signed by the duke in October 1832. After inspection, Phillpotts agreed to license the building, and the documents were sent to the duke a week later. The licence was granted on 9 November 1832.[20] With all obstacles now overcome, John Edwards, the vicar of Berry Pomeroy, appointed his curate, James Shore, as curate of Bridgetown Chapel (at the suggestion of the duke), and the building was opened for worship.[21]

A workable compromise was now in place, albeit one fraught with potential hazards. Phillpotts believed that the stipulations contained within the petition and licence furnished adequate incentive for the duke to endow the building as quickly as possible, and also to restrict its services to the rites of the Established Church.[22] The duke saw matters differently. As patron of Berry Pomeroy, he believed that he could exert sufficient influence upon the vicar to nominate whomsoever he wished as curate, granting

[19] Frank Vaughan suggests that the chapel was first licensed by Phillpotts for a two-year period. See Vaughan, *A History of the Free Church of England*, 2nd edn., 30.

[20] Ellis, *Queen's Bench Reports*, 650.

[21] One member of Shore's congregation testified before the Court of Arches that the chapel was licensed by the bishop in November 1832 and that Shore was licensed to officiate there in April 1833. See Robertson, *Reports of Cases*, 394. Shore was paid £200 a year by the duke for serving at the chapel and lived with his family at 1 Seymour Place, Bridgetown. See MSS 1392 M/L19 46/15; 1392 M/L39/3, Devon County RO, Exeter; '1851 Religious Census, Devonshire', Devon County RO.

[22] Davies, *Henry Phillpotts Bishop of Exeter, 1778–1869*, 222.

him the benefits of the patronage of Bridgetown Chapel without the necessity of providing a further endowment. Additionally, while the language of the licence ensured that the building must always be used for 'religious worship', the duke apparently did not realize (probably because no clear precedent existed in ecclesiastical law) that this would present an obstacle to its being removed from the jurisdiction of the Established Church, if need should arise. These misapprehensions soon embroiled the duke, the members of his family, the bishop, and, most significantly, James Shore, in a most acrimonious and complicated legal entanglement.

John Edwards died in 1834.[23] The duke then nominated the Revd Edward Brown as his successor as vicar of Berry Pomeroy, with the understanding that Shore would continue as curate at Bridgetown Chapel. Brown's service in the parish continued until 1843, when he received the duke's sanction to exchange the living for that of Monkton Farleigh, Wiltshire, held by the Tractarian William Burrough Cosens.[24] After the duke had agreed to this exchange, and after some private consultations between Cosens and Phillpotts, it was disclosed that in 1834 Brown had not provided the bishop's registrar with the required nomination for Shore to serve as curate at Bridgetown.[25] As the result of this omission, which Phillpotts characterized as a 'very rare occurrence', it came to light that Shore had technically been serving at the chapel for the past nine years without a valid licence.[26] When this development was brought to Brown's attention, he denied Phillpotts's allegation and claimed that he had, in fact, completed the necessary paperwork at the time of his arrival in the parish. Under pressure, Phillpotts produced a nomination which had been signed by Brown in 1834. It did not, however, pertain to Shore, but to a mysterious stranger by the name of Dusautoy.[27] Shore was then informed by the bishop that he could only continue at Bridgetown

[23] He served as vicar of Berry Pomeroy from 1781 to 1834. During this time, he resided at Blagdon, some two miles away, and performed no clerical duties, leaving such matters to his curate. See Cooke, *The Diocese of Exeter in 1821*, ii.19.

[24] Cosens was the son of William Cosens of Ipplepen, Devon. He matriculated at Magdalen Hall, Oxford, 10 Mar. 1818, age 26, and was made BA in 1824 and MA in 1825. See *Al. Ox.*, ii.300. Cosens published a rather one-sided account of the affair which made little or no impact upon the religious public. See W. B. Cosens, *The Case of the Revd James Shore, as Between the Patron and the Vicar, in a Letter to his Parishioners* (Exeter, 1849).

[25] *EC* (1848), 270.

[26] Phillpotts, *The Case of the Revd James Shore*, 15.

[27] See letter of Brown, 29 Dec. 1848, in *ER* (1849), 617–18.

by acquiring a new nomination from Cosens. This predicament, not anticipated by the duke when the exchange was agreed to, placed Shore in a most precarious position, for no formal arrangement had been made with Cosens to continue his services, and since Cosens now held the cure of souls he had complete power over all Anglican ministry within the parish. Ultimately this legal entanglement, created by the duke's approval of the exchange between Brown and Cosens as well as by Shore's unlicensed status, presented Phillpotts with the opportunity to institute a doctrinally suitable clergyman at Berry Pomeroy, while simultaneously removing what he considered to be a troublesome and unsound curate from Bridgetown.

Phillpotts's antipathy towards Shore had been developing ever since 1841. In that year, the patrons of the parish of Cudleigh had held an election in order to determine the parishioners' choice of a new incumbent, and Shore had put himself forward as one of the initial four candidates.[28] He withdrew prior to the election, but was, soon afterwards, publicly accused of publishing a handbill supporting Wilmont Palk, the Evangelical candidate opposed by the bishop. Phillpotts was outraged by Shore's behaviour, which he characterized as an 'extremely indecent and improper thing',[29] and summoned him to be admonished for his open disloyalty. Palk was duly elected and nominated by the trustees to become the new incumbent. Phillpotts, yet to be defeated in the matter, refused to institute Palk, alleging that the deed of trusteeship was faulty and the election irregular.[30] Hoping to delay matters until the right of presentation lapsed, he abandoned his scheme only when the trustees procured a court order requiring him to institute Palk and to pay costs. Phillpotts suffered a severe public humiliation in this affair, and was quick to place the blame for it on Shore's disingenuous behaviour—a factor which, he later admitted, almost induced him to withdraw his licence.[31]

Cosens, meanwhile, took up residence at Berry Pomeroy on 14 October 1843 and Shore called on him two days later. During this meeting, Cosens informed Shore that the matter of a new nomination had now been taken out of his hands, since he had previ-

[28] Lambert, *The Cobbett of the West*, 132–3. The terms of the trust required the trustees to hold an election in the parish and to nominate the successful candidate as incumbent.

[29] Ibid. 133.

[30] Ibid.

[31] Testimony by the bishop in *Phillpotts* v. *Latimer*. See *ER* (1849), 613.

ously engaged with the bishop to replace Shore as curate of Bridgetown Chapel.[32] This came as a great surprise to Shore, for he had just received two separate appeals from Phillpotts urging him to secure the nomination from Cosens as soon as possible. Shore then realized that he was being deceived by both Cosens and Phillpotts who, it now appeared, had conspired to prevent him from obtaining the nomination and remaining at Bridgetown Chapel.[33] Later that same day, Shore received a note from the bishop prohibiting any further services at Bridgetown. He obeyed the order and closed the chapel; it remained closed for the next five months.[34]

During this time Shore received offers of preferment elsewhere, but as insinuations about the nature of his character had begun to surface locally he concluded that he could not withdraw without suffering a permanent blemish on his reputation.[35] Shore instead consulted the Duke of Somerset, who offered to remove the chapel from the jurisdiction of the Church of England if doing so would make it possible for Shore to continue as curate.[36] Although sincerely attached to the Anglican Church, Shore admitted that with pain and reluctance he was willing to secede from it out of concern for the continued spiritual welfare of his congregation, especially as they were now under the care of a Tractarian incumbent. In addition, he believed that Phillpotts would use his influence to prevent his securing a position in this or any other diocese, thus subjecting his family to the consequences of unemployment and poverty.[37] Because of these factors, rather than from any serious objections to Church order or doctrine, Shore informed Phillpotts that he intended to continue at Bridgetown Chapel with or without a new nomination, even if this required his reluctant secession from the Establishment. Phillpotts responded to this implied threat by stating that he was no longer in communion with Shore. Moreover, he warned Shore

[32] James Shore, *A Statement of the Proceedings of the Bishop of Exeter* (1848), 5.

[33] Ibid. This was denied by Phillpotts, however, who claimed that he gave Cosens no encouragement on the question, and 'made him understand that he must act altogether on his own judgment' in the matter of allowing Shore to continue as minister of Bridgetown Chapel. See Phillpotts, *The Case of the Revd James Shore*, 17.

[34] Culling Eardley, *An Appeal to the Country*, 2nd edn. (Torquay, 1849), 4.

[35] The *Free Church of England Magazine* (1869), 28–9.

[36] Shore to Phillpotts, 13 Nov. 1843, in Phillpotts, *The Case of the Revd James Shore*, 21.

[37] Shore to Phillpotts, 11 Nov. 1843, ibid. 20–1.

that both canon and civil law forbade the secession of any clergyman who had been episcopally ordained.[38] Perplexed by the bishop's response, Shore disregarded this thinly veiled threat to prosecute him if he attempted to secede, and prepared to reinstitute services at Bridgetown.

In February 1844 a petition signed by eight hundred members of the Bridgetown congregation was presented to the duke urging him to reopen the chapel as soon as possible.[39] The duke appeared only too willing to comply with the wishes of the signatories, and, on the twenty-sixth of that month, had the building registered under the provisions of the Toleration Act[40] as a Dissenting meeting house.[41] Two days later, Shore informed Phillpotts that he now considered himself outside the jurisdiction and authority of the Church and no longer subject to his discipline.[42] Phillpotts responded by revoking Shore's licence to officiate in the diocese.[43] Three days later, in order to remove any possible doubts about his new status, Shore recited the oaths and signed the required declarations under the Toleration Act of 1689.[44] On 22 March 1844 Shore again notified Phillpotts that he no longer considered himself to be a member of the establishment. He politely inquired of the bishop whether additional procedures were necessary for a clergyman lawfully to secede from the Church,[45] but

[38] Phillpotts to Shore, 13 Nov. 1843, in Phillpotts, *The Case of the Revd James Shore*, 22.

[39] Culling Eardley, *An Appeal to the Country*, 4; Merryweather, *History of the Free Church of England*, 67. Little is known about the identity of these petitioners. Presumably they were members of Shore's congregation which allegedly numbered around 800. It remains uncertain whether prior to attending Bridgetown Chapel the petitioners worshipped at the parish Church at Berry Pomeroy (two miles away), the parish Church at Totnes (across the river), or at a local Dissenting meeting-house. In any case, the number of signatures on this petition bears testimony to the extent of Shore's popularity in the community. Between 1834 and 1853 the pew rents from Bridgetown Chapel averaged approximately £140 per year. See MS 1392 M/L Rentals 5, Devon County RO, Exeter.

[40] 52 Geo. III. Cap. 155.

[41] *EC* (1848), 270; Robertson, *Reports of Cases*, 388; Shore, *A Statement of the Proceedings of the Bishop of Exeter*, 7. Davies, *Henry Phillpotts Bishop of Exeter*, 224, incorrectly identifies the date as 16 Feb.

[42] Shore to Phillpotts, 28 Feb. 1844, in Culling Eardley, *An Appeal to the Country*, Appendix A; *EC* (1848), 270.

[43] On 7 Mar.; served on 13 Mar. See Robertson, *Reports of Cases*, 388; Ellis, *Queen's Bench Reports*, 643, 650.

[44] 1 William & Mary, Cap. 18; later, 52 Geo. III. Cap. 155, sections 4 and 5. See Robertson, *Reports of Cases*, 388; Shore, *A Statement of the Proceedings of the Bishop of Exeter*, 7.

[45] Shore to Barnes, 22 Mar. 1844, in James Shore, *The Case of the Revd James Shore, M.A., by Himself* (1849), 65.

this was ignored and he was simply informed by the bishop's secretary that he could not 'officiate as a clergyman *in any place* without the licence of the bishop'.[46] Disregarding these admonitions, on 14 April 1844, Shore reopened Bridgetown Chapel as the first congregation of the Free Church of England.[47]

II

Phillpotts's provocative response to Shore's inquiry was prompted by his belief that the seventy-sixth canon prevented any clergyman from voluntarily renouncing his orders in the Church. This read: 'no man being admitted a deacon or minister shall from thenceforth voluntarily relinquish the same, nor afterwards use himself in the course of his life as a layman, upon pain of excommunication.'[48] The legal implications of this canon at the time of Shore's secession are difficult to determine. In its original, early seventeenth-century context, it appears that it was intended to bind the clergy for life to the Church and to the jurisdiction of their diocesan. Such a restriction would prevent indiscriminate secessions, undertaken in an attempt to escape episcopal discipline, and would help to avoid the creation of rival religious bodies within a parish. Perhaps because of the Anglican bishops' reluctance to interpret the canons strictly during the eighteenth century, no attempt to enforce the canon had ever been made. Although in some ways Phillpotts was an episcopal autocrat, even his record on canonical enforcement was inconsistent, as W. J. Conybeare pointed out in the pages of the *Edinburgh Review*. The bishop, Conybeare claimed, violated the rubric 'every time he confirms, and disobeys the canons of the universal church, by deserting his episcopal residence in the cathedral city';[49] he habitually altered the wording of services to suit his fancy, bestowed lavish patronage upon his relations and partisans, and repeatedly usurped patronage rights belonging to others.[50] A prominent example of Phillpotts's inconsistency was exposed in the case of *Escott* v. *Mastin* in 1842. This involved the refusal of an Anglican clergyman to perform the burial service over a child who had been

[46] Barnes to Shore, 6 Apr. 1844, ibid. 66. (italics added)

[47] The *Free Church of England Magazine* (1869), 28–9.

[48] C. H. Davis, *The English Church Canons of 1604* (1869), 75. If violated, the canons also carried civil penalties (fine or imprisonment), which could be inflicted by the ecclesiastical courts.

[49] Conybeare, 'Bishop Phillpotts', 75.

[50] Ibid. 75–9, 83–4.

baptized by a Wesleyan minister, an action which the Judicial Committee of the Privy Council held to be in violation of canon law, suspending the offending clergyman from his duties for three months.[51] In his *Charge* of 1842, Phillpotts expressed his fervent opposition to the ruling, denouncing it from his cathedral pulpit as *ipso facto* void, for any canon 'purporting to extinguish a right created or recognized by the law of the land, is not worth the paper on which it is printed'.[52] Accordingly, heretics and schismatics, as he characterized Nonconformists, should by law and in practice be regarded as *ipso facto* excommunicated and ineligible to receive the sacraments of the Church.[53]

III

As the direct result of Shore's continued ministry at Bridgetown without licence and against the monition of his diocesan, charges were instituted against him in the ecclesiastical courts at the instruction of Bishop Phillpotts.[54] On 14 June 1844, he received a summons ordering him to appear before a Preliminary Commission of Inquiry.[55] Shore considered ignoring the summons, but naïvely concluded that if he did he might be committed for contempt, thus preventing his case from being tried on its merits.[56] He therefore appeared, under protest, before the commission which was held on 6 August 1844 at the Seven Stars, Totnes,[57] and argued that as the result of his secession and his declarations under the provisions of the Toleration Act he was now a Dissenter and exempt from episcopal discipline. The commission, however, denied this claim, countering that a clergyman could not 'divest himself of the character which had been impressed upon him by his ordination', unless he was released under the same authority by which the obligation was imposed. In other words, a clergy-

[51] Brodrick and Fremantle, *A Collection of the Judgments of the Judicial Committee of the Privy Council*, 4–29. See also the case of *Titchmarch* v. *Chapman*, 1844.

[52] Henry Lord Bishop of Exeter, *A Charge Delivered to the Clergy of the Diocese of Exeter* (1842), 58–9.

[53] Ibid. 68–9.

[54] The case was officially known as *Barnes* v. *Shore.*

[55] The diocesan court had been amended by the Church Discipline Act of 1840 (3–4 Vict. Cap. 86). After being charged, a clergyman was required to appear before a preliminary commission, where the bishop would either hear the case in person with three assessors (one of whom must be a lawyer), or send it by letter of request to a provincial court. See S. L. Ollard (ed.), *A Dictionary of English Church History*, 2nd edn. (1919), 157.

[56] Culling Eardley, *An Appeal to the Country*, 5.

[57] Shore, *The Case of the Revd James Shore, M.A., by Himself*, 31.

man could be deposed from his orders, but he could not voluntarily relinquish them.[58]

Shore was convicted by the commission of violating canon law and of disobeying his ecclesiastical superiors. He appealed against its decision to the Court of Arches, which issued its initial judgment on 5 August 1845.[59] Sir Herbert Jenner Fust, the Dean of Arches, dismissed Shore's conscientious grounds for seceding as palpably absurd, and claimed that both the spirit of the canons and common sense opposed the notion that a clergyman could voluntarily renounce his orders.[60] Is it meant, Fust asked, that 'one being guilty of immorality, can exempt himself from the censures of the Church, by saying he had taken certain oaths, and qualified himself as a Dissenting Preacher? Were that so, there would be an end to all Church discipline; the notion is too preposterous.'[61] Shore appealed the decision to the Court of Queen's Bench, which found against him.[62] Finally, on 20 June 1846, Fust issued a subsequent ruling in the Court of Arches.[63] Although exempting Shore from answering for the offence of seceding from the Church, for which 'there must be other proceedings, in order to procure additional punishment'; he found him guilty of 'publicly reading prayers, according to the form prescribed by the Prayer Book, and of preaching in an unconsecrated chapel without a licence'.[64] Shore was then admonished to refrain in the future from such ecclesiastical offences, which not only violated the dictates of his diocesan, but would now also violate those of the court; finally came the reminder that he was still a clergyman, 'from which office he cannot of his own authority relieve himself'.[65]

Three days after Fust's subsequent ruling, Lord Brougham introduced a petition on Shore's behalf in the House of Lords.

[58] *CO* (1846), 349–50.

[59] Robertson, *Reports of Cases*, 388–90; Brodrick and Fremantle, *A Collection of the Judgments of the Judicial Committee of the Privy Council*, 45.

[60] Robertson, *Reports of Cases*, 388–9. Fust (1778–1852) was Dean of the Arches, a Privy Councillor, and Master of Trinity Hall, Cambridge.

[61] Ibid. 389–90; *The English Reports* (Edinburgh, 1900–30), clxiii.1,074–80.

[62] Brodrick and Fremantle, *A Collection of the Judgments of the Judicial Committee of the Privy Council*, 45; *EC* (1848), 270; Robertson, *Reports of Cases*, 390.

[63] Ibid. 390–9; Brodrick and Fremantle, *A Collection of the Judgments of the Judicial Committee of the Privy Council*, 46–9.

[64] Robertson, *Reports of Cases*, 398–9; Brodrick and Fremantle, *A Collection of the Judgments of the Judicial Committee of the Privy Council*, 48–9.

[65] Robertson, *Reports of Cases*, 399; Brodrick and Fremantle, *A Collection of the Judgments of the Judicial Committee of the Privy Council*, 49.

Phillpotts responded by denying any wrongdoing in the affair and by dismissing Shore as a disobedient malcontent of little significance. If blame must be accorded, he argued, it should fall upon the shoulders of the Duke of Somerset who had failed to keep his promise to endow Bridgetown Chapel. Such an attack upon the absent and ailing duke did little to divert criticism from Phillpotts, or to diminish his growing reputation for litigiousness.[66]

IV

The focus of the debate then returned to the West Country. Lord Seymour, the duke's son and Liberal MP for Totnes, leapt to the defence of his aged father at a local rally, claiming that Phillpotts's attack was a deliberate falsehood and that no such engagement to endow the chapel had ever been made.[67] The bishop's statement was diametrically opposed to the truth and a malicious charge which had left a false imputation upon the duke.[68] The press was quick to take up Shore's case, particularly the *Western Times*, whose radical and fervently Protestant editor Thomas Latimer (an old and bitter opponent of clericalism, who pursued Phillpotts with determination) now seized a golden opportunity to ridicule Tory and High Church intolerance. Latimer characterized Phillpotts as 'cunning rather than clever' and as one who is 'everlastingly in hot water, but never clean'. He was a 'careless perverter of facts' who 'does no credit to the mitre, which he is paid £200 a week . . . to wear', and 'so notorious as a brawler, that any story respecting his rule and discipline . . . is received without question, and circulated from mouth to mouth as Gospel'.[69]

The contest escalated as Phillpotts responded to this attack by filing a claim for libel and defamation against Latimer.[70] Although securing an impartial jury proved difficult, the trial eventually

[66] *Hansard's Parliamentary Debates: Third Series*, lxxxvii.869–70.

[67] Edward Adolphus Seymour, the twelth Duke of Somerset (1804–85) was Liberal MP for Totnes between 1834 and 1855. He served as First Lord of the Admiralty between 1859 and 1866. See W. D. Mallock and G. Ramsden (eds.), *Letters, Remains, and Memoirs of Edward Adolphus Seymour, Twelfth Duke of Somerset, KG* (1893); *DNB*, xvii.1,253–4. In religious matters as in politics he was a determined liberal and author of the work, *Christian Theology and Modern Scepticism* (1872), which was attacked by (among others) Joseph M'Caul in *The Duke of Somerset's Recent Attack upon the Bible Criticized* (1872).

[68] Lambert, *The Cobbett of the West*, 138.

[69] Ibid. 139, citing the *Western Times*, 25 July 1846.

[70] Because of the seriousness of the case, Latimer would have been guilty of criminal charges if the jury had found for Phillpotts.

opened in Exeter in March 1848. After hearing the testimony, Baron Platt, the trial judge, instructed the jury to find for Phillpotts; ignoring this, they instead found for Latimer, ruling that the duke had not violated his engagement over the endowment and that Latimer was innocent of issuing libel or of making defamatory statements.[71] Phillpotts avoided paying costs only through a legal technicality, the accompanying publicity helping further to damage his reputation in the local community.

V

Although the eighth section of the Toleration Act of 1689[72] appeared to provide refuge for clergymen seceding into the Nonconformist ministry,[73] a number of subsequent legal opinions disputed this. As early as 1742, for instance, in the case of *Trebec* v. *Keith*, Lord Hardwicke insisted that although the Toleration Act was made to 'protect persons of tender consciences, and to exempt them from penalties', to extend it to clergymen who had acted contrary to the Church's rules and discipline would be to introduce the utmost confusion.[74] The fourth section of the Toleration Act of 1689 appeared to provide similar refuge. In November 1845, the Court of Queen's Bench decreed that the fourth section exempted both laymen and clergy who took the oaths and subscribed to the relevant declarations from prosecution in the ecclesiastical court for not conforming to the Church of England. To claim this exemption, it was probably sufficient for the party simply to declare himself publicly to be a Dissenter. This did not, however, apply to Anglican clergymen who could not, in this manner, or otherwise at their own pleasure, divest themselves of their orders so as to exempt themselves from correction by their bishops for breach of ecclesiastical discipline.[75] Even if Shore proved that he had been sued in the ecclesiastical court for Nonconformity, this would not absolve him, as an episcopally ordained clergyman, from canonical obedience in those things which accorded to the rites and ceremonies of the Established Church.[76] The wording of the

[71] Davies, *Henry Phillpotts Bishop of Exeter, 1778–1869*, 226–9.

[72] 1 William & Mary, Cap. 18.

[73] See E. Neville Williams, *The Eighteenth-Century Constitution* (Cambridge, 1960), 44.

[74] Robertson, *Reports of Cases*, 389; *QR* (1849), 43.

[75] Brodrick and Fremantle, *A Collection of the Judgments of the Judicial Committee of the Privy Council*, 45.

[76] Ibid. 49 n.

Dissenters' Relief Act of 1779 also contributed to the obscurity of this point of law.[77] Because in describing those eligible for protection it employed similar language to that of the eighth section of the Toleration Act, it appeared to exempt Anglicans who made the necessary declarations from penalty or imprisonment for officiating as Nonconformists. This argument, however, was also rejected by the courts. In 1812, another statute[78] extended the relief of the Toleration Act to 'every person who shall teach or preach at or officiate in or shall resort to any congregation of Protestants'.[79] This ambiguous wording was modified two years later by Sir John Nicholl in the case of *Carr* v. *Marsh*, in which the court restricted the statute's application to laymen and denied the extension of its benefits to anyone who had been episcopally ordained.[80]

VI

Shore appealed against the decision of the Court of Arches to the Judicial Committee of the Privy Council, which rendered its decision on 24 August 1848. The denial of his appeal was based on four points: that secession does not shield a clergyman from ecclesiastical censures for breach of discipline; that an unconsecrated proprietary chapel, to which strangers are admitted, is not a private house; that in order to be convicted under ecclesiastical law, it is not necessary that all the charges be proved; and, that the court in awarding a penalty is not bound by the request of the accusing party.[81] Three documents were then issued against Shore: a prohibition against officiating or preaching within the province of Canterbury, a writ to pay Phillpotts's costs in the Court of Arches, and another writ to pay the bishop's costs in the

[77] It read 'That every person dissenting from the Church . . . and in holy orders . . . being a preacher . . . of any congregation of Dissenting Protestants, who, if he scruple to declare and subscribe a declaration . . . shall be . . . hereby declared to be, entitled to all exemptions, benefits, privileges, and advantages granted to Protestant Dissenting ministers . . . and shall also be exempted from any imprisonment . . . for preaching or officiating in any congregation of Protestant Dissenters'. See Williams, *The Eighteenth-Century Constitution*, 345–6.

[78] 52 Geo. III, Cap. 155, section 4.

[79] *QR* (1849), 43.

[80] *Carr* v. *Marsh* involved proceedings against a clergyman for preaching in a parish church without the incumbent's permission. See *QR* (1849), 44; Robertson, *Reports of Cases*, 389.

[81] Brodrick and Fremantle, *A Collection of the Judgments of the Judicial Committee of the Privy Council*, 44.

Privy Council.[82] In the judgment Sir John Dodson declared that a priest, although a seceder from the Church, may be '*committed to prison* for contempt of court for preaching as a Dissenting minister'. Furthermore, neither deposition, degradation, nor excommunication, 'can confer on a clergyman a legal right to officiate or preach as a Dissenting minister'.[83] Dodson's insistence that clergymen could not voluntarily renounce their orders left Shore with few options. Reform of canon law could only be undertaken by act of Convocation (which had been in a state of suspension since 1717) or Parliament.[84] Only Shore's willingness to abandon his ministry at Bridgetown, or, conversely, Phillpotts's willingness to set aside the judgments of the ecclesiastical courts, could now prevent Shore from being arrested and imprisoned.

VII

During 1848, churchmen and Dissenters alike mounted a public campaign to protest against Shore's prosecution and to encourage Parliament to enact relief for seceding clergymen. On 13 April, five thousand of Shore's supporters attended the first of several rallies at Exeter Hall, London,[85] and other large gatherings were held in great towns up and down England and Scotland.[86] After the Court of Arches issued its prohibition against his engaging in clerical activity,[87] Shore expected to receive a warrant for his arrest as the result of his refusal to abandon his ministry at Bridgetown. Phillpotts, however, was content to await the outcome of the Privy Council's decision before proceeding, and, at least for the moment, Shore remained free to preach and to speak at public meetings in support of his case.

[82] Culling Eardley, *An Appeal to the Country*, 6–7.

[83] *EdR* (1849), 148–9; *Non* (1848), 668. Sir John also referred to the case of Horne Tooke which involved the legality of a clergyman sitting in the House of Commons. Prior to 1801, there was a widely understood convention barring clergy from sitting in the Commons. In that year, the Revd Horne Tooke was elected MP for the rotten borough of Old Sarum. Shortly after taking his seat, a bill was rushed through both Houses enacting a statute prohibiting clergymen from becoming members of parliament. Uncharacteristically, Horne Tooke resigned his seat without protest at the end of the session. See *Hansard*, xxxv.1,323–1,420.

[84] Convocation had been suspended by George I as a result of the so-called 'Bangorian controversy' in 1717. It did not meet again, except formally, until 1852. The English canons continued in their unreformed state until 1865.

[85] *EC* (1848), 269; *Non* (1848), 268.

[86] Phillpotts, *The Case of the Revd James Shore*, 30; *EC* (1849), 254, 262. Cf. *Non* (1849), 59.

[87] In June 1846.

During this time there was much speculation and debate in the religious press over the Shore affair. That this episode of ecclesiastical tyranny and oppression was better suited to the times of Laud than those of Sumner was painfully obvious to the Dissenting editor of the *Evangelical Magazine*; equally obvious was the bishop's enmity towards the Evangelical clergy which 'lay at the foundation of all the cruel and unmanly proceedings against Mr Shore'.[88] High Churchmen were equally fierce in their pronouncements. The *English Churchman* dismissed Evangelicalism as little more than implicit Dissent, while Shore was condemned as a deserter and traitor to the Establishment cause, and as a 'pertinacious and ingenious speculator upon popular credulity'.[89] It went on to claim, without the slightest hint of shame or regret, that the primary motivation behind Phillpotts's and Cosens's persecution of Shore had been their determined opposition to the continued presence of an Evangelical clergyman at Bridgetown Chapel.[90]

Shore's legal status was dealt a significant set-back by the Privy Council's confirmation of the decision of the Court of Arches.[91] He had hoped that the case's extensive publicity might lead the Privy Council to overturn the ruling of the Court of Arches; he also hoped that, if the Council upheld this ruling, the various delays accompanying it might ultimately prevent his incarceration. But this was not to be. In early 1849 a warrant was issued for his arrest on the grounds of failing to pay £186 14*s*. 2*d*. in costs to the Privy Council.

Issuing a warrant for Shore's arrest was one thing, apprehending him was quite another, for the ecclesiastical authorities shrewdly concluded that any attempt to arrest him at Bridgetown was likely to result in a violent confrontation between the officers of the court and Shore's local supporters. Some weeks passed in this unsettled state, and Shore continued defiantly to proclaim his right to preach wherever he was called by God. In early March he tested this assertion by accepting an invitation to preach at the Countess of Huntingdon's chapel at Spa Fields. The ecclesiastical authorities were alerted that Shore was finally venturing outside the protection of Bridgetown, and a plan was devised to capture him in the act of preaching. During the evening service

[88] *EM* (1849), 201, 253. [89] *EC* (1848), 766; (1849), 181. [90] Ibid.

[91] See Brodrick and Fremantle, *A Collection of the Judgments of the Judicial Committee of the Privy Council*, 44–9.

on 9 March 1849, two officers of the Court of Arches quietly slipped into the back of Spa Fields Chapel, and, in one of the more dramatic religious confrontations of modern times, waited until Shore had finished his sermon and had begun to descend from the pulpit. Then, in near riotous conditions, they pushed through the shocked and protesting onlookers to arrest and transport him to Exeter gaol.[92] In a quickly written note to the Revd Thomas Elisha Thoresby, the minister of Spa Fields, Shore confirmed his arrest and declared that this had nothing at all to do with his refusal to pay the bishop's costs, as the warrant claimed, but was solely the result of his unwillingness to cease from preaching outside the establishment. He did not have the means of paying these costs, and even if he had, he would still be in contempt of court for preaching and would again be committed to prison.[93] Thoresby rushed off to place an announcement of the arrest in the next edition of *The Times*, including a reiteration of Shore's claims.[94] Phillpotts was greatly angered by this public rebuke and the subsequent sensation, and ordered Barnes to issue a statement denying Shore's allegations and assuring the public that the arrest involved nothing more than Shore's refusal to pay the outstanding court costs.[95] This claim, however, was publicly denied on a number of occasions.[96]

The details and complexity of Shore's case had by now become lost on the religious public. What seemed clear, however, was that Shore had seceded over a matter of conscience, that Phillpotts had concocted a series of legal obstacles in a Jesuitical attempt to prevent this from occurring, and that officers of the court had invaded the sanctity of a Nonconformist chapel to arrest and imprison Shore for nothing more than preaching the Gospel. Furthermore, in spite of the bishop's assurances, the rulings of the various courts clearly indicated that, even if Shore were persuaded to pay the costs in question, he would still be subject to arrest and imprisonment if he continued to preach without a licence.

[92] Vaughan, *A History of the Free Church of England*, 24; Price, *The Organization of the Free Church of England*, 11.

[93] Shore to Thoresby, 9 Mar. 1849, in Vaughan, *A History of the Free Church of England*, 24; Thoresby, *The Free Church of England*, 57.

[94] *The Times*, 10 Mar. 1849.

[95] Barnes to *The Times*, 12 Mar. 1849.

[96] Including E. P. Bouverie, who denounced it on the floor of the House of Commons on 21 Mar. 1849. See *Hansard: Third Series*, ciii.1,073; John Fitzgerald, *An Appeal to Pious and Devoted Clergymen* (1851), 33–4.

The public outcry accompanying Shore's imprisonment forced Archbishop Sumner to press Phillpotts for an immediate and thorough explanation. The bishop's response, however, which he quickly published, failed to satisfy his numerous critics.[97] Instead, it produced even wider public interest in the case and even greater public condemnation of himself. Phillpotts denied wishing to chain any member of the clergy to the Church's communion if he conscientiously believed that it was his duty to withdraw from it. The true churchman, he wrote, would instead urge clergymen quietly to withdraw, rather than 'to persist in the performance of offices which they can no longer perform without peril to their own souls, and a serious offence to the souls of others'. He went on to claim that, on more than one occasion, he himself had acted on this principle, and had, in fact, offered Shore the same courtesy.[98] Phillpotts then offered a most disingenuous suggestion. He denied that Shore had properly seceded from the Church and cited extracts from his correspondence in an attempt to substantiate this allegation. If Shore had in fact seceded, as the chancellor had strongly advised him to do, and proclaimed himself a Dissenter, he would have been speedily released from his obligations with little or no cost to anyone.[99]

From his cell in Exeter gaol, Shore defended himself against the bishop's allegations by publishing a strong attack upon Phillpotts and upon the discrepancies contained within his explanation.[100] The bishop, Shore claimed, had mutilated and suppressed many of his most important letters and had laboured to trap and crush a powerless opponent in an attempt to drive him from his congregation and out of the Church.[101] The discrepancies between Shore's account of his correspondence and Phillpotts's earlier one were now blatantly obvious, and their public disclosure did little to advance the bishop's already tarnished reputation. Shore, on the other hand, benefited from the publicity aroused by these revelations, and his reputation as a poor curate suffering at the hands of a powerful and unscrupulous episcopal tyrant was substantially advanced by Phillpotts's apparent duplicity.

As the weeks passed, Shore's health began to deteriorate and pressure increased for his friends and supporters (by now banded

[97] Phillpotts, *The Case of the Revd James Shore.*
[98] Ibid. 3–4. [99] Ibid. 30.
[100] Shore, *The Case of the Revd James Shore, M.A., by Himself.* [101] Ibid. 6–11.

together in a London committee) to pay his costs and to secure his release from gaol. The religious press urged payment by public subscription;[102] Shore, however, refused to consider any such suggestion. Declaring himself a prisoner for the sake of conscience, he announced that 'he would rather remain in prison for life, or until such measures of religious liberty were obtained as to leave all men free', than come out because concessions had been made in his own case.[103] By 2 May, however, Shore's health had worsened to the point where his committee decided that securing his prompt release was imperative.[104] The sum was soon collected and, on 23 May, a cheque for £186 14*s.* 2*d.* was drawn and presented to the sheriff of Exeter. The courier was then informed, however, that Phillpotts insisted that Shore also pay an attachment for additional costs in the Privy Council in the amount of £124 1*s.* 10*d.*[105] Although furious at the bishop's uncharitable behaviour, the committee had no choice but to submit. A week later the additional amount was sent and Shore was released.

VIII

In spite of repeated warnings from the various courts, Shore was determined to continue at Bridgetown Chapel. 'I shall occupy the same ground and preach the Gospel as I did before,' he defiantly declared upon being released, and 'if the bishop feels it to be his conscientious duty to carry out the laws of his Church, I shall, of course, be soon committed to prison again. I hope (D.V.) I shall be able to preach to my congregation . . . next Sunday.'[106] Shore returned to Bridgetown and remained there, unmolested by either the ecclesiastical courts or Bishop Phillpotts, for some years.[107] He also continued to appear at public meetings up and down the country bemoaning his ill-treatment, but gradually he abandoned this activity and returned to full-time ministry.[108] In January 1850 *The Times* announced the disbanding of Shore's London committee. During its lifetime, it had raised £614 2*s.* 7*d.* by public

[102] *Non* (1849), 198; the *Record*, 15 Mar. 1849.

[103] Ibid. 299; *ER* (1849), 777. Phillpotts, however, stated that he gave no direction for enforcing the decrees of the courts; neither did he do anything to prevent their being enforced. See Phillpotts, *The Case of the Revd James Shore*, 31.

[104] *The Times*, 5 May 1849.

[105] *Non* (1849), 418.

[106] Ibid. 438; the *Record*, 14 June 1849.

[107] MSS 1392 M/L54/3; 1392 M/L52/5, Devon County RO, Exeter.

[108] Lambert, *The Cobbet of the West*, 171.

subscription, £525 15*s.* 10*d.* being spent on the case (including the £310 16*s.* 4*d.* that had been paid to Phillpotts for his costs); the remaining £88 6*s.* 9*d.* being presented to Shore after his release from gaol.[109]

Although Shore was allowed to continue at Bridgetown, it appears that he became locally something of a marked man.[110] At the time Totnes was notoriously fractured by political conflict. As one contemporary account put it, 'Near the church is the Guildhall. Well would it be for the place if it were at the bottom of Torbay, could it only convey with it the feelings of gall and bitterness, engendered by the genius of the spot. Probably the strife of politics is sterner, and more incessant, in Totnes, than in any other town.'[111] Shore cannot have been *persona grata* to many strong Tories or Anglican partisans.

Shore continued to labour in this fractious atmosphere until the middle of 1862 when he moved to Matlock, Derbyshire.[112] The reasons which lay behind this move are not entirely clear. It may have been, as several accounts have suggested, that he was attracted to Matlock to seek a cure for his chronic rheumatism in the now fashionable 'waters'.[113] Alternatively, he may have been motivated by a religious end, for it is clear that at Matlock he became associated with the celebrated spa owner and philanthropist John Smedley (1803–74).[114]

Smedley had acquired substantial wealth through producing high quality woollen goods and through his proprietorship of Smedley's Hydro in Matlock, one of the largest and most luxurious spa hotels in England.[115] At much the same time as Shore's imprisonment, Smedley seceded from the Church of England and formed his own Evangelical connexion, publishing a revised Prayer Book and writing extensively on religious matters, espe-

[109] *The Times*, 10 Jan. 1850. [110] *High Peak News*, 15 Aug. 1874.

[111] Jack Simmons (ed.), *A Devon Anthology* (1971), 185.

[112] See MS Baptismal Records, Bridgetown Chapel, Devon County RO, Exeter. Afterwards, Shore continued as minister in name, returning to Bridgetown for occasional services. He resigned formally in Apr. 1869.

[113] The *Totnes Times*, 17 Apr. 1869; D. Taylor and D. Bush, *The Golden Age of Hotels* (1974), 52.

[114] Joseph Buckley, *Modern Buxton* (1886), 34–6; John Leach, *The Book of Buxton* (Buckingham, 1987), 77.

[115] Which was opened in 1852. See Joseph Buckley, *Recollections of the Late John Smedley* (Manchester and London, 1888); *Matlock Bath as it Was, and Is . . . With a Short Sketch of the Personal History of John Smedley* (1866).

cially concerning his objections to both Anglicanism and Nonconformity.[116] So extensive was Smedley's spiritual influence, and so numerous were the Free Methodist chapels that he founded, that he soon became known throughout the area as the 'Prophet of the Peaks'.

While at Matlock, Shore became, according to one account, 'a great believer in homeopathy' and a qualified practitioner in the art of hydropathy (cold-water treatments combined with a strict diet).[117] This interest found expression at Smedley's Hydro and at the Matlock House Hydropathic, described as a 'beautiful and extensive structure', which Shore operated until around 1865.[118] Perhaps sensing greater opportunities elsewhere, Shore then opened the Malvern House Hydropathic Hotel on Hartington Road, Buxton, one of the town's first lodging houses to offer hydropathy.[119] Here he made an immediate mark upon the local commercial scene, his hotel enjoying considerable success in the town's highly competitive spa market.[120] Upon opening, it could accommodate forty patients; quickly, however, in 1872, 1881, and 1883, extensions had to be built; by 1884 the hotel, now operated by Shore's son-in-law, could accommodate some one hundred and eighty patients.[121] Shore also operated the Royal Hotel in Spring Gardens, Buxton, as a hydropathic spa in conjunction with Malvern House,[122] as well as Street House Farm, some five miles south of Buxton, where he produced a constant supply of meat and fresh vegetables for his rapidly expanding spa business.[123] As

[116] John Smedley, *Historical Sketch of the Ancient and Modern Church of Britain* (Derby, 1854); *The Ministerial Office and Mode of Worship of the Nonconformists, and That of the Church of England Considered* (Derby, 1854); *Remarks on the Deficient Mode in Which the Bible is Read in the Church of England* (1855).

[117] Buckley, *Modern Buxton*, 35.

[118] Ibid.; Trevor Marchington, 'The Development of Buxton and Matlock Since 1800', MA thesis (London, 1960), 108–9.

[119] Taylor and Bush, *The Golden Age of Hotels*, 52; *Harrod's Directory of Derbyshire*, (1870); *White's Directory of Derbyshire* (Sheffield, 1872); '1871 Religious Census, Derbyshire', Derby County RO, Matlock. Hydropathy was first practised in England at Ben Rhydding near Ilkley, West Riding, where Smedley was cured of typhoid; afterwards he became an ardent practitioner himself. See Leach, *The Book of Buxton*, 77. The Malvern House Hotel was later known as the Buxton Hydropathic Ltd., and still later as the Spa Hotel.

[120] Mike Langham and Colin Wells, *Buxton, a Pictorial History* (Guildford, 1993), 93–4.

[121] Marchington, 'The Development of Buxton and Matlock Since 1800', 108–9.

[122] *White's Directory of Derbyshire*, 1872.

[123] Then in the parish of Hartington Middle Quarter. See *Kelly's Directory of Derbyshire* (1876).

at Smedley's Hydro, divine worship was regarded at Malvern House as something of an integral part of the water therapy. As a final string to his bow Shore (beginning in 1868, or perhaps even earlier), organized and presided over services of the Free Church of England, which continued to be held at Malvern House until 1882.[124]

Shore's curious career as a Derbyshire hotel owner, hydropathy practitioner, and Free Church of England minister, however prosperous and successful, was nevertheless destined to be short-lived. On Wednesday 12 August 1874, while riding near Street House Farm with members of his family, he was thrown from his horse. Sustaining serious injuries he was quickly moved to the nearby Duke of York inn where he was pronounced dead. He was in his seventieth year.[125] He was buried, amidst much local mourning and ceremony, on 16 August in the churchyard of Bridgetown Chapel.[126] A memorial stone was subsequently placed by his descendants on the spot where he fell.[127] Bishop Phillpotts had died five years earlier. After Shore's departure from Devon, Bridgetown Chapel continued to be owned by the Duke of Somerset and continued to function as a chapel of the Free Church of England, but without, until 1870, the benefit of a permanent minister.[128] Ironically, on 30 July 1888, it was consecrated by Edward Bickersteth, Bishop of Exeter, as a chapel-of-ease to the parish of Berry Pomeroy and dedicated in honour of St. John the Evangelist.[129]

The high drama of the Shore case had a number of repercussions which made it, as with the Gorham affair, more than a tussle between an authoritarian bishop and an obstinate clergyman. It played a part in the formation of the Free Church of England; it

[124] See the *Free Church of England Magazine* (July 1867), 202; (Aug. 1868), 223; Buckley, *Matlock Bath*, 21–2, 72–3. It remains uncertain who presided at these services after Shore's death. See the *Free Church of England Magazine* (1881), 146; (1882), 165; (1883), 180.

[125] The *Buxton Advertiser*, 15 Aug. 1874; *High Peak News*, 15 Aug. 1874; the *Free Church of England Magazine* (1874), 177. His wife, Susannah, died in July 1868 and was buried in Bridgetown. See MS Burial Records, Bridgetown Chapel, Devon County RO, Exeter.

[126] The *Buxton Advertiser*, 19 Aug. 1874; *High Peak News*, 22 Aug. 1874.

[127] It has now been moved into an adjacent field owned by Street House Farm.

[128] See MSS Baptismal and Burial Records, Bridgetown Chapel, Devon County RO, Exeter.

[129] This occurred three years after the death of the twelfth Duke of Somerset and was undertaken by his son, the thirteenth Duke. The church now lies within the benefice of Totnes.

excited an acrimonious debate over the question of the indelibility of Anglican orders, and it prompted the introduction of the ill-fated Clergy Relief Bill in Parliament.

IX

With his secession from the Church of England in 1844, Shore helped set in motion what would soon be known as the Free Church of England.[130] Like a number of other bodies who left (or were forced out of) the Established Church, the Free Church of England continued to use the Prayer Book and adhere to the Thirty-Nine Articles, although it restricted the use of vestments, eliminated any reference to the doctrine of baptismal regeneration, and forbade any practice which diminished the clergy's freedom of conscience.[131] Alongside its sister organization, the Countess of Huntingdon's Connexion, it experienced quiet growth throughout its early years and a number of new congregations were organized in the West Country, including Exeter and Ilfracombe (1844), Southernhay (1845), Babbacombe (1852), and Bovey Tracey (1857).[132] Its members, both clerical and lay, were drawn largely from Anglican Evangelicalism, relatively few being gathered out of the ranks of Protestant Dissent. It remains uncertain whether the foundation and extension of the Free Church of England was primarily motivated by anti-Phillpotts sentiment, or was more broadly based. Its growth, however, was unquestionably aided by the tensions which developed between Phillpotts and the Evangelicals in the diocese of Exeter.

Within the Countess of Huntingdon's Connexion, on the other hand, during the 1850s there emerged a growing party of clergy and laity drawn not from Anglicanism but from the increasing number of free liturgical churches, or those Nonconformist bodies which continued to use some (or all) of the Anglican Prayer Book. Although these individuals looked to the Connexion for their ministry and fellowship, they nevertheless maintained a sturdy independence of spirit; they were, moreover, destined to become a definite political party within the Connexion. Despite numerous attempts to forge a formal union between the Free Church of England and the Connexion, by 1863 this had proved impossible.

[130] Merryweather, *History of the Free Church of England*, 68; Peaston, *The Prayer Book Tradition*, 71.

[131] Ibid. 80–7.

[132] See Brockett, *Nonconformity in Exeter*, 212–13.

Consequently, the Connexion to all intents and purposes, split apart: its 'Anglican' elements helping to form the new denomination which was registered in Chancery in August 1863 as the Free Church of England; its more traditional and conservative Nonconformist, Calvinistic, and connexional elements remaining as a small denomination which exists to this day.[133]

In 1873, the Free Church of England opened discussions with the recently founded Reformed Episcopal Church in America, and something resembling a federal union between the two bodies was soon effected.[134] Three years later, Benjamin Price was consecrated by Edward Cridge, the former Dean of Victoria, British Columbia, who had earlier been consecrated by George David Cummins, the former assistant Bishop of Kentucky in the Episcopal Church and presiding bishop of the Reformed Episcopal Church in America.[135] Five days later, Cridge and Price consecrated John Sugden as the second bishop in the Free Church of England.[136]

It was perhaps ironic that a Church whose origins can be traced back to a bitter struggle of an apostolically ordained clergyman to renounce his sacred orders should, in turn, become so concerned about apostolicity. A further paradox can be found in the fact that Shore, although clearly regarded by the Free Church of England as its principal founder, and despite his remaining a minister in its connexion for the rest of his life, had little to do with its formal administration after his release from prison. At an early stage, in 1844, when Pusey's appearance in the pulpit of the parish church at Ilfracombe while under the 'ban' of Oxford had provoked a considerable anti-Tractarian backlash in the town, Shore established a congregation of the Free Church of England in Ilfracombe and regularly preached there until a permanent minister could be secured.[137] He also made at least one generous contribution to the Free Church while proprietor of the Malvern House Hotel in Buxton.[138] Beyond this, however, it appears that Shore

[133] See Richard David Fenwick, 'The Free Church of England, Otherwise Known as the Reformed Episcopal Church, *c.*1845–*c.*1927: A Study in Church Growth and Development', Ph.D. thesis (Lampeter, 1995).

[134] Vaughan, *A History of the Free Church of England*, 70–1.

[135] Peaston, *The Prayer Book Tradition*, 72.

[136] Vaughan, *A History of the Free Church of England*, 267.

[137] The *Circular of the Free Church of England* (Jan. 1864), 81–97.

[138] The *Free Church of England Magazine* (1868), 344.

remained firmly outside the organizational structure of the Church, pursuing instead contacts with other Evangelical seceders such as Henry Bulteel, the former high Calvinist curate of St. Ebbe's, Oxford, who now lived in Devon.[139] Nor did Shore become involved in one of the principal campaigns of the Free Church of England's early life: its attempt to enact liturgical reform by purging the Prayer Book of those elements deemed to encourage sacerdotalism, Ritualism, and Anglo-Catholicism.[140]

X

From the outset, questions about the indelibility of holy orders cast a shadow over the Shore affair. The origins of this doctrine, which involved the essential nature of the Anglican priesthood, as distinct from its role or function, lay in patristic teaching and had been upheld by the Council of Trent.[141] In 1597, the doctrine of indelibility was brought into mainstream Anglican teaching through the publication of Book V of Hooker's *Ecclesiastical Polity*. This argued that once ordination had occurred a priest's clerical function might be suspended or degraded, but the ties binding him to its sacred and lasting character could not be severed by voluntary renunciation.[142] In 1604, the adoption of the seventy-sixth canon appeared to incorporate the doctrine of indelibility into the body of Anglican law. In theory, this would have applied to all episcopally ordained clergymen who had abandoned the Church of England since 1604, which would include a portion of the nearly two thousand Puritans who were ejected (or who withdrew) from their livings at the Restoration, the Nonjurors, the eighteenth-century Anglican rationalists who moved into Unitarianism, some of the Evangelicals who became Methodists, as well as the Tractarians (like John Henry Newman and Henry Edward Manning) who seceded to the Church of Rome.

Why all Shore's seceding predecessors had been spared prosecution under the seventy-sixth canon is not clear. The tolerance of eighteenth-century bishops offers a partial explanation. It is

[139] Bulteel's son married one of Shore's daughters in 1852. He also officiated at Bridgetown at the wedding of another one of Shore's daughters in 1858, and at the funeral of yet another of Shore's daughters in 1860. See MSS Marriage and Burial Records, Bridgetown Chapel, Devon County RO, Exeter.

[140] Peaston, *The Prayer Book Tradition*, 75.

[141] *EdR* (1849), 151.

[142] Richard Hooker, *Of the Laws of Ecclesiastical Politie* (1611), 411.

likely that the absence of any previous prosecution of this kind had diverted attention from the possibilities of the canon in the minds of modern bishops, less litigious and crusty than the notorious Phillpotts. Secessions to the obscurer corners of Protestant Dissent may have seemed too trivial to warrant provocative legal action in an era of advancing political liberalism: such action might also be construed as persecution and play into the hands of the Liberation Society. It is also possible that some High Churchmen would not have welcomed a lawsuit which could conceivably have been applied to those who seceded Romewards, though in such instances of succession from one branch of the Catholic Church to another, the issue of indelibility would presumably not have applied.

Phillpotts himself was too astute to become embroiled in a debate over the indelibility of Anglican orders. He consistently evaded the claims of some critics that he was advocating the doctrine of indelibility through judicial intimidation by simply asserting that he was engaged in nothing more than the proper enforcement of Church discipline and canon law. His prosecution of Shore was nevertheless unprecedented in the nearly two hundred and fifty years since the enactment of the canons, and, at the very least, it suggested that Phillpotts's understanding of a clergyman's ability to set aside his priestly character differed widely from common Anglican practice.

Some of Shore's predecessors in the Evangelical movement, like John Wesley, who had lived before the Oxford Movement precipitated a reaction away from High Church principles, spoke in favour of indelibility.[143] Even the Calvinistic Thomas Scott, a generation later than Wesley, writing in response to the secession of the Irish Evangelical John Walker, claimed that the ancient church 'considered the ministerial office and character as abiding . . . Even if', he asked, a clergyman 'should on any account be removed from his original charge; does not his office and character remain indelible; except taken away by him who delegated them?'[144] Shore's Evangelical contemporaries, however, qualified (or rejected outright) such claims. The *Christian Observer* argued that the propriety of a clergyman renouncing his orders depended

[143] See John Wesley, *A Farther Appeal to Men of Reason and Religion*, 4th edn. (Bristol, 1758), 88.

[144] Thomas Scott, *A Letter to the Revd Peter Roe* (Kilkenny, 1816), 26–7.

upon whether he had initially been called by God into the Church's ministry. If he had, then he could not renounce his status, for 'the call given by the Holy Spirit may not be dispensed with at the individual's pleasure'.[145] If, on the other hand, a clergyman came to believe that his initial call into the ministry had not been of God, and that he now believed he was being called to leave the Church or to serve in another pasture; or, conversely, that the Church had come to believe that its act of ordaining a person had been in error, both must remain free to act: the clergyman to renounce, and the Church to dispose.[146]

The related principle of apostolic succession was also endorsed by several Evangelical leaders of the post-Tractarian era who took pleasure in the apostolic descent of the Anglican priesthood.[147] The normative position of Evangelicals, however, was to accept the ministry of most other, non-episcopal Protestant churches as valid. Episcopacy was ancient and apostolical but not *jure divino*: it might pertain to the *bene esse* of the Church, but not to the *esse*.[148] Ultimately it was the Holy Spirit, not the terrestrial church, which called men to the ministry, and the conversion of sinners which validated its authenticity.

Phillpotts's prosecution of Shore was regarded as more than a high-handed disciplinary act by an authoritarian bishop. From the Evangelical point of view it possessed a theological dimension, relating it to the Gorham issue as yet another act of aggression against Reformation principles instigated by a Tractarian sympathizer. It was noted that Phillpotts had failed to proceed against seceders to Rome in his own diocese, among them his own chaplain William Maskell who seceded in 1850. This implied that the Bishop of Exeter placed Romeward secession in a different category from secession into Dissent, and saw it as a transition from one branch of the Catholic Church to another. Whether this is true or not is difficult to determine. When Henry Edward Manning, who had been in close and constant consultation with Phillpotts during and after the Gorham affair, subsequently seceded to Rome, the bishop was so shocked and angered that he denounced it as a public disgrace. Phillpotts, however, later

[145] *CO* (1846), 351. [146] *CO* (1849), 216, 287, 288, 360.

[147] See *CO* (1804), 482–3; (1836), 562; Thomas Gisborne, *A Familiar Survey of the Christian Religion, and of History* (1799), 538–40.

[148] See Norman Sykes, *Old Priest and New Presbyter* (Cambridge, 1956).

apologized to Manning saying that, distracted by the Shore case, he had spoken in sorrow as much as in anger.[149] None the less, it might well have appeared to Evangelicals that indelibility was being smuggled into official Anglican teaching through the ecclesiastical courts in the Shore case, much as attempts were being made in the Gorham case to force baptismal regeneration as the only acceptable interpretation of the baptismal rubric. If High Church bishops continued in this campaign, the Church's tradition of internal accommodation, by which Broad, High, and Evangelical churchmen co-existed in mutual tolerance, might be destroyed. The Shore case helped to sharpen up the internal party divisions of the Established Church and to intensify the alarm created by the secession of Newman and others. Moreover, fears of High Church intransigence were not confined to Evangelicals,[150] for Broad Churchmen also expressed alarm at the rigidity of Phillpotts's construction of Anglicanism which they perceived as a threat to the comprehensiveness of the National Church.[151]

XI

It is not surprising that moves were made to resolve the ambiguities of the canon by act of Parliament. In 1846, the Whigs, led by Lord John Russell, had taken office, and liberalism was in the ascendant.[152] In February 1849, E. P. Bouverie introduced the Clergy Relief Bill (as it was quickly labelled) in Parliament, in direct response to Shore's impending imprisonment. This proposed that seceding clergymen, after subscribing to the normal oaths required under the Toleration Act, should declare their dissent from the Articles of the Anglican Church. A copy of each declaration would then be forwarded to the local bishop and registered. This action would have the full force and effect of deprivation, the declarers being relieved of all burdens and liabilities as clergymen, and of all pains or penalties for acting as Dissent-

[149] Edmund Sheridan Purcell, *The Life of Cardinal Manning* (1896), i.629; ii.692 n.

[150] See Julian Charles Hare, 'Archdeacon Hare's Letter to the Hon. Richard Cavendish', 1850, in *Miscellaneous Pamphlets* (Cambridge, 1855).

[151] See Thomas Musgrave, *A Charge Delivered to the Clergy of the Diocese of York* (1849); John Kaye, *A Charge to the Clergy of the Diocese of Lincoln* (1852); Edward Coplestone, *A Charge Delivered to the Clergy of the Diocese of Llandaff* (1848).

[152] See G. I. T. Machin, *Politics and the Churches in Great Britain 1832 to 1868* (Oxford, 1977), 181–228.

ing ministers. They would also be allowed to sit in Parliament.[153] On 14 and 21 March and 2 May 1849, the Clergy Relief Bill provoked sharp debates in the Commons.[154] If Shore himself was a minor personage, many of those who debated his case were not, for they included Gladstone, Roundell Palmer, John Bright, Sir George Grey, and Joseph Hume.[155] MPs showed understandable confusion about some of the issues involved. The attorney general himself, when asked whether it was true that a clergyman leaving the Church of England for the Roman Church was free from all penalty, while one seceding to a Protestant Dissenting denomination was not, replied evasively that the question put to him was 'a point about which great difficulty existed both in the civil and the ecclesiastical courts', and that he 'must decline, without further consideration, to answer it'.[156] Understandably, this apparent inequity worried several members.

Though the debate produced the usual crop of red herrings (for example, should a seceding clergyman be allowed to stand for Parliament?) the issues which most concerned MPs were fairly clear, whatever the complexities of the law.[157] Would the official sanctioning by a Clergy Relief Bill of secession like Shore's not make exodus from the Church all too easy, thus devaluing the sacred and established character of the Anglican priesthood? It was one of the paradoxes of the Shore affair that an exponent of this view was none other than Henry Drummond, the former abettor of the Western Schism and the Catholic Apostolic Church, whose establishmentarian Toryism now came to the fore. How, asked Drummond, could ecclesiastical discipline be maintained by the Church if it abrogated the right to inflict civil penalties? Could the army and navy be run effectively if the House repealed the Mutiny Act? Passage of the Clergy Relief Bill in his view would amount to a virtual separation of Church and State.[158] Others agreed that it was important to keep some kind of strict formal control over exit from the Church, as well as entry into it. What

[153] See *Hansard: Third Series*, cii.1,128–33. Bouverie (1818–89) was the Liberal MP for Kilmarnock and the second son of the third Earl of Radnor, W. P. Bouverie, the distinguished Whig politician. He later served on the Ecclesiastical Commission for England and supported the disestablishment of the Irish Church.

[154] Ibid. 696–702, 1,072–5; civ.1,120–39.

[155] Ibid., cii.701, 1,074, 1,132–3; ciii.697–8, 700–1, 1,075; civ.1,126–8, 1,131–9.

[156] Ibid., cii.701. [157] Ibid. 1,075. [158] Ibid., ciii.699–700.

otherwise was to stop a clergyman from popping in and out of his sacred—and established—office as the whim took him? If the terms of egress were totally relaxed, H. C. Lacy argued, then 'a man might say he was a Dissenter now, and the next day say he was not a Dissenter.'[159] Why could some legal machinery not be created 'by which a clergyman might be divested of his office by the same authority which invested him with it?'[160] Should not some disciplinary controls be kept to stop a rascally cleric from seceding in order to avoid censure and punishment for immorality, or from a casual desire to take up some more profitable secular employment? Behind this argument lay, perhaps, some consciousness of the growing assimilation of the clerical profession to others like medicine and the law, which for some time had been tightening up their standards and procedural requirements.

On the other side was the liberal argument that the existing canon, if enforced on Shore, would encourage hypocrisy and make clergymen insincere by compulsion; although they conscientiously dissented from the doctrines of the Church, they must at present, apparently, remain in it, or subject themselves to penalties for preaching what they believed to be the truth in a building unlicensed by a bishop. The radical Joseph Hume wholeheartedly agreed with this argument: any other course, he claimed, would force parsons into insincerity and prevarication, and he hoped that Parliament 'would place every facility in the way of a clergyman's leaving the Church under such circumstances'.[161] On this construction what was at stake, in Shore's case, was liberty of conscience and the right of private judgment, themes repeatedly championed by liberals and Protestant Dissenters.

The Clergy Relief Bill passed out of the Commons on 25 July 1849,[162] and its first reading was held, without debate, in the Lords on the same day.[163] The parliamentary session ended on 1 August, however, and the bill died without a final reading. It was not reintroduced in the next session. It is difficult to determine precisely why a Relief Bill of some description was not enacted as the immediate result of the Shore case. When Bouverie's bill was introduced, it had received a warm reception from Evangelicals

[159] Ibid. ciii.697. [160] Ibid. 1,073–4.
[161] Ibid. 1,074. [162] Ibid. cvii.951–3. [163] Ibid. 949–53.

and Dissenters alike, who lauded its aims and pressed for its swift enactment.[164] The bill may not have been reintroduced, however, because public interest in the case diminished after Shore's release from prison, or, more likely, because the amended and watered-down version had been severely criticized by both churchmen and Dissenters, prompting Bouverie and his supporters to conclude that no bill was better than a bad bill.[165] It was not until 1870 that relief was definitively granted to seceding clergymen. The Clerical Disabilities Act[166] provided that after resignation clergymen should execute a deed of relinquishment abandoning all privileges and obligations acquired at ordination, which was to be enrolled in the Court of Chancery.[167] They would then be free to act as laymen, or as Dissenting ministers, without penalty or encumbrance from their former character as priests in holy orders. This statute was later modified by the Incumbents Resignation Act of 1871,[168] and by the Burial Laws Amendment Act of 1880.[169]

XII

The Shore case is one of the more curious and tangled episodes in the legal history of the Victorian Church. Its timing contributed much to the perplexity and anger surrounding it. The extension of Tractarianism and the weakening of Evangelical confidence and leadership meant that it would not pass unnoticed in high places. The furore over the recent secession of Newman and the Gorham case focused attention on its outcome, while Phillpotts, the chief combatant, was already much in the public eye, both locally and nationally, for his numerous acts of episcopal high-handedness. In the Shore case, as in Gorham's, two unusually strong-minded clergymen, each convinced of their rectitude, collided head on. Each was no doubt motivated by party spirit as

[164] See *CO* (1849), 216, 287, 288, 360; *Non* (1849), 222, 229; Culling Eardley, *An Appeal to the Country*, 23.

[165] Both Shore and Baptist Noel had criticized the amended bill for requiring seceders to suffer deprivation from the Christian (as opposed to Anglican) ministry, to which they had been called. See the *Record* (23 Apr. 1849); *EC* (1849), 294.

[166] 33 and 34 Vict. Cap. 91.

[167] See Benjamin Whitehead, *Statutes Relating to Church and Clergy* (1894), 187–9.

[168] 34 and 35 Vict. CH 44 SS 15.

[169] 43 and 44 Vict. CH 41 SS 14. See John Henry Blunt, *The Book of Church Law* (1921), 213–14.

well as conscientious religious principle. Shore was convinced that it was God's will for him to continue at Bridgetown and, as Phillpotts painfully discovered, no amount of ecclesiastical pressure, discipline, or intimidation could alter this conviction.

No doubt Shore acted contumaciously in disregarding the command of his diocesan to cease from officiating as a clergyman in the diocese of Exeter. Had he wished, he could have reduced the tension of the affair and saved his Church and bishop from adverse publicity by securing preferment elsewhere, from some Evangelical patron. His public campaign of vengeance against Phillpotts and the Tractarians tended to deteriorate into a personal vendetta. It certainly exacerbated the conflict of what were now becoming recognizably rival Church parties.[170] The Shore affair presented both antagonists with dilemmas and a tension between principles to which they held dear. In Shore's case, it was the tension which we have seen recurring in other parallel cases: that between loyalty to the Anglican establishment and loyalty to the 'Gospel principles' of the Reformation, which appeared increasingly threatened nationally as well as in the diocese of Exeter. It also presented the Evangelical party with an *embarras du choix*: condemnation of the Privy Council's ruling compromised their own Erastianism; conversely, submission to it encouraged heretical doctrine and the violation of Shore's right of private judgement.

Phillpotts too had a tightrope to walk between his obligation to maintain the unity of his diocese—and the comprehensive National Church of which it was a part—and his inbred desire to enforce obedience and uniformity among the clergy under his control. When reminiscing with Henry Edward Manning about the Shore affair some years later, Phillpotts asked the Cardinal how the Roman Catholic Church dealt with recalcitrant priests. 'We have a ready remedy for a priest who disobeys his bishop,' came the reply. 'We suspend him *a divinis* by withdrawing the "faculties" given to him on taking charge of a mission.' 'I envy the Church of Rome', Phillpotts responded, 'for its possession of such an effective weapon.'[171] Paradoxically, Phillpotts's passion for censure and litigation helped to undermine the very unity of

[170] See Walter Farquhar Hook, *Letter to the Bishop of Ripon, on the State of Parties in the Church of England* (1841); F. D. Maurice, *Reasons for Not Joining a Party in the Church* (1841).

[171] Purcell, *Life of Cardinal Manning*, ii.692 n.

Church and State which (as with other High Churchmen) he sought to maintain.

Questions remain as to Phillpotts's primary motivation in prosecuting Shore. He may have wished to uphold an uncompromising enforcement of episcopal authority as recognized in canon law, but this seems inconsistent with his behaviour during the case of *Escott* v. *Mastin*. He may have believed that all seceders into the Nonconformist ministry should be prosecuted, but this is inconsistent with his practice elsewhere, since other Evangelical seceders within his diocese escaped ecclesiastical censure and prosecution. It is possible that Shore was used as an example in the expectation that the threat of arrest, ruinous prosecution, and a lengthy prison sentence would sufficiently deter all but the most determined seceder from following his example.[172] On the other hand, Phillpotts may have been less concerned about ecclesiastical discipline and authority, or the secession of an unimportant Evangelical, than about the loss of Bridgetown Chapel to the Church of England. He alluded to this point on a number of occasions, and his provocative outburst upon the absent Duke of Somerset during the debate over the Clergy Relief Bill suggests that the animosity created by the unsatisfactory conclusion of the endowment negotiations remained a prime force behind his actions.

The reverberations of the Shore case, however strong, did not match those of the Gorham affair. Its implications were less serious because it affected only those clergymen who actively chose to secede into Dissent, and not the great mass of Evangelical clergy. Moreover, it did not go to the very heart of Anglican theological and doctrinal identity as did the debate on baptismal regeneration. Though the issue of indelibility lurked beneath the surface, it was not made fully explicit. The right of a priest in the Established Church to transfer his clerical functions elsewhere was—unlike many doctrinal issues—at least a soluble question, which could be laid to rest by a simple Act of Parliament. Shore was a lone and obscure individual, not a natural leader, nor the head of a group; moreover, he was not as well-established in the Evangelical party as Gorham, and not as likely to set in motion a landslide of similar secessions.

[172] See *Non* (1849), 299.

At the same time his case was important. It disturbed the already troubled consciences of Evangelical clergymen. Richard Spooner, speaking in the Commons on Shore's behalf, described how he had received a heavy pile of mail from sympathetic clerics, expressing 'regret that any person should be exposed to ecclesiastical censures on account of their Dissent from the doctrines of the Established Church.'[173] The Bridgetown Chapel affair was yet another ingredient in the few, critical years which saw publication of Tract 90 in 1841, the Scottish Disruption in 1843, Newman's secession in 1845, Gorham's legal ordeal between 1847 and 1850, and Baptist Noel's dramatic secession in 1848. There can be little doubt that the Shore case added to the crisis of confidence which seized not only Evangelicalism, but Anglicanism itself, in the mid-nineteenth century.

[173] *Hansard: Third Series*, ciii.699.

Conclusion

Despite all the polemic and publicity which accompanied the various Evangelical secessions, the number of clergymen who formally seceded from the Church of England in the first half of the nineteenth century was relatively small. This does not mean, however, that their secessions were without significance. As we have seen, they were an unsettling influence on many of their brethren and on the Church of England as a whole. Their role in sharpening up party conflict within the Church was not negligible. The existence of various groups of 'ultras' in the Evangelical ranks helped to confirm suspicious High Churchmen in their stereotyped views about the dangers inherent in extreme Protestantism. Here, it seemed, was evidence of the tendency of religious individualism—the belief in 'private judgement'—to produce schism and anarchy. The seceders were living proofs that Evangelicals were unsound in their churchmanship, and had a dangerous proclivity to Dissent. Men like Henry Drummond and Edward Irving, trusting in the imaginary prompting of the Holy Spirit, showed the folly of evangelical religious 'enthusiasm'. Groups like those around John Walker and John Nelson Darby showed the consequences of attempting rash and radical biblical exegesis, without reliance on the accumulated wisdom of tradition. The seceders underlined the need for a fixed, objective, dogmatic creed, which could only be provided by a tradition-based faith, founded on the accumulated wisdom of the Church Catholic.

There is little doubt that the great mass of Evangelicals who remained loyal to the Church of England were often gravely embarrassed by these well-publicized secessions from their ranks. Their claim to be not only good churchmen, but the only *true* churchmen, was undermined by the exodus of their disgruntled colleagues, angrily shaking the dust of Anglicanism off their feet as they departed. The seceders compromised the efforts of men like Charles Simeon and William Goode to build up a sensible, orderly Evangelical party in the Church, which was moderate enough to attract intelligent and respectable converts. They were perhaps even more disturbing because they articulated ideas and anxieties which existed in the minds of a large number of respectable Evangelicals, and gave them dangerous publicity. The seceders also brought into unwanted salience half-concealed doubts—doubts about the purity of the liturgy, for example, about the value of the Church–State connection, and (in the case of the pre-millennialists) doubts about the spiritual state of the present-day Evangelical party. By publicizing their views they provided ammunition not only for the opponents of 'vital religion', but also for the rivals of the Church of England itself. The secessions were clearly a godsend to critics of the Establishment, who delighted in showing up the corruptions of the State Church. Seceders like Henry Bulteel, J. C. Philpot, and Baptist Noel, who published violent attacks on the apostasy of the Church which they had abandoned, provided propaganda for the cause of disestablishment.

Nonconformist leaders entertained the hope that there might one day be large-scale secessions of Evangelicals to Protestant Dissent, precipitated perhaps by some great *cause célèbre*. As we have seen, the Gorham and Shore cases, and the Noel secession, had all aroused excitement and expectation in Dissenting circles. But there was to be no English equivalent to the Scottish Disruption of 1843. The almost simultaneous crises produced by Gorham, Shore, and Noel shook Anglican Evangelicals, but the shudder was brief. While appeals calling for mass secession from the Church were occasionally offered during the 1850s—such as that of the wealthy and eccentric spa owner John Smedley (himself a seceder from the Church)—Evangelical alarm was short-lived.[1] Perhaps remarkably, the period succeeding that which is examined in this study produced no group secessions equivalent to those of the 'Kellyites', the 'Walkerites', the Western Schismatics, the Catholic Apostolicals, and the Christian Brethren.

This is perhaps surprising. The later decades of the nineteenth century were marked by recurrent party conflict and crisis. The Church was racked by the storm over publication of *The Origin of Species* (1859) and *Essay and Reviews* (1860), by the Colenso affair

[1] See John Smedley, *A Letter Addressed to the Ministers and Members of the Section of the Church of England Denominated Evangelical* (Derby, c.1855).

(1863–5), and by the long, drawn-out warfare between outraged Evangelicals and militant Ritualists. In the late nineteenth century, the High Church wing of the Established Church increased its numerical strength, often at the expense of the 'Gospel clergy'. Yet the trickle of Evangelical seceders seems almost to have dried up. There were no more group secessions, and individual withdrawals, such as those in protest against Ritualism, appear to have occurred less often, mostly involving clergy who seceded into the Free Church of England or one of its related connexions.[2]

Why was this? Events that did not happen are notoriously more difficult to explain than those that did, so any answer must be highly speculative, especially since the late nineteenth century lies well beyond the period on which this study has focused. Moreover, despite the appearance of several valuable monographic studies, the history of late Victorian Evangelicalism contains much unmapped territory.[3] Nevertheless, one or two highly tentative suggestions can be offered.

The Gorham case might provide a clue to the relative absence of secessions in the 1850s and 1860s. If the case threatened to trigger off mass secessions in its early stage, when Bishop Phillpotts had gained the initial, favourable verdict in the Court of Arches, the final judgment could be construed as something of an Evangelical victory. The highest tribunal had now declared that the Evangelical interpretation of the baptismal service was valid, or at least not inconsistent with the formularies of the Church of England. If the contest was indeed what some claimed it to be, namely a battle for the survival of Reformation principles in the Church of England, then the Reformers appeared to have triumphed. Moreover, the knowledge that the Judicial Committee of the Privy Council was henceforth always in play as an arbiter in such cases, may have comforted anxious Evangelicals who feared for the future of the Gospel at the hands of autocratic High

[2] See Richard David Fenwick, 'The Free Church of England, Otherwise Known as the Reformed Episcopal Church, c.1845–c.1927: A Study in Church Growth and Development', Ph.D. thesis (Lampeter, 1995).

[3] For details on this period see B. E. Hardman, 'The Evangelical Party in the Church of England 1855–65', Ph.D. thesis (Cambridge, 1963); K. J. Heasman, 'The Influence of the Evangelicals Upon . . . Voluntary Charitable Institutions in the Second Half of the Nineteenth Century', Ph.D. thesis (London, 1959); Martin Wellings, 'Aspects of Late Nineteenth Century Anglican Evangelicalism: The Response to Ritualism, Darwinism, and Theological Liberalism', D.Phil. thesis (Oxford, 1989).

Church prelates like Phillpotts. It was now less probable that any bishop would attempt high-handedly to winkle Evangelicals out of his diocese, or to impose partisan views of the Anglican formularies on his clergy.

It is possible too that the departure of the most advanced, 'Romanizing' Tractarians with Newman in 1845, and with Manning in the wake of the Gorham judgment around 1850, helped to relieve some of the anxiety experienced by Evangelicals at the progress of the Oxford Movement. Provocative figures like W. G. Ward and Frederick Oakeley, who had shocked Protestants by attacking the Reformers in the *British Critic*, seemed now to have revealed themselves in their true colours by apostatizing openly to Rome. Did the Romeward secessions clear the air and lower the tension? Though the Anglo-Catholics retained a formidable presence in the Church, they were perhaps no longer so alarming. They were now under the tutelage of Pusey, whose loyalty to the Church was deep and who did not share the root and branch antipathy to Evangelicals displayed by some of the Romanizers.[4] Despite the continued threat of Ritualism, it seemed to some 'Gospel clergy' that the energies of the Oxford Movement were now directed less to controversy than to quiet work in the parishes.[5] By this time, moreover, Evangelicals had had time to organize their counter-attack. They were more secure. In apologists like William Goode and Francis Close, they produced a formidable defence of the Evangelical position and of their claim to a rightful place in the Church of England.[6]

It is likely that, by the 1860s, the spectre of Roman subversion within the Church, though still alive, did not arouse quite the same anxiety: with the arrival of Cardinal Wiseman and the furore over Ecclesiastical Titles, it was the rejuvenated Roman Church itself which was the chief target of Evangelical hostility, more than the Anglo-Catholic wing of the Church of England.[7] The external enemy drew most (but not all) of the 'no popery' fire. Though Evangelicals remained ever watchful of Catholic activity in the

[4] David Forrester, *Young Doctor Pusey* (1989), 108–34.

[5] See James Bentley, *Ritualism and Politics in Victorian Britain* (Oxford, 1978); George William Herring, 'Tractarianism to Ritualism', D.Phil. thesis (Oxford, 1984).

[6] See Peter Toon, *Evangelical Theology, 1833–56. A Response to Tractarianism* (1979).

[7] See John Wolffe, *The Protestant Crusade in Great Britain, 1829–1860* (Oxford, 1991).

Church, they learned in time to come to terms with its existence as a strong and permanent element in the Establishment.

Evangelical loyalty to the Church may also have been enhanced during this period by the continued extension of sympathetic patronage; of 'spheres of influence' which provided employment (often in influential livings) for a number of Evangelicals. This enhanced profile sometimes led to further preferment in the Church. In 1826, for example, Francis Close was appointed (by Charles Simeon) to the perpetual curacy of Holy Trinity, Cheltenham, where he exercised a powerful and wide-ranging ministry until his elevation to the deanery of Carlisle in 1856. At Carlisle, where he was universally recognized as one of the leaders of the 'Gospel cause' in the north, he was able to employ his now considerable influence on behalf of the movement until his retirement in 1881.

Another factor which may have diminished the supply of Evangelical seceders was the continued Nonconformist campaign to enact disestablishment. During the mid-nineteenth century, the liberation movement, in an effort to bolster support, became more militant and more closely identified with the forces of liberalism—factors which hardly encouraged Evangelicals (however indifferent they might have become about their own Church) to abandon the *via media*. Hence, secession may have appeared less attractive, the advantages of the Anglican Establishment more obvious.

If religious anxiety lay behind some Evangelical secessions during the first half of the nineteenth century, so too did social and political tensions. By the mid-1850s, these too had largely subsided. The fears of atheistical radicalism which had alarmed churchmen from the 1790s through the 'Hungry Forties' and the Chartist era, had lost much of their force. Churchmen had come to terms with the traumatic crisis of 1829–32. The shock of Catholic Emancipation and the Reform Bill, which had intensified the millennial expectations of men like Drummond and Irving, was now water under the bridge. The Whigs turned out not to be the anti-clerical Erastians that many Tory churchmen of the Drummond type had feared. It was, in fact, the Whig Lord John Russell who appointed John Bird Sumner to the see of Canterbury in 1848. Indeed, between 1855 and 1860, Lord Palmerston used his patronage to appoint a row of Evangelicals to the episcopate.[8] The acute 'Church in danger' crisis of the early 1830s had, by now, subsided. The Established Church met the challenge to its hegemony by a massive programme of church and school building, and regained much of the confidence which had ebbed away in earlier decades. By the early 1850s, Britain was moving into the period of the mid-Victorian economic boom. Politically we are in what W. L. Burn has termed the 'Age of Equipoise'.[9] Chartism had collapsed. The Corn Laws were repealed. Liberalism was in the ascendant, and a high degree of social and political consensus was, to some extent, replacing the sharp class conflicts of the 1830s and 1840s. By the 1850s and 1860s, the eschatological anxiety which gripped many Evangelicals in the early decades, and had contributed to the unease and psychic anxiety which encouraged secession, had largely subsided.

Moreover, in the later decades of the century, the Church of England began to cope more effectively with the problems of 'spiritual destitution' in the cities. Church extension funded by private contributions showed that the Establishment was now outstripping its denominational rivals in the field of evangelism and pastoral care. Significant relaxations in the law now made it easier for clergymen to copy the evangelistic methods of Dissenters and Methodists. In 1855, thanks to Lord Shaftesbury, the law prohibiting the assembly of more than twenty persons outside the church for Anglican worship, was repealed: it was now possible to hold services in the open air, or in the public halls.[10] Had Baptist Noel still been an Anglican clergyman in 1860, it is possible that he would no longer have despaired of the ability of the Established Church to tackle the problems of metropolitan irreligion as effectively as the Nonconformists.

A final factor may have been the realization that the various seceders, for all the publicity which their departures generated, rarely attained considerable success as Nonconformist ministers, at least in the eyes of the world. Few attracted great followings, or established buoyant congregations which prospered beyond their retirement or death. Some, like George Baring and James Shore, abandoned the ministry altogether. And those who were relatively successful, such as James Harington Evans, Joseph Charles

[8] See Owen Chadwick, *The Victorian Church*, 3rd edn. (1971), i.468–76.

[9] See W. L. Burn, *The Age of Equipoise* (1964).

[10] Chadwick, *The Victorian Church*, i.524–5.

Philpot, and Baptist Noel, all seemed somewhat diminished in stature and of less concern to the public, as a consequence of their secession from the Established Church. Of the more than one hundred clergy who abandoned the Anglican fold during the first half of the nineteenth century, perhaps only John Nelson Darby attained considerable—and lasting—influence, and that indirectly (and in spite of his own shortcomings) through the enduring popularity of dispensational theology in North America.

But this is to stray into the realm of conjecture. The fact remains that Evangelical group secessions seem to have dried up after the middle of the nineteenth century. The exodus of bodies like the 'Walkerites' or 'Irvingites' has not been repeated during the last one hundred and fifty years. At the climax of the furore against Ritualism in the 1890s and in the early years of the present century, attempts were made to organize a collective secession of Evangelical clergy, who were disgusted at the legal protection which had been accorded to those using novel 'Catholic' rituals. The response to these upheavals was negligible. While at least three Evangelical clergymen publicly seceded from the Church at various times, together with a small number of lay secessions, the leaders of the party remained resolute against any such step. As J. C. Ryle, perhaps the most influential Evangelical of the late nineteenth century, argued fiercely in 1891, 'secession is not necessary. So long as the Articles and Prayer Book are not altered we occupy an impregnable position. We have an open Bible and our pulpits are free . . . Above all, secession would be cowardly. To launch the lifeboat and forsake the ship because she had carried away her masts and lost her rudder and is at present helpless—to leave an innocent body of passengers to the charge of a mutinous and unfaithful crew . . . would be an unworthy and disastrous mistake.'[11] Evangelicals realized that a large-scale secession would only leave the Church more securely in Ritualist hands, and might, disastrously, provoke disestablishment by an angry and Protestant-dominated Parliament.

None the less, the threat of Evangelical secessions has continued to plague the Church of England from time to time. At the onset of a new millennium, for example, members of the Evangelical pressure group *Reform* are threatening to secede from the

[11] See J. C. Ryle, *Is All Scripture Inspired?* (1891), 62–3.

Church over such issues as the ordination of women to the priesthood, the elevation of women to the episcopate, and (especially) the acceptance of practising homosexuals in the ministry. Moreover, in the wider Anglican Communion conflict between Evangelicals (mainly from England, Australia, and the Third World) and revisionists (mainly from North America) is mounting over similar issues, threatening a major schism. Fortunately, any further consideration of these issues lies outside the remit of this investigation.

APPENDIX

Evangelical Seceders from the Church of England, *c.*1730–1900

1. Clerical secessions to Protestant Nonconformity

Robert Aitken: *c.*1836 ('Aitkenite'; later returned to the Church of England)
Mr Arnold: *c.*1818 (Western Schism)[1]
Nicholas Armstrong: 1832 (Catholic Apostolic Church)
Charles Tamberlane Astley: *c.*1878 (Presbyterian)
James Babb: *c.*1844 (Supralapsarian Calvinist)
James Scott Baker: 1832 (Nondenominational)
Frederick Bannister: *c.*1840s (Plymouth Brethren)
George Baring: 1816 (Western Schism)
Henry Battiscombe: 1828 (Baptist)
George Bevan: 1816 (Western Schism)
Henry Birch: *c.*1838 (Huntingtonian/Strict Baptist)
Mr Bird: *c.*1840s (Nondenominational)
Henry Borlase: 1832 (Plymouth Brethren)
John Bradford: 1778 (Countess of Huntingdon's Connexion)
Charles L. Brenton: 1831 (Strict and Particular Baptist; later Plymouth Brethren)
Isaac Bridgman: 1822 (Nondenominational)
William John Brook: 1803/4 (Calvinistic Baptist)
H. F. Bruder: *c.*1835 (Nondenominational)
Henry B. Bulteel: 1831 (Catholic Apostolic Church; later Strict and Particular Baptist; later Nondenominational with possibly some Plymouth Brethren connection)
William Marriott Caldecott: 1831 (Plymouth Brethren)
James T. Campbell: 1832 (Congregationalist)
Robert Harkness Carne: 1820 (Independent Calvinist)
Edward Carr: 1811 (Nondenominational)
George Carr: 1830s (Plymouth Brethren)
Edward Warren Caulfield: 1849 (Nondenominational)
Charles Chapman: 1850 (Baptist)

[1] Possibly the Revd Henry Arnold, vicar of Longstock, Hampshire.

Thomas Charles: 1811 (Welsh Calvinistic Methodist)
George Chute: 1874 (Free Church of England)
John Marsden Code: 1836 (Plymouth Brethren)
Mr Cole: *c.*1831 (Strict and Particular Baptist)
John Corser: *c.*1830 (Nondenominational; later possible Plymouth Brethren connections)
Thomas C. Cowan: 1817 (Western Schism; later Baptist)
James Creighton: 1783 (Wesleyan Methodist)
Edward Crowley: n.d. (Plymouth Brethren)
Thomas Tennison Cuffe: 1850 (Countess of Huntingdon's Connexion)
Henry Dalton: 1835 (Cathlic Apostolic Church)
Raymond Samuel Daniell: 1873 (Free Church of England)
John Nelson Darby: 1828/33 (Plymouth Brethren)
Mr Digby: *c.*1840s (Nondenominational)
Robert Crawford Dillon: 1840 (Reformed Church of England)
John Dodson: 1849 (Baptist)
James Harington Evans: 1815 (Western Schism; later Baptist)
John Gambold: 1742 (Moravian)
Robert Gibson: 1833 (Nondenominational)
Bernard Gilpin: 1835 (Congregationalist)
Robert Govett: *c.*1844 (Strict and Particular Baptist)
Richard Greaves: 1836 (Unitarianism/Theosophy)
Thomas Hubberd Gregg: 1860s (Reformed Episcopal Church)
Samuel Hall: 1833 (Independent Calvinist; later returns to the Church of England)
George Hamilton: *c.*1770 (Irish Nondenominational)
Henry Anthony Hammond: *c.*1883 (Plymouth Brethren)
Edward Hardman: 1834 (Catholic Apostolic Church)
Charles Frearson Hargrove: 1835 (Plymouth Brethren)
James Lampen Harris: 1832 (Plymouth Brethren)
John Hawker: *c.*1830 (Eldad Chapel)
J. B. Heard: n.d. (Nondenominational)
Richard Hill: *c.*1835 (Plymouth Brethren)
Roger Hitchcock: 1826 (Strict and Particular Baptist)
Richard Holden: n.d. (Plymouth Brethren)[2]
Thomas Housman: 1837 (Strict and Particular Baptist)
Thomas Hughes: *c.*1830s (Trinity Chapel, Hackney)
William Hurn: 1822 (Congregationalist)
Thomas Husband: 1833 (Strict and Particular Baptist)
John Hutchins: *c.*1740s (Moravian; later Quaker)
Benjamin Ingham: *c.*1736 (Moravian; later 'Inghamite'; later 'Sandamanian')

[2] Possibly of the diocese of Manchester, who drops off the *Clergy List* after 1888.

Andrew J. Jukes: 1844 (Baptist)
John Kay: 1834 (Strict and Particular Baptist)
Thomas Kelly: 1803 (Kellyites)
William George Lambert: *c.*1831 (Nondenominational; possibly Plymouth Brethren)
William Lush: *c.*1850s (Strict and Particular Baptist)
Timothy R. Matthews: 1832 (Primitive Episcopal; later, Catholic Apostolic Church; later, Latter Day Saint)
Robert Meek: *c.*1830 (Presbyterian; later returned to the Church of England)
Capel Molyneux: 1872 (Nondenominational)
William Morshead: 1832 (Independent; Plymouth Brethren sympathies)
Christopher Neville: 1870 (Nondenominational)
Isaac Nicholson: 1792 (Congregationalist)
Hon. Baptist W. Noel: 1848 (Baptist)
Robert Norton: 1854 (Catholic Apostolic Church)
C. H. O'Donoghue: 1832 (Baptist)
Francis Okely: 1740 (Baptist; later Moravian)
A. C. Ord: n.d. (Plymouth Brethren)[3]
Henry John Owen: 1833 (Catholic Apostolic Church)
John William Peters: 1834 (Nondenominational)
Joseph Charles Philpot: 1835 (Strict and Particular Baptist)
Henry James Prince: *c.*1843 (Princeites; Agapemonites)
Charles Raby: *c.*1811 (Independent Calvinist)
Arthur Augustus Rees: 1840s (Nondenominational)
John Richardson: 1762 (Wesleyan Methodist)
Mr Robinson: 1804 (Walkerites)
Mr Robinson: 1830s (Plymouth Brethren)
Jacob Rogers: 1740 (Baptist; later Moravian)
Daniel Rowland: 1763 (Welsh Calvinistic Methodist)
Richard Burdon Sanderson: *c.*1830s (Baptist)
Mr Seager: *c.*1840s (Nondenominational)
Dr Shaw: 1870 (Free Church of England)
James Shore: 1844 (Free Church of England)
Isaac Slee: 1779 (Baptist)
Thomas Snow: 1815 (Western Schism; later returned to the Church of England)
Charles Stirling: *c.*1900 (Nondenominational)
James B. Stoney: 1834 (Plymouth Brethren)
Leonard Strong: *c.*1827 (Nondenominational; later Plymouth Brethren)

[3] Of Bournemouth.

Robert Taylor: 1818 (Deism)
William Taylor: 1783 (Countess of Huntingdon's Connexion)
William Tiptaft: 1831 (Strict and Particular Baptist)
Frederick Tryon: 1839 (Strict and Particular Baptist)
Walter Thomas Turpin: *c.*1830s (Plymouth Brethren)
Thomas Tweedy: *c.*1833 (Plymouth Brethren)
John Walker: 1804 (Walkerites)
Lewis Way: 1824 (English Protestant Chapel, Marboeuf, Paris)
George Vicesimus Wigram: 1831 (Plymouth Brethren)
Thomas Wills: 1783 (Countess of Huntingdon's Connexion)

2. *Some notable 'irregulars'/'half-regulars' in the Church of England/Ireland*

John Berridge: *c.*1750s (parish of Everton)
Walter Chapman: *c.*1750s (Countess of Huntingdon's Connexion)
Thomas Coke: *c.*1778 (Wesleyan Methodist)
Brian Bury Collins: 1780s (Wesleyan Methodist)
Henry Draper: *c.*1809 (Countess of Huntingdon's Connexion)
Sir Culling Eardley: *c.*1850 (Nondenominational)
John Eyre: 1775 (Nondenominational)
John Fletcher: 1768 (Wesleyan Methodist)
Henry Gauntlett: 1805 (St. Mary's Chapel, Reading)
Thomas Haweis: 1768 (Countess of Huntingdon's Connexion)
Rowland Hill: 1769/1770 (Surrey Chapel, London)
Griffith Jones: *c.*1716 (Welsh Calvinistic Methodist)
Charles Kinchin: 1739 (Wesleyan Methodist; later Moravian)
William Mann: 1786 (Bethesda Chapel, Dublin)
Henry Piers: 1742 (Wesleyan Methodist)
John Simpson: *c.*1740s (Moravian)[4]
Edward Smyth: 1786 (Irish Wesleyan Methodist; Bethesda Chapel, Dublin)
John Wesley: 1739 (Wesleyan Methodism)
George Whitefield: 1739 (Calvinistic Methodist)
William Williams: 1743 (Welsh Calvinistic Methodist)

3. *Some notable lay seceders to Protestant Nonconformity*

Baroness Barham: 1813 (Welsh Calvinistic Methodism)
Sir Thomas Baring: 1815 (Western Schism; later returned to the Church of England)
John Bayford: *c.*1833 (Catholic Apostolic Church)
John Gifford Bellett: 1827/8 (Plymouth Brethren)

[4] Simpson or Sympson.

Robert Mackenzie Beverley: *c.*1840s (Plymouth Brethren)
John Bate Cardale: 1831 (Catholic Apostolic Church)
Henry Drummond: 1815 (Western Schism; later Catholic Apostolic Church)
James Pierrepont Greaves: 1817 (Theosophy)
Anthony Norris Groves: 1827 (Plymouth Brethren)
Percy Francis Hall: *c.*1830 (Plymouth Brethren)
Howell Harris: 1736 (Welsh Calvinistic Methodist)
Lady Selina Hastings: *c.*1761 (Countess of Huntingdon's Connexion)
Grey Hazlerigg: *c.*1850s (Strict and Particular Baptist)
Thomas Read Kemp: 1816 (Western Schism)
William George Lambert: 1832 (Plymouth Brethren)
John Mason: *c.*1806 (Baptist; later Western Schism; later Baptist)
Francis W. Newman: *c.*1830 (Nondenominational; later Unitarian)
Benjamin Wills Newton: 1832 (Plymouth Brethren)
Spencer Perceval: 1834 (Catholic Apostolic Church)
Lady Theodosia Powerscourt: *c.*1833 (Plymouth Brethren)
Thomas H. Reynolds: *c.*1848 (Plymouth Brethren)
John Smedley: *c.*1850 (Free Methodism)
Henry William Soltau: 1837 (Plymouth Brethren)
Thomas Vasey: 1788 (Wesleyan Methodist)
Granville Augustus William Waldegrave, third Lord Radstock: *c.*1860s (Plymouth Brethren)
Francis Valentine Woodhouse: *c.*1833 (Catholic Apostolic Church)

4. *Some notable seceders (former Evangelicals) who became High Churchmen/Tractarians prior to seceding to the Church of Rome*

William Dodsworth: 1850
Frederick William Faber: 1845
Henry Edward Manning: 1851
John Henry Newman: 1845
George Dudley Ryder: 1846
Richard Waldo Sibthorp: 1841
George Spencer: 1830
Sir Harry Trelawny: 1810
Henry William Wilberforce: 1850
Robert Isaac Wilberforce: 1854
William Wilberforce: 1863

BIBLIOGRAPHY

PRIMARY SOURCES

Alnwick Castle, Northumberland, MSS 'Drummond Papers'.

Baring Brothers, 8 Bishopsgate, London, MSS 'Northbrook Papers'.

Bodleian Library, Oxford:

MS Add. c.290, 'The Principal Clergy of London', 1844.

MSS 'Annual Reports of the Oxford and Oxfordshire Auxiliary Society for Promoting Christianity among the Jews'.

MSS St. Edmund Hall 67 1–20, 'The Diary of the Revd John Hill'.

MSS Eng. Misc. e. 351–60, 'The Diary of the Revd John Rashdall'.

MS No. G.A. Oxon. 4° 271.

MSS Letters, 'Gorham Letters'.

MSS Phillips-Robinson, c.514, 60–2.

MSS 'Topographical Oxfordshire'.

Bristol City Record Office, Bristol, MSS 'Bishop's Transcripts, Parish of St. Thomas', Bristol'.

Bristol City Record Office, Bristol, MSS 'Records of the Diocese of Bristol, Act Book', 1810–36.

Cambridge University Library, Hulsean Prize Essay, 1962, MS 'Evangelicalism 1785–1835', by Haddon Wilmer.

Cambridge University Library, Thornton Family Papers, MS 7674.

Derbyshire County Record Office, Matlock, MS '1871 Religious Census, Derbyshire'.

Devon Record Office, Exeter, MSS 'Berry Pomeroy (St. John's, Bridgetown), PR1, Baptism Records'.

Devon Record Office, Exeter, MSS 'Berry Pomeroy (St. John's, Bridgetown), PR6, Burial Records'.

Devon Record Office, Exeter, MS 'Minute Book', Bartholomew Street Chapel.

Devon Record Office, Exeter, MSS 'Papers of the Seymour Family of Berry Pomeroy'.

Devon Record Office, Exeter, MS '1851 Religious Census, Devonshire'.

Edinburgh, MSS 'Letters of Henry Bulteel', in possession of the Revd. Iain H. Murray.

Essex, MSS 'Noel Family Papers', in the possession of Captain Gerard Noel.

Exeter Cathedral Library, Exeter, MSS 'Bishop Phillpotts Correspondence'.

Hampshire Record Office, Winchester, MSS 'Ashburton Estate Deeds'.

Hampshire Record Office, Winchester, MSS 'Records of the Diocese of Winchester'.

Henry E. Huntington Library, San Marino, Calif., MSS Macaulay Family Papers, 'Journal of Selina Macaulay'.

The John Rylands University Library, Manchester, The Christian Brethren Archive, MS 'Diary of Alfred C. Fry'.

Lambeth Palace Library, London, MSS 'Blomfield Papers'.

Leicestershire County Record Office, Leicester, MSS 'Noel Family Papers'.

Lincolnshire County Record Office, Lincoln, MSS 'Bishop Kaye Correspondence'.

New Road Baptist Church Archives, Oxford, MS 'Church Book'.

Oxfordshire Record Office, Oxford, MSS 'Oxford Diocesan Papers'.

Oxfordshire Record Office, Oxford, MSS 'Parish Records of St. Ebbe's'.

Somerset Local Studies Library, Taunton, MS 'Octagon Chapel'.

Surrey Record Centre, Woking, MS PSH/ALB/2/2.

Surrey Record Centre, Woking, MS PSH/ALB/3/1.

Surrey Record Centre, Woking, MS 1322.

Wiltshire Record Office, Trowbridge, MSS 'Records of the Diocese of Salisbury'.

SECONDARY SOURCES

Unpublished Books, Articles, and Theses

Acheson, Alan R., 'The Evangelicals in the Church of Ireland, 1784–1859', Ph.D. thesis (Queen's University Belfast, 1967).

Adams, A., 'Converts to the Roman Catholic Church in England, circa 1830–70', B.Litt. thesis (Oxford, 1977).

Balda, W. D., '"Spheres of Influence": Simeon's Trust and its Implications for Evangelical Patronage', Ph.D. thesis (Cambridge, 1981).

Bass, C. B., 'The Doctrine of the Church in the Theology of J. N. Darby', Ph.D. thesis (Edinburgh, 1952).

Bradley, Ian, 'The Politics of Godliness: Evangelicals in Parliament, 1784–1832', D.Phil. thesis (Oxford, 1974).

Burnham, Jonathan David, 'The Controversial Relationship between Benjamin Wills Newton and John Nelson Darby', D.Phil. thesis (Oxford, 2000).

Burns, R. Arthur, 'The Diocesan Revival in the Church of England, *c.*1825–1865', D.Phil. thesis (Oxford, 1990).

Casbard, Retta T. L., 'Henry Drummond of Albury', Albury Historical Society, Albury, Surrey.

Clarke, D. F., 'Benjamin Ingham (1712–1772), with Special Reference to His Relations with the Churches . . . of His Time', M.Phil. thesis (Leeds, 1971).

Embley, Peter L., 'The Origins and Early Development of the Plymouth Brethren', Ph.D. thesis (Cambridge, 1966).

Ervine, W. J. C., 'Doctrine and Diplomacy: Some Aspects of the Life and Thought of the Anglican Evangelical Clergy, 1797 to 1837', Ph.D. thesis (Cambridge, 1979).

Fenwick, Richard David, 'The Free Church of England, Otherwise Known as the Reformed Episcopal Church, *c.*1845–*c.*1927: A Study in Church Growth and Development', Ph.D. thesis (Lampeter, 1995).

Fox, L. Pamela, 'The Work of the Reverend Thomas Tregenna Biddulph With Special Reference to His Influence on the Evangelical Movement in the West of England', Ph.D. thesis (Cambridge, 1953).

Grass, Tim, 'The Church's Ruin and Restoration: The Development of Ecclesiology in the Plymouth Brethren and the Catholic Apostolic Church, *c.*1825–*c.*1866', Ph.D. thesis (King's College London, 1997).

Hardman, B. E., 'The Evangelical Party in the Church of England 1855–65', Ph.D. thesis (Cambridge, 1963).

Heasman, K. J., 'The Influence of the Evangelicals Upon . . . Voluntary Charitable Institutions in the Second Half of the Nineteenth Century', Ph.D. thesis (London, 1959).

Hehir, Irene, 'New Lights and Old Enemies: The Second Reformation and the Catholics of Ireland, 1800–35', MA diss. (Wisconsin, 1983).

Herring, George W., 'Tractarianism to Ritualism', D.Phil. thesis (Oxford, 1984).

Hill, Myrtle, 'Evangelicalism and the Churches in Ulster Society: 1770–1850', Ph.D. thesis (Queen's University Belfast, 1987).

Kochav, Sarah, 'Britain and the Holy Land: Prophecy, the Evangelical Movement, and the Conversion and Restoration of the Jews 1790–1845', D.Phil. thesis (Oxford, 1989).

Lamb, Charles Edward, 'A Brief History of Kemptown', http://www.kemptown.co.uk/history.htm.

Lancaster, J., 'John Bate Cardale, Pillar of Apostles: A Quest for Catholicity', B.Phil. thesis (St. Andrews, 1978).

Liechty, Joseph, 'Irish Evangelicalism, Trinity College Dublin, and the Mission of the Church of Ireland at the End of the Eighteenth Century', Ph.D. thesis (Maynooth, 1987).

Linnan, John E., 'The Evangelical Background of John Henry Newman, 1816–26', Th.D. thesis (Louvain, 1965).

Lively, Robert Lee, Jr., 'The Catholic Apostolic Church and the Church of Jesus Christ of Latter Day Saints: A Comparative Study of Two

Minority Millenarian Groups in Nineteenth Century England', D.Phil. thesis (Oxford, 1977).
Marchington, Trevor, 'The Development of Buxton and Matlock Since 1800', MA thesis (London, 1960).
Murray, N., 'The Influence of the French Revolution on the Church of England and its Rivals, 1789–1803', D.Phil. thesis (Oxford, 1975).
Oliver, Robert W., 'The Emergence of a Strict and Particular Baptist Community Among the English Calvinistic Baptists, 1770–1850', Ph.D. thesis (CNAA, 1986).
Rennie, Ian S., 'Evangelicalism and English Public Life, 1832–50', Ph.D. thesis (Toronto, 1962).
Sangster, E., 'The Life of the Revd Rowland Hill (1744–1833) and His Position in the Evangelical Revival', D.Phil. thesis (Oxford, 1964).
Stevenson, Kenneth W., 'The Catholic Apostolic Eucharist', Ph.D. thesis (Southampton, 1975).
Stewart, K. J., 'Restoring the Reformation: British Evangelicalism and the "Réveil" at Geneva 1816–1849', Ph.D. thesis (Edinburgh, 1992).
Thompson, Joshua, 'Baptists in Ireland, 1792–1922: A Dimension of Protestant Dissent', D.Phil. thesis (Oxford, 1988).
Walsh, J. D., 'The Yorkshire Evangelicals in the Eighteenth Century: With Especial Reference to Methodism', Ph.D. thesis (Cambridge, 1956).
—— 'Calvinism' (Oxford, n.d.).
Wellings, M., 'Aspects of Late Nineteenth Century Anglican Evangelicalism: The Response to Ritualism, Darwinism and Theological Liberalism', D.Phil. thesis (Oxford, 1989).
Young, Howard V. Jr., 'The Evangelical Clergy in the Church of England, 1790–1850', Ph.D. diss. (Brown University, 1958).

Printed Sources: A

Adelphos, 'A Letter to the Hon. and Revd Baptist Noel', in *EM* (1849).
Adolphus, John Leycester and Ellis, Thomas Flower, *Queen's Bench Reports* (1848).
Allibone, S. Austin, *A Critical Dictionary of English Literature and British and American Authors Living and Deceased*, 3 vols. (Philadelphia, 1877).
Allon, Henry, *Memoir of the Revd James Sherman* (1863).
The Annual Register.
Anon., *Interesting Reminiscences of the Early History of 'Brethren'*, with letter from J. G. Bellett (n.d.).
Anti-Schism: A Review of the Principles Contained in the Hon. and Revd B. W. Noel's Tract 'The Unity of the Church' (by 'a Layman') (1838).
Archer, Thomas, *William Ewart Gladstone and his Contemporaries*, 4 vols. (1898).

Atkins, J. B., *Life of Sir William Howard Russell*, 2 vols. (1911).
Baildon, W. P. (ed.), *The Records of the Honourable Society of Lincoln's Inn* (1897–1902).
Ball, J. T., *The Reformed Church of Ireland*, 2nd edn. (London and Dublin, 1890).
The *Baptist Magazine.*
The *Baptist Messenger.*
The *Baptist Quarterly.*
The *Baptist Reporter.*
Barber, J. R., *A Letter to the Revd H. B. Bulteel* (1831).
Baring-Gould, S., *The Church Revival* (1914).
Barry, Edward, *The Friendly Call of Truth and Reason to a New Species of Dissenters* (Reading, 1799).
Bateman, Josiah, *The Life of the Right Revd Daniel Wilson, D.D.*, 2 vols. (1860).
Baxter, Richard, *Five Disputations of Church-Government and Worship* (1659).
Bean, James, *Zeal Without Innovation* (1808).
Ben-Ezra, Juan Josafat [Manuel Lacunza Y Diaz], *Venida del Mesias en gloria y majestad* (Mexico, 1825).
Bentinck, Lady Norah, *My Wanderings and Memories*, 2nd edn. (1924).
Berridge, John, *The Works of the Revd John Berridge, A.M.*, ed. Richard Wittingham (1838).
Bevan, George [Anon], 'God in Christ', in *Two Letters* (1818).
——*A Ready Reply to a Pamphlet Entitled 'Human Deity Developed or, Familiar Remarks on a Pamphlet Entitled God in Christ'* (1819).
Bickers, H. E., *A Brief History of the Baptist Church now Meeting in South Street Chapel, Exeter, From the Year 1656* (Exeter, 1906).
Bickersteth, Edward. *Practical Remarks on the Prophecies* (1824).
——'Practical Remarks on the Prophecies', in *A Scriptural Help*, 12th edn. (1825).
——*Preparedness for the Day of Christ Urged on all Christians* (1833).
——'The Coming of Christ', in *The Book of Private Devotions* (1839).
——*The Signs of the Times in the East* (1845).
Biddulph, T. T., *Baptism, Essays on Some Select Parts of the Liturgy of the Church of England* (Bristol, 1798).
——*A Seal of the Christian Covenant* (1816).
——*Search After Truth* (Bristol, 1818).
Binney, Thomas [Anon], *The Great Gorham Case* (1850).
Birks, T. R., *The Christian State: Or the First Principles of National Religion* (1847).
——*Memoir of the Revd Edward Bickersteth, Late Rector of Watton, Herts*, 2nd edn., 2 vols. (1852).
——*The Present Crisis* (1854).

Blunt, John Henry, *The Book of Church Law* (1921).
Boase, Charles William, *Register of the Rectors and Fellows, Scholars, Exhibitioners, and Bible Clerks of Exeter College, Oxford* (Oxford, 1879).
Bogue, David, and Bennett, James, *History of Dissenters, 1688–1808*, 4 vols. (1808–12).
Borlase, Henry, *Reasons for Withdrawing from the Ministry of the Church of England* (Plymouth, 1833).
——'Separation from Apostasy not Schism', in the *Christian Witness*, 1834.
——*Papers by the Late Henry Borlase, Connected with the Present State of the Church* (1836).
Boys, Thomas, *The Suppressed Evidence* (1832).
Brainwood, William, *Letters on a Variety of Subjects* (1808).
Braithwaite, Joseph Bevan, *Memoirs of Joseph John Gurney*, 2 vols. (Norwich, 1855).
Bransby, James Hews, *Evans' Sketch of the Various Denominations of the Christian World*, 18th edn. (1841).
Brenton, L. C. L., *Memoir of Jahleel Brenton; Reasons for Not Ceasing to Teach and Preach the Lord Jesus Christ* (Bath, 1832).
——*The Septuagint Translated into English*, 2 vols. (1844).
——'A Sermon on Revelations XIV:13', in the *North British Review* (1848–9).
——*A Sermon on Revelations XIV:13*, 2nd edn. (1849).
——*Diaconia: Or, Thoughts on Ministry* (1852).
——*Alas, My Brother!* (1854).
——*Memoir of Vice-Admiral Sir Jahleel Brenton, Baronet, K.C.B.* (1855).
——*The Bible and Prayer Book Versions of the Psalms* (1860).
——*Thoughts on Self-examination* (1862).
'A Brief Account of the Revd James Harington Evans, M.A.', in James Harington Evans (ed.), *Three Funeral Sermons* (1850).
A Brief Memoir of the Revd William Richardson, 2nd edn. (1822).
A Brief Reply to the Reverend Mr Tiptaft's Letter to the Bishop of Salisbury (by 'a Member of the Church of England') (Reading, 1831).
The *Bristol Gazette*.
The *Bristol Mirror*.
The *British Banner*.
The *British Critic*.
Brocas, T., *God: No Respecter of Persons* (1808).
Brock, William, *Memorial Sermon for Baptist W. Noel* (1873).
Brodrick, George C. and Fremantle, William H. (eds.), *A Collection of the Judgments of the Judicial Committee of the Privy Council in Ecclesiastical Cases Related to Doctrine and Discipline* (1865).
Brooke, Richard Sinclair, *Recollections of the Irish Church* (1877).

Broome, Edward W., *The Revd Rowland Hill: Preacher and Wit* (1881).
Brown, Abner William, *Recollections of the Conversation Parties of the Revd Charles Simeon, MA* (1863).
Buchan, John, *Brasenose College* (1898).
Buck, Charles (ed.), *A Theological Dictionary*, 2nd edn. (1833).
Buckley, Joseph, *Matlock Bath as it Was, and Is . . . With a Short Sketch of the Personal History of John Smedley* (1866).
——*Modern Buxton* (1886).
——*Recollections of the Late John Smedley* (Manchester and London, 1888).
Bugg, George, *Spiritual Regeneration, Not Necessarily Connected With Baptism* (Kettering, 1816).
Bulteel, Henry, *A Sermon on 1 Cor. 2:12*, 6th edn. (Oxford, 1831).
——*A Reply to Dr Burton's Remarks* (Oxford, 1831).
——'Sermon for the Continental Society, 10 May 1831', in the *Preacher*, 8 vols. (London, 1830–5), ii: 162–74.
——*The Doctrine of the Miraculous Interferences of Jesus on Behalf of Believers*, 2nd edn. (Oxford, 1832).
——*To All that Love Truth and Consistency* (Oxford, 1841).
——*An Address Delivered on the Opening of a Free Episcopal Church, in the City of Exeter, on the 26th of September, 1844* (Oxford, 1844).
——[Anon.], *Oxford Argo* (1845).
Burgh, William, *Dissent From the Church of England Shewn to be Unwarrantable*, 2nd edn. (Dublin, 1833).
Burgon, John William, *Lives of Twelve Good Men*, 2 vols. (1888).
Burton, Edward, *Remarks Upon a Sermon Preached at St. Mary's on Sunday, February 6, 1831* (Oxford, 1831).
——*One Reason for Not Entering Into Controversy With An Anonymous Author of Strictures* (Oxford, 1831).
The *Buxton Advertiser.*
The Calm Observer: Or Remarks on the Sermons Lately Preached in the Parish Church of St. Helen's, Abingdon, by the Revd W. Tiptaft, Vicar of Sutton, and J. Hewlett, Head Master of the Grammar School, Abingdon (Abingdon, 1830).
Calvin, John, *Institutes of Christian Religion*, 2 vols. (Philadelphia, 1932).
Cameron, Charles A., *History of the Royal College of Surgeons* (Dublin, London, and Edinburgh, 1886).
Campbell John, *Memoirs of David Nasmith* (1844).
Cardale, John Bate, *Readings Upon the Liturgy and Other Divine Offices of the Church*, 2 vols. (1848–78).
Carne, Robert Harkness, *The Proper Deity, and Distinct Personality, Agency, and Worship, of the Holy Spirit, Vindicated, Against the Recent Evils of Messieurs Baring, Bevan, Cowan, etc* (Exeter, 1818).
——*Reasons for Withdrawing from the National Establishment* (1820).

——*A Defense and Explication of the Sinlessness, Immortality, and Incorruptibility of the Humanity of the Son of God* (1829).
Carus, William, *Memoirs of the Life of the Revd Charles Simeon, M.A.* (1847).
——*Memoirs of the Life of the Revd Charles Simeon, M.A.*, 3rd edn. (1848).
Caston, M., *Independency in Bristol* (London and Bristol, 1860).
'Cautions to Clergymen Seceding from the Episcopal Church' (by 'a Dissenter') in *BMag* (1850).
Cecil, Richard, *Memories of the Hon and Revd W. B. Cadogan, M.A., John Bacon, Esq, RA, and the Revd John Newton* (1812).
——*Remains of the Revd Richard Cecil, M.A.*, ed. Josiah Pratt, 8th edn. (1825).
Chalmers, Thomas, *The Christian and Civic Economy of Large Towns*, 3 vols. (Glasgow, 1821–6).
——*On the Use and Abuse of Literary and Ecclesiastical Endowments* (Glasgow, 1827).
——'On Religious Endowments', in *The Collected Works of Thomas Chalmers*, xi (1829)
——*The Cause of Church Extension* (Edinburgh, 1835).
——*The Collected Works of Thomas Chalmers*, 25 vols. (Glasgow, 1835–42).
——*Lectures on the Establishment and Extension of National Churches* (Glasgow, 1838).
Chapman, Charles, 'Address Delivered at his Baptism, July 7, 1850', in *BMag* (1850).
Charlesworth, V. J., *Rowland Hill* (1876).
The *Christian Guardian.*
The *Christian Herald.*
The *Christian Observer.*
The *Christian Remembrancer.*
The *Christian Times.*
The *Christian Witness.*
The *Church and State Gazette.*
Church, R. W., *The Oxford Movement*, 3rd edn. (1892).
The Church of England Vindicated (by 'a Layman') (Exeter, 1818).
Cole, Henry, *A Letter to the Revd Edward Irving* (1827).
The *Congregational Magazine.*
The *Contemporary Review.*
Conybeare, W. J., 'Bishop Phillpotts', in *EdR* (1852).
——'Church Parties', in *EdR* (1853).
Cooper, William, *An Address to the Church Assembling in Plunket-Street, Dublin* (Dublin, 1805).
——*A Letter to Mr John Walker* (Dublin, 1808).
Coplestone, Edward, *A Charge Delivered to the Clergy of the Diocese of Llandaff* (1848).

Cosens, W. B., *The Case of the Revd James Shore, as Between the Patron and the Vicar, in a Letter to His Parishioners* (Exeter, 1849).

Cottle, Joseph, *Strictures on the Plymouth Antinomians*, 2nd edn. (1824).

Courtney, John ['Clericus Surriensis'], *An Earnest Protest* (1837).

Cowan, Thomas C., *A Brief Account of the Reasons Which Have Induced the Rev. T. C. Cowan to Secede From the Established Church*, 2nd edn. (Bristol, 1817).

Cox, G. V., *Recollections of Oxford* (1868).

Cox, Robert, *Secession Considered* (1832).

Craik, Henry, *Passages from the Diary and Letters of Henry Craik*, ed. W. E. Tayler (Bristol, 1866).

Crane, Jane Miriam, *Records of the Life of the Revd Wm. H. Havergal, M.A.*, 2nd edn. (1882).

Cripps, C. A., *A Practical Treatise on the Law Relating to Church and Clergy*, 6th edn. (1886).

Crookshank, C. H., *Memorable Women of Irish Methodism in the Last Century* (1882).

——*History of Methodism in Ireland*, 3 vols. (1886).

Croskery, Thomas, *Plymouth-Brethrenism: A Refutation of its Principles and Doctrines* (1879).

Crossley, E. and Ardrews, A., *Extracts from the Writings of the Late Henry Borlase on subjects connected with the Present State of the Church* (1892).

Cuffe, T. T., *Reasons for Secession: Or, Objections to Remaining in the Established Church* (1851).

Darby, John Nelson, 'Considerations Addressed to the Archbishop of Dublin and the Clergy Who Signed the Petition to the House of Commons For Protection' (Dublin, 1827), in *CW* (1956).

——*Considerations on the Nature and Unity of the Church of Christ* (Dublin, 1828).

——'Reflections upon the Prophetic Inquiry and the Views Advanced in it' (1829), in *CW* (1956).

——[Oudies], *The Doctrine of the Church of England at the Time of the Reformation, of the Reformation Itself, of Scripture, and of the Church of Rome, Briefly Compared With the Remarks of the Regius Professor of Divinity* (Oxford, 1831).

——'A Letter on a Serious Question Connected with the Irish Education Measures of 1832' (1832), in *CW* (1956).

——'The Dispensation of the Kingdom of Heaven—Matt. XIII', in the *Christian Witness* (1834).

——'The Notion of a Clergyman, Dispensationally the Sin Against the Holy Ghost' (*c.*1834), in *CW* (1956).

——'The Apostasy of the Successive Dispensations' (1836), in *CW* (1956).

——'On the Apostasy: What is Succession a Succession of?' (1840), in *CW* (1956).
——'On the Formation of Churches' (1840), in *CW* (1956).
——'Progress of Evil on the Earth' (1840), in *CW* (1956).
——'A Glance at Various Ecclesiastical Principles, and Examination of the Foundations on Which the Institutions of the Church on Earth are Sought to be Based—In Reply to Various Writings' (1846), in *CW* (1956).
——'What is the Church?' (1849), in *CW* (1956).
——'The Dispensation of the Fullness of Times' (1850), in *CW* (1956).
——*Analysis of Dr Newman's* Apologia Pro Vita Sua (1866).
——*On Ecclesiastical Independency* (1880).
——*Disendowment—Disestablishment: A Word to the Protestants of Ireland, in a Letter to the Ven. Archdeacon Stopford* (Dublin, 1869), in *CW* (1956).
——*Letters of John Nelson Darby*, ed. J. A. Trench, 3 vols. (1886).
——*The Church—What is it?—Her Power, Hopes, Calling, Present Position and Occupation* (1887), in *CW* (1956).
——*The Collected Writings of J. N. Darby*, 2nd edn., ed. William Kelly, 32 vols. (Kingston-on-Thames, 1956).
——'Brief Remarks on the Work of the Revd David Brown' (n.d.), in *CW* (1956).
——'A Letter to a Clergyman on the Claims and Doctrines of Newman Street' (n.d.), in *CW* (1956).
——'On Ministry: Its Nature, Source, Power and Responsibility' (n.d.), in *CW* (1956).
——'Parochial Arrangements Destructive of Order in the Church', (1834), in *CW* (1956).
——'Remarks on a Tract Circulated by the Irvingites Entitled, "A Word of Instruction"' (n.d.), in *CW* (1956).
——'Studies on the Book of Daniel' (n.d.), in *CW* (1956).
——'Substance of a Reading on Ephesians' (n.d.), in *CW* (1956).
——'What the Christian Has Amid the Ruin of the Church' (n.d.), in *CW* (1956).
——'Who is a Priest and What is a Priest?' (n.d.), in *CW* (1956).
Daubeny, Charles, *A Guide to the Church* (1798).
——*Vindiciae Ecclesiae Anglicane* (1803).
——*A Guide to the Church*, 2nd edn., 2 vols. (1804).
——*A Word in Season On the Nature of the Christian Church* (Bath, 1817).
——*On the Nature, Progress and Consequences of Schism* (1818).
Dealtry, William, *The Importance of the Established Church* (1832).
——*Religious Establishments Tried by the Word of God* (1833).
Dix, John, *Pen and Ink Sketches of Poets, Preachers, and Politicians* (1846).

Dix, John, *Pen Portraits; or Pen-Pictures of . . . Eminent British Preachers* (Boston, 1854).

Dodson, John, *Brief Reasons for Leaving the English Establishment* (1849).

Doyle, James. [J. K. L.], *Vindication of the Religious and Civil Principles of the Irish Catholics in a Letter Addressed to Marquis Wellesley by J. K. L.* (Dublin, 1823).

——*Letters on the State of Ireland Addressed by J. K. L. to a Friend in England* (Dublin, 1825).

Drummond, Henry, *A Defence of the Students of Prophecy* (1828).

——*Dialogues on Prophecy*, 3 vols. (1828–9).

——[Layman] *Candid Examination of the Controversy Between Messrs Irving, A. Thomson, and J. Haldane* (1829).

——[A Tory of the Old School] *A Letter to the King Against Repeal of the Test Act by a Tory of the Old School* (1829).

——[Layman] *Supplement to the Candid Examination of the Controversy* (1830).

——*Social Duties on Christian Principles* (1830).

——*Reform Not a New Constitution* (1831).

——*Abstract Principles of Revealed Religion* (1845).

——*Discourses on the True Definition of the Church* (1858).

——*Speeches in Parliament and Some Miscellaneous Pamphlets of the Late Henry Drummond, Esq.*, ed. Lord Lovaine, 2 vols. (1860).

Dublin University Magazine.

Eardley, Culling, *An Appeal to the Country on Behalf of the Revd James Shore*, 2nd edn. (Torquay, 1849).

Ecclesiastical Intelligence.

The *Eclectic Review.*

The *Edinburgh Review.*

Edward, Mervyn, Seventh Viscount Powerscourt, *Muniments of the Ancient Saron Family of Wingfield* (1894).

Elliott, Edward Bishop, *Horae Apocalypticae*, 4th edn., 4 vols. (1851).

The *English Churchman.*

The English Reports (Edinburgh, 1900).

The Englishman's Greek Concordance to the New Testament (1839).

Eton School Lists.

The Evangelical Alliance: Proceedings of the Conference held at Freemasons' Hall, London, from Aug. 19th to September 2nd 1846 (1847).

The *Evangelical Magazine.*

Evans, James Harington, *A Series of Dialogues on Important Subjects* (1819).

——*Letters to a Friend* (1826).

——*Three Funeral Sermons* (1850).

Evans, James Joyce, *Memoir and Remains of the Revd James Harington Evans* (1852).

Evil of Separation from the Church of England Considered in a Series of Letters Addressed Chiefly to the Revd Peter Roe, Minister of St. Mary's, Kilkenny (Kilkenny, 1815).
An Examination of the Record's Twelve Articles on Mr Noel's Work (by 'a Presbyter') (1849).
First Report of the Continental Society For the Diffusion of Religious Knowledge (1819).
Fish, Henry C., *Pulpit Eloquence of the Nineteenth Century* (New York, 1857).
Fitzgerald, John, *The Apostolic Minister's Preparation for Departure* (1847).
——*An Appeal to Pious and Devoted Clergymen* (1851).
Flavel, John, *A Blow at the Root* (1818).
Fleming, James, *The Life and Writings of the Revd Edward Irving, MA* (1923).
Foster, Joseph (ed.), *Alumni Oxonienses, 1715–1886*, 4 vols. (Oxford, 1888).
——(ed.), *Index Ecclesiasticus* (Oxford, 1890).
Fourth Report of the Continental Society (1822).
Fowler, Henry, *Letters to the Revd H. B. Bulteel* (1831).
Fowler, J., *Richard Waldo Sibthorp: A Biography* (1880).
Fox, The Hon. Henry Edward, *The Journal of the Hon. Henry Edward Fox*, ed. the Earl of Ilchester (1946).
Fraser's Magazine.
The *Free Church of England Magazine.*
Friend, A., *Memoirs of the Life of the Revd Thomas Wills, A.B.* (1804).
Froude, James Anthony (ed.), *Reminiscences by Thomas Carlyle*, 2 vols. (1881).
Froude, Richard Hurrell, *Remains*, 4 vols. (1838–9).
Fuller, Andrew, 'Strictures on Sandemanianism', in *Twelve Letters to a Friend* (Nottingham, 1810).
Garbett, James, *Diocesan Synods and Convocation* (1852).
Garratt, Evelyn R., *Life and Personal Recollections of Samuel Garratt* (1908).
Gauntlett, Henry [Detector], *Letters to the Stranger in Reading* (1810).
——*Sermons: By the Late Henry Gauntlett, Vicar of Olney, Bucks. With a Memoir of the Author*, ed. C. T. Gauntlett, 2 vols. (1835).
The *Gentleman's Magazine.*
Gibson, E. C. S., 'Henry Phillpotts', in William Edward Collins (ed.), *Typical English Churchmen: From Parker to Maurice* (1902).
Gill, John, *A Body of Doctrinal Divinity*, 3 vols. (1769–70).
Gilmour, Clotworthy, *A Reply to the Hon. and Revd Baptist Wriothesley Noel's Essay on the Union of Church and State* (1849).
Gindey, W. T., *The History of the London Society for Promoting Christianity amongst the Jews* (1908).
Girdlestone, Charles, *Three Letters on Church Reform* (1832–4).
——*Church Rates Lawful, But Not Always Expedient* (1833).
Gisborne, Thomas, *A Familiar Survey of the Christian Religion, and of History* (1799).

Gladstone, William E., *The State in its Relations with the Church* (1838).
——'The Evangelical Movement; its Parentage, Progress, and Issue', in *QR* (1879).
——*Gleanings of Past Years*, 7 vols. (1879).
——*The Gladstone Diaries*, ed. M. R. D. Foot and H. C. G. Matthew, 11 vols. (Oxford, 1968–90).
Glas, John, *The Works of Mr. John Glas*, 4 vols. (Edinburgh, 1761).
Godkin, James, *Ireland and Her Churches* (1867).
Goode, William, *The Doctrine of the Church of England as to the Effects of Baptism in the Case of Infants* (1849).
——*A Letter to the Bishop of Exeter* (1850).
——*The Case of Archdeacon Wilberforce Compared with That of Mr. Gorham* (1854).
——*Rome's Tactics* (1867).
The *Gospel Ministry.*
The *Gospel Pulpit.*
The *Gospel Standard.*
Grace, Thomas, 'A Letter', in Peter Roe (ed.), *The Evil of Separation from the Church of England Considered* (Kilkenny, 1815).
Grant, James, *The Plymouth Brethren: Their History and Heresies* (1875).
Groves, Edward Kennaway, *George Müller and His Successors* (Bristol, 1906).
Groves, Henry, *Darbyism: its Rise and Development* (1866).
——*Memoir of Lord Congleton* (1884).
Groves, Mrs, *Memoir of the Late Anthony Norris Groves* (1856).
Haldane, Alexander, *Memoirs of the Lives of Robert Haldane of Airthrey, and of His Brother, James Alexander Haldane* (1852).
Haldane, James, *A Refutation of the Heretical Doctrine Promulgated by the Revd Edward Irving* (Edinburgh, 1828).
——*Answer to Mr. Henry Drummond's Defence of the Heretical Doctrine Promulgated by Mr. Irving* (Edinburgh, 1830).
——*Reply to Mr Henry Drummond's Supplement to the Candid Examination* (Edinburgh, 1830).
Hall, John, *The Memory of the Just: A Tribute to the Memory of the Late Thomas Kelly* (Dublin, 1855).
Hall Peter, *A Candid and Respectful Letter to the Revd William Tiptaft* (Salisbury, 1832).
——*Congregational Reform, According to the Liturgy of the Church of England* (1835).
——*A Memoir of the Revd Thomas Robinson, M.A.* (1837).
The *Hampshire Chronicle.*
Hanbury, Benjamin, *My Baptized One: Thoughts for Thinking Parents* (1850).
Hannah, W., *Memories of Dr Chalmers*, 4 vols. (Edinburgh, 1849–52).

Hansard, The Parliamentary History of England From the Earliest Period to the Year 1803 (1819). *The Parliamentary Debates: Forming a Continuation of the Work Entitled 'The Parliamentary History of England From the Earliest Period to the Year 1803'* (1820–30).

Hansard's Parliamentary Debates: Third Series, Commencing with the Accession of William IV (1831–91).

Harding, William Henry, *The Life of George Müller* (1914).

Hare, Julian Charles, 'Archdeacon Hare's Letter to the Hon. Richard Cavendish' (1850), in *Miscellaneous Pamphlets* (Cambridge, 1855).

Harris, J. H., *Address to the Parishioners of Plymstock* (Plymouth, 1832).

—— *What is a Church? or, Reasons for Withdrawing from the Ministry of the Establishment* (Plymouth, 1832).

Harrod's Directory of Derbyshire, 1870.

Hart, Joseph, *Hymns* (1759).

Hawker, Robert, *The Works of the Revd Robert Hawker, DD*, ed. J. Williams, 10 vols. (1831).

Hawkins, Edmund, *A Sermon Upon the Way of Salvation* (Oxford, 1831).

Hewlett, Joseph, *A Sermon Preached at Abingdon, on Sunday, December 27, 1829* (Abingdon, 1830).

Hibernian Evangelical Magazine.

High Peak News.

Hill, Richard, *An Apology for Brotherly Love, and for the Doctrines of the Church of England* (1798).

—— *Pietas Oxoniensis: Or, a Full and Impartial Account of the Expulsion of Six Students from St. Edmund Hall, Oxford* (1768).

Hill, Rowland, *Journal of a Tour Through the North of England and Parts of Scotland* (1799).

—— *Spiritual Characteristics Represented in an Account of a Most Curious Sale of Curates by Public Auction* (1803).

—— *A Letter* (Manchester and London, 1835).

Hinton, James, *A Vindication of the Dissenters in Oxford* (1792).

—— *A Nut Cracker* (Oxford, 1832).

Hoare, W. D., 'Extract of a Letter', in Peter Roe (ed.), *The Evil of Separation from the Church of England Considered* (Kilkenny, 1815).

Hodgson, Robert, *Life of Beilby Porteus* (1811).

Hole, Charles, *The Life of the Reverend and Venerable William Whitmarsh Phelps M.A.*, 2 vols. (1871).

—— *A Manual of English Church History* (1910).

Holland, Margaret Jean (ed.), *Life and Letters of Zachary Macaulay* (1900).

Hook, W. F., *Letter to the Right Reverend the Lord Bishop of Ripon, on the State of Parties in the Church of England* (1841).

Hooker, Richard, *Of the Laws of Ecclesiastical Politie* (1611).

Hoppus, J. [Schism], *An Examination of the Principles Contained in the Hon. B. W. Noel's Tract 'On the Unity of the Church'* (1838).

Horne, C. S., *Nonconformity in the XIXth Century* (1905).

Howard, K. H. W., *A Complete Textual Index of the Published Sermons and Pulpit Expositions of Joseph Charles Philpot* (Stamford, 1972).

Howe, John, *Christian Union* (1839).

Human Deity Developed or, Familiar Remarks on a Pamphlet Entitled 'God in Christ' (1818).

Huntingford, George Isaac, *A Call for Union with the Established Church* (Winchester, 1800).

Hutcheson, C., *Tidings from the Mountains* (1845).

Ince, W., *The Past History and Present Duties of the Faculty of Theology in Oxford* (Oxford, 1878).

'Incidents in the Life of John Thornton, Esq, the Philanthropist', in the *Congregational Magazine* (1842).

Ingham, Benjamin, *Diary of an Oxford Methodist, Benjamin Ingham, 1733–1734*, ed. Richard Heitzenrater (Durham, NC, 1985).

The *Inquirer.*

Ireland's Mirror, or A Chronicle of the Times, 2 vols. (Dublin, 1804–5).

Irons, William Josiah [Oxoniensis], *Strictures on the Revd Mr Bulteel's Sermon and on the Revd Dr Burton's Remarks* (Oxford, 1831).

Irving, Edward [Juan Josafat Ben-Ezra], *The Coming of Messiah in Glory and Majesty*, 2 vols. (1827).

—— *A Letter to the King, On the Repeal of the Test and Corporation Laws* (1828).

—— 'Sermons, Lectures and Occasional Discourses', in *The Doctrine of the Incarnation Opened in Six Sermons* (1828).

—— *The Church and State Responsible to Christ, and to One Another* (1829).

—— *The Orthodox and Catholic Doctrine of Our Lord's Human Nature* (1830).

Is a Decision of the Privy Council a Reason for Secession? A Letter to a Clergyman of the Evangelical School (by 'another Clergyman') (1850).

Jackson's Oxford Journal.

Jenkins, D. E., *The Life of the Revd Thomas Charles B.A. of Bala* (Denbigh, 1908).

Jerram, Charles, *Secession From the Church of England Considered in a Letter to a Friend* (1836).

The *Jewish Expositor.*

John Bull.

Judd, Gerrit P. (ed.), *Members of Parliament 1734–1832*, 2nd edn. (Hamden, Conn., 1972).

Julian's Dictionary of Hymnology (1892).

Kaye, John, *A Charge to the Clergy of the Diocese of Lincoln* (1852).

Keane, Edward P., Phair, Beryl, and Sadler, Thomas U. (eds.), *King's Inn Admission Papers 1607–1867* (Dublin, 1982).

Kelly, Thomas, *Hymns on Various Passages of Scripture* (Dublin, 1804).
——*Hymns Adapted for Social Worship* (Dublin, 1811).
——*Hymns Not Before Published* (Dublin, 1815).
——*A Plea for Primitive Christianity* (Dublin, 1815).
——*A Letter to the Revd William Burgh* (Dublin, 1833).
Kelly's Directory of Derbyshire, 1876.
Kelly's Directory of Oxford, 1964.
Killen, W. D., *The Ecclesiastical History of Ireland*, 2 vols. (1875).
Kipling, Thomas, *The Articles of the Church of England Proved Not to be Calvinistic* (Cambridge, 1802).
Knox, Alexander, *Remarks on an Expostulatory Address to the Members of the Methodist Society* (Dublin, 1802).
——*Remains of Alexander Knox, Esq*, 4 vols. (1834–7).
A Letter to the Hon. and Revd Baptist W. Noel (by 'M.A.') (1837).
Ley, T. H. [A Clergyman], *A Letter to the Late Perpetual Curate of Plymstock* (Devonport, 1832).
The Life and Letters of William Urwick, D.D., of Dublin (1870).
Lindsey, Theophilus, *The Apologia of Theophilus Lindsey* (1774).
Lister, T. H., 'State of the Irish Church', in *EdR* (1835).
The *London City Mission Magazine.*
The *London Literary Gazette.*
Macaulay, Thomas Babington. *The Letters of T. B. Macaulay*, ed. T. Pinney (1974–81).
M'Caul, Joseph, *The Duke of Somerset's Recent Attack Upon the Bible Criticized* (1872).
M'Clean, Archibald, *The Works of Archibald M'Clean*, ed. W. Jones, 6 vols. (1823).
McNeile, Hugh, *A Sermon* (1826).
——'The True Scriptural Ground and Limits of Church Authority' (1830), in the *Pulpit*, 14.
——'Church Reform' (1832), in the *Pulpit*, 19.
——'The Danger of the Church of Ireland' (1832), in the *Pulpit*, 19.
——*Miracles and Spiritual Gifts* (1832).
——'Church Endowments Defended Both Upon Scriptural and Secular Grounds' (1834), in the *Pulpit*, 23.
——'The Constitutional and Ritual of the Church of England Defended' (1834), in the *Pulpit*, 23.
——'Church Endowments Defended' (1834), in the *Pulpit*, 30.
——*Letters to a Friend* (1834).
——*The Church Establishment* (1837).
——'The Scriptural Warrant for an Established Church' (1837), in the *Pulpit*, 30.
——*Lectures on the Church of England* (1840).

McNeile, Hugh, *Speech* (Edinburgh, 1844).

——*The Church and the Churches* (1846).

——*The Royal Supremacy Discussed in a Correspondence Between Archdeacon [Robert] Wilberforce and the Revd Hugh McNeile* (1850).

Madden, Mrs Hamilton [An Old Pensioner], *Personal Recollections of the Right Revd Robert Daly, D.D.* (Dublin, 1872).

——*Memoir of the Late Right Revd Robert Daly, D.D., Lord Bishop of Cashel* (1875).

Madden, Samuel, *Memoir of the Life of the Late Peter Roe, A.M.* (Dublin, 1842).

Magee, William, *A Charge to the Clergy* (Dublin, 1822).

——*The Evidence of His Grace the Archbishop of Dublin, Before the Select Committee of the House of Lords, on the State of Ireland* (Dublin, 1825).

——*A Charge Delivered at His Triennial and Metropolitan Visitation* (Dublin, 1827).

——*The Works of the Most Reverend William Magee, D.D*, ed. A. H. Kenny (1842).

Mallock, W. D. and Ramsden, G. (eds.), *Letters, Remains, and Memoirs of Edward Adolphus Seymour, Twelfth Duke of Somerset, KG* (1893).

Mann, Horace, *Report on the Religious Worship in England and Wales* (1851).

Mann, John, *The Stranger in Reading* (Reading, 1810).

Dr Mant's Sermon on Regeneration Vindicated from the Remarks of T. T. Biddulph (Shrewsbury, 1816).

Mant, Richard, *An Appeal to the Gospel* (Oxford, 1812).

——*Two Tracts* (1815).

——*History of the Church of Ireland*, 2 vols. (1840).

Mant, Walter Bishop, *Memoirs of the Right Reverend Richard Mant* (Dublin, 1857).

Marked Separation in All Religious Meetings . . . Considered (by 'a Member of the Church of Christ in Sligo') (Dublin, 1805).

Marsh, Catherine, *The Life of the Revd William Marsh, D.D.*, 6th edn. (1867).

Marsh, William. *A Few Plain Thoughts on Prophecy* (Colchester, 1840).

——*Passages from Letters by a Clergyman on Jewish, Prophetical and Scriptural Subjects* (1845).

——*The Church and the State* (1849).

Martin, R. W., *Ireland Before and After the Union* (1848).

Mason, John, 'Reasons for Withdrawing From a Church Not Constituted Agreeably to the Rule of the Word of God', in the *New Baptist Magazine* (1825).

——*On the Godhead, Distinction, Unity and Worship of the Father, the Son, and the Spirit* (Exeter, 1826).

Maurice, F. D., *Reasons for Not Joining a Party in the Church of England* (1841).

Mayhew, Henry, *London Labour and the London Poor* (1851).

Memoir of the Revd Samuel Kiplin (Exeter, 1832).
Merryweather, F. S., *History of the Free Church of England* (1873).
Middelton, John White, *An Ecclesiastical Memoir of the First Four Decades of the Reign of George the Third* (1822).
Miller, Edward, *The History and Doctrines of Irvingism*, 2 vols. (1878).
Milne, Robert, *An Attempt to Defend the Church of England* (Dublin, 1817).
Milner, Joseph, *The History of the Church of Christ*, 6 vols. (York and Cambridge, 1794–1809).
The Moderator Between the Hon. B. W. Noel and 'Clericus Surriensis' (by 'Christianus Episcopus') (1838).
Modern Fanaticism Unveiled (1831).
Moncreiff, G. A., *Remains of Thomas Byrth D.D., F.A.S.* (1851).
Moore, James, *Earlier and Later Nonconformity in Oxford* (Oxford, 1875).
——*Pictorial and Historical Gossiping Guide to Oxford* (Oxford, 1882).
More, Hannah, *An Estimate of the Religion of the Fashionable World*, 3rd edn. (1791).
——*Remarks on the Speech of M. Dupont* (1793).
——*Hints Towards Forming the Character of a Young Princess* (1805).
——*Moral Sketches of Prevailing Opinions and Manners* (1819).
——*The Works of Hannah More*, 6 vols. (1834).
Morison, John, *The Fathers and Founders of the London Missionary Society*, 2nd edn. (1844).
Morley, John, *The Life of William Ewart Gladstone*, 2 vols. (1903).
The *Morning Watch.*
Morris, R., *Faith, Prayer, and Work* (1866).
Motherwell, Maiben C., *A Memoir of The Late Albert Blest* (Dublin, 1843).
Mozley, J. B., *Letters of the Revd J. B. Mozley, D.D*, ed. Anne Mozley (1885).
Mozley, Thomas, *Reminiscences Chiefly of Oriel College and the Oxford Movement*, 2 vols. (1882).
Müller, George, *A Narrative of Some of the Lord's Dealings With George Müller, Minister of Christ* (Bristol, 1837).
Murray, R., *Murray's Compendium of Logic* (1847).
Mursell, Arthur, *Baptist W. Noel: A Tribute and a Memorial* (1873).
Musgrave, Thomas, *A Charge Delivered to the Clergy of the Diocese of York* (1849).
Neatby, William Blair, *A History of the Plymouth Brethren* (1901).
Needham, R. W., *The Church and the Synod* (1851).
The *New Baptist Magazine.*
The *New Evangelical Magazine.*
The *New York Independent.*
Newman, Francis William, *Phases of Faith*, 6th edn. (1860).
Newman, John Henry, 'The Life and Times of Selina, Countess of Huntingdon', in the *British Critic* (1840).

Newman, John Henry, *Two Essays on Scriptural Miracles and On Ecclesiastical*, 2nd edn. (1870).
——[A Master of Arts], 'Suggestions Respectfully Offered to Individual Resident Clergymen of the University in Behalf of the Church Missionary Society', in *The Via Media*, 3rd edn., 2 vols. (1877).
——*Apologia Pro Vita Sua* (1879).
——*Letters and Correspondence of John Henry Newman*, ed. Anne Mozley, 2 vols. (1891).
Newman, John Henry, *The Letters and Diaries of John Henry Newman*, 12 vols., ed. Charles Stephen Dessain (1962).
——*The Letters and Diaries of John Henry Newman*, 2 vols., ed. Ian Ker and Thomas Gornall, SJ (Oxford, 1979).
Newton, B. W., 'Doctrines of the Church in Newman Street', in the *Christian Witness* (1835).
——and Borlase, Henry, *Answers to the Questions Considered at a Meeting Held in Plymouth*, 2nd edn. (Plymouth, 1847).
Newton, John, 'The Lord Reigneth', in *The Works of the Revd John Newton*, 6 vols., ed. Richard Cecil (1824).
Nicholson, Samuel, *Select Remains of the Revd John Mason, Late Pastor of the Church of Christ in Bartholomew Terrace, Exeter, with a Memoir of his Life* (1836).
Nineteenth Report of the Continental Society (1837).
Noel, Baptist W., *Remarks on the Revival of Miraculous Powers in the Church* (1831).
——*The State of the Metropolis Considered*, 2nd edn. (1835).
——*The Spiritual Claims of the Metropolis* (1836).
——*The Unity of the Church* (1837).
——*A Defence of a Tract Entitled, 'The Unity of the Church'* (1837).
——'An Established Religion', in *The Important Influence* (1837).
——*A Letter to the Right Honourable Lord Viscount Melbourne, on Church Extension* (1839).
——'What is Christianity?', in *Lectures Against Socialism* (1840).
——*A Plea for the Poor* (1841).
——*Christian Missions to Heathen Nations* (1842).
——*The Case of the Free Church of Scotland* (1844).
——*The Doctrine of the Word of God Respecting Union Among Christians* (1844).
——*The Catholic Claims Considered* (Dublin, 1845).
——*The Proposed Increase in the Grant to Maynooth* (1845).
——*Protestant Thoughts in Rhyme* (1845).
——'The Morning Sermon', in *Sermons Preached by Eminent Divines* (1847).
——*Notes of a Tour in Switzerland in the Summer of 1847* (1848).
——*Sermons Preached at the Chapels Royal* (1848).

—— *The Substance of Two Sermons* (1848).
——'Address of the Hon. and Revd B. W. Noel on the Occasion of His Baptism at John Street Chapel, August 9, 1849', in the *Pulpit*, 56.
——'The Church and the World', in *Lectures Delivered Before the Young Men's Christian Association, 1848–1849* (1849).
——'The Effects of Infant Baptism', in *BMag* (1849).
——'Essay on Christian Baptism', in *BMag* (1849).
——*A Letter to the Bishop of London on the Clergy Relief Bill* (1849).
——*A Selection of Psalms and Hymns, Adopted Chiefly for Congregational and Social Worship* (1853).
——*Freedom and Slavery in the United States of America* (1863).
——*A Letter to the Revd C. H. Spurgeon* (1864).
——*The Case of W. Gordon, Esq* (1866).
——*Hymns about Jesus* (1868).
Noel, Emilia F., *Some Letters and Records of the Noel Family* (1910).
Noel, Napoleon, *The History of the Brethren*, 2 vols. (Denver, 1936).
Noel, Sidney, *Ernest Noel* (1932).
The *Nonconformist*.
Norris, H. H., *The Origin, Progress and Existing Circumstances of the London Society for Promoting Christianity Amongst the Jews* (1825).
The *North British Review*.
Notorious, G., *Two Letters* (1816).
Nowell, Thomas, *An Answer to a Pamphlet, Entitled Pietas Oxoniensis* (Oxford, 1768).
'Obituary for Baptist W. Noel', in the *Baptist Messenger* (1873).
O'Donnoghue, H. C., *A Familiar and Practical Exposition of the Thirty-Nine Articles of Religion of the United Church of England and Ireland* (1816).
Oliphant, Mrs, *The Life of Edward Irving*, 6th edn. (*c*.1900).
Ollard, S. L., *The Six Students of St. Edmund Hall Expelled From the University of Oxford in 1768* (1911).
Overton, John, *The True Churchmen Ascertained* (York, 1801).
——*The Books of Genesis and Daniel Defended* (1820).
Overton, John H., *The English Church in the Nineteenth Century* (1894).
The *Oxford Chronicle*.
The *Oxford University, City, and County Herald*.
Palmer, William, *A Hard Nut to Crack, or a Word in Season for Mr Bulteel* (Oxford, 1831).
——*At Him Again! Or a Fox Without a Tail, Being Another Word for Mr Bulteel* (Oxford, 1832).
The *Pamphleteer*.
Pattison, Mark, *Essays by the Late Mark Pattison*, ed. Henry Nettleship (Oxford, 1889).
The *Penny Pulpit*.

Peters, J. W., *A Few Words on the Sinful Position of the Evangelical Clergy in the Church of England* (1835).
Petty, John, *The History of the Primitive Methodist Connexion* (1880).
Phelan, William, *The Bible, Not the Bible Society* (Dublin, 1817).
Philippus Anti-Osiander, *A Friendly Letter, Addressed to the Revd Mr Bulteel, in Consideration of His Late University Sermon* (Oxford, 1831).
Phillimore, Sir Robert, *The Ecclesiastical Law of the Church of England*, 2 vols. (1873).
Phillips, Walter Alison, *History of the Church of Ireland From the Earliest Times to the Present Day*, 3 vols. (Oxford, 1933).
'Dr. Phillpotts the Bishop', in *Fraser's Magazine* (1831).
Phillpotts, Henry, *A Charge Delivered to the Clergy of the Diocese of Exeter* (1842).
—— *The Case of the Revd James Shore*, 4th edn. (1849).
—— *A Letter to Sir Robert Inglis* (1852).
Philpot, Joseph Charles, *A Letter to the Provost of Worcester College* (1835).
—— *A Letter to the Provost of Worcester College, Oxford*, 6th edn. (1835).
—— *Secession From the Church of England Defended*, 3rd edn. (1836).
—— *The Heir of Heaven Walking in Darkness, and the Heir of Hell Walking in Light* (1837).
—— *What is it That Saves a Soul?* (1837).
—— *The True and Proper, and Eternal Sonship of the Lord Jesus Christ, the Only-begotten Son of God* (1861).
—— 'Obituary of William Tiptaft', in *GS* (1864).
—— *The Advance of Popery in this Country* (1869).
—— *Letters of the Late Joseph Charles Philpot, With a Brief Memoir of His Life and Labours*, ed. W. C. Clayton and S. L. Philpot (1871).
—— 'Preface', in John Warburton, *The Mercies of a Covenant God*, 2nd edn. (1878).
—— *Early Sermons*, 4 vols. (1906).
—— *William Tiptaft*, 3rd edn. (Leicester, 1972).
Philpot, J. H., *The Seceders*, 2nd edn., 2 vols. (1931).
Pickering, Henry, *Chief Men Among the Brethren*, 2nd edn. (London and Glasgow, 1931).
Pierson, Arthur T., *George Müller of Bristol* (1899).
'The Plymouth Brethren', in *ER* (1839).
Plymouth Brethrenism: Its Ecclesiastical and Doctrinal Teachings; With a Sketch of its History, 2nd edn. (1874).
Powerscourt, Theodosia, *Letters and Papers by the Late Theodosia A. Viscountess Powerscourt*, ed. Robert Daly (Dublin, 1838).
Powerscourt, Viscount, *A Description and History of Powerscourt* (1903).
Pratt, John H., *The Thought of the Evangelical Leaders: Notes of the Discussions of the Eclectic Society Eclectic Notes* (1856; repr. Edinburgh, 1978).

The *Preachers in Print.*
The *Presbyterian Review.*
Price, A. E., *The Oganization of the Free Church of England*, 2nd edn. (1908).
Proby, W. H. B., *Annals of the 'Low Church' Party in England, Down to the Death of Archbishop Tait*, 2 vols. (1888).
Proceedings of the Continental Society . . . Twelfth Year, 1829–1830 (1830).
The *Pulpit.*
Purcell, Edmund Sheridan, *The Life of Cardinal Manning*, 2 vols. (1896).
—— *Life and Letters of A. P. De Lisle* (1900).
The *Quarterly Review.*
Quiller Couch, Lilian M., *Reminiscences of Oxford* (Oxford, 1892).
Randolph, John, *A Charge Delivered to the Clergy of the Diocese of London* (1810).
The *Record.*
Redford, George, *Christianity Against Coercion* (1840).
Reid, Wemyss, *The Life of William Ewart Gladstone* (1899).
Religious Life in the Established Church (by 'a Friend') (1849).
Remarks on A Sermon (by 'a Presbyter') (Stamford, 1837).
Reminiscences and Sayings of the Late Mr William Tiptaft, 2nd edn. (Oxford, 1875).
Returns of the Religious Census of 1851 for the County of Rutland, Microfilm 142, Leicestershire County RO.
Robertson, J. E. P., *Reports of Cases Argued and Determined in the Ecclesiastical Courts at Doctors' Commons* (1845).
Robinson, Robert, *Select Works of the Revd Robert Robinson of Cambridge*, ed. William Robinson (1861).
Robinson, Thomas, *The Christian System*, 3rd edn., 3 vols. (1825).
Roe, Peter (ed.), *The Evil of Separation from the Church of England Considered* (Kilkenny, 1815).
Ross, David Robert, *A Reply to the Author of an Article Entitled 'Sandemanian Theology, John Walker' Which Appeared in the Eclectic Review of November 1838* (Dublin, 1839).
The *Royal Devonport Telegraph and Plymouth Chronicle.*
Russell Borker, G. F. and Stenning, Alan H. (eds.), *The Westminster School Register from 1764 to 1883* (1892).
—— *The Record of Old Westminsters*, 2 vols. (1928).
Ryder, Henry, *A Farewell Sermon* (Lutterworth, 1815).
—— *Charge to the Clergy of Gloucester* (Gloucester, 1816).
—— *A Charge* (Stafford, 1828).
Ryland, John, *Serious Remarks on the Different Representations of the Evangelical Doctrine* (Bristol, 1818).
Ryle, J. C., *Is All Scripture Inspired?* (1891).
The *Salisbury and Winchester Journal.*

Sandeman, Robert, *Letters on Theron and Aspasio*, 2 vols. (Edinburgh, 1761).
Savage, James, *History of Taunton* (Taunton, 1822).
Scholefield, James, *An Argument for a Church Establishment* (Cambridge, 1833).
Scott, John, *An Inquiry Into the Effects of Baptism* (1815).
—— *The Life of the Revd Thomas Scott* (1822).
—— *Reformation, Not Subversion* (1831).
Scott, Thomas, *A Treatise on Growth in Grace* (1795).
—— *Remarks on the Refutation of Calvinism by George Tomline*, 2 vols. (1811).
—— 'A Letter' (1815), in Peter Roe (ed.), *The Evil of Separation From the Church of England Considered* (Kilkenny, 1815).
—— *A Letter to the Revd Peter Roe* (Kilkenny, 1816).
—— *Essays on the Most Important Subjects in Religion*, 10th edn. (1823).
—— *Letters and Papers of the Late Revd Thomas Scott, D.D.*, ed. John Scott (New Haven, 1826).
Seeley, R. B., *Essays on the Church* (1834).
Seymour, A. C. H., *The Life and Times of Selina Countess of Huntingdon*, 2 vols. (1839); 6th edn., 2 vols. (1844).
Seymour, Edward Adolphus, *Christian Theology and Modern Scepticism* (1872).
Shakespear, H. W. A., *A Refutation of the Falsehoods contained in Mr Tryon's Letter to J. C. Philpot* (1847).
Shaw, Robert, 'A Letter', in Peter Roe (ed.), *The Evil of Separation from the Church of England Considered* (Kilkenny, 1815).
Sherle, Ambrose, *Charis: Or, Reflections, Chiefly, Upon the Office of the Holy Spirit in the Salvation of Men* (1803).
Shore, James, *A Statement of the Proceedings of the Bishop of Exeter in the Case of the Revd James Shore, M.A.* (1848).
—— *The Case of the Revd James Shore, M.A., by Himself* (1849).
Sidney, Edwin, *The Life of the Revd Rowland Hill* (1834).
—— *The Life, Ministry, and Selections from the Remains, of the Revd Samuel Walker, B.A.* (1835).
Simeon, Charles, *Helps to Composition, or One-Hundred Skeleton Sermons* (Cambridge, 1801).
—— *The Excellency of the Liturgy* (Cambridge, 1812).
—— *The True Test of Religion in the Soul* (Cambridge, 1817).
Simons, John, *A Letter to a Highly Respected Friend* (1818).
Simpson, David, *A Plea for the Church* (1797).
—— *A Plea for Religion and the Sacred Scriptures*, 5th edn. (1808).
Sinclair, John, *Synodal Action in the Church Unreasonable and Perilous* (1852).
Singer, J. H., *Brief Memorials of . . . B. W. Mathias* (Dublin, 1842).
Sirr, Joseph D'Arcy, *A Memoir of the Honourable and Most Reverend Power Le Poer Trench* (Dublin, 1845).

Skeats, Herbert S. and Miall, Charles S., *History of the Free Churches of England, 1688–1891* (1891).
Smedley, John, *Historical Sketch of the Ancient and Modern Church of Britain* (Derby, 1854).
—— *The Ministerial Office and Mode of Worship of the Nonconformists, and that of the Church of England Considered* (Derby, 1854).
—— *A Letter to the Ministers and Members of the Section of the Church of England Denominated Evangelical* (Derby, *c.*1855).
—— *Remarks on the Deficient Mode in Which the Bible is Read in the Church of England* (1855).
Smith, Sydney, *Selected Letters of Sydney Smith*, ed. Nowell C. Smith (Oxford, 1981).
Snow, Thomas, *A Reply to a Letter Written by the Revd John Simons* (1818).
—— *Two Letters From the Rt Revd the Lord Bishop of Bristol, John Kaye, to the Revd Thomas Snow and His Reply to Each* (Blandford, 1826).
Stafford, James Charles, *An Earnest Persuasive to Unity* (Oxford, 1840).
Stanhope, George, *Advice to the Religious Societies* (1730).
Stephen, C. E., *Sir James Stephen* (Gloucester, 1906).
Stokes, George T., 'John Nelson Darby', in the *Contemporary Review* (1885).
Stowell, Hugh, 'Speech' (1843), in the *Pulpit*, 43.
—— *The Excellencies of the English Liturgy* (1865).
Strictures on a Pamphlet, Entitled the Monstrosities of Methodism (by 'a Beneficed Clergyman') (Dublin, 1808).
Stride, W. K., *Exeter College* (1900).
Summers, William Henry, *History of Congregational Churches* (Newbury, 1905).
Sumner, John Bird, *Apostolic Preaching Considered* (1815).
—— *A Charge Delivered to the Clergy of the Diocese of Chester in 1849* (1849).
—— *Apostolic Preaching Considered*, 9th edn. (1850).
—— *Practical Reflections on Select Passages of the New Testament* (1859).
Synge, John, *Observations on A Call to the Converted* (Teignmouth, 1831).
Tatham, Edward, *Letters to the Right Honourable Edmund Burke on Politics* (Oxford, 1791).
The *Taunton Courier.*
Teignmouth, Lord, *Reminiscences of Many Years* (Edinburgh, 1878).
Teodor, John and DeChylinski, Dobrogost, *The Misfortunes of Baptist W. Noel* (1851).
The *Times.*
Thomas, V., *Memorials of Malignant Cholera in Oxford* (Oxford, 1855).
Thoresby, T. E., *The Free Church of England: Its Origin, Constitution, Doctrines, and Objects* (1873).
Thornton, Thomas (ed.), *Notes of Cases in Ecclesiastical and Maritime Courts*, 7 vols. (1843–50).

Tiptaft, William, *A Sermon Preached in the Parish Church of St. Helen, Abingdon, on Christmas Day, 1829, at the Appointment of the Masters and Governors of Christ's Hospital* (Abingdon, 1830).
——*A Letter Addressed to the Bishop of Salisbury*, 2nd edn. (Abingdon, 1831).
——*Two Letters Addressed to the Bishop of Salisbury* (Abingdon, 1832).
The *Totnes Times.*
Toulmin, Joshua, *The History of Taunton*, 3rd edn. (Taunton, 1874).
Towgood, Michaijah, *Dissenting Gentleman's Letters* (1746–8).
Tregelles, S. P., *Three Letters to the Author of a Retrospect of Events that Have Taken Place Among the Brethren*, 2nd edn. (1894).
Trollope, Anthony, *The McDermots of Ballycloran*, 3 vols. (1847).
——*Clergymen of the Church of England* (1866).
Try the Spirits (1831).
Tryon, Frederick, *Old Paths and New* (1847).
——*A Reply to a Letter* (Peterborough, 1847).
——*The Single Eye* (1847).
Tuckwell, W., *Reminiscences of Oxford* (1900).
——*Pre-Tractarian Oxford* (1909).
Tyerman, L., *The Life of the Revd George Whitefield* (1876).
The Unknown Tongues!! Or, the Reverend Edward Irving Arraigned at the Bar of the Scriptures of Truth, and Found 'Guilty', to Which is Added, a Letter, by the Revd H. B. Bulteel, M.A., 6th edn. (1832).
Urwick, William, *Brief Sketch of the Religious State of Ireland* (Dublin, 1852).
——'Memoir of the Late Revd Thomas Kelly, of Dublin', in *EM* (1856).
Vaughan, Edward Thomas, *Some Account of the Reverend Thomas Robinson, M.A.* (1815).
Venn, Henry, *The Life and a Selection of the Letters of the Late Revd Henry Venn, M.A.*, ed. Henry Venn, 2nd edn. (1835).
——*Annals of a Clerical Family* (1904).
The Views on Baptism of the Honorable and Revd Baptist Noel, M.A. (Leeds, 1849).
Vinet, A., *An Essay on the Profession of Personal Religious Conviction, and Upon the Separation of Church and State, Considered* (1843).
The *Voluntary Church Magazine.*
Walker, John, *The Church in Danger* (Dublin, 1796).
——*Substance of a Charity Sermon* (Dublin, 1796).
——*A Sermon, General Fast* (Dublin, 1800).
——*An Expostulatory Address to the Members of the Methodist Society in Ireland* (Dublin, 1802).
——*A Series of Letters to Alexander Knox* (Dublin, 1802).
——*An Address to Believers of the Gospel of Christ* (Dublin, 1804).
——*Hints on Christian Fellowship* (Dublin, 1804).
——'Thoughts on Baptism' (1805), in *WE* (1838).

——'An Essay on the Divine Authority of the Apostolic Traditions' (1807), in *WE* (1838).
——'Observations on a Letter Addressed to the Author' (1809), in *WE* (1838).
——'Remarks on Certain Questions' (1810), in *WE* (1838).
——'Thoughts on Religious Establishments' (1810), in *WE* (1838).
——'A Brief Account of the People Called Separatists' (1821), in *WE* (1838).
——'A Sufficient Reply to Mr Haldane's Late Strictures Upon the Author's Letters on Primitive Christianity' (1821), in *WE* (1838).
——'The Petition of Certain Christian People Resident in London' (1822), in *WE* (1838).
——*Supplementary Annotations on Livy* (Glasgow, 1822).
——'Statement of the Interruption of Christian Connexion Between the Church in London and the Church in Dublin' (1829), in *WE* (1838).
——'Remarks Corrective of Occasional Mistranslations in the English Version of the Sacred Scriptures' (1831), in *WE* (1838).
——*Seven Letters to a Friend on Primitive Christianity* (1834).
——*Essays and Correspondence, Chiefly on Spiritual Subjects, by the Late John Walker*, ed. William Burton, 2 vols. (1838).
Warburton, John, *Mercies of a Covenant God* (1837).
——*Mercies of a Covenant God*, 2nd edn. (1878).
Wardlaw, Ralph, *National Church Establishments Examined* (1839).
Ware, Alfred (ed.), *A Compendium of Irish Biography* (Dublin, 1878).
Warne, Frederick G., *George Müller: the Modern Apostle of Faith* (1898).
Warner, Richard, *All the Counsel of God* (Bath, 1817).
——*Considerations on the Doctrines of the Evangelical Clergy* (Bath, 1817).
——*Old Church of England Principles Opposed to the 'New Light'* (Bath, 1817).
——*The Claims of the Church of England* (Bath, 1819).
Watson, C. E., *Rodborough* 'Tabernacle: An Account by John Knight, Written in 1844', in Albert Peel (ed.), *Transactions of the Congregational Historical Society* (1927–9).
Watson, J. H., *Year Book of St. John the Evangelist, Bridgetown* (Totnes, 1952).
Webster's Oxford Directory, 1869.
Wesley, John, *A Farther Appeal to Men of Reason and Religion* (1745).
——*A Plain Account of the People Called Methodists* (Bristol, 1749).
——*A Farther Appeal to Men of Reason and Religion*, 4th edn. (Bristol, 1758).
——'Reasons Against a Separation From the Church of England' (1758), in *CO* (1805).
——'The Consequence Proved' (n.d.), in Thomas Jackson (ed.), *The Works of John Wesley*, 3rd edn., 14 vols. (1829–31).
——*The Letters of the Revd John Wesley, A.M.*, ed. John Telford, 8 vols. (1931).

Wesley, John, *The Journal of the Revd John Wesley*, ed. Nehemiah Curnock, 8 vols. (1938).
—— *The Journal of the Revd John Wesley*, 2nd edn., ed. Nehemiah Curnock (1967).
The *Western Times.*
Weylland, John Matthias, *These Fifty Years* (1884).
Whitaker, T. D., *An History of Whalley*, 4th edn. (1872–6).
Whitehead, Benjamin, *Statutes Relating to Church and Clergy* (1894).
White's Directory of Derbyshire, 1872.
Wigram, George, *The Englishman's Greek Concordance to the New Testament* (1839).
Wilberforce, Robert Isaac and Wilberforce, Samuel, *The Life of William Wilberforce*, 5 vols. (1838).
Wilks, Samuel Charles, *Correlative Claims and Duties* (1821).
Wilks, Washington, *Edward Irving: An Ecclesiastical and Literary Biography* (1854).
Williams, J. B., *A Plea for Religion and the Sacred Writings* (*c.*1774).
Willis, Arthur J. (ed.), *Winchester Ordinations, 1660–1829*, 2 vols. (Folkestone, 1964–5).
Wills, James and Wills, Freeman, *The Irish Nation: Its History and Its Biography*, 4 vols. (Edinburgh, London, and Dublin, 1875).
Wilson, Daniel, *The Doctrine of Regeneration Practically Considered* (1817).
—— *The Character of the Good Man as a Christian Minister, a Sermon Occasioned by the Death of the Revd Basil Woodd, M.A., to Which are Subjoined Notes on the Controversy Between the Professor of Divinity at Oxford and the Revd Mr. Bulteel* (1831).
—— *A Farewell Charge*, 2nd edn. (1845).
Wilson, Thomas, *The Works of the Right Reverend Father In God Thomas Wilson*, ed. C. Cruttwell, 2 vols. (Bath, 1781).
Woodd, Basil, *The Excellence of the Liturgy* (1810).
Woolmer's Exeter and Plymouth Gazette.
Wright, Thomas, *The Life of William Huntington, SS* (1909).
The *Zoar Chapel Pulpit.*

Printed Sources: B

Abbey, C. J. and Overton, J. H., *The English Church in the Eighteenth Century*, 2nd edn. (1902).
Acheson, Alan R., *A History of the Church of Ireland, 1691–1996* (Dublin, 1997).
Agnew, J. and Palmer, R., 'Report on the Papers of Henry Drummond of Albury (1786–1860) and Members of his Family (1670–1865)', in *Royal Commission on Historic Manuscripts* (1977).
Akenson, Donald H., *The Church of Ireland* (New Haven, Conn., 1971).

Anderson, Ray S., 'Fundamentalism', in Alister E. McGrath (ed.), *The Blackwell Encyclopedia of Modern Christian Thought* (Oxford, 1995).
Baird, R. G., 'Some Reminiscences of Drummond's Bank', in *Three Banks Review* (1950).
Baker, Frank, *William Grimshaw 1708–63* (1963).
——*John Wesley and the Church of England* (1970).
Baker, William F., *Beyond Port and Prejudice, Charles Lloyd of Oxford, 1784–1829* (Orono, Me., 1981).
Bartlett, Thomas, *The Fall and Rise of the Irish Nation: The Catholic Question, 1690–1830* (Savage, Md., 1992).
Baylis, Robert, *My People* (Wheaton, Ill., 1995).
Beattie, David, J., *Brethren: The Story of a Great Recovery* (Kilmarnock, 1940).
Bebbington, D. W., 'The Life of Baptist Noel: Its Setting and Significance', in *BQ* (1972).
——*Evangelicalism in Modern Britain* (1989).
——*William Ewart Gladstone: Faith and Politics in Victorian Britain* (Grand Rapids, Mich., 1993).
Beckett, J. C., *The Making of Modern Ireland 1603–1923* (1966).
Bentley, James, *Ritualism and Politics in Victorian Britain* (Oxford, 1978).
Best, G. F. A., 'The Evangelicals and the Established Church in the Early Nineteenth Century', in the *Journal of Theological Studies* (1959).
——*Temporal Pillars* (Cambridge, 1964).
Binfield, Clyde, *George Williams and the YMCA* (1973).
Blake, Steven T., *Cheltenham's Churches and Chapels, AD 733–1883* (Cheltenham, 1979).
Boase Frederic, *Modern English Biography* (Truro, 1897).
——*Modern English Biography*, 2nd edn., 2 vols. (1965).
Bolitho, H. and Peel, D., *The Drummonds of Charing Cross* (1967).
Bowen, Desmond, *The Idea of the Victorian Church* (Montreal, 1968).
——*The Protestant Crusade in Ireland, 1800–70* (Dublin, 1978).
——*History and Shaping of Irish Protestantism* (New York, 1995).
Boylan, Henry (ed.), *A Dictionary of Irish Biography*, 2nd edn. (Dublin, 1979).
Bradley, Ian, *The Call to Seriousness* (New York, 1976).
Brady, David, *The Christian Brethren Archive in the John Rylands University Library of Manchester* (Florence, 1988).
Bray, Gerald, *The Anglican Canons 1529–1947* (1998).
Brierly, Peter William and Johnstone, Patrick J. (eds.), *World Churches Handbook* (1997).
Brilioth Yngve, *The Anglican Revival* (1925).
Broadbent, E. H., *The Pilgrim Church*, 3rd edn. (1945).
Brockett, Allan, *Nonconformity in Exeter, 1650–1875* (Manchester, 1962).
Brown, C. G., 'Itinerancy and Loyalty: A Study in Eighteenth Century Evangelicalism', in *JRH* (1971).

Brown, C. K. F., *A History of the English Clergy, 1800–1900* (1953).

Brown, Ford K., *Fathers of the Victorians* (Cambridge, 1961).

Brown, Stewart J., *Thomas Chalmers and the Godly Commonwealth in Scotland* (Oxford, 1982).

Burke's Landed Gentry, 18th edn., 3 vols. (1965).

Burke's Peerage and Baronetage, 10th edn. (1980).

Burne, W. L., *The Age of Equipoise* (1964).

Burtchaell, George Dames and Sadleir, Thomas Ulick (eds.), *Alumni Dublinenses* (Dublin, 1924).

Callaghan, James Patrick, *Primitivist Piety: The Ecclesiology of the Early Plymouth Brethren* (Lanham, Md., 1996).

Cameron, George C., *The Scots Kirk in London* (Oxford, 1979).

Carter, Grayson, 'Baptist Wriothesley Noel', in *New DNB*.

——'Baroness Barham', in *New DNB*.

——'George Baring', in *New DNB*.

——'Harriet Wall', in *New DNB*.

——'Henry Drummond', in *BDE*.

——'James Harington Evans', in *New DNB*.

——'James Shore', in *New DNB*.

——'Joseph Charles Philpot', in *New DNB*.

——'Robert Harkness Carne', in *New DNB*.

——'Robert Hawker', in *New DNB*.

Chadwick, Owen, *The Victorian Church*, 3rd edn., 2 vols. (1971).

——'Chalmers and the State', in A. C. Cheyne (ed.), *The Practical and the Pious* (Edinburgh, 1985).

Chambers, Ralph F. and Oliver, Robert W., *The Strict Baptist Chapels of England*, 5 vols. (1952–63).

Clarke, Basil F. L., *The Building of the Eighteenth-Century Church* (1963).

Clegg, Herbert, 'Evangelicals and Tractarians', in the *Historical Magazine of the Protestant Episcopal Church* (1966–7).

Coad, F. Roy, *A History of the Brethren Movement* (Exeter, 1968).

Cohn, N., *The Pursuit of the Millennium*, 3rd edn. (1970).

Coleman, Bruce, 'The Nineteenth Century: Nonconformity', in Nicholas Orme (ed.), *Unity and Variety: A History of the Church in Devon and Cornwall* (Exeter, 1991).

Coles, Sarah, 'The Grange in the 19th Century', in the *Hampshire Magazine* (1983).

Collinson, Patrick, 'The English Conventicle', in W. J. Sheils and Diana Wood (eds.), *Studies in Church History: Voluntary Religion* (Oxford, 1986).

Cooke, Michael, 'The Diocese of Exeter in 1821', in the *Report of the Devon and Cornwall Record Society* (1960).

Crone, John S. (ed.), *A Concise Dictionary of Irish Biography*, 2nd edn. (Dublin, 1937).

Crossley, Alan (ed.), 'A History of the County of Oxford: The City of Oxford', in *The Victorian History of the Counties of England* (Oxford, 1979).
Davenport, Rowland, *Albury Apostles*, 2nd edn. (1973).
Davies, G. C. B., *Henry Phillpotts Bishop of Exeter, 1778–1869* (1954).
—— *The First Evangelical Bishop* (1957).
Davis, C. H., *The English Church Canons of 1604* (1869).
Doe, Norman, *Canon Law in the Anglican Communion* (Oxford, 1998).
Doubleday, H. R. (ed.), 'Hampshire and the Isle of Wight', in *The Victorian History of the Counties of England*, 2nd edn. (1973).
Downer, A. C., *A Century of Evangelical Religion in Oxford* (1938).
Drummond, Andrew Landale, *Edward Irving and His Circle* (1938).
Edgerley, J. T. (ed.), *Ecclesiastical Law* (rep. from Halsbury's *Laws of England*) (1957).
Elliott, Marianne, 'Ireland and the French Revolution', in H. T. Dickinson (ed.), *Britain and the French Revolution* (1989).
Elliott-Binns, L. E., *Religion in the Victorian Era* (1963).
Embley, Peter L., 'The Early Development of the Plymouth Brethren', in Bryan R. Wilson (ed.), *Patterns of Sectarianism* (1967).
Evans, Eifion, *Daniel Rowland and the Great Evangelical Awakening in Wales* (Edinburgh, 1985).
Ferguson, Sinclair B. and Wright, David F. (eds.), *New Dictionary of Theology* (Leicester, 1988).
Flegg, Columba Graham, *'Gathered Under Apostles': A Study of the Catholic Apostolic Church* (Oxford, 1992).
Forrester, David, *Young Doctor Pusey* (1989).
Forster, E. M., *Marianne Thornton* (1956).
Froom, Le Roy E., *The Prophetic Faith of Our Fathers*, 4 vols. (Washington, 1946–54).
Froude, James Anthony, *The English in Ireland in the Eighteenth Century*, 3 vols. (1872–4).
Gabb, Arthur, *A History of Baptist Beginnings with an Account of the Rise of Baptist Witness in Exeter, and the Founding of South Street Church* (Exeter, 1954).
Gash, Norman, *Aristocracy and People*, 3rd edn. (1983).
Gilley, Sheridan, 'Newman and Prophecy', in the *Journal of the United Reformed Church Historical Society* (1985).
——*Newman and his Age* (1990).
Good, James I., *History of the Swiss Reformed Church Since the Reformation* (Philadelphia, 1913).
Grass, Tim, '"The Restoration of a Congregation of Baptists": Baptists and Irvingism in Oxfordshire', in *BQ* (forthcoming).
Greaves, R. W., 'Golightly to Newman, 1824–45', in *JEH* (1958).
Green, V. H. H., *Religion at Oxford and Cambridge* (1964).

Harrison, B., *Drink and the Victorians* (1971).
Harrison, J. F. C., *The Second Coming* (1979).
Hempton, D. N., 'Evangelicalism and Eschatology', in *JEH* (1980).
——*Methodism and Politics in British Society 1750–1850* (1984).
——'Methodism in Irish Society, 1770–1830', in *Transactions of the Royal Historical Society* (1986).
——*Religion and Political Culture in Britain and Ireland* (Cambridge, 1996).
Hill, Christopher, 'Dr Tobias Crisp, 1600–1643', in John Prest (ed.), *Balliol Studies* (Oxford, 1982).
Hilton, Boyd, *The Age of Atonement* (Oxford, 1988).
Hopkins, Hugh Evans, *Charles Simeon of Cambridge* (1977).
Jagger, Peter J., *Gladstone: The Making of a Christian Politician* (Allison Park, Pa., 1991).
Johnson, Thomas J., Robinson, John L., and Jackson, Robert Wyse, *A History of the Church of Ireland* (Dublin, 1953).
Jones, A. N., *Gower Memories of William Griffiths* (Aberayron, 1957).
Jones, Iorwerth Hughes, 'Lady Barham in Gower', in the *Journal of the Gower Society* (1956).
Kapman, A. E., *A History of St. Thomas' Baptist Church, Exeter, 1817–1967* (Exeter, 1967).
Lambert, Richard S., *The Cobbett of the West* (1939).
Langham, Mike and Wells, Colin, *Buxton: A Pictorial History* (Guildford, 1993).
Leach, John, *The Book of Buxton* (Buckingham, 1987).
Lewis, Donald M., *Lighten their Darkness* (New York, 1986).
——(ed.), *The Blackwell Dictionary of Evangelical Biography* (Oxford, 1995).
Liechty, Joseph, 'The Popular Reformation Comes to Ireland: The Case of John Walker and the Foundation of the Church of God, 1804', in R. V. Comerford (ed.), *Religion, Conflict and Coexistence in Ireland* (Dublin, 1990).
——'The Problem of Sectarianism and the Church of Ireland', in Alan Ford, James McGuire, and Kenneth Milne (eds.), *As by Law Established: The Church of Ireland Since the Reformation* (Dublin, 1995).
Loane, Marcus, *Cambridge and the Evangelical Secession* (1952).
Long, G. H., *Anthony Norris Groves: Saint and Pioneer* (1939).
McDonnell, Sir Michael (ed.), *The Registers of St. Paul's School* (1997).
Machin, G. I. T., *Politics and the Churches in Great Britain 1832 to 1868* (Oxford, 1977).
Mackintosh, William H., *Disestablishment and Liberation* (1972).
Manning, Bernard Lord, *The Protestant Dissenting Deputies* (Cambridge, 1952).
Martin, Roger H., *Evangelicals United: Ecumenical Stirrings in Pre-Victorian Britain, 1795–1830* (1983).

Matthew, H. C. G. (ed.), *The New Dictionary of National Biography* (Oxford, in preparation).
Merchant Taylor's School Register.
Middleton, R. D., *Magdalen Studies* (1936).
Murray, Iain H., *The Puritan Hope*, 3rd edn. (Edinburgh, 1984).
Newsome, David, 'Justification and Sanctification: Newman and the Evangelicals', in the *Journal of Theological Studies* (1964).
—— *The Parting of Friends* (1966).
Nias, J. C. S., *Gorham and the Bishop of Exeter* (1951).
Nockles, Peter, *The Oxford Movement in Context* (Cambridge, 1994).
—— 'Church or Protestant Sect? The Church of Ireland, High Churchmanship, and the Oxford Movement, 1822–1869', in the *Historical Journal* (1998).
—— '"Lost Causes and . . . Impossible Loyalties": The Oxford Movement and the University', in M. G. Brock and M. C. Curthoys (eds.), *The History of the University of Oxford: Nineteenth Century Oxford* (Oxford, 1997).
Oakes, John, 'Lewis Way', in *BDE*.
Oliver, Robert W., *The Strict Baptist Chapels of England* (1968).
Oliver, W. H., *Prophets and Millennialists* (Auckland and Oxford, 1978).
Ollard, S. L. (ed.), *A Dictionary of English Church History*, 2nd edn. (1919).
Paul, S. F., *The Story of the Gospel in England*, 4 vols. (Ilfracombe, 1948–50).
—— *Further History of the Gospel Standard Baptists*, 5 vols. (Brighton, 1951–66).
—— *The Seceders*, iii (Letchworth, 1960).
Peacock, Barbara, 'Reprieve for The Grange', in the *Hampshire Magazine* (1974).
Pearson, Hesketh, *The Smith of Smiths*, 5th edn. (1945).
Peaston, A. Elliott, *The Prayer Book Revisions of the Victorian Evangelicals* (Dublin, 1963).
—— *The Prayer Book Tradition in the Free Churches* (1964).
Phillips, Walter Alison (ed.), *History of the Church of Ireland, From the Earliest Times to the Present Day*, 3 vols. (Oxford and London, 1933).
Pollard, Arthur and Hennell, Michael (eds.), *Charles Simeon* (1959).
Reynolds, J. S., *The Evangelicals at Oxford 1735–1871*, 2nd edn. (Appleford, 1975).
Rijke, Jon de., *Schijin en zijn: Een onderzoek naar de prediking van Joseph Charles Philpot* (Maassluis, 1994).
Robbins, William, *The Newman Brothers* (1966).
Rodes, Robert E., *Law and Modernization in the Church of England* (South Bend, Ind., 1991).
Rosman, Doreen, *Evangelicals and Culture* (1984).

Rowdon, Harold H., 'Secession From the Established Church in the Early Nineteenth Century', in *VE* (1964).
—— *The Origins of the Brethren 1825–50* (1967).
Saarberg, J. A., *Der pelgrims metgezel* (Houten, 1987).
Sandeen, E. R., *The Roots of Fundamentalism* (Chicago, 1970).
Scotland, Nigel, *The Life and Work of John Bird Sumner* (Leominster, 1995).
Sewell, Gordon and Sewell Constance, 'When Carlyle Found Love at The Grange', in the *Hampshire Magazine* (1960).
Shipley, Cecil Edgar, *The Baptists of Yorkshire* (Bradford, 1912).
Short, K. R., 'Baptist Wriothesley Noel', in *BQ* (1963).
Shuff, Roger N., 'Open to Closed: The Growth of Exclusivism Among Brethren in Britain, 1848–1953', in the *Brethren Archivists and Historians Network Review* (1997).
Simmons, Jack (ed.), *A Devon Anthology* (1971).
Smyth, Charles, *Simeon and Church Order* (Cambridge, 1940).
—— *The Church and the Nation* (1962).
Standring, George Lancelot, *Albury and the Catholic Apostolic Church* (Albury, Surrey, 1985).
Starr, Edward C., *A Baptist Bibliography* (Rochester, NY, 1976).
Stephen, Leslie (ed.), *The Dictionary of National Biography*, 63 vols. (1885–1900).
Strachan, C. Gordon, *The Pentecostal Theology of Edward Irving* (1973).
Stunt, T. C. F., 'Irvingite Pentecostalism and the Early Brethren', in the *Christian Brethren Research Fellowship Journal* (1965).
—— 'Two Nineteenth Century Movements', in the *Evangelical Quarterly* (1965).
—— '*A Bibliographic History of Dispensationalism* by Arnold D. Ehlert—a review', in the *Christian Brethren Research Fellowship Journal* (1968).
—— 'Early Brethren and the Society of Friends', in the *Christian Brethren Research Fellowship Occasional Paper* (1970).
—— 'John Henry Newman and the Evangelicals', in *JEH* (1970).
—— 'Prophetics, Pentecostals and the Church', in the *Harvester* (1975).
—— 'John Synge and the Early Brethren', in the *Christian Brethren Research Fellowship Journal* (1976).
—— 'Geneva and British Evangelicals in the Early Nineteenth Century', in *JEH* (1981).
—— '"Trying the Spirits:" the Case of the Gloucestershire Clergyman (1831)', in *JEH* (1988).
—— 'Henry Bulteel', in *New DNB*.
—— 'John Bate Cardale', in *New DNB*.
—— 'John Nelson Darby', in *New DNB*.
Sykes, Christopher, *Two Studies in Virtue* (1953).

Sykes, Norman, *Church and State in England in the XVIII Century* (Cambridge, 1934).
—— *Old Priest and New Presbyter* (Cambridge, 1956).
Symons, A. J. A., *Essays and Biographies* (1969).
Taylor, D. and Bush, D., *The Golden Age of Hotels* (1974).
Thompson, David M., 'Scottish Influence on the English Churches in the Nineteenth Century', in the *Journal of the United Reformed Church History Society* (1978).
Tiller, Kate (ed.), *Church and Chapel in Oxfordshire 1851* (Oxford, 1987).
Tolley, Christopher, *Domestic Biography* (Oxford, 1997).
Toon, Peter, *The Emergence of Hyper-Calvinism in English Nonconformity 1689–1765* (1967).
—— *Evangelical Theology, 1833–56: A Response to Tractarianism* (1979).
Turner, W. G., *John Nelson Darby* (1926).
Underwood, A. C., *A History of the English Baptists* (1st edn. 1947; repr., 1961).
Varley, Joan, 'A Bedfordshire Clergyman of the Reform Era and His Bishop', in *Worthington George Smith and Other Studies*, Bedfordshire Historical Record Society (Bedford, 1978).
Vaughan, Frank, *A History of the Free Church of England* (Bath, 1938); 2nd edn. (Wallasey, 1960).
Veitch, Thomas Stewart, *The Story of the Brethren Movement* (*c.*1920).
Venn, John and Venn, J. A. (eds.), *Alumni Cantabrigienses*, pt. II, 6 vols. (Cambridge, 1940).
Virgin, Peter, *Church in an Age of Negligence* (Cambridge, 1989).
Votruba, M. J., 'Observations Concerning Practices of the Lord's Supper', in *Discipliana* (1962).
Waddams, S. W., *Law, Politics and the Church of England* (Cambridge, 1992).
Wallace, Dewey D., Jr., *Puritans and Predestination: Grace in English Protestant Theology, 1525–1695* (Chapel Hill, NC, 1982).
Walsh, J. D., 'Joseph Milner's Evangelical Church History', in *JEH* (1959).
—— 'The Anglican Evangelicals in the Eighteenth Century', in M. Simon (ed.), *Aspects de l'Anglicanisme* (Paris, 1974).
—— 'Religious Societies, Methodist and Evangelical, 1738–1800', in W. J. Sheils and Diana Wood (eds.), *Studies in Church History: Voluntary Religion* (Oxford, 1986).
Walsh, John, Haydon, Colin, and Taylor, Stephen (eds.), *The Church of England,* c.*1689*–c.*1833: From Toleration to Tractarianism* (Cambridge, 1993).
Ward, M., *Young Mr Newman* (1948).
Ward, W. R., *Victorian Oxford* (1965).
Weber, Timothy P., *Living in the Shadow of the Second Coming* (Oxford, 1979).
Welch, Edwin (ed.), *Two Calvinistic Methodist Chapels, 1734–1811* (1975).

Welch, Edwin, *Spiritual Pilgrim: A Reassessment of the Life of the Countess of Huntingdon* (Cardiff, 1995).

Weremchuk, Max S., *John Nelson Darby* (Neptune, NJ, 1992).

Whitley, H. C., *Blinded Eagle: An Introduction to the Life and Teaching of Edward Irving* (1955).

Wickes, Michael J. L., *Devon in the Religious Census of 1851* (Appledore, 1990).

Williams, E. Neville, *The Eighteenth-Century Constitution* (Cambridge, 1960).

Wolffe, John, 'Bishop Henry Phillpotts and the Administration of the Diocese of Exeter, 1830–1868', in *Transactions of the Devonshire Association* (1982).

—— *The Protestant Crusade in Great Britain, 1829–1860* (Oxford, 1991).

Wood, Arthur Skevington, *Thomas Haweis, 1734–1820* (1957).

Ziegler, Philip, *The Sixth Great Power* (1988).

INDEX

Index